Past Human Migrations
in East Asia

This book examines the history of the peopling of East Asia, drawing upon the latest evidence in genetics, linguistics and archaeology. It investigates the ways in which we can detect migration, and its different markers in these fields of inquiry. Results from each sphere of academic investigation are compared and reinterpreted in the light of evidence from others. A methodological section reviews key issues in the integration of disciplines and possible pitfalls in developing a synthesis of prehistory. Amongst many original chapters, fresh contributions by Chinese archaeologists and geneticists present challenging views on rice domestication and a reconstruction of the history of yak pastoralism in Central Asia. A series of papers review the language phyla of the region, alerting readers to current issues in their classification and interrelations. A further theme is that of the Austronesian dispersal and controversies over the pattern of its expansion. Other chapters focus on the West and North Asian regions from north-east India to Siberia and the role of demography in driving linguistic and genetic variation. The book should be of great interest to advanced students and researchers in all disciplines working on the prehistory of East Asia and adjacent regions.

Alicia Sanchez-Mazas is Professor of Population Genetics at the University of Geneva, where she chairs the Department of Anthropology. Her main interest is the study of human genetic diversity and evolution. She has published many book chapters and papers, and co-edited *The Peopling of East Asia* (2005).

Roger Blench is the Managing Director of a consultancy and research company, Mallam Dendo Ltd, specialising in development anthropology, especially pastoralism. He has long-term research interests in the interface of archaeology and linguistics, and has co-edited diverse volumes, including *Language, Archaeology, and the African Past* (2006).

Malcolm Ross was Professor of Linguistics at the Australian National University until his retirement in 2007 and is co-director of the Oceanic Lexicon Project. His interests include the histories of Austronesian and Papuan languages. He was a co-author of *The Oceanic Languages* (2002) and has published many articles on Australian and Papuan languages.

Ilia Peiros is Visiting Professor at the Santa Fe Institute, USA. His main interest is the comparative linguistics of East and south-east Asia. He has published several books and numerous articles. His current activity is to compile electronic etymological databases for the *Evolution of Human Languages* project.

Marie Lin is the Director of the Transfusion Medicine and Anthropology Research laboratory at the Taipei Mackay Memorial Hospital and a professor at the Institute of Forensic Medicine of National Taiwan University. She has published on blood groups, HLA, mtDNA and the Y-chromosome in Taiwanese aboriginal populations.

Routledge Studies in the Early History of Asia

1 **Imperial Tombs in Tang China, 618–907**
   The politics of paradise
   Tonia Eckfeld

2 **Elite Theatre in Ming China, 1368–1644**
   Grant Guangren Shen

3 **Marco Polo's China**
   A Venetian in the realm of Khubilai Khan
   Stephen G Haw

4 **The Diary of a Manchu Soldier in Seventeenth-Century China**
   "My Service in the Army", by Dzengeo
   Introduction, Translation and Notes by Nicola Di Cosmo

5 **Past Human Migrations in East Asia**
   Matching archaeology, linguistics and genetics
   Edited by Alicia Sanchez-Mazas, Roger Blench, Malcolm D. Ross, Ilia Peiros and Marie Lin

Past Human Migrations in East Asia

Matching archaeology, linguistics and genetics

**Edited by
Alicia Sanchez-Mazas, Roger Blench,
Malcolm D. Ross, Ilia Peiros and
Marie Lin**

Routledge
Taylor & Francis Group
LONDON AND NEW YORK

First published 2008
by Routledge
2 Park Square, Milton Park, Abingdon, Oxon OX14 4RN

Simultaneously published in the USA and Canada
by Routledge
270 Madison Ave, New York, NY 10016

Routledge is an imprint of the Taylor & Francis Group, an informa business

© 2008 Editorial selection and matter: Alicia Sanchez-Mazas, Roger Blench, Malcolm D. Ross, Ilia Peiros and Marie Lin; individual chapters the contributors

Reprinted 2009

Typeset in Times New Roman by
HWA Text and Data Management, London

All rights reserved. No part of this book may be reprinted or reproduced or utilised in any form or by any electronic, mechanical, or other means, now known or hereafter invented, including photocopying and recording, or in any information storage or retrieval system, without permission in writing from the publishers.

British Library Cataloguing in Publication Data
A catalogue record for this book is available from the British Library

Library of Congress Cataloging-in-Publication Data
A catalog record for this book has been requested

ISBN13: 978–0–415–39923–4 (hbk)
ISBN13: 978–0–203–92678–9 (ebk)

ISBN10: 0–415–39923–8 (hbk)
ISBN10: 0–203–92678–1 (ebk)

Contents

List of plates   viii
List of figures   ix
List of maps   xii
List of tables   xiii
List of contributors   xv
Obituaries   xxiv
Preface   xxviii
Acknowledgements   xxx
List of abbreviations   xxxi

Introduction   1

Methodological issues: linking genetic, linguistic and archaeological evidence   3
ROGER BLENCH, MALCOLM ROSS, AND ALICIA SANCHEZ-MAZAS

PART I
Archaeology and prehistory   21

1. Austronesian cultural origins: out of Taiwan, via the Batanes Islands, and onwards to Western Polynesia   23
PETER BELLWOOD AND EUSEBIO DIZON

2. Evidence for a late onset of agriculture in the Lower Yangtze region and challenges for an archaeobotany of rice   40
DORIAN Q. FULLER, LING QIN, AND EMMA HARVEY

3. Livestock in ancient China: an archaeozoological perspective   84
JING YUAN, HAN JIAN-LIN, AND ROGER BLENCH

vi Contents

  4 Stratification in the peopling of China: how far does the linguistic evidence match genetics and archaeology?   105
ROGER BLENCH

  5 The expansion of *Setaria* farmers in East Asia: a linguistic and archaeological model   133
LAURENT SAGART

PART II
Linguistics   159

  6 The integrity of the Austronesian language family: from Taiwan to Oceania   161
MALCOLM ROSS

  7 The Formosan language family   182
ILIA PEIROS

  8 Time perspective of Formosan Aborigines   211
PAUL JEN-KUEI LI

  9 To which language family does Chinese belong, or what's in a name?   219
GEORGE VAN DRIEM

10 Altaic loans in Old Chinese   254
SERGEI A. STAROSTIN, WITH AN INTRODUCTION BY ILIA PEIROS

11 Comparing Japanese and Korean   263
ROY ANDREW MILLER

12 The speed of language change, typology and history: languages, speakers and demography in North-East India   287
FRANÇOIS JACQUESSON

PART III
Genetics   **311**

13 The GM genetic polymorphism in Taiwan aborigines: new data revealing remarkable differentiation patterns   313
ALICIA SANCHEZ-MAZAS, LUDMILLA OSIPOVA, JEAN-MICHEL DUGOUJON, LAURENT SAGART, AND ESTELLA S. POLONI

14 Maternal lineage ancestry of Taiwan Aborigines shared with the Polynesians   334
JEAN A. TREJAUT, TOOMAS KIVISILD, JUN HUN LOO, CHIEN LIANG LEE, CHUN LIN HE, CHEN CHUNG CHU, HUI LIN LEE, AND MARIE LIN

15 Mitochondrial DNA diversity of Tao-Yami and Batan islanders: relationships with other Taiwanese aborigines   349
JUN HUN LOO, JEAN TREJAUT, CHEN-CHUNG CHU, AND MARIE LIN

16 A genetic perspective on the origins and dispersal of the Austronesians: mitochondrial DNA variation from Madagascar to Easter Island   356
ERIKA HAGELBERG, MURRAY COX, WULF SCHIEFENHÖVEL, AND IAN FRAME

17 A DNA signature for the expansion of irrigation in Bali?   376
J. STEPHEN LANSING, TATIANA M. KARAFET, JOHN SCHOENFELDER, AND MICHAEL F. HAMMER

18 The effect of history and life-style on genetic structure of North Asian populations   395
TATIANA M. KARAFET, LUDMILA P. OSIPOVA, AND MICHAEL F. HAMMER

19 Y-chromosome phylogeography in Asia: inferring haplogroup origins and polarity of haplogroup dispersion   416
PETER A. UNDERHILL

20 Understanding yak pastoralism in Central Asian Highlands: mitochondrial DNA evidence for origin, domestication and dispersal of domestic yak   427
XUE-BIN QI, HAN JIANLIN, ROGER BLENCH, J. EDWARD O. REGE, AND OLIVIER HANOTTE

Index   443

Plates

1.I Red-slipped bowl sherds decorated with friezes of circle-stamped meanders, from Sunget
1.II A selection of Taiwan nephrite artifacts recovered in 2005 from Anaro
5.I The AN settlement of Taiwan with the Malayo-Polynesian and Tai-Kadai migrations
7.I Lexicostatistical classification of Formosan languages
8.I Map of the dispersal of the Formosan Aborigines in Taiwan
12.I Schematic representations of language groupings
13.I Map of Taiwan showing GM haplotype frequencies and plot of the gene diversity in each Aboriginal population
13.II Multidimensional scaling analysis among 113 populations from Southeast Asia based on GM frequencies
14.I Tree drawn from a median-joining network of 96 mtDNA haplotypes observed in nine indigenous Taiwanese populations
14.II Most parsimonious tree reconstruction relating Taiwanese aboriginal, Asian and Oceanian complete mtDNA sequences of haplogroup B4a
15.I Median-joining networks of three major haplogroups (F, B, E) in nine indigenous Taiwanese populations and Batanes from the Philippines
15.II Phylogenetic tree of nine indigenous Taiwanese Populations, Batan and other populations of Asia
16.I Map of Madagascar showing the ethnic groups and the composition of maternal (mtDNA) and paternal (Y chromosome) types.
16.II Map of the Pacific showing the frequency of mitochondrial DNA haplogroups
17.Ia Median-joining microsatellite networks for haplogroup O-M95 in Gunung Kawi in older *subaks*
17.Ib Median-joining microsatellite networks for haplogroup O-M95 in Gunung Kawi in younger *subaks*.

Figures

1.1	Pottery from Torongan and Reranum caves	30
1.2	Vessel rims from Sunget. Dotted lines indicate red slip	32
1.3	A graph to show Austronesian dispersal distance	36
2.1	A phylogenetic representation of modern rice cultivars and wild populations based on SINE genetics	43
2.2	A scatter plot of length and width of grains measured in modern populations	46
2.3	Rice husk lens in situ during Hemudu excavations	48
2.4	The idealized evolutionary spectrum from pure foraging to agriculture based on domesticated crops	52
2.5	Rice panicle maturation and harvest yields assuming wild type grain shedding	55
2.6	Chart of japonica rice grain metrical development in terms of length, width and thickness measures	56
2.7	Graph of grain length and width over the course of development	56
2.8	Counts of rice find types from Kuahuqiao	58
2.9	The proportions of rice grains and spikelets within given shape ranges based on length-to-width ratios	59
2.10	A scatter plot of grain measurements from selected Neolithic sites	60
2.11	Size increase in Lower Yangzte rice phytoliths	62
2.12	A concentration of acorns at the base of pit H27 at Hemudu	63
2.13	Plan of dug features of early paddy fields from Caioxieshan, late Majiabang period (4500–4000 BC)	68
2.14	A synthetic chronology of Neolithic China	71
3.1	Complete skeletons of cows excavated at Shantaisi (Longshan culture), Zhecheng county, Henan Province	87
3.2	Pigs and human buried together at Xinglongwa	90
3.3	Group of animal skulls excavated from a house at Xinglonggou	90
3.4	Pig skull with an artificial hole in the forehead	91
3.5	Significantly twisted dentition of pig jaw excavated at Kuahuqiao	92
3.6	A pit with one carriage and two horses at Yinxu, Anyang city, Henan Province	97
3.7	A pit with two horses at Yinxu, Anyang city, Henan Province	98

x List of figures

4.1	Elements in reconstructing China's prehistory	106
4.2	Sino-Tibetan according to Matisoff (2001)	107
4.3	'Fallen leaves' model of Sino-Tibetan according to Driem (2005)	108
4.4	Family tree of Sinitic languages	109
4.5	Hmong-Mien languages according to Niederer (2004)	113
4.6	Altaic and Macro-Altaic	114
4.7	Daic according to Edmondson and Solnit (1997b)	117
4.8	Austroasiatic with calibrated time-depths according to Diffloth (2005)	118
4.9	Austronesian according to Blust (1999)	120
5.1	Skulls from China with ritual tooth evulsion	140
5.2	Genealogy of language entities (capitalized) within STAN and related archaeological sites	144
5.3	Nested isoglosses for the numerals '5' to '10' in Formosan languages	148
5.4	Higher AN phylogeny based on numerals from '5' to '10'	149
6.1	Blust's Austronesian family tree	165
6.2	A small part of the genealogical tree of Oceanic languages	166
6.3	An elaborated Austronesian genealogical tree	170
7.1	The consonants of Proto-Atayal	183
7.2	The Proto-Saisiyat consonant system	183
7.3	The proto-language consonant system of Bunun	184
7.4	A reconstruction of the Proto-Tsouic consonant system	184
7.5	A reconstruction of Proto-Rukai consonants	185
7.6	The reconstruction of 17 proto-consonants for Puyuma	185
7.7	The Proto-Paiwan consonantal system	186
8.1	Proto-Austronesian subgrouping according to Starosta (1995)	213
8.2	Proto-Austronesian subgrouping according to Blust (1999)	214
8.3	Proto-Austronesian subgrouping according to Li (present study)	214
9.1	One of the language families identified by Julius Heinrich von Klaproth in his polyphyletic view of Asian linguistic stocks	220
9.2	Tibeto-Burman subgroups identified since Julius von Klaproth	222
9.3	The Indo-Chinese or Sino-Tibetan theory (2005)	223
9.4	Sagart's Sino-Austronesian theory (2005)	239
9.5	Starostin's Sino-Caucasian and Dene-Daic theories	232
9.6	Starosta's Proto-East-Asian	241
12.1	Population densities by district, Assam 1931	291
12.2	Densities are not explained only by village territory.	294
12.3	The four variants in North-Eastern India	295
12.4	Distinct reticulation patterns	299
13.1	Multidimensional scaling analysis among 15 populations from Taiwan and China	321
13.2	Multidimensional scaling analysis among 63 populations from Southeast Asia	324

List of figures xi

13.3	Average genetic distances between each aboriginal population from Taiwan and the populations belonging to different linguistically defined groups of Southeast Asia	325
14.1	Principal component analysis map obtained from a matrix of haplogroup frequencies in nine Taiwan indigenous tribes	339
16.1	Diagram of human mitochondrial DNA	360
17.1	Irrigation systems originating from springs at Gunung Kawi Sebatu	379
17.2	Aerial photograph with outline of the Gunung Kawi water temple	381
17.3	Relationship of the location of a farmer's fields to his views on the relative importance of losses from pests or water shortages	383
17.4	Aggregate responses of 90 farmers in three upstream *subaks* and three downstream *subaks*	384
18.1	Evolutionary tree for the 50 Y-chromosome lineages	400
18.2	MDS plot of 30 populations based on Φ_{ST} genetic distances	402
18.3	Spatial autocorrelation plots	404
18.4	Heterozygosity (h) versus distance from centroid (rii)	405
19.1	Representation of numbers of shared and independent Y-chromosome haplogroups in India, Pakistan and East Asia	420
19.2	Spatial south towards north cline of associated 10 loci microsatellite mean variance of haplogroup J2 chromosomes in Turkey	421
19.3	Spatial frequency distribution map of haplogroup H2-M52 chromosomes and spatial distribution map of haplogroup H2	423
19.4	Spatial frequency distribution map of haplogroup L-M20 chromosomes and spatial distribution map of sub-haplogroup L1-M76 chromosomes	424
20.1	The current distribution of yak pastoralism in Central Asian Highlands	429
20.2	The sampling sites for the study of the distribution of three yak mtDNA lineages in domestic yak populations	431
20.3	Unrooted neighbour-joining phylogeny of domestic yak	432
20.4	The mtDNA D-loop haplotype diversity (Hd) observed in 29 domestic yak populations	434
20.5	Regression of mtDNA D-loop haplotype diversities versus geographic distances in domestic yak populations	438

Maps

1.I	The distribution of Austronesian languages, together with archaeological dates for the spread of Neolithic cultures	24
1.II	The location of the Batanes Islands between Taiwan and Luzon	27
2.I	Map of the Middle and Lower Yangtze showing archaeological sites	42
2.II	A map of wild rice distribution and likely zones of domestication	45
5.I	Archaeological sites with *Setaria italica* 5000 BP and earlier	135
6.I	The Austronesian family and major Austronesian language groups	162
12.I	Sketch map of North-East India	288
12.II	East and North-East India: Tibeto-Burman language sub-groups	297
12.III	Rivers with a Boro-Garo name are depicted with a thick line	298
12.IV	Arunachal Pradesh now, with the main district limits	300
12.V	Sketch map of 'Naga' languages	302
13.I	Map of Taiwan showing the areas settled by the aboriginal populations	314
17.I	Map of Bali showing locations of Gunung Kawi (Gianyar) and Tabanan *subaks*, site of archaeological study (Sebatu)	378
18.I	Map showing the approximate geographic positions of 30 populations sampled	398

Tables

1.1	Radiocarbon dates older than 1000 BC for assemblages from Itbayat, Batan and Sabtang Islands, 2002 to 2006 fieldwork	31
2.1	Plant species identified from Hemudu and Kua-Hua-Qiao from fruit remains	64
3.1	Evidence for early pig-rearing in China	88
3.2	Subspecies of *Sus scrofa* in China	88
4.1	Language phyla of China	106
4.2	Horse terms in East Asia	115
4.3	Physical types and linguistic affiliation of Tarim Basin mummies	122
4.4	What drove the expansion of East Asian language phyla?	126
5.1	Examples of sound correspondences	136
5.2	The numerals from five to ten in Formosan and PMP	147
5.3	Disyllabic AN words in Buyang	151
6.1	Selected words in scattered Austronesian languages	163
6.2	An English vowel change	167
6.3	Sound correspondences in two languages of New Britain (Bismarck Archipelago)	167
6.4	Cognate vocabulary in selected Oceanic languages	168
6.5	Sound correspondences in selected Oceanic languages	169
6.6	Sound correspondences from Table 6.1	173
7.1	Some correspondences in the Tsouic group	184
7.2	Proto-Tsou consonantal correspondences	185
7.3	Phonetic correspondences between the Formosan languages	187
7.4	Reconstructed consonants	188
7.5	Using Formosan languages to reconstruct a consonant system	188
7.6	Correlation between Blust's less conservative languages and major groups in Dyen's lexicostatistical classification	190
7.7	Lexicostatistical matrix for Formosan languages	191
7.8	Ages suggested for several well-known families	192
10.1	Lexical matches between Chinese and Altaic	258
12.1	The 1931 British Census: Assam and its surroundings	289
12.2	Population densities in 1931 Assam	290
12.3	Mishing immigration	292

12.4	Rural population (lower densities)	293
12.5	Low-density rural population, grouped	294
12.6	Rural population (higher densities)	296
12.7	Some tribes in Arunachal Pradesh	299
12.8	Three words in Tani dialects	301
12.9	Three words in 27 'Naga' languages	305
12.10	'Sparse' and 'dense' extremes	306
13.1	GM frequencies in Aborigines and some other populations of East Asia	318
14.1	Mitochondrial haplogroup frequencies among Taiwan Aborigines, Northern and Southern Han populations	338
14.2	Coalescence dates for haplogroups	343
16.1	List of the population samples of this study, with the number of individuals and observed mitochondrial haplogroups	364
16.2	Summary of the population statistics calculated in each population on mtDNA sequences between positions 16,081 and 16,380	366
17.1	Comparison of average measured irrigation flows	382
17.2	Genetic diversity parameters based on Y-SNP haplogroups, Y-STR haplotypes and mtDNA HVS1 sequences for individual populations	388
17.3	Fst parameters for Y-SNP haplogroups, Y-STR haplotypes and mtDNA HVS1 sequences	390
17.4	Mantel test: correlation between geography and genetics, and between mtDNA and Y-chromosome genetic distances	391
18.1	Sample composition, linguistic affiliations, and genetic diversity for 30 populations	399
18.2	Analysis of molecular variance (AMOVA)	402
18.3	Correlation and partial correlation coefficients between genetics, geography, and linguistic distances	403
20.1	Mean mtDNA D-loop sequence divergences within and between yak mtDNA lineages and their approximate divergence time	433
20.2	The mtDNA diversity in four geographic areas of domestic yak	434

Contributors

Peter Bellwood (PhD, Cambridge University) is Professor of Archaeology in the School of Archaeology and Anthropology, Australian National University. He has written or edited *Man's Conquest of the Pacific* (1978), *The Polynesians* (2nd edn 1987), *Archaeological Research in South-eastern Sabah* (1988), *The Austronesians* (ed. with J. Fox and D. Tryon, 1995), *Prehistory of the Indo-Malaysian Archipelago* (2nd edn 1997, published online by ANU E-Press 2007), *Examining the Farming/Language Dispersal Hypothesis* (ed. with C. Renfrew), *Southeast Asia: From Prehistory to History* (2004: ed. with Ian Glover), and *First Farmers* (2005). The latter won the 2006 Book Award of the Society for American Archaeology.

Roger Blench (PhD, Cambridge University) is a social anthropologist and director of a company undertaking development consultancy. He has a long involvement with the interface of linguistics and archaeology, and has published four edited volumes with Routledge in this area (*Archaeology and Language*, vols 1–4). He has been co-editor of a book on the history of African livestock, and of *The Peopling of East Asia* (Routledge 2005) and most recently, the author of *Language, Archaeology, and the African Past* (2006) integrating archaeology and linguistics in Africa.

Murray Cox (PhD, University of Otago) is a post-doctoral research associate in molecular anthropology in Dr Michael Hammer's research group at the University of Arizona. His research interests are the reconstruction of human demographic history using genetic markers, with special emphasis on populations of the Indo-Pacific region.

Eusebio Dizon (PhD, University of Pennsylvania) is Head of the Underwater Archaeology Section and Curator I in the Archaeology Division, National Museum, Manila. He is also a Professorial Lecturer at the University of the Philippines, Diliman, the Ateneo de Manila University, Quezon City and the University of Santo Tomas, Manila. He has carried out extensive fieldwork in both land and underwater archaeology in the Philippines, the United States, India, and Southeast Asia, and is currently co-directing an archaeological project in the Batanes Islands, northern Philippines, with Peter Bellwood. He has published many papers on Philippine archaeology, and a book co-authored with Rey Santiago, *Faces of Maitum* (Capitol Press, 1996).

Jean-Michel Dugoujon is Director of Research at the Centre National de la Recherche Scientifique in Paris, and head of the Laboratory of Anthropobiology in Toulouse. His main research interest is the evolution and genetic history of human populations, with a main focus on the GM markers of immunoglobulins. He is currently coordinating several interdisciplinary projects on the peopling of North Africa, the Mediterranean region and South America. He analyses both mtDNA and nuclear (microsatellites and SNPs) markers in samples from linguistically defined populations.

Ian Frame is a computer officer at the University of Cambridge. His work includes the promotion of advanced computer methods for environmental science applications. Using computing techniques, he has researched the structure and evolution of retrotransposons, genetic structures similar to retroviruses such as HIV, the human immunodeficiency virus. He has extensive experience in the computer analysis of human genetic information, particularly mitochondrial DNA sequence data. In addition, he has performed ancient bone DNA typing on human and animal bones from archaeological contexts, including the *Mary Rose* ship.

Dorian Q. Fuller is Lecturer in Archaeobotany at the Institute of Archaeology, University College London. He was educated at Yale University and Cambridge, where he completed his PhD on the emergence of agriculture in South India (2000). He has conducted archaeological fieldwork in India, Pakistan, Sudan, Morocco and more recently China. He has published numerous scholarly articles on the archaeobotany of plant domestication, early agriculture in South Asia and Nubian archaeology. His is co-author with Eleni Asouti of *Trees and Woodlands in South India: An Archaeological Perspective* (Left Coast Press, 2007).

Erika Hagelberg is Professor of Evolutionary Biology at the University of Oslo. She has developed techniques for the analysis of genetic information from ancient human bones, and worked on the first applications of bone DNA typing in archaeology and forensic identification. Her current research includes the analysis of DNA from ancient and modern humans to infer patterns of partial population migrations and expansions in the Indo-Pacific region.

Michael F. Hammer is a research scientist at the University of Arizona. He received his PhD degree at the University of California, Berkeley. His primary research goals are to better understand the genomic and evolutionary factors shaping patterns of human variation and to test models of human origins. Over the last decade he has pursued studies of variation on the Y chromosome as a model system to explore human evolution. Now his studies involve comparing patterns of genetic variation on the Y chromosome, mitochondrial DNA,

X chromosome, and autosomes to distinguish the genomic footprint of natural selection from the signatures of demographic processes.

Han Jian-Lin is a molecular geneticist working on molecular characterization of domestic animal genetic resources. After graduating from Gansu Agricultural University (GAU) in 1984, he was an associate professor of animal genetics and breeding in the Department of Animal Science at GAU until 2000. He focused on molecular genetic diversity in Old World camelids at Giessen University and the International Livestock Research Institute in 1997–2000, proceeding to a PhD in molecular ecology and ecological genetics at Lanzhou University in 2000. He set up the INRI International Yak Information Center in 1994, now hosted at GAU. His research interests are animal husbandry in the extreme ecological environments of the high Hindu-Kush Himalayan and Qinghai-Tibetan Plateau region and the central Asian steppes (yak) and of the low central Asian deserts (Bactrian camels).

Olivier Hanotte is a molecular geneticist. He received his PhD and postdoctoral training at the University of Leicester. He is currently a senior scientist and Project Leader in Animal Genetic Resources at the International Livestock Research Institute, with responsibility for establishing, developing and leading a programme on the genetic characterization of indigenous livestock genetic resources from the developing world in cattle, sheep, goat, chicken, yak and camels. He is also responsible for the livestock quantitative traits loci mapping projects, ensuring coordination of international and collaborative mapping efforts aiming to identify the chromosomal regions associated with trypanosomiasis (sleeping sickness) tolerance in cattle and resistance to gastro-intestinal parasite (nematodes) in sheep.

Emma Harvey was educated at the University of Bradford and University College London where she completed her PhD on early agricultural communities in northern and eastern India (2006). Her research involved extensive comparative studies of rice grains and phytoliths, and she has published articles on the archaeobotany of India and the use of phytoliths in the study of rice crop-processing.

Chun Lin He obtained his master's degree in aquaculture at the National Taiwan Ocean University. He then specialised in molecular endocrinology where he spent some time analysing steroid receptors expression during sex changes in fish. Recently he concentrated his efforts toward molecular genetics and population studies. He is now a research assistant in the Department of Medicine at the Mackay Memorial Hospital in Taipei. In his current work, he utilizes SNP and STR markers techniques to determine variation in the non-recombining (NR) region of the Y chromosome, and analyses the distribution of paternal lineages in the Taiwan Han and Aboriginal populations and other populations of Southeast Asia. He is also working in collaboration with Richard Villems from the Estonian Biocentre of Tartu to find new NR SNP markers that may have a more relevant practical value in analysing populations of Asia.

François Jacquesson is a researcher in linguistics in Centre National de la Recherche Scientifique, Paris. Since 1984, he has being studying languages in north-east India. He has published a number of papers arising from his linguistic research and on multidisciplinary topics such as demography and linguistics and relative speed of language change in different linguistic areas. He is the author of *Le Deuri, langue tibéto-birmane d'Assam* (2005). He coordinates the Brahmaputra Project, an interdisciplinary and international project for the study of north-east India.

Tatiana M. Karafet is an associate research scientist at the University of Arizona, and Senior Research Scientist of the Institute of Cytology and Genetics, Novosibirsk. She completed her PhD at the University in Novosibirsk in 1986, specializing in the human population genetics of indigenous Siberian populations. She has taken part in numerous field trips to different parts of Siberia and has published papers on various aspects of the population structure of native groups in Siberia based on classical genetic markers. Since 1994, when she moved to Tucson, Arizona, her research has involved the molecular analysis of human genetic variation, mostly Y-chromosome studies.

Toomas Kivisild is a lecturer in human evolutionary genetics at the Leverhulme Centre for Human Evolutionary Studies in the University of Cambridge. His main interest is the integration of multidisciplinary studies into the reconstruction of human evolution. During his professorship as a molecular anthropologist at the Estonian Biocentre and the Department of Evolutionary Biology, IMCB of Tartu University where he graduated, he worked on prehistoric human demography of Africa, Asia (India) and East Asia as inferred from mitochondrial DNA and Y-non-recombining chromosome regions.

J. Stephen Lansing is a professor of anthropology at the University of Arizona, with a joint appointment in ecology and evolutionary biology. He is also a research professor at the Santa Fe Institute, and Director of Yayasan Somia Pretiwi, an Indonesian foundation promoting collaborative research on environmental problems in the tropics. He is the author of *Evil in the Morning of the World: Phenomenological Approaches to a Balinese Community* (1974), *The Three Worlds of Bali* (1983), *Priests and Programmers: Technologies of Power in the Engineered Landscape of Bali* (1991), *The Balinese* (1994), and *Perfect Order: Recognizing Complexity in Bali* (2006). Documentary films include *The Three Worlds of Bali* (1981), *The Goddess and the Computer* (1988), and a segment of *The Sacred Balance*.

Chien Liang Lee studied food sciences at the Tunghai University and obtained his master's degree in biological science and technology from Chiao Tung University in Taiwan. He is now a research assistant in the Transfusion Medicine Research Laboratory, Mackay Memorial Hospital, Taipei. His research focuses on population genetics where he primarily studies mitochondrial DNA of regional populations. As a student of Professor Alan Cooper, he gained great expertise in the molecular DNA analysis of ancient human remains. He is now finalizing the setting up of the national 'ancient DNA molecular laboratory' as part of a multidisciplinary project on the origin of Austronesian speakers that includes archaeology, anthropology and linguistics.

Hui Lin Lee holds a master's degree from the Tamkang University. She has gained most of her experience while working at the blood bank in Mackay Memorial Hospital, Taipei. She has also participated in many research projects such as serological associations of human platelet antigens (HPA) and neutrophil antigens (NA). She is currently a research assistant in the Transfusion Medicine Research Laboratory of the same hospital, where her main research revolves around studying population genetics and disease associations using HLA and other systems of the major histocompatibility complex. She has contributed in the discovery of many new alleles and is a participating author of many articles on HLA.

Paul Jen-kuei Li is a research fellow of the Institute of Linguistics, Academia Sinica, Taipei, and was Professor of Linguistics at National Taiwan University (1974–84) and National Tsing Hua University (1986–94). He is interested in the Austronesian and Sino-Tibetan language families, and has done extensive fieldwork on Formosan languages. He has published several monographs on Formosan languages, including *Rukai Structure* (1973), *The History of Formosan Aborigines: Linguistics* (1999, in Chinese), *Pazih Dictionary* (2001), and *Pazih Texts and Songs* (2003), both with Shigeru Tsuchida. He edited *Austronesian Studies Relating to Taiwan* (1995), and his *Selected Papers on Formosan Languages* appeared in 2004.

Marie Lin is the Director of the Transfusion Medicine and Anthropology Research Laboratory at the Mackay Memorial Hospital, Taipei and a professor at the Institute of Forensic Medicine of National Taiwan University. She has conducted pioneer research on blood groups and is the instigator and developer of the Taiwan National Blood program. She has worked on inferring demography from blood groups, HLA data and more recently from mtDNA sequencing and the non-recombining haploid Y-chromosome. She has embarked on a study of ancient DNA from human remains using mitochondrial DNA variation to reconstruct prehistoric human demography of Taiwan and East and Southeast Asia.

Jun-Hun Loo is a research associate at the Transfusion Medicine and Anthropology Research Laboratory at the Mackay Memorial Hospital, Taipei. She holds a master's degree in public health from UCLA with a major in biostatistics. She coordinates laboratory research in molecular anthropology using mtDNA and non-recombinant Y-chromosome analysis, including work on DNA from ancient human remains. She is currently seeking to associate her findings on the genetic relationships between Batanes Islanders and Taiwan Aborigines with neighbouring insular populations and analysing possible northward and southward genetic flows that would better describe the genetic profile of Batanes islanders. She is actively involved in a multidisciplinary project, a cooperation between linguistics, archaeology and anthropology aiming to analyse the relationship between Austronesian speakers and the pre-Holocene settlers in Taiwan.

Roy Andrew Miller (PhD, Columbia University 1953). Retired since 1989, but has held faculty appointments at International Christian University Tokyo, Yale, and University of Washington; visiting appointments at Stanford, Stockholm, Oslo and Vienna. Publications include: *The Japanese Language* (Chicago, 1967; Japanese translation 1972; German 1993); *Japanese and the Other Altaic Languages* (Chicago, 1971; Jap. trans. 1981); *Studies in the Grammatical Tradition in Tibet* (Amsterdam, 1976); *Origins of the Japanese Language* (Korean trans. 1985); *Prolegomena to the First Two Tibetan Grammatical Treatises* (Vienna, 1993); and *Languages and History: Japanese, Korean and Altaic* (Oslo, 1996).

Ludmila Osipova is the Chief of Laboratory at the Institute of Cytology and Genetics, Novosibirsk, Russia. She graduated from the Novosibirsk State University in 1971. Her PhD thesis (1988) concerned immunoglobulin polymorphism in northern Siberian populations. She is a specialist in the human population genetics of native Siberian peoples. During over 60 field trips in Siberia she has created a unique collection of blood and DNA samples from 16 ethnic groups, accompanied by demographic and genealogical data. This collection is used for Gm-RFLP, Y chromosome, mtDNA and other studies in collaboration with colleagues from France, USA, Estonia and other countries.

Ilia Peiros is a visiting professor in the Evolution of Human Languages Program at the Santa Fe Institute. He has published four books: *A Comparative Vocabulary of Five Sino-Tibetan Languages* (6 vols, with S. Starostin) (1996); *Katuic Comparative Dictionary* (1996); *Comparative Linguistics in Southeast Asia* (1998); and *A Genetic Classification of Austroasiatic Languages* (in Russian, 2004). His main linguistic interests include the etymological study of the languages of Southeast Asia and the investigation of the linguistic prehistory of the Indo-Pacific and Australia.

Estella S. Poloni teaches and conducts research at the Laboratory of Genetics and Biometry of the University of Geneva. She is a population geneticist mainly interested in anthropology and evolution. Her research focuses on the variability of gender-specific molecular markers in human populations, and the relationships between genetic and linguistic differentiation in human populations. Her recent contributions to journal articles have appeared in *Annals of Human Genetics*, *European Journal of Human Genetics*, *American Journal of Physical Anthropology* and *American Journal of Human Genetics*. She recently participated in a review article on the genetic diversity of Europe (M.H. Crawford ed.), *Anthropological Genetics: Theory, Methods and Applications* (Cambridge University Press, 2007).

List of contributors xxi

Qi Xue-bin is currently a postdoctoral fellow at Kunming Institute of Zoology, Chinese Academy of Sciences, working on the molecular evolution of genes involved in the function and development of primate brains, and also on the genetic diversity of lactase- and high-altitude-related genes among Chinese ethnic populations. He received his MSc from Gansu Agricultural University, Lanzhou, in 2000, and his PhD from Lanzhou University, in 2004. During his MSc and PhD studies he conducted a large-scale study of the phylogeography of the domestic yak by characterizing genetic variations on milk protein loci, autosomal and Y-chromosome microsatellite loci and mitochondrial DNA sequences.

Qin Ling is a lecturer at the School of Archaeology and Museology at Beijing University. She completed her PhD on Neolithic social structure in the Taihu Lake area. She has worked extensively on Neolithic excavations around China and has jointly directed fieldwork in Zhejiang, Shandong and Henan. She has published articles on Lower Yangzte Neolithic burial customs, settlement patterns, jade artefacts, and subsistence.

J. Edward O. Rege is an animal scientist with a strong background in animal genetics and breeding. He is currently the Director of the Biotechnology Theme of International Livestock Research Institute (ILRI), where his current research includes the development of vaccines and diagnostic tools for tropical livestock diseases, gene discovery and the delivery of genetic change, and the characterization and conservation of animal genetic resources. Previously he was the initiator and Head of the Animal Genetic Resources programme at ILRI and coordinated global activities on the characterization and conservation of indigenous animal genetic resources of developing countries for over 12 years. He has for many years been a keen researcher in conservation, improvement and utilization of indigenous agro-biodiversity in the context of livestock development in developing countries and has extensive experience in sub-Saharan Africa and Asia.

Malcolm Ross was Professor of Linguistics in the Research School of Pacific and Asian Studies at the Australian National University until his retirement in 2007 and is currently a co-director of the Oceanic Lexicon Project. He is a co-author with John Lynch and Terry Crowley of *The Oceanic Languages*, a major reference work published by Curzon Press in 2002. His interests include the histories of Austronesian and Papuan languages, focusing especially on New Guinea and north-west Island Melanesia and on Taiwan. He is also a student of processes of language change, including those brought about by contact. He has published book chapters and papers on each of these topics.

Laurent Sagart is a senior researcher with the Centre National de la Recherche Scientifique, Paris. He received his education in Bordeaux, Paris and Nanjing, and his PhD from the University of Aix-Marseille in 1990. He has published extensively in Chinese dialectology, Old Chinese phonology and morphology, comparative Chinese linguistics, and the Austronesian languages. He has been a visiting scholar in Hawaii, Melbourne and Beijing and a visiting professor in Taiwan and in the USA. He has organized research projects in phonetics, historical phonology, and language contact. His is the author of *The Roots of Old Chinese*, published by John Benjamins in 1999, and a co-editor of *The Peopling of East Asia*, published by RoutledgeCurzon in 2005.

Alicia Sanchez-Mazas is Professor of Population Genetics and head of the Laboratory of Anthropology, Genetics and Peopling History (AGP) at the University of Geneva, where she conducts research projects related to the history of modern humans. She coordinates laboratory and biostatistics analyses in molecular anthropology, with a special focus on the major histocompatibility complex (MHC) in humans (HLA). Her current investigation is mainly devoted to African and East Asian genetic history and possible relationships between genetic and linguistic variation. She has published numerous book chapters and papers on these topics and worldwide human genetic diversity. She was a co-editor of *The Peopling of East Asia* published by RoutledgeCurzon in 2005.

John Schoenfelder received his PhD from UCLA and is currently a research associate both at the University of Arizona Department of Anthropology and at the Cotsen Institute of Archaeology at UCLA. His research has explored the development of polities and coexisting institutions in Bali and in Hawaii. Themes of particular interest include agricultural technology, the role of irrigation agriculture in sociopolitical evolution, the ideological use of indexical signs, the relationship between population movement and cultural change, and cartography and geographic information systems.

Sergei Starostin, who passed away in 2005 while this volume was in preparation, was the Head of Center of Comparative Linguistics at the Russian State University of the Humanities in Moscow and the Director of the Evolution of Human Languages programme at the Santa Fe Institute. His major books (some co-authored) include: *Hurro-Urartian as an Eastern Caucasian Language* (1986), *Reconstruction of the Old Chinese Phonological System* (in Russian, 1989), *The Altaic Problem and the Origin of Japanese* (in Russian, 1991), *A North Caucasian Etymological Dictionary* (1994), *A Comparative Vocabulary of Five Sino-Tibetan Languages* (6 vols, 1996) and *An Etymological Dictionary of Altaic Languages* (3 vols, 2003). His linguistic interests included the investigation of distant relationships among languages, including the Sino-Caucasian, Nostratic and Austric super-families. His etymological databases are available at <http://starling.rinet.ru>.

Jean Trejaut is a research fellow at the Transfusion Medicine and Anthropology Research laboratory at the Mackay Memorial Hospital, Taipei. There he conducts mitochondrial and Y-chromosome studies of populations from Taiwan, East Asia and Island Southeast Asia. He is about to start analysis of the genetic variation of ancient DNA obtained from human remains from various regions of Taiwan and will compare the results with present-day patterns to provide a well-defined population-genetics background for better understanding the genetic complexity seen in the demography of Taiwan and Island Southeast Asia. He conducted HLA studies for the Australian Red Cross for 26 years.

Peter A. Underhill is a senior research scientist in the Department of Genetics at Stanford University. His research involves the molecular analysis of human genetic variation in human populations. In 1995, he co-invented DHPLC technology, which greatly accelerated the discovery of genetic markers on the human Y chromosome. This pioneering work has led to the development of a phylogeny, which defines numerous Y-chromosome lineages with distinctive geographic appellation, providing considerable transparency concerning paternal biogeographical ancestry. He has co-authored numerous peer-reviewed publications, most of which provide genetic perspectives to human population structure and history.

George van Driem, Professor of Linguistics at Leiden University, writes grammars of previously undocumented languages in the Himalayas. He directs the Himalayan Languages Project and conceived the research programme Languages and Genes of the Greater Himalayan Region. In addition to several reference grammars, he has written a two-volume handbook, *The Languages of the Himalayas* (Brill, 2001). He is currently completing grammars of the three most endangered languages of Bhutan.

Jing Yuan is an archaeologist working on zooarchaeology, the relationship between human beings and the environment and the association between animals and humans in prehistory. He obtained his PhD in 1993 from Chiba University, Japan. He is currently a professor at the Institute of Archaeology of Chinese Academy of Social Sciences in Beijing and is also a guest professor at Beijing University. He serves as a member of the Executive Committee of the International Council of Archaeology and is a standing member of the Committee of Quaternary Research in China, as well as a member of the editorial board of Acta Archaeologica Sinica.

Obituaries

Sergei Starostin

(1953–2005)

Sergei Starostin's sudden death shocked everyone who was fortunate enough to know him. We have lost a great friend and probably the most gifted and productive comparative linguist of the last few decades.

Sergei was born and spent most of his life in Moscow. He began to study languages, both classical—Latin, Greek and Sanskrit—and modern, ranging from Polish to Swahili, while he was still in primary school, and soon entered Indo-European linguistics. By the time he left school, his attention had been drawn to the study of Nostratic, the only super-family known at that time, and while still a teenager attended a course on Nostratic taught by Dolgopolski at Moscow State University in 1965–1966.

As a student at Moscow State University, Sergei learned Japanese and in his first year (1972) published his first paper, on Japanese historical phonology. As Japanese is heavily influenced by Chinese, he began to study Chinese and its history, later becoming a respected specialist in Classical Chinese. His reconstruction of Old Chinese phonology, which later became his 1979 PhD thesis and finally a 1989 book, was the first of Sergei's major discoveries and provided tools for breakthroughs in several related fields. At the university, Sergei participated in several trips to the Caucasus and learned the excitement of fieldwork. Not surprisingly, the linguistic history of that region quickly became a major interest. After graduation, Sergei became a PhD student and then a researcher at the Institute of Oriental Studies of the Soviet Academy of Science (IVAN), where he worked for the next 15 years.

By the mid-1970s, Sergei's views on comparative linguistics had been shaped. Although never published, they clearly show in his work. These views, as I understand them, state that a theory must be based on solid facts, to be presented before any theoretical statement is made. Hence collecting new data is the main priority of any research. This obsession with facts is seen in the data-heavy style of all Sergei's papers and books. He believed that the main goal of comparative linguistics is to reconstruct proto-languages, especially their phonologies and lexicons. Compiling the dictionary of a proto-language requires a detailed search for etymologies in all available languages, not a random extraction of forms. Reconstruction must proceed step by step from recent times to prehistory. First proto-languages are reconstructed from recorded sources, then these proto-languages are used for deeper reconstructions. The comparative method, he believed, is applicable to any language family regardless of its typological or sociolinguistic features. The only restriction is lack of data. And he believed that all data should be available to everyone, a principle embodied in his website (http://starling.rinet.ru). Sergei could not understand people who did not want to share their data.

During his time at IVAN, working together with his friends and colleagues, Sergei compiled three etymological dictionaries. In the late 1970s and early 1980s he compiled a Sino-Tibetan comparative dictionary, finally published in 1996. His 1994 reconstruction of Northern Caucasian phonology and an etymological dictionary of the proto-language were based on a study of all available languages and major dialects, with reconstructions of the proto-languages of several younger families which were used in the reconstruction of Proto-Northern Caucasian. This was followed by his 1982 reconstruction of Proto-Yenisseian and an etymological dictionary. To compile just one such dictionary would be a life-time achievement for many linguists. But in addition to his dictionaries, Sergei published books and articles and gave talks on various other languages: Hurrian, Indo-European, Old Chinese grammar, Tangut reconstruction, Korean dialects, Nivkh tones, tones in languages of the Caucasus and so on. One group of articles describes prehistoric linguistic contacts between Northern Caucasian and Afroasiatic, Sino-Tibetan and Austronesian, Chinese and Tai, among others. In 1982, Sergei put forward the Sino-Caucasian theory, linking Northern Caucasian, Sino-Tibetan and Yenisseian, and later Basque and Burushaski, into a single super-family culminating in the first draft of a book finished in 2005.

At about the same time Sergei became interested in lexicostatistics and glottochronology. At first he rejected these methods, but under the influence of Yakhontov, began to investigate them. He focused on the use and improvement of lexicostatistical lists and their application in the search for language relationships as well as inferring absolute dates from lexicostatistics (glottochronology).

Sergei's first attempts at lexicostatistics were done with a calculator and were very time-consuming and not entirely accurate. Only when he gained access to an IVAN computer around 1985 did his achievements in this field accelerate. Computers opened a new chapter in Sergei's life, as he began to create programs for comparative linguistics. This task required him to become expert in programming and database management. After several years he produced the STARLING system, an important tool for this type of research. With STARLING, available on the Internet, linguists can create etymological databases and link them together, establish phonological correspondences and conduct lexicostatistical studies.

In the late 1980s, Sergei returned to Japanese and published a book justifying its Altaic origin, primarily using his modified version of lexicostatistics. This led to his 1992 PhD. Another ten years of work with various colleagues produced the

Etymological Dictionary of the Altaic Languages, a detailed study of relations between Turkic, Mongolian, Tungus-Manchu, Korean and Japanese.

After this Sergei started to prepare an assault on the main problem of comparative linguistics: the issue of the monogenesis of human languages. At this stage Russian linguists recognised two superfamilies: Nostratic and Sino-Caucasian. With new data, it became possible to re-examine the Nostratic hypothesis. Sergei considered that the Nostratic languages formed two related superfamilies: Afroasiatic and Euroasiatic (Indo-European, Uralic, Altaic, Kartvelian and Dravidian) and that an etymological dictionary of Euroasiatic was needed, based on etymological dictionaries of its daughter-languages. This work has started and provisional results are available on the Internet.

From 1992, Sergei worked at the Russian State University of the Humanities, Moscow as Director of the Centre for Comparative Linguistics. In 1998, he was elected a Corresponding Member of the Russian Academy of Sciences.

In 2002, Sergei became a director of the Evolution of Human languages project initiated by Murray Gell-Mann at the Santa Fe Institute. The project matched his dream of a search for deep relations among the world's languages. Here Sergei formulated his most exciting hypothesis, sometimes referred as 'Borean', according to which most languages of Eurasia, Northern Africa and some parts of Oceania belong to a single Borean super-super-family, formed by two ancient branches: (i) Western (Afroasiatic and Euroasiatic) and (ii) Eastern (Sino-Caucasian and Austric). Again the etymologies are available on Internet.

From 2006, Sergei had planned to launch a full-scale survey of other language families (New Guinea, Australia, the Americas and Africa) and to evaluate their relationship with Borean. Now this must be done without him. And this will be very, very difficult...

Ilia Peiros

Satoshi Horai
(1946–2004)

We were very sad to learn that Professor Satoshi Horai passed away unexpectedly on August 10, 2004 at the age of 58. We were told that he had a lung abscess. Professor Horai's last international talk "Genetic origins of the Ainu inferred from combined DNA analyses of maternal and paternal lineages" was given in our meeting in Geneva *Human migrations in continental East Asia and Taiwan: genetic, linguistic and archaeological evidence* in June 2004.

Professor Horai was born in1946; he graduated with an MD/PhD from the Nara Medical University, in Japan in 1977. He worked in the Department of Biological Sciences at the University of Tokyo from 1976 to 1982, and in the Department of Immunohematology and Blood Bank at the University Hospital of Leiden in the Netherlands (1979-1981) just before he moved to Laboratory of Human Genetics at the National Institute of Genetics of Shizuoka in Japan from 1982 to 1998. From 1998 he was Professor at the Department of Biosystem Sciences of the Graduate University for Advanced Studies at Kanagawa.

We all feel his departure is an immense loss to the scientific community as he published so many important articles concerning population genetics, especially on the polymorphism of mitochondrial DNA and Y chromosome, and contributed greatly to the understanding of the peopling of Japan and East Asia.

The editors

Preface

This volume arose out of an international conference, 'Human Migrations in Continental East Asia and Taiwan', organized by Alicia Sanchez-Mazas, Marie Lin and Ilia Peiros in Geneva, Switzerland, 10–13 June 2004. Twenty-five geneticists, linguists and archaeologists were invited to present their most recent results, and about twenty additional researchers and students came of their own accord to listen to the talks and participate in the discussions. The idea of an inter-disciplinary conference on this topic was not new; it followed a workshop organized three years earlier (29–31 August 2001) by Laurent Sagart and the late Stanley Starosta in Périgueux, which also gave birth to a major publication, *The Peopling of East Asia: Putting Together Archaeology, Linguistics and Genetics* (ed. Sagart, Blench and Sanchez-Mazas, RoutledgeCurzon, 2005). Many of the researchers present in Périgueux were also at the Geneva conference, and this was particularly appreciated, as participants could gain an awareness of the scholarly progress made in the meantime. We are thus much indebted to Laurent Sagart, as the Geneva conference was able to benefit from that earlier experience and because he initiated an international inter-disciplinary network of researchers interested in the peopling of East Asia. We are also sincerely grateful to Estella Poloni, who was the promoter of a fruitful collaboration funded by the French Centre National de la Recherche Scientifique (CNRS) Action *Origine de l'Homme, du Langage et des Langues (OHLL)* between Paris and Geneva, and who also contributed to the success of the Geneva meeting.

The successful organization of the Geneva conference owed much to the technical and administrative members of the Department of Anthropology and Ecology of the University of Geneva: Marisa Andosilla, Leila Gaudé, Jean-Gabriel Elia and David Roessli, and its head, André Langaney, who encouraged the meeting because of his ongoing interest in crossing disciplinary boundaries in order to understand the history of modern humans. The department owes this precious legacy to him, and we dedicate this book to him with the hope that this was only the first conference of its kind in Geneva, and will be followed by many others in the future.

Some participants in the Geneva conference, archaeologists Cheng-hwa Tsang and Henry Wright and geneticist Jin Li, were unable to contribute papers to this book, and we sincerely regret this. We appreciate on the other hand the fact that Dorian Fuller and his co-workers, George van Driem, and also Xue-bin Qi and his co-workers, who were not conference speakers, kindly agreed to send contributions respectively for archaeology, linguistics and genetics.

Finally, we were saddened during the preparation of this volume by the sudden passing of Sergei Starostin and Satoshi Horai, who had both participated in the Geneva conference. Our sadness is more than personal, as their deaths are significant losses to science. Thanks to Ilia Peiros, it has been possible to include Sergei's contribution in the book and we regret that this has not been feasible for Satoshi's paper.

Acknowledgements

The Geneva conference was held, and this volume was published, with the generous assistance of the International Relationship Service of the Swiss National Foundation (SNF conference grant #IB3220-101318 to A.S.-M.), the Division of Biology and Medicine of the Swiss National Foundation (SNF research grant #3100A0-112651 to A.S.-M.), the authorities of the University of Geneva (Switzerland), the Faculty of Science and the Department of Anthropology of Ecology of the University of Geneva (Switzerland), the Academic Society of Geneva (Switzerland), the Mackay Memorial Hospital in Taipei (Taiwan), the Ministry of Education of Taiwan, the Council of Indigenous People in Taiwan, the National Science Council of Taiwan, Meditech Biotechnology (Taiwan), the Santa Fe Institute (USA), the French Centre National de la Recherche Scientifique (CNRS) and its Origine de l'Homme, du Langage et des Langues (OHLL) programme. The organizers and editors gratefully acknowledge the financial help of these institutions.

We warmly thank collaborators in the Department of Anthropology and Ecology of the University of Geneva for their assistance during the preparation and the conduct of the meeting held in Geneva and the preparation of the typescript of this book: Marisa Andosilla, Jean-Gabriel Elia, Leila Gaudé, David Roessli, Stephan Weber and Professor André Langaney for his support.

We also thank the authorities of the University of Geneva and anonymous reviewers for their support for the publication of this book.

Abbreviations

AD	anno Domini
AGP	Laboratory of Anthropology, Genetics and Peopling History
AMS	accelerator mass spectroscopy
AN	Austronesian
BC	before Christ
BCE	before common era
bp	base pair
BP	before present
cal.	calibrated
CAS	Central Asia
CASS	Chinese Academy of Social Sciences
CE	common era
CEMP	Central/Eastern Malayo-Polynesian
CI	confidence interval
CNRS	Centre National pour la Recherche Scientifique
CR	coding region
CSS	Central-South Siberia
del	deletion
EAS	East Asia
EDAL	*Etymological Dictionary of the Altaic Languages* (
F&R	forward and reverse
FAMP	Formosan ancestor of Malayo-Polynesian
FATK	Formosan ancestor of Tai-Kadai
HLA	human leucocyte antigens
HVRI	hyper-variable region I
HWE	Hardy-Weinberg equilibrium
LGB	Laboratory of Genetics and Biometry
LZ	Low Zhou
MC	Middle Chinese
MDS	multi-dimensional scaling analysis
MP	Malayo-Polynesian
mtDNA	mitochondrial DNA
NES	Northeast Siberia

np(s)	nucleotide position(s)
NRY	non-recombining portion of the Y chromosome
NWS	Northwest Siberia
OC	Old Chinese
OHLL	Origine de l'Homme, du Langage et des Langues
PAN	Proto-Austronesian
PCA	principal component analysis
PM	Polynesian motif
PMP	Proto-Malayo-Polynesian
PNG	Papua New Guinea
PST	Proto-Sino-Tibetan
PSTAN	Proto-Sino-Tibetan-Austronesian
PTB	Proto-Tibeto-Burman
PTK	Proto-Tai-Kadai
RFLP	restriction fragment length polymorphism
SHWNG	South Halmahera/West New Guinea
SNP	single nucleotide polymorphism
ST	Sino-Tibetan
STAN	Sino-Tibetan-Austronesian
STRs	short tandem repeats
SWS	Southwest Siberia
TB	Tibeto-Burman
TBL	*A Tibeto-Burman Lexicon*
TK	Tai-Kadai
TMRCA	time to the most recent common ancestor
Y-STR	Y-chromosome short tandem repeat

Introduction

Methodological issues

Linking genetic, linguistic and archaeological evidence

Roger Blench, Malcolm Ross, and Alicia Sanchez-Mazas

1. The problem: linking linguistics, archaeology and genetics

The concept of linking linguistics, archaeology and genetics in the reconstruction of the past is becoming a commonplace at certain types of academic conference, but the reality is that each discipline largely pursues its own methods and what little interaction there is remains marginal. Generally, despite much talk of interdisciplinary work, many of the questions asked are internal to the individual discipline, are addressed to colleagues and do not concern the larger sphere of understanding the past.

Some of the talk of interdisciplinary work seems to imply that one day there will be a super-discipline investigating the early human past in which the disciplines of archaeology, historical linguistics and genetics will somehow be merged. This is a misunderstanding. The methods and data of these disciplines are distinct and, importantly, they provide independent support for hypotheses about the past. For example, interdisciplinary work on the history of Austronesian speakers has been reasonably successful, especially where archaeology and linguistics are concerned. This success came, however, only when members of the two disciplines stopped piecing together their findings in a multidisciplinary jigsaw. Archaeologists who prior to the 1980s accepted the glottochronological findings of linguists (e.g. Bellwood 1979) found themselves led up the garden path. It was only when scholars in the two disciplines correlated the results of their single-discipline researches that cross-disciplinary work began to make real sense (Spriggs 1989). Such correlation of course entails some understanding of the status of results in the other discipline.

Since the middle of the 20th century two sets of reasoning procedures have been used by historical linguists, and both are used to produce phylogenetic trees. The comparative method dates from the 19th century, and identifies groups of related languages by reconstructing shared innovations (Ross, Chapter 6, this volume): it is inferred that a set of languages forms a subgroup, i.e. shares a common ancestor, if they share innovations. The members of such a subgroup may appear quite dissimilar: this is irrelevant to subgrouping. On the other hand, a set of languages may appear rather similar, and yet not form a subgroup within the family because their similarities are shared retentions from the protolanguage of the entire family. The comparative method establishes groups of related languages, and subgroups within groups, and subsubgroups within subgroups, and so on recursively. It thereby provides a chronological sequence of language splits. It typically relies on the correlation of its results with those of archaeology for absolute dating.

The second set of reasoning procedures consists of lexicostatistics and glottochronology and is due to Morris Swadesh (1952). Here similarity is king. One takes a list of perhaps 200 basic meanings and finds the words representing these in the languages to be compared. It is assumed that basic vocabulary changes at a constant rate, and that the percentage of meanings that are represented by similar words in a pair of languages is a measure of the phylogenetic relationship between them. Glottochronology builds on the constant-rate assumption and calibrates the lexicostatistics-based tree against time-depth (Peiros, Chapter 7, this volume).

Practitioners of both sets of procedures would regard these accounts as oversimplifications, and rightly so. The point, however, is that there is an underlying difference in reasoning between the two approaches, and they may generate quite different results. This fact is not infrequently overlooked by linguists (let alone practitioners of neighbouring disciplines), who attempt to combine what are in essence logically incompatible procedures.

We referred above to 'methods' and 'data' in linguistics. There is an important distinction within 'methods', however, between reasoning procedures and the tools used to apply them. This is another source of confusion. For example, a team led by Russell Gray employs wordlists to generate dated phylogenetic trees of language relationships, and there is a widespread misapprehension that this is an application of lexicostatistics and glottochronology. Its practitioners insist, however, that they are performing a computational simulation of the comparative method, identifying probable shared innovations, and using archaeological datings to calibrate time depth (Greenhill and Gray 2005; Atkinson and Gray 2006). Computation based on a collection of wordlists, typically associated with lexicostatistics, is being used as a tool in the application not of lexicostatistics but of the comparative method.

Geneticists also use two distinct sets of reasoning procedures. These deal with different data types and lead to different kinds of interpretation. Population genetics applies to gene frequencies estimated at the population level from the genetic typing of representative individuals. Population genetics theory allows one to predict the evolution of such frequencies under both neutral and selective models, by taking account of the effect of gene flow due to population migration, of genetic drift during periods of isolation, of demographic expansion or contraction, and also, in the case of selective models, of the different selective forces which may affect genetic evolution (Cavalli-Sforza and Bodmer 1999). By applying specific methods such as multivariate analyses and analyses of genetic variance, the genetic variation observed in a set of presently living populations may then be interpreted backwards in relation to their history, once significant selective effects have been ruled out (Cavalli-Sforza *et al.* 1994).

The second approach is commonly known as phylogeography (e.g. Underhill, Chapter 19, this volume). It is based on the reconstruction of molecular genealogies – phylogenetic trees – of DNA haplotypes identified in a set of individuals from different populations. Here, gene frequencies are only estimated in a second step, when groups of phylogenetically related haplotypes, known as haplogroups, are inferred from the tree. Unlike haplotypes, such haplogroups may reach significant frequencies. Then a relationship is sought between the molecular genealogy of each haplotype and the geographic area(s) where the corresponding haplogroup is at a high incidence; hence the term phylogeography.

There is a major contrast between the ways results in population genetics and phylogeography are interpreted. Molecularly remote haplotypes are sometimes found within a single population while closely related ones are observed in distantly related populations. Therefore, the genealogy of a set of observed haplotypes does not necessarily (and generally does not) reflect the genealogy of the populations represented in the study (Nei 1987). A simple manifestation of this is that different genetic markers may reveal different genealogies even though the genealogy of the populations must be unique. The link between the history of peoples (i.e. groups of individuals) and the history of genes is thus not straightforward. Genes can be transmitted paternally or maternally, or both, and may appear in a given population through migration or recurrent mutation. A consequence is that estimated dates for the common ancestors of DNA haplotypes in a given genealogy do not generally correspond to the actual times of population migrations or differentiations (see section 3.1).

2. Congruence

A key assumption of the trans-disciplinary enterprise, at least with regard to linguistics and archaeology, is that results can be matched. Patterns of language distribution are, in principle, congruent with archaeology. There is some departure from congruence when a community shifts from one language to another, but this incongruence is often greatly overestimated. As Ross (Chapter 6, this volume) notes, a majority of instances of language shift during the Austronesian dispersal were associated with a shift from foraging to agriculture, resulting in an incongruence between genetics and archaeology/linguistics, but not between archaeology and linguistics.

Incongruence between archaeology and linguistics arises, superficially at least, where, for example, an Austronesian language and culture have been sinicized or papuanized. The Tsat of Hainan island speak an Austronesian language, but it has gone through two stages of transformation; first austroasiaticization as a consequence of long residence in Vietnam, and then sinicization through a millennium of bilingualism with Chinese on Hainan (Thurgood and Li 2003). The Takia of Karkar Island speak an Austronesian language with singularly Papuan grammar reflecting past bilingualism in a Trans New Guinea language (Ross 1996). From a macro-perspective, the Takia speak an Austronesian language but culturally resemble Papuan speakers. However, when one looks at the language in detail, there is no real incongruence: the Takia speak a papuanized language and have a papuanized culture.

Regrettably, the possibility of congruence between archaeology and linguistics is rejected by many archaeologists, for whom linguistics is simply a separate discipline and for whom 'the makers of the pots must remain silent'. For them a local incongruence resulting from contact appears to vitiate the broader congruence between the two disciplines. We argue, however, that since both archaeology and linguistics are direct reflections of human activities, they must, in some way, be congruent. One good reason for thinking this is that there is a clear congruence in the present; culture and language *are* clearly linked and divergences can be explained by relatively simple sociolinguistic processes.[1] The single biggest problem in linking various approaches is that within a discipline it is neither fashionable nor popular to frame hypotheses to be tested in terms of the questions asked by another discipline. So archaeologists give almost no time to matching the patterns of the cultures they delineate with historical linguistics and linguists are often uninterested in reconstructing terms and concepts that could illuminate historical hypotheses. Austronesian and Papuan scholarship constitutes an honourable exception to this in the level of cooperation between some historical linguists and archaeologists (Bellwood *et al.* 1995; Pawley *et al.* 2005).

The potential for congruence between genetics and either archaeology or linguistics is much less. The two different genetic approaches outlined above need to be considered separately. Genes are not peoples, and they have a distributional logic quite different from languages and cultures. The diffusion of a given gene does not necessarily reflect the geographic expansion of a given population or population group, nor the diffusion of a given culture or language, as it may simply represent a diffusion through population contact. Hence the tendency of phylogeographers to consider a given haplotype or haplogroup as a marker of the diffusion of a cultural complex is unfounded; like the proposal, for example, to make this link for Upper Palaeolithic cultures such as the Gravettian or Aurignacian (Semino *et al.* 2000). Rather, genes reflect extensive and complex patterns of human interaction with each other and with the environment in one-to-one and one-to-many relationships. A lesson to be learned from population geneticists is that maps of different genetic markers generally reflect geography rather than ethnicity, with gradients of allele frequencies extending over the entire world (Serre and Pääbo 2004). Global genetic discontinuities are often the result of geographic barriers (Barbujani and Belle 2006), while cultural differences may not be an obstacle to intermarriages (Blanc *et al.* 1990); cultural boundaries are more permeable to genetic exchanges.

Where geography can be eliminated as the reason for congruence, a match between genetic maps and linguistics (or archaeology) implies that cultural boundaries may also influence the extent of gene flow among populations. Such a match is sometimes detectable at the world scale (Chen *et al.* 1995; Poloni *et al.* 1997; Belle and Barbujani 2007) and is particularly meaningful when independent genetic markers converge to give similar results. However, on any large land mass, contiguous populations interact in such an intensive and complex fashion as to oblige researchers to analyse congruence in much greater depth, seeking to explain why and how cultural and genetic patterns share common histories (e.g. Karafet *et al.*, Chapter 18, this volume). But a major difficulty is discriminating between different contributing factors – e.g. between geography and linguistics – when a genetic structure corresponds with both of them. Typical examples arise when the distribution of linguistic families itself is geographically structured, as in most of Eurasia (with the exception of some isolated linguistic groups like the Basques, who live in the midst of Indo-European-speaking populations). In Africa, speakers of unrelated language phyla live adjacent to one another, for example, Khoesan and Niger-Congo in the south, Nilo-Saharan, Niger-Congo and Afroasiatic in the north-east. Therefore, while genetic structures cannot be tested against well-differentiated geographic or linguistic structures in East Asia (Sanchez-Mazas *et al.* 2005), an integrated account may prove more successful in Africa (Excoffier *et al.* 1991). In reality, many of the recent successes in genetics have more to do with geographic and demographic than with cultural parameters. For example, geneticists have emphasized the role of fragmented environments, such as islands or other isolated locales, in explaining the genetic heterogeneity observed among related populations throughout large geographic areas, like Oceania (Hagelberg, Chapter 16, this volume; Sanchez-Mazas *et al.* 2005). They have been able to demarcate possible migration routes in the first expansion of modern humans from a single origin, even though there is still much debate on their relative importance and dating (Forster and Matsumara 2005; Mellars 2006). Movements associated with cultural processes, on the other hand, have been much more difficult to isolate genetically.

A related issue often raised by geneticists is that of language diversity. Genetics can often put a quantitative measure on diversity and wonder whether this can be mapped against linguistic diversity. This seems as if it ought to work, but it does not, because languages diversify in different ways. The Australian and Trans New Guinea language areas are well-known for being highly diverse lexically and extremely uniform phonologically. Daic languages are quite uniform lexically but extremely diverse tonally. Khoesan and Nilo-Saharan languages are diverse in almost every conceivable way. Mountain *et al.* (1992) report on measures of diversity within Sinitic, but show that different categories of linguistic feature show different levels of diversity. This is not to say that diversity carries no information at all. The diversity within the Australian and Trans New Guinea regions clearly reflects their long-term settlement, but whether anything more precise can be extracted from this variety is open to question.

3. Dating

3.1. Genetic dating

Another aspect of genetics that is difficult to match to the other disciplines is dating. Absolute dates for population divergence are usually proposed on the basis of molecular phylogenies. To construct a molecular phylogeny implies that a molecular 'clock' measuring a constant speed of genetic divergence is accepted a priori. The constancy of the molecular clock is of course an approximation (Ho and Larson 2006), and is more valuable for greater time depths, except in the case of rapidly evolving genes for which recurrent mutations, or homoplasies, will be too frequent (e.g. mtDNA). Molecular clocks are usually calibrated against absolute dates for the common ancestors of humans and chimpanzees based on the fossil record. But this raises at least two major problems: (1) the lack of well-documented palaeontological evidence for these dates (Stauffer *et al*. 2001); and (2) the arbitrary choice of the 'outgroup', i.e. the ape DNA used to calibrate the tree. This second point is important because apes exhibit a much higher level of intra-specific genetic divergence than humans (Gagneux *et al*. 1999; Kaessmann *et al*. 1999). What is more, genetic dates are usually inferred with such large confidence intervals that they can easily match multiple historical or cultural events and thus satisfy any hypothesis defended *a priori* by the researcher. Then we can only take the lower and upper limits of confidence intervals as the time-frame for the events under study.

There is a further important obstacle to dating historical events through a genetic approach; phylogenies give times for the most tecent common ancestors (TMRCA) of a set of haplotypes or haplogroups, i.e. molecules. As mentioned above, genes are not peoples and there is no reason for the nodes of a phylogenetic tree (the MRCA) to correspond to identifiable events in population history, such as migrations or differentiations. In reality, genetic tree nodes are usually older than population events. For example, phylogenetic trees in genetics usually describe events that happened long before the putative origins of the language groups under discussion. This also explains why genealogies obtained for independent sets of genetic markers, like mtDNA (172,000 years, Ingman *et al*. 2000) and Y chromosome (59,000 years, Underhill *et al*. 2000) do not match (or match only thanks to the huge confidence intervals of their TMRCA): each gene has its own history. It is not surprising, therefore, that acute contradictions between published results sometimes appear. Two chapters in Bellwood and Renfrew (2002) provide a spectacular example of such a contradiction, with Oppenheimer and Richards (Chapter 22) interpreting the so-called 'Polynesian motif' in mtDNA as utterly inconsistent with the Austronesianist archaeology/linguistics consensus, and Hurles (Chapter 23) presenting an opposing view. Indeed the writings of Oppenheimer constitute a broader problem for the credibility of genetic dating for this region since his 'findings' are so completely at odds with any standard archaeological consensus (Oppenheimer 2004; Oppenheimer and Richards 2001a, 2001b).

Coming back to population genetics approaches, one cannot superpose any time scale on genetic maps of population differentiations, for the simple reason that the rate of evolution of gene frequencies is not constant. It depends on demography (rapid in small populations, slow or null in large populations). Here again, different genetic markers (when transmitted independently from one generation to the other through different chromosomes or distant regions on the same chromosome) often provide heterogeneous information on population history. They may tell stories related to different periods. Interestingly, however, plausible scenarios for the peopling history of given geographic areas may now be proposed through simulation approaches (e.g. Currat and Excoffier 2005). Basically, real genetic data are compared to virtual data obtained by simulating alternative evolutionary scenarios based on different parameters chosen a priori. These parameters include time elapsed since a population origin or differentiation, demographic parameters such as population size and migration rate, and intensity of selection for the marker under study. One or several scenarios – and hence, sets of parameters – will finally be favoured according to their greater likelihood in explaining real data. This field of research has developed recently thanks to the increasing power of computer processors. But, of course, while these methods may offer interesting applications, the arbitrary choice of different sets of parameters remains open to discussion.

3.2. Lexicostatistics and glottochronology

Lexicostatistics and glottochronology are held by most linguists to have been largely discredited, but they have undergone a major revival recently. The late Sergei Starostin (Chapter 10, this volume) devised a new series of algorithms that provided dates for the major language phyla studied by his group (including Sino-Tibetan and Altaic) and these dates are assigned to phyla on the Santa Fe website as well as in their publications. Greenberg (1987) also proposed new methods to calculate glottochronological dates. Two volumes of edited papers published by the McDonald Institute (Renfrew *et al.* 2000) consider dating issues at some length, but individual authors reach very contradictory conclusions. Ehret (2000), for example, finds the glottochronology of Bantu in harmony with his own projections of south-east African history, but without more cogent links to the findings of other archaeologists this can only be given limited credence.

To its adherents, there is something very persuasive about glottochronology, as it seems to be a magical shortcut to dates that linguists otherwise cannot provide. However, it relies on the exceedingly shaky assumption that basic vocabulary changes at a constant rate. This is so obviously false that we believe the temptations of glottochronology should be resisted. The new enthusiasts for glottochronology have one feature in common: a disdain for the hard work of trawling the archaeological literature. For example, Starostin *et al.* (2003) reconstruct a number of crop names in proto-Altaic, yet they date the break-up of Altaic some millennia prior to the inception of agriculture in this region.

4. When linguists disagree on classification

A key issue in linguistics that can be very perplexing for outsiders in the East Asian region is the matter of macrophylic schemas. A number of scholars consider that many of the language phyla of East Asia are related to one another. Unfortunately, their maps of these relationships are very diverse. The affiliation of Sino-Tibetan has been a particular problem, with a more 'conventional' view linking it with Miao-Yao or Daic, as well as wider hypotheses that bring in Caucasian or

Austronesian. Similarly, Austronesian, Austroasiatic and Daic are often linked. Indeed, some authors seem to think that all these phyla will ultimately prove to be related. When working on the problem of correlation with other disciplines it is best to retain a minimalist view; namely that while these views *may* reach a consensus among scholars in the future, at present we need to look for the interdisciplinary correlates of agreed groupings.

At least from the perspective of the comparative method, the detection of a language phylum entails a different reasoning procedure from the identification of subgroups within an already known phylum. The procedure for identifying a phylum is outlined by Nichols (2006) and entails what she calls individual-identifying evidence, i.e. formal parallels across languages that could not have arisen by chance. The parallel forms may be paradigms of affixes, lexical morphemes of three or more syllables, or collections of lexical items. There are two problems in applying this procedure in East Asia, the first of which is limited to the mainland South-east Asian region.

Languages of mainland South-east Asia are typically isolating in morphological type and tend to have monosyllabic lexical morphemes of a particular phonological type (which among other things includes tone). This makes the application of Nichols's procedure difficult, and perhaps impossible, as neither the required paradigms of affixes nor lexical morphemes of three or more syllables exist, and one is thrown back on collections of lexical items with regular sound correspondences as the only evidence of phylic relationship.

This leads to a question which is not specific to East Asia: when is such a collection of lexical items large enough to demonstrate a relationship?[2] Sagart (Chapter 5, this volume) defends the Sino-Tibetan/Austronesian macrophylum hypothesis. He has argued for this elsewhere (see his references) on the basis of lexical items with regular sound correspondences. This evidence has been criticized both for insufficiency and for considerable meaning differences among allegedly cognate items. Our purpose here is not to assert a position with regard to Sagart's claim, but to point to the level to which historical linguists do not agree, although in principle Nichols provides pointers to statistical procedures for determining whether such evidence is probative.

This problem means that even some formerly established groupings are now disputed, Altaic being the most salient example. Altaic is taken in its most extensive form to include Turkic, Mongolic, Tungusic and Korean-Japonic, which share a more or less common morphological type: they are agglutinative, verb-final and suffixing, and should offer ample material for individual-identifying evidence. The weak form of Altaic (excluding Japonic) was long held by most scholars following the work of Poppe (1965) and Miller (1996, and Chapter 11, this volume). However, the coherence of Altaic was questioned by Janhunen (1994), for whom the resemblances between its branches are a mosaic of loanwords. More recently, Starostin *et al.* (2003) have published a very large number of Altaic etymologies (over 2,000), and it has yet to be shown that these are all false, but the integrity of Altaic remains controversial, as debate in the pages of the journal *Diachronica* has shown (Georg 2004, 2005; Starostin 2005).

The tiny Korean-Japonic family is also controversial. Korean has most commonly been claimed as part of Altaic (Martin 1991a, b), although it shares many typological features with Japanese. For Janhunen (1994: 10–13) this is most probably the result of intensive interaction over an extended period rather than evidence for a genetic relationship between the languages. For Whitman and Frellesvig (Whitman 1985; Frellesvig 2001; Frellesvig and Whitman forthcoming) it is because Korean and Japonic form a family.

Languages in East Asia have often been classified together on the grounds of common morphological type, be it isolating or agglutinative, but shared morphological type (and a corresponding shared lexical organization) may result from long-standing and at times intense contact (Enfield 2003). It does not necessarily reflect linguistic phylogeny. On the other hand, if recent work by Ostapirat (2005) and Sagart (2004) is headed in the right direction (and we remain agnostic on this topic) Daic is in fact a branch of Austronesian, the phylic origins of which have been obfuscated by contact-induced change in morphological type in the better described Daic languages. Typology and phylic affiliation must be kept absolutely distinct.

The identification of macrophyla is a problem because their postulation entails great time depths. Changes in lexicon and in other language features at time depths over, say, 8,000 years are so great that the search for individual-identifying features (and the more stringent form of lexicostatistics that demands the analysis of sound correspondences) becomes impossible. In this context Nichols (1997) adds the term 'quasi-stock' to the vocabulary of historical linguistics. A quasi-stock is a grouping of well-supported groups into a larger grouping with promising markers of relatedness but with no regular sound correspondences and few clear cognates. Nichols's example of a quasi-stock is Afro-Asiatic.[3] By her rough rubric Trans New Guinea and Sino-Tibetan are also quasi-stocks. They are groupings which lie at the very limit of the reach of the comparative method. Perhaps Reid's (1999, 2005) arguments for an Austronesian/Austroasiatic nexus place it in this category, too: there is cognate bound morphology and apparently a certain amount of cognate basic vocabulary – promising, but in need of further research.

Outside Asia, Joseph Greenberg has used a different set of reasoning procedures, dubbed 'mass comparison', to identify language phyla in three areas, Africa (1963), the languages of the Andaman Islands, New Guinea and Tasmania (1971), and the Americas (1987). Despite claims that mass comparison is an application of the comparative method (e.g. Greenberg and Ruhlen 1992), it is not the linguistic comparative method as understood by most historical linguists. The initial steps of the linguistic comparative method are (1) the diagnosis of a family by individual-identifying evidence; (2) collecting sets of cognate words and affixes; and (3) working out the sound correspondences of the cognate sets (Ross and Durie 1996). Step 3 provides a validation of step 1, establishing the possible existence of a group (and a benchmark for finding the innovations that identify subgroups). It shows that present-day languages belonging to the family are descended through regular sound changes from a common protolanguage. Mass comparison conflates steps 1 and 2: resemblant words and morphemes with similar meanings are assumed to be outcomes of relatedness, but they do not reach the individual-identifying threshold and so relatedness remains undemonstrated (Ringe 1992). Worse, validation through step 3 is omitted.

Ironically, Greenberg's (1963) identification of phyla in Africa has been accepted by Africanist historical linguists, apparently because some of the materials he used could be validated by an application of step 3 (Nichols 1992: 5). This is not quite the triumph it has been represented as, because three of the four phyla he named existed *de facto* in the literature, and much of his work on internal groupings has been extensively revisited (Blench 2006). Greenberg's 1971 application of mass comparison to the 'Indo-Pacific' has drawn little attention and been largely supplanted, and his identification of American phyla has provoked a torrent of criticism of the method.

Geography can often play a role in the classification of languages; thus the proximity of two language phyla leads them to be regarded as related. For example, Daic (Thai) was long held to be related to Chinese partly because of its similar morphology, but also because its most diverse members were geographically embedded in Chinese populations. George van Driem (Chapter 9, this volume) has regularly pointed out that the classic internal structure of Sino-Tibetan (a primary branching between Sinitic and Tibeto-Burman) is not based on linguistic arguments, but rather a perception of the geographic and cultural separateness of China from the Himalayas. Even the recent conspectus of Sino-Tibetan (Thurgood and La Polla 2003) presents no arguments for the primary split of Sinitic, simply assuming it without evidence (Blench, Chapter 4, this volume). It is for linguists to insist that this is an incoherent approach. Linguistic classifications must be entirely based on linguistic arguments. It is noted above that there are good geographic and archaeological arguments for assuming the pre-Austronesians came from the Chinese mainland, but we should be methodologically wary of calling any mainland culture Austronesian without a single fragment of linguistic evidence.

5. Trees, rakes and linkages: internal classification of language phyla

Historical linguists tend to work with 'tree' models, where languages split, usually in binary fashion, and this is evidently convenient when trying to fashion a correspondence with archaeology, as a chronology can be developed. But some linguists are sceptical of these models and it is clear that languages do not always develop in such a convenient fashion. There are at least two major sources of 'inconvenient' patterns.

One is that, at a certain stage in the history of a family, a language may diversify into a dialect network, some of the dialects of which become geographically isolated through their speakers' emigration and develop into distinct subgroups of languages, whilst the stay-at-home dialects continue both to diversify and to interact with each other, acquiring a pattern of overlapping innovations but having no exclusively shared innovation that identify them as a subgroup.

The other source of inconvenient patterns is contact with languages that belong to another phylum or a more or less distantly related part of the same phylum. As we noted above, it is likely that the common pattern of mainland East Asian languages with reduced morphology, complex tones and simplified word structures represents massive convergence between different language phyla. However, the fine-grained description of contact in a particular language or group of languages can tell us a good deal about the culture history of its speakers and help us to correlate linguistic and archaeological findings.

It is difficult to work with non-trees, because they present no sense of chronology, and it is for this reason that a distinction is made in Austronesian linguistics between innovation-defined subgroups like Oceanic (the conventional subgroups of the comparative method) and innovation-linked subgroups or linkages like Western Malayo-Polynesian, the member languages of which are linked by overlapping patterns of innovations.[4] Both can be incorporated into a tree of sorts (see Ross, Chapter 6, this volume).

6. Sampling frames in genetics

An important but little-discussed aspect of the methodology of genetics is the targeting of sample collection. The hard-science aspect of genetics has often blinded journal referees to the highly unscientific nature of the samples that are analysed. Thus we can find 'West or South Africans' compared to 'Caucasians', the latter term being simply a euphemism for 'white race', a concept that is nowadays unacceptable. Even now, many studies depend on 'out of the freezer' materials, often exchanged between laboratories, where samples really collected within a serious anthropological or ethnolinguistic framework are often a minority. Moreover, sample sizes are generally too low to be statistically representative, and this crucial issue – the ABC of population genetics – is almost never addressed. The problem is all the more serious now that DNA typing technologies allow us to define haplotypes at a much more precise level than before, such that the number of detectable haplotypes is always much higher than the number of individuals sampled (which was not the case with studies based on blood groups or proteins). If we are really to solve some of the major problems of correlating genes and language, then what is required is targeted sampling; i.e. collecting samples that are statistically valid and reflect closely the particular groups that are the focus of the study. It is thus unacceptable to make claims about – to take an extreme but common example – 'Africans' (versus 'non-Africans', e.g. Yu *et al.* 2002) when in fact a handful of population samples are supposed to represent the huge diversity of African ethnic and linguistic groups (not to mention the nonsensicality of 'non-Africans'). Ethnolinguistically targeted sample collections, such as the Taiwanese (Sanchez-Mazas *et al.*, Chapter 13, and Trejaut *et al.*, Chapter 14, this volume) or those planned within the framework of the Languages and Genes of the Greater Himalayan Region project headed by George van Driem and co-workers, are presently under way and more coherent results may emerge within a few years.

7. Local factors that may confuse results

7.1. Teleology in archaeology

Linguistics and archaeology are not driven by the spirit of pure enquiry; archaeology in particular is often prone to hijacking by nationalist agendas. This is not a new point, but the development of the nation state in the 20th century has resulted in a bizarre framing of accounts of the past in terms of the boundaries of the present. It encourages archaeological accounts to view the horizons of the past as leading inexorably towards those of the present. Typically, in China, ancient cultures become precursors of the Han state, rather than, perhaps, dead ends.[5] This is persuasive but misleading: most of what we know about Sinitic suggests that the Han expansion is quite recent and therefore almost any older archaeological culture is *not* likely to associated with Sinitic speakers.

7.2. Confusion associated with written texts

The reconstruction of some parts of Sino-Tibetan has been confused by the existence of archaic written texts. Much historical scholarship has gone into the reconstruction of Old Chinese, a language that would consistently account for the system of ancient texts. But there is, and can be, no evidence that such a language was ever spoken, and no necessary link with proto-Sinitic, a language reconstructed from the wide range of modern dialects. Similar problems have arisen by confusing Sanskrit with proto-Indo-Aryan, as Turner (1966) does in his magisterial volumes. Probably if we had a better reconstruction of proto-Sinitic, there would fewer problems about its place within the larger Sino-Tibetan schema.

8. Conclusion

The collection of methodological problems raised in this introductory chapter may seem to give a rather negative impression of the interdisciplinary enterprise. But if this were our thinking we would not have put together this volume. Rather our purpose has been to enter some caveats about simplistic models of congruence and to help each disciplinary specialist to be aware of the pitfalls of reading literature outside their immediate ambit (and sometimes even within it). But demonstrations that researchers are increasingly becoming aware of the need to read around their subject in a geographical and historical frame are found in recent publications: see, for example, Pawley (2002) on the Austronesian dispersal or the interdisciplinary collection edited by Pawley *et al.* (2005) on the Papuan peoples.

Notes

1 English is the most intensively studied language in the world, and recent explorations of its varieties make it perfectly possible to account for both variation and the congruence or otherwise of the cultures of those who speak it.

2 As Starostin (this volume) notes, regular sound correspondences, preferably in basic vocabulary, are essential if shared inheritance is to be demonstrated and the possibility of borrowing eliminated.
3 This is also an example of the curiously inconsistent way outsiders evaluate evidence for the existence of particular phyla. Compared with Trans New Guinea, Afro-Asiatic has hundreds of proposed etymologies, and some well-established and distinctive phonological and morphological features.
4 There are other ways in which a linkage may come into being, but detailed discussion would require at least a paper to itself.
5 It is interesting to compare these with Stephen J. Gould's strictures on models of evolution that are structured so as they always finish with the evolution of modern humans, rather than being full of byways and forking paths that lead nowhere.

References

Atkinson, Q.D. and Gray, R.D. (2006) 'How old is the Indo-European language family? Progress or more moths to the flame?', in P. Forster and C. Renfrew (eds) *Phylogenetic Methods and the Prehistory of Languages*, pp. 91–110, Cambridge: McDonald Institute for Archaeological Research.

Barbujani, G. and Belle, E.M. (2006) 'Genomic boundaries between human populations', *Human Heredity*, 61: 15–21.

Belle, E.M. and Barbujani, G. (2007) 'Worldwide analysis of multiple microsatellites: language diversity has a detectable influence on DNA diversity', *American Journal of Physical Anthropology*, 133 [Epub 16 May 2007].

Bellwood, P. (1979) *Man's Conquest of the Pacific*, New York, NY: Oxford University Press.

Bellwood, P. and Renfrew, C. (eds) (2002) *Examining the Farming/Language Dispersal Hypothesis*, Cambridge: McDonald Institute of Archaeological Research.

Bellwood, P., Fox, J. and Tryon, D. (eds) (1995) *The Austronesians: Historical and Comparative Perspectives*, Canberra: Department of Anthropology, Research School of Pacific and Asian Studies, Australian National University.

Blanc, M., Sanchez-Mazas, A., Hubert van Blyenburgh, N., Sevin, A., Pison, G. and Langaney, A. (1990) 'Inter-ethnic genetic differentiation: Gm polymorphism in eastern Senegal', *American Journal of Human Genetics*, 46: 383–92.

Blench, R.M. (2006) *Archaeology, Language and the African Past*, Lanham, MD: Altamira Press.

Cavalli-Sforza, L.L. and Bodmer, W.F. (1999) *The Genetics of Human Populations*, Mineola, NY: Dover Publications.

Cavalli-Sforza L.L., Menozzi, P. and Piazza, A. (1994) *The History and Geography of Human Genes*, Princeton, NJ: Princeton University Press.

Chen J., Sokal, R.R. and Ruhlen, M. (1995) 'Worldwide analysis of genetic and linguistic relationships of human populations', *Human Biology*, 67: 595–612.

Currat, M. and Excoffier, L. (2005) 'The effect of the Neolithic expansion on European molecular diversity', *Proceedings: Biological Science*, 272: 679–88.

Ehret, C. (2000) 'Testing the expectations of glottochronology against the correlations of language and archaeology in Africa', in C. Renfrew, A. McMahon and L. Trask (eds) *Time Depth in Historical Linguistics*, 2 vols, Cambridge: McDonald Institute for Archaeological Research.

Enfield, N.J. (2003) *Linguistic Epidemiology: Semantics and Grammar of Language Contact in Mainland Southeast Asia*, London and New York, NY: RoutledgeCurzon.

Excoffier, L., Harding, R.M., Sokal, R.R., Pellegrini, B. and Sanchez-Mazas, A. (1991) 'Spatial differentiation of RH and GM haplotype frequencies in Sub-Saharan Africa and its relation to linguistic affinities', *Human Biology*, 63: 273–307.

Forster, P. and Matsumura, S. (2005) 'Did early humans go north or south?', *Science*, 308: 965–6.

Frellesvig, B. (2001) 'A common Korean and Japanese copula', *Journal of East Asian Linguistics*, 10: 1–35.

Frellesvig, B. and Whitman, J. (forthcoming) 'The Japanese-Korean vowel correspondences', in M. Endo Simon and P. Sells (eds) *Japanese/Korean Linguistics*, Stanford, CA: CSLI.

Gagneux, P., Wills, C., Gerloff, U., Tautz, D., Morin, P.A., Boesch, C., Fruth, B., Hohmann, G., Ryder, O.A. and Woodruff, D.S. (1999) 'Mitochondrial sequences show diverse evolutionary histories of African hominoids', *Proceedings of the National Academy of Science USA*, 96: 5077–82.

Georg, S. (2004) Review of Starostin *et al.* (2003), *Diachronica*, 21: 445–50.

Georg, S. (2005) Reply to Starostin (2005), *Diachronica*, 22: 455–7.

Greenberg, J.H. (1963) *The Languages of Africa*, Bloomington, IN: Indiana University Press.

Greenberg, J.H. (1971) 'The Indo-Pacific hypothesis', in T.A. Sebeok (ed.) *Current Trends in Linguistics*, 8: *Linguistics in Oceania*, pp. 807–71, The Hague: Mouton.

Greenberg, J.H. (1987) *Language in the Americas*, Stanford, CA: Stanford University Press.

Greenberg, J.H. and Ruhlen, M. (1992) 'Linguistic origins of native Americans', *Scientific American* (Nov.): 60–5.

Greenhill, S.J. and Gray, R.D. (2005) 'Testing population dispersal hypotheses: Pacific settlement, phylogenetic trees, and Austronesian languages', in R. Mace, C.J. Holden and S. Shennan (eds) *The Evolution of Cultural Diversity: Phylogenetic Approaches*, pp. 31–52, London: UCL Press.

Ho, S.Y. and Larson, G. (2006) 'Molecular clocks: When times are a-changin'', *Trends in Genetics*, 22: 79–83.

Hurles, M. (2002) 'Can the hypothesis of language/agriculture co-dispersal be tested with archaeogenetics?', in P. Bellwood and C. Renfrew (eds) *Examining the Farming/Language Dispersal Hypothesis*, pp. 299–309, Cambridge: McDonald Institute of Archaeological Research, ch. 23.

Ingman M., Kaessmann, H., Paabo, S. and Gyllensten, U. (2000) 'Mitochondrial genome variation and the origin of modern humans', *Nature*, 408: 708–13.

Janhunen, J. (1994) 'Additional notes on Japanese and Altaic', *Journal de la Société Finno-Ougrienne*, 85: 236–40, 256–60.

Kaessmann, H., Wiebe, V. and Paabo, S. (1999) 'Extensive nuclear DNA sequence diversity among chimpanzees', *Science*, 286: 1159–62.

Martin, S.E. (1991a) 'Morphological clues to the relationships of Japanese and Korean', in P. Baldi (ed.) *Patterns of Change, Change of Patterns: Linguistic Change and Reconstruction Methodology*, pp. 235–62, Berlin: Mouton de Gruyter.

Martin, S.E. (1991b) 'Recent research on the relationships of Japanese and Korean', in S. Lamb (ed.) *Sprung from Some Common Source*, pp. 269–92, Stanford, CA: Stanford University Press.

Mellars P. (2006) 'Going east: New genetic and archaeological perspectives on the modern human colonization of Eurasia', *Science*, 313: 796–800.
Miller, R.A. (1996) *Languages and History: Japanese, Korean and Altaic*, Bangkok: White Orchid Press.
Mountain, J.K., Wang, W.S.-Y., Du, R., Yuan, Y. and Cavalli-Sforza, L.L. (1992) 'Congruence of genetic and linguistic evolution in China', *Journal of Chinese Linguistics*, 20: 315–30.
Nei, M. (1987) *Molecular Evolutionary Genetics*, New York, NY: Columbia University Press.
Nichols, J. (1992) *Linguistic Diversity in Space and Time*, Chicago, IL: University of Chicago Press.
Nichols, J. (1997) 'Modeling ancient population structures and movement in linguistics', *Annual Review of Anthropology*, 26: 359–84.
Nichols, J. (2006) 'The comparative method as heuristic', in M. Durie and M. Ross (eds) *The Comparative Method Reviewed: Irregularity and Regularity in Linguistic Change*, pp. 39–71. New York: Oxford University Press.
Oppenheimer, S.J. (2004) 'The "Express Train from Taiwan to Polynesia"; on the congruence of proxy lines of evidence', *World Archaeology*, 36: 591–600.
Oppenheimer, S.J. and Richards, M. (2001a) 'Slow boat to Melanesia?', *Nature*, 410: 166–7.
Oppenheimer, S.J. and Richards, M. (2001b) 'Fast trains, slow boats, and the ancestry of the Polynesian islanders', *Science Progress*, 84: 157–81.
Oppenheimer, S.J. and Richards, M. (2002) 'Polynesians: Devolved Taiwanese rice farmers or Wallacean maritime traders with fishing, foraging and horticultural skills?', in P. Bellwood and C. Renfrew (eds) *Examining the Farming/Language Dispersal Hypothesis*, pp. 287–97, Cambridge: McDonald Institute of Archaeological Research.
Ostapirat, W. (2005) 'Kra-Dai and Austronesian: Notes on phonological correspondences and vocabulary distribution', in L. Sagart, R. Blench and A. Sanchez-Mazas (eds) *The Peopling of East Asia: Putting Together Archaeology, Linguistics and Genetics*, London: RoutledgeCurzon.
Pawley, A.K. (2002) 'The Austronesian dispersal: Languages, technologies and people', in P. Bellwood and C. Renfrew (eds) *Examining the Farming/Language Dispersal Hypothesis*, Cambridge: McDonald Institute of Archaeological Research.
Pawley, A.K., Attenborough, R., Golson, J. and Hide, R. (eds) (2005) *Papuan Pasts: Cultural, Linguistic and Biological Histories of Papuan-speaking Peoples*, PL 572, Canberra: ANU.
Poloni, E.S., Semino, O., Passarino, G., Santachiara-Benerecetti, A.S., Dupanloup, I., Langaney, A. and Excoffier, L. (1997) 'Human genetic affinities for Y-chromosome P49a,f/TaqI haplotypes show strong correspondence with linguistics', *American Journal of Human Genetics*, 61: 1015–35.
Poppe, N.N. (1965) *Introduction to Altaic linguistics*, Wiesbaden: Otto Harrassowitz.
Reid, L.A. (1999) 'New linguistic evidence for the Austric hypothesis', in E. Zeitoun and P.J. Li (eds) *Selected Papers from the Eighth International Conference on Austronesian Linguistics*, pp. 1–30, Taipei: Institute of Linguistics (Preparatory Office), Academia Sinica.
Reid, LA. (2005) 'The current status of Austric: A review and evaluation of the lexical and morphosyntactic evidence', in L. Sagart, R. Blench and A. Sanchez-Mazas (eds) *The Peopling of East Asia: Putting Together Archaeology, Linguistics and Genetics*, pp. 132–60, London: RoutledgeCurzon.

Renfrew, C., McMahon, A. and Trask, L. (eds) (2000) *Time Depth in Historical Linguistics*, 2 vols, Cambridge: McDonald Institute for Archaeological Research.

Ringe, D.A. (1992) 'On calculating the factor of chance in language comparison', *Transactions of the American Philosophical Society*, 82: 1–110.

Ross, M. (1996) 'Contact-induced change and the comparative method: cases from Papua New Guinea', in M. Durie and M. Ross (eds) *The Comparative Method Reviewed: Regularity and Irregularity in Language Change*, pp. 180–217, New York, NY: Oxford University Press.

Ross, M. and Durie, M. (1996) 'Introduction', in M. Durie and M. Ross (eds) *The Comparative Method Reviewed: Regularity and Irregularity in Language Change*, pp. 3–38, New York, NY: Oxford University Press.

Sagart, L. (2004) 'The higher phylogeny of Austronesian and the position of Tai-Kadai', *Oceanic Linguistics*, 43: 411–44.

Sanchez-Mazas A., Poloni, E.S., Jacques, G. and Sagart, L. (2005) 'HLA genetic diversity and linguistic variation in East Asia', in L. Sagart, R. Blench and A. Sanchez-Mazas (eds) *The Peopling of East Asia: Putting Together Archaeology, Linguistics and Genetics*, pp. 273–96, London and New York, NY: RoutledgeCurzon.

Semino, O., Passarino, G., Oefner, P.J., Lin, A.A., Arbuzova, S., Beckman, L.E., De Benedictis, G., Francalacci, P., Kouvatsi, A., Limborska, S., Marcikiae, M., Mika, A., Mika, B., Primorac, D., Santachiara-Benerecetti, A.S., Cavalli-Sforza, L.L. and Underhill, P.A. (2000) 'The genetic legacy of Paleolithic Homo sapiens sapiens in extant Europeans: a Y chromosome perspective', *Science*, 290: 1155–9.

Serre, D. and Pääbo, S. (2004) 'Evidence for gradients of human genetic diversity within and among continents', *Genome Research*, 14: 1679–85.

Spriggs, M. (1989) 'The dating of the Island Southeast Asian Neolithic: an attempt at chronometric hygiene and linguistic correlation', *Antiquity*, 63: 587–613.

Starostin, S. (2005) 'Response to Stefan Georg's review of the Etymological Dictionary of the Altaic Languages', *Diachronica*, 22: 451–4.

Starostin, S.A., Dybo, A. and Mudrak, O. (2003) *Etymological Dictionary of the Altaic Languages*, 3 vols, Leiden: Brill.

Stauffer, R.L., Walker, A., Ryder, O.A., Lyons-Weiler, M. and Hedges, S.B. (2001) 'Human and ape molecular clocks and constraints on paleontological hypotheses', *Journal of Heredity*, 92: 469–74.

Swadesh, M. (1952) 'Lexicostatistic dating of prehistoric ethnic contacts', *Proceedings of the American Philosophical Society*, 96: 453–62.

Thurgood, G. and LaPolla, R.J. (eds) (2003) *The Sino-Tibetan Languages*. London and New York, NY: Routledge.

Thurgood, G. and Li, F. (2003) 'Contact induced variation and syntactic change in the Tsat of Hainan', in D. Bradley, R. LaPolla, B. Michailovsky and G. Thurgood (eds) *Language Variation: Papers on Variation and Change in the Sinosphere and in the Indosphere in honour of James A. Matisoff*, Canberra: Pacific Linguistics.

Turner, R.L. (1966) *A Comparative Dictionary of the Indo-Aryan Languages*, London: Oxford University Press.

Underhill, P.A., Shen, P., Lin, A.A., Jin, L., Passarino, G., Yang, W.H., Kauffman, E., Bonne-Tamir, B., Bertranpetit, J., Francalacci, P., Ibrahim, M., Jenkins, T., Kidd, J.R., Mehdi, S.Q., Seielstad, M.T., Wells, R.S., Piazza, A., Davis, R.W., Feldman, M.W., Cavalli-Sforza, L.L. and Oefner, P.J. (2000) 'Y chromosome sequence variation and the history of human populations', *Nature Genetics*, 26: 358–61.

Whitman, J.B. (1985) 'The phonological basis for the comparison of Japanese and Korean', Ph.D. dissertation, Harvard University.
Yu, N., Fu, Y.X. and Li, W.H. (2002) 'DNA polymorphism in a worldwide sample of human X chromosomes', *Molecular Biology and Evolution*, 19: 2131–41.

Part I
Archaeology and prehistory

1 Austronesian cultural origins

Out of Taiwan, via the Batanes Islands, and onwards to Western Polynesia

Peter Bellwood and Eusebio Dizon

The 'Express Train' and 'Out of Taiwan' models for Austronesian origins

In 1988, Jared Diamond wrote a much-quoted article in which he compared the Austronesian dispersal from South-east Asia into Oceania to the rapid movement of an express train (Diamond 1988). This view was based on archaeological evidence, and Diamond did not specify a particular homeland for the Austronesians. He noted that any suggestion of China or Taiwan could, at that time, only be speculative. Since 1988, a large literature has arisen in which the chronological concept of an 'express train' has somehow become conflated with the geographical concept of an Austronesian homeland in Taiwan. This circumstance, for which Diamond cannot be blamed, has led to a situation of confusion. The term 'Express Train' should now be dropped from the Austronesian debate. The hypothesis that we espouse is better termed the 'Out of Taiwan hypothesis for Austronesian dispersal' (Bellwood and Dizon 2005).

We know today that the Austronesian dispersal *in its totality* was not really an express train – it required over 3000 years from the Neolithic settlement of Taiwan before settlers reached New Zealand (Map 1.1). Certainly, Austronesian dispersal involved some very rapid movements, but they were interspersed with long pauses. We agree that Diamond's metaphor was a useful one that has encouraged much productive debate, but the time has come to put the 'Express Train' firmly in its place as a description of the velocity of only one episode of Austronesian dispersal: the Lapita movement through Melanesia into western Polynesia. We need now to focus on the real issue of where Austronesian languages and cultures originated.

From an overall perspective, the only sensible way to understand the genesis of the Austronesian-speaking peoples is multidisciplinary, involving, at the very least, comparative linguistics, archaeology and biological anthropology (Bellwood 1997, 2005). This chapter focuses on the archaeological record of the initial period of Neolithic dispersal from Taiwan into the northern Philippines, about 4000 years ago. This archaeological movement was remarkably similar in its geographical directionality to the linguistic movement that gave rise to the Malayo-Polynesian subgroup, which includes all Austronesian languages spoken outside Taiwan (see

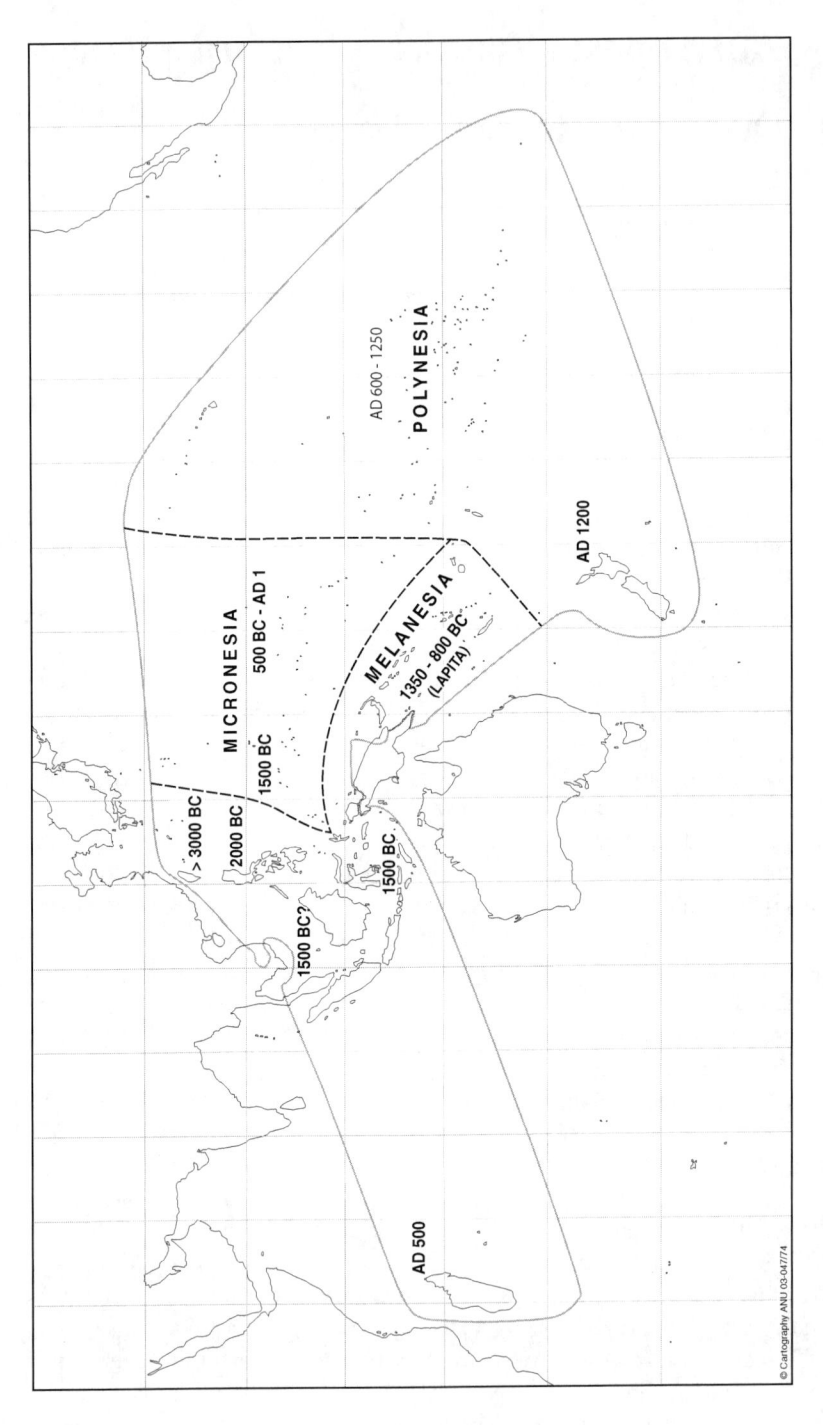

Map 1.1 The distribution of Austronesian languages, together with archaeological dates for the spread of Neolithic cultures. Beyond the Solomon Islands, Austronesian speakers appear to have been the first human populations.

Malcolm Ross, Chapter 6, this volume, also Ross 2005; Blust 1995, 1999; Pawley 2002). This differentiation probably took place a little after the break-up of Proto-Austronesian linguistic unity within Taiwan, and involved population movement from this island towards the south. Thus, Malayo-Polynesian might be a secondary subgroup of one of the several Taiwan primary subgroups, rather than a primary subgroup in its own right, but its significance as a record of Austronesian dispersal during the past 4000 years, more than halfway around the world, is immense.

Linguistically, the Malayo-Polynesian subgroup includes all of the 1000 or so Austronesian languages, apart from the 13 survivors in Formosan Taiwan. Archaeologically, it has been claimed by Bellwood (1997, 2004a) that the late third and second millennium BC distribution of red-slipped pottery and associated Neolithic material culture over a vast region including parts of Taiwan, the Philippines, Sabah, eastern Indonesia, Island Melanesia (Lapita), to as far as western Polynesia (Tonga, Samoa), records one of the major stages in the dispersal of the speakers of Malayo-Polynesian languages. This chapter investigates the archaeological commencement of this dispersal.

New discoveries in Taiwan and Northern Philippine archaeology relevant for Neolithic population dispersal into Indonesia and Oceania

The intention in this chapter is to discuss the new archaeological findings that are coming to light as a result of a major project on Itbayat Island and Batan Island, both in the Batanes Islands, northern Philippines, and to put them in perspective within the total picture of Neolithic spread in Island South-east Asia and Oceania. We also comment on some new archaeological data from Taiwan and the Cagayan Valley of northern Luzon. These new data make a 4000 BP Neolithic movement out of Taiwan into the northern Philippines a virtual certainty.

In south-western Taiwan, discoveries at Nanguanli in the Tainan Science Based Industrial Park take the Taiwan Neolithic (Dabenkeng culture) back to *at least* 3000 BC, with ample evidence of incised, cord-marked and red painted pottery, rice and foxtail millet cultivation (carbonized grains), and pig and dog domestication (Tsang Cheng-hwa 2005). The current date of perhaps 3500 BC for the Neolithic settlement of Taiwan, a little younger than some previous estimates (for instance Bellwood 2000: 350), is nevertheless at least one millennium earlier than any well-dated Neolithic assemblages in Island South-east Asia. Clearly, Neolithic dispersal underwent a pause in Taiwan, perhaps for a thousand years.

Recent research in many regions of Taiwan, especially the southeast, indicates that the cord marked and incised pottery of the Dabenkeng phase had been virtually replaced by plain but red-slipped pottery by 2000 BC, with only lingering quantities of fine cord-marking after this date. This is particularly clear at Chaolaiqiao (c.2200 BC) and other sites along the southeastern coastline of the island (Hung 2005, 2008). It is from this phase, with red-slipped pottery predominating, and a utilization of Taiwan nephrite from the Fengtian source, that the first Malayo-

Polynesian populations left Taiwan for the islands to the south, travelling possibly via the small islands of Ludao and Lanyu off southern Taiwan.

The overall Neolithic radiocarbon chronology for Island South-east Asia, prior to 3000 radiocarbon years ago, has been examined by Matthew Spriggs (2003). Chronological implications are that the Neolithic expansion into the northern Philippines was under way before 2000 BC, and by at least 1500 BC into eastern Indonesia, western Melanesia and the Mariana Islands of Micronesia. The latter movement, across 2000 km of open sea, was perhaps the first long-distance oceanic voyage recorded in human history. In northern Luzon, the possible source region for the movement to the Marianas, the existing Neolithic sequence in the open sites in the Cagayan Valley goes back to about 2000 BC (Hung 2005).

Of course, in talking about archaeological dates for earliest human settlement, there exists the question of how long, in statistical average terms, it will take archaeologists to find the oldest sites in any given area. Common sense dictates that early immigrant populations would have been small. Pioneer archaeologists will not find the oldest sites immediately unless they are extremely lucky, and will often be led astray by spuriously old C^{14} dates from peripheral locations that have been blessed with strong research profiles. An example of this comes from the record of Lapita discovery in western Oceania, with the early claim by biological anthropologist William Howells (1973) that ancestral Polynesians migrated through Micronesia into Fiji and Western Polynesia, avoiding most of Melanesia at first, partly because the C^{14} dates were oldest in Fiji at that time (Howells also, of course, relied on biological evidence to support his views). But now, after several decades of very intensive Lapita research, it has become clear that Lapita began in the far west of Melanesia (Bismarck Archipelago) at about 1350 BC, and only in actuality reached Fiji about 1000 BC or later (Green 2003). Radiocarbon dates can sometimes be misleading in cultural terms.

What of regions like the northern Philippines, where the relevant research is much newer? Have we found the very oldest sites here? Surely, we need to allow a couple of centuries in most South-east Asian regions to allow populations to grow to archaeologically visible sizes, particularly on very large islands such as Luzon, Sulawesi and Borneo. This, combined with the younger dating that has occurred with the increasing density of research on much smaller islands in western Polynesia and Fiji expands the dispersal chronology considerably, moving the dates backwards (older) before 2000 BC for the northern Philippines, but forwards (younger) towards 1000 BC for Fiji and Tonga (Spriggs 2003; Green 2003). This suggests a total time span of about 1000 years for Neolithic spread from Taiwan to western Polynesia, perhaps not quite an express train, although our suspicion from available C^{14} dates is that movement could have been very rapid indeed in some parts of the range. This step-like progression is discussed further below.

The Batanes Islands

The Batanes Islands lie 150 km from the southern tip of Taiwan and 200 km from the north coast of Luzon (Map 1.II). The open sea distance from Lanyu (off south-

Austronesians cultural origins 27

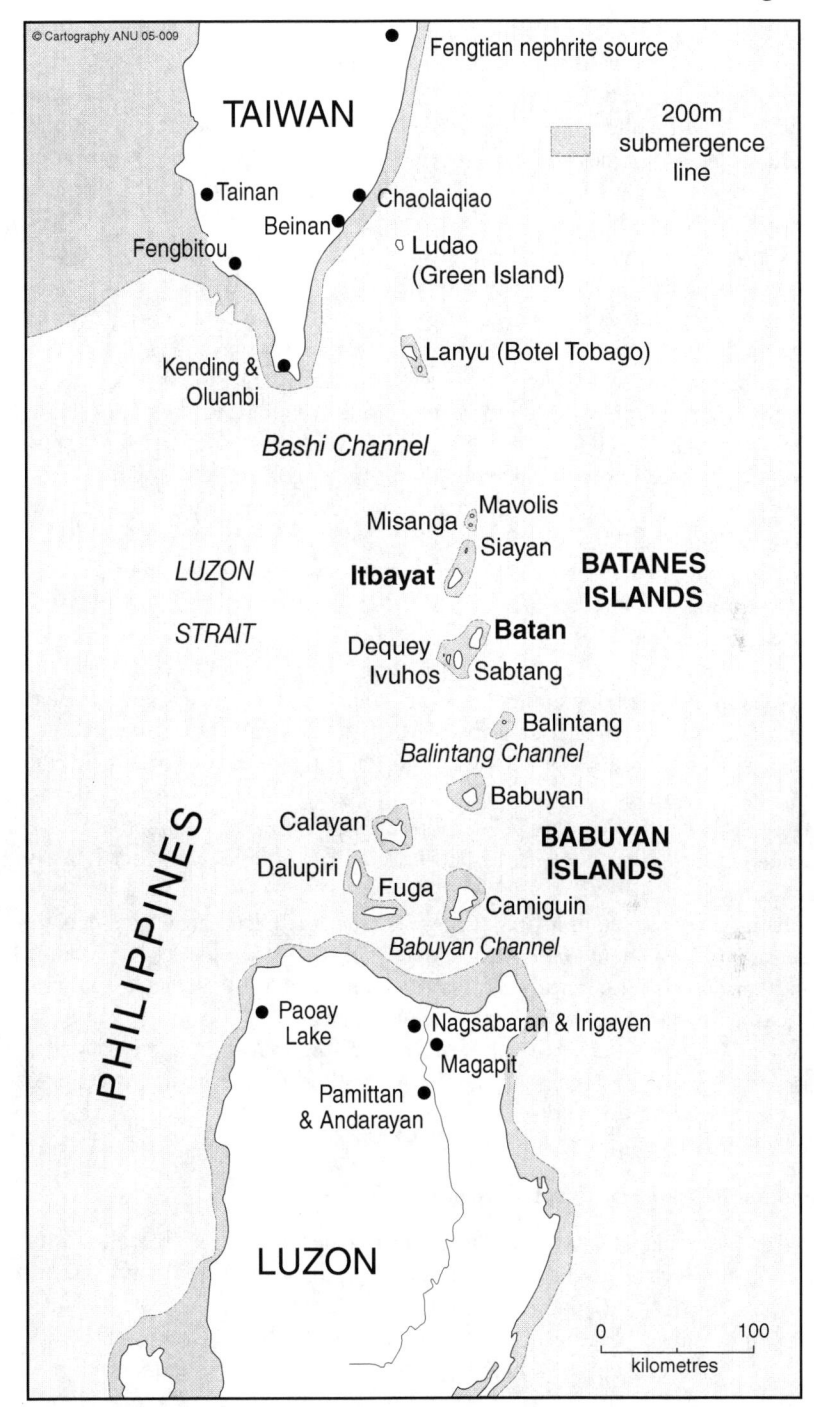

Map 1.II The location of the Batanes Islands between Taiwan and Luzon.

eastern Taiwan) to Mavolis (northern Batanes) is about 100 km, and once this point was reached all other islands of the Batanes would have been intervisible. Since 2002, the two authors have been conducting archaeological research in these islands, with colleagues from the Australian National University, National Museum of the Philippines and the University of the Philippines (Bellwood *et al.* 2003; Bellwood and Dizon 2005).[1] This research has focused mainly on Batan and Itbayat Islands and takes us back to about 2000 BC.

As discussed elsewhere (Bellwood *et al.* 2003: 142), there was never a Pleistocene land bridge from Taiwan to Luzon via the Batanes because the intervening sea passages are too deep. So it comes as no surprise that, during four seasons of archaeological fieldwork in the Batanes, excavations in six caves and rock shelters (amongst other sites) have failed *absolutely* to give any sign of pre-ceramic occupation. All sites are sterile culturally below the lowest potsherds, and the islands have no trace of a pre-ceramic lithic industry. The Batanes were seemingly first settled by Neolithic populations moving from Taiwan with pottery, polished stone and developed maritime technologies, presumably the ancestors of the present Ivatan and Itbayaten populations.

This circumstance means that the Batanes have a very different kind of prehistory from, for instance, Luzon, or other islands in the Philippines and Indonesia where there were Pleistocene populations of hunter-gatherers using flaked lithics. In the Cagayan Valley on Luzon we have an interesting situation of interaction between incoming Neolithic and presumed indigenous hunter-gatherer populations. Archaeology reveals the roots of this interaction, because a hunter-gatherer (presumably ancestral Agta) human presence is attested in the Peñablanca Caves in the Cagayan Valley from at least 25,000 BP (Mijares 2005). In the Batanes, however, Neolithic populations arrived to find an apparently pristine landscape untouched by humans, as did the first Austronesians to enter Remote Oceania several centuries later.

As far as Batanes Neolithic archaeology is concerned, we now have a number of sites dating from about 4000 years ago and onwards, the older ones revealing some rather surprising connections with Taiwan. Because the Batanes cultural sequence has been discussed in some detail elsewhere (Bellwood *et al.* 2003; Bellwood and Dizon 2005), we only refer here to the four most significant sites that illustrate initial settlement from Taiwan, followed by continuing contacts afterwards for almost three millennia.

Torongan and Reranum Caves, Itbayat Island

The oldest assemblages known so far in the Batanes come from the interior of the Torongan sea cave on the east coast of Itbayat, and from Reranum Cave at the northern tip of the island. Torongan is about 100 m long, and was probably of great significance because it allowed access out to the sea from the interior of the island (the coastal cliffs here rise sheer about 80 m above the sea). The archaeological deposit is located about 13 m above the base of the cave, near the top of a high cone of fallen rock and soil piled against the south-western wall of the inland mouth. The basal horizon contained sherds of plain and red-slipped pottery, otherwise undecorated, with everted and slightly concave rims paralleled closely in the site of Chaolaiqiao in south-eastern Taiwan (Figure 1.1). Reranum Cave, only excavated in 2006, has very similar pottery, together with a few fine cord-marked sherds, but we have been unable to get secure dating for this site owing to disturbance. Chaolaiqiao, securely dated by AMS C^{14} to 2200 BC, is a very important discovery because it establishes the presence of this horizon of predominantly red-slipped pottery in eastern Taiwan, here associated with nephrite working, close to the offshore stepping-stone islands of Ludao and Lanyu. It also represents the virtual end of the fine cord-marked pottery tradition in south-eastern Taiwan (Hung 2005, 2008). The assemblage from Nagsabaran in the Cagayan Valley also has similar everted and concave rims to those from Chaolaiqiao (Figure 1.1).

The C^{14} dates on food residues and marine shells from Torongan Cave (Table 1.1) point to a chronology for initial occupation of Itbayat at about *cal.* 2000 BC, although there are younger dates from higher in the profile suggesting that the site was visited over a long period, indeed into the Ming dynasty according to a coin of the emperor Wan Li (AD 1583–1620) found just below the surface. Torongan also has four circle-stamped sherds with white lime or clay infilling amongst the otherwise undecorated plain and red-slipped sherds, similar to the sherds with stamped circles from Sunget and Anaro (below). However, these appear to be relatively late in the Torongan sequence. One specific item from Torongan with Taiwan affinity, found amongst the early pottery, is a waisted stone hoe of igneous or metamorphic rock.

Sunget, Batan Island

The Sunget site behind Mahatao on Batan Island (Site 56 in Koomoto 1983: 55) was discovered as a result of road construction in 1982. Excavations in 2002, 2003 and 2004 have shown that the cultural deposit lies about 10–30 cm below the surface of an old palaeosol, buried by ash from an eruption of Mt Iraya that occurred about 1000 years ago. We have two almost identical AMS dates on food residues inside potsherds that indicate a calibrated date for the assemblage between 1250 and 1000 BC, although charcoal dates also extend into the first millennium BC. The pottery style is quite unified in terms of rim forms and vessel shapes, so major use of the site might have been relatively short-lived, with occupation followed by cultivation of the site, as occurs today.

The Sunget material found by the Kumamoto University team in 1982 relates to assemblages of later Neolithic date in Taiwan, especially the Yuanshan and Beinan cultures of northern and eastern Taiwan (Tsang 2000: 75). The everted concave rims that continue from the older Torongan assemblage also relate to continuing assemblages of stamped and red-slipped pottery in the Cagayan Valley of northern Luzon (e.g. Magapit, Nagsabaran and Irigayen: see Hung 2005). All of these linkages fall generally into the period 1500–1000 BC. The Sunget pottery is mainly red-slipped and includes globular restricted vessels with everted

30 *Peter Bellwood and Eusebio Dizon*

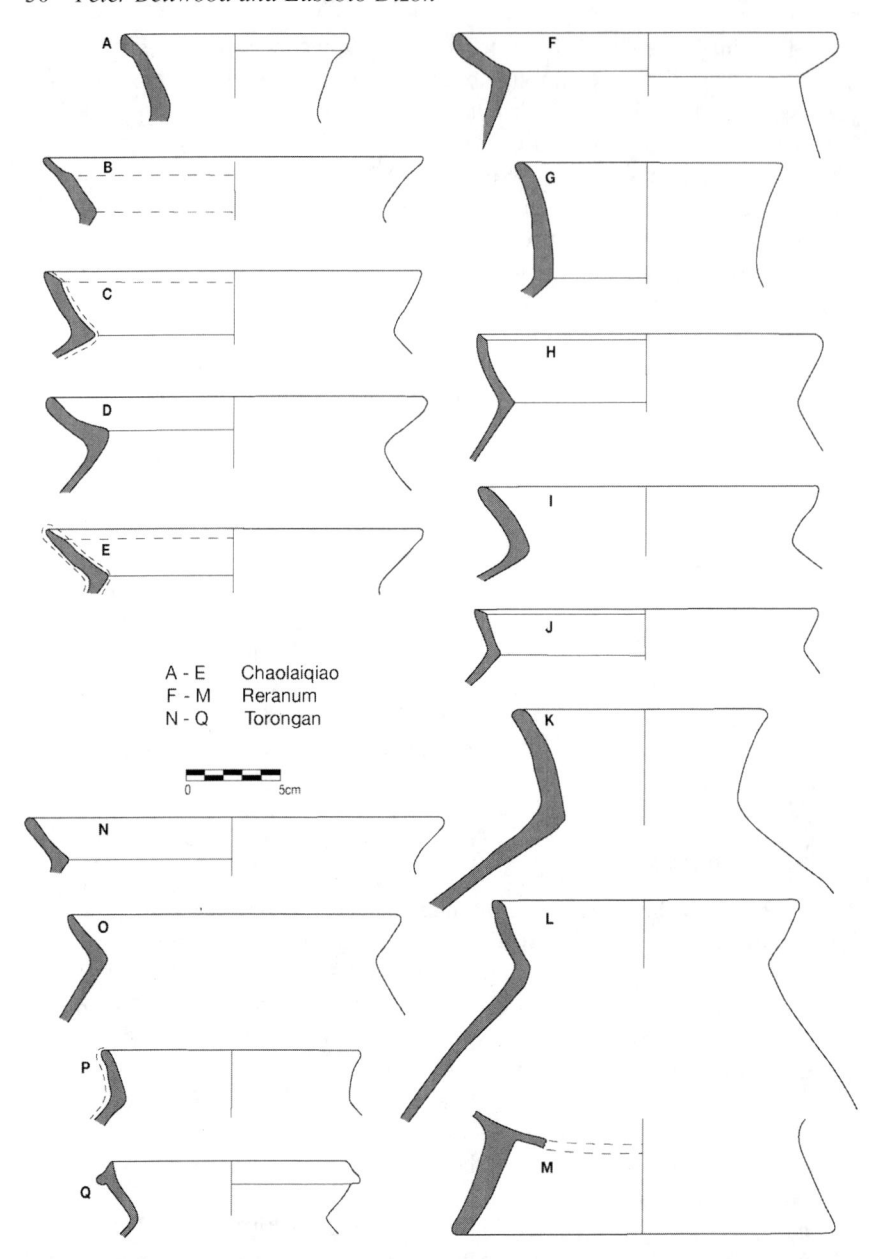

A - E Chaolaiqiao
F - M Reranum
N - Q Torongan

Figure 1.1 Pottery from Torongan and Reranum caves, together with similar pottery from Chaolaiqiao, north of Taidong, southeastern Taiwan (*cal.* 2000 BC); dotted lines indicate red slip.

Table 1.1 Radiocarbon dates older than 1000 BC for assemblages from Itbayat, Batan and Sabtang Islands, 2002 to 2006 fieldwork

LOCATION, SITE	CONTEXT	DATE BP	LAB NO.	OXCAL, 2 SIGMA
ITBAYAT ISLAND	*TORONGAN AND ANARO PHASES*			
Torongan Cave*	Food residue on sherd at 55–60 cm (base of cultural layer)	3860±70	OZH 771	2500–2130 BC
Torongan Cave*	Tectarius shell at 55–60 cm	3880±40	OZH772	2025–1721 BC
Torongan Cave*	Food residue on sherd at 55–60 cm	3320±40	Wk 14642	1690–1510 BC
Torongan Cave*	Turbo shell at 50–55 cm	3352±35	Wk 14641	1384–1095 BC
Torongan Cave*	Thais shell at 45–50 cm	3663±41	Wk 15794	1737–1456 BC
Torongan Cave*	Marine shell at 40–45 cm	3470±50	OZH773	1522–1217 BC
Reranum Cave*	Square A, 25–30 cm, Turbo argyrostomus marine shell	3253±47	Wk 19715	1390–900 BC
Anaro hilltop site*	Area 3, 95–105 cm, food residue on sherd	2770±50	OZH774	1040–810 BC
BATAN and SABTANG ISLANDS	*SUNGET PHASE*			
Sunget Top Terrace*	Layer 5, 15–20 cm within layer, resin coating on sherd exterior	5790±150	OZH776	Not calibrated (fossil resin)
Sunget Top Terrace*	Layer 5, 20–30 cm within layer, food residue in pottery	2910±190	ANU 11817	1700–500 BC
Sunget Main Terrace*	Layer 5, 15–20 cm within layer, food residue in pottery	2915±49	Wk 14640	1270–970 BC
Savidug Jar Burial Site*	Layer 4, 180 cm below surface, charcoal with Sunget style pottery	2828±37	Wk 19711	1120–900 BC

Waikato dates have been calibrated by the laboratory using Oxcal versions 3.8 and 3.10. For the other Batanes dates we have used Calib Rev. 5.0.1, with a delta R for marine shells of 18±34 from coral core data, Xisha Island, Paracel Islands (Fiona Petchey, Waikato C14 Lab., pers. comm. 20/11/06). Asterisked dates are AMS.

tall and unthickened rims (Figures 1.2a–d, f–h), some placed on tall ring feet and provided with vertical handles, together with open bowls with direct rims decorated externally with zones of close-set stamped circles (Plate 1.I), forming what appear to have been rectangular meanders in horizontal bands.

Sunget has also produced two biconical spindle whorls, one decorated with stamped circles, perhaps used to spin strong fibres such as those from the leaves and hard leaf stems of *Musa textilis* (*abaca*, Manila hemp) or ramie (*Boehmeria nivea*) (Judith Cameron personal communication). The biconical morphology links the whorls to many contemporary Neolithic sites in northern and eastern Taiwan. Rare but similar biconical whorls also occur in 2nd millennium BC Cagayan Valley sites such as Andarayan (Cameron 2002).

Other Sunget artefacts include large numbers of notched and flat ovate pebble 'sinkers' of a type also common all over Taiwan from Dabenkeng times onwards; a Fengtian (eastern Taiwan) nephrite adze and a slate projectile point, and a few stone adzes of shouldered and stepped types. However, as noted above, one remarkable virtual absence from Sunget, indeed everywhere in the Batanes, is any evidence for flaked stone tools – presumably chert-like materials were so scarce that the community depended entirely on polished stone. It is also of course likely that these people belonged to a cultural tradition that had long since lost interest in purely flaked stone technology, as in much of Neolithic China and Taiwan. To

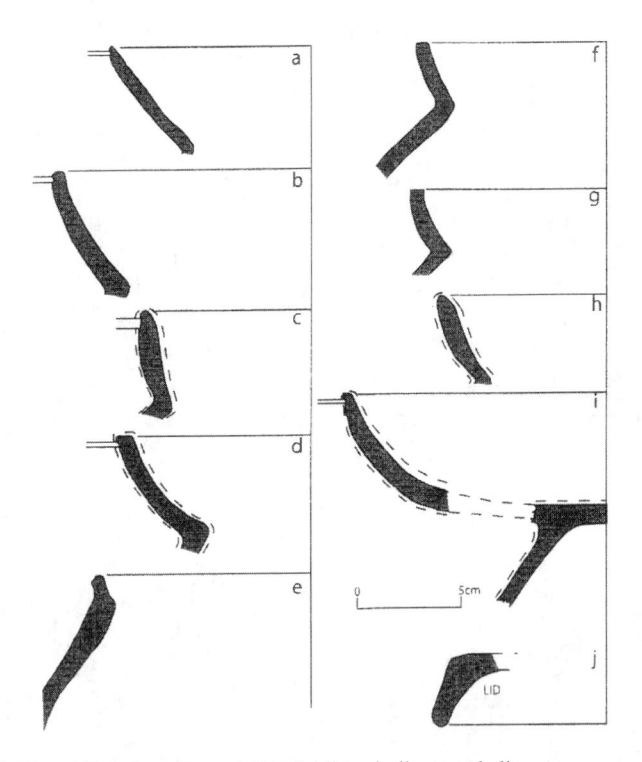

Figure 1.2 Vessel rims from Sunget. Dotted lines indicate red slip.

those accustomed to excavating Neolithic sites in eastern Indonesia or Melanesia this absence of flaked lithics seems strange, and it obviously emphasizes that in the latter areas there was considerable carry-over of indigenous technology into the Neolithic.

Anaro, Itbayat Island

The Anaro site runs on terraces around the summit of the Anaro flat-topped limestone 'mesa', about 200 m long and 20 m wide, left upstanding between a series of surrounding incised valleys. The archaeological deposits have been heavily eroded in some places, and on the lower slopes of the hill a remarkable density of strewn artefacts can be found in a number of fields cleared for cultivation. These surface artefacts include pottery sherds (some with stamped circle patterns like Sunget), many broken adzes of pale grey metamorphic rock (some tanged), stone barkcloth beaters, pottery spindle whorls, pig bones, broken tools of Taiwan slate, and pieces of drilled and cut Fengtian nephrite (Plate 1.II).

Several locations around the top of Anaro have been excavated since 2004, and we now have (including surface finds) a remarkable number of items imported from Taiwan; pieces of Taiwan slate probably used to groove and snap nephrite using quartz sand, nephrite adzes, nephrite discs and an array of shaped nephrite debitage that appears to represent a full reduction sequence for the manufacture of the *lingling-o* type of jade earring with three circumferential projections (Bellwood and Dizon 2005; Hung 2005: figure 8). All of the nephrite analysed so far from Anaro has been sourced to the Fengtian source near Hualien, in eastern Taiwan (Iizuka et al. 2005; Hung et al. 2007). The slate and nephrite pieces excavated from the locations termed Anaro 2 and 3 are associated with C^{14} dates which extend from AD 700 back to almost 1000 BC, and further dates are in process.

Much of the Anaro slate and nephrite is of Early Metal Phase (Iron Age) date, and thus not relevant for Neolithic dispersal issues. We do not yet have nephrite or slate items from Torongan, but a small Fengtian nephrite adze and a slate point were found in 1982 at Sunget, presumably dated to *cal*.1000 BC (see Koomoto 1983: figure 25). The basal spit of Anaro 3 also produced an ear pendant of shell of a very precise Beinan type (south-eastern Taiwan), also C^{14} dated to almost 1000 BC. So, there can be little doubt that both slate and nephrite were in circulation in the Batanes by at least 1000 BC, if not before.

The real significance of all the Anaro slate and nephrite is that it demonstrates *direct* contact between the Batanes and Taiwan, perhaps via Ludao and Lanyu, starting by at least 3000 years ago. This observation matters, because artefacts of Taiwan slate have not been found in northern Luzon, and Taiwan nephrite artefacts here are rare. So it is impossible to believe that this nephrite and slate all travelled from Taiwan to Luzon, then back northwards to the Batanes. Both Solheim (1984–5) and Anderson (2005) have suggested that direct sailing from Taiwan to the Batanes would have been very difficult for Neolithic populations, owing to the presence of the north-flowing Kuroshio Current. The Sunget and Anaro nephrite and slate evidence tends to refute this view.

Hung Hsiao-chun (2005, 2008) has also been able to show that artefacts of Taiwan nephrite, such as bracelets and beads, occur in a number of Neolithic sites in Luzon dating back as far as 1800–1500 BC, including Nagsabaran in the Cagayan Valley, sites in Batangas Province, and possibly Dimolit in Isabela. The movement of Taiwan nephrite into the Philippines was thus occurring potentially as early as 2000 BC on a wide scale, and might have continued, expressed in changing artefact fashions, for three millennia. But none of these Luzon sites have anything like the quantity of nephrite found in Anaro, and they lack slate. They do not indicate colonizing movements from Taiwan to the Batanes via Luzon.

From Taiwan to the Batanes

The evidence from Torongan, Reranum and Sunget, dated to between 2,500 and 500 BC at outer limits, makes an eastern Taiwan to the Batanes (and Luzon) north-to-south directionality of the Neolithic colonization process very likely. This evidence includes:

(1) the red-slipped pottery from Torongan and Reranum Caves, dated to *cal.* 2000 BC, which resembles in rim forms the pottery from Chaolaiqiao in south-eastern Taiwan, dated to *cal.* 2200 BC;
(2) the fine cord-marked sherds from Reranum Cave
(3) the Sunget vertical handles, biconical baked clay spindle whorls, notched stone sinkers and the artefacts of slate and Fengtian nephrite, indicating direct contact with Taiwan at about 1000 BC;
(4) the large quantities of Taiwan slate and Fengtian nephrite from Anaro, plus some Anaro stone adzes that appear also to be imports from Taiwan, all dating from 1000 BC onwards;
(5) the bones of domesticated pigs from at least 3000 BP in Sunget (Torongan and Reranum have no preserved animal bone). The Batanes have no evidence for a pre-human wild pig population, and the wild pig of Luzon, *Sus philippensis*, was apparently never domesticated (Groves 1997).

Evidence for contemporary contact with northern Luzon, which was presumably reached by Neolithic settlers from Taiwan at about the same time as the Batanes Islands, includes many of the Anaro stone adzes with trapezoidal cross-sections (some tanged), mostly of pale grey metamorphic rock. These are parallelled closely in some Cagayan Valley sites with red-slipped pottery, such as Irigayen. Also of non-Taiwan origin may be the habit of decorating pottery with zones of stamped circles (from Sunget and Anaro onwards, but apparently not yet innovated in the basal layer at Torongan). Indeed, one wonders if this Batanes circle stamping formed the background to the development of both circle and dentate stamping in the Neolithic of the Cagayan Valley, and ultimately to the early Marianas and Lapita dentate- and circle-stamping traditions. At present, the chronology is not tight enough to resolve this issue, and it is, of course, quite possible that innovations flowed back as frontiers extended, as in the case of the Talasea obsidian from New Britain found in the early red-slipped pottery assemblage at Bukit Tengkorak in Sabah (Bellwood and Koon 1989). However, derivation of the whole Neolithic complex present in the Batanes and Cagayan *from the south* is to our minds completely impossible. We now have enough C^{14} dates from the Batanes and Cagayan, detailed in Table 1.1, to give this region an edge of at least 500 years over the beginning of the Lapita sequence in western Melanesia.

The movement of population from eastern Taiwan into the northern Philippines, probably between 2500 and 2000 BC on present evidence (Hung 2005), formed the first stage in an astounding spread of a Neolithic population that reached western Polynesia by only a millennium or so later, traversing a maritime distance of almost 10,000 km (Bellwood 1997, 2004a, 2004b, 2005). Until now, it has been possible to argue *in vacuo* that many Austronesian-speaking populations, such as Polynesians, could not have originated in Taiwan because there is no relevant archaeological record in support (Oppenheimer 2004; Oppenheimer and Richards 2001). Such arguments can only be made if one ignores the linguistic and archaeological records altogether, or makes the historically unsupportable assumption that the Austronesian languages spread as 'trade languages', without native speaker transmission (see Malcolm Ross's chapter in this volume for a firm statement against this possibility). Clearly, it is true that not all Austronesian-speaking populations originated *genetically* in Taiwan – no one would make this claim, for instance, for many eastern Indonesian or Melanesian populations, or even for the Agta of northern Luzon. But to extend this argument to the languages and material cultures of Austronesian prehistory and to deny Taiwan's role in their origins, as done by Oppenheimer (2004), is completely counter-productive. Indeed, Oppenheimer's only genetic weapon, his assumption based on mtDNA molecular clock calculations that Polynesians are derived from Palaeolithic eastern Indonesians, is now under very strong attack (Cox 2005; Trejaut *et al.* 2005; Pierson *et al.* 2006; Penny 2005). The relationships between the archaeological and linguistic data pertinent to Malayo-Polynesian dispersal are not the results of circular reasoning, as Oppenheimer (2004) asserts, but of the independent analytical strengths of the relevant databases and the determination of other scholars to take these databases into account.

The timing of Neolithic spread: southern China to Taiwan, then to Polynesia

In actuality, Diamond's Express Train metaphor fits well when applied to a part of the Austronesian dispersal, especially the region from eastern Taiwan, through the Philippines and eastern Indonesia, into the western part of Polynesia (Tonga and Samoa). It fits the archaeological and linguistic records, which are unanimous in reflecting rapid dispersal in some regions, as for instance the route from Sulawesi through the Moluccas into Island Melanesia. This dispersal appears to have taken place in under a millennium.

In his 1997 book, Bellwood reconstructed the chronology of Austronesian dispersal from Taiwan into the western Pacific as follows:

> During the late fifth or fourth millennium BC colonists from the mainland of southern China (probably Zhejiang or Fujian) settled Taiwan ... During the third millennium BC colonists moved into Luzon, and the Malayo-Polynesian subgroup now began its separation from the other primary subgroups of Austronesian which remained on Taiwan ... By at least 2000 BC Proto-Malayo-Polynesian began to break up, probably with settlement expanding in various directions into the southern Philippines, Borneo, Sulawesi and the Moluccas.
>
> (Bellwood 1997: 241–2)

Since the above was written, many new excavations have been carried out in Taiwan and the northern Philippines, reinforcing this general pattern very strongly. Matthew Spriggs updated the C^{14} evidence in 2003 to suggest Neolithic settlement of Taiwan between 3500 and 3000 BC, followed by movement to the Philippines about 2000 BC, to Talaud and Sulawesi by 1600 BC, and to the Moluccas and East Timor by 1500 BC. According to Spriggs (2003), the beginnings of Lapita in the Bismarcks occurred between 1500 and 1350 BC, and reached the Solomons by 1050 BC. Western Polynesia appears to have been reached by 1000–800 BC.

In 2004, Bellwood published a graph to illustrate just such a chronology (Bellwood 2004b: figure 3.2), and this is reproduced here as Figure 1.3. No attempt is made to 'smooth' this graph by imposing a curve over the points, and it is intended to illustrate what in reality could have been a very step-like progression of human colonization, with periods of relative stasis interspersed with periods

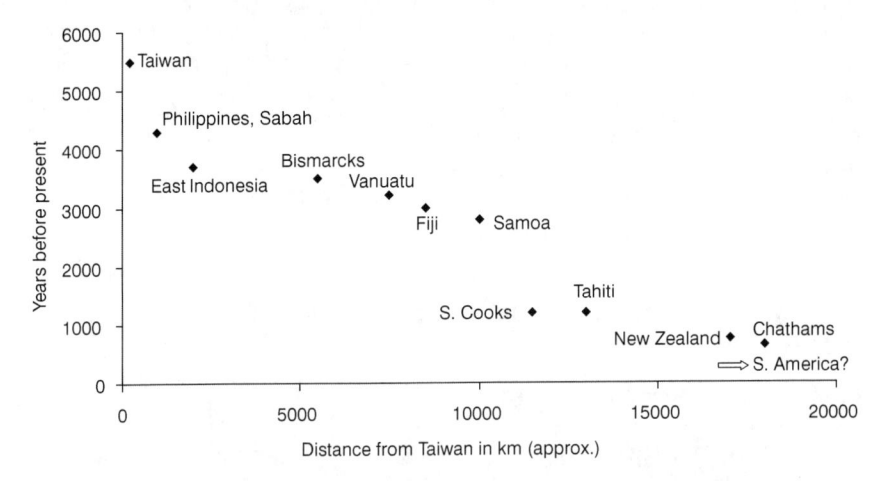

Figure 1.3 A graph to show Austronesian dispersal distance (in thousands of km) out of Taiwan, versus C14 dates for initial settlement (Reproduced from Bellwood 2004b, with permission from the McDonald Institute for Archaeological Research, Cambridge).

of rapid and far-flung movement. We can see that two periods of relative stasis occurred: in Taiwan between 3500 and 2500/2000 BC, and in western Polynesia between 800 BC and about AD 600. In between, rapid moves occurred from the Philippines to the Bismarcks between about 2000 and 1350 BC, and on to Samoa by 800 BC. Later on, movement occurred from western Polynesia through the whole of eastern Polynesia between AD 600 and 1250 (this progression is also detailed in Map 1.I).

Bellwood (2005: 276) has recently summarized the Neolithic movement from the Philippines to Samoa as occurring over a period of 1000 years, between approximately 1800 and 800 BC, involving an average spread rate of 8.5 km per year, obviously mostly over water and hence very fast in world terms. That book was written before the new dates were acquired from the Batanes, and if the settlement of the Batanes is pushed back beyond 2000 BC, the rate of spread correspondingly slows down a little over the total haul. But the movement from Sulawesi to the Bismarcks, about 3500 km, could on present evidence have taken place within a couple of centuries, between 1500 and 1300 BC, and this gives a very rapid rate indeed: 18 km per year on average.

Demic diffusion as a process of population movement has been out of fashion amongst archaeologists for a long time now. In the Austronesian arena we need to bring it back, in moderation, as a process that postulates periodic increases and movements of population reflecting technological, economic or social stimuli, combined with continuous population admixture along an expanding migration front (as discussed clearly by Cavalli-Sforza 2002 and in modified form by Renfrew 2002). As postulated by Cavalli-Sforza, demic diffusion theory should apply very well to tribal, Neolithic, illiterate, pre-bureaucratic and pre-globalized populations undergoing demographic increase in a situation of finite resources in their home territories. The rate of expansion of Neolithic cultures discussed above can be equated reasonably with a process of demic diffusion: generation by generation population increase, combined with movements that were sometimes slow, sometimes saltatory as people jumped water gaps. Were the Austronesian/Neolithic expansion to have been the result of no more than mere trade or 'cultural diffusion', without movement of people, then we might expect the process to have been far quicker – Taiwan to Tonga in a few centuries perhaps, rather than a millennium. But, of course, it did not happen that way.

Acknowledgements

This research has been funded by the National Geographic Society, the Australian Research Council, and the Australian Institute for Nuclear Sciences and Engineering. The Batanes Islands research is supported by the National Museum of the Philippines and by the Archaeological Studies Program in the University of the Philippines.

References

Anderson, A. (2005) 'The archaeological chronology of the Batanes Islands, Philippines, and the regional sequence of Neolithic dispersal', *Journal of Austronesian Studies*, 1(2): 25–45.

Bellwood, P. (1997) *Prehistory of the Indo-Malaysian Archipelago* (2nd edn), Honolulu, HI: University of Hawaii Press.

Bellwood, P. (2000) 'Formosan prehistory and Austronesian dispersal', in D. Blundell (ed.) *Austronesian Taiwan*, pp. 337–65, Berkeley, CA: Phoebe A. Hearst Museum of Anthropology.

Bellwood, P. (2004a) 'The origins and dispersals of agricultural communities in Southeast Asia', in I. Glover and P. Bellwood (eds) *Southeast Asia: From Prehistory to History*, pp. 21–40, London: RoutledgeCurzon.

Bellwood, P. (2004b) 'Colin Renfrew's emerging synthesis', in M. Jones (ed.) *Traces of Ancestry*, pp. 31–9, Cambridge: McDonald Institute.

Bellwood, P. (2005) *First Farmers: The Origins of Agricultural Societies*, Oxford: Blackwell.

Bellwood, P. and Dizon, E. (2005) 'The Batanes archaeological project and the "Out of Taiwan" hypothesis for Austronesian dispersal', *Journal of Austronesian Studies* (Taitung, Taiwan), 1(1): 1–33.

Bellwood, P. and Koon, P. (1989) '"Lapita colonists leave boats unburned!" The question of Lapita links with Island Southeast Asia', *Antiquity*, 63: 613–22.

Bellwood, P., Stevenson, J., Anderson, A. and Dizon, E. (2003) 'Archaeological and palaeoenvironmental research in Batanes and Ilocos Norte Provinces, northern Philippines', *Bulletin of the Indo-Pacific Prehistory Association*, 23: 141–61.

Blust, R. (1995) 'The prehistory of the Austronesian-speaking peoples', *Journal of World Prehistory*, 9: 453–510.

Blust, R. (1999) 'Subgrouping, circularity and extinction: some issues in Austronesian comparative linguistics', in E. Zeitoun and P.J.-K. Li (eds) *Selected Papers from the 8th International Conference on Austronesian Linguistics*, pp. 31–94, Taipei: Institute of Linguistics, Academia Sinica.

Cameron, J. (2002) 'Textile technology and Austronesian dispersals', in G. Clark, A. Anderson and T. Vunidilo (eds) *The Archaeology of Lapita Dispersal in Oceania*, pp. 177–81, Canberra: Pandanus Books.

Cavalli-Sforza, L.L. (2002) 'Demic diffusion as the basic process of human expansions', in P. Bellwood and C. Renfrew (eds) *Examining the Farming/Language Dispersal Hypothesis*, pp. 79–88, Cambridge: McDonald Institute for Archaeological Research.

Cox, M. (2005) 'Indonesian mitochondrial DNA and its opposition to a Pleistocene-era origin of Proto-Polynesians in Island Southeast Asia', *Human Biology*, 77: 179–88.

Diamond, J. (1988) 'Express train to Polynesia', *Nature*, 336: 307–8.

Green, R. (2003) 'The Lapita horizon and traditions: Signature for one set of Oceanic migrations', in C. Sand (ed.) *Pacific Archaeology: Assessments and Prospects*, pp. 95–120, Nouméa: Cahiers de l'Archéologie en Nouvelle-Calédonie, 15.

Groves, Colin (1997) 'Taxonomy of wild pigs (*Sus*) of the Philippines', *Zoological Journal of the Linnaean Society of London*, 120: 163–91.

Howells, W.W. (1973) *The Pacific Islanders*, New York: Scribner's Sons.

Hung, H.-C. (2005) 'Neolithic interaction between Taiwan and northern Luzon', *Journal of Austronesian Studies* (Taitung, Taiwan), 1(1): 109–33.

Hung, H.-C. (2008) 'Migration and Cultural Interaction in Southern Coastal China, Taiwan and the Northern Philippines, 3000 BC to AD 1: The Early History of the Austronesian-speaking Populations'. Unpublished PhD thesis, Australian National University.

Hung, H.-C., Iizuka, Y. and Santiago, R. (2004) 'Lost treasure from beyond the sea: A prehistoric jade bell-shaped bead excavated from the Philippines', *The National Palace Museum Research Quarterly*, 21: 43–56 (in Chinese with English abstract).

Hung, H.-C., Iizuka, Y., Bellwood, P., Nguyen Kim Dung, Bellina, B., Silapanth, P., Dizon, E., Santiago, R., Datan, I. and Manton, J. (2007) 'Ancient jades map 3000 years of prehistoric exchange in Southeast Asia'.*Proceedings of the National Academy of Sciences* (USA) 104: 19745-50

Iizuka, Y., Bellwood, P., Hung, H.-C. and Dizon, E. (2005) 'A non-destructive mineralogical study of nephritic artefacts from Itbayat Island, Batanes, northern Philippines', *Journal of Austronesian Studies* (Taitung, Taiwan), 1(1): 83–108.

Koomoto, M. (1983) 'General survey in Batan Island', in University of Kumamoto, *Batan Island and Northern Luzon*, pp. 17–68, Japan: University of Kumamoto, Faculty of Letters.

Mijares, A. (2005) 'The archaeology of Peñablanca Cave sites, northern Luzon, Philippines', *Journal of Austronesian Studies* (Taitung, Taiwan), 1(2): 65–93.

Oppenheimer, S. (2004) 'The "Express Train from Taiwan to Polynesia"; on the congruence of proxy lines of evidence', *World Archaeology*, 36: 591–600.

Oppenheimer, S. and Richards, M. (2001) 'Fast trains, slow boats, and the ancestry of the Polynesian islanders', *Science Progress*, 84: 157–81.

Pawley, A. (2002) 'The Austronesian dispersal: Languages, technologies and people', in P. Bellwood and C. Renfrew (eds) *Examining the Farming/Language Dispersal Hypothesis*, pp. 251–74, Cambridge: McDonald Institute for Archaeological Research.

Penny, D. (2005) 'Relativity for molecular clocks', *Nature*, 436: 183–4.

Pierson, M., Martinez-Arias, R., Holland, B., Gemmell, N., Hurles, M. and Penny, D. (2006) 'Deciphering past human population movements in Oceania: provably optimal trees of 127 mtDNA genomes', *Molecular Biology and Evolution*, 23: 1966–75.

Renfrew, C. (2002) '"The emerging synthesis": The archaeogenetics of language/farming dispersals and other spread zones', in P. Bellwood and C. Renfrew (eds) *Examining the Farming/Language Dispersal Hypothesis*, pp. 3–16, Cambridge: McDonald Institute for Archaeological Research.

Ross, M. (2005) 'The Batanic languages in relation to the early history of the Malayo-Polynesian subgroup of Austronesian', *Journal of Austronesian Studies* (Taitung, Taiwan), 1(2): 1–24.

Solheim, W.G. II (1984–5) 'The Nusantao Hypothesis', *Asian Perspectives*, 26: 77–88.

Spriggs, M. (2003) 'Chronology of the Neolithic transition in Island Southeast Asia and the western Pacific', *Review of Archaeology*, 24(2): 57–80.

Trejaut, J., Kivisild, T., Loo, J.-H., Lee, C.-L., Hsu, C.-J., Li, Z.-Y. and Lin, M. (2005) 'Traces of archaic mitochondrial lineages persist in Austronesian-speaking Formosan populations', *Public Library of Science (PLoS) Biology* 3(8): e247.

Tsang Cheng-hwa (2000) *The Archaeology of Taiwan*, Taipei: Council for Cultural Affairs, Executive Yuan.

Tsang, C-H. (2005) 'Recent discoveries at a Tapenkeng culture site in Taiwan: implications for the problem of Austronesian origins', in L. Sagart, R. Blench and A. Sanchez-Mazas (eds) *The Peopling of East Asia*, pp. 63–73, London: RoutledgeCurzon.

2 Evidence for a late onset of agriculture in the Lower Yangtze region and challenges for an archaeobotany of rice

Dorian Q. Fuller, Ling Qin, and Emma Harvey

Introduction

The origin of agriculture represents a particularly important transition in human prehistory. By producing food through cultivating plants, and to a lesser degree by herding animals, it became possible to store surpluses which could support larger settled populations (sedentism and increased population density), and specialist occupations (non-food producers). Agriculture created the potential for much greater rates of population increase. The demographic differentiation between the idealized early farmer and hunter-gatherer has been a fundamental assumption for many powerful models of prehistoric population change, genetic change and language spread (e.g. Bellwood 2005). Within this context, rice agriculture is usually considered to be an essential factor underlying the Holocene migrations that are supposed to have created cultural geography of much of China as well as Southeast Asia (e.g. Bellwood 2005; Higham 2003). The hard evidence for the timing, geography and evolutionary processes involved in the establishment of rice agriculture is, however, rather limited and ambiguous. Such evidence will be crucial to any story of agricultural origins and dispersal in East Asia. This chapter considers an alternative hypothesis, the late domestication of rice, which sees much of the evidence for early rice as reflecting foraging and a long period of incipient cultivation of still wild plants.

Below we summarize and critically assess the evidence from plant remains, storage features, and tools relating to the plant economy at Hemudu and Kuahuqiao, based on the final monographs published in Chinese (Zhejiang Provincial Institute 2003; 2004), with comments on available comparative data from other sites in China. The hard evidence indicates an economy based heavily on the seasonal collection and storage of nuts, especially acorns, and calls into question textbook descriptions of well-developed rice agriculture. We will focus on the evidence relating to rice at these sites and consider how an understanding of rice evolution under cultivation towards non-shattering, larger-grained and more even-ripening morphotypes requires new analytical approaches to archaeological rice remains. The evidence suggests morphologically wild rice under incipient cultivation through the Hemudu/Majiabang period (5000–4000 BC). This is then situated within a longer-term regional sequence from the Kuahuqiao through the Liangzhu period (6000–2200 BC), where the evolution of clearly domesticated rice forms and the development of field systems and tillage indicates a rapid but late development of intensive rice agriculture, alongside animal husbandry, craft production and fiber crop cultivation. It remains possible that some parts of the Middle Yangtze valley had earlier, but separate, trajectories leading to domesticated rice, although our review also argues for reassessing claims in this region. This case study raises questions that remain to be addressed through new research, including systematic archaeobotany and quantitative morphometrics.

Recent discussions on rice domestication

Increasing interest in the origins of agriculture in East Asia has drawn particular attention to the Yangtze basin region as one area of probable rice domestication (Map 2.I). In particular, the site of Bashidang (Pengtoushan culture) on the Lishui river (Hunan Province) and Chengbeixi on the middle Yangtze river (Hubei Province) provide some of the earliest dated rice grain assemblages from the sites of settled village communities by 6500–6000 BC (Pei 1998; Crawford and Shen 1998; Lu 1999; Crawford 2005; Higham 2005; Bellwood 2005). An important later assemblage comes from Chengtoushan, Daxi culture, from c.4500 BC (Pei 1998; Zhang and Wang 1998; Nasu et al. 2006). An earlier process of rice domestication is attributed to presumably seasonal cave sites south of the Yangtze, although the evidence consists of a few finds of rice grains, and a statistical change in phytoliths through time at the Poyang Lake area cave sites, Diaotonghuan and Xianrendong (Zhao 1998; see reviews by Lu 1999: 93–7 and 2006; Yan 2002; Yasuda 2002; Higham 2005; Crawford 2005). These limited data have been assembled in theoretical models that compare the process of agricultural origins in South China to that in the better documented Near East, including timing and causation related to the Younger Dryas and terminal Pleistocene climate change (Cohen 1998; Harris 2005; Yasuda 2002; Yasuda and Negendank 2003; Higham 2005: 235). The implicit assumption is that plant cultivation must precede animal domestication. No attempt has been made to identify a series of progressive subsistence system changes equivalent to that in the Near East in which pre-domestication cultivation has been identified (Hillman 2000; Hillman et al. 2001; Colledge 1998, 2001; Willcox 1999, 2002). Such an evolutionary sequence can be hypothesized for the Lower Yangtze, and probably elsewhere.

Unfortunately, the hard evidence for a transition from wild plant gathering to cultivation remains exiguous. The contrast with the large bodies of data in regions like Southwest Asia (e.g. Colledge 2001; Willcox 2002, 2004, 2005; Bar-Yosef 2003) or North America (e.g. Smith 1992; Brownman et al. 2005) is stark. As the review by Crawford (2005) emphasizes, systematic, problem-oriented archaeobotanical research into agricultural origins is relatively new in Chinese archaeology. Indeed, the first clear exposition of archaeobotanical field sampling methodology (flotation) in Chinese is quite recent (Zhao, Z. 2004). Other recent articles have addressed identification criteria (Liu, C. 2004; Crawford and Lee

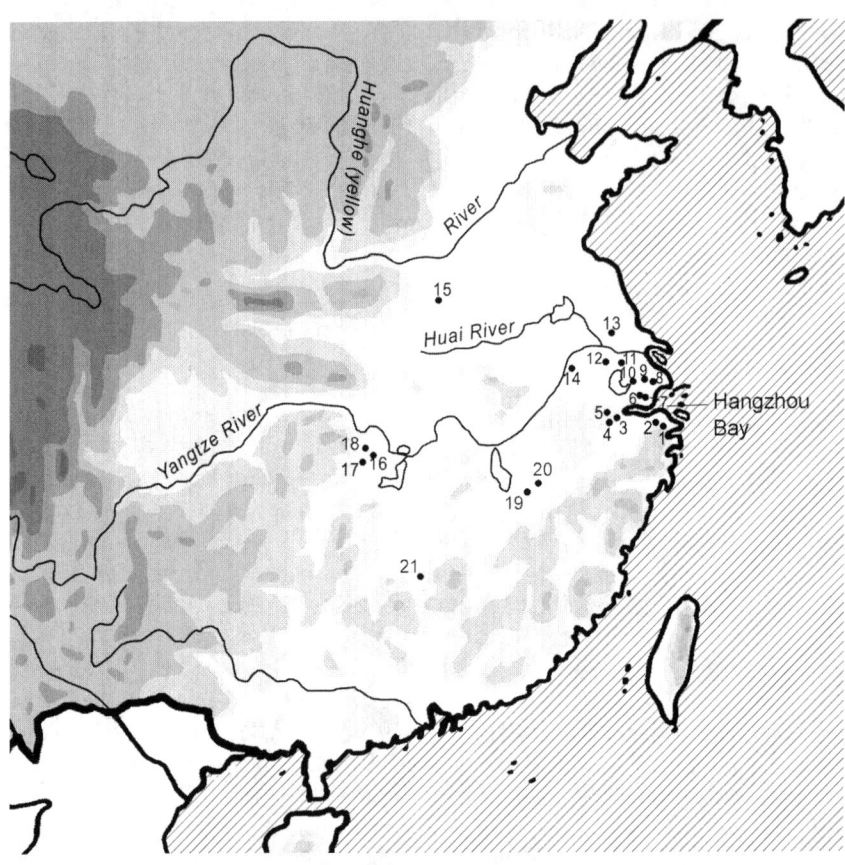

Map 2.1 Map of the Middle and Lower Yangtze showing archaeological sites mentioned in text: 1. Hemudu 河姆渡; 2. Tianluoshan 田螺山; 3. Kuahuqiao 跨湖桥; 4. Shangshan 上山; 5. Liangzhu 良渚; 6. Majiabang 马家浜; 7. Nanhebang 南河浜; 8. Maqiao 马桥; 9. Songze 崧泽; 10. Longnan 龙南, Caoxieshan 草鞋山, and Chuodun 绰墩; 11. Weidun 圩墩; 12. Sanxingcun 三星村; 13. Longqiuzhuang 龙虬庄; 14. Lingjiatan 凌家滩; 15. Jiahu 贾湖; 16. Bashidang 八十挡; 17. Pengtoushan 彭头山; 18. Chengtoushan 城头山; 19. Diaotonghuan 吊桶环; 20. Xianrendong 仙人洞; 21. Yuchanyan 玉蟾岩

2003; Nasu *et al.* 2006), and the potential contributions of archaeobotany to cultural history (Zhao, Z. 2001; Crawford *et al.* 2005).

In the present chapter, we draw attention to the need for greater sophistication in producing detailed models for pathways towards plant domestication and for the systematic collection and study of archaeobotanical data. We do this through a reassessment of the evidence for early rice exploitation and supposed agriculture in the Lower Yangtze region, with some comments on adjacent regions. Evidence from the final report on the well-known site of Hemudu (Zhejiang Provincial Institute 2003) is reconsidered together with Kuahuqiao site (Zhejiang Provincial

Institute 2004), both in northern Zhejiang province near the southern margin of Yangtze river delta. The first occupation at the site of Hemudu (layer 4) dates from *c*. 5000–4900 BC, with the main village occupation ceasing by *cal*. 4600 BC. Subsequent use is indicated by a few storage pits for nuts from 4400–4000 BC (layer 3B). These earlier layers define Hemudu culture, which is roughly contemporary with the early Majiabang culture north of Hangzhou Bay. After 4000 BC, the site has yielded Songze period burials and a well (layer 2). Meanwhile Kuahuqiao has dates that fall between 6000 BC and 5400 BC (based on the authors' calibration of the radiocarbon data in the final reports). While the time span of these two sites is considerably later than the dates for the beginnings of agriculture now widely accepted for the Middle Yangtze region, these sites illustrate some of the challenges in studying early rice cultivation and the pitfalls in the assumption that rice grain finds imply rice agriculture, and dependence on rice.

Situating Chinese rice: evolutionary biology and geography

Chinese botanical scholarship has a long history of studying rice, although new insights into its origins have come from genetic studies in the last decade. Variation between cultivated forms and within wild populations has been important, both

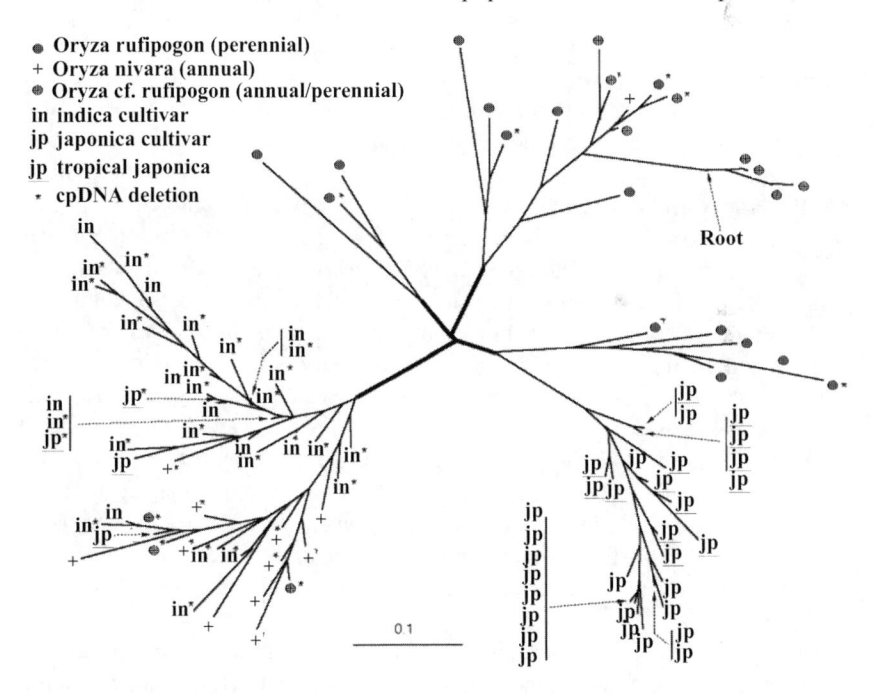

Figure 2.1 A phylogenetic representation of modern rice cultivars and wild populations based on SINE genetics (after Cheng *et al*. 2003; taxonomy revised to follow Vaughan 1994). This shows the clearly distinct lineages of *japonica* (including tropical forms, sometimes called *javanica*) and indica cultivars, which are interspersed with the annual wild populations (*Oryza nivara*).

for modern rice improvement programs and for providing insights into the origins of rice (Wang *et al.* 1999; Vaughan *et al.* 2003). Genetic findings in recent years have overturned the widely held presumption of a single Chinese origin for rice. There now is substantial evidence for genetic distinctions between *indica* and *japonica* from a range of data (Sato *et al.* 1990; Sano and Morishima 1992; Chen *et al.* 1993; Sato 2002; Cheng *et al.* 2003; Vaughan *et al.* 2003; Li *et al.* 2004; Londo *et al.* 2006). Most significant is genetic evidence from the chloroplast and nuclear DNA variants called SINEs. A sequence deletion in the chloroplast DNA of *indica* cultivars links them with wild annual '*O. rufipogon*' (i.e. *O. nivara* in modern taxonomy) (Chen *et al.* 1993; Cheng *et al.* 2003; for current rice taxonomy see Vaughan 1989, 1994). Meanwhile, there are some seven SINEs that separate the *nivara-indica* group from the *rufipogon-japonica* (see Figure 2.1; based on Cheng *et al.* 2003). These genetic data, together with biogeography, argue that rice in China was domesticated from perennial wild plants that grew in wetland environments, in contrast to the annual monsoonal rainwater wild rice domesticated in India (Map 2.II). The phylogeny of Cheng *et al.* (2003) also put tropical *japonica* cultivars (including long-grained *javanica*) towards the base of the *japonica* phylogeny. We would not expect there to have been an ancient 'intermediate' form of rice, but rather two separate trajectories towards domestic rices in Asia, each with distinct morphological tendencies in grain shape and with differing ecological settings. Ecologically, the fundamental contrast is between the perennial *O. rufipogon* in marshy environments, and the annual *O. nivara* in seasonal monsoon puddles (Sato 2002).

Morphometric data from modern rice populations suggest distinct tendencies in morphological evolution in these two groups. Grain measurements indicate substantial overlap within the *Oryza sativa* 'complex', including *O. rufipogon*, *O. nivara*, cultivars, and *O. spontanea* that results from hybridization between cultivated and wild rices (Figure 2.2). *Oryza sativa* is a spectrum, from short plump *japonica* to long thin *indica*. The domestication process for rice in China should therefore lead evolutionarily from thin *O. rufipogon* towards the short-grained and plump *japonica*, with a possible early offshoot of long-grained *javanica* development. Tropical *indica* rices represent a completely separate evolutionary sequence from shorter, relatively plumper-grained *O. nivara* towards the long and thin-grained *Oryza sativa indica*, although many *indica* populations fall within the range of variation of wild populations. Thus in general there has been more grain morphological evolution in *japonica*, which may be explained in part by the absence of the wild progenitor from most of the core *japonica* range, at least for the past few thousand years, as well as adaptation to more temperate environments.

Another important biogeographic observation is that the actual wild progenitor populations of Yangtze rice domestication(s) are today extinct. This statement is a logical corollary of basic observations in historical biogeography and evolutionary biology. Species vary, genetically and morphologically, across their geographic distribution and this variation is likely to be greater in widespread species or in species that are divided into smaller 'islands' of distribution, and thus are more

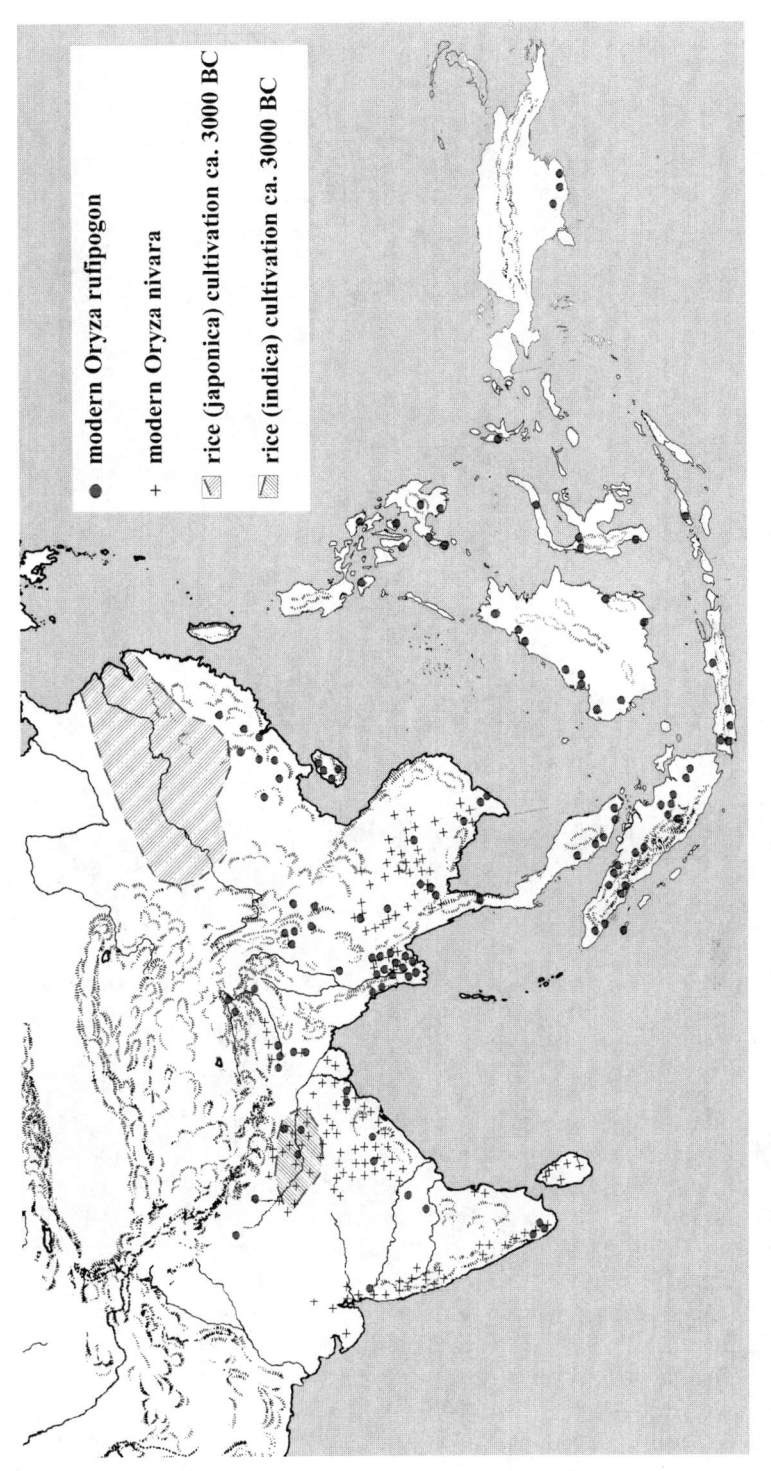

Map 2.11 A map of wild rice distribution and likely zones of domestication. The distribution of the two wild progenitors of rice is plotted after Vaughan (1994). The extent of rice cultivation *cal.*3000 BC is indicated based on archaeological evidence (for China, after Yan 2002; for India, based on Fuller 2002 but updated).

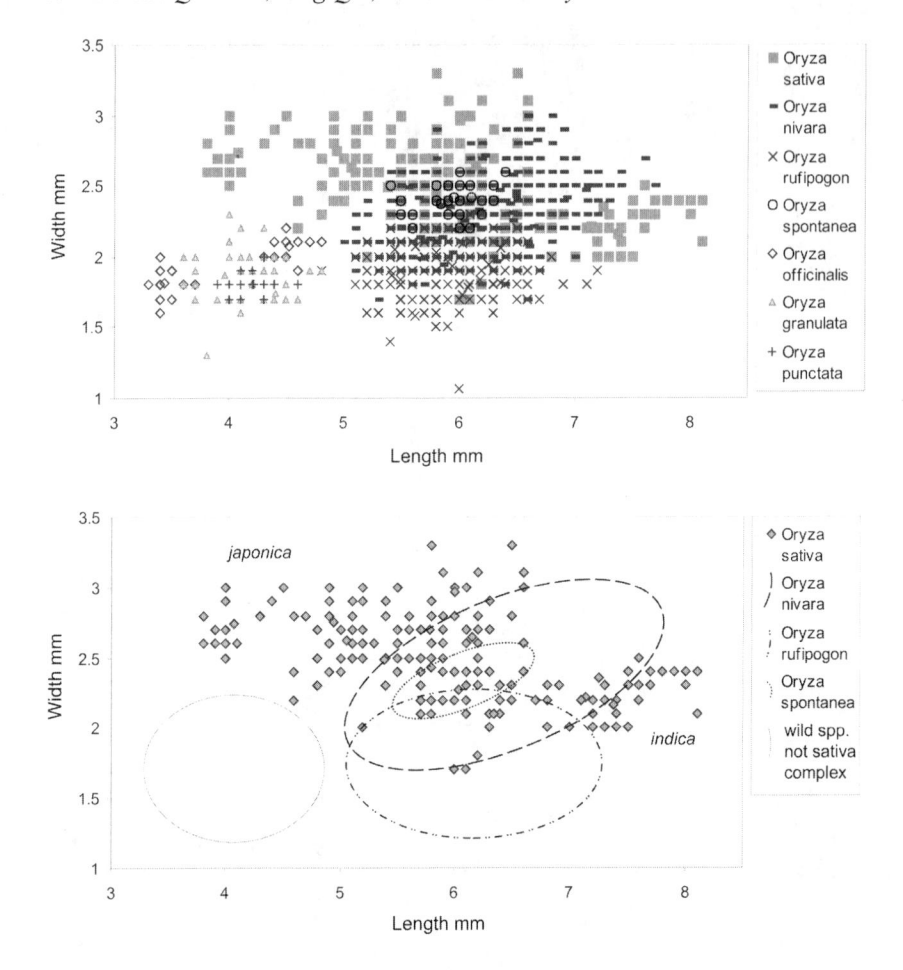

Figure 2.2 A scatter plot of length and width of grains measured in modern populations (measured by E. Harvey on 72 populations). The top graph shows individual grain measurements for a range of species, whereas these are replaced by ovoid distributions for wild species in the lower graph.

prone to genetic drift effects. Therefore we would expect there to have been some genetic and morphological variation in ancient Yangtze wild rice. Wild rice must have extended northwards to this region under warmer climatic conditions, first during the terminal Pleistocene and then once again after the Younger Dryas, during the early and middle Holocene (on climatic change in the region, e.g. Yu *et al.* 2000; Yi *et al.* 2003; Tao *et al.* 2006). Thus we would expect wild rice to have been present in the Lower Yangtze when Kuahuqiao and Hemudu were occupied. Persistence of wild rice, however, is likely to have ended during later Holocene climatic cooling, although there are apparent textual references from the first millennium BC (Chang 1983). This implies that some of the variation between Yangtze wild rice populations has been lost, and may not be represented in modern populations, which are restricted to southernmost China, Southeast Asia, and South Asia. Indeed, one of the genetic lineages of *japonica* rice identified by Londo *et al.* (2006) is not represented by any modern wild populations. The rice of Kuahuqiao might represent some of this lost genetic diversity, but what is needed is much larger sampling of morphometric data for ancient rice.

This perspective also raises the possibility that some populations of wild ancestors had unique traits they transmitted to their cultivated descendants but that differ from existing wild specimens in modern collections. Actual wild progenitor populations were part of now extinct radiations of wild rice that persist only in their domesticated form. This is important to keep in mind in the case of traits like husk phytolith morphology, which are not demonstrably connected to the domestication syndrome. For such traits, differences between modern cultivars and wild populations may represent the historical contingencies of phylogenetics.

Hemudu: claims and underlying assumptions

Hemudu occupies a central position in the archaeological syntheses of early Chinese agriculture and accounts of the dispersal of agriculture in world prehistory. Whatever concerns and debates persist around earlier Chinese Neolithic sites, all authors assume that Hemudu represents a village based on established rice agriculture: 'the earliest group reliant on domesticated rice is represented by the Hemudu site' (Crawford 2005: 84; see also, Chang 1986: 210; Barnes 1993: 94; Higham 1995, 2005: 247; Bellwood 2005: 125). We will, however, raise some questions about the status of rice at Hemudu, both in terms of its domestication status and of its importance in diet. Attention is also normally drawn to the pig and water buffalo remains from Hemudu as implying animal herding (Chang 1986: 211; Bellwood 1997: 208), although archaeozoological criteria in support of herding and morphological domestication of these animals are not discussed in any detail and also deserve careful reassessment.

When first discovered, Hemudu had the earliest rice in the world (Yan 1982; Liu 1985; Zhao and Wu 1987). Attention was drawn to large quantities of rice remains, including culms (straw), panicles and chaff together with some grains, which formed in a distinct layer in the waterlogged stratigraphy of the site. The material is clearly dominated by chaff, judging by available excavation photographs (e.g. Figure 2.3), and similar material has been seen by the authors from current excavations at nearby Tianluoshan. This was taken to represent a large quantity of rice, and was interpreted as the remains of a threshing floor (Bellwood 1997: 208). It was estimated that the rice would be equivalent to 120 tonnes (e.g. Yan 1982: 22), although this assumes a continuous deposit of rice. Published photographs (Zhejiang Provincial Institute 2003) and the finds from Tianluoshan indicate that the rice husk was deposited in discontinuous lenses, as if dehusking (not threshing) waste had been periodically dumped from elsewhere. The distinction between dehusking and threshing is potentially significant as dehusking is a necessary processing activity for wild or domesticated rice, as opposed to threshing which is only necessary for non-shattering domesticated plants.

Figure 2.3 Rice husk lens in situ during Hemudu excavations (reproduction from Zhejiang Province Institute 2003: pl. XLI.2)

Studies of the Hemudu rice have invariably assumed that it represents domesticated rice. Previous studies have focused largely on determining the varietal category of this rice based on ratios of grain measurements (e.g. You 1976, 2003; Zhou 1981, 2003; Liu 1985; Oka 1988), husk (lemma/palea) tubercles (Zhang 1996; Zhang and Wang 1998; Zhang 2000, 2002; Tang *et al.* 2003), and bulliform phytoliths (Zheng *et al.* 2004a). Different workers and different techniques have produced apparently contradictory results, with claims for differentiated *indica* and *japonica* at Hemudu (Zhou 1981; Liu 1985; Bellwood 1997: 206), or inferences of just *indica* types (You 1976; Oka 1988), or the definition of an unique 'ancient' rice that preceded the differentiation of these two types (Zhang 1996; Zhang and Wang 1998; Zhang 2000, 2002; Higham 2005: 244). Similarly, rice assemblages from other Neolithic sites in China have also been suggested to indicate the existence of distinctive, extinct 'ancient' cultivars that do not fit into modern categories (e.g. Zhang 2000, 2002; Pei 1998). At Kuahuqiao it is reported that grain measurements suggest *indica* rice, while bulliform phytoliths indicate *japonica*, a contradiction which is not explained (Zheng *et al.* 2004b; Zhejiang Provincial Institute 2004). These conclusions raise the question as to whether the assumptions on which comparative studies have been based are valid. These centre on the large quantities of rice, and the presence of bone 'spades', but not on careful consideration of what might be expected to be different about rice gathered by foragers as opposed to that cultivated or genetically transformed by cultivation.

Working from recent advances in genetic research, including that which indicates that Indian and Chinese rice domestications were separate, Sato (2002) argued that all the rice must be of *japonica* type, since a number later ancient DNA samples from the region were entirely of the *rufipogon-japonica* lineage, and *indica* was expected to have come from India (see also Crawford and Shen 1998: 864; Fuller 2002: 297–300).

The published descriptions of the rice from Hemudu contain indications that the rice may not have been fully domesticated. Much of the rice was found in the form of spikelets, and many spikelets lack grains or have incipient unformed grains. This implies that the spikelets were harvested before maturity, which implies a rice population that is not fully domesticated. While some of the spikelets are reported as awnless, some have awns, a trait of the wild rice. SEM examination by Sato (2002) suggests that many awns have reduced hairs by comparison with modern wild materials. Sato also considered spikelet bases, although the criteria were not reported in detail (on a sample-by-sample basis), nor was the sampling procedure from which eighty-one spikelets were obtained clear. Sato (2002) reports five of wild type and seventy-six of 'domestic' type, the latter including some that were 'intermediate between wild and cultivated strains'.

Herders or hunters?

The situation with animals also is rather more ambiguous than often assumed. Hemudu has figured prominently in discussions of East Asian animal domestication, with both water buffalo and pig herding assumed by several textbooks (e.g. Chang 1986: 211; Smith 1995; Bellwood 1997: 208; 2005). Following some earlier exaggerated reports, Bellwood (1997: 208) was misled into believing that pigs represented 90 per cent of the animal assemblage, which was taken to indicate major reliance on pig-keeping. This misrepresents the data, since of specimens identified in the final report, 75 per cent are from birds, fish, and reptiles (e.g. turtles). Of the quarter that are mammals (NISP = 1135), water buffalo account for only 8 per cent and pigs 26 per cent (Zhejiang Provincial Institute 2003: 156–216). This is hardly comparable to the 60–90 per cent of domestic/pro-domestic fauna (sheep/goat/cattle) at early pastoral sites in Southwest Asia or Pakistan (cf. Meadow 1993; Bar-Yosef 2000). At Kuahuqiao, mammals are more prominent, representing 62.5 per cent of the reported bones (Zhejiang Provincial Institute 2004: 260–3). Of these pigs account for only 10.1 per cent, while water buffalo are an impressive 32 per cent. The age profiles for water buffalo are consistent with hunting (Liu *et al.* 2004). Amongst the pigs it has been suggested that some of the third molars are small enough to be domesticated and a few mandibles are deformed, another feature of domestication. These domesticated morphotypes, however, are represented by just a few specimens, suggesting little reliance on pig-keeping. This could therefore be indicative of a special role for kept pigs, such as for periodic feasts, rather than a crucial subsistence role. The subsequent increase in pigs at Hemudu could indicate greater reliance, and indeed the proportion here is comparable to later sites in the region, from the Majiabang to the Liangzhu period, where pigs range between 21 and 34 per cent of mammalian fauna (Huang 2001; Zhang, M. 1999; Longqiuzhuang Site Archaeology Team 1999: 465–92; Administration of Cultural Heritage of Shanghai 1987: 111–13; 2002: 347–66). At all sites, even into the third millennium BC (Liangzhu period), mammal bone assemblages are dominated by deer (41–72%). The Kuahuqiao and Hemudu periods thus show a reliance on hunting and fishing with some supplemental pig-keeping, established as the Lower Yangtze Neolithic pattern.

One of the surprising things about the Neolithic of the Lower Yangtze is how insignificant water buffalo appear to be. Amongst post-Hemudu sites, water buffalo make up only 4 per cent of the bone assemblage from Majiabang period Lonqiuzhuang (Longqiuzhuang Site Archaeology Team 1999), whereas at other, later sites (Weidun, Longqiuzhuang, Songze, Maqiao) their bones appear to be completely absent (Huang 2001; Zhang, M. 1999; Administration of Cultural Heritage 1987: 111–13; 2002: 347–66). This is particularly surprising as we would expect water buffalo to have been used for ploughing in the Lower Yangtze, and evidence in the form of stone plough tips occurs from the Mid–Late Songze, with the earliest from a burial at Tangmiaosun (Administration of Cultural Heritage 1985). This might suggest that water buffalo were brought under domestication, or adopted, specifically for ploughing rather than initially as a food source. If so, this represents a significant difference from the process inferred from Southwest Asia and Europe for a transition from cattle as meat animals to a wider utility for secondary products including traction (see Sherratt 1981).

Current evidence argues for a predominance of deer-hunting and fishing throughout the Lower Yangtze Neolithic. While some pigs were apparently reared, these are a consistent minority of bones, suggesting a special status for these animals, such as for feasting. Elsewhere in China, early domestic pigs have been inferred from the same general time horizon as Kuahuqiao, as at Cishan in the Yellow River valley (Yuan and Flad 2002; Yuan 2003) and at Xinglonggou in northeast China (Yuan personal communication). These other sites come from a very different environmental and cultural context, from amongst early millet cultivators, and it is not yet possible to determine whether pigs had multiple origins within China (but several domestications across Eurasia are clear, Larson *et al.* 2005). The lack of material cultural evidence for diffusion prior to the Songze–Middle Dawenkou time horizon might favour separate regional processes

Evolutionary expectations: the making of domestic rice

The basis of food production is a direct involvement of humans in the management of the lives and life cycles of certain plant and animal species, termed 'domesticated'. It is the management of these species, over hundreds of years, that led to the evolutionary changes of domestication. A very real archaeological challenge is to identify the beginnings of cultivation amongst morphologically wild rice, and track the gradual biological changes this incurred. Theoretically this could be a much longer stage than that for wheat and barley due to the cross-pollination common amongst wild rices. In Southwest Asian archaeology, this challenge has been met over the past ten years as evidence for pre-domestication cultivation has been recognized through the statistical composition of wild seed assemblages, which document the inferred emergence of weed ecologies (Harris 1998; Colledge 1998; Hillman 2000; Hillman *et al.* 2001; Willcox 1999, 2002). Also important is a growing morphometric database from the Near East (Willcox 2004; Colledge 2001, 2004) which indicates that wheat and barley grains increased in size starting in the Pre-Pottery Neolithic A and earliest Pre-Pottery Neolithic B, prior to evidence for the emergence of domestic type seed dispersal (tough rachis dominance of archaeological chaff assemblages). This implies that grain size increased under the selection of early cultivation, prior to the evolution of the full domestication syndrome in Near Eastern cereals (cf. Willcox 2004). In summary, Near Eastern archaeobotany now presents an outline of a phased evolutionary process through which changes in human practices (cultivation) and changes in plant morphology (seed size increase and domestic-type seed dispersal) evolved over an extended period of perhaps 1000–3000 years (Figure 2.4; also Tanno and Willcox 2006; Weiss *et al.* 2006). Future research in China needs similar evidence if we are to understand the processes of agricultural emergence in this region. More flotation, more seeds, and more quantification of their composition is needed, alongside increased attention to quantitative patterns of morphology and size in the crops themselves.

While much data has been published on early Chinese rice, most of it has been seen through the lens of modern variation within domesticated rice. In short, authors have assumed that finds of rice are cultivated and domesticated and that research needs only decide whether the rice is *indica* or *japonica*. As already noted, there is no consistency or consensus, which has led some scholars to reject the utility of measuring grains at all, preferring phytoliths (Zheng *et al.* 2004a) or ancient DNA (e.g. Sato 2002), although the latter is yet to be shown to survive in the most ancient samples. But ancient rice remains, whether of grains, spikelets, or phytoliths, should be studied and characterized in their own right. Then morphometric traits of ancient populations, often represented by a few simple measurements, can be used to look at variations between sites, or between periods. This variation can then be interpreted through evolutionary models and morphometric expectations based on modern comparative materials and principles of the 'domestication syndrome'.

The 'domestication syndrome' consists of a number of traits that tend to be found in domesticated plants, but that differ from their wild relatives (Gepts 2004). These are traits which evolve under the conditions of cultivation selected by cycles of harvesting and sowing from harvested stores, and may also be influenced by the new soil conditions of tilled fields (Harlan *et al.* 1973). This implies that the human behavioural change, cultivation, necessarily precedes the morphogenetic

52 *Dorian Q. Fuller, Ling Qin, and Emma Harvey*

→ Increasing labour input per land unit

→ Increasing size, density and duration of settlements

→ Increasing population density

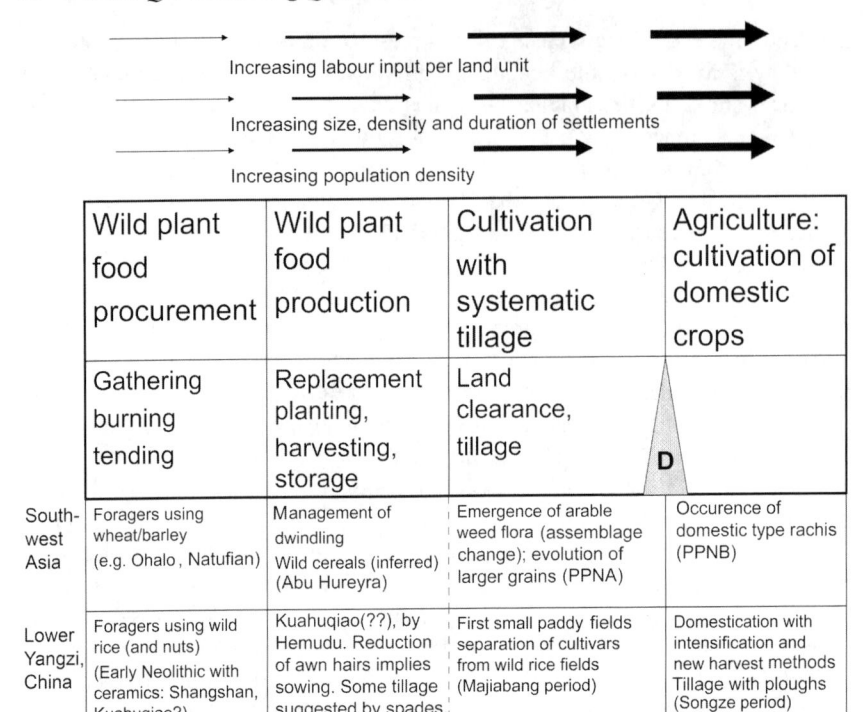

	Wild plant food procurement	Wild plant food production	Cultivation with systematic tillage	Agriculture: cultivation of domestic crops
	Gathering burning tending	Replacement planting, harvesting, storage	Land clearance, tillage	D
South-west Asia	Foragers using wheat/barley (e.g. Ohalo, Natufian)	Management of dwindling Wild cereals (inferred) (Abu Hureyra)	Emergence of arable weed flora (assemblage change); evolution of larger grains (PPNA)	Occurence of domestic type rachis (PPNB)
Lower Yangzi, China	Foragers using wild rice (and nuts) (Early Neolithic with ceramics: Shangshan, Kuahuqiao?)	Kuahuqiao(??), by Hemudu. Reduction of awn hairs implies sowing. Some tillage suggested by spades.	First small paddy fields separation of cultivars from wild rice fields (Majiabang period)	Domestication with intensification and new harvest methods Tillage with ploughs (Songze period)

Figure 2.4   The idealized evolutionary spectrum from pure foraging to agriculture based on domesticated crops, indicating the significant stages of wild plant food production and pre-domestication cultivation (after Harris 1996). On the rows at the base of the chart the inferred presence of these stages in the Near East is indicated and our suggested identification of these stages in the Lower Yangtze River area.

change in plants (Figure 2.4). As was first realized by Helbaek (1960) and has become increasingly discussed amongst those who study plant domestication, this means there is an essential distinction between cultivation (human activity) and domestication (change in the plant), and that we should expect there to be a phase, however brief, of pre-domestication cultivation (Harlan 1975; Wilke *et al.* 1972; Hillman and Davies 1990a, 1990b; Harris 1989, 1996; Gepts 2004).

One quintessential characteristic of domesticated grain crops is the loss of natural seed dispersal (Zohary and Hopf 1973; 2000; Hillman and Davies 1990a, 1990b). This is achieved in rice by a toughening of the attachment of the spikelet base to the rachilla and, as shown by Thompson (1996), this is accompanied by a subtle change in the cross-section of the rachilla attachment scar (also Sato 2002). The evolution of this toughened attachment is readily explained by natural selection and population genetics under circumstances of cultivation and harvesting, as has been demonstrated in wild wheats (Hillman and Davies 1990a, 1990b; Willcox 1999). However, this implies that tough rachis mutants already exist in very small frequencies in wild populations and thus change must be documented at a populational level (Kislev 1997: 226–8). What is more, cereals that are harvested green, i.e. immature, may also mimic this domestic trait as the natural grain-shedding mechanism will not yet have set in. In other words, tough rachis characters may be present in green-harvested plants as well as coming to dominate mature plants of the domesticated morphotype. Under the circumstances of cultivation and harvesting in which human harvesting is through cutting or uprooting, there is a bias towards collection of toughened mutants, which therefore enter subsequent generations in larger numbers through sowing.

Of importance is modelling the rate of change and the time that would be expected to fix the domestic type mutants in a population, which depends on the strength of the selective force as well as the extent of continued gene flow from wild types into the seed of subsequent generations (Hillman and Davies 1990a, 1990b). Unlike wheat and barley, which are almost exclusively self-pollinating, wild rice has been shown to have significant out-breeding on the order of 40–60 per cent of fertilized florets (Oka and Morishima 1967). Thus in contrast to self-pollinating species in which, under strong selection from harvesting and sowing, 'domestication', the populational process of fixing the tough-rachis mutants, could happen in 20–30 years, strong selection in cross-pollinating rice should double this to *ca.* 50 years. But crucial to this model is the selection pressure favouring the domestic type mutant. If this is reduced to 10 or 5 per cent then domestication slows down, even in self-pollinating species, taking on the order of 200–400 years. With reduced selection pressure in a cross-pollinating species this can slow to more than 1,000 years. Thus it is crucial to consider how human activities set up this selection pressure: this includes harvesting by methods that favour tough mutants, saving a large proportion of the harvest for sowing the following year, and sowing in areas without natural wild seeds of the species. If the same wild stand areas are resown, and the quantity of resown grain is equal to or less than the natural seed dispersal by the wild population, there will be essentially no selection for domestication. Other factors that might greatly reduce any selection for domesticated morphotypes are methods of harvesting, such as paddle and basket harvesting, widely used ethnographically for gathering wild grass seeds (Harris 1984; Harlan 1989). In addition, and probably quite significant, is that if wild cereals are harvested somewhat green, i.e. before most of the grains are mature, or if individual wild plants have a long period during which grains gradually come into maturity (which is the case with wild rice), grain loss to the harvester may be lessened, but selection for the domesticated type will also be reduced.

An important issue to consider is how these traits relate to the evolution of the domestication syndrome in rice. Both traits relate to the reduction of the wild-type dispersal adaptation, which is reduced or removed through domestication. But they relate to the domestication syndrome differently in terms of the kind of selection under which they can be expected to evolve. The non-shedding spikelet trait should be strongly selected by harvesting of (mature) panicles with a sickle or knife, followed by subsequent cycles of sowing and harvesting. By contrast, longer, heavily haired awns and hairy husks are selected for by natural seed dispersal as these appendages, like those in other wild cereals, help to bore into the soil and keep the spikelet there until germination. Thus the reduction in number or size of these appendages is caused by the reduction of natural selection for efficient seed dispersal brought about by human sowing. The directional reduction in hairs suggests that the removal of selection for hairs is sufficient. This change may be brought about by a decrease in metabolic developmental costs involved in producing so many hairs.

Another contrast between domesticated and wild cereals that might slow down the domestication process as well as complicate archaeological detection is evenness of ripening. One characteristic of most crops is that their flowering and production of seed is timed almost synchronously across the entire plant (and indeed population). This contrasts with wild relatives which tend to have a much more extended period of seed production, which means that at any particular time a large proportion of the grains are immature or have already been shed. This has been experimentally confirmed in wild rice by Lu (2006), who found extremely low yields when harvesting wild rice with sickles upon maturation, at which time most grain was lost or had already been shed. When seed dispersal is still by natural shattering, we might expect gatherers to target more immature plants to decrease seed loss during the harvest process. The implication for archaeobotanists is that ancient wild, and early cultivated, populations would most likely be harvested fairly immature, and would produce a mixture of mature and immature grains. This means we must take seriously the presence, perhaps even predominance, of the immature grain in early assemblages.

This problem is also highlighted by ethnographic parallels. In parts of aboriginal Australia where hunter-gatherers intensively used wild millet grains, grasses might be stripped by hand in a wooden or bark dish, before natural maturation and seed shedding (Allen 1974; Harris 1984: 64). Alternatively they could be uprooted while still green to minimize the loss of seed. These were stacked, left to dry, and then burnt, serving to separate the grain and parch the husks. Where the burnt stacks were small, heaps of hulled millet grains were available for dehusking, cooking, and consumption. Wild grasses may also be harvested by paddling or with baskets (e.g. Harris 1984; Harlan 1989; Lu 1998), in which case timing must be chosen so as to maximize those grains which are still on the plant and near maturity. This means targeting them early in the cycle of grain maturation when many grains on the plant will still be immature. In modern domesticated rice, individual plants take about fifteen days for all grains to mature (Hoshikawa 1993), and we might expect this window to have been even longer in wild or early cultivated populations. In wild-type shattering plants this means that in order to avoid massive loss of grains, especially nearly mature grains, panicles need to be harvested early. This means large proportions, or at least half or more, of grains harvested will be immature (Figure 2.5). We might expect these substandard grains to be more readily lost through processing and thus to be over-represented archaeologically.

Immature grains will differ in the size and shape from their mature counterparts, and will complicate attempts to identify wild or domestic status from grain size and shape. The way the grains mature is that first they lengthen and then gradually

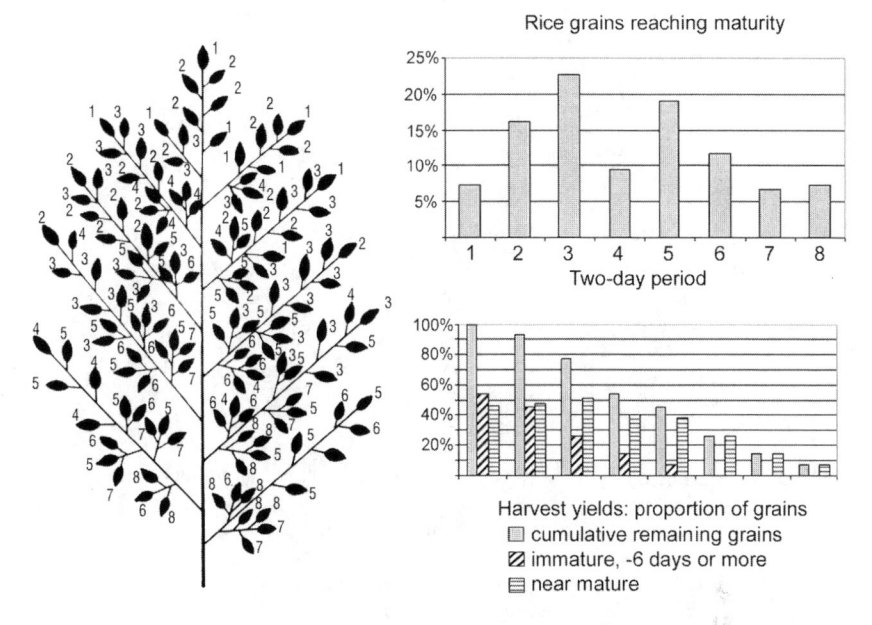

Figure 2.5 Rice panicle maturation and harvest yields assuming wild type grain shedding. The diagram on the left indicates the stage of pollen shed, and by extension grain initiation on an individual rice plant (after Hoshikawa 1993). The graph at the top right converts this into the percentage of grains that are expected to come into maturity at each of these stages, approximately two days each, i.e. a total of 16 days for the grains of an entire plant to mature. The graph on the lower right indicates that total number of grains remaining on the plant at each stage and the proportions that are near mature and substantially immature (by six days or more).

thicken in the final days of maturing (Figure 2.6). This means that immature grains have exaggerated length to width ratios (Figure 2.7). As conventional studies of modern material always focus on fully mature grains, the simple extension of these ancient materials is flawed. The difficulty is highlighted by the fact that measured ancient rices in China match neither modern varieties nor wild forms but fall in an intermediate zone, the basis for proposals of a distinctive 'ancient cultivated rice' variety (e.g. Pei 1998; Zhejiang Provincial Institute 2003: 439; Zhang 2000, 2002). Ancient rice grains match neither the wild *rufipogon* rices of modern south China/Southeast Asia nor the *japonica* cultivars that were domesticated there, but often come closer, in ratio, to *indica* rices. Actual measurements, however, even allowing for probable size changes due to carbonization, do not match *indica*. This situation is readily explained if we consider these grains to be immature, i.e. harvested green.

As a starting point, we still must consider morphometric variation amongst the mature grains of modern rice. There is great variability in the size and proportions of domesticated rice species today, encompassed by the several wild species that occur in South and Southeast Asia (Figure 2.2). A survey of this overlap

56 Dorian Q. Fuller, Ling Qin, and Emma Harvey

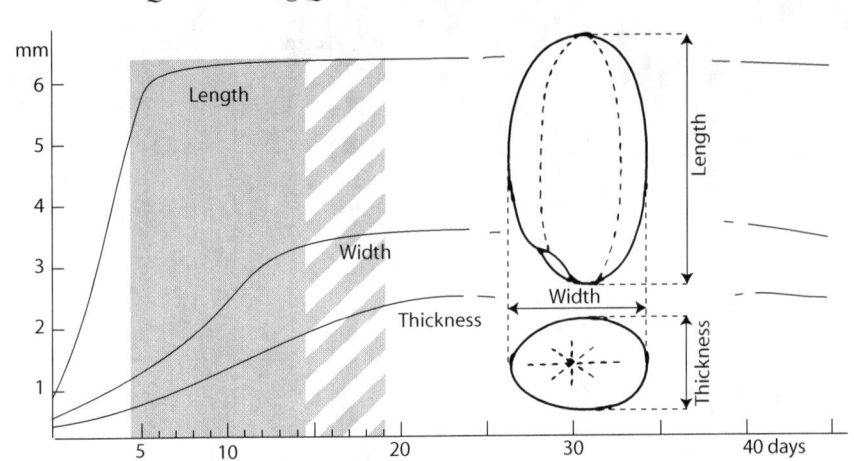

Figure 2.6 Chart of *japonica* rice grain metrical development in terms of length, width and thickness measures (after Hoshikawa 1993), on which is shaded the period of grain immaturity in which grain proportions differ from those of standards based on the mature grain. Shown in solid grey is an approximate 10-day window during which immature grain proportions will be biased towards length, and thus closer to *indica* or *rufipogon*, rather than *japonica*.

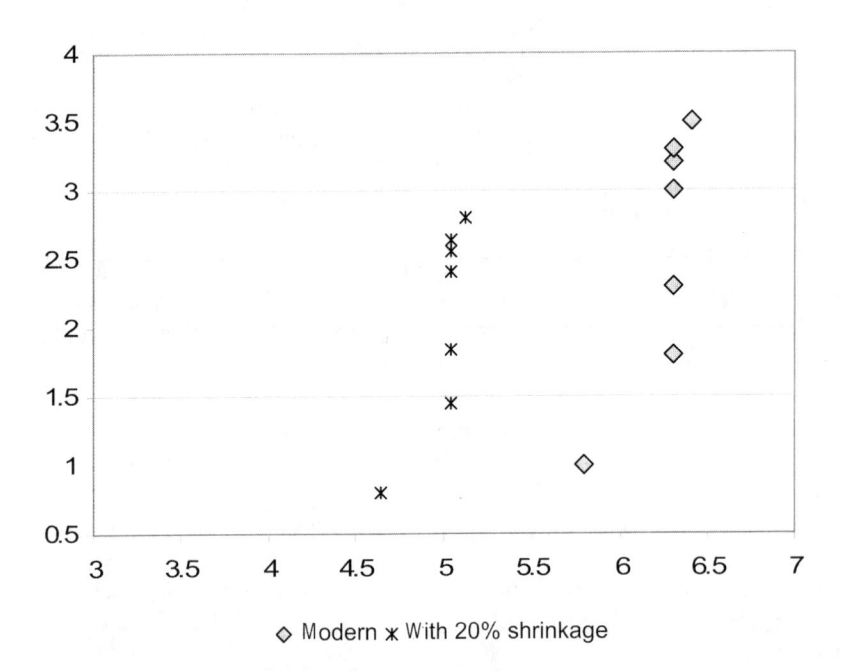

◇ Modern ✶ With 20% shrinkage

Figure 2.7 Graph of grain length and width over the course of development, based on Figure 2.5. This trajectory is also adjusted for 20 per cent reduction to account for the likely effects of charring.

makes it difficult to assign one or a few grains to any given population (Harvey 2006; see also Thompson 1996: 176). This problem is made more difficult by the changes, including shrinkage and distortion, during charring, as well as the problem of varying maturity levels. The few studies which have been conducted on the effects of charring on rice grains (Garton 1979; Lone *et al.* 1993), as well as those studying this effect on other cereals (Nesbitt 2006: 21; Willcox 2004), suggest that reductions in length and breadth are normally 10–20 per cent but can be potentially as much as 30 per cent. Reduction to length is normally greater, making grains tend towards rounder shapes. While further studies are certainly warranted on this issue, we will consider a 20 per cent reduction a useful rule of thumb for the present discussion.

Another factor that has particular relevance is the harvesting of wild rice. In regions such as China and India, where populations of wild rice would have been abundant, we cannot assume that the rice found on an archaeological site is domestic. Wild rice harvesting is still a fairly common economic strategy for non-agricultural and semi-agricultural groups, for example in parts of southern Orissa (India) (Watt 1889–93) or in North America, where *Zizania aquatica* was seasonally collected by native groups like the Ojibwa (Jenks 1900). The shattering nature of wild rice means that grains need to be harvested before they are fully mature to avoid grain loss (cf. experimental results of Lu 2006), thus adding immature grains to the harvest, which might even be dominated by immature grains. This will complicate identifications from sites before or during the process of domestication, when accurate identification is most important. Therefore the morphometric identification of archaeological rice assemblages to species or subspecies is far more complicated than is often assumed.

The rice of Hemudu and beyond: harvesting unripe

The prominent rice deposits at Hemudu are unlikely to represent threshing floors. They consist mainly of husk material, as if they were disposed waste from dehusking episodes (Figure 2.3), with little evidence of the straw and leaves that would be expected from threshing of domesticated rice or the primary waste from threshing floors. As noted in the Hemudu report, most of the remains consisted of empty rice husks (Zhou 2003: 430), also evident from photographs (Figure 2.3). These included not just dehusking waste but some with immature or indeed unformed grains. At Kuahuqiao similar material was found and quantified (Figure 2.8), indicating a predominance of immature spikelets, including many in which the grain had not yet formed. One implication of this is that, if rice plants were harvested when immature, spikelet bases may appear tough if threshed, as they were harvested before the abscission layers had matured. This means that spikelet base data is necessary but not sufficient to infer domestication status. Rather what is needed is evidence for mature spikelets/grains, together with tough, domestic-type, abscission scars.

In many reports, rice grains and spikelets have been considered in terms of length to width ratios, as a means to assigning them to ether the *indica* or *japonica*

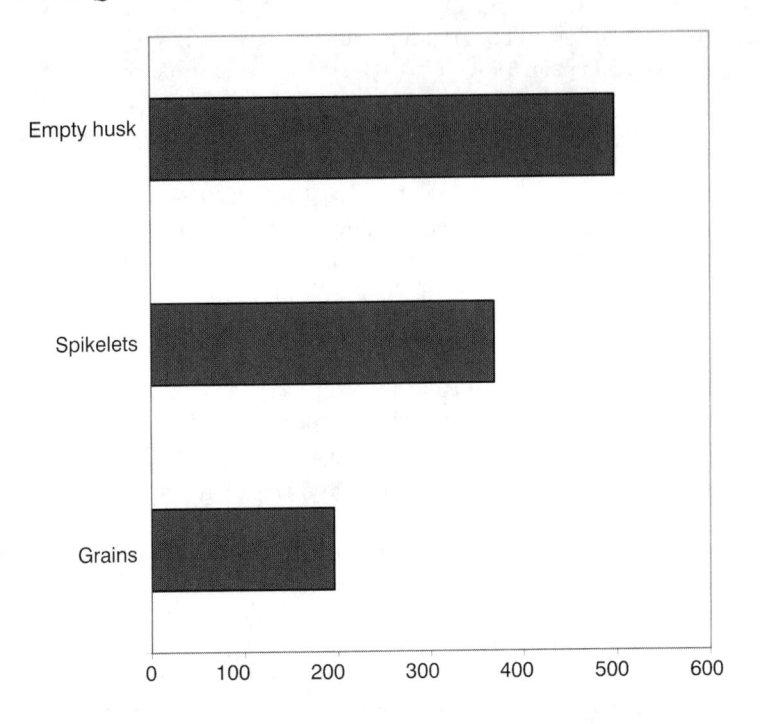

Figure 2.8 Counts of rice find types from Kuahuqiao (after Zheng 2004).

subspecies, and in some cases to distinct 'ancient' varieties of rice. This approach is misleading when a wide range of wild species are taken into account (Figure 2.9). As implied by the developmental trajectory of rice (Figure 2.6), these ratios will also differ in immature rice, which is how hunter-gatherers presumably gathered most of their rice. Therefore, rice morphometrics need to be approached through actual scatter-plots of measurements rather than through the use of ratios.

While data on raw measurements are still relatively scarce, the available patterns appear significant (Figure 2.10). The morphometric data available from Kuahuqiao and Longqiuzhuang (mainly of the Majiabang period, which succeeds Hemudu chronologically) suggest that grain assemblages are dominated by immature grains. This assumes that the mature grains would have been in the range of modern domesticates. This is plausible if we consider the likelihood that early pre-domestication cultivation has already begun to select for larger grains, as was the case in the Near East with wheat and barley (cf. Willcox 2004). In addition, the reduction in hairs on the awns of rice recovered from Hemudu (Sato 2002) implies relaxation of natural selection for seed dispersal aids, which we would expect under cultivation. Thus the evidence from Kuahuqiao (6000–5400 BC) and from the earlier Majiabang period (from 5000–4,400 BC) both suggest pre-domestication cultivation. The rice at this stage can be regarded as a 'pro-domesticate' as some aspects of the domestication syndrome had begun to evolve but the key change, in terms of seed dispersal, had not.

Agriculture in the Lower Yangtze region 59

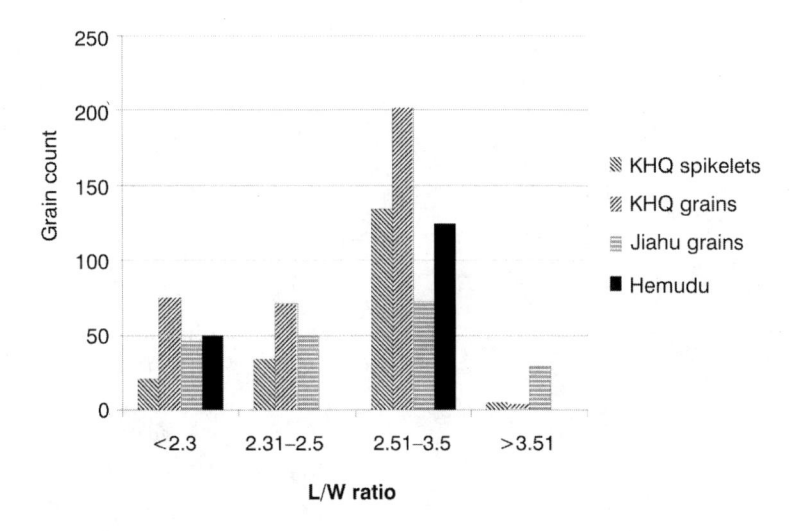

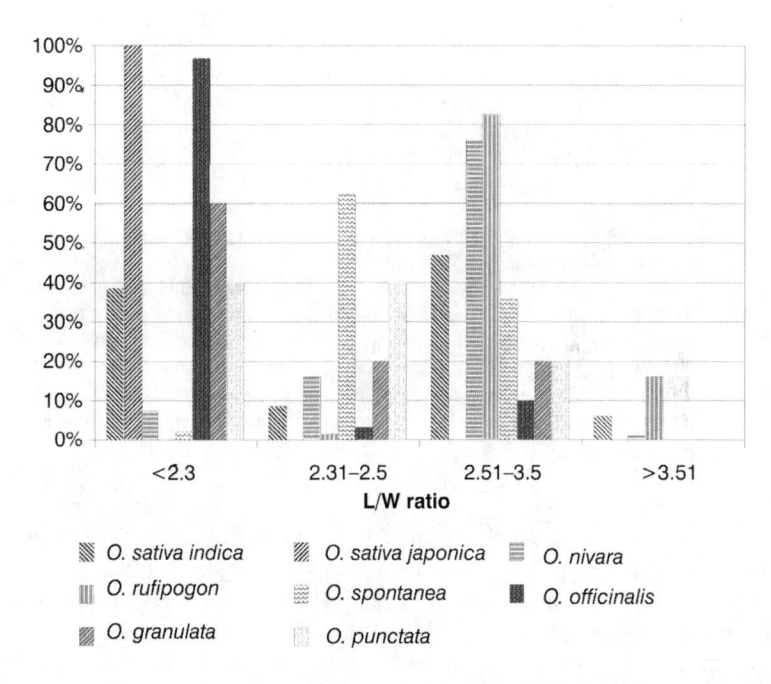

Figure 2.9 The proportions of rice grains and spikelets within given shape ranges based on length-to-width ratios, from selected Chinese Neolithic sites (top), and from modern measured rice populations (dataset the same as Figure 2.2). While such data have traditionally been used to arrive at the mix of *indica* and *japonica* grains on Neolithic sites, this clearly only has validity if the presence of any wild rice species can be ruled out, and ancient grains are assumed to be fully mature.

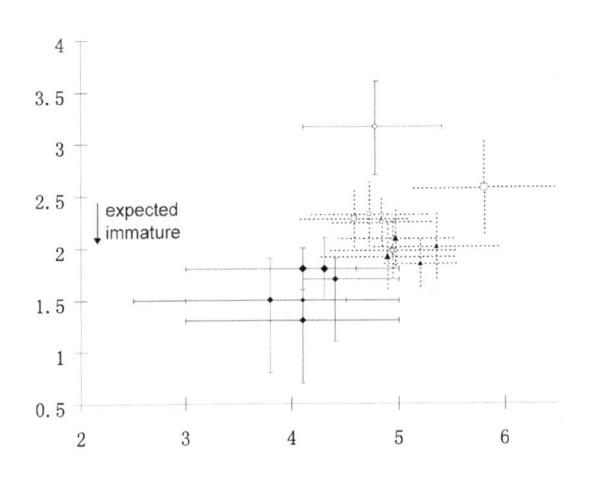

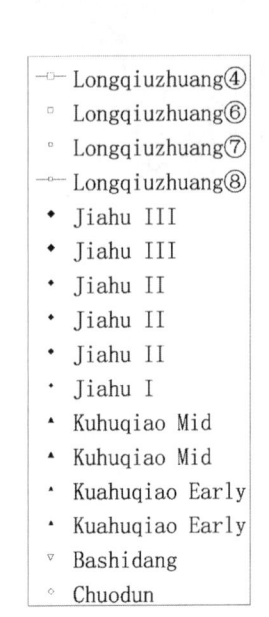

Figure 2.10 A scatter plot of grain measurements from selected Neolithic sites, including Kuahuqiao (after Zheng *et al.* 2004b), Longqiuzhuang (after Huang and Zhang 2000) and Chuodun (Tang 2003). Cases where only spikelets (with husk) appear to have been measured, as at Hemudu, have been excluded. Notice that grains from Kuahuqiao and the lower (Majiabang period) levels (8–6) at Longqiuzhuang fall largely or entirely in the expected immature grain proportions (compare Figure 2.6), while the latest Majiabang period grains from Longqiuzhuang (level 4) indicate a clear shift towards longer and fatter grains that can be regarded as fully mature, and thus domesticated. Published averages from selected Middle Yangtze sites are also shown, including individual sample means from Jiahu (Henan Provincial Institute of Archaeology 1999), reported site average from Bashidang (from Pei 1998) and for the three rice types ('*japonica*', '*indica*' and 'ancient rice') from Chengtoushan (from Zhang and Wang 1998). Middle Yangtze site Bashidang also suggests wild and/or immature grains, while the later Chengtoushn suggests domestication. Jiahu measurements may be more comparable to a different wild species, such as *O. officinalis*.

A clear contrast is seen with the latest assemblage from Longqiuzhuang (late Majiabang period, *cal.* 4000 BC), in which grains are longer, plumper (2.5–3 mm) and most likely fully mature. Also significantly plumper grains have been recovered from Chuoden (also late Majiabang), which has evidence for a possible paddy field (Gu 2003). This suggests that an important morphological shift in archaeological rice occurred in the Lower Yangtze region during the later 4th millennium BC. This seems most likely to be due to a shift towards harvesting of mature panicles as opposed to immature panicles, rather than an evolutionary development in grain shape. This would imply that it became feasible to allow grains to mature on the plant without loss, or in other words that tough, domesticated type rachises had evolved to dominate the rice populations being harvested.

Some rice samples from elsewhere, such as the Middle Yangtze region, can also be taken into account. Rice measurements from Bashidang, 6400–6000 BC (Pei 1998) fall in the midst of the wild/immature 'pro-domesticate' range of Kuahuqiao. Reported measurements from Jiahu (Henan Provincial Institute 1999) are remarkably small, by comparison with either modern cultivars or Lower Yangtze Neolithic immature grains. This suggests that they come closest to a wild rice, perhaps *Oryza rufipogon* (taking into account c. 20 per cent shrinkage due to charring, and possible immaturity), or more likely *O. officinalis*, a prolific grain-producer. Intriguingly, measurements from Chengtoushan, which were only reported as averages of three modal types (Zhang and Wang 1998), include some which suggest immature pro-domesticates and others fully mature domesticated types. Domesticated rice may have been harvested at this site. When considered in comparison to contemporary and later sites elsewhere in the Yangtze this raises the possibility that fully domesticated rice may have evolved more than once at different Yangtze localities, and at different periods. While all of these sites have been assumed in most literature to be agricultural, they may represent different degrees of cultivation of morphologically wild rice (Bashidang and the Pengtoushan culture) as well as some pure gathering of wild rice (at Jiahu). Jiahu also has acorns, water chestnuts and soybean (possibly cultivated but still wild in terms of size criteria), and sickles. Thus the dynamics of agricultural origins would appear to be complex, with various subsistence strategies involving various wild and pro-domesticates playing a role. This highlights a need for more systematic archaeobotanical sampling and quantitative analysis, to improve upon earlier unquestioned assumptions that rice (or millet) present on a site equates with full-blown agriculture.

There is an additional source of evidence that can be used to assess rice plant maturity. A recent study of morphometric variation in rice bulliform phytoliths (produced in the leaves of rice) has suggested that aspects of this form are under genetic control, in particular the proportions of the 'stalk' which has been used to differentiate *japonica* from *indica* varieties (Zheng *et al.* 2003, 2004a, 2004b). This study also examined other proportions, but found that the size of bulliforms, especially horizontal (HL) and vertical length (VL) show a strong correlation with plant maturity (Figure 2.11, Zheng *et al.* 2003: 1217, fig. 3). In other words, more mature plants produce larger bulliforms. Recent metrical data from sites in the Lower Yangtze indicates a significant shift towards larger bulliforms through time (Figure 2.10). These data therefore agree with the evidence of grain morphometrics that earlier rice, e.g. of the Majiabang period, was being harvested substantially less mature than later, presumably domesticated, rice of the Songze and Liangzhu phases. Phytolith morphometrics might also provide a means for assessing variation between populations of ancient wild rice. As is clear from Figure 2.10, the Lower Yangtze sequence from Majiabang through Liangzhu shows a clear regression that suggests one morphological population. A complicating factor that requires consideration is the possible presence of other *Oryza* spp. in the region during the earlier Holocene. We can have little doubt that the *Oryza sativa* complex was present. What are needed are more comparative data on the range

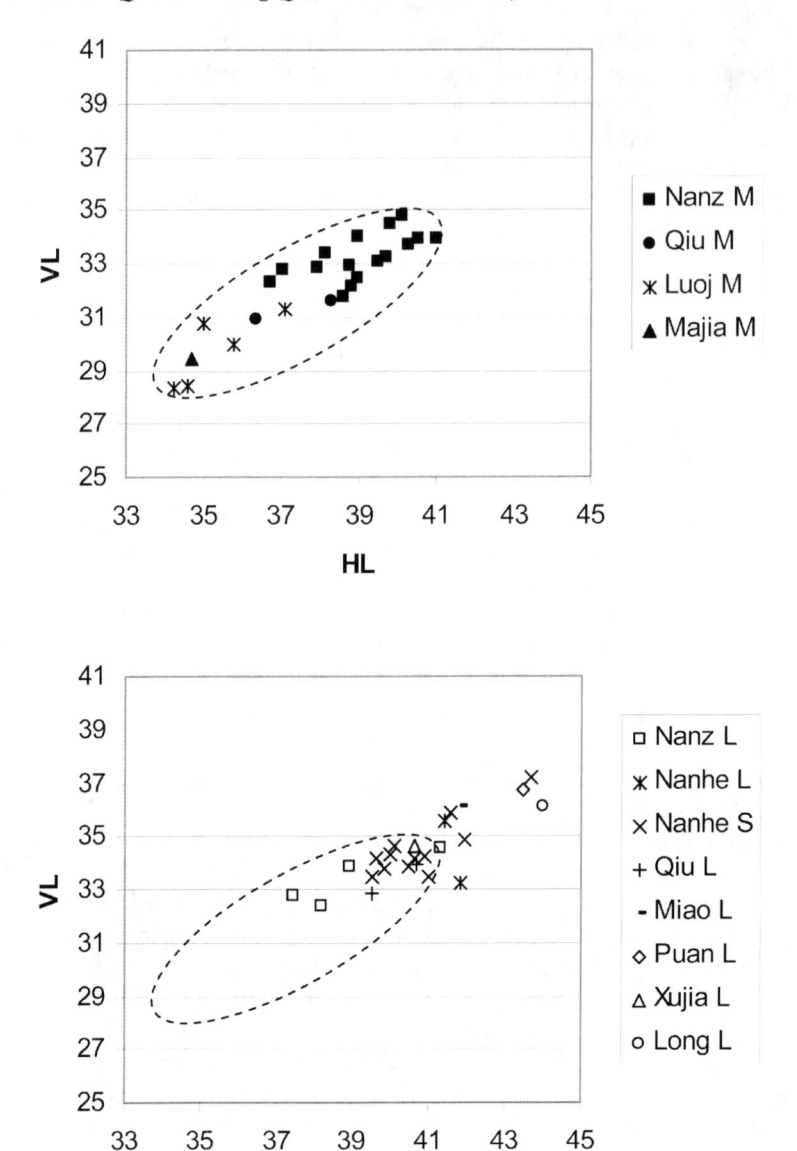

Figure 2.11 Size increase in Lower Yangzte rice phytoliths. The upper graph shows measured horizontal length (HL) and vertical length (VL) of rice bulliform phytoliths from Majiabang period samples (M), while the lower graph shows measurements from samples of the subsequent Songze (S) and Liangzhu (L) phases. The dashed oval represents the distribution of the Majiabang measurements. Data replotted from Zheng *et al*. 2004a. Site names abbreviated: Nanzhuangqiao, Nanhebang, Qiucheng, Luojiajiao, Miaoqian, Puanqiao, Xujiawan, Longnan, Majiabang.

of morphometrics in bulliforms across Asian *Oryza* spp. as well as untransformed raw archaeological measurements so that the population-level metric characters can be compared across time and space rather than being simply pigeonholed as '*indica*' or '*japonica*'.

Rice in a nut-based economy

The rice used at Hemudu and Kuahuqiao should be considered in the context of a broader plant economy. Despite the lack of flotation or systematic efforts at sieving for plant remains, both Hemudu and Kuahuqiao produced substantial quantities of plant remains, thanks in large part to waterlogged preservation. While preliminary reports and secondary literature has tended to focus exclusively on the rice remains, this can be seen as a small component of a broader subsistence base with a focus on nuts. Table 2.1 summarizes the species present at these sites based on the final reports (Zhejiang Province Institute 2003, 2004). What is striking about this list of taxa is the wide range of nuts, in particular acorns (Figure 2.12), but also foxnuts (*Euryale ferox*), peach and apricot stones (which contain almond

Figure 2.12 A concentration of acorns at the base of pit H27 at Hemudu (from Zhejiang Provincial Institute of Archaeology 2003).

Table 2.1 Plant species identified from Hemudu and Kuahuqiao from fruit remains, and their possible uses, taken from the final reports

Taxa; Common names (English, Chinese)		Probable use[1]
Lagenaria siceria Eng. Bottle gourd; Ch. 葫芦 *Hu lu*	H K	Containers, fishing net floats, seeds can be processed for oily kernal
Quercus spp. Eng. Oaks, acorns; Ch. 橡子 *Xiang zi*	H K	Potential carbohydrate staple (storable)
Choerospondias axillaris Eng. "Southern Sour Jujube", Ch. 南酸枣 *Nan suan zao*	H K	Edible fruits, rich in vitamin C; also medicinal
Amygdalus davidiana (syn *Prunus davidiana*)[2] Eng. Chinese mountain peach, Ch. 山桃 *shan tao*	H	Edible seasonal fruits, seeds can be eaten roasted (like almonds), and stored in stone
Amygdalus (Prunus) persica [Rosaceae], Eng. True peach Ch. 毛桃 *Mao tao*; probably *A. davidiana*	K	As above
Prunus mume Eng. Mume apricot; Ch. 酸梅 *Suan mei*	K	Edible seasonal fruits, seeds can be eaten roasted (like almonds), and stored in stone
Prunus armeniaca Eng. Apricot; Ch. 杏 *Xing*	K	Edible seasonal fruits, seeds can be eaten roasted (like almonds), and stored in stone
Euryale forox Eng. Foxnut, "gorgon seeds"; Ch. 芡实 *qian shi*	H K	Seeds dried to make starchy flour (storable); stems and roots eaten as vegetable
Sophora sp. Eng. Sophora; Ch. 槐 *Huai*	H	Leaves or roots used medicinally (Sophora spp.); pods used as a yellow dyestuff (S. japonica)
Coix sp. Eng. Job's tears Ch. 薏苡 *Yi yi*	H	Grains edible as cereal (storable)
Trapa sp. Eng. Water chestnut Ch. 菱角 *Ling jiao*	K	Edible nut
Polygonaceae Eng. Knotweed (family) Ch. 蓼科	K	Edible with roasting; species in this family known to have been used in aboriginal North America and Jomon Japan (Crawford 1983, 1997)
Oryza rufipogon/sativa[3] [Poaceae] Eng. Rice; Ch. 稻 *Dao*	H K	Potential carbohydrate staple (storable)

Source: Zhejiang Provinicial Institute of Archaeology (2003; 2004).

Notes
1 Ethnographically documented uses based on Usher (1974); Menninger (1977)
2 Not recorded in report, but included amongst unidentified fruit seeds, examined by the authors at the Hemudu museum, Nov. 2004. This species was identified in the report of the basis of leaf remains.
3 On the specific identify and domestication status of rice, see discussion in text.

like seeds that can be made edible by roasting), and water chestnuts. Polygonaceae nutlets (knotgrasses) are also a potential food source. All of these taxa are known from archaeological or ethnographic sources as storable food sources that are potential staples or second-tier resources used by hunter-gatherers. Rather than merely being present, acorns were stored in large quantities. At Hemudu, a number of straight-sided to bell-shaped pits were excavated. While these have probably been truncated, their profiles suggest storage pits. In several cases, these contained vast stores of acorns, and in one case foxnuts, and peach pits. From the 2004 excavations of the Zhejiang Provincial Institute of Archaeology at Tianluoshan (directed by Sun Guoping), a contemporaneous site near to Hemudu, vast quantities of nuts, including acorns (probably *Cyclobalanopsis* sp.), water chestnuts (*Trapa bispinosa*), and foxnuts (*Euryale ferox*), have been once again recovered. The authors are currently collaborating in archaeobotanical studies of this material, and it is clear that in addition to storage pits with nuts, nutshell fragments are ubiquitous across samples. Rice spikelet bases and chaff fragments are also widespread.

Nuts potentially provide an important staple resource for hunter-gatherer groups, which may be intensifiable through storage, but is unlikely to lead to cultivation (Harris 1977). Nuts have played the role of subsistence staples across a wide range of hunter-gatherer societies, from the mongongo nuts of !Kung bushmen of southern Africa, which contributed about one-third of the traditional diet (Lee 1968), to the acorn starch staples of aboriginal Californian tribes (Heizer and Elsasser 1980: 82–114). In the case of California, aboveground granaries were constructed to store large autumn harvests for use through the winter and early spring. Together with substantial fishing and hunting, California hunter-gatherers reached substantial population densities in late prehistory, including some village settlements (Fagan 1995: 231–56). Archaeologically, the advent of Californian nut-use is associated with quantities of milling stones, more substantial and long-term occupations with substantial middens and burial grounds that become widespread between 6000 and 3000 BC (Wallace 1978; Fagan 1995: 219–30). In eastern North America, nuts were the staple food of Holocene hunter-gatherers, and even once cultivation and domestication of local seed crops had occurred (*cal.* 2500 BC), nuts continued to predominate in archaeobotanical assemblages for the next 2500 years (Johanessen 1988; Milner 2004: 86–7). It has been suggested that the cultivation of small-seeded crops in eastern North America may have played a role of risk-buffering and providing dietary breadth to nut-focused subsistence, and thus food production remained small-scale (Winterhalder and Goland 1997; Gardner 1997; Smith 2001). Acorns were also important alongside wild cereals and grasses in the Late Pleistocene pre-agricultural Near East, as evident at Ohalo II (Kislev *et al.* 1992; Weiss *et al.* 2004). For this region, estimates of foraging and processing efficiency suggest that acorns ought to have been preferred resources, even by comparison to wild wheat and barley if they are available in sufficient quantity within a 25 km radius of sites (Barlow and Heck 2002). Elsewhere in East Asia, amongst the Jomon tradition of the Japanese archipelago, nuts, including acorns and toxic horse chestnuts, were staple resources stored, and in part detoxified, in subterranean pits dug into wetlands (Imamura 1996; Takahashi and Hosoya 2002; Kobayashi *et al.* 2004). In some parts of Jomon Japan, such as southern Hokkaido, some groups began to cultivate local plants, such as barnyard millet, which served as a supplement to, but did not replace, wild nuts in the diet (Crawford 1983).

We believe that the substantial evidence for stored acorns and other nuts at Kuahuqiao and Hemudu argues for including the early to middle Neolithic of the Lower Yangtze amongst these comparisons. Elsewhere, sites such as Jiahu have produced quantities of acorns and water chestnuts as well (Henan Provincial Institute 1999; Z. Zhao personal communication), suggesting this pattern might be more widespread in southern China than previously recognized. As demonstrated by the Jomon and in parts of prehistoric North America, substantial social complexity and artistic traditions can be supported on a nut-based foraging economy. It was, nevertheless, within such an economy that some communities, such as Hemudu, began to tend, plant, and till wild plants, notably rice. These practices gradually ended in agricultural dependence and morphological domestication.

Economic developments after Hemudu

Other archaeological evidence, both tools and excavated features, suggest that techniques of cultivation underwent development through time during the course of the Hemudu, Majiabang, and Songze cultural phases. Hemudu yielded a great many hafted or haftable bone scapula artefacts, which are regarded as spades or hoes, as well as some wooden spade blades (Liu 1985; Chang 1986: 212; Zhejiang Province Institute 2003). This strongly suggests manipulation of the soil through tillage. Coupled with the evidence that rice grains were largely immature we regard this as a strong case for wild plant food production (see Figure 2.4). This hypothesis may be testable through future systematic sampling of seeds and phytoliths for evidence of an emergent weed flora. In addition, we should expect a protracted period during which the proportions of domesticated type rice spikelet bases increased in proportion to wild or immature type.

These practices may have had somewhat earlier origins, as spades were also found at Kuahuqiao (Zhejiang Provincial Institute 2004). However, they were not necessarily used for cultivation, as the excavators noted that the spades from Kuahuqiao were very poorly hafted by comparison to the later Hemudu material and may not have been very practical for tilling mud (Zhejiang Provincial Institute 2004: 176–7). At Kuahuqiao, only four possible bone 'spades' were recovered, accounting for just 4.4 per cent among all bone and horn tools. By contrast, the later Hemudu site yielded 192 bone spades, 6.6 per cent among all bone and horn tools. There are also significant differences between Kuahuqiao and Hemudu spades in terms of how they were hafted. At Kuahuqiao, these have small holes drilled near the top of the tool, 9–10 cm in depth, 2.4–2.8 cm in diameter. This would have made for very weak hafting, inadequate for working heavy mud. The bone spades of Hemudu have elaborate features, including large holes lower down the blade within a groove, all of which would have stabilized the hafting, making them effective digging tools. This may indicate the bone scapula 'spades' were initially developed for some other function and were subsequently transferred (exapted) to managing soils in rice marshes, which would have necessitated refinements in hafting. Tillage, perhaps with replanting, probably began in the 6th millennium BC, and had perhaps begun on a small scale by Kuahuqiao. Certainly by the time of Hemudu and/or Majiabang replanting and tillage had become the norm, as this would account for the reduction in awn hairs which implies the relaxation of natural selection as a seed dispersal aid. This period therefore involved wild plant food production, or pre-domestication cultivation, of rice.

The somewhat thicker grains from lower Longqiuzhuang, compared to Kuahuqiao, could suggest some selection for more domesticated plants, including more harvestable mature individuals as well as the thicker grains which characterize *japonica* domesticates as opposed to wild *rufipogon*. It is from the Majiabang period, however, that the first documented evidence for field systems occurs. At the site of Caoxieshan (Jiangshu province), a network of channels and dug-out features suggests small-scale wetland farming plots (Zou *et al.* 2000), with intensive cultivation of small plots (Figure 2.13). This development would prevent the cultivated wild rice from cross-pollination with free-growing populations. The creation of separate rice paddy fields could have sped up the selection for domesticated types in the cultivated populations.

In addition, the small and concentrated populations of rice in these fields might have encouraged experimentation with harvesting and harvesting efficiency. This would have involved both timing, to obtain larger quantities of mature grain, and techniques such as uprooting and cutting, which taken together could have increased selective pressure for non-shattering fully domesticated morphotypes. As evident from the measured grains of the upper level at Longqiuzhuang and the Songze and Liangzhu bulliforms, there appears to have been a shift towards harvesting more, or largely, mature rice plants during the latest Majiabang phase and the Songze, and certainly by Liangzhu times. This could only be readily achieved if the plants were domesticated.

In the later Songze period and Liangzhu phase, the first stone plough tips occur, indicating more intensive cultivation methods. The earliest plough tip is from a mid-to-late Songze period cemetery (see Administration of Cultural Heritage 1985), which suggests a minimum age for water buffalo domestication, as these are the only plausible energy source for pulling early ploughs. Archaeozoological analyses at Kuahuqiao are consistent with hunting of wild buffalo (Liu *et al.* 2004), and clear bone evidence for changing patterns of manipulation of this species or morphological change is so far lacking. While the domestication of this animal should be sought through systematic archaeozoology in assemblages dating between Kuahuqiao (5400 BC) to the Songze (3500 BC), the surprising lack of bones of *Bubalus* remains a challenge.

The evidence for harvesting tools also supports the evolutionary scheme hypothesized here. Stone sickles or harvesting knives are well-known from Middle Neolithic sites in northern China in millet-growing traditions, such as the Cishan, Beixin and Dawenkou cultures (Chang 1986: 93, 160; Barnes 1995: 100). Such tools are, however, unknown from Kuahuqiao, Hemudu and Majiabang periods

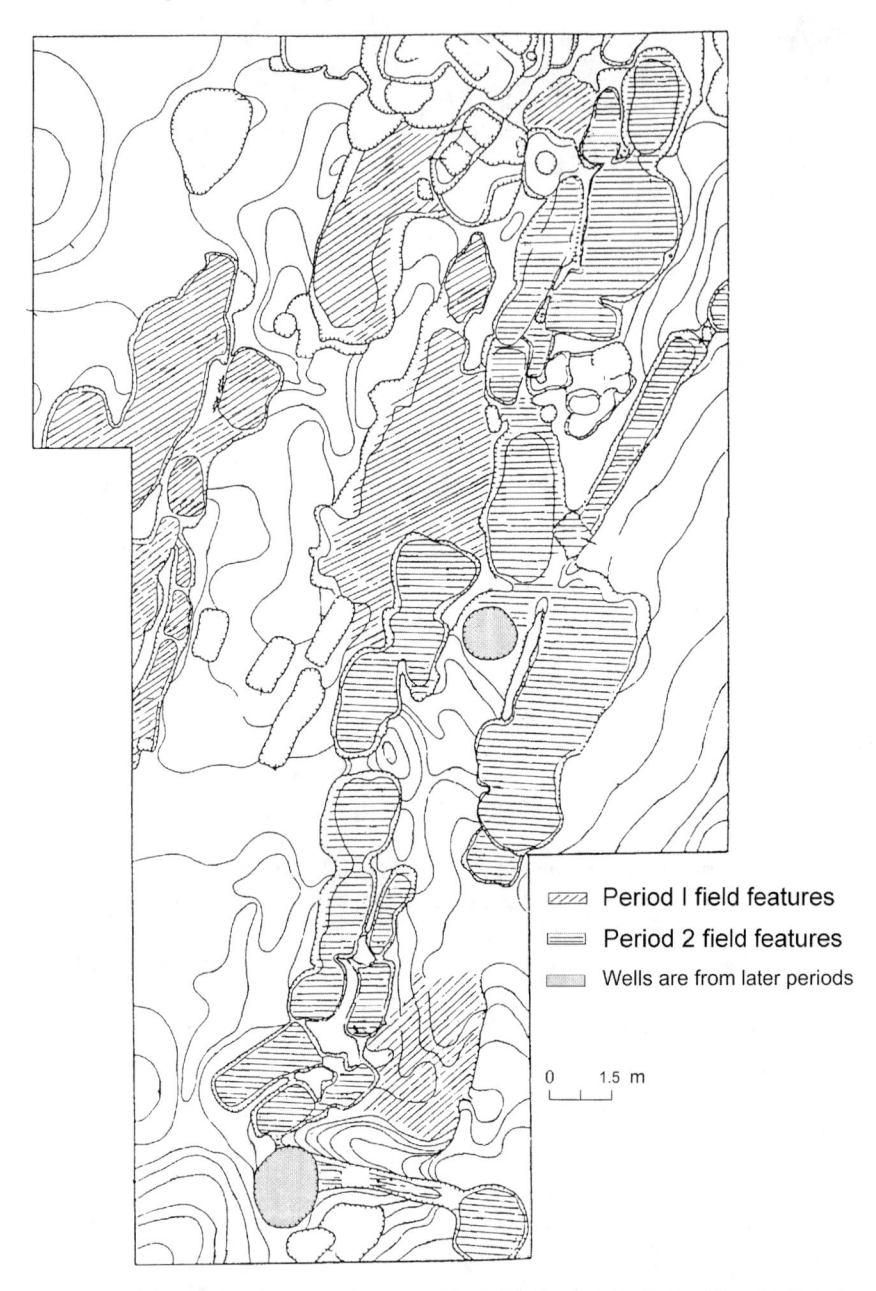

Figure 2.13 Plan of dug features of early paddy fields from Caioxieshan, late Majiabang period (4500–4000 BC), Jiangsu Province, China (after Zou *et al.* 2000).

in the Lower Yangtze, suggesting that harvesting during those periods did not involve sickling. Uprooting, or some other form of cutting or beating, while plants were still in their early stages of grain formation must be assumed. The first clear sickles or harvest knives in the Lower Yangtze date from the Liangzhu period (Chang 1986: 256–2; Barnes 1995: 100). Thus an intensification of wild plant food production (pre-domestication cultivation) focused on rice can be inferred for the Kuahuqiao–Hemudu–Majiabang sequence, for a period of at least one millennium (if beginning from Hemudu) or two millennia (if, from Kuahuqiao). This phase of pre-domestication cultivation of 1000–2000 years is comparable to that suggested by recent research in the Near East (e.g. Hillman 2000; Willcox 1999, 2002, 2004, 2005; Fuller 2005). When subsequent domestication occurred (by Late Majiabang/Songze, *c*. 4000 BC), it may have been in part based on a newly adopted harvesting technology of sickles, which had been long-established elsewhere in China.

Cultural and social developments

The sequence of agricultural evolution in the Lower Yangtze makes sense in terms of cultural and social developments in the region during the course of the Neolithic. While earlier sites comparable to Kuahuqiao and Hemudu are still few and far between, from the Majiabang, Songze and Liangzhu phase considerable numbers are known. This includes not only settlement sites but numerous cemeteries, which provide a useful window into aspects of social organization and complexity (Qin 2000, 2003). From the Majiabang period through to the earlier Songze, large cemeteries are known, with the largest ones known having some hundreds to more than a thousand burials, as at Weidun (e.g. Changzhou Museum 1974, 1984, 2001) and Sanxingcun (Sanxingcun Archaeology Team 2004). While finds in these graves include some of the earliest objects of craft production, including jade *Jue* and *Huang*, there is little evidence for major stratification within cemeteries in terms of access to wealth nor differences between cemeteries. One exception is the site of Lingjiatan, early Songze period (Anhui Provincial Institute 2000), which is markedly richer than any other site, and included the distinctive object types known as jade figurines, tortoise-with-plaque, dragon, eagle-bear-shaped-ornaments, and so on. While this may have been a significant centre of craft production and wealth accumulation, it did not continue in this way into subsequent periods.

By the later Songze period (*cal.* 3500–3300 BC), important social changes suggest developing social stratification. Cemeteries are smaller than the previous period, with grave counts numbering around 100 graves per cemetery, such as Songze (Administration of Cultural Heritage 1987) and Nanhebang (Zhejiang Provincial Institute 2005a). Within these cemeteries there is recurring evidence for internal social differentiation suggested by access to prestige objects such as jade ornaments and stone axes, and the total number of ceramic vessels deposited in graves (Qin 2003). The emergence of small paddy fields during the late Majiabang period would have provided a new means of producing a controllable form of wealth in terms of grain surpluses, and would have necessitated increased territoriality and a system of land ownership. It was the more productive and intensive agriculture made possible by full morphological domestication that would have provided for increased production of wealth objects. Agricultural intensification, in terms of increased labour input and increased productivity per unit of land (cf. Boserup 1965; Morrison 1994), occurred during the Songze period as indicated by the first appearance of stone plough tips (Administration of Cultural Heritage 1985), implying the emergence of animal (buffalo) traction. As argued in the context of the Near East and Europe (Sherratt 1981, 1999) this 'secondary product revolution' would have enhanced the production of wealth differentials and changes in social organization relating to status difference between families and probably between genders. The increasing size of plough heads through the course of the subsequent Liangzhu period suggests a further trend towards more intensive and probably more productive rice agriculture.

Social differentiation became increasingly marked during the course of the Liangzhu period (from 3300 BC), with increasing regional population density and craft specialization, especially evident in the production of prestige jade objects (Qin 2003). Cemeteries in this period became significantly smaller and more exclusive. Groups of graves generally number between 20 and 40. The cemeteries occur in two types, those dug into specially prepared clay platforms (e.g. Luodun site, see Suzhou Museum 1999) and those dug adjacent to houses (e.g. Puanqiao site, see Archaeology Department of Peking University 1998). By the mid Liangzhu period (3000 BC) it is clear from burial objects that the platform cemeteries have particular access to wealth, including large numbers of jade objects produced by a very limited number of specialized production centres that were probably linked to distinct, and controlled, geological jade sources (e.g. Fanshan site, see Zhejiang Province Institute 2005b; Qin 2003). The richest platform cemeteries are clearly located at the key regional centres, much as Liangzhu itself (Zhejiang Province Institute 2005c). By this period, sites were widely distributed across the landscape, and with quite small habitation structures located on low anthropogenic mounds. This pattern suggests a high density of farmers practising rice plough agriculture.

A wider context of rice production and domestication in Neolithic China

The revised model for the development of agriculture in Lower Yangtze needs to be understood in a wider comparative context of Neolithic economies in China. Figure 2.14 provides a synthetic chronological framework for various regional Neolithic traditions in China on which we have charted our revised model for the evolution of plant cultivation and domestication in the Lower Yangtze and suggested equivalent hypotheses for other regions. For virtually all of these regions, published archaeobotanical data is not yet adequate to chart these developments unambiguously. Nevertheless a coherent framework emergences, in which agriculture based on domesticated rice is much later than generally assumed. This

Agriculture in the Lower Yangtze region 71

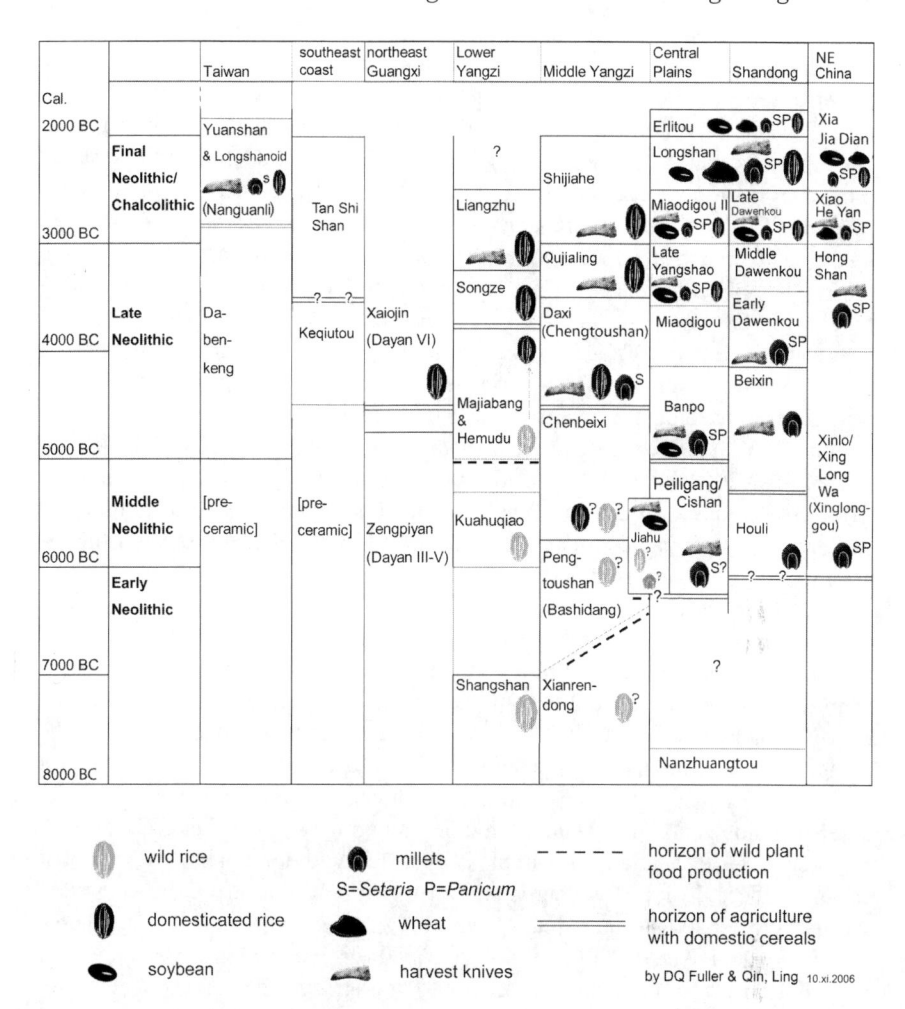

Cal.	Taiwan	southeast coast	northeast Guangxi	Lower Yangzi	Middle Yangzi	Central Plains	Shandong	NE China
2000 BC	Final Neolithic/ Chalcolithic	Yuanshan & Longshanoid (Nanguanli)	Tan Shi Shan	? Liangzhu	Shijiahe	Erlitou Longshan Miaodigou II	Late Dawenkou	Xia Jia Dian Xiao He Yan
3000 BC					Qujialing	Late Yangshao	Middle Dawenkou	Hong Shan
4000 BC	Late Neolithic	Da-ben-keng	—?—?— Xaiojin Keqiutou (Dayan VI)	Songze	Daxi (Chengtoushan)	Miaodigou	Early Dawenkou	
5000 BC				Majiabang & Hemudu	Chenbeixi	Banpo	Beixin	Xinlo/ Xing Long Wa (Xinglong-gou)
6000 BC	Middle Neolithic	[pre-ceramic]	[pre-ceramic] Zengpiyan (Dayan III-V)	Kuahuqiao Peng- toushan (Bashidang)	? Jiahu ?	Peiligang/ Cishan	Houli	
7000 BC	Early Neolithic			Shangshan	Xianren-dong ?	?		
8000 BC					Nanzhuangtou			

Legend:
- wild rice
- domesticated rice
- soybean
- millets (S=*Setaria* P=*Panicum*)
- wheat
- harvest knives
- ----- horizon of wild plant food production
- ═══ horizon of agriculture with domestic cereals

by DQ Fuller & Qin, Ling 10.xi.2006

Figure 2.14 A synthetic chronology of Neolithic China based on evidence for major crops and the transitions to cultivation and domestication.

succeeds lengthy traditions of wild plant food production (of 1,000–2,000 years) and presumably an even longer period of wild rice collecting by Early Holocene (and Late Pleistocene) hunter-gatherers. Sites with wild plant food production tend to have abundant evidence for gathered plant foods, most notably nuts and acorns. Elsewhere in China, in the Yellow River basin and further north, millet cultivation and harvesting with sickles were already well established.

These broad chronological patterns may correlate with important aspects of environmental change. A number of recent palaeoenvironmental studies from Lower Yangtze region provide well-dated information on Holocene climate and vegetation (Yu *et al.* 2000; Yi *et al.* 2003; Lu *et al.* 2003; Tao *et al.* 2006) and in broad outline these correlate with data from the South China Sea, suggesting that these indeed reflect primarily regional climate change. After 15,000 BP, East Asia warmed, reflected in chemical analyses of South China Sea sediments (Wang *et al.* 1999) and in pollen diagrams from the broader region, such as Japan (Yasuda 2002; Yasuda and Negendank 2003), which indicate the decline (or northward retreat) of coniferous taxa and the increase of broad-leaved taxa, including oaks (*Quercus/Cyclobalanopsis/Lithocarpus*) and chestnuts (*Castanopsis/Castanea*). Under such circumstance we would expect wild rice species to have migrated into the Yangtze basin for the first time (and perhaps further north). This is probably reflected in the first occurrence of rice bulliforms at 14,000–13,000 BP in a core in the palaeo-estuary of the Yangtze (Lu *et al.* 2003), although identification of these phytoliths with domesticated rice is doubtful. After this period, the earliest reports of archaeological rice grains and phytoliths occur in cave sites south of the middle Yangtze region, e.g. Yuchanyan, Xianrengdong, Diaotunghuan (Zhao 1998; Zhang 2002; Yuan 2002; Yasuda 2002), which we would interpret as hunter-gatherers beginning to add this newly available species group to their foraging strategy. This favourable climate was interrupted by the Younger Dryas which is clear in most palaeoenvironmental datasets.

In the Early Holocene a climatic optimum favoured once again the spread of subtropical/warm-temperate broad-leaved trees, including nut-bearing oaks and chestnuts, as well as wild rice. Rice phytoliths reappear in the offshore core from *cal.* 9000 BP (Lu *et al.* 2003). In the Lower Yangtze region much of today's low-lying land area had not yet formed – this occurred subsequently due to the combination of alluvial sedimentation and sea-level fall. Kuahuqiao lies in a slightly higher topographic position than Hemudu or Majiabang, which is likely to reflect colonization in the later periods of emerging low-lying land. These areas are likely to have had many favourable habitats for wild rice. An important habitat change, reflected in pollen diagrams, is a marked decline in nut-bearing trees shortly before 5000 BC, including *Quercus*, *Cyclobalanopsis*, and in some cores *Castanonpsis* (Tao *et al.* 2006; Yu *et al.* 2000). This is reflected in a broader pattern of declines in arboreal pollen (Yi *et al.* 2003). It is striking that this correlates with the period of the emergence of the Hemudu culture. Nut-using foragers of the region may have responded by relying increasingly on available wild rice and they therefore began to bolster rice supplies through cultivation. One issue which is still not clear is how these climatic changes of the mid-Holocene would have impacted wild rice stands, which may also have influenced the strategies of the Kuahuqiao–Hemudu nut-foragers.

Conclusion

The reappraisal of the archaeobotany and archaeology of the Lower Yangtze in this chapter should provide a new framework for problem-oriented research. We have proposed some explicit and testable hypotheses about the nature of rice and rice use in the Lower Yangtze from the period 6000 to 2500 BC, with implications for earlier periods and other regions of China (such as the middle Yangtze). Our model of rice-use by nut-focused forager-hunter-fishers until the 6th millennium BC, followed by a long period of 1,000–2,000 years of initial pre-domestication cultivation, differs from previous descriptions of the archaeological cultures in this region. Our model fits with available archaeobotanical data and predicts what further systematic sampling should find: grains with morphometrics in the wild/immature range that become mature and domesticated over the course of the 6th and 5th millennia BC and rice populations that shift statistically from immature and wild type shattering to predominantly mature and non-shattering. This is congruent with causal factors that incorporate regional environmental change. New samples of rice spikelet bases and rice grains provide an opportunity to assess this hypothesis, and indeed recent excavations at Tianluoshan (a Hemudu culture site), provide such an opportunity. The authors' current collaborative research on archaeobotany of Tianluoshan has been designed specifically with these problems in mind and so far there are indications of not only great quantities of water chestnuts and acorns but also rice spikelet bases. Initial results suggest that we can distinguish the presence of mature wild, immature wild and domesticated abscission scar types, and the proportions of these will indicate where along the evolutionary trajectory of domestication this site lies.

Our revised model of late rice domestication in the Lower Yangzte also makes sense in terms of social inferences from the region's archaeology. If, as some have suggested, rice cultivation (and domestication) were indeed present from the Late Pleistocene, where are the agricultural village sites between the Pleistocene and mid-Holocene? Rice agriculture is highly productive and would be expected to promote marked population density increase in the region, but large numbers and densities of sites do not occur before the late Majiabang, Songze and Liangzhu periods, i.e. from the late 5th millennium BC. Our model provides a framework which explains this demographic transition and the lack of substantial numbers of earlier settlement sites. One of the contributing factors to previous misconceptions has been an anachronistic emphasis on rice agriculture, with little research effort expended on understanding the role of nuts, fish and other wild resources. A contrast can be drawn with Early Holocene archaeology in Japan, where more emphasis has been laid on nut-use, because rice domestication is not an issue. Indeed, as noted by Crawford (2005: 84), early ceramic-producing societies are conventionally interpreted in contrasting ways in the archaeological research traditions of China and Japan, with the assumption that they represent agriculturalists in China and hunter-gatherers in Japan. The archaeobotanical evidence from the Lower Yangtze suggests that it is time to emphasize the importance of nuts and hunter-gatherer practices in the formation of early village cultures in southern China.

Acknowledgements

The authors would like to thank our Zhejiang province colleagues, especially Sun Guoping and Zheng Yunfei, who introduced the first author to the material of the Hemudu museum and other sites under research by the provincial institute. We have also benefited from discussions with Zhao Zhijun. Our current archaeobotanical collaboration at Tianluoshan has been made possible by Sun, Zheng, Zhao and the provincial director, Cao Jin Yan. The authors' involvement in this project is supported by grants from the Sino-British Trust of the British Academy and China National Education Ministry Project Grant for the Center for the Study of Chinese Archaeology at Peking University. Research on the morphometrics of modern rice species was conducted by E. Harvey as a research student supported by an Arts and Humanities Research Board studentship.

References

Administration of Cultural Heritage of Shanghai (1985) 'Shanghai Songjiang xian Tangmiaocun yizhi' 上海松江县汤庙村遗址 (Tangmiaocun site in Songjiang county of Shanghai), *Kaogu* 考古 (Archaeology), 1985(7): 590.

Administration of Cultural Heritage of Shanghai (1987) *Songze: xinshiqi shidai yizhi fajue baogao* 崧泽：新石器时代遗址发掘报告 (Songze: Excavation Report of a Neolithic Site), Beijing: Cultural Relics Publishing House.

Administration of Cultural Heritage of Shanghai (2002) *Maqiao: 1993–1997 fajue baogao* 马桥: *1993–1997 年发掘报告* (Maqiao Site: 1993–1997 Excavation Report), Shanghai: Shanghai Calligraphy and Painting Press.

Administration of Cultural Heritage of Zhejiang (1978) 'Hemudu yizhi diyici fajue baogao' 河姆渡遗址第一次发掘报告 (First season's excavation report of Hemudu site), *Kaogu xueba* 考古学报 (Acta Archaeologia Sinica), 1978(1): 39–108.

Allen, H. (1974) 'The Bagundji of the Darling Basin: Cereal gatherers in an uncertain environment', *World Archaeology*, 5: 309–22.

Anhui Provincial Institute of Archaeology (2000) *Lingjiatan yuqi* 凌家滩玉器 (The Jade Wares from Liangjiatan Site), Beijing: Cultural Relics Publishing House.

Archaeology Department of Peking University (1998) 'Zhejiang Tongxiang Pu'anqiao yizhi fajue jianbao' 浙江桐乡普安桥遗址发掘简报 (Brief report of the excavation of Puanqiao site in Tongxiang of Zhejiang province), *Wenwu* 文物 (Cultural Relics), 1998(4): 1–74.

Barlow, K.R. and Heck, M. (2002) 'More on acorn eating during the Natufian: Expected patterning in diet and the archaeological record of subsistence', in S.L.R. Mason and J. Hather (eds) *Hunter-gatherer Archaeobotany: Perspectives from the Northern Temperate Zone*, pp. 128–45, London: Institute of Archaeology, University College London.

Barnes, G.L. (1993) *China, Korea and Japan: The Rise of Civilization in East Asia*, London: Thames & Hudson.

Bar-Yosef, O. (2000) 'The context of animal domestication in Southwestern Asia', in M. Mashkour, A.M. Choyke, H. Buitenhuis and F. Poplin (eds) *Archaeozoology of the Near East IVA: Proceedings of the Fourth International Symposium on the Archaeozoology of Southwestern Asia and Adjacent Areas*, pp. 185–95, Groningen: ARC.

Bar-Yosef, O. (2003) 'The Natufian and the Early Neolithic: Social and economic trends in Southwestern Asia', in P. Bellwood and C. Renfrews (eds) *Examining the Farming/Language Dispersal Hypothesis*, pp. 113–26, Cambridge: McDonald Institute for Archaeological Research.

Bellwood, P. (1997) *Prehistory of the Indo-Malaysian Archipelago*, 2nd edn, Honolulu, HI: University of Hawaii Press.

Bellwood, P. (2005) *First Farmers: The Origins of Agricultural Societies*, Oxford: Blackwell.

Boserup, E. (1965) *The Conditions of Agricultural Growth: The Economics of Agrarian Change under Population Pressure*, Chicago, IL: Aldine.

Brownman, D.L., Fritz, G.J. and Watson, P.J. (2005) 'Origins of food-producing societies in the Americas', in C. Scarre (ed.) *The Human Past: World Prehistory and the Development of Human Societies*, pp. 306–49, London: Thames & Hudson.

Chang, K.-C. (1986) *The Archaeology of Ancient China*, New Haven, CT: Yale University Press.

Chang, T.T. (1983) 'The origins and early cultures of the cereal grains and food legumes', in D.N. Keightley (ed.) *The Origins of Chinese Civilization*, pp. 65–93, Berkeley, CA: University of California Press.

Chang, T.T. (1995) 'Rice', in J. Smartt and N.W. Simmonds (eds) *Evolution of Crop Plants*, pp. 147–55, Harlow: Longman Scientific.

Chang, T.T. (2000) 'Rice', in K.F. Kiple and K.C. Ornelas (eds) *The Cambridge World History of Food*, pp. 132–49, Cambridge: Cambridge University Press.

Changzhou Museum (1974) 'Jiangsu Changzhou Weidun cun xinshiqi shidai yizhi de diaocha yu shijue' 江苏常州圩墩村新石器时代遗址的调查与试掘 (The Survey and Testing Excavation of Weidun Neolithic Site in Changzhou in Jiangsu Province), *Kaogu* 考古 (Archaeology), 1974(2): 109–15.

Changzhou Museum (1984) 'Changzhou Weidun xinshiqi shidai yizhi disanci fajue jianbao' 常州圩墩新石器时代遗址第三次发掘简报 (The brief report for the third season's excavation of Weidun Neolithic site in Changzhou), *Shiqian yanjiu* 史前研究 (Prehistoric Studies), 1984(2): 69–81.

Changzhou Museum (2001) '1985nian Jiangsu Changzhou Weidun yizhi de fajue' 1985年江苏常州圩墩遗址的发掘 (1985's excavation of Weidun site), *Kaogu xueba* 考古学报 (Acta Archaeologia Sinica), 2001(1): 73–110.

Chen, W.-B., Ikuo, N., Yo-Ichiro, S. and Nakai, H. (1993) '*Indica* and *Japonica* differentiation in Chinese landraces', *Euphytica*, 74: 195–201.

Cheng, C., Motohashi, R., Tchuchimoto, S., Fukuta, Y., Ohtsubo, H. and Ohtsubo E. (2003) 'Polyphyletic origin of cultivated rice: based on the interspersion patterns of SINEs', *Molecular Biology and Evolution*, 20: 67–75.

Cohen, D.J. (1998) 'The origins of domesticated cereals and the Pleistocene–Holocene transition in East Asia', *Review of Archaeology*, 19: 22–9.

Cohen, D.J. (2002) 'New perspectives on the transition to agriculture in China', in Y. Yasuda (ed.) *The Origins of Pottery and Agriculture*, pp. 217–27, New Delhi: Lustre Press and Roli Books.

Colledge, S. (1998) 'Identifying pre-domestication cultivation using multivariate analysis', in A.B. Damania, J. Valkoun, G. Willcox and C.O. Qualset (eds) *The Origins of Agriculture and Crop Domestication*, pp. 121–31, Aleppo, Syria: ICARDA.

Colledge, S. (2001) *Plant Exploitation on Epipalaeolithic and Early Neolithic Sites in the Levant*, Oxford: British Archaeological Reports.

Colledge, S. (2004) 'Reappraisal of the archaeobotanical evidence for the emergence and dispersal of the "founder crops"', in E. Peltenberg and A. Wasse (eds) *Neolithic Revolution: New Perspectives on Southwest Asia in Light of Recent Discoveries on Cyprus*, pp. 49–60, Oxford: Oxbow Books.

Crawford, G.W. (1983) *Paleoethnobotany of the Kameda Peninsula Jomon*, Anthropological Papers, Museum of Anthropology, University of Michegan No. 73. Ann Arbor, MI: University of Michigan.

Crawford, G. (2005) 'East Asian Plant Domestication', in M.T. Stark (ed.) *Archaeology of Asia*, pp. 77–95, Oxford: Blackwell Publishing.

Crawford, G. and Lee, G.-A. (2003) 'Agricultural origins in the Korean Peninsula', *Antiquity*, 77: 87–95.

Crawford, G. and Shen, C. (1998) 'The origins of rice agriculture: recent progress in East Asia', *Antiquity*, 72: 858–66.

Crawford, G., Underhill, A., Zhijun Zhao, Gyoung-ah Lee, Feinman, G., Nicholas, L., Fengshi Luan, Haiguang Yu, Hui Fang and Fengshu Cai (2005) 'Late Neolithic plant remains from northern China: preliminary results from Liangchengzhen, Shandong', *Current Anthropology*, 46: 309–17.

Diamond, J., and Bellwood, P. (2003) 'Farmers and their languages: the first expansions', *Science*, 300: 597–603.

Fagan, B.M. (1995) *Ancient North America: The Archaeology of a Continent*, London: Thames & Hudson.

Fei, H. and Min Zhang (2000) 'Pollen and phytolith evidence for rice cultivation during the Neolithic at Longqiuzhuang, eastern Jianghuai, China', *Vegetation History and Archaeobotany*, 9: 161–8.

Fuller, D.Q. (2002) 'Fifty years of archaeobotanical studies in India: laying a solid foundation', in S. Settar and R. Korisettar (eds) *Indian Archaeology in Retrospect*, vol. 3, *Archaeology and Interactive Disciplines*, pp. 247–363, Delhi: Manohar.

Fuller, D.Q. [= Fu Daolian 傅稻镰] (2005) 'A comparative study on the origins of agriculture', *Gudai Wenming* 古代文明 (Ancient Civilizations), 4: 317–38 (in Chinese, trans Qin Ling).

Gardner, P.S. (1997) 'The ecological structure and behavioral implications of mast exploitation strategies', in K.J. Gremillion (ed.) *People, Plants, and Landscapes: Studies in Paleoethnobotany*, pp. 161–78, Tuscaloosa, AL: University of Alabama Press.

Garton, D. (1979). 'A study of the effects of charring in rice grains', BA dissertation, Institute of Archaeology, University of London.

Gepts, P. (2004) 'Crop domestication as a long-term selection experiment', *Plant Breeding Reviews*, 24: 1–44.

Gu Jianxiang (2003) 'Chuodun Yizhi Majiabang Wenhua Shiqi Shuidao Tian' 绰墩遗址马家浜时期水稻田 (The rice paddy land from Chuodun site of Majiabang period), Chuodun Shan site: Collected papers, *Dongnan Wenhua* (South-east Culture), 2003 (special issue 1): 42–5 (in Chinese).

Harlan, J.R. (1975) *Crops and Man*, Madison, WI: American Society for Agronomy.

Harlan, J.R. (1989) 'Wild grass-seed harvesting in the Sahara and sub-Sahara of Africa', in D.R. Harris and G.C. Hillman (eds) *Foraging and Farming: The Exploitation of Plant Resources*, pp. 79–98, London: Unwin & Hyman.

Harlan, J.R., De Wet, J.M.J. and Price, E.G. (1973) 'Comparative evolution of cereals', *Evolution*, 27: 311–25.

Harris, D.R. (1977) 'Alternative pathways towards agriculture', in C.A. Reed (ed.) *Origins of Agriculture*, pp. 179–243, The Hague: Mouton.

Harris, D.R. (1984) 'Ethnohistorical evidence for the exploitation of wild grasses and forbs: Its scope and archaeological implications', in W.A. van Zeist and W.C. Casparie (eds) *Plants and Ancient Man: Studies in Palaeoethnobotany*, pp. 63–9, Rotterdam: Balkema.

Harris, D.R. (1989) 'An evolutionary continuum of people-plant interaction', in D.R. Harris and G.C. Hillman (eds) *Foraging and Farming: The Evolution of Plant Exploitation*, pp. 11–26, London: Routledge.

Harris, D.R. (1996) 'Introduction: themes and concepts in the study of early agriculture', in D.R. Harris (ed.) *The Origins and Spread of Agriculture and Pastoralism in Eurasia*, pp. 1–9, London: UCL Press.

Harris D.R. (1998) 'The origins of agriculture in southwest Asia', *The Review of Archaeology*, 19: 5–11.

Harris, D.R. (2005) 'Origins and spread of agriculture', in G. Prance and M. Nesbitt (eds) *The Cultural History of Plants*, pp. 13–26, London: Routledge.

Harvey, E.L. (2006) 'Early agricultural communities in northern and eastern India: an archaeobotanical investigation', PhD dissertation, University College London.

Heizer, R.F. and Elsasser, A.B. (1980) *The Natural World of the California Indians*, Berkeley, CA: University of California Press.

Helbaek, H. (1960) 'The palaeoethnobotany of the Near East and Europe', in R.J. Braidwood and B. Howe (eds) *Prehistoric Investigations in Iraqi Kurdistan*, pp. 99–108, Chicago, IL: University of Chicago Press.

Henan Provincial Institute of Archaeology (1999) *Wuyang jiahu* 舞阳贾湖 (Jiahu Site in Wuyang), Beijing: Science Press.

Higham, C.F.W. (1995) 'The transition to rice cultivation in Southeast Asia', in T.D. Price and A. Gebauer (eds) *Last Hunters – First Farmers: New Perspectives on the Prehistoric Transition to Agriculture*, pp. 127–56, Santa Fe, NM: School of American Research.

Higham, C.F.W. (2003) 'Languages and farming dispersals: Austroasiatic languages and rice cultivation', in P. Bellwood and C. Renfrew (eds) *Examining the Language/Farming Dispersal Hypothesis*, pp. 223–32, Cambridge: McDonald Institute for Archaeological Research.

Higham, C.F.W. (2005) 'East Asian agriculture and its impact', in C. Scarre (ed.) *The Human Past: World Prehistory and the Development of Human Societies*, pp. 234–63, London: Thames & Hudson.

Hillman, G.C. (2000) 'Abu Hureyra 1: the Epipalaeolithic', in A.M.T. Moore, G.C. Hillman and A.J. Legge (eds) *Village on the Euphrates: From Foraging to Farming at Abu Hureyra*, pp. 327–98, New York: Oxford University Press.

Hillman, G., and Davies, M.S. (1990a) 'Measured domestication rates in wild wheats and barley under primitive cultivation and their archaeological implications', *Journal of World Prehistory*, 4: 157–222.

Hillman, G., and Davies, M.S. (1990b) 'Domestication rates in wild wheats and barley under primitive cultivation', *Biological Journal of the Linnean Society*, 39: 39–78.

Hillman, G.C., Hedges, R., Moore, A.M.T., Colledge, S. and Pettitt, P. (2001) 'New evidence of Late Glacial cereal cultivation at Abu Hureyra on the Euphrates', *The Holocene*, 11: 383–93.

Hoshikawa, K. (1993) 'Anthesis, Fertilization and Development of Caryopsis', in T. Matsuo and K. Hoshikawa (eds) *Science of the Rice Plant*, vol. 1, *Morphology*, pp. 339–76, Tokyo: Food and Agriculture Policy Research Center.

Huang, Xianghong (2001) 'Weidun yizhi chutu dongwu yihai jianding' 圩墩遗址出土动物遗骸鉴定 (The identification of animal remains from Weidun Site), *Kaogu xueba* 考古学报 (Acta Archaeologia Sinica), 2001(1): 108.

Huang, F., and Min Zhang (2000) 'Pollen and phytolith evidence for rice cultivation during the Neolithic at Longqiuzhuang, eastern Jainghuai, China', *Vegetation History and Archaeobotany*, 9: 161–8.

Imamura, K. (1996) *Prehistoric Japan: New Perspectives on Insular East Asia*, London: UCL Press.

Jenks, A.E. (1900) *The Wild Rice Gatherers of the Upper Lakes: A Study in American Primitive Economics* (Annual report of the Bureau of American Ethnology to the Secretary of the Smithsonian Institution, 19/2), Washington, DC: Government Printing Office.

Jiarong, Y. (2002) 'Rice and pottery 10,000 yrs BP at Yuchanyan, Dao County, Hunan Province', in Y. Yasuda (ed.) *The Origins of Pottery and Agriculture*, pp. 157–66, New Delhi: Lustre Press and Roli Books.

Johannessen, S. (1988) 'Plant remains and culture change: Are Paleoethnobotanical data better than we think?', in C.A. Hatorf and V.S. Popper (eds) *Current Paleoethnobotany: Analytical Methods and Cultural Interpretations of Archaeological Plant Remains*, pp. 145–66, Chicago, IL: University of Chicago Press.

Kharakwal, J.S., Yano, A., Yasuda, Y., Shinde, V.S. and Osada T. (2004) 'Cord impressed ware and rice cultivation in South Asia, China and Japan: possibilities of inter-links', *Quaternary International*, 123–5: 105–15.

Kislev, M.E. (1997) 'Early agriculture and paleoecology of Netiv Hagdud', in O. Bar-Yosef and A. Gopher (eds) *An Early Neolithic Village in the Jordan Valley*, part 1, *The Archaeology of Netiv Hagdud*, pp. 209–36, Cambridge, MA: Peabody Museum of Archaeology and Ethnology, Harvard University.

Kislev, M.E., Nadel, D. and Carmi, I. (1992) 'Epipalaeolithic (19,000 BP) cereal and fruit diet at Ohalu II, Sea of Galilee, Israel', *Review of Palaeobotany and Palynology*, 73: 161–6.

Kobayashi, T., Kaner, S. and Nakamura, O. (2004) *Jomon Reflections: Forager Life and Culture in the Prehistoric Japanese Archipelago*, Oxford: Oxbow Books.

Larson, G., Dobney, K., Albarella, U., Fang, M., Matisoo-Smith, E., Robins, J., Lowden, S., Finlayson, H., Brand, T., Willerslev, E., Rowley-Conwy, P., Andersson, L. and Cooper, A. (2005) 'Worldwide phylogeography of wild boar reveals multiple centers of pig domestication', *Science*, 307: 1618–21.

Lee, R.B. (1968) 'What hunters do for a living, or, how to make out on scarce resources', in R.B. Lee and I. de Vore (eds) *Man the Hunter*, pp. 30–48, Chicago, IL: Aldine.

Li, Can, Yu Zhang, Kai Ying, Xiang Liang and Bin Han (2004) 'Sequence variation of simple sequence repeats on chromosome-4 in two subspecies of Asian cultivated rice', *Theoretical and Applied Genetics*, 108: 392–400.

Liu, Changjiang (2004) 'Su, Shu zili de xingtai bijiao jiqi zai kaogu jianding zhong de yiyi' 粟、黍籽粒的形态比较及其在考古鉴定中的意义 (Morphological comparison of foxtail millet and broomcorn millet and its significance in archaeological identification), *Kaogu* 考古 (Archaeology), 2004(8): 76–83.

Liu, Li, X. Chen et al. (2004) 'Kuahuqiao yizhi de shuiniu yicun fenxi' 跨湖桥遗址的水牛遗存分析 (Investigation of water buffalo from Kuahuqiao site), in Zhejiang Provincial Institute of Cultural Relics and Archaeology (ed.) *Kuahuqiao*, pp. 344–8, Beijing: Cultural Relics Publishing House.

Liu, J. (1985) 'Some observations on the archaeological site of Hemudu, Zhejiang Province, China', *Bulletin of the Indo-Pacific Prehistory Association*, 6: 40–5.

Londo, J.P., Chiang, Y.-C., Hung, K.-H., Chiang, T.-Y., and Schaal, B.A. (2006) 'Phylogeography of Asian wild rice, *Oryza rufipogon*, reveals multiple independent domestications of cultivated rice, *Oryza sativa*', *Proceedings of the National Academy of Sciences (USA)*, 103: 9578–83.

Lone, F.A., Khan, M. and Buth, G.M. (1993) *Palaeoethnobotany: Plants and Ancient Man in Kashmir*, Rotterdam: Balkema.

Longqiuzhuang Site Archaeology Team (1999) *Longqiuzhuang* 龙虬庄 (Longqiuzhuang Site), Beijing: Science Press.
Lu, T.L.D. (1998) 'A green foxtail (*Setaria viridis*) cultivation experiment in the Middle Yellow River Valley and some related issues', *Asian Perspectives*, 41: 1–14.
Lu, T.L.D. (1999) *The Transition from Foraging to Farming and the Origin of Agriculture in China*, Oxford: BAR.
Lu, T.L.D. (2006) 'The occurrence of cereal cultivation in China', *Asian Perspectives*, 45: 129–58.
Lu, H., Liu, Z., Wu, N., Berne, S., Saito, Y., Liu, B. and Wang, L. (2003) 'Rice domestication and climatic change: phytolith evidence from East China', *Boreas*, 31: 378–85.
Luojiajiao Archaeology Team (1981) *Tongxiang xian Luojiajiao yizhi fajue baogao* 桐乡县罗家角遗址发掘报告 (Excavations at Luojiajiao Site in Tongxiang County of Zhejiang Province), Beijing: Cultural Relics Publishing House.
Meadow, R. (1993) 'Animal domestication in the Middle East: A revised view from the eastern Margin', in G. Possehl (ed.) *Harappan Civilization: A Recent Perspective*, pp. 295–320, New Delhi: Oxford and IBH.
Menninger, E.A. (1977) *Edible Nuts of the World*, Stuart, FL: Horticultural Books.
Milner, G.R. (2004) *The Moundbuilders: Ancient Peoples of Eastern North America*, London: Thames & Hudson.
Morrison, K.D. (1994) 'Intensification of production: archaeological approaches', *Journal of Archaeological Method and Theory,* 1: 111–59.
Nasu, H., Momohara, A., Yasuda, Y., and He, J. (2006) 'The occurrence and identification of Setaria italica (L.) P. Beauv. (foxtail millet) grains from the Chengtoushan site (ca. 5800 cal BP) in central China, with reference to the domestication centre in Asia', *Vegetation History and Archaeobotany* (online first: DOI 10.1007/s00334-006-0068-4).
Nesbitt, M.N. (2006) *Identification Guide for Near Eastern Grass Seeds*, London: Institute of Archaeology, University College London.
Oka, H.I. (1988) *Origin of Cultivated Rice*, Tokyo: Japanese Scientific Societies Press.
Oka, H.-I. and Morishima, H. (1967) 'Variations in the breeding systems of a wild rice, *Oryza perennis*', *Evolution*, 21: 249–58.
Pei, A. (1998) 'Notes on new advancements and revelations in the agricultural archaeology of early rice domestication in the Dongting Lake region', *Antiquity*, 72: 878–85.
Qin, L. (2000) 'Liangzhu wenhua de yanjiu xianzhuang ji xiangguan wenti' 良渚文化的研究现状及相关问题 (Review of the history and issues in the study on Liangzhu culture), *Kaoguxue yanjiu* 考古学研究 (Archaeology Studies), 4: 77–100.
Qin, Ling (2003) 'Huantaihu diqu shiqian shehui jiegou de tansuo' 环太湖地区史前社会结构的探索 (A study of prehistoric social structure in Taihu area), PhD dissertation, Peking University, Beijing.
Sano, R., and Morishima, H. (1992) '*Indica-Japonica* differentiation of rice cultivars viewed from variations in key characters of isozyme, with species reference to Himalayan hilly areas', *Theoretical and Applied Genetics*, 84: 266–74.
Sanxingcun Archaeology Team (2004) 'Jiangsu jintan sanxingcun xinshiqi shidai yizhi' 江苏金坛三星村新石器时代遗址 (Sanxingcun, a Neolithic site in Jintan of Jiangsu Province)', in Zhejaing Provincial Institute (ed.) *Majiabang wenhua* 马家浜文化 (Majiabang Culture), pp. 193ff, Hangzhou: Zhejiang Photography Press.
Sato, Y.-I. (2002) 'Origin of rice cultivation in the Yangtze River Basin', in Y. Yasuda (ed.) *The Origins of Pottery and Agriculture*, pp. 143–50, New Delhi: Lustre Press and Roli Books.

Sato, Yo-Ichiro, Ryuuji Ishikawa and Hiroko Morishima (1990) 'Nonrandom association of genes and characters found in *indica x japonica* hybrids of rice', *Heredity*, 65: 75–9.

Sherratt, A. (1981) 'Plough and pastoralism: aspects of the secondary products revolution', in I. Hodder, G. Isaac and N. Hammond (eds) *Pattern of the Past: Studies in Honour Of David Clarke*, pp. 261–305, Cambridge: Cambridge University Press.

Sherratt, A. (1999) 'Cash-crops before cash: organic consumables and trade', in C. Gosden and J. Hather (eds) *The Prehistory of Food: Appetites For Change*, pp. 13–34, London: Routledge.

Smith, B.D. (1992) *Rivers of Change: Essays on Early Agriculture in Eastern North America*, Washington, DC: Smithsonian Press.

Smith, B. D. (1995) *The Emergence of Agriculture*, New York: Scientific American Library.

Smith, B.D. (2001) 'Low-level food production', *Journal of Archaeological Research*, 9: 1–43.

Suzhou Museum (1999) 'Jiangsu Changshu Luodun yizhi fajue jianbao' 江苏常熟罗墩遗址发掘简报 (Brief report of excavation at Luodun site in Changshu of Jiangsu province), *Wenwu* 文物 (Cultural Relics), 1999(7): 40–55.

Takahashi, R. and Hosoya, L.A. (2002) 'Nut exploitation in Jomon society', in S.L.R. Mason and J. Hather (eds) *Hunter-gatherer Archaeobotany: Perspectives from the Northern Temperate Zone*, pp. 146–55, London: Institute of Archaeology, University College London.

Tang, Linghua (2003) 'Chuodun Yizhi de Yuanshi Daozuo Yicun' 绰墩遗址的原始稻作遗存 (The primitive rice remains from Chuodun site)', Chuodun Shan site: Collected papers, *Dongnan Wenhua* (South-east Culture) (special issue 1): 46–9 (in Chinese).

Tang, Shengxiang *et al.* (2003) 'Hemudu Luojiajiao chutu daogu waifu shuangfeng rutu de saomiao dianjing guancha yanjiu' 河姆渡、罗家角出土稻谷外稃双峰乳突的扫描电镜观察研究 (SEM study of bi-peak-tubercle of lemma in Hemudu and Luojiajiao ancient rice), in Zhejiang Provincial Institute (ed.) *Hemudu: xinshiqi shidai yizhi kaogu fajue baogao* 河姆渡：新石器时代遗址考古发掘报告 (Hemudu: an excavation report of the Neolithic site), pp. 431–9, Beijing: Cultural Relics Publishing House.

Tanno, K.-I., and Willcox, G. (2006) 'How fast was wild wheat domesticated?', *Science*, 311: 1886.

Tao, J., Min-Te Chen, and Shiyuan Xu (2006) 'A Holocene environmental record from the southern Yangtze River delta, eastern China', *Palaeogeography, Palaeoclimatology, Palaeoecology*, 230: 204–29.

Thompson, G.B. (1996) *The Excavations of Khok Phanom Di, a Prehistoric Site in Central Thailand*, vol. 4, *Subsistence and Environment: The Botanical Evidence. The Biological Remains Part III*, London: Society of Antiquaries of London.

Thompson, G.B. (1997) 'Archaeobotanical indicators of rice domestication: A critical evaluation of diagnostic criteria', in R. Ciarla and F. Rispoli (eds) *South-East Asian Archaeology 1992*, pp. 159–74, Rome: Instituto Italiano per L'Africa e L'Orient.

Usher, G. (1974) *Dictionary of Plants Used by Man*, New York: Hafner Press.

Vaughan, D.A. (1989) *The Genus Oryza L.: Current Status of Taxonomy*, Los Banos: International Rice Research Institute.

Vaughan, D.A. (1994) *The Wild Relatives of Rice: A Genetic Resources Handbook*, Los Banos: International Rice Research Institute.

Vaughan, D.A., Morishima, H. and Kadowaki, K. (2003) 'Diversity in the *Oryza* genus', *Current Opinion in Plant Biology*, 6: 139–46.

Veasey, E.A., Karasawa, M.G., Santos, P.P., Rosa, M.S., Mamani, E. and Oliveira, G.C.X. (2004) 'Variation in the loss of seed dormancy during after-ripening of wild and cultivated rice species', *Annals of Botany*, 94: 875–82.

Wallace, W.J. (1978) 'Post-Pleistocene archaeology, 9000–2000 BC', in R.F. Heizer (ed.) *Handbook of North American Indian*, vol. 8, *California*, pp. 25–36, Washington, DC: Smithsonian Press.

Wan, J. and Ikehashi, H. (1997) 'Identification of two types of differentiation in cultivated rice (*Oryza sativa* L.) detected by polymorphism of isozymes and hybrid sterility', *Euphytica*, 94: 151–61.

Wang, X., Chuanqing Sun, Hongwei Cai and Juzhong Zhang (1999) 'Origin of the Chinese cultivated rice (*Oryza sativa* L.)', *Chinese Science Bulletin*, 44: 295–304.

Wang, L., Sarnthein, M., Erlenkeuser, H., Grootes, P.M., Grimalt, J.O., Pelejero, C. and Linck, G. (1999) 'Holocene variations in Asian monsoon moisture: A bidecadal sediment record from the South China Sea', *Geophysical Research Letters*, 26: 2889–92.

Watt, G. (1889–93) *Dictionary of the Economic Products of India*, 8 vols, London: W.H. Allen & Co.

Weiss, E., Wetterstrom, W., Nadel, D. and Bar-Yosef, O. (2004) 'The broad spectrum revisited: Evidence from plant remains', *Proceedings of the National Academy of Science (USA)*, 101: 9551–5.

Weiss, E., Kislev, M.E. and Hartmann, A. (2006) 'Autonomous cultivation before domestication', *Science*, 312: 1608–10.

Wilke, P.J., Bettinger, R., King, T.F. and O'Connell, J.-F. (1972) 'Harvest selection and domestication in seed plants', *Antiquity*, 46: 203–9.

Willcox, G. (1999) 'Agrarian change and the beginnings of cultivation in the Near East: Evidence from wild progenitors, experimental cultivation and archaeobotanical data', in C. Gosden and J. Hather (eds) *The Prehistory of Food: Appetites for Change*, pp. 478–500, London: Routledge.

Willcox, G. (2002) 'Geographical variation in major cereal components and evidence for independent domestication events in Western Asia', in R.T.J. Cappers and S. Bottema (eds) *The Dawn of Farming in the Near East*, pp. 133–40, Berlin: Ex Oriente.

Willcox, G. (2004) 'Measuring grain size and identifying Near Eastern cereal domestication: Evidence from the Euphrates valley', *Journal of Archaeological Science*, 31: 145–50.

Willcox, G. (2005) 'The distribution, natural habitats and availability of wild cereals in relation to their domestication in the Near East: Multiple events, multiple centres', *Vegetation History and Archaeobotany*, 14: 534–41.

Winterhalder, B. and Golland (1997) 'An evolutionary ecology: Perspective on diet choice, risk, and plant domestication', in K.J. Gremillion (ed.) *People, Plants and Landscapes: Studies in Paleoethnobotany*, pp. 123–60, Tuscaloosa, AL: University of Alabama Press.

Yan, Wenming (1982) 'Zhongguo daozuo nongye de qiyuan (yi)' 中国稻作农业的起源 (The origin of Chinese rice agriculture. 1), *Nongye kaogu* 农业考古 (Agriculture Archaeology), 1: 22.

Yan, Wenming (2002) 'The origins of rice agriculture, pottery and cities', in Y. Yasuda (ed.) *The Origins of Pottery and Agriculture*, pp. 151–6, New Delhi: Lustre Press and Roli Books.

Yasuda, Y. (2002) 'Origins of pottery and agriculture in East Asia', in Y. Yasuda (ed.) *The Origins of Pottery and Agriculture*, pp. 119–42, New Delhi: Lustre Press and Roli Books.

Yasuda, Y. and Negendank, J.F.W. (2003) 'Environmental variability in East and West Eurasia', *Quaternary International*, 105: 1–6.

Yi, S., Saito, Y., Zhao, Q. and Wang, P. (2003) 'Vegetation and climate changes in the Changjiang (Yangtze Rover) Delta, China, during the past 13,000 years inferred from pollen records', *Quaternary Science Reviews*, 22: 1501–19.

You X. (1976) 'Dui hemudu disi wenhuaceng chutu daogu he gusi de jidian kanfa' 对河姆渡第四文化层出土稻谷和骨耜的几点看法 (Some issues on rice grains and bone-spade *si* unearthed from layer 4 of Hemudu site), *Wenwu* 文物 (Cultural Relics), 1976(8): 20–3.

You, X. (2003) reprint of You (1976) included in Zhejiang Provincial Institute of Archaeology and Cultural Relics Hemudu: xinshiqi shidai yizhi kaogu fajui baogao.

Yu, S.Y., Zhu, C., Song, J., and Qu, W.Z. (2000) 'Role of climate in the rise and fall of Neolithic cultures on the Yangtze Delta', *Boreas*, 29: 157–65.

Yuan, J. (2002) 'Rice and pottery 10,000 yrs BP at Yuchanyan, Dao County, Hunan Province', in Y. Yasuda (ed.) *The Origins of Pottery and Agriculture*, pp. 157–66, New Delhi: Lustre Press and Roli Books

Yuan, J. (2003) 'The problem of the origin domestic animals in Neolithic China', *Chinese Archaeology*, 3: 154–6.

Yuan, J. and Rowan Flad (2002) 'Pig domestication in ancient China', *Antiquity*, 76: 724–32.

Zhang, J. and Wang, X. (1998) 'Notes on the recent discovery of ancient cultivated rice at Jiahu, Henan Province: A new theory concerning the origin of *Oryza japonica* in China', *Antiquity*, 72: 897–901.

Zhang, M. (1999) 'Tongxiang xinqiao yizhi shijue baogao' 桐乡新桥遗址试掘报告 (Primary report of the test excavation at Xinqiao site of Tongxiang), *Nongye kaogu* 农业考古 (Agriculture Archaeology), 1999(3): 70–6.

Zhang, W. (1996) 'Hemudu chutu daogu waifu biaomian shuangfeng rutu de yanjiu' 河姆渡出土稻谷外稃乳突的扫描电镜观察 (The study on bi-peak-tubercle of lemma in Hemudu ancient rice), in Xiongkun Wang and Chuanqing Sun (eds) *Zhongguo zaipeidao qiyuan yu yanhua yanjiu zhuanji* 中国栽培稻起源与演化研究专集 (Origin and Differentiation of Chinese Cultivated Rice), pp. 42–6, Beijing: China Agricultural University Press.

Zhang, Wenxu (2000) 'Shuidao de shuangfeng rutu, gudao tezheng he zaipei shuidao de qiyuan' 水稻的双峰乳突、古稻特征和栽培水稻的起源 (the bi-peak-tubercle structure of rice, features of ancient rice and the origin of rice cultivation), in Y. Yasuda and W. Yan (eds) *Daozuo taoqi he dushi de qiyuan* 稻作 陶器和都市的起源 (The Origins of Rice Agriculture, Pottery and Cities), pp. 115–28, Beijing: Cultural Relics Publishing House.

Zhang, W. (2002) 'The bi-peak tubercle of rice, the character of ancient rice and the origin of cultivated rice', in Y. Yasuda (ed.) *The Origins of Pottery and Agriculture*, pp. 205–16, New Delhi: Lustre Press/Roli Books.

Zhao, S. and Wu, W.-t. (1987) 'Early Neolithic Hemudu culture along the Hangzhou estuary and the origin of domestic paddy rice in China', *Asian Perspectives*, 27: 29–34.

Zhao, Z. (1998) 'The Middle Yangtze region in China is one place where rice was domesticated: Phytolith evidence from the Diaotonghuan Cave, Northern Jaingxi', *Antiquity*, 72: 885–97.

Zhao, Z. (2001) 'Zhiwu kaoguxue de xueke dingwei yu yanjiu neirong' 植物考古学的学科定位与研究内容 (Disciplinary Position and Research Content of Paleoethnobotany), *Kaogu* 考古 (Archaeology), 2001(7): 55–61.

Zhao Zhijun (2004) 'Zhiwu kaoguxue de tianye gongzuo fangfa – fuxuan fa' 植物考古学的田野工作方法—浮选法 (Flotation: a paleobotanic method in field archaeology), *Kaogu* 考古 (Archaeology), 2004(3): 80–7.

Zhao, Z., Pearsall, D.M., Jr., Benfer, R.A. and Piperno D.R. (1998) 'Distinguishing rice (*Oryza sativa* Poaceae) from wild *Oryza* species through phytolith analysis, II: Finalized method', *Economic Botany*, 52: 134–45.

Zhejiang Provincial Institute of Cultural Relics and Archaeology (2003) *Hemudu: xinshiqi shidai yizhi kaogu fajue baogao* 河姆渡：新石器时代遗址考古发掘报告 (Hemudu: An Excavation Report of the Neolithic Site), Beijing: Cultural Relics Publishing House.

Zhejiang Provincial Institute of Cultural Relics and Archaeology (2004) *Kuahuqiao* 跨湖桥 (Kuahuqiao Site Report), Beijing: Cultural Relics Publishing House.

Zhejiang Provincial Institute of Cultural Relics and Archaeology (2005a) *Nanhebang: Songze wenhua yizhi fajue baogao* 南河浜：崧泽文化遗址发掘报告 (Nanhebang: Excavation Report of a Songze Culture Site), Beijing: Cultural Relics Publishing House.

Zhejiang Provincial Institute of Cultural Relics and Archaeology (2005b) *Fanshan* 反山 (Fanshan Excavation Report), Beijing: Cultural Relics Publishing House.

Zhejiang Provincial Institute of Cultural Relics and Archaeology (2005c) *Liangzhu yizhiqun* 良渚遗址群 (Liangzhu Sites Group), Beijing: Cultural Relics Publishing House.

Zheng, Y., Yanjun Dong, Akira Matsui, Tetsuro Udatsu, Hiroshi Fujiwara (2003) 'Molecular genetic basis of determining subspecies of ancient rice using shape of phytoliths', *Journal of Archaeological Science*, 30: 1215–21.

Zheng, Y., Matsui, A., and Fujiwara, H. (2004a) 'Phytoliths of rice detected in the Neolithic sites in the Valley of the Taihu Lake in China', *Environmental Archaeology*, 8: 177–83.

Zheng, Y., Jaing, L.-p., and Zheng, J.-m. (2004b) 'Study on the remains of ancient rice from Kuahuqiao site in Zhejiang Province', *Chinese Journal of Rice Science*, 18: 119–24 (in Chinese).

Zhou, Jiwei (1981) 'Changjiang zhongxiayou chutu gudao kaocha baogao' 长江中下游出土古稻考察报告 (Investigation of ancient rice from Mid and Lower Yangtze River) *Yunnan nongye keji* 云南农业科技 (Yunnan Agricultural Science and Techniques), 1981(6): 1–6.

Zhou, Jiwei (2003) 'Zhejiang yuyao Hemudu xinshiqi shidai yizhi chutu daoli xingtai fenxi jianding' 浙江余姚河姆渡新石器时代遗址出土稻粒形态分析鉴定 (The morphological investigation and identification of rice grain from Hemudu Site)', in Zhejiang Provincial Institute (ed.) *Hemudu: xinshiqi shidai yizhi kaogu fajue baogao* 河姆渡：新石器时代遗址考古发掘报告 (Hemudu: An Excavation Report of the Neolithic Site), pp. 429–30, Beijing: Cultural Relics Publishing House.

Zohary, D. and Hopf, M. (1973) 'Domestication of pulses in the Old World', *Science*, 182: 887–94.

Zohary, D. and Hopf, M. (2000) *Domestication of Plants in the Old World*, 3rd edn, Oxford: Oxford University Press.

Zou, H., Gu, J., Li, M., Tang, L., Ding, J. and Yao, Q. (2000) 'Findings of paddies of Majiabang Culture at Caoxieshan, Jiangsu Province', in W. Yan and Y. Yasuda (eds) *The Origins of Rice Agriculture, Pottery and Cities*, pp. 97–114, Beijing: Cultural Relics Publishing House [in Chinese]

3 Livestock in ancient China

An archaeozoological perspective

*Jing Yuan, Han Jian-Lin, and
Roger Blench*

1. Introduction

Archaeologists working on animal domestication must assess the significance of bones excavated from archaeological sites. In ancient China, there are references to the 'harvest of abundant five crops and flourishing with six livestock species'. The 'six species' were horse, cow, sheep/goat, pig, dog and chicken (Shao 2003). This review introduces the methodology used to identify bones of ancient livestock, to estimate the time-depth and origins of the six livestock species and to discuss in detail recent research on the origins of pigs and horses. Epstein (1969) is an overall view of the livestock species and breeds kept in China.

There are two models to explain the origin of livestock in ancient China: one is the domestication of certain indigenous species from the Neolithic times through interacting with, controlling and taming the wild stocks, e.g. the domestic pig. Olsen (1993) believed that China was a centre for early animal domestication. The other is the introduction of an exotic, already domesticated species from another geographic area by exchange with other ancient, outside residents, for example, the horse.

2. Methodology used to identify bones of ancient livestock in China

Four criteria can be applied to determine if bones recovered from an archaeological site were those of domesticated animals. The first is the traditional technique of morphological observations and measurements on the skeleton, in particular the size of the teeth. If the age and sex structure of the remains deviate significantly from those expected in a wild species, indicating human manipulation, then the bones may well be of animals tamed and/or kept by ancient humans.

The second criterion is the abrupt appearance of a species not previously present in the area, usually an indicator of a human introduction.

The third criterion is the associated cultural material at archaeological sites. At Chinese Neolithic sites, full or partial skeletons of two animal species often occur, intentionally entombed together or as funerary accompaniments to human skeletons. Pigs, for example, frequently occur in different geographic locations throughout Neolithic times. Dogs are confined to eastern China, although they are also found in all Neolithic periods. Other animals are seldom found at such sites and it is believed that these two species were selected due to their particular association with humans. This association was established over time through taming and rearing of the animals, thereby implying that the buried pigs and dogs were domestic.

The fourth strategy is the application of new technologies: diet composition analysis and DNA phylogeny. Domesticated animals were given feed that often included residues of the skins or shells of crops and vegetables, and also the leftovers of human meals. Analyses of stable isotopes of C^{13} and N^{15}, and trace elements in animal bones point to the diet composition and thus the relevant feed sources. Further comparison with human bones excavated at the same site can provide indicators as to the domestic status of animal remains. Similarly, the study of mitochondrial DNA retrieved from animal bones may allow us to establish the relationship between animal bones at different sites within varying time frames. This will eventually help reconstruct the phylogeny and relationships of domesticated animals, leading to a better understanding of their origin and also of the domestication process.

As far as the origin of domesticated animals is concerned, reliable conclusions can only be drawn if the archaeological context is taken into account *before* the observation and measurement of the bones. This is because the body conformation of animals does not change at the initial phase of domestication; in particular, tooth morphology is very conservative. They are the most stable part of an animal skeleton and take a long time to adapt to a new feeding regime. The teeth of primitive forms of domesticated animals can more closely resemble their direct wild ancestors than their later descendants.

In the initial phase of domestication, numbers of domesticated animals are too limited to demonstrate a typical sex and age structure. Hence the special association of humans with pigs and dogs at certain archaeological sites is used to argue for their domesticated status. In addition, the analysis and comparison of diet in the bodies of human and animal species using stable isotopes and trace elements will show whether they shared the same or similar foodstuffs. DNA analysis over a broad geographical area and on a large sample size is of great importance in elucidating the phylogenetic relationship of animals. With the development and greater use of modern approaches, archaeological research will attain more precise scientific results.

3. Estimated time and location of origins of the six livestock species in ancient China

The oldest known remains of silica bodies of rice, pottery, and stone and animal bone tools used for rice cultivation occur at the archaeological sites of Xianrendong and Diaotonghuan in Wannian county (N 28°41′, E 117°05′; 14,000–11,000 BP), Jiangxi Province (Yan 1997). Remains of pottery and tools made of animal bones and stones were also found at Zengpiyan site (N 25°12′, E 110°16′; 12,000–7000 BP) in Guilin, Guangxi Province (Institute of Archaeology 2003). All these are evidence for crop cultivation and pottery-making as early as 12,000 BP (although see Fuller et al., Chapter 2, this volume, for queries as to the domestic status of early rice findings). All of the bone tools were from wild animals as this period is far prior to domestication (Yuan 2001).

Dog was probably the earliest domesticated animal to appear in China. Dog remains have been found at Nanzhuangtou (N 39°7'12", E 115°39'19"; 10,500–9700 BP; Li et al. 2000) in Xushui county, Hebei Province (Baoding Institute of Cultural Relic Management et al. 1992). Yuan et al. (unpublished) found that the dentition length of mandible of the dog remains at this site was 79.9 mm, shorter than the 90 mm of modern wolf specimens collected in the Institute of Vertebrate Paleontology and Paleoanthropology of Chinese Academy of Sciences. Presumably the history of dog keeping in China goes further back still, as by this time the teeth had already undergone significant changes.

The second domesticated animal in China was the pig. The remains of pig mandibles are found at Kuahuqiao (N 30°9'34", E 120°13'53"; 8200–7000 BP in Zhejiang Provincial Institute and Xiaoshan Museum 2004) in Xiaoshan county, Zhejiang Province. The teeth were significantly distorted, indicating domestic pigs (Yuan and Yang 2004). By analogy, these changes in body conformation imply that the domestication of pigs should be dated still further back (also see section on pig domestication).

Skeletons of cattle (Figure 3.1) were discovered in a pit at Shantaisi site (4500–4200 BP) in Zhecheng county (N 34°04', E 115°18'), Henan Province (Zhang and Zhang 1997). These are the earliest domesticated cattle in the area along the middle to lower reaches of the Yellow River. However, it is not possible to analyse evidence for changes in their body conformation due to a very limited comparative sample.

Sheep and goat remains also appear around 4400 BP along the middle to lower reaches of the Yellow River (Yuan unpublished). There is almost no sheep/goat bone at sites older than 4400 BP, but they abruptly appear in abundance at almost every site after this date. As with cattle, further investigation of changes in body conformation based on the excavated skeletal materials need to be conducted.

The pattern for horses is similar to sheep/goat and cattle (section 4). They are first recorded at the Yinxu site (N 36°8', E 114°17'; 3300–3050 BP) in Anyang city, Henan Province (Yuan 2004).

The date of chicken domestication in China has remained controversial despite the many measurements that have been made on bones excavated at various sites. However, the results are not easy to sort out. Based on historical records, domestic chickens may be as recent as 3300 BP. Inscriptions on cattle scapulas or tortoise shells of the late Shang Dynasty (3300–3050 BP) excavated at Yingxu refer to chickens used for sacrifice by the kings. Sacrifice was an important activity in the Shang era and the kings used both humans and domestic animals.

Figure 3.1 Complete skeletons of cows excavated at Shantaisi (Longshan culture), Zhecheng county, Henan Province.

4. Origin of domestic pigs in China

Archaeological excavations in the 1920s provided the evidence for the long history of pig keeping in China. A relatively high proportion of pig bones among the total mammal materials, paintings of pigs on the pottery and/or pottery of pigs were excavated in the third and fourth layers at Hemudu site. Other early and middle Neolithic sites in Guangdong Province also support pig keeping in southern China as early as 6000 BP (Zhang *et al.* 1986; Bo 1994). Table 3.1 presents the main relevant findings. New findings of pigs at archaeological sites in Inner Mongolia, northern China and the Yangtze River delta areas appear to push back the domestication process still further and are discussed in more detail below.

Larson *et al.* (2005) analysed the mtDNA sequences of 686 samples (362 wild and feral boars and 324 domestic pigs) and proposed multiple centres of pig domestication in Eurasia with at least one in south-eastern Asia. A number of subspecies of *Sus scrofa* occur in China (Table 3.2).

There are another three subspecies including *S. s. ussuricus* in far north-eastern China, *S. s. raddeanus* in southern Mongolia and Chinese Inner Mongolia, and *S. s. nigripes* in far north-western China. All indigenous Chinese pigs are classified into six major geographic groups spanning northern China, southern China, central China, south-eastern China, south-western China and Qinghai-Tibetan Plateau.

Table 3.1 Evidence for early pig-rearing in China

Site	County	Province	Map reference	Date	Material	Reference
Yangshao	Mianchi	Henan	N 34°76' E 111°75'	6800–5000 BP	Bones	Zhang et al. 1986; Su 2006
Banpo	Xi'an	Shaanxi	N 34°27' E 108°95'	5600 ± 105 – 6640 ± 105a BP	Bones	Zhang et al. 1986; Li 2004
Hemudu	Yuyang	Zhejiang	N 30°4' E 121°16'	6780 ± 90 BP	Bones	Zhong 1976; Zheng et al. 1994
Luojiajiao	Tongxiang	Zhejiang	N 30°37' E 120°28'	7040 ± 130 BP; or 7170–6890 BP	Bones	Excavation team for Luojiajiao Site 1981; Tang et al. 1999

Table 3.2 Subspecies of *Sus scrofa* in China

Subspecies	Ancestor of domestic pigs in:
S. s. chirodontus	southern China including Hainan Island
S. s. taivanus	contributed to the gene pool of small-eared miniature pigs in Taiwan
S. s. moupinensis	northern China
S. s. leucomystax	partially contributed to the gene pool in northeastern China
S. s. salvanius	miniature pigs in southwestern China

Each group has its unique morphological, productive, adaptive and historical background (Zhang 1980; Zhang et al. 1986). Archaeology also favours multiple origins for domesticated pigs within China. There is no present evidence for cultural exchanges between the three archaeological sites mentioned above, and pig-keeping activities may therefore have originated and evolved independently.

Dobney et al. (2006), using the protocol for recording linear enamel hypoplasia (Dobney and Ervynck 2004), examined 377 pig molars excavated at six archaeological sites[1] in China and compared them with modern Chinese wild boars in museums in Europe and USA. The index of linear enamel hypoplasia of modern Chinese wild boars was low and similar to modern and ancient European wild boars. All six sites demonstrated a high hypoplasia index that supports domesticated individuals.

In particular, Zengpiyan was the earliest archaeological site, where 65 per cent of the pig bones were estimated to come from individuals at 1–2 years old, and were therefore considered as domestic (Guangxi Provincial Working Group and Guilin Committee 1976; Li and Han 1978; Tan 1984; Zhang et al. 1986). This was challenged by evidence that the average length of the third cheek tooth was longer than 40 mm and pigs constituted less than 5 per cent of the total mammals at this site, although the proportion of pigs >2.5 years was more than 40 per cent of all suid remains, and thus they were possibly not domesticated. However, the re-examination of the specimens for linear enamel hypoplasia shows that the index of this site was similar to other younger sites such as Jiahu site (N 33°37′, E 113°39′; Chen 2001) in Wuyang county, Henan Province, Yuchisi site (Zhang, A.B. 2004) in Mengcheng (N 33°17′, E 116°32′), Anhui Province, and Huayuanzhuang site in Anyang (N 36°7′, E 114°22′), Henan Province, but was significantly higher than that of the modern wild boars. No final conclusion can be drawn as to the presence of domesticated pigs at this site based on a single observation and because of its range of dates spanning 5000 years (Dobney *et al.* 2006).

4.1 Xinglongwa site in Chifeng city, Inner Mongolia Autonomous Region

Xinglongwa (N 41°56′ and E 118°42′) is dated to 8200–7000 BP. It is divided into three phases: the first phase is 8200–8000 BP, the second 8000–7400 BP and the third 7400–7000 BP (Inner Mongolian Team 1997). Observation and measurement of the structure and change of the tooth morphology in the pig remains showed that more than 65 per cent of individuals had a third cheek tooth longer than 40 mm and that this proportion increased to 90 per cent in phase III, a character typical of wild boars. Age structure was also similar to wild boars. The proportion of bones ascribed to pigs among the total mammals was 42.9 per cent in phase I, 14.4 per cent in phase II and 22.5 per cent in phase III. In contrast, proportions of cervids were greater than pigs in phases II and III but lower in phase I. Hence most suid remains at this site were probably wild boars (Yuan and Yang unpublished).

However, there were some exceptions. In the phase II tombs, an adult male human was laid out fully extended, with a male pig and a female pig placed one side of the dead person (Figure 3.2). The pigs' legs were twisted together, probably indicating that they were bound prior to burial (Inner Mongolian Team 1997). In addition, in a settlement at Xinglonggou, some 10 km from Xinglongwa and similar to Xinglongwa phase II in date, some 15 animal skulls were recovered, of which 12 were of pigs and 3 red deer (Figure 3.3). In most skulls, there was an artificial hole in the forehead (Figure 3.4) (Inner Mongolian Team 2002). The burial of skulls, predominantly pigs, first occurs in Xinglongwa phase I, but the complete excavation report remains to be published.

For three reasons, the findings at both Xinglongwa and Xinglonggou sites point to domestic pigs in limited numbers:

(1) Suid bones were present with a reduced third cheek tooth approximately 34 mm long at Xinglongwa site (Yuan and Yang unpublished).
(2) The majority of the bones of 17 mammalian species unearthed at the Xinglongwa site were red and roe deer, but only a small proportion were pig bones. However, only pigs were buried together with humans, an indication of a unique connection between pigs and humans.

Figure 3.2 Pigs and human buried together at Xinglongwa.

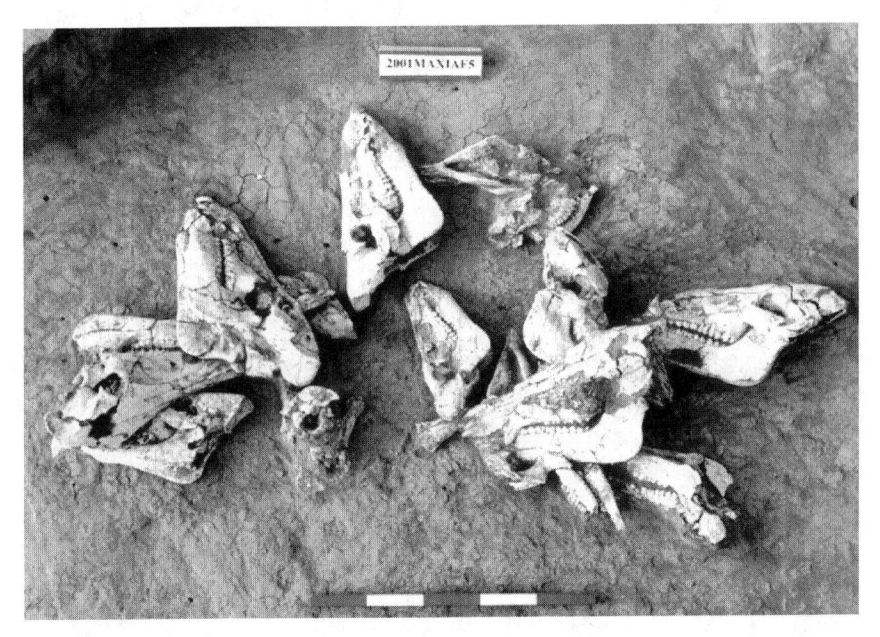

Figure 3.3 Group of animal skulls excavated from a house at Xinglonggou.

(3) Pigs predominate in the animal skulls at Xinglonggou and unpublished data suggest this is also true at Xinglongwa.

The percentage of pig bones among the total of mammals excavated at Xinglongwa phase I was 42.9 per cent, double that of red deer (20.1 per cent). It falls to 14.4 and 22.5 per cent, not significantly different from red deer (16.7 and 20 per cent), in phases II and III (Yuan and Yang unpublished). These figures do not reflect the ratios of pigs to red deer in the groups of animal skulls, where pigs predominate.

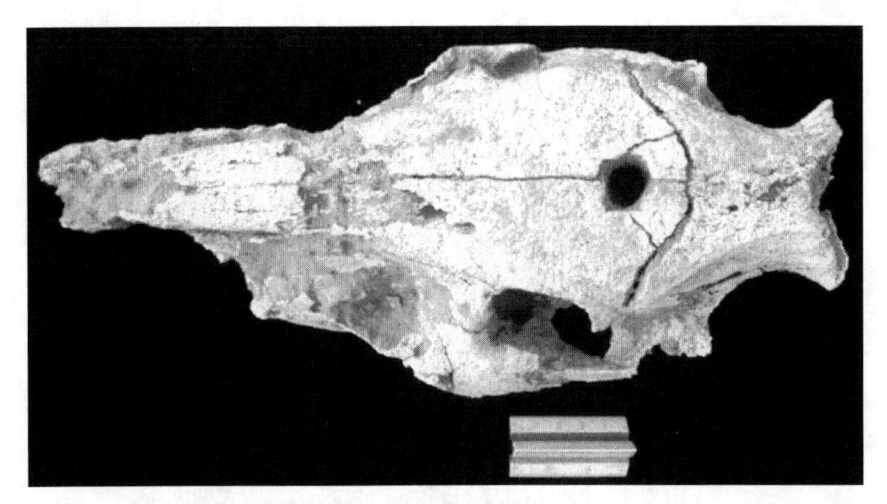

Figure 3.4 Pig skull with an artificial hole in the forehead.

This either implies that domesticated pigs were already kept in the Inner Mongolian area 8200–7000 BP, or that wild boars were favoured for cultural reasons.

There is further circumstantial evidence. Foxtail and broomcorn millets were excavated at Xinglonggou and they are dated to about 8000 BP (Zhao 2004). Observation and measurement of samples of these millets showed that they retained basic ancestral characteristics of their wild relatives. The upper reaches of the Xiliao river where the Xinglonggou site is located may have been a centre of domestication of these two millet species and a nucleus of the arid agriculture in northern China with these two millet species as staple food crops. The proto-domestication of millets may be related to the importance of pigs in this zone.

4.2 Cishan site in Wu'an county, Hebei Province

Cishan (N 36°43' and E 114°12') is dated to approximately 8000 BP (Hebei Provincial Institute and Handan Institute 1981). Pig bones were excavated at this site. The average length of the third cheek tooth of the lower jaw is 41.4 mm and the average width 18.3 mm. More than 60 per cent of the pigs discovered at this site were slaughtered between six months and one year old. Among the 186 pits excavated, there were two pigs in the bottom of H5, and one pig each in H12, H14 and H265. A dog was also found in H107. All these animal bones were covered in carbonized millet grains (Hebei Provincial Institute and Handan Institute 1981).

The data on this site were published in 1980 and the animal bones were identified without comment; it is therefore hard to be sure that the pigs were domestic. However, the limited measurements of the third cheek tooth of the lower jaw do seem to match the proposed criteria for domestic pig remains. The age structure of these pigs was different from a sample of those being hunted and presumably a result of human interference. All the complete pig skeletons excavated in the four pits were covered with millet grains, a clear marker of intentionality. This does strongly suggest the presence of domestic pigs around 8000 BP at this site. Furthermore, the excavation of animal bones at sites younger than Cishan indicates a gradual expansion of domestic pig keeping in this area (Zhou 1981; Yuan and Flad 2002).

4.3 Kuahuqiao site in Xiaoshan city, Zhejiang Province

Kuahuqiao (N 30°9′34″, E 120°13′53″) is dated to 8200–7000 BP (Zhejiang Provincial Institute and Xiaoshan Museum 2004). It is further divided into the first, second and third phases at 8200–7800 BP, 7700–7300 BP and 7300–7000 BP (Zhejiang Provincial Institute and Xiaoshan Museum 2004).

In all phases at this site, the dentition of the pig jaws was significantly twisted (Figure 3.5) and the teeth were disordered due to a shortened lower jaw, evidence for domestication.

In terms of size, there were six measurements of the third cheek tooth in phase I. Three of them were > 42 mm but the other three were < 40 mm. All three measurements of the cheek tooth in phase II were below 40 mm. Among the four measurements of the cheek tooth in phase III, one was 40.96 mm and the rest of three were below 38 mm. The three measurements > 42 mm were probably of wild pigs, but all the other 10 specimens fall within the range of domesticated pigs. The gradual reduction in size of the cheek tooth over time is a characteristic of domestication. From the age structure, pigs aged 2.5 years or above fell from

Figure 3.5 Significantly twisted dentition of pig jaw excavated at Kuahuqiao.

87.5 per cent in phase I to 45 per cent in phase II. The average age was 4.6 years in phase I, 3.5 years in phase II and 2.9 years in phase III. From the ratio of suid bones to all mammals present at this site, the percentages ascribed to pigs were 22.6, 12.2 and 8 per cent in the early, middle and late phases (Yuan and Yang 2004).

Since the pig jaws in the early phase at Kuahuqiao already had disordered dentition and individuals with a third cheek tooth smaller than 40 mm were on the increase, these morphological changes almost certainly reflect a regime of human captivity and feeding. It is therefore likely that domestic pigs are present at Kuahuqiao by 8200 BP. Despite this, the excavation at Kuahuqiao requires further careful interpretation as pigs were only 15 per cent of all mammals (Yuan and Yang 2004). This is the reverse of the process of a gradual increase of the proportion of pigs against other mammals at all other Neolithic sites in northern China (Yuan 1999). This is a pattern very specific to the Neolithic sites of the Yangtze River delta. In an important literary reference of the early Qin Dynasty (221–206 BC) the *Zhou Li – Zhifangshi*, it states that 'In the town called Huiji of Yangzhou in south-western China, birds and mammals were hunted and rice was used as crop' (Anonymous 1979). Until the pre-Qin Dynasty times, rice was planted, but meat was still obtained from hunting birds and wild animals. It may well be that there was a relative limited number of livestock, if any, present in the Yangtze River delta in the pre-Qin Dynasty. If Kuahuqiao has been correctly interpreted, the history of pig keeping in southern China may be older than 8200 years BP. This reduces the gap in dates between China and south-east Anatolia (Hongo and Meadow 1998).

5. Origin of domestic horse in ancient China

The horse used to be considered the first among the six livestock species in ancient China as an administration system for horse management was established over 3000 years ago (Shao 2003). The system played an important role in transport for administration, military purposes and also cultural exchanges (Xie 1986; Xie *et al.* 1986). For the origin of the domestic horse in China, there are three different views:

(1) Olsen (1984) suggested an origin of the domestic horse in China from the mid-Neolithic period.
(2) Zhou (1984), Xie (1986), Wang (1998) and Wang and Song (2001) proposed the presence of the domestic horse from the Longshan culture (4350–3950 BP).
(3) Yuan and An (1997) and Chen (1999) believed that domesticated horses were introduced into the areas along the middle and lower reaches of the Yellow River during the late Shang Dynasty (3300–3050 BP).

Kong (1994) and Gong (2003) have also reviewed the history of introduction of horse chariot and carriage from and/or through western Asia into China.

The major differences on the issue of origin of the domestic horse and its domestication in ancient China is whether the domesticated horse was introduced together with the chariot/carriage from the pastoral area around the Black and Caspian Seas and when this took place; or if there was an indigenous, independent origin of the domesticated horse within China and if so, when and where (Chen 1999). The last view was argued by C.S. Zhang (2004) who claimed that it is hard to imagine horses being used only for draught purposes because almost all of the archaeological evidence from the late Shang Dynasty derives from excavations at sites with horse and chariots/carriages. It is probable that horse riding took place prior to the use of the horse as a draught animal and that this helped establish a special connection between humans and horses. The horse would then have been treated as a special sacrifice after the death of its owner. Thus the domesticated horse was possibly kept in the areas along the Yellow River from the Xia Dynasty onwards (4000–3600 BP). Although rock art representing the herding and riding of horses is found in northern China at dates prior to the Shang Dynasty, the horse may well have been domesticated independently and possibly at a later date in northern Asia. This section will present the discoveries of horse bones in ancient China and their distribution.

5.1. Late Pleistocene

Horse bones occur at 32 late Pleistocene sites in China, of which one site is located each in Helongjiang, Guizhou and Sichuan Provinces and Xinjiang Uigur Autonomous Region, two each in Yunnan Province and Inner Mongolian Autonomous Region, three each in Jilin and Shaanxi Provinces, four in Liaoning Province, and seven each in Shanxi and Gansu Provinces (Han and Xu 1989; Qi 1989).

This pattern of distribution has three characteristics:

(1) Most sites are concentrated in north-eastern, northern and north-western China – 28 out of 32, with only four sites present in south-western China.
(2) All the horse bones excavated in northern China are assigned to the species *Equus caballus przewalskii*. Those bones found in south-western China remain unclassified.
(3) The numbers of bones excavated at each site are very different, as the majority are present at sites in northern China, with the Palaeolithic Siyu site (28,945 ± 1370 BP) (Institute of Archaeology 1977) in Shuozhou city (around N 39°19′, E 112°26′), Shanxi Province being the most abundant. Based on the counting of the third cheek teeth, there were approximately 120 horses at this site (Jia *et al.* 1972). In contrast, the record of horse bones in south-western China is sparse, with only one or two third cheek teeth per site.

5.2. Neolithic China

Although Neolithic sites in China have abundant animal remains, horse bones are scarce. Two pieces of horse teeth and one phalange were found in the culture layer at Banpo Neolithic site (5600 ± 105–6640 ± 105 BP; Li 2004) in Xi'an (N 34°27', E 108°95'), Shaanxi Province. This site has a deep accumulation of cultural materials, ranging from 6000 to 2000 BP but concentrated within the 6000 to 5000 BP period (Li and Han 1959). Two complete horse skeletons were unearthed from a pit at Nanshacun site (4000 BP) in Hua county (N 34°53', E 109°77'), Shaanxi Province (Wang 1998). Horse bones were present in the culture layer at Baiying site (4160 BP) in Tangyin county (N 35°92', E 114°35'), Henan Province (Zhou 1983) and horse phalanges were also discovered at Chengziya site (4000 BP) in Zhangqiu county (N 36°72', E 117°53'), Shandong Province (Liang 1934).

One horse tooth was discovered in the culture layer at Fujiamen site (5000 BP) in Wushan county (N 34°69', E 104°88') along the upper reaches of the Yellow River, Gansu Province (Yuan unpublished). At Dahezhuang site (3700 BP) in Yongjing county (N 35°97', E 103°34'), Gansu Province, three lower jaws of horses were present (Gansu Team 1974). Qinweijia-Qijia cemetery in the Yongjing county has similar dates to Dahezhuang and a few fragments of horse bones were reported, but with unknown positions and numbers due to breakage (Gansu Team 1975). There is a report of horse bones at Dashanqian site (4000–3500 BP; Institute of Archaeology *et al.* 1998) in Chifeng city (N 41°56' and E 118°42'), Inner Mongolia (Cai *et al.* 2007).

Five specimens of ancient horse bones excavated at Dashanqian and four pieces of horse bones at the nearby Jinggouzhi site (2115 ± 65 BP) (Research Centre Jilin University and Inner Mongolian Regional Institute 2004) were recently characterized using mitochondrial DNA D-loop sequences (Cai *et al.* 2007). Three samples from Dashanqian shared one mutation with the cluster (A2) to which the *Equus caballus przewalskii* sequences belong and other six specimens from both sites were grouped into A, E and F clusters of modern horses according to the phylogenetic network established by Jansen *et al.* (2002). This result does not rule out *Equus caballus przewalskii* as the probable source for the ancient horse bones excavated 4000 BP in northern China.

Queries remain concerning excavations of this period. Because all mammal bones excavated at Banpo were treated as one single excavation unit but not sorted based on the stratigraphy, the horse bones found at this site might be dated to anywhere between 6000 and 2600 BP. No horse bone occurs in cultural layers at other sites of similar date (6000–5000 BP) to Banpo (Yuan and An 1997). Records of the horse bones at both Baiying and Chengziya sites were very plain, in particular at Baiying, with its few broken equid specimens, unknown positions and no clear explanation as to why they were assigned to horses. Again, no horse bone was present at other sites dating to about 4000 BP similar to Baiying and Chengziya along the Yellow River (Yuan and An 1997). There is no detailed excavation report on Nanshacun, but a brief publication indicated there were horse bones present in the pit. However, without reference to cultural context, its dating remains suspect (Wang and Song 2001). These questionable materials may have to be put to one side at present. Equid bones excavated at sites in the area along the Yellow River were probably *Equus caballus przewalskii*.

Horse bones were also recorded at Fujiamen, Dahezhuang and Qinweijia-Qijia along the upper reaches of the Yellow River but the sparse specimens at Fujiamen and Qinweijia-Qijia and lack of detailed description of the three equid lower jaws recorded at Dahezhuang make further analysis problematic. The specimens were not preserved; further investigation is therefore impossible.

5.3. Shang Dynasty

By the early Shang Dynasty, numerous sites have been excavated. Sites with animal bones are limited and only a few have been sorted out properly. Fortunately, some important Shang Dynasty sites of different periods have been worked on and the situation can be summarized as follows.

Bones of pig, cattle, sheep, deer, dog and fish but no horse were excavated in the sacrificial place at the Shang walled-town site (3600–3400 BP) in Yanshi city (N 34°73', E 112°77'), Henan Province (Shangcheng Team 2001). Similarly, bones of cattle, dog, pig, deer and crane as well as elephant's cheek tooth and clam shell were present at the sacrifice place at Xiaoshuangqiao site (3435–3410 BP) in Zhengzhou city (N 34°73', E 112°77'), Henan Province, but again none of horse (Song *et al.* 1995). There were bones of herring, chicken, field mouse, dog, rhinoceros, pig, elk, cattle, buffalo and sheep, and clam shell, but no horse at Huanbei Shang walled-town site (around N 36°7', E 114°22'; 3370–3220 BP) in Anyang, Henan Province (Yuan and Tang 2000).

A number of pits with carriages and horses, in general, one carriage with two horses (Figure 3.6), were excavated at Yinxu site (N 36°8', E 114°17'; dated to 3300–3050 BP) in Anyang city, Henan Province (Yuan 2004).

In addition, another 20 pits with horses were discovered between autumn of 1934 and autumn of 1935 in Xibeigang at Yinxu. Each pit had 1–37 horses, with 2 horses per pit being most common. In spring 1978, more than a hundred square pits lined up together were detected using a probe shovel in the south-eastern part of the M1550 large tomb at this site. Forty of them were excavated, with 1–8 horses per pit and 2 horses per pit present in 12 out of the 40 pits (Figure 3.7), 6 horses per pit in 11 of the 40 pits as well as 2 horses and one man per pit in 3 of the 40 pits. These horses were probably used for sacrifices. Apart from these horse pits concentrated in one place, there were also cattle and pig pits scattered around the tombs at this site (Chen 1994).

Laoniupo site (3250–3050 BP) in Xi'an (N 34°27', E 108°95'), Shaanxi Province, has radiocarbon dates similar to the late Shang Dynasty Yinxu site. There was one pit with a man, horse and dog entombed together, one pit with a horse alone, and one pit with a chariot and two horses (Department of History 1988). Qianzhangda site in Tengzhou (N 35°7', E 117°8'), Shandong Province, is dated to between the late Shang and early Zhou Dynasties (3300–2900 BP), a bit later than Yinxu and a

Livestock in ancient China 97

number of pits with one chariot and two horses were also found there (Institute of Archaeology 1995). It seems probable that there were no domesticated horses in the early Shang Dynasty, but they have been present in China since the late Shang (3300 BP).

Figure 3.6 A pit with one carriage and two horses at Yinxu, Anyang city, Henan Province.

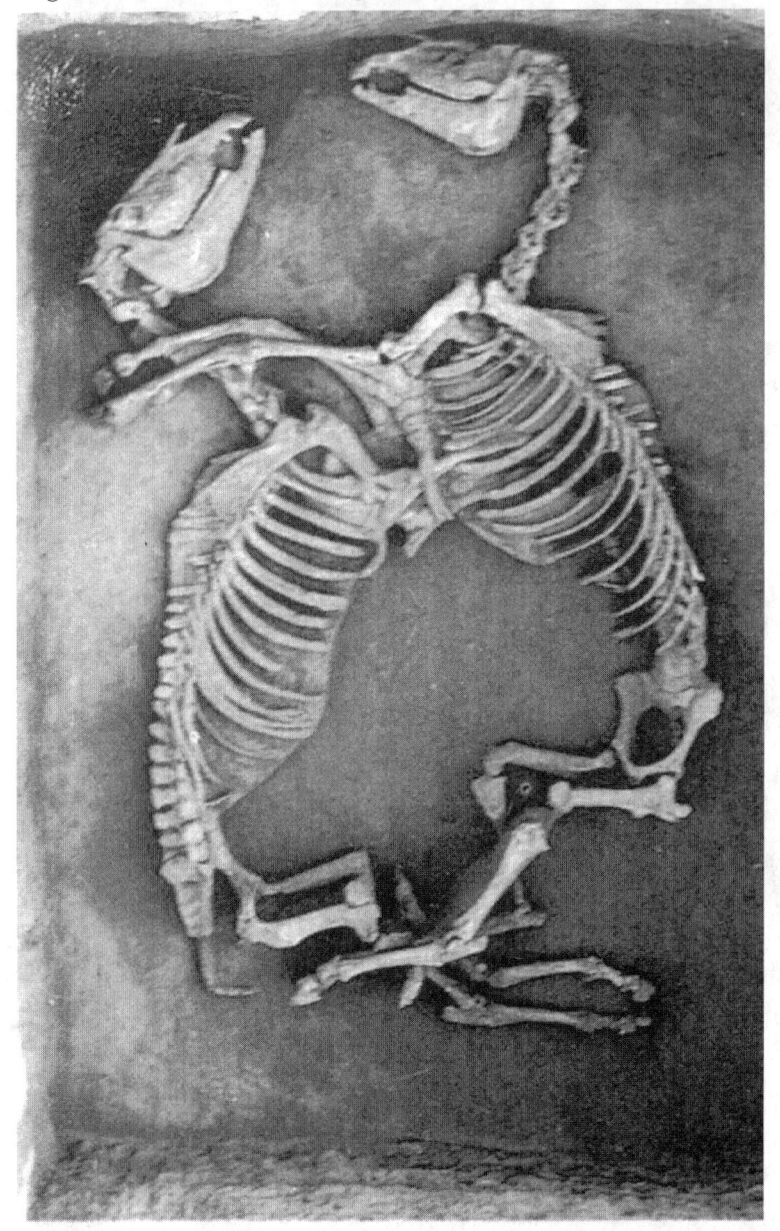

Figure 3.7 A pit with two horses at Yinxu, Anyang city, Henan Province.

5.4. Discussion

Archaeologists have found horses entombed in pits containing chariots with horses or horses alone at Yinxu, a clear indication that domesticated horses were used for sacrifices. However, no horse bone was present at early Shang Dynasty sites and in the sacrificial place, culture layer and pit of Huanbei Shang walled-town business site (late Shang). There could be two explanations for this: limited excavation of Shang Dynasty sites has yet to recover equids; or the horse was not present until late Shang times. The horse was treated as a special animal and they were owned only by the royal families or aristocracy of the Shang Dynasty. Horses were used for chariots or sacrifices when their owners were alive and then entombed with their owners after death. They were not used as a meat animal. This could be a reason why there was no horse at Huanbei Shang walled-town site. Chickens, dogs, pigs, cattle, sheep and goats were treated differently. In the oracle inscriptions on tortoiseshells or cattle scapulae, there were records of these species also used for sacrifices. There were bones of these animals present in both the culture layer and also the ashpits. They were believed to have been thrown out after human meals.

Research on ancient inscriptions gives us another line of evidence that we can use. While some oracle bones record the inscription "The king fed horses in the stables" (Institute of History 1981), no such inscriptions describing the king feeding cattle, sheep, dogs, chickens, or pigs have ever been identified. We believe that this oracle bone inscription concerning the king feeding horses highlights the importance of horses to the Shang Dynasty. Obviously, it is highly unlikely that the king personally raised horses, but the phrase itself probably refers to the symbolic role that the king once played in horse rearing. It is, however, just this sort of symbolic participation by the king in raising the horses that demonstrated its significance. Therefore possession of a horse had a specific social status in this period. The sudden appearance of the horse in the late Shang Dynasty along the middle and lower reaches of the Yellow River was probably associated with arrival of a foreign culture and/or commerce.

6. Conclusions

In summary, we proposed four criteria to analyse excavated animal bones in China and to determine their status as livestock. The probable time and location of presence of dog, pig, cattle, sheep, horse and chicken in ancient China have been reviewed and the origins of domesticated pig and horse discussed in detail. We believe that there are two different patterns of origin of livestock in ancient China: the first is the process of domestication since the Neolithic period by the inhabitants through their direct, long-term interaction with the wild relatives of livestock, e.g. the pig; the second is the late introduction of domesticated animals from another part of the world through exchange and interaction of culture and commerce, e.g. the case of horse introduction into the middle and lower reaches of the Yellow River.

Note

1 These were: 12,000–7000 BP at Zengpiyan site in Guilin, Guangxi Province, 9000–7000 BP at Jiahu site in Wuyang, Henan Province, 4800–4000 BP at Yuichisi site in Mengcheng, Anhui Province, 4000 BP at Dongguan site in Yuanqu, Shanxi Province, 3400 BP at Huayuanzhuang site in Anyang, Henan Province and 2900–2500 BP at Fengxi site in Chang'an, Shaanxi Province.

References

Anonymous (1979) *'Annotation of Shisanjing'* (十三经注疏), photocopy by Zhonghua Book Co., Beijing, pp. 861–3 (in Chinese).

Baoding Institute of Cultural Relic Management, Xushui Institute of Cultural Relic Management, Department of Archaeology of Beijing University, and Department of Archaeology of Hebei University (1992) 'Preliminary report on the trial excavation at Nanzhuangtou site, Xushui county, Hebei Province', *Archaeology*, 11: 961–6 (in Chinese).

Bo, W.C. (1994) 'Investigation of origin of domesticated pigs in China', *Agricultural Archaeology*, 3: 278–80 (in Chinese).

Cai, D.W., Han, L., Xie, C.Z., Li, S.N., Zhou, H. and Zhu, H. (2007) 'Characterization of Bronze Age horse remains excavated in Chifeng, Inner Mongolia, using mitochondrial DNA marker', *Progress in Natural Science*, 3: 385–390 (in Chinese).

Chen, B.Z. (2001) 'Phytolith assemblages of the Neolithic site at Jiahu, Henan Province, and its significance in environmental archaeology', *Acta Micropalaeontologica Sinica*, 18: 211–16 (in Chinese).

Chen, X.C. (1999) 'Re-visit of the origin of domesticated horse and other relevant issues', *Chinese Cultural Relic Newspaper*, 23 June 1999 (in Chinese).

Chen, Z.D. (1994) 'Natural relic', in Institute of Archaeology, CASS (eds.) *Discovery and Research at Yinxu* (殷墟的发现与研究), pp. 415–18, Beijing: Science Press (in Chinese).

Department of History and Archaeology, Northwest University (1988) 'Excavations at a cemetery of Shang Dynasty in Laoniupo, Xi'an, Shaanxi Province', *Cultural Relic*, 6: 1–22 (in Chinese).

Dobney, K. and Ervynck, A. (2004) 'A protocol for recording linear enamel hypoplasia on archaeological pig teeth', *International Journal of Osteoarchaeology*, 8: 263–73.

Dobney, K., Yuan, J., Ervynck, A., Albarella, U., Rowley-Conwy, P., Yang, M.F. and Luo, Y.B. (2006) 'A new angle of view on the investigation of origin of domesticated pigs in China', *Archaeology*, 11: 1034–40 (in Chinese).

Epstein, H. (1969) *Domestic Animals of China*, Farnham Royal, Bucks: Commonwealth Agricultural Bureau.

Excavation Team for Luojiajiao Site (1981) 'Animal fauna at Luojiajiao site', in *Report on Luojiajiao Site in Tongxiang: Proceedings of Zhejiang Provincial Institute of Cultural Relic and Archaeology* (浙江省文物考古研究所学刊), pp. 1–42, Beijing: Cultural Relic Publishing House (in Chinese).

Gansu Team of Institute of Archaeology, CASS (1974) 'Report on excavation at Dahezhuang site in Yongjing, Gansu Province', *Acta Archaeologica Sinica*, 2: 29–61 (in Chinese).

Gansu Team of Institute of Archaeology, CASS (1975) 'The Qijia culture cemetery at Qinweijia-Qijia site in Yongjing, Gansu Province', *Acta Archaeologica Sinica*, 2: 57–96 (in Chinese).

Gong, Y.Y. (2003) 'Chariot: Its evolution and introduction', *Journal of Zhejiang University (Humanities and Social Sciences)*, 33(3): 21–31 (in Chinese).

Guangxi Provincial Working Group on Cultural Relic and Guilin Committee of Cultural Relic (1976) 'Excavation of caves at Zengpiyan site in Guilin, Guangxi Province', *Archaeology*, 3: 177 (in Chinese).

Han, D.F. and Xu, C.H. (1989) 'Concurrent discussion on the mammalian fauna and the living environment of early humans during Quaternary Period in southern China', in R.K. Wu, S.Z. Wu and S.S. Zhang (eds) *China's Early Hominids* (中国远古人类), pp. 338–91, Beijing: Science Press (in Chinese).

Hebei Provincial Institute of Antiquity Management and Handan Institute of Antiquity Management (1981) 'Cishan site in Wu'an, Hebei Province', *Acta Archaeologica Sinica*, 3: 303–38 (in Chinese).

Hongo, H. and Meadow, R.H. (1998) 'Pig exploitation at Neolithic Çayönü Tepesi (Southeastern Anatolia)', in S.M. Nelson (ed.) *Ancestors for the Pigs: Pigs in Prehistory* (MASCA Research Papers in Science and Archaeology, 15), pp. 77–98, Philadelphia, PA: University of Pennsylvania, Museum of Archaeology and Anthropology.

Inner Mongolian Team of Institute of Archaeology, CASS (1997) '1992's report on excavation of a settlement location at Xinglongwa site in Aohan, Inner Mongolia', *Archaeology*, 1: 1–26 (in Chinese).

Inner Mongolian Team of Institute of Archaeology, CASS (2002) 'Significant achievements in excavation at Xinglongwa site in Aohan, Inner Mongolia', *Newsletters of Research Centre of Ancient Civilization of Chinese Academy of Social Sciences* (Jan.): 64-7 (in Chinese).

Institute of Archaeology, CASS (1977) 'Report on dating using radiocarbon – IV', *Archaeology*, 3: 201 (in Chinese).

Institute of History, CASS (1981) *Compilation of Oracle Bone Inscriptions* (甲骨文合集), 9: 3603, no. 29415. Beijing: Zhonghua Book Co. (in Chinese).

Institute of Archaeology, CASS (1995) 'Significant findings at Qianzhangda site in Tengzhou, Shandong Province', *Chinese Cultural Relic Newspaper*, 8 Jan. (in Chinese).

Institute of Archaeology, CASS, Inner Mongolian Regional Institute of Cultural Relic and Archaeology and Chifeng Team of Department of Archaeology of Jilin University (1998) 'Report of 1996's excavation at Dashanqian site in Kalaqin, Inner Mongolia', *Archaeology*, 9: 43–49 (in Chinese).

Institute of Archaeology, CASS, Guangxi Provincial Working Group on Cultural Relic, Zengpiyan Muzeum in Guilin and Guilin Working Group on Cultural Relic (2003) *Zengpiyan Site in Guilin* (桂林甑皮岩), Beijing: Cultural Relic Publishing House (in Chinese).

Jansen, T., Foster, P., Levine, M.A., Oelke, H., Hurles, M., Renfrew, C., Weber, J. and Olek, K. (2002) 'Mitochondrial DNA and the origins of the domestic horse', *Proceedings of the National Academy of Sciences of the United States of America*, 99: 10905–10.

Jia, L.B., Gai, P. and You, Y.Z. (1972) 'Excavation report from the Paleolithic site in Shiyu, Shanxi Province', *Acta Archaeologica Sinica*, 1: 38–58 (in Chinese).

Kong, J. P. (1994) 'Origin of carriage and its evolution', *Chinese Cultural Relic Newspaper*, 12 June (in Chinese).

Larson, G., Dobney, K., Albarella, U., Fang, M., Matisoo-Smith, E., Robins, J., Lowden, S., Finlayson, H., Brand, T., Willerslev, E., Rowley-Conwy, P., Andersson, L. and Cooper, A. (2005) 'Worldwide phylogeography of wild boar reveals multiple centres of pig domestication', *Science*, 307: 1618–21.

Li, B.C. (2004) 'Discussion on Holocene palaeoclimate environment in the ruins of Banpo in Xi'an', *Journal of Northwest University (Natural Science Edition)*, 34(4): 485–8 (in Chinese).

Li, Y.C., Wang, K.F. and Zhang, Y.L. (2000) 'The evolution of Paleo-vegetation and Paleo-environment in Nanzhuangtou site and their relationship with man activities', *Marine Geology and Quaternary Geology*, 20(3): 23–30 (in Chinese).

Li, Y.H. and Han, D.F. (1959) 'Faunal remains from a Neolithic site of Banpo in Xi'an, Shaanxi Province', *Vertebrate Paleontology and Paleoanthropology*, 1(4): 173–85 (in Chinese).

Li, Y.H. and Han, D.F. (1978) 'Animal fauna at the Zengpiyan site in Guilin, Guangxi Province', *Vertebrate Paleontology and Paleoanthropology*, 4: 244–54 (in Chinese).

Liang, S.Y. (1934) 'Bone remains of animals and birds and shell remains from gastropods', in Institute of Historical Linguistics, National Central Research Academy (eds.) *Chengziyan*, pp. 90–1 (in Chinese).

Olsen, S.J. (1984) 'The early domestication of the horse in North China', *Archaeology*, 37: 62–3.

Olsen, S.J. (1993) 'China as a centre for early animal domestication', *Acta Anthropologica Sinica*, 12(2): 120–9 (in both Chinese and English).

Qi, G.Q. (1989) 'Concurrent discussion on the mammalian fauna and the living environment of early humans during Quaternary Period in northern China', in R.K. Wu, S.Z. Wu and S.S. Zhang (eds) *China's Early Hominids* (中国远古人类), pp. 277–337, Beijing: Science Press (in Chinese).

Research Centre for Chinese Frontier Archaeology of Jilin University and Inner Mongolian Regional Institute of Cultural Relic and Archaeology (2004) 'Summary of 2002's excavation of tomes in western Jinggouzhi site in Linxi county, Inner Mongolia', *Antiquity and Cultural Relic*, 1: 6–18 (in Chinese).

Shangcheng Team of Institute of Archaeology, CASS (2001) 'Sacrificial place of early Shang Dynasty at the walled-town site in Yanshi, Henan Province', *Chinese Cultural Relic Newspaper*, 5 Aug. (in Chinese).

Shao, B.Y. (2003) 'Six livestock species and society in early Qin Dynasty', *Agricultural Archaeology*, 1: 239–54 (in Chinese).

Song, G.D., Xie, W. and Chen, X. (1995) 'Significant excavations at Xiaoshuangqiao site in Zhengzhou, Henan Province', *Chinese Cultural Relic Newspaper*, 13 Aug. (in Chinese).

Su, J. (2006) 'Yangshao culture and Banpo site', *History of Publication*, 1: 1 (in Chinese).

Tan, S.M. (1984) 'Origin of domesticated pigs based on the excavation of pig bones at Zengpiyan site', *Agricultural Archaeology*, 2: 339 (in Chinese).

Tang, S.X., Zhang, W.X., and Liu, J. (1999) 'The study on the bi-peak-tubercle on lemma of Hemudu and Luojiajho ancient excavated rice grains with electric scanning microscope', *Acta Agronomica Sinica*, 25(3): 320–7 (in Chinese).

Wang, Y.T. (1998) 'Re-visit of history of horse keeping and related issues in China', *Chinese Cultural Relic Newspaper*, 12 Aug. (in Chinese).

Wang, Z.J., and Song, P. (2001) 'Probes on origin of domesticated horses in northern China', *Archaeology and Cultural Relic*, 2: 26–30 (in Chinese).

Xie, C.X. (1986) 'History of utilization of horse in ancient China', in Z.G. Zhang and X.H. Zhu (eds) *Compilation of Historical Information of Livestock in China* (中国畜牧史料集), pp. 103–22, Beijing: Science Press (in Chinese).

Xie, C.X., Wang, T.Q., and Yang, J.S. (eds) (1986) *The Horse and Ass Breeds in China* (中国马驴品种志), pp. 1–17, Shanghai: Shanghai Scientific and Technical Publishers (in Chinese).

Yan, W.M. (1997) 'New progress on investigation of history of rice cultivation in China', *Archaeology*, 9: 71–6 (in Chinese).

Yuan, J. (1999) 'Man's meat-acquiring patterns in Neolithic China', *Acta Archaeologica Sinica*, 1: 1–22 (in Chinese).

Yuan, J. (2001) 'Issues on investigation of origin of domesticated animals in Neolithic China', *Cultural Relic*, 5: 51–8 (in Chinese).

Yuan, J. (2004) 'Two thoughts on zooarchaeological reseach at Yinxu site, Anyang, Henan Province', *Review of Archaeology* (考古学集刊) (Beijing: Cultural Relic Publishing House), 15: 236–42 (in Chinese).

Yuan, J. and Flad, R. (2002) 'Pig domestication in ancient China', *Antiquity*, 76: 724–32.

Yuan, J. and An, J.A. (1997) 'Two issues on of China's zooarchaeological research', *Chinese Cultural Relic Newspaper*, 26 April (in Chinese).

Yuan, J. and Tang J.G. (2000) 'Report on investigation of animal bones excavated at Huayuanzhuang site in Huanbei of Anyang, Henan Province', *Archaeology*, 11: 75–81 (in Chinese).

Yuan, J. and Yang, M.F. (2004) 'Investigation of animal fauna', in Zhejiang Provincial Institute of Cultural Relic and Archaeology and Xiaoshan Muzeum (eds) *Kuahuqiao* (跨湖桥), pp. 241–70, Beijing: Cultural Relic Publishing House (in Chinese).

Zhang, A.B. (2004) 'A preliminary view on the prehistoric animal domestication in Huaihe River valley', *Agricultural History of China*, 23(2): 51–4 (in Chinese).

Zhang, C.S., and Zhang, G.Z. (1997) 'Preliminary report on investigations and excavations at sites of Shang Dynasty's culture in Shangqiu, Henan Province', *Archaeology*, 4: 24–31 (in Chinese).

Zhang, C.S. (2004) 'Wild horse, domestic horse and eastern Asian center of horse keeping', *Agricultural Archeology*, 1: 252–4 (in Chinese).

Zhang, Z.G. (1980) 'Origin and development of Chinese pig breeds', *Journal of Beijing Agricultural University*, 3: 45–55 (in Chinese).

Zhang, Z.G., Li, B.T., and Chen, X.H. (eds) (1986) *Pig breeds in China* (中国猪品种志), pp. 1–24, Shanghai: Shanghai Scientific and Technical Publishers (in Chinese).

Zhao, Z.J. (2004) 'New probes on investigation of history of arid agriculture in northern China', *Chinese Cultural Relic Newspaper*, 11 Oct. (in Chinese).

Zhejiang Provincial Institute of Cultural Relic and Archaeology and Xiaoshan Museum (2004) *Kuahuqiao* (跨湖桥), pp. 241–70, Beijing: Cultural Relic Publishing House (in Chinese).

Zheng, Y.F., You, X.L., Xu, J.M., Bian, O.J. and Yu, W.J. (1994) 'Silica body analysis on rice remains at Hemudu site', *Journal of Zhejiang Agricultural University*, 20(1): 81–5 (in Chinese).

Zhong, X. (1976) 'Probe of origin of pig in China based on the bones and pottery pigs excavated at Hemudu site', *Cultural Relic*, 8: 24–6 (in Chinese).

Zhou, B.X. (1981) 'Animal remains found at Cishan site, Wu'an, Hebei Province', *Acta Archaeologica Sinica*, 3: 339–46 (in Chinese).

Zhou, B.X. (1983) 'Animal skeletal remains at Longshan culture site of Baiying in Tangyin, Henan Province', *Review of Archaeology* (考古学集刊) (Beijing: Chinese Social Science Press), 3: 48–50 (in Chinese).

Zhou, B.X. (1984) 'Domesticated animals in Neolithic China', in Institute of Archaeology, Chinese Academy of Social Sciences (ed.) *Archaeological Findings and Research in China* (新中国的考古发现与研究), pp. 194–9, Beijing: Cultural Relics Publishing House (in Chinese).

4 Stratification in the peopling of China

How far does the linguistic evidence match genetics and archaeology?

Roger Blench

1. Introduction

1.1 The problem: synthesizing linguistics, archaeology and genetics

The concept of synthesizing linguistics, archaeology and genetics in the reconstruction of the past is becoming a commonplace; but the reality is that each discipline largely pursues its own methods and what little interaction there is remains marginal. Hence many of the questions asked are internal to the discipline, addressed to colleagues, not the larger sphere of understanding the past. China and East Asia in general represent a particularly difficult case because so much of the linguistics and archaeology is driven by an emphasis on high culture. Major archaeological texts refer neither to linguistics nor genetics and speculation about the identity of non-Chinese groups mentioned in the texts tends to be unanchored. In addition, ideology surrounding the definition of minorities in China has confused the analysis in genetics papers. This situation has begun to change and a review of the current situation may be useful.[1]

A preliminary outline of an agenda for interdisciplinary study is set out in Wang (1998) who characterized linguistics, archaeology and genetics as 'three windows on the past'. This model should be expanded by separating out the potential information in written documents from the results of comparative linguistics based on spoken language. In addition, comparative ethnography has so far only featured in the archaeology 'window'. But, especially in Taiwan, information on the distribution of material and cultural traits is rich and can potentially be incorporated into larger models. Figure 4.1 represents a potential multidisciplinary framework for reconstructing China's past.

2. The linguistic pattern of present-day China

2.1. General

Although dominated numerically by languages of the Sino-Tibetan phylum, China is highly diverse linguistically (Ramsey 1987). Table 4.1 shows the main language phyla represented.

106   *Roger Blench*

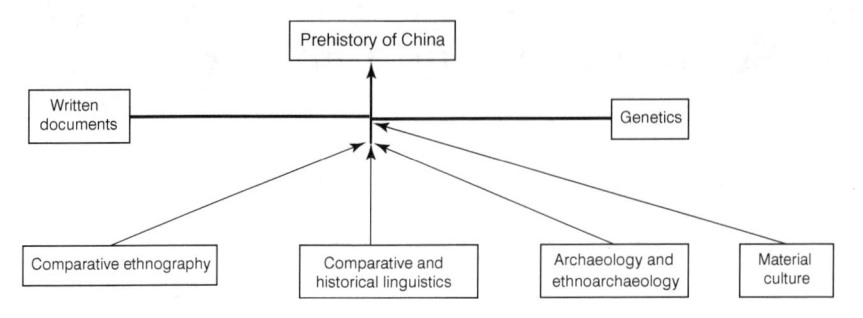

Figure 4.1   Elements in reconstructing China's prehistory.

Table 4.1 Language phyla of China

Phylum	Examples
Sino-Tibetan/Tibeto-Burman	Chinese, Yi, Pumi, Naxi, Bai, Tujia
Hmong-Mien = Miao-Yao	Ho Te, Hmong, Pa Hng
Altaic (Turkic, Mongolic, Tungusic)	Ili Turko, Monguor, Evenki
Daic= Tai-Kadai = Kra-Dai	Zhuang, E
Austroasiatic	Blang, Mang, U
Austronesian (Chamic)	Tsat
Indo-European	Tajik, Wakhi, Russian, Macanese
Korean	
Unclassified	Waxianghua, Wutunhua

Ethnologue 2005 estimates lists 236 languages for China, but this includes 13 dialects of Chinese and Chinese sign language. However, new languages are regularly being recorded, such as the Austroasiatic Bugan, yet to be classified within Mon-Khmer. This figure contrasts with the official count of 56 (55 + Han), which includes all the minorities of Taiwan under a single name, Gaoshan (Yin 1989). Despite the unlikely nature of the official figure, it continues to be propagated on websites and official documents. According to 1990 data, minorities constitute some 91 million or 6.5 per cent of the population, so they are relatively numerous compared with other countries in the region (MacKerras 1997). Despite this official view, Chinese linguistic sources do provide data on the highly diverse languages subsumed under the official minorities, and survey programmes continue to record new languages. Even so, this is probably a fraction of the number of languages that used to exist; the spread of the Han over the last 3,000 years has probably eliminated a once still greater diversity.

2.2. Sino-Tibetan

Sino-Tibetan is the phylum with the second largest number of speakers after Indo-European, largely because of the size of the Chinese population. Current estimates put their number at c.1.3 billion (Ethnologue 2005). Apart from Burmese and Tibetan, most other languages in the phylum are small and remain little-known, partly because of their inaccessibility. The name Sino-Tibetan carries with it heavy historical baggage. Originating as 'Indo-Chinese' in the middle of the 19th century, it originally carried racial connotations (Van Driem 2002). The first recognition of the phylum probably dates to Julius von Klaproth (1823) who recognized three parallel branches: Chinese, Burmese and Tibetan (Van Driem, Chapter 9, this volume). Von Klaproth also explicitly excluded Austroasiatic and Daic, unlike many later classifiers, who sequentially brought in almost all the phyla in this region, in a series of now discarded phylogenies. Strangely, the notion that the Sinitic branch (i.e. the varieties of Chinese) is not related to the rest of Tibeto-Burman is still held in some quarters and even recent conspectuses (e.g. Thurgood and La Polla 2003) feel the obligation to refer to this view.

Considering the importance of Sino-Tibetan and its history of scholarship, there is a striking lack of agreement as to its internal classification. Broadly speaking, the opposing camps are those who consider Sinitic as a primary subgroup of Sino-Tibetan (Benedict 1972, 1976; Bodman 1980; Matisoff 2003; Bradley 1997; Thurgood and La Polla 2003) and those who would place it at some lower node within the remaining languages, thereby applying the name Tibeto-Burman to the whole phylum (Shafer 1974; Van Driem 1997). Under the second proposal, Sinitic would thus be incorporated within the group conventionally defined in opposition to Sinitic. These two views are reflected in Figure 4.2 and Figure 4.3. Figure 4.2 shows the internal structure of Sino-Tibetan according to Matisoff (2001: 297), which can be taken to represent the mainstream.

The groups represented here are by and large 'geographic' categories; Kamarupan and Himalayan have no genetic status. Even this view has never been justified in print, despite the space afforded by the 800 pages of Matisoff (2003). Moreover, the exclusion by Matisoff of many small branches of Sino-Tibetan and the branching of others from a single node does not suggest this is a fully

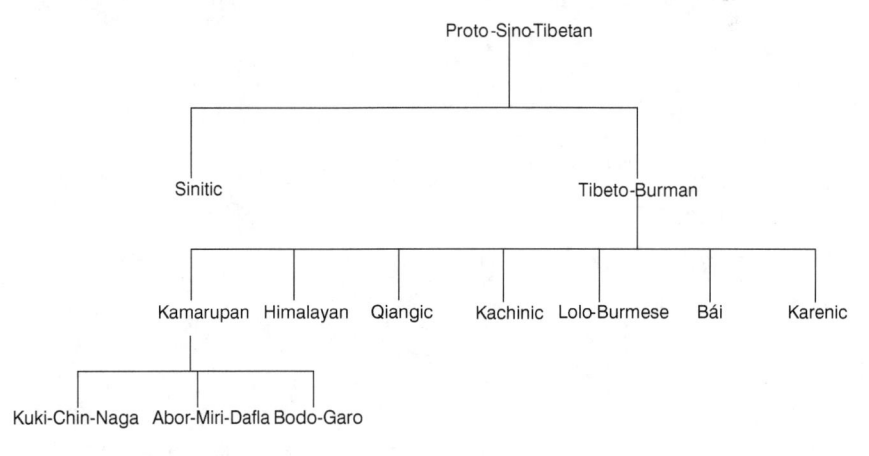

Figure 4.2 Sino-Tibetan according to Matisoff (2001).

108 *Roger Blench*

worked-out theory. The equally agnostic alternative is represented in the view of Van Driem (2005), in his 'fallen leaves' schema (Figure 4.3).

Van Driem's model presents no assumptions at all about subgrouping but simply maps already well-recognized groups. This is an entirely geographical model, which places generally agreed subgroups in proximity, with the area of the ellipse representing their size, but advances no hypothesis about their ultimate relationships. Whether this represents progress is debatable, but the 'fallen leaves' model has the virtue of treating all branches of Sino-Tibetan as of equal status and requiring that their position be ultimately defined. Van Driem would argue that this is a fair representation of the current state of our knowledge.

It is hard not to gain the impression that a state of academic warfare exists between the various camps. Languages given prominence by one side are ignored by the other. For example, Gongduk, first drawn attention to in Van Driem (2001), appears to be a highly divergent Himalayan language that may be of great significance for the reconstruction of the phylum. However, no mention of this language is made in either Matisoff (2003) or Thurgood and LaPolla (2003).

Sinitic

Sinitic is a general term for all the languages deemed to be part of the Chinese subgroup. This label is not uncontroversial, as the Bái language has been analysed

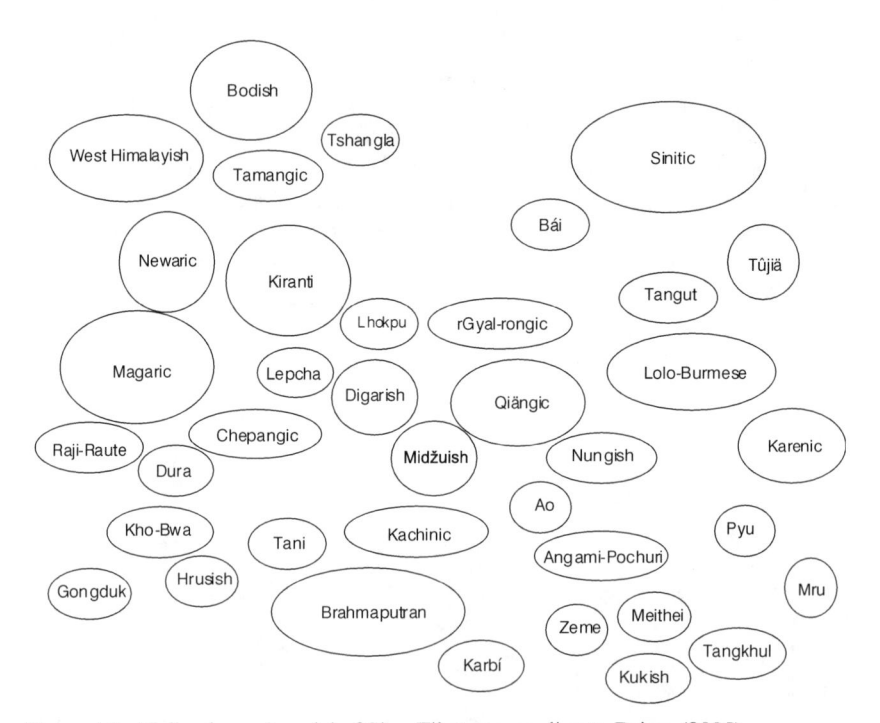

Figure 4.3 'Fallen leaves' model of Sino-Tibetan according to Driem (2005).

as a remote relative of Chinese, or as a distinct Sino-Tibetan language heavily influenced by Chinese (see summary in Norman 2003: 73). Sinitic is generally divided into some seven recognized dialect groups, Mandarin, Mǐn, Hakka, Yuè, Gàn, Wú and Xiāng, but Norman (2003: 72) argues that these are ill-defined and that the unity of groups such as Wú is far from proven. Moreover, the Mǐn dialects are distinct from the other branches of Sinitic, and presumably represent a primary split. Modern-day Sinitic lects can be reconstructed to a proto-language, referred to as 'Common Chinese'. However, Chinese is exceptional in that there are decipherable records going back at least to the Shang oracle bones, roughly the 13th century BC (Herforth 2003: 59). By the Warring States period (475–221 BC) a corpus of prose texts allows us to undertake a reasonable analysis of phonology and grammar of what is usually called Zhou Chinese (Baxter and Hubbard 1992; Sagart 1999). It appears that the morphology and grammar of this language are strikingly different from Modern Chinese and rather resemble other branches of Sino-Tibetan. Figure 4.4 shows the historical relation between these groups as presently understood;

A figure such as this suggests a unidirectional evolution of Chinese, but, rather like Sanskrit, early written materials presumably represented one lect among many spoken forms of which no record remains.

China also has intriguing 'remnant' languages such as Tujia (Brassett and Brassett 2005), hard to classify because they have been so heavily Sinicized. The Tujia[2] are likely to be the modern descendants of the Ba people, whose kingdom (near modern-day Chongqing) flourished between 600 and 400 BC but fell to the Qin in 316 BC. The Ba appear in historical records as the Tujia from about AD 1300 onwards. Written Chinese texts also contain material on other Sino-Tibetan languages that can provide rather fragmentary insights into language diversity in the past (Wang 1998). Bái words are recorded in the *Manshu*, a work of the Tang Dynasty, while the Han Dynasty *Bailangge* (= Pai-Lang) is written in a Tibeto-Burman language, probably related to Yi. The Bái language is spoken around Dali in north-western Yunnan by some 1,250,000 people (Ethnologue 2005). Although

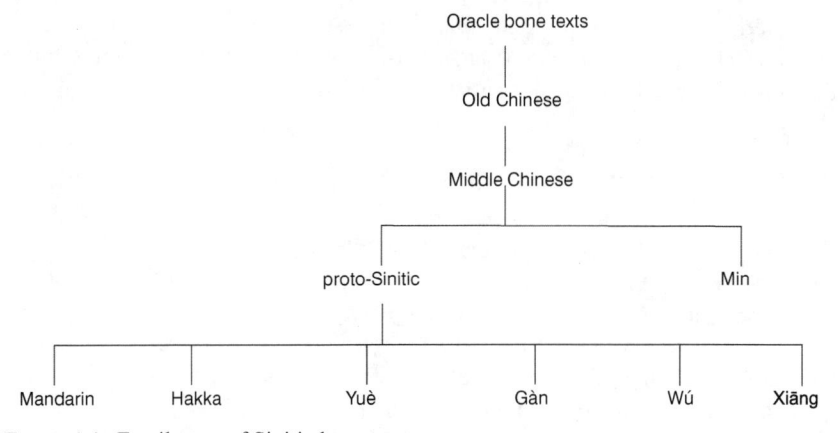

Figure 4.4 Family tree of Sinitic languages.

officially classified as Tibeto-Burman, evidence for this is problematic because of the complex layers of ancient loans from Chinese and other languages (Wiersma 2003). These two languages are now generally considered to be Sino-Tibetan, although the many layers of Sinitic loanwords make it difficult to extract their core vocabulary. It may be that Tujia and Bái are traces of a much more diverse earlier Sino-Tibetan population largely eliminated by the spread of Sinitic. The notion that Bái is co-ordinate with Sinitic would have to be squared with the new understanding of the place of Chinese in the Tibeto-Burman 'tree'.

A language that is still puzzling is Waxianghua, spoken by 300,000 people (in 1995) in a 6,000 km^2 area in western Hunan Province, Wuling Mountains, including Yuanling, Chunxi, Jishou, Guzhang and Dayong counties. It differs greatly from both South-western Mandarin (Xinan Guanhua) and Xiang Chinese (Hunanese), but is relatively uniform within itself. It has so far remained unclassified. Similarly, the Wutun language with some 2,000 speakers in Eastern Qinghai Province, Huangnan Tibetan Autonomous Prefecture, mixes elements of Chinese, Tibetan and Mongolian, but its ultimate genetic affiliation remains unknown.

External affiliations of Sino-Tibetan

The external affiliations of Sino-Tibetan are also controversial. Sino-Tibetan has been linked with almost every phylum in East Asia (and the New World) and it is hard to make a judgement on this potential for promiscuous cohabitation. Most scholars consider the similarities in lexicon and phonology between Sino-Tibetan and the other phyla with which it is in geographical proximity to be the result of contact. Two macrophylic models have been argued for in recent times; Sino-Caucasian and Sino-Austronesian. Sino-Caucasian has been principally promoted by the late Sergei Starostin (1991) and Sino-(Tibetan)-Austronesian by Laurent Sagart (1994, 2005). Van Driem (Chapter 9, this volume) has reviewed these models and finds the case for Sino-Caucasian flawed by irregular correspondences and wayward semantics. Sino-Austronesian is altogether more promising and most of those who have considered the evidence conclude that Sagart has made a case for links between the two phyla. The issue is whether it can be demonstrated that this is the result of genetic affiliation as opposed to contact.

Archaeological and genetic correlates of Sino-Tibetan expansion

Is it therefore worth trying to make proposals for the pattern of Sino-Tibetan expansion within this mosaic of uncertainty? Probably only generalizations of a very broad kind are useful. The first is that Sino-Tibetan may well be substantially older than is usually thought. The overall pattern seems to be some well-defined groups that have expanded in the last few thousand years and a scatter of archaic languages with unusual features that are very different one from another. This suggests that the source populations could have been the fragmented hunter-gatherer groups spread over a wide area between the Himalayan Plateau and North

China, at least 10,000–12,000 years ago. This period is very poorly known in the archaeology of mainland China but perhaps can be identified with the Shengwen (= 'cord-marked') pottery found between the Yangzi and Yellow rivers. Better known is the Chulmun pottery of the Korean peninsula, which is associated with an alternation between land-mammal hunting and exploitation of marine resources. If this is so, a model that has populations migrating down river valleys, popular in explaining phylic expansion in this region, is inappropriate; these were probably hunters spreading across open terrain. Once agriculture began, the early adopters gained a massive advantage and some groups spread preferentially, most notably the Sinitic speakers. The topography allowed the survival of archaic groups in montane areas; hence the pattern of fragmentation of Sino-Tibetan.

A quite different view is canvassed by Matisoff on the STEDT website.[3] He says:

> The Proto-Sino-Tibetan (PST) homeland seems to have been somewhere on the Himalayan plateau, where the great rivers of East and Southeast Asia (including the Yellow, Yangzi, Mekong, Brahmaputra, Salween, and Irrawaddy) have their source. The time of hypothetical ST unity, when the Proto-Han (= Proto-Chinese) and Proto-Tibeto-Burman (PTB) peoples formed a relatively undifferentiated linguistic community, must have been at least as remote as the Proto-Indo-European period, perhaps around 4000 BC. The TB peoples slowly fanned outward along these river valleys, but only in the middle of the first millennium AD did they penetrate into peninsular Southeast Asia, where speakers of Austronesian (= Malayo-Polynesian) and Mon-Khmer (Austroasiatic) languages had already established themselves by prehistoric times. The Tai peoples began filtering down from the north at about the same time as the TB's. The most recent arrivals to the area south of China have been the Hmong-Mien (Miao-Yao), most of whom still live in China itself.

This model does not seem to account for the internal diversity of Sino-Tibetan, nor the relative internal diversity of individual branches. If Sinitic and Tibeto-Burman are a primary split, why is Tibeto-Burman so much more internally divided? Six thousand years seems a short period to arrive at the present diversity when compared to Austronesian, which should be of comparable antiquity.

Wherever Sinitic originates within Sino-Tibetan, there is a broad consensus that its main spread has been north–south, from the millet-growing to the rice-growing areas and that it has assimilated or overwhelmed a diverse *in situ* population (e.g. Fitzgerald 1972; Lee 1978; LaPolla 2001). It is therefore *unlikely* that Sinitic can be identified with the earliest Neolithic communities in north China such as the Péilígǎng or Císhān (6500 BP onwards) and it is more helpful to think of Sinitic as one of Barnes's (1993: 108) 'Late Neolithic Elites' emerging between 3500 and 2000 BC. The notable feature of the end of this period is the appearance of bronze vessels in the archaeological record and it easy to imagine the inception of the Shang as marking the take-off of Sinitic. Presumably, a major element in the *in situ* population was Hmong-Mien-speaking, but unless these groups were considerably north of their present location, the agriculturists of Císhān were not Hmong-Mien either. Van Driem (1998) has canvassed Sichuān as the likely original homeland of Sino-Tibetan (Tibeto-Burman in his terms). A comparable view is supported in a study of Y chromosome haplotypes reported in Su *et al.* (2000) who argue that proto-Sino-Tibetan was spoken in northern Sichuān and dispersed westwards to the Himalayas and east and south to create the Chinese dialects. However, they also argue that this nucleus was the lineal descendant of early Neolithic millet-growers, which seems highly unlikely. There is no obvious candidate for the ethnolinguistic identity of the millet-growers of Péilígǎng and it may be that they have no linguistic descendants.

An interesting example of the politicization of archaeological narratives is the description by Da-Shun (1995) of the Hongshan culture of Liaoning Province, north-east of Beijing. This is usually dated to 4000–3000 BC, i.e. roughly contemporaneous with the Yangshao. Despite it being well outside the imperial boundaries, Da-Shun sees this as 'the dawn of Chinese civilization' and attempts to link it with that civilization through a series of typological indicators, a writing system, bronze metallurgy, etc. A particular type of altar, also found elsewhere in China, is part of the thread that links this region with the later Ming Dynasty. The reality is that there is no evidence that this region would have been Sinitic-speaking at this period; it is much more credible that the inhabitants would have been Altaic speakers, either speaking pre-Mongolic or Koreanic languages.

2.3. Hmong-Mien

The Hmong-Mien (= Miao-Yao)[4] languages are spoken mostly in China with some groups also in Laos, Việt Nam and Thailand. Their centre of gravity is between the Yangzi and the Mekong rivers. Hmong-Mien languages are quite close to one another, and although Ethnologue (2005) lists some 35 languages, many of these are mutually intelligible lects. There have been various comparative overviews of the group, starting with Purnell (1970), Wang (1994), Wang and Mao (1995) and Niederer (1998). Tapp *et al.* (2004) have edited a comprehensive overview of recent scholarship that includes much valuable bibliography.

The internal structure of the family is still very much in flux as new information becomes available. Of particular interest is the Pa-Hng language which has evidence of features of both main branches, although it is apparently closer to the Hmongic (Niederer 2004). Still debated is the place Ho Te, or She, a language spoken in South-eastern Guangdong Province by less than 1,000 speakers. Figure 4.5 shows the internal classification of Hmong-Mien according to Niederer (2004: 141).

The Hmong-Mien languages have been linked with almost all the East Asian language phyla, but never conclusively. Despite sharing much common vocabulary with their neighbours, evidence for a genetic link is lacking and these languages probably constitute a small but independent phylum. All the Hmong-Mien languages are relatively close to one another and the date of their overall

Stratification in the peopling in China 113

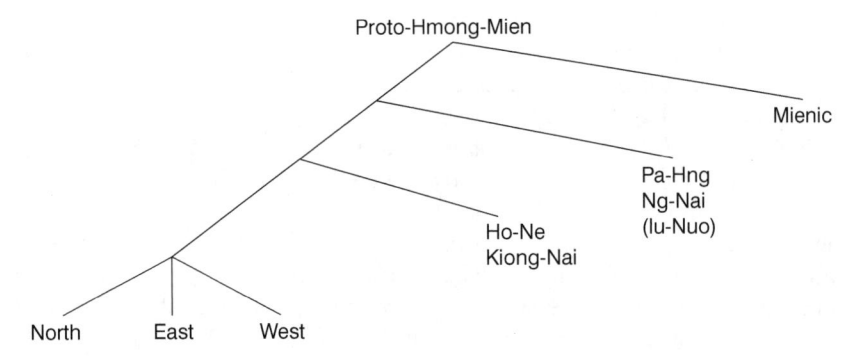

```
                    Proto-Hmong-Mien
                    /              \
                   /                \
                  /                   Mienic
                 /  \
                /    \
               /      \              Pa-Hng
              /        \             Ng-Nai
             /          Ho-Ne        (Iu-Nuo)
            /\          Kiong-Nai
           /  |  \
          /   |   \
       North East  West
```

Figure 4.5 Hmong-Mien languages according to Niederer (2004).

dispersal is quite recent. This suggests that one bottleneck brought the phylum into existence, and Mienic at least went through another bottleneck, as it appears to be far more uniform than Hmongic.

The linguistic geography of the Hmong-Mien suggests very strongly that they were scattered by the incoming Han and probably forced southwards into modern Laos and Thailand, probably in the last 3,000–4,000 years. This has sparked a number of debates on the relative antiquity of these groups; if Hmong-Mien preceded Chinese, should it not be more diverse? Sagart (personal communication) has put forward the suggestion that pre-Mien was adopted by the Chu state (500 BC onwards) which would have had a Sinicized bureaucracy. The northern distribution of Mien would then represent the boundary of this state. Yao, the more southerly languages, must have escaped Chu at some stage but were perhaps incorporated within another state, as Yao languages have a unique set of Sinitic loans.

Ratliff (2004) has made use of the reconstructions of proto-Hmong-Mien by Wang and Mao (1995) to explore the likely environment of the putative homeland of these people. Two valuable conclusions can be drawn from this: the Hmong-Mien were already established farmers prior to their dispersal and animals and plants reconstructible to proto-Hmong-Mien point to a homeland south of the Yangzi River.[5]

Despite the lack of internal diversity in Hmong-Mien, it seems difficult to imagine that pre-Hmong-Mien are not ancient inhabitants of the East Asian area. It seems as if the other more diverse relatives of Hmong-Mien must have been eliminated by the Han expansion and the languages still in existence are a secondary expansion. The pre-Hmong-Mien may therefore be identified with one of the Neolithic pottery horizons, but it seems unlikely that the present diaspora would have any direct correlate, since their dispersal is based on a pattern of refuge rather than positive expansion.

2.4. *Altaic*

The minimal set of Altaic languages consists of Turkic, Mongolic and Tungusic, spread from Turkey to Siberia, and all attested in China. However, the macrophylum, Macro-Altaic, including Korean and Japanese, remains controversial. Most scholars accept the membership of Korean, fewer Japanese (see Martin 1991; Miller 1996 and Chapter 11, this volume). Figure 4.6 shows a tree representing the Altaic and Macro-Altaic groupings.

Starostin *et al.* (2003) have published a major etymological dictionary of comparative Altaic, which provides rich material for interpreting its prehistory. Compared with the other phyla discussed here, Altaic has a very unusual substructure. Each of its branches is internally very close-knit, but they are very different from one another. Indeed the dispersal of Turkic has largely taken place in historical time (Golden 1998). The pattern of the phylum points to the likely loss of other branches of Altaic intermediate between those still in existence. The differences between branches have led some scholars to claim that Altaic is not a phylum but a bundling of languages that have interacted (Janhunen 1994).

Today the Turkic languages are spread across Central Asia from Sakha (Yakutia) to the Turkish republic, with their centre of gravity in Asian Russia. They are represented in China by Salar, related to Crimean Turkish, and the Uyghur languages and are probably a relatively recent intrusion. The principal sources on the languages and history of this group are Menges (1995) and Johanson and Csató (1998). Generally speaking, the Turkic languages are very closely related and are consistent with a pattern of expansion from the present-day region of modern Mongolia, both westwards to Turkey and north to Sakha.

Mongolic languages are spoken throughout much of modern Mongolia, with outlying Mongolic languages spoken in China and Afghanistan (Janhunen 2003). Much of the region today is dominated by Khalkh Mongol, but the relative uniformity of Mongolic can be attributed to the empire founded by Chinggis Khan (AD 1,200 to 1,400) which grew to control the largest land empire ever recorded and probably eliminated earlier ethnic and linguistic diversity. Janhunen

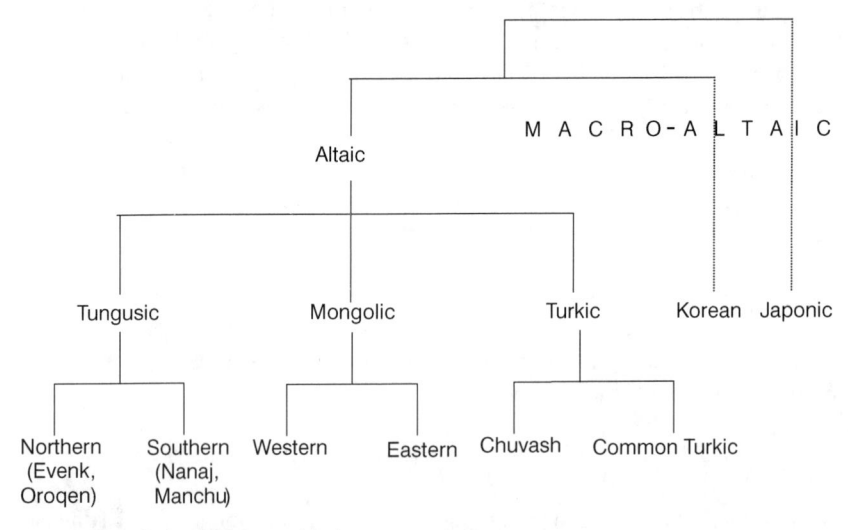

Figure 4.6 Altaic and Macro-Altaic.

Stratification in the peopling in China 115

(1993) has analysed lexical elements borrowed from Mongolic into Manchurian Tungusic to argue that the family formerly exhibited much greater diversity. Some of the isolated Mongolic languages in China may well be remnants of military expeditions rather than traces of earlier expansions. Kolman *et al.* (1996) sampled the mtDNA of Mongolian populations within Mongolia extensively, and found a high degree of genetic homogeneity, as well as a close link to New World populations. Whether such homogeneity would be reproduced if the sample were extended to Mongolic populations outside Mongolia is unclear, since this may simply reflect the recent dominance of the Khalkh.

The region of Mongolia had a much warmer climate in the early Holocene, and much of the high plateau was heavily forested. As a consequence, subsistence strategies were quite diverse and it is assumed there was agriculture in this period, although this is an inference from Yangshao pottery finds rather than direct evidence (Barnes 1993: 154). Reconstructions in Starostin *et al.* (2003) also point to an important agricultural component in early Altaic, although the glottochronological dates they attribute to the phylum make no sense in terms of known archaeology. When the climate became more arid in the 3rd millennium BC, there was a development of nomadic pastoralism. At the same time, rock-engravings show horse-drawn chariots and these are presumably ancestral to the carts essential to transhumance in Mongolia today. It would not be unreasonable to link this evolution of pastoralism with the expansion of the Mongolic languages. Although today Mongolic is quite undiverse, this is the result of the spread of Khalkh Mongol following the establishment of the Khanates in the medieval period. But there is every reason to think that pastoral peoples, herding horses and other species, have been on the northern borders of China for a long period. Janhunen (1998) has explored the vocabulary of the horse in Central Asia and points out that the terms are all related in almost all the phyla of this region (Table 4.2).

This suggests that horse culture was spread rapidly by a single group; linguistic geography points strongly to Mongolic speakers. As Janhunen (1998) points out, the absence of this root for horse in Turkic suggests that it is not an Altaic root, but a series of ancient loanwords. Norman (1988: 18) identifies some loanwords from Altaic into Old Chinese, for example OC *duk, 'calf' and Starostin (Chapter 10, this volume) proposes others such as 粒 *rə p* 'cereals, grain as food'.

Table 4.2 Horse terms in East Asia

Language group	Proto-form
Mongolic	morin
Tungusic	murin
Korean	mar (말)
Japanese	uma (うま)
Chinese	mǎ (馬)

Source: Janhunen (1998).

Apart from Manchu, the Tungusic languages all have a small number of speakers whose populations were until recently hunter-gatherers (Doerfer 1978). Starostin *et al.* (2003) propose that speakers may have undergone a reversion to foraging, as Tungusic shares names for crops with other Altaic languages. The Tungusic languages are not highly diverse compared with other Siberian populations, suggesting recent expansion. However, what remains of Tungusic today does not reflect its previous importance. Manchu was the language of the ruling class in China until recently, although it has now almost disappeared (Svanberg 1988). Tungusic groups were probably spread more widely across northern Heilongjiang Province and the adjacent Mongol-speaking area, and were in early interaction with Koreanic speakers. Tungusic speakers may have introduced the Northern Bronze Complex into the Korean peninsula during the 1st millennium BC, while the Rong people, associated with the Upper Xiajiadian in south-eastern Mongolia, might be a southern intrusion of Tungusic (Barnes 1993: 165).

2.5. Daic

The Daic or Tai-Kadai languages, of which Thai is the most well-known and widespread representative, are spoken from southern Thailand into Burma, Laos, Vietnam and China. Up-to-date maps of their distribution are given in Edmondson and Solnit (1997a) who estimate the number of speakers of these languages as at least 80 million. Overviews of the phylum are given in Edmondson and Solnit (1988, 1997a). Figure 4.7 shows the view of the internal relationships of Daic given by Edmondson and Solnit (1997b).

All the diversity of Daic languages is in China; despite the highly visible southward extension of Thai today, the likely origin of Daic is in Kweichow. The external affiliations of Daic have remained highly controversial, sharing as it does many features with surrounding language phyla, notably Austroasiatic, Hmong-Mien and Sino-Tibetan. These were used by Benedict (1975, 1990a) to erect 'Austro-Tai', a macrophylum that would unite Austroasiatic, Hmong-Mien, Daic and Austronesian. The general trend, however, has been in the opposite direction, to regard each of these phyla as distinct and unrelated. Thurgood (1994) has demonstrated that much of the evidence for hypotheses that link together the major language phyla of South-east Asia, such as Benedict's Austro-Tai, derive from ancient loanwords rather than genuine cognacy.

Ostapirat (2005) has recently proposed a series of regular correspondences linking Daic with Austronesian. Ostapirat assumes a simple model of a primary split, with Daic being the Austronesians who stayed at home. But this seems unlikely as Daic looks more like a branch of proto-Philippines and does not share the complexities of Formosan. Sagart (2005) has fleshed out a proposal which has proto-Daic speakers migrating back across from the northern Philippines to the region of Hainan island; hence the distinctiveness of Hlai, Be and Daic, resulting from radical restructuring following contact with Hmong-Mien and Sinitic. If so, such a migration would be around 4000 BP, in conformity with current dates for the first incursions in the northern Philippines.

Stratification in the peopling in China 117

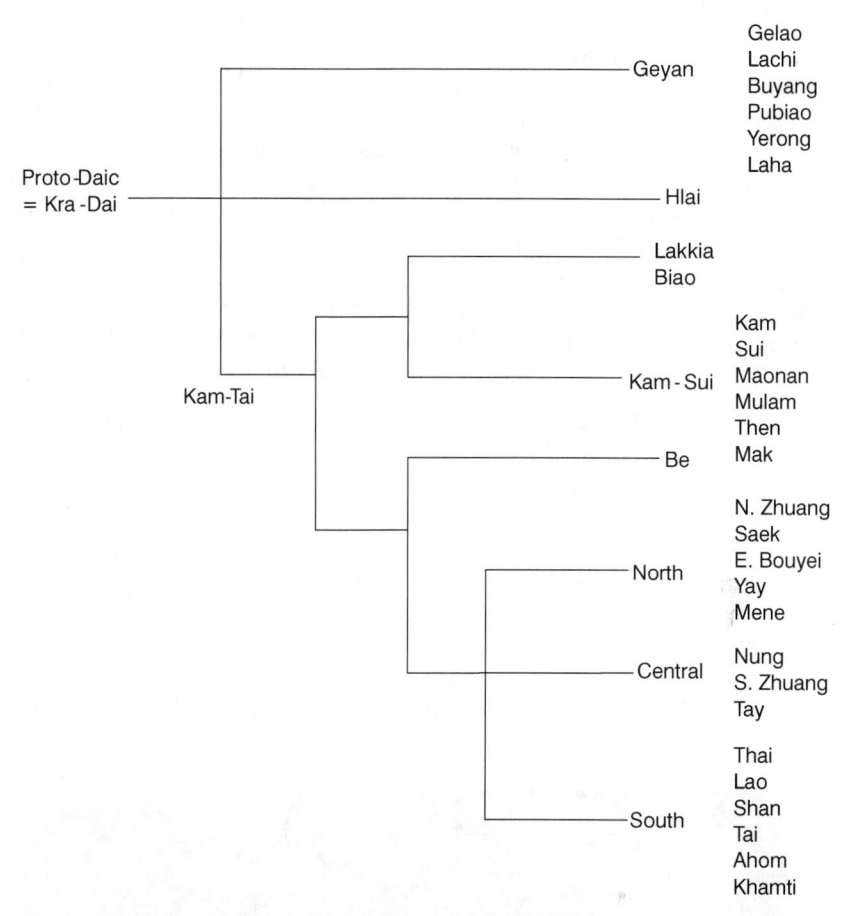

```
                                              Gelao
                                              Lachi
                              ┌─── Geyan      Buyang
                              │               Pubiao
                              │               Yerong
Proto-Daic  ──────────────────┤               Laha
= Kra-Dai                     │
                              └─── Hlai

                                   ┌─── Lakkia
                                   │    Biao
                                   │
                                   │              Kam
                                   │              Sui
                                   ├─── Kam-Sui   Maonan
              Kam-Tai               │             Mulam
                                    │             Then
                                    ├─── Be       Mak
                                    │
                                    │              N. Zhuang
                                    │              Saek
                                    │              E. Bouyei
                                    ├─── North     Yay
                                    │              Mene
                                    │
                                    │              Nung
                                    ├─── Central   S. Zhuang
                                    │              Tay
                                    │
                                    │              Thai
                                    │              Lao
                                    └─── South     Shan
                                                   Tai
                                                   Ahom
                                                   Khamti
```

Figure 4.7 Daic according to Edmondson and Solnit (1997b)

Daic languages are not all that diverse and almost certainly a candidate for a major agricultural expansion. Despite this, there is no obvious archaeological correlate. Blench (2005) has presented some evidence for thinking that speakers of proto-Daic were not originally rice-cultivators, but borrowed these techniques from Austroasiatic speakers. Reconstruction has yet to produce evidence for their subsistence strategies, and it may be that they were originally cultivators of tubers such as taro, which would fit with the links with the islands. But without a deeper knowledge of the pattern of Daic dispersal, it is hard to link them directly with any of the known archaeological horizons of south China.

2.6. Austroasiatic

Austroasiatic languages are the most poorly researched of all those under discussion. Many are not documented at all and some recently discovered in China are effectively not classified. The genetics of Austroasiatic speakers are

118 *Roger Blench*

almost unresearched. Austroasiatic is conventionally divided into two families, Mon-Khmer (in SE Asia) and Muṇḍā (in India). Diffloth (2005: 79) now considers Austroasiatic to have three primary branches but no evidence for these realignments has been published. Indeed Austroasiatic classification has been dogged by a failure to publish data, making any evaluation of competing hypotheses by outsiders a merely speculative exercise. With these reservations, therefore, Figure 4.8 shows this most recent 'tree' of Austro-Asiatic.

The main branch of Austroasiatic in China is Western Palaungic, a cluster of languages such as Hu and Kon Keu and some of the Waic languages close to the Burmese border. Palyu, a branch of Austroasiatic, consists of two languages, Bogan and Bolyu. The latter, also known as Lai, is found isolated from the remainder of Austroasiatic in Guangxi and is probably a migrant group from

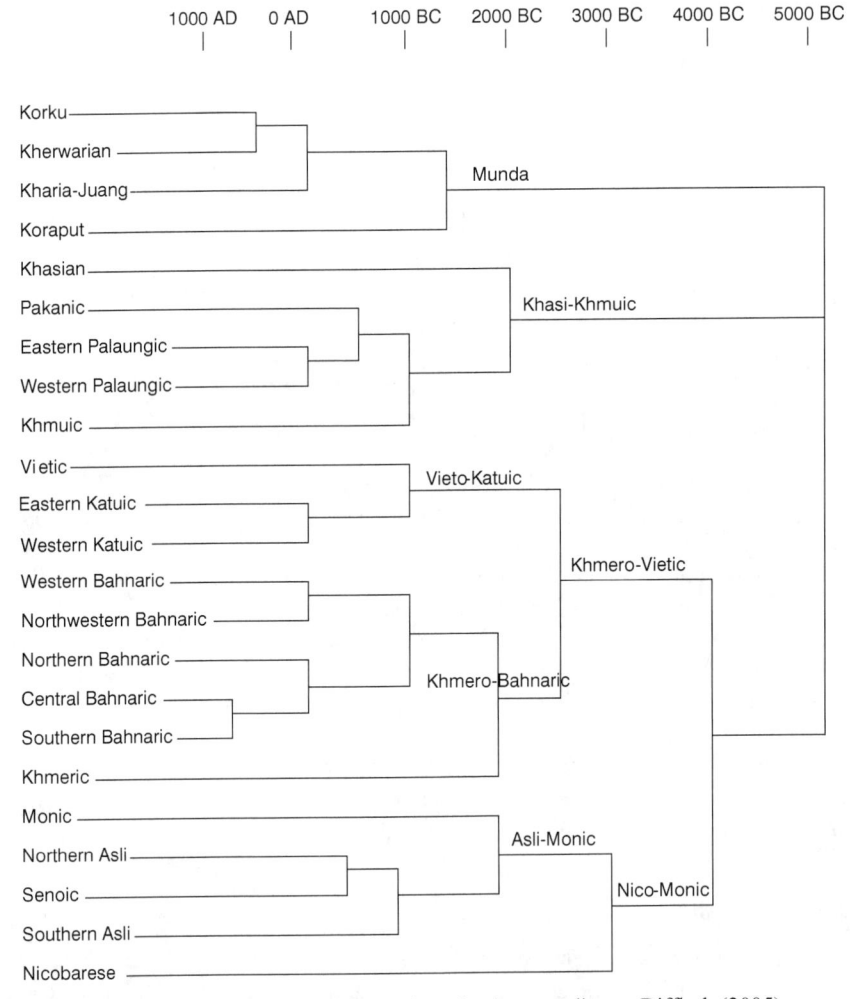

Figure 4.8 Austroasiatic with calibrated time-depths according to Diffloth (2005).

further south (Benedict 1990b). There are also four unclassified Austroasiatic languages in China listed as Pakanic: Bugan, Buxinhua, Kemiehua and Kuanhua spoken by very small populations in south-western Yunnan.

It has long been argued that Austroasiatic was once much more widespread in China and was driven south by the expansion of the Han (Norman and Mei 1976). Some names of zodiacal animals, the Old Chinese words for 'river' and 'tiger' appear to be borrowings (Norman 1988: 18). This has been related to a more general identification of northern regions as the homeland of Austroasiatic. Van Driem (2001) describes a number of theories including the 'northern shores of the Bay of Bengal'. Blust (1996) put forward the idea that the homeland of proto-Austric (a hypothetical macrophylum uniting Austronesian and Austroasiatic) was in Leaping Tiger Gorge in Yunnan but this has been left adrift by doubts about the validity of Austric. Diffloth's (2005) claim that Austroasiatic speakers typically spread along river valleys seems to be justified, although they obviously became seagoing at some point. Austroasiatic languages are very fragmented; the spread of Austronesian, Sino-Tibetan and Daic in more recent times has isolated its populations among other phyla.

Although there have been many promises, there are *no* justified proto-Austroasiatic reconstructions. The dictionary of Shorto (2006) provides preliminary lexical evidence for some reconstructions but it is based on a limited dataset. It is impossible to see whether faunal or crop names are really supported by a reconstructed proto-language. Diffloth (2005: 78) has claimed that faunal reconstructions point to a tropical origin and that an elaborated rice terminology indicates an already agricultural society, but the evidence for this remains unpublished and without a chronology, so it is difficult to relate to a dated palaeoenvironment. South China/Myanmar/Laos is an important area of biodiversity and there is evidence that Austroasiatic languages were once more widespread in China. Is it likely that southern China was the homeland area of Austroasiatic?

A possible archaeological correlation is the geometric cord-marked pottery that is found in south China prior to 5000 BC (Chang 1986: 95). Pottery has been recovered from sites such Hsien-jen-tung and Tseng-p'i-yen dated by thermoluminescence to >7,000 BP, which makes it the earliest pottery in China. This was originally assumed to be similar to the 'Neolithic' represented by Spirit Cave in north-east Thailand, but the notion that this represented early farmers has now been discredited (Higham and Thosarat 1998). Nonetheless, similarities between the artefacts do suggest they represent a related culture, unless the pottery in Spirit Cave is intrusive. This distribution area also correlates with Daic speakers but if our sense of the coherence of Daic is correct, it is too early to represent their expansion. Such a date would approximately correlate with that advanced by Diffloth although he canvasses quite a different area of origin for Austroasiatic.

2.7. Austronesian

Austronesian is the second-largest language phylum in the world after Niger-Congo and certainly one of the most widespread, stretching from Easter Island to Madagascar (Bellwood *et al.* 1995). Compared with many of the other phyla in this region, its internal structure is relatively transparent and there are few doubts about the languages it includes (with the exception of Daic, see above). Its possible external affiliations are numerous and almost all language phyla of the adjacent mainland have been canvassed. China is presently on the very edge of its distribution and the sole Austronesian language, Tsat, spoken in China today, is not a representative of an older stratum of Austronesian connected to Formosan, but a later migration from insular South-east Asia (Thurgood 1999). Tsat is a close relative of Roglai, a Chamic language found in Vietnam and the founders of the Utsat community probably fled to Hainan after break-up of the Cham Empire.

The usual view of Austronesian is that Formosan forms one branch opposed to the remainder, Malayo-Polynesian. Blust (1999) has challenged this by suggesting that Formosan languages are so diverse as to form a series of high-level primary branches. Figure 4.9 shows the top-level structure of Austronesian according to Blust (1999).

Sagart (2004; Chapter 5, this volume) has been active in arguing for a 'Sino-Tibetan-Austronesian' and has argued that the Formosan languages diversified in a chain around the island before expanding southwards, which would explain why there is a significant chronological gap between settlement from the mainland and further expansion towards the Philippines.

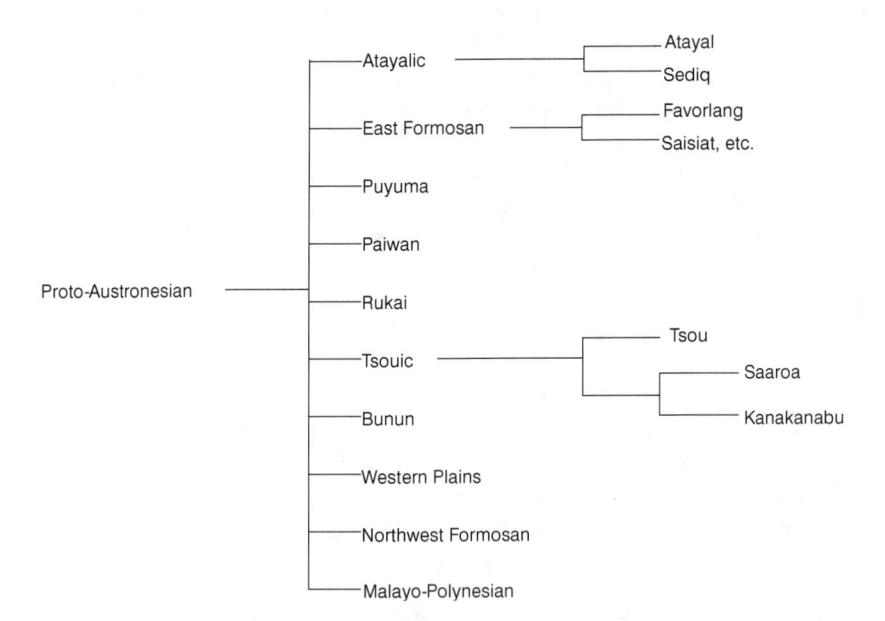

Figure 4.9 Austronesian according to Blust (1999).

Although there are no Formosan-type languages spoken in China today, it is widely accepted that the ancestors of the Austronesian peoples crossed from the mainland. At that period, the population would have consisted of Pleistocene hunter-gatherers represented by the cave site at Ch'ang-pin on the eastern coast and the sites of O-luan-pi II and Lung-K'eng on the southern coast. A link with the Ta Peng Keng, or Corded Ware culture, was first proposed in Ferrell (1966: 124) and was later taken up by a variety of authors, most recently Tsang (2005). The Hemudu site in Zhejian, south of Shanghai, north of Taiwan, is usually identified as a typical source area (Chang 1981). The inhabitants of Hemudu were rice-growers, with advanced woodworking and maritime technology. The pottery at Hemudu is black, cord-marked ware that shares designs with the Ta Peng Keng, but is obviously at the extreme margin of its distribution. Tsang (2005: 71) argues that the most likely source area is the Pearl River Delta and that recent finds show close affinities with the Neolithic of Hongkong.

Genetics broadly supports these conclusions; Melton *et al.* (1998) argued from an analysis of Taiwanese DNA for an Austronesian homeland on the mainland. Capelli *et al.* (2001) explored the patterns of paternal DNA, using 10 haplogroups, in Austronesian, Papuan and south China populations. Although the authors seem more interested in demonstrating the absence of a contribution from *Homo erectus*, the distribution of their haplogroups H and L has some interesting stories to tell about the Austronesian expansion. L is dominant in south China populations, common in Amis, the Philippines and parts of Indonesia, virtually disappearing in Melanesia and reappearing markedly in Polynesia. Haplogroup H is present in south China but becomes dominant in most of the Formosan groups, and is present throughout Indonesia. Haplogroup C looks rather as if it represents the Papuan-related Pleistocene hunter-gatherers of Indonesia, although one would expect these to be also present in the Philippines.

2.8. Indo-European

North-west China also has Indo-European outliers, notably Tajik (Sarikoli) and the Wakhi, Iranian languages of the Pamir branch spoken around Xinjiang, relatively recent intrusions, relics of the Silk Route trade. China is the home of Tocharian, a language attested in manuscripts found in the Täklimakan desert. The linguistic features of Tocharian link it to Celtic and Italic, rather than the closer Indo-Iranian languages. A further impetus to these discoveries has been given by the mummies first uncovered in Xinjiang in 1988, which have been recorded at various sites, all representing linked but distinct historical layers, dating back to 4000 BP (Mair 1998; Barber 1999; Mallory and Mair 2000). The features of the mummies are surprising by any standards, since the figures are up to 2m in height, with European features including marked beards, wearing cloths apparently woven in plaid patterns and with women wearing tall 'Welsh' conical hats. Needless to say, this hardly squares with nationalist ideologies about Chinese origins, but these images have also sparked a bout of speculation from the European side, with

122 *Roger Blench*

wandering tribes of Celts setting up camp in north-west China and bringing all good things to inner Asia.

Tocharian documents date from the 7th–8th centuries; the Tarim Basin mummies from 2000 BC. So the question has been, did the mummies 'speak' an Indo-European language? Assuming we are not dealing with stray Celtic supporters, it is reasonable to assume that at least some were Indo-European speakers and that they were hunter-gatherers who somehow wandered this long distance in pursuit of animals. But we cannot prove this and indeed various claims have been made for other affiliations, including Uyghur. But thinking of these people as the ancestors of the Tocharians and possibly the people who transmitted some early Indo-European loans in Sinitic[6] would be the simplest solution.

Mallory and Mair (2000: 302) consider the problems at some length and conclude there is probably no unitary solution. Without unwinding the whole argument, they conclude the mummies probably fall into four different groups in terms of physical type and that these are partly correlated with locations and dates. Table 4.3 shows their assignments.

The general conclusion is that there are two distinct layers of Europoid populations represented among the Tarim mummies, one representing Tocharian and thus affiliated to far western populations, the other more closely relating to the Indo-Iranian languages and the peoples of the Hindu Kush.

2.9 Korean

China is on the very edge of the Korean-speaking area, in Jilin Province, adjacent to the North Korean border. Korean today is an isolated language, linked to Altaic, but not closely. However, in an earlier period there must have been a linguistic family, Koreanic, with more diversity than is apparent today, and probably spread over a broader area of north-east China. Accounts of the 'Neolithic' in Jilin (Zhen-hua 1995) and Heilongjiang Provinces (Ying-jie 1995) suggest they shared a similar culture with strong links to the Korean peninsula, dating to >4000 to >2000 BC. Fish and aquatic resources were apparently of major importance in their diet and are characterized by incised and impressed pottery with geometric

Table 4.3 Physical types and linguistic affiliation of Tarim Basin mummies

Location	Hypothetical language	Physical type	Date
Chärchän	Prākrit, Koränian	?	1000 BC
Lopnur	Prākrit, Koränian	Proto-Europoid, Indo-Afghan	1800 BC
Qumul	? Tocharian A	Proto-Europoid	1000 BC
Turpan	? Tocharian A	Proto-Europoid	4–5th centuries BC
	Tocharian B	Indo-Afghan, Pamir-Ferghana	

Source: Mallory and Mair (2000: 302).

markings. It is possible that these regions were originally populated by Koreanic speakers.

3. Contributions from genetics

Recent years have seen an explosion of publications on molecular biology in relation to East Asian populations. Although some of these address the question of the peopling of China, it is often difficult to match their conclusions with archaeology and linguistics. Chu *et al.* (1998) exemplify the rather worrying tendencies of 'official' genetics. They start with the figure of 55 minorities, which includes Taiwanese populations, and conclude:

> Genetic profiles of 28 populations sampled in China supported the distinction between southern and northern populations, while the latter are biphyletic. Linguistic boundaries are often transgressed across language families studied, reflecting substantial gene flow between populations.

From this they jump to an amazing map of the peopling of China which certainly makes no sense in relation to any archaeological or linguistic data. Ding *et al.* (2000) then directly contradict this:

> Archaeological, anatomical, linguistic, and genetic data have suggested that there is an old and significant boundary between the populations of north and south China. We use three human genetic marker systems and one human-carried virus to examine the North–south distinction. We find no support for a major north–south division in these markers; rather, the marker patterns suggest simple isolation by distance.

By contrast, Guo *et al.* (1998) who looked at the types of JC polyomavirus, found that it subdivides into four major types in China, and that there is a very distinctive Mongolian type, B1-b, not found in Han populations, whereas other minor Mongolian types are. In China itself, the CY type was characteristic of North China and SC of the South. These differences are attributed to extensive mixing with minorities in the south and rather less with Altaic populations further north.

The approach taken by Mountain *et al.* (1992) to the evolution of Sinitic is quite innovative. Because Chinese surnames are extremely conservative they were used as a proxy for genetic affiliation. The linguistic traits of seven main dialect groups of Sinitic were compared with the patterning of surnames in the same geographic areas. Interestingly, the correspondence with lexical features was much greater than with phonological features.

Kivisild *et al.* (2002) confirm the geographical rather than ethnolinguistic specificity of East Asian DNA, although the distribution of the M7 haplogroup 'branch' and its 'twigs' suggests specificity in the case of isolated or island populations, such as Korea, Japan and insular South-east Asia. This strongly suggests that, in a sense, as with languages, large, contiguous mainland areas lead to massive interchange, whether genetically or linguistically.

Oota *et al.* (2002) compared mtDNA variation in continental Asia. They studied

> mtDNA HV1 sequences for 84 Xi'an and 82 Changsha Han Chinese, 89 Honshu Japanese, and 35 Vietnamese. Comparison of these sequences with other Asian mtDNA sequences reveals high variability within populations, but extremely low differentiation among Asian populations. Correlations between genetic distance and geographic distance, based on mtDNA and Y chromosome variation, indicate a higher migration rate in females than in males. This may reflect patrilocality, as suggested previously, but another plausible hypothesis is that the demographic expansion associated with the spread of agriculture in Asia may be responsible for the extreme genetic homogeneity in Asia.

This seems highly unlikely. Sampling large urbanized groups will probably show evidence of large-scale genetic interchange; to be convincing, the sample would have to include a wide scatter of minorities.

A more assimilable scenario is that exemplified in Wen *et al.* (2004a, b) which looks at sex-biased admixture in 'Southern Tibeto-Burmans' (Bái, Lolo-Burmese, Tûjiä, etc.). Haplotype group distributions of Y-chromosome and mtDNA markers indicate that the genetic structure of these populations was 'primarily formed by two parental groups: northern immigrants and native southerners'. The implication is that a key element of ethnolinguistic group formation may have been the migration of males, who took wives among *in situ* populations. This may be a useful model for the process of Sinicization and in particular it can be mapped against the deep influence of Sinitic on Bái and Tûjiä. Nonetheless, it is unclear what social and migratory process this reflects; perhaps the movement of soldiers or seasonal hunters or cultivators. Zhang *et al.* (2006) compared CCR2 allele polymorphisms in 15 Chinese ethnic populations distributed widely across the country and taking in all the main language phyla. They found significant allelic variation, principally between the Tungusic and Mongolic populations in the north-east and the southern groups, but much less variation between those in the north-west (Xinjiang, etc.). They attribute this to a significant founder effect from this region, which would certainly agree with the linguistic evidence.

4. The peopling of China

Many questions about the dating of the language phyla of China remain unresearched and therefore potential answers are inevitably highly tentative. But it may be useful to clarify the useful questions.

4.1. What populations underlay the Sinitic/Han Chinese?

The underlying population was probably ethnolinguistically highly diverse but would have consisted of Tungusic-Koreanic speakers in the north, Hmong-Mien in the centre, intertwined with other Sino-Tibetan groups, and Austroasiatic and Austronesian speakers in the south. There may well have been more language isolates, especially in coastal areas representing the type of phylic diversity seen in Siberia. In the far north-west, where Chinese expansion is more recent, there would have been at least two different resident Indo-European groups.

4.2. When and from which direction was the Sinitic expansion?

This expansion was from north to south, from millet cultivating in the dry zone to the humid areas where irrigated rice was possible. However, Sinitic languages underwent a significant bottleneck some >2000 years ago and records of the language prior to that are highly idiosyncratic. Knowledge of the expansion of Sinitic prior to this event will remain restricted.

4.3. What populations came after the Chinese?

The Turkic speakers in the Xinjiang region represent a late incursion. Pre-Mongolic speakers would have made incursions on the settled villages in northern China as nomadic pastoralism developed. It is also possible that Tungusic is a recent expansion following a bottleneck. The expansion of Daic would have roughly coincided with the expansion of Sinitic and may represent a remigration of Austronesian from insular South-east Asia.

4.4. What drove the expansion of different phyla or groupings?

Table 4.4 shows some very speculative motives for the expansion of East Asian language phyla with even more speculative dates.

An unsatisfactory aspect is the attribution of approximate dates to phyla on the basis of synchronic diversity. But the present form of Hmong-Mien cannot be very old because existing languages are so tightly knit. This is probably an artefact of the assimilation of much of its prior diversity by Sinitic and its roots will lie much deeper. Similarly, with Sino-Tibetan, the languages that reflect an earlier diversity have become not only isolated but heavily Sinicized, making it difficult to analyse the extent to which they reflect an older stratum of dispersal.

Table 4.4 What drove the expansion of East Asian language phyla?

Phylum	Comment	Date BP
Early Sino-Tibetan	? Dialect diversification typical of hunter-gatherers	>6000
Sinitic	Neolithic agriculture	3500
Mongolic	Development of horse culture and nomadic pastoralism	4500
Tungusic	Dialect diversification typical of hunter-gatherers [excepting Manchu]	?
Hmong-Mien	Not relevant since present distribution is a late artefact of Sinitic expansion	3000
Daic	Agriculture [but of what type?]	3500
Austroasiatic	? Tuber and fruit-based agriculture in river valleys	7000
Austronesian	Fishing and rice based subsistence [although to what extent there was an expansion in China is unknown]	7000

5. Where next?

The chapter sets out recent evidence for the distribution of the different language phyla in China and their possible archaeological and genetic correlates. But:

- The linkage between archaeological cultures and ethnolinguistic groupings remains sketchy.
- The antiquity of these groupings is highly controversial.
- The internal classification of Sino-Tibetan is very unsettled, although this is essential to making a rational model.
- Genetics input has been more effective at higher levels in establishing the overall affinities of the mainland populations and less in terms of particular language phyla. Indeed the evidence is that genetic variation is determined more by geography than by linguistic affiliation. This is probably to be expected, given the high levels of interaction between speakers of different languages.

The reasons for this are:

- Historical linguistics has a very long way to go, especially in reconstructing lexical items that could be linked to subsistence and thence to archaeology. Some phyla remain very poorly served (and it is common for unsubstantiated proto-forms to be published).
- Archaeology remains very patchy, with some areas well-known, others not.
- Genetics is solving some large-scale problems in the human settlement of the region, but whether it can contribute to the interface between linguistics and archaeology is less certain. More reliable sampling frames would help.

Genetics and archaeology are proceeding apace in China and the coming years are likely to generate significant new data which will certainly clarify some of the issues raised in this chapter.

Notes

1 Paper presented at the Symposium 'Human migrations in continental East Asia and Taiwan: Genetic, linguistic and archaeological evidence', Geneva, 10–13 June 2004. Université de Genève. The revision of April 2006 has benefited from two subsequent fieldtrips to China, and I would particularly like to thank my colleagues at the Institute of Zoology in Kunming, especially Qi Xuebin and Su Bing, for extensive discussion on some of these issues. I would also like to acknowledge the input of Laurent Sagart and George van Driem, who have strongly influenced my views on some issues set out here.
2 A valuable website on Tujia language and culture is http://www.brassett.org.uk/tujia/ehome.html.
3 At http://stedt.berkeley.edu/.
4 This formulation is also not uncontroversial since it privileges the names of two particular dominant groups influential in the United States (Tapp *et al.* 2004: n. 11)
5 This might seem evident, given their present location, but Hmong oral traditions have been widely held to point to environments much further north, in Siberia (see Tapp *et al.* 2004).
6 The much cited example of 'honey', Old Chinese *mit < Tocharian B *mit*. See Pulleyblank (1983). Sinitic also borrows from Indo-Aryan, e.g. the words for 'grape' and 'jasmine' (Norman 1988: 19).

References

Barber, E.W. (1999) *The Mummies of Urumqi*, London: Macmillan.
Barnes, G.L. (1993) *China, Korea and Japan: The Rise of Civilization in East Asia*, London: Thames & Hudson.
Baxter, I.I.I., and Hubbard, W. (1992) *A Handbook of Old Chinese Phonology*, Berlin: Mouton de Gruyter.
Bellwood, P., Fox, J.J. and Tryon, D. (eds) (1995) *The Austronesians*, Canberra: Australian National University.
Benedict, P.K. (1972) *Sino-Tibetan: A Conspectus*, Cambridge: Cambridge University Press.
Benedict, P.K. (1975) *Austro-Thai: Language and Culture, with a Glossary of Roots*, New Haven: Human Relations Areas Files Press.
Benedict, P.K. (1976) 'Sino-Tibetan: another look', *Journal of the American Oriental Society*, 96(2): 167–97.
Benedict, P.K. (1990a) *Japanese/Austro-Tai* (Linguistica Extranea Studia, 20), Ann Arbor, MI: Karoma Publishers.
Benedict, P.K. (1990b) 'How to tell Lai: An exercise in classification', *Linguistics of the Tibeto-Burman Area*, 13: 1–26.
Blench, R.M. (2005) 'From the mountains to the valleys: understanding ethnolinguistic geography in SE Asia', in L. Sagart, R.M. Blench and A. Sanchez-Mazas (eds) *The Peopling of East Asia: Putting Together Archaeology, Linguistics and Genetics*, pp. 31–50, London: Routledge.

Blust, R.A. (1996) 'Beyond the Austronesian homeland: the Austric hypothesis and its implications for archaeology', in W.H. Goodenough (ed.) *Prehistoric Settlement of the Pacific* (Transactions of the American Philosophical Society, 86/5), Philadelphia: American Philosophical Society.

Blust, R. (1999) 'Subgrouping, circularity and extinction: Some issues in Austronesian comparative linguistics', in E. Zeitoun and P.J.-K. Li (eds) *Selected Papers from Eighth International Conference on Austronesian Linguistics*, pp. 31–94, Taipei: Academica Sinica.

Bodman, N.C. (1980) 'Proto-Chinese and Sino-Tibetan: Data towards establishing the nature of the relationship', in F. van Coetsem and L.R. Waugh (eds) *Contributions to Historical Linguistics: Issues and Materials*, pp. 34–199, Leiden: E.J. Brill.

Bradley, D. (1997) 'Tibeto-Burman languages and classification', in D. Bradley (ed.) *Tibeto-Burman Languages of the Himalayas*, Pacific Linguistics A-86, pp. 1–72. Canberra: Australian National University.

Brassett, P. and Brassett, C. (2005) *Imperial Tiger Hunters: An Introduction to the Tujia People of China*, Eastbourne, UK: Antony Rowe Publishing Services.

Capelli C., Wilson, J.F., Richards, M., Stumpf, M.P., Gratrix, F., Oppenheimer, S., Underhill, P., Pascali, V.L., Ko, T.M., and Goldstein, D.B. (2001) 'A predominantly indigenous paternal heritage for the Austronesian-speaking peoples of insular Southeast Asia and Oceania', *American Journal of Human Genetics*, 68: 432–43.

Chang, K.-C. (1981) 'The affluent foragers in the coast areas of China: Extrapolation from evidence on transition to agriculture', in *SENRI Ethnological Studies* (Osaka, National Museum of Ethnology), 9: 177–86.

Chang, K.-C. (= Zhāng Guāngzhí) (1986) *The Archaeology of Ancient China*, 4th edn, New Haven, CT: Yale University Press.

Chu, J.Y., Huang, W., Kuang, S.Q., Wang, J.M., Xu, J.J., Chu, Z.T., Yang, Z.Q., Lin, K.Q., Li, P., Wu, M., Geng, Z.C., Tan, C.C., Du, R.F.,and Jin, L. (1998) 'Genetic relationship of populations in China', *Proceedings of the National Academy of Sciences USA*, 95: 11763–8.

Da-Shun, G. (1995) 'Hongshan and related cultures', in S.M. Nelson (ed.) *The Archaeology of Northeast China: Beyond the Great Wall*, pp. 21–64, London and New York, NY: Routledge.

Diffloth, G. (2005) 'The contribution of linguistic palaeontology and Austroasiatic', in L. Sagart, R.M. Blench and A. Sanchez-Mazas (eds) *The Peopling of East Asia: Putting Together Archaeology, Linguistics and Genetics*, pp. 77–80, London: RoutledgeCurzon.

Ding, Y.C., Wooding, S., Harpending H.C., Chi, H.C., Li, H.P., Fu, Y.X., Pang, J.F., Yao, Y.G., Yu, J.G., Moyzis, R. and Zhang, Y. (2000) 'Population structure and history in East Asia', *Proceedings of the National Academy of Sciences USA*, 97: 14003–6.

Doerfer, G. (1978) 'Classification problems of Tungus: Beiträge zur nordasiatischen Kulturgeschichte', *Tungusica* (Wiesbaden: Otto Harrassowitz), 1: 1–26.

Driem, G. van (1997) 'Sino-Bodic', *Bulletin of the School of Oriental and African Studies*, 60: 455–88.

Driem, G. van (1998) "Neolithic correlates of ancient Tibeto-Burman migrations', in R.M. Blench and M. Spriggs (eds) *Archaeology and Language II*, pp. 67–102, London: Routledge.

Driem, G. van (2001) *Languages of the Himalayas: An Ethnolinguistic Handbook of the Greater Himalayan Region Containing an Introduction to the Symbiotic Theory of Language*, 2 vols, Leiden: Brill.

Driem, G. van (2002) 'Tibeto-Burman replaces Indo-Chinese in the 1990s: review of a decade of scholarship', *Lingua*, 111: 79–102.

Driem, G. van (2005) 'The contribution of linguistic palaeontology and Austroasiatic', in L. Sagart, R.M. Blench and A. Sanchez-Mazas (eds) *The Peopling of East Asia: Putting Together Archaeology, Linguistics and Genetics*, pp. 77–80, London: Routledge Curzon

Edmondson, J.A. and Solnit, D.B. (eds) (1988) *Comparative Kadai: Linguistic Studies beyond Tai*, Dallas, TX: Summer Institute of Linguistics and the University of Texas at Arlington.

Edmondson, J.A. and Solnit, D.B. (eds) (1997a) *Comparative Kadai: The Tai Branch*, Dallas, TX: Summer Institute of Linguistics and the University of Texas at Arlington.

Edmondson, J.A. and Solnit, D.B. (1997b) 'Introduction', in J.A. Edmondson and D.B. Solnit (eds) *Comparative Kadai: The Tai Branch*, pp. 1–32, Dallas, TX: Summer Institute of Linguistics and the University of Texas at Arlington.

Ferrell, R. (1966) 'The Formosan tribes: a preliminary linguistic, archaeological and cultural synthesis', *Bulletin of Institute of Ethnology*, 21: 97–130.

Fitzgerald, C.P. (1972) *The Southern Expansion of the Chinese People: Southern Fields and Southern Oceans*, London: Barrie & Jenkins.

Golden, P.B. (1998) 'The Turkic peoples, a historical sketch', in L. Johanson and E.A. Csató (eds) *The Turkic Languages*, pp. 16–29, London: Routledge.

Guo, J., Sugimoto, C., Kitamura, T., Ebihara, H., Kato, A., Guo, Z., Liu, J., Zheng, S.P., Wang, Y.L., Na, Y.Q., Suzuki, M., Taguchi, F. and Yogo, Y. (1998) 'Four geographically distinct genotypes of JC virus are prevalent in China and Mongolia: implications for the racial composition of modern China', *Journal of Genetic Virology*, 79: 2499–505.

Herforth, D. (2003) 'A sketch of late Zhou Chinese grammar', in G. Thurgood and R.J. LaPolla (eds) *The Sino-Tibetan Languages*, Routledge Language Family Series, pp. 57–71, London and New York, NY: Routledge.

Higham, C., and Thosarat, R. (1998) *Prehistoric Thailand: From Early Settlement to Sukhothai*, Bangkok: River Books.

Janhunen, J. (1993) 'The teens in Jurchen and Manchu revisited', *Mémoires de la Société Finno-Ougrienne*, 215: 169–84 (Festschrift für Raija Bartens).

Janhunen, J. (1994) 'Additional notes on Japanese and Altaic [1 and 2]', *Journal de la Société Finno-Ougrienne*, 85: 236–40, 256–60.

Janhunen, J. (1998) 'Ethnicity and Language in Prehistoric Northeast Asia', in R.M. Blench and M. Spriggs (eds) *Archaeology and Language II*, pp. 195–208, London: Routledge.

Janhunen, J. (2003) *The Mongolic Languages*, London: Routledge.

Johanson, L., and Csató, E.A. (eds) (1998) *The Turkic Languages*, London: Routledge.

Kivisild, T., Tolk, H.-V., Parik, J., Wang, Y., Papiha, S.S., Bandelt, H.-J. and Villems, R. (2002) 'The emerging limbs and twigs of the East Asian mtDNA tree', *Molecular and Biological Evolution*, 19: 1737–51.

Klaproth, J.H. von (1823) *Asia Polyglotta*, Paris: A. Schubart.

Kolman, C.J., Nyamkhishig, S. and Eldredge, B. (1996) 'Mitochondrial DNA Analysis of Mongolian Populations and Implications for the Origin of New World Founders', *Genetics*, 142: 1321–34.

LaPolla, R.J. (2001) 'The role of migration and language contact in the development of the Sino-Tibetan language family', in A.Y. Aikhenvald and R.M.W. Dixon (eds) *Areal Diffusion and Genetic Inheritance*, pp. 225–54, Oxford: Oxford University Press.

Lee, J. (1978) 'Migration and expansion in Chinese history', in W.H. McNeill and R.S. Adams (eds) *Human Migration: Patterns and Policies*, pp. 20–47, Bloomington, IN and London: Indiana University Press.

MacKerras, C. (1997) *China's Minorities: Integration and Modernization in the Twentieth Century*, Oxford: Oxford University Press.

Mair, V. (ed.) (1998) *The Bronze Age and Early Iron Age Peoples of Eastern Central Asia*, 2 vols, Washington, DC, and Philadelphia, PA: Institute for the Study of Man and University of Pennsylvania.

Mallory, J.P., and Mair, V.H. (2000) *The Tarim Mummies*, London: Thames & Hudson.

Martin, S.E. (1991) 'Recent research on the relationships of Japanese and Korean', in S. Lamb (ed.) *Sprung from Some Common Source*, pp. 269–92, Stanford, CA: Stanford University Press.

Matisoff, J.A. (2001) 'Prosodic diffusibility in South-East Asia', in A.Y. Aikhenvald and R.M.W. Dixon (eds) *Areal Diffusion and Genetic Inheritance*, pp. 291–327, Oxford: Oxford University Press.

Matisoff, J.A. (2003) *Handbook of Proto-Tibeto-Burman*, Berkeley, CA: University of California Press.

Melton, T., Clifford, S., Martinson, J., Batzer, M. and Stoneking M. (1998) 'Genetic evidence for the proto-Austronesian homeland in Asia: MtDNA and nuclear DNA variation in Taiwanese aboriginal tribes', *American Journal of Human Genetics*, 63: 1807–23.

Menges, K.H. (1995) *The Turkic Peoples and Languages*, 2nd edn, Wiesbaden: Harrassowitz.

Miller, R.A. (1996) *Languages and history: Japanese, Korean and Altaic*, Bangkok: White Orchid Press.

Mountain, J.K., Wang, W.S.Y., Du, R, Yuan, Y., and Cavalli-Sforza, L.L. (1992) 'Congruence of genetic and linguistic evolution in China', *Journal of Chinese Linguistics*, 20: 315–32.

Niederer, B. (1998) *Les langues Hmong–Mjen (Miáo–Yáo): Phonologie Historique* (Lincom Studies in Asian Linguistics, 7), Munich: Lincom Europa.

Niederer, B. (2004) 'Pa-hng and the classification of the Hmong-Mien languages', in N. Tapp, J. Michaud, C. Culas and G.Y. Lee (eds) *Hmong/Miao in Asia*, pp. 129–46, Bangkok: Silkworm Books.

Norman, J. (1988) *Chinese* (Cambridge Language Surveys), Cambridge and New York, NY: Cambridge University Press.

Norman, J. (2003) 'The Chinese dialects: Phonology', in G. Thurgood and R.J. LaPolla (eds) *The Sino-Tibetan Languages* (Routledge Language Family Series), pp. 72–83, London and New York, NY: Routledge.

Norman, J. and Mei, T. (1976) 'The Austroasiatics in ancient south China: some lexical evidence', *Monumenta Serica*, 32: 274–301.

Oota, H., Kitano, J., Jin, F., Yuasa, I., Wang, L., Ueda, S., Saitou, N. and Stoneking, M. (2002) 'Extreme mtDNA homogeneity in continental Asian populations', *American Journal of Physical Anthropology*, 118: 146–53.

Ostapirat, W. (2005) 'Kra-Dai and Austronesian: notes on phonological correspondences and vocabulary distribution', in L. Sagart, R.M. Blench and A. Sanchez-Mazas (eds) *The Peopling of East Asia: Putting Together Archaeology, Linguistics and Genetics*, pp. 107–31, London: RoutledgeCurzon.

Pulleyblank, E.G. (1983) 'The Chinese and their neighbours in prehistoric and early historic times', in D.N. Keightley (ed.) *The Origins of Chinese Civilization*, pp. 411–66, Berkeley, CA: University of California Press.

Purnell, H.C. Jr. (1970) 'Towards a reconstruction of Proto-Miao-Yao', PhD, Cornell University.

Ramsey, S.R. (1987) *The Languages of China*, Princeton, NJ: Princeton University Press.

Ratliff, M. (2004) 'Vocabulary of environment and subsistence in the Hmong-Mien proto-language', in N. Tapp, J. Michaud, C. Culas and G.Y. Lee (eds) *Hmong/Miao in Asia*, pp. 147–6, Bangkok: Silkworm Books6.

Sagart, L. (1994) 'Proto-Austronesian and Old Chinese evidence for Sino-Austronesian', *Oceanic Linguistics*, 33: 271–308.

Sagart, L. (1999) *The Roots of Old Chinese*, Amsterdam: John Benjamins.

Sagart, L. (2004) 'The higher phylogeny of Austronesian and the position of Tai-Kadai', *Oceanic Linguistics*, 43: 411–44.

Sagart, L. (2005) 'Sino-Tibetan-Austronesian: An updated and improved argument', in L. Sagart, R.M. Blench and A. Sanchez-Mazas (eds) *The Peopling of East Asia: Putting Together Archaeology, Linguistics and Genetics*, pp. 161–76, London: Routledge Curzon.

Shafer, R. (1974) *Introduction to Sino-Tibetan*, Wiesbaden: Otto Harrassowitz.

Shorto, H. (2006) *A Mon–Khmer Comparative Dictionary*, ed. Paul Sidwell, Doug Cooper and Christian Bauer (PL 579), Canberra: ANU.

Starostin, S.A. (1991) 'On the hypothesis of a genetic connection between the Sino-Tibetan languages and the Yenisseian and North Caucasian languages', in V. Sheveroshkin (ed.) *Dene-Sino-Caucasian*, pp. 12–42, Bochum: Universitätsverlag Dr N. Brockmeyer.

Starostin, S.A., Dybo, A. and Mudrak, O. (2003) *Etymological Dictionary of the Altaic Languages*, 3 vols, Leiden and Boston, MA: Brill.

Su, B., Xiao, C., Deka, R., Seielstad, M.T., Kangwanpong, D., Xiao, J., Lu, D., Underhill, P., Cavalli-Sforza, L.L., Chakraborty, R. and Jin, L. (2000) 'Y chromosome haplotypes reveal prehistorical migrations to the Himalayas', *Human Genetics*, 107: 582–90.

Svanberg, I. (1988) *The Altaic Speakers of China: Numbers and Distribution*, Uppsala: Uppsala University.

Tapp, N., Michaud, J., Culas, C. and Lee, G.Y. (eds) (2004) *Hmong/Miao in Asia*, Bangkok: Silkworm Books.

Thurgood, G. (1994) 'Tai-Kadai and Austronesian: the nature of the relationship', *Oceanic Linguistics*, 33: 345–68.

Thurgood, G. (1999) *From Ancient Cham to Modern Dialects: Two Thousand Years of Language Contact and Change*, Honolulu, HI: University of Hawai'i Press.

Thurgood, G., and LaPolla, R.J. (eds) (2003) *The Sino-Tibetan Languages* (Routledge Language Family Series), London and New York, NY: Routledge.

Tsang, C.H. (2005) 'Recent discoveries of the Tap'enkeng culture in Taiwan: Implications for the problem of Austronesian origins', in L. Sagart, R.M. Blench and A. Sanchez-Mazas (eds) *The Peopling of East Asia: Putting Together Archaeology, Linguistics and Genetics*, pp. 63–73, London: Curzon Press.

Wang, F. (1994) *Reconstruction of the Proto-Miao Language*, Tokyo: Institute for the Study of the Languages and Cultures of Asia and Africa (in Chinese and English).

Wang, F. and Mao, Z. (1995) *Miao-yao yu guyin gouni*, Beijing: Zhongguo Shehui Kexue.

Wang, W.S.-Y. (1998) 'Three windows on the past', in V. Mair (ed.) *The Bronze Age and Early Iron Age Peoples of Eastern Central Asia*, pp. 508–34, 2 vols, Washington, DC, and Philadelphia, PA: Institute for the Study of Man and University of Pennsylvania.

Wen, B., Li, H., Lu, D., Song, X., Zhang, F., He, Y., Li, F., Gao, Y., Mao, X., Zhang, L., Qian, J., Tan, J., Jin, J., Huang, W., Deka, R., Su, B., Chakraborty, R. and Jin, L. (2004a) 'Genetic evidence supports demic diffusion of Han culture', *Nature*, 431: 302–5.

Wen, B., Xie, X., Gao, S., Li, H., Shi, H., Song, X., Qian, T., Xiao, C., Jin, J., Su, B., Lu, D., Chakraborty, R. and Jin, L. (2004b) 'Analyses of genetic structure of Tibeto-Burman populations reveals sex-biased admixture in southern Tibeto-Burmans', *American Journal of Human Genetics*, 74: 856–65.

Wiersma, G. (2003) 'Yunnan Bai', in G. Thurgood and R.J. LaPolla (eds) *The Sino-Tibetan Languages* (Routledge Language Family Series), pp. 651–73, London and New York, NY: Routledge.

Yin, M. (ed.) (1989) *China's Minority Nationalities*, Beijing: Foreign Languages Press.

Ying-jie, T. (1995) 'The Neolithic in Heilongjiang Province', in S.M. Nelson (ed.) *The Archaeology of Northeast China: Beyond the Great Wall*, pp. 118–44, London and New York, NY: Routledge.

Zhang, X.L., Zhang, C.Y., Yu, Y., Chen, F., Li, P. and Fu, S.B. (2006) 'CCR2 allele polymorphisms in 15 Chinese ethnic populations', *International Journal of Immunogenetics*, 33: 45–8.

Zhen-hua (1995) 'Recent Neolithic discoveries in Jilin Province', in S.M. Nelson (ed.) *The Archaeology of Northeast China: Beyond the Great Wall*, pp. 89–117, London and New York, NY: Routledge.

5 The expansion of *Setaria* farmers in East Asia

A linguistic and archaeological model

Laurent Sagart

1. The farming/language dispersal hypothesis

The farming/language dispersal hypothesis (Bellwood 2001; Renfrew 1996; Bellwood and Renfrew 2003) claims that the formation of some of the world's major language families followed from the establishment of sustainable agricultural economies: a resulting increase in population densities led to founding dispersals by populations originally speaking dialects of the same language seeking new agricultural lands; in time these dialects evolved into diversified language families. The farming/language dispersal hypothesis – which should not be taken as an absolutist theory claiming that *all* language families have their origins in an agricultural dispersal, or that all agricultural dispersals result in identifiable families (see Bellwood 2005) – is an attractive explanatory mechanism, because shift to agriculture will normally produce an increase in population densities, because farming populations with expanding demographics and plenty of available land around them will normally expand to occupy this land, and because once-homogeneous languages will normally undergo distance-based linguistic differentiations when spoken over large geographical areas.

In East Asia, at least two of the world's major cereals, foxtail millet (*Setaria italica*) and rice, were domesticated. With rice, there appear to have been two distinct domestication events, one leading to *Oryza sativa japonica* and another to *Oryza sativa indica*. Can these domestications be linked to the formation of one or more East Asian language families?

Excluding north-eastern Eurasia, five families are commonly recognized in East Asia: Sino-Tibetan, Hmong-Mien (aka Miao-Yao), Tai-Kadai, Austroasiatic and Austronesian, with estimated time depths of 7000 BP for Austroasiatic, 7,000–6000 BP for Sino-Tibetan, 5500 BP for Austronesian, 4000–3000 BP for Tai-Kadai, and 2500 BP for Hmong-Mien (see Sagart *et al.*, 2005: 2). Domestication of rice (*Oryza sativa*) had occurred by 8500~9000 BP in the mid-Yángzi Basin (Lu 2005: 51; Bellwood 2005: 21),[1] and even earlier, around 10,000 BP, at the Shangshan site in the Lower Yángzi (Jiang and Liu 2006). Domesticated foxtail millet (*Setaria italica*) appears in the Yellow Valley around 8500 BP (Lu 2005: 51). Overall, the dates for the language families appear to be more recent than those for the cereals, suggesting that the language/farming hypothesis will be more helpful in explaining the formation of macrofamilies than of currently recognized language families.

Bellwood (2005) has examined the question from an archaeologist's point of view, noting that the Austroasiatic and Miao-Yao families, either singly or together as a macrophylum, may have developed out of the first rice-farming societies of the mid-Yángzi valley. With foxtail millet, he has detected 'the germs of a scenario' whereby foxtail millet would have been domesticated as a second cereal by early rice farmers from the Yángzi area in the process of expanding north, where rice was less successful because of drier conditions. In this chapter I will take Bellwood's hint and present linguistic evidence to suggest that a rice-and-foxtail farming expansion is at the root of the linguistic macrophylum I have called Sino-Tibetan-Austronesian.

2. Foxtail millet and the STAN hypothesis

Since 1990 I have been claiming that Chinese and AN are genetically related. Originally the proposed relationship left the other ST languages out of the picture, but I have now (Sagart 2005b) accepted that ST is a valid taxon, and argued that ST as a whole is a sister group to AN within a macrophylum I call STAN. The evidence is of the usual kind: at least 12 per cent shared vocabulary on a Swadesh 100-word list, with sound correspondences,[2] and shared morphology, including in particular the heart of AN verbal morphology (Sagart 2005b, for the most recent statement). In contrast, the Austric theory, which claims that the Austronesian and Austroasiatic families form a macrophylum, lacks a body of lexical comparisons constrained by recurrent sound correspondences (Diffloth 1994; Reid 2005). The Austric theory is almost exclusively based on claims of shared morphology (Schmidt 1906; Reid 1994, 2005). This in turn makes a claim that Austric is a monophyletic taxon difficult to maintain, especially since some of the 'Austric' morphology is also found in Sino-Tibetan (Sagart 1995). The STAN and Austric theories are not necessarily incompatible: an old macrophylum with a proto-language in excess of 10,000 years BP, having STAN as one of its branches and Austroasiatic as the other, would explain the shared 'Austric' morphology as well as the scarcity of attractive lexical comparisons between Austroasiatic and the STAN languages (Sagart 1994, 1995; Reid 2005).

I have argued (1994: 216, 1995, 2005b) that foxtail millet is coterminous with the STAN macrophylum. This makes sense of the geographical distribution of *Setaria* before 5000 BP. Archaeologically, foxtail millet has been found in sites distributed over north China, Tibet and Táiwān at dates between 8500 and 5000 BP (Map 5.I), but hardly anywhere else before 5000 BP. North China, the Tibetan and Himalayan regions and Táiwān are also the main areas where STAN languages were spoken before 5000 BP under my theory. Apparent lack of geographical continuity between these three areas may reflect little more than regional gaps in the current archaeological record.

My hypothesis will also explain the sharing of a term for *Setaria* by AN and ST. A term for foxtail millet is reconstructed to PAN: *beCeŋ (Blust 1980).

Setaria *farmers in East Asia* 135

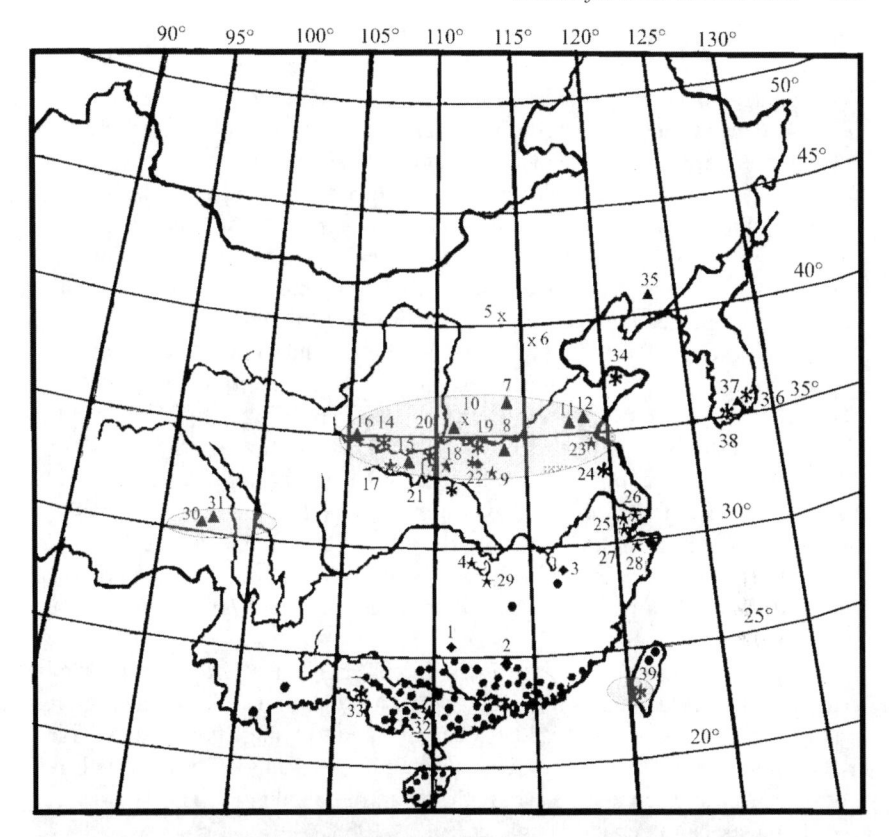

Map 5.1 Archaeological sites with *Setaria italica* 5000 BP and earlier (Source: Tracey Lu 2005: 53, with added shaded ellipses).

Legend
• Current loci of common wild rice (*Oryza rufipogon*) apart from the major distribution
♦ Prehistoric loci of common wild rice
x Archaeological sites of the upper Palaeolithic
■ Archaeological sites where cultivated rice (*O. sativa*) is found
✸ Archaeological sites where both cultivated rice and millet are found
▲ Archaeological sites where cultivated millets are found

Sites: 1. Yuchanyan 14,000–10,000 BP? 2. Niulian Cave 12,000–10,000 BP? 3. Xianrendong/ Diaotonghuan 14,000–12,000 BP? 4. Pengtoushan/Bashidang 9500–8000 BP. 5. Hutouliang 11,000 BP. 6. Nanzhuangtou 11,000–9000 BP. 7. Cishan *cal.* 8000–7500 BP. 8. Peiligang cal. 8000–7500 BP. 9. Jiahu *cal.* 8400–7600 BP. 10. Xiachuan 18,000–13,000 BP. 11. Běixīn 7400–6400 BP.12. Dadunzi *cal.* 6800–6360 BP. 13. Huaxian 5000–4000 BP. 14. Anban *cal.* 4852–4487 BP. 15. Banpo 6065–5490 BP. 16. Dadiwan 7150–4900 BP. 17. Lijiacun *cal.* 7179–6796 BP. 18. Xiawangguang *cal.* 7210–4490 BP. 19. Dahecun cal. 5500–4400 BP. 20. Xiyincun 7000–5000 BP. 21. Qinglongquan cal. 5350–4148 BP. 22. Lilou *cal.* 4142–3725 BP. 23. Lianyungang about 7000 BP. 24. Longqiuzhuang 7000–5500 BP. 25. Xudun 5605–4610 BP. 26. Songze 5330–4550 BP. 27. Luojiajiao 6220–6080 BP. 28. Hémǔdù *cal.* 7200–6400 BP. 29. Chengtoushan 6500 BP. 30. Chengdou Karuo 5555–4750 BP. 31. Changguogou 3370 BP. 32. Dingsishan 6500 BP. 33. Gantuoyan approximately 4000 BP. 34. Qixia *cal.* 4873–3780 BP. 35. Xinle 6620–6150 BP. 36. Daundong 2510 BP. 37. Tongsamdong 4590 BP. 38. Nam River localities 4060–2800 BP. 39. Nan-kuan-li approx. 5000 BP.

I have pointed out (2003) that the Old Chinese[3] term 稷 *ᵇtsïk 'foxtail millet' corresponds to PAN *beCeŋ. In that paper I did not cite any cognate of 稷 *ᵇtsïk in a ST language outside of Chinese: I had missed the word tɕaʔ⁵⁵ 'millet' in Trung (TBL 417; what kind of millet is unclear), again corresponding regularly with the Chinese word. More recently, a second cognate has turned up: cək '*Setaria italica*' in geographically and phylogenetically distant Lhokpu, an unclassified ST language of southwest Bhutan.[4] The sound correspondences which link the PAN and Chinese forms are recurrent ones in my analysis, despite the unpredictable – though widely recognized[5] – alternation between final -ŋ and -k *within* Sino-Tibetan, as illustrated in the examples for 'horn' and 'rib, bone'.

Given the geographical distance between Lhokpu and Chinese on the one hand and the appearance of phonological regularity between the forms for *Setaria* in Chinese, Trung and Lhokpu on the other hand, a loan will not easily explain the Lhokpu word for *Setaria*. A word something like *tsək 'foxtail millet = *Setaria italica*' can now be firmly assigned to an early stage of the ST family, possibly PST itself. This indicates that at least from an early stage in the development of the family, ST speakers knew – probably grew – foxtail millet. The finding at mKhar-ro (Chinese Karuo, point 30 on Map 5.I) in Eastern Tibet of grains of *Setaria italica* with a calibrated C-14 date range of 5555–4750 BP (Fu Daxiong 2001: 66) is consonant with this.

Likewise, the recent find in Nan-Kuan-Li, a Dàpénkēng 大盆坑 culture site in south-west Táiwān dating to 4500–5000 BP, of large quantities of carbonized grains of millet, apparently foxtail, together with rice grains (Tsang 2005), has provided archaeological proof that the Dàpénkēng culture – usually associated with the proto-Austronesian language – had both foxtail millet and rice. This is precisely what linguists had been claiming: see Blust (1988: 61) for a reconstruction of the floral environment of PAN speakers including domesticated rice and foxtail millet.

In recognition of the importance of foxtail millet for both Sino-Tibetan and Austronesian, both as a staple and as a sacred plant, I have proposed (1995) that the origin of the PSTAN macrophylum is in the area of the earliest foxtail-cultivating villages: the Císhān-Péilǐgāng culture area of northern China, mainly in Héběi, Hénán and south Shānxī,[6] beginning *cal.* 8500 BP. I think of Proto-STAN as the language of these earliest foxtail farmers.

Table 5.1 Examples of sound correspondences

	PAN	OC	Garo	Other ST languages
Foxtail millet	beCeŋ	稷 ᵇtsïk		Trung tɕaʔ⁵⁵, Lhokpu cək
Horn	quRuŋ	角 ᵃk-rok	groŋ	
Rib, bone	ta-[q,k]eRaŋ	骼 ᵃk-rak	greŋ	Burmese khraŋ

3. Rice and the STAN hypothesis

At least some of the earliest farmers in the Císhān-Péilǐgāng culture area cultivated rice. This was true of Jiǎhú in the Huái River basin, *cal.* 8500 BP, where rice was abundant, while *Setaria* was marginal[7] if it was there at all; and of Héxī in north Shāndōng, *cal.* 8000 BP (Wright 2004). Rice had been domesticated in the Yángzi Valley at least a millennium before foxtail millet. In view of the huge impact of rice on the subsistence of East Asian populations, it would be astonishing if the domestication of this cereal had not left its signature in the linguistic record.

The first issue to be considered here is whether there were distinct Neolithic transitions for rice and for *Setaria*. The focal area for *Setaria* is in the Císhān-Péilǐgāng culture, some 800 km north of the Yángzi valley. Lu (2005), citing continuities in the toolkit of Mesolithic hunter-gatherers and of early farmers in north China, argues for an independent Neolithic domestication of *Setaria*. Instead, Bellwood (2005), noting the suddenness of the appearance of farming villages in the core *Setaria* area, suggests that *Setaria* was domesticated as a second cereal when rice farmers expanding from the south encountered a drier climate in which rice, an aquatic plant, did not do as well as in the Yángzi valley. Although cultivated rice has not been found together with *Setaria* in many of the classical Císhān-Péilǐgāng sites, Bellwood's idea explains the suddenness of the Neolithic transition in the *Setaria* area, and the fact that rice is present in *some* of the earliest Císhān-Péilǐgāng sites like Jiǎhú or Héxī.

One complication comes from the well-accepted division of domesticated rice into two subspecies, *Oryza indica* and *Oryza japonica*, differentiated by morphological features such as grain shape, leaf colour, hair length, etc. In geographical terms, *indica* are lowland rices grown throughout tropical Asia (south-east and south), while *japonica* are found in temperate East Asia, upland areas of south-east Asia, and high elevations in south Asia. Analyses of genetic divergence between *indica* and *japonica* cultivars have yielded divergence times of ~440,000 years ago and 86,000–200,000 years ago, strongly supporting the view that the two subspecies are 'derived from independent domestication events from an ancestral rice that had already differentiated into (at least) two gene pools' (Garris et al. 2005 and references therein).

In view of the south-east and south Asian distribution of both modern *Oryza indica* landraces and of the Austroasiatic languages, it is tempting to associate the *indica* transition with the Austroasiatic language family. Recently Londo et al. (2006) have placed the domestication of *indica* south of the Himalayas; however, both linguistically and in terms of population genetics, the Austroasiatic peoples appear to fit more easily in south-east Asia than in south Asia. If Londo et al. are right about the place of domestication of *indica*, the good overall match between the distribution of *indica* and of the Austroasiatic languages must be considered coincidental. Different locations were proposed by Zhang Juzhong and Wang Xiangkun (1998): based on measurements of the length/width ratio of archaeologically derived rice grains, they argued that *indica* was domesticated in the mid-Yángzi valley, while *Japonica* was domesticated further north, in the upper Huái valley, with Jiǎhú as an early and characteristic site. At first sight, the theory of Wang and Zhang appears more attractive than that of Londo *et al.* because archaeological evidence for very early rice cultivation is available at Jiǎhú and in the mid-Yángzi valley. However, pre-domestication differentiation of wild *Oryza rufipogon* into wild *japonica* and *indica* types requires a more important natural barrier than that offered by the lowland plain between the mid-Yángzi and the upper Huai valley (Susan McCouch, pers. comm., March 2007).

Placing domestication of *japonica* in the mid-Yángzi and domestication of *indica* somewhere in present-day south-west China seems preferable: that theory would provide the requisite natural barriers between *japonica* and *indica*; it would allow us to place the Austroasiatic homeland on the East Asian side of the Tibetan plateau; finally, it would be consistent with Diffloth's proposal, based on reconstructed faunal terms, of a tropical homeland for Austroasiatic (Diffloth 2005).

Since in terms of material culture Jiǎhú clearly belongs to the Císhān-Péilǐgāng culture, which is otherwise known for its association with *Setaria italica*, the new theory would lead us to recognizing two independent Neolithic transitions in China: one in the north-east for *japonica*-cum-*Setaria italica*, and one in the south-west for *indica*. Bellwood's scenario of a secondary domestication of *Setaria* by rice farmers would apply to the former transition. I will tentatively accept the new theory. Like others before me, I will suppose that the rice-based Austroasiatic expansion out of East Asia led to the introduction of *indica* rice cultivation into India.

I have shown above (Map 5.1 and text) that there exists a geographical association in the distribution of foxtail millet at 5000 BP and the macrophylum I call STAN, and that the name of foxtail millet is shared by Sino-Tibetan and Austronesian. What of rice? If it is true that the earliest north Chinese farmers cultivated rice, we would expect that, as with foxtail millet, elements of the vocabulary of rice cultivation will be found in the descendants of the language of these earliest northern Chinese farmers: the Sino-Tibetan and Austronesian peoples, in my theory. Indeed, there are at least two good rice-related lexical comparisons between ST and AN. I will now summarize the evidence in Sagart (2003).

First, PAN *Semay 'rice as food, cooked rice' corresponds well to an ST set consisting of Old Chinese 米 ᵃCə-mijʔ (where C was some voiceless consonant responsible for the high tone in some modern reflexes) 'husked grain', Bodo-Garo *mey or *may 'paddy', Karen (Benedict 1972) *me* < *may* 'boiled rice', and especially rGyalrong *sməy* 'grain' (meaning inferred from *sməy khri* 'rice', see Sagart 2003). Second, PAN *beRas 'husked rice' opposite OC 糲 ᵇmə-rat-s 'husked rice', WT *mbras* < *m-ras* 'rice', Lushai raʔ 'fruit, to bear fruit', is likely to have meant 'husked rice', possibly as part of a broader meaning such as 'fruit'. These comparisons suggest that PSTAN speakers were acquainted not just with *Setaria*, but also with rice. This increases the likelihood that the equation Císhān-Péilǐgāng = PSTAN is meaningful, and reinforces the case for the STAN expansion being based on rice- and *Setaria*-farming. Supposing two separate Neolithic transitions for the Austroasiatic family and for my STAN macrophylum will account neatly for the absence, noted in Sagart (2003), of any shared agricultural vocabulary between these two groups of languages.

With these observations in mind, I present below a linguistic and archaeological model of the expansion of my hypothesized rice-and-*Setaria*-farming, STAN-speaking populations.[8]

4. A model of the STAN expansion

4.1. 8500–7000 BP: first expansion and first split

Subsequent to the establishment of an agriculture based on *Oryza sativa japonica* and *Setaria italica* in the Císhān-Péilígāng culture area of north and noth-east China around 8500 BP, I hypothesize that the PSTAN-speaking population increased in density and expanded out of its original homeland, splitting into a western group, probably corresponding to the Yǎngsháo culture, and an eastern group, corresponding to the Běixīn-Dàwènkǒu culture complex (from 7000 BP). Out of the western group ST would eventually evolve. I will not examine its development here as the linguistic subgrouping of ST is still poorly understood (Sagart 2006a) and attempts at matching linguistic groups with archaeologically derived entities are premature. I will focus instead on the development of the eastern group, which in my view leads to Austronesian. The eastern group was centred in an area in the eastern lowlands and coastal regions of northern China, including present-day Shāndōng, north Jiāngsū and perhaps the eastern fringes of Hénán and Ānhuī, a region characterized at the time by a wetter, warmer, marshy and lacustrine environment (Chang 1986: 162), as indicated by pollen grains and fauna (notably *Alligator sinensis*). One of the earliest sites in the region is Běixīn in east Shāndōng,[9] which Chang (1986: 160) regards as intermediate between Péilígāng and Dàwènkǒu. Radiocarbon dates are concentrated in the 7500–6500 BP range. Běixīn was a culture of millet farmers who raised pigs, cattle and chicken. The Dàwènkǒu culture, whose late phases continued until 4000 BP, is known through many sites in the Shāndōng–north Jiāngsū area. It too was a culture of millet farmers (Chang 1986: 160). It is in the earliest phase of the Dàwènkǒu culture that the custom of tooth evulsion – the ritual ablation of the upper lateral incisors, in adolescent boys and girls (Figure 5.1) – began around 6500 BP, apparently as a local development (Han and Nakahashi 1996).

Much later, in the course of their eastward expansion in the first millennium BCE, the early Chinese of the Zhōu dynasty encountered in that same region a complex of peoples they called Yí 夷 *^{b}lïj, whom they subjugated. The Yí languages became extinct perhaps 2,000–1,500 years ago, the entire Yí-speaking population shifting to Chinese. Almost nothing is known of the Yí languages apart from a few place names. It is possible, and indeed likely, that the Yí languages were those of the descendants of the early rice and millet farmers of coastal east China. If so, they would have formed an eastern sister group to Sino-Tibetan, and the stock out of which the Austronesian languages later arose.

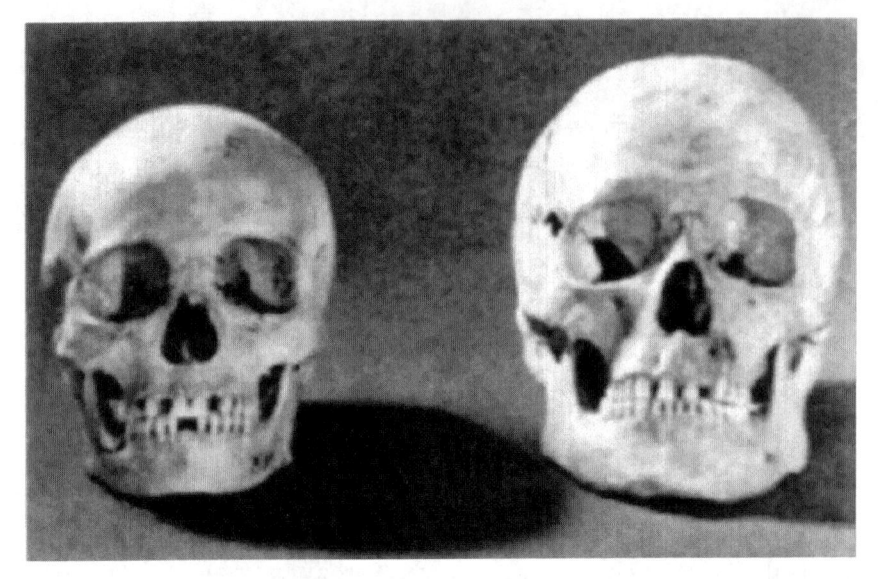

Figure 5.1 Skulls from China with ritual tooth evulsion (courtesy Roger Blench).

It can be supposed that the eastern seaboard farmers, who continued to rely on hunting and gathering to supplement their diet, began to specialize in the direction of their new 'wet' environment and to acquire elements of a way of life based on a combination of coastal foraging, hunting and sea fishing with rice and foxtail millet agriculture, which characterizes the early Austronesians.[10] With these skills, these groups found coastal environments particularly attractive, and they started expanding southward along the China coast.

4.2. 7000–5500 BP: *coastal expansion*

Major Neolithic cultures have been brought to light in coastal Jiāngsū and Zhéjiāng, in particular the Mǎjiābāng culture of south Jiāngsū and the Hémǔdù culture in Hángzhōu Bay, both dating back to *cal.* 7000 BP (Chang 1986). The question immediately arises as to how these cultures relate to the Běixīn-Dàwènkǒu cultures: do they represent their southern expansion, or a distinct Neolithic tradition? The early dates for Mǎjiābāng and Hémǔdù, the fact that these cultures relied on rice agriculture, with suggestions of irrigation techniques at Hémǔdù, the lack of evidence for foxtail millet, together with the fact that tooth evulsion was apparently not practised at Hémǔdù, hint that they may represent a distinct Neolithic tradition from Běixīn-Dàwènkǒu, perhaps going back to the earliest rice sites in the lower Yángzi valley, like the 10,000 BP site described by Jiang and Liu (2006), 150 km inland from Hémǔdù. If this is correct, the southward-expanding Běixīn-Dàwènkǒu people must have passed early Mǎjiābāng-Hémǔdù sites, with the possibility of cultural contact and exchange between the two cultures. It is possible that some of the elements which we have come to view as part of early

Austronesian material culture, such as stilt houses, were acquired at the contact with the Mǎjiābāng-Hémǔdù cultures.

We pick up the trace of our expanding tooth-extracting farmers again in Tánshíshān and Xītóu on or near the north Fújiàn coast. Although foxtail has so far not been found in these and related sites, it should be kept in mind that millet grains are extremely small and hard to identify unless flotation techniques are used. Tánshíshān was a farming culture that also made use of marine, riverine and forest resources (Chang 1986: 290), and practised tooth evulsion (Yan Wenming, pers. comm., Oct. 1998). Chang (1986: 290) argues that its middle stratum culture is earlier than 4000 BP, and its lower stratum earlier still. From Tánshíshān on, cord-marked pottery, probably acquired through contact with inland cultures, becomes a prominent archaeological marker.

Further expansion of these people along the narrow south-east China coast may have led them as far as the Pearl River delta, where the Hedang site, *cal.* 5000–3000 BP, has tooth evulsion (Higham 1996: 84).

4.3. The Yuè language: Austroasiatic, TK or what?

What languages did the Tánshíshān and Pearl River delta people speak? Again we lack the evidence of modern languages, as most of the indigenous languages of the region went extinct in the 1st millennium CE, or shortly thereafter, as a result of Chinese expansion and large-scale shift to Chinese among indigenous populations. Today the only non-Chinese language spoken in the region is Ho Nte (also Shē 畬), a Hmong-Mien language of eastern Guǎngdōng. These people in all probability originate further inland, where the main Hmong-Mien concentrations, historical attestations and centre of diversity are located: they cannot easily be equated with the Tánshíshān Neolithic tradition.

Before the Chinese conquest of the south, the region of the Fújiàn and Guǎngdōng coast was inhabited by a people, or peoples, known to the Chinese as Yuè 越 (OC *^{b}wat), whose language became extinct probably in the early 1st millennium CE. Because of the geographical agreement between them, it is possible that the Yuè language was descended from the language(s) of the Tánshíshān culture people. There are scattered observations on the Yuè language in early Chinese texts, including in some cases Yuè words transcribed phonetically in Chinese characters. In one case, an entire Yuè text: the 'Song of the Yuè boat woman' 越人歌, discussed below, was transmitted to us. I discuss below two claims concerning the linguistic identity of the Yuè peoples.

4.3.1. Yuè as Austroasiatic: Norman and Mei

In an oft-cited paper, Norman and Mei (1976: 295) claimed that the Yuè peoples of ancient south-eastern China spoke an Austroasiatic language closely related to Vietnamese. Their claim relies on a few Yuè words recorded in late Hàn Chinese texts (1st and 2nd centuries CE), as well as on modern Mǐn (Fújiàn) dialect words viewed by them as substratum words: relics of the old indigenous language in the colloquial layer of the Mǐn dialects. I discuss here four of the principal ones.

TO DIE

A Yuè word meaning 'die' was recorded in Zhèng Xuán's commentary to the *Zhōu Lǐ*. Zhèng Xuán, a Hàn-time commentator, transcribed it by means of the character 札, MC tsreat. Norman and Mei compared this word with VN *chêt* 'to die'. However 札 is a well-attested Chinese word also meaning 'to die (of external causes/prematurely/in an epidemic)', a fact overlooked by Norman and Mei. It occurs extensively in the classical literature in contexts that do not particularly imply a Yuè or southern connection. That this word occurred in the Yuè language in Hàn times could be because Yuè borrowed it from Chinese; alternatively the form recorded by Zhèng Xuán could have been the regular word for 'die' in a variety of *Chinese* spoken in the Yuè region. The resemblance of this Chinese word to an Austroasiatic word is probably accidental.

SHAMAN

A Chinese word 童 tóng 'child; servant', is used in the Buddhist literature in the extended meaning 'servant or messenger of a god' (Soothill and Hodous n.d.). It occurs widely in late 19th- and early 20th-century China as a colloquial word for 'magician, sorcerer' (Doré 1926: 39, 42, 55, 144, 214), in the Mǐn dialects of Fújiàn: Fúzhōu *tøyŋ₂*, Amoy *taŋ₂* 'shaman, spirit healer, medium', but also in Jiāngsū, Ānhuī and Shāndōng where varieties of Mandarin are spoken. Pointing out that shamans are usually grown men, not children, and oblivious of the secondary meaning of 童 as 'servant' in Chinese, Norman and Mei rejected the identity of the Mǐn word with the character 童, and compared the Mǐn dialect forms with VN *đông* 'to shamanize, to communicate with spirits' and other Austroasiatic forms. The resemblance between the Mǐn and Austroasiatic terms is undoubtedly fortuitous.

TO KNOW

A Chinese word 別 bié, MC pjet 'to separate', with secondary cognitive meanings such as 'to distinguish, discriminate' and even as 'to recognize, to know' in the *Zuǒ Zhuàn* (6th year of Duke Xiang), has become the regular word for 'to know, to recognize' both in Mǐn (Fúzhōu *pai?₇*, Amoy *bat₇*) and, as a Chinese loanword, in Vietnamese too (*biết*). Unaware that the Mǐn and Vietnamese forms reflect a rare but attested meaning of a good Chinese word, Norman and Mei took the Mǐn forms to belong to their putative pre-Chinese Austroasiatic substratum.

DOG

A southern Yuè word for 'dog' is recorded in the *Shuō Wén*, a dictionary of Chinese characters published about 100 CE, as 獶獀. The pronunciation of this binomial at the time must have been something like *ou-sou* or *ou-ṣou*. This may have transcribed a foreign *oso* or *oṣo*, since in Hàn transcriptions the rhyme /-ou/ frequently served to represent undiphthongized foreign /o/. This disyllable is actually closer in sound to PAN *asu, *u-asu 'dog' than to the palatal-initialled Austroasiatic monosyllable VN *cho*, Old Mon *clüw*, etc. 'dog' to which Norman and Mei compare it. This comparison actually supports the view that the southern Yuè language was Austronesian-related, rather than Austroasiatic-related.

Other comparisons presented by Norman and Mei in their paper appear to be either East Asian areal words if not Chinese words in disguise ('duckweed', 'wet'), and long shots ('kind of fish'). I will not discuss them here. In general, while Norman and Mei cannot be blamed for not offering sound correspondences to support their claims, it must be borne in mind that lexical comparisons not constrained by sound correspondences cannot easily be distinguished from chance resemblances. In conclusion, there is no convincing evidence, linguistic or other, of an early Austroasiatic presence on the south-east China coast. The cradle of the Vietic branch of Austroasiatic is very likely in north Vietnam, at least 1000 km to the south-west of coastal Fújiàn, and the Austroasiatic homeland itself is in all likelihood situated a good deal further to the west, in view of the early Austroasiatic migration to north India.

4.3.2. *Yuè as proto-Tai: Zhèngzhāng*

Scholars in China often automatically equate the Yuè language with an early form of Tai-Kadai. However, the core of the Tai-Kadai area geographically, in Hǎinán and in the region of the present-day China–Vietnam boundary, is beyond the extreme southern end of the Yuè area, so this is far from self-evident. An attempt to link them on linguistic grounds is due to Zhèngzhāng (1991). The 'Song of the Yuè boat-woman' 越人歌 is the text of a song in the Yuè language, reportedly collected and transcribed phonetically in Chinese characters by a Chinese traveller from Chǔ 楚 in 528 BCE. It is included in the *Shàn-shuō* 善說 chapter of the *Shuō Yuàn* 說苑, a Hàn-dynasty work by 劉向 Liú Xiàng, accompanied by a Chinese version which is not necessarily a direct translation. Zhèngzhāng (1991) hypothesized that the underlying language was an early form of Tai, and proposed an interpretation of the text in terms of Written Thai words and sentence patterns. This is anachronistic, however, as Thai was reduced to writing only after the 13th century CE, and almost 2000 years separate it from the time when the song was recorded. Thai, moreover, is a member of the south-west branch of Tai, which is itself a subgroup within Kam-Tai, a branch of Tai-Kadai. It is possible that Kam-Tai was already individualized in the 6th century BCE, but Proto-Kam-Tai would have sounded significantly different from Written Thai. Zhèngzhāng's proposal has remained controversial.

144 *Laurent Sagart*

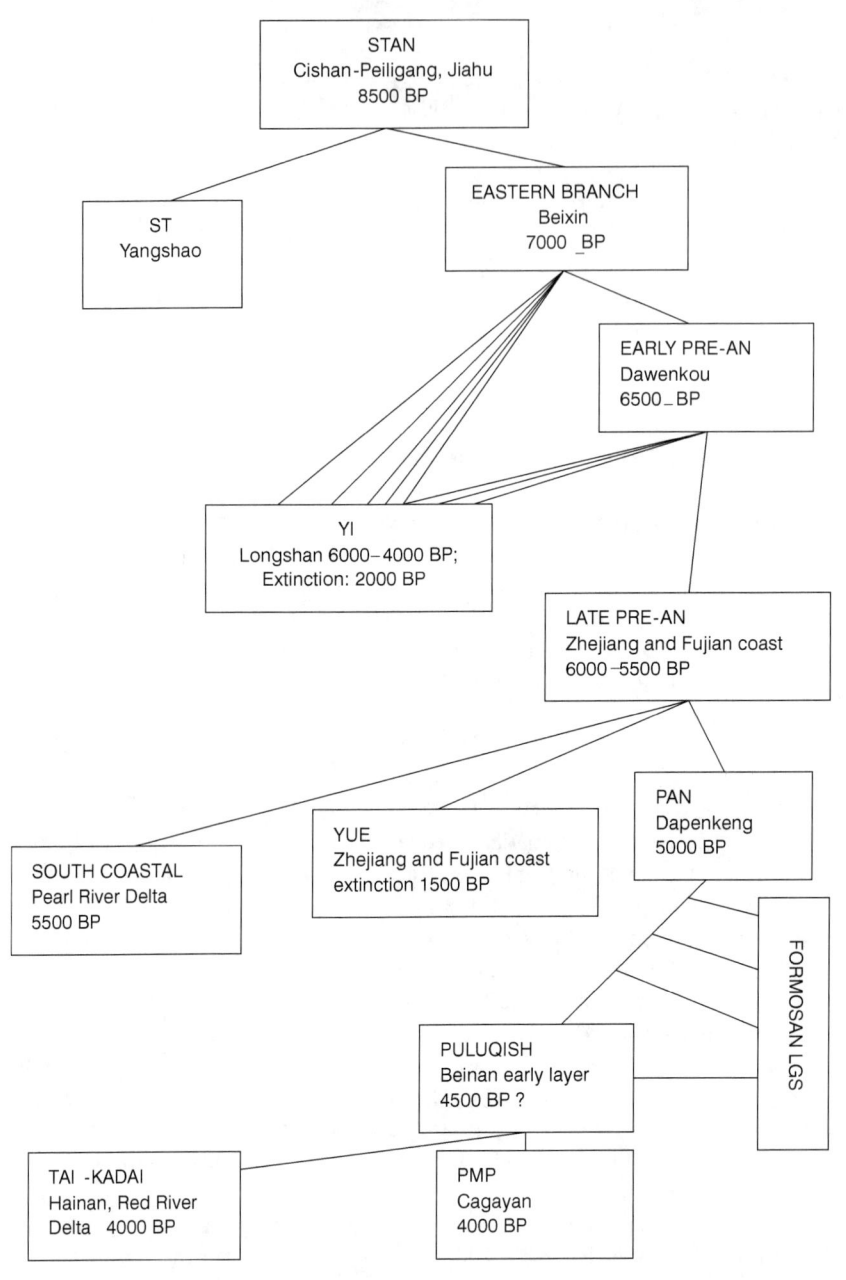

Figure 5.2 Genealogy of language entities (capitalized) within STAN and related archaeological sites.

Unfortunately the evidence is too scarce to permit a direct identification of the affiliation of the Yuè language. My guess is that it, like PAN, was descended from the language or languages of the Tánshíshān-Xītóu culture complex. This would make it an extinct group within the eastern branch of the wider STAN phylum.

4.4. 5500 BP: passage to Táiwān

From the hills of Nánrì 南日 and Píngtán 平潭, two islands just off the north Fújiàn coast, in the immediate vicinity of Xītóu, a Tánshíshān culture site, the top of Mt. Xuěshān, the highest peak in northern Táiwān, can be seen with the naked eye (Christophe Coupé, pers. comm., May 2004). The passage to Táiwān of a group of Tánshíshān culture people (who clearly had sea-voyaging capabilities), presumably in search of new coastal lands, was probably purposeful. Leaving from the Nánrì or Píngtán islands, then, and heading straight toward Mt. Xuěshān across the 130 km-wide Táiwān straits, the explorers would probably have made landfall in the region of present-day Hsinchu or Miaoli in the north-west of Táiwān. Their arrival in Táiwān, and their installation there is matched in the archaeological record by the appearance in the 4th millennium BCE on the west coast of Táiwān of a diversified Neolithic culture, the Dàpénkēng culture, with a strong resemblance to the contemporary culture on the other side of the straits. In Táiwān, the newcomers found a pre-existing population of hunter-gatherers whose existence is known from a few pre-ceramic assemblages (Changpinian) on the east coast and at the southern tip of Táiwān, as well as from the oral literature of the Austronesian peoples on Táiwān. According to a story told by the Tsou and recorded by Segawa in the early 20th century (see Yuasa 2000: 87), these 'small people' had no anus, hence they could not eat rice.

In Táiwān, readily interpretable linguistic evidence again becomes available, as fourteen indigenous languages survive to this day. All are Austronesian. Probably a majority of Austronesianists now accept that the Austronesian homeland was in Táiwān. The appearance in the 4th millennium BCE of the Dàpénkēng culture, the oldest Neolithic culture in the Austronesian world, is regarded since Chang Kwang-chih (1987, 1989) as the founding event of the Austronesian culture and language family. In general it can be said that the match between the elements of Dàpénkēng material culture identified from archaeology and the independently reconstructed PAN cultural lexicon (Blust 1996) is good, and that the recent archaeological finds near Táinán (Tsang 2005) have made it even better, with the discovery of carbonized grains of rice and foxtail millet *cal.* 5000 BP.

Cultural traits that continued from the Císhān-Péilǐgāng down to Dàpénkēng are: urn burials for children; semi-subterranean houses, seen in Císhān-Péilǐgāng, Dàwènkǒu and among the modern-day Atayal (Ferrell 1969: 30), although in Dàwènkǒu and among the Atayal the semi-subterranean house is only one of many house types. Tooth evulsion, which as we have seen arose in the Dàwènkǒu culture and was practised at Tánshíshān in Fújiàn, was also practised by the rice-and-millet agriculturists at Nan-kuan-li in south-west Táiwān *cal.* 5000–4500 BP. It was still practised in much the same way as in Dàwènkǒu (pulling out of the

146 Laurent Sagart

upper lateral incisors, in boys and girls) by the modern Austronesians of Táiwān until the 20th century (Yuasa 2000: 61 for photographic documentation).[11]

4.5. 5500–4000 BP: diversification in Táiwān

The genealogy of Austronesian languages is a matter of controversy, even among those Austronesianists who regard Táiwān as the AN homeland: there is general agreement that the first diversification must have occurred on Táiwān, and that the AN languages outside of Táiwān form a monophyletic taxon ('Malayo-Polynesian') but opinions differ as to the shape of the tree (rake-like with many primary branches, or tree-like with only two or three?) and as to the position of the MP languages (primary branch or lower-order subgroup?). Blust's phylogeny (1999) is based on phonological mergers. He argues for a rake-like tree with as many as nine primary branches on Táiwān and a tenth, Malayo-Polynesian, outside Táiwān. For him, the island was circled with Neolithic settlers 'in one ethnographic instant' (1999: 53). Another line of research (Harvey 1979) treats Malayo-Polynesian as a subgroup within a larger taxon also including some, but not all, languages of Táiwān.

My own interpretation (Sagart 2004, slightly modified in Sagart 2006b)[12] belongs to the second tradition. It is based on innovations in the basic vocabulary, less sensitive to contact than sound changes. Its backbone is a series of six innovations in numerals from '5' to '10', resulting in the widespread words *lima '5', *enem '6', *pitu '7', *walu '8', *Siwa '9' and *puluq '10', all of which are usually – but incorrectly – assigned to PAN. In my interpretation, the PAN numeral system had stable numerals only up to '5'; numbers between '5' and '10' were made up on the spot using additive, subtractive or multiplicative strategies; for instance '8' could be expressed as '5 plus 3' or '2 times 4', and '9' as '5 plus 4' or '1 taken out of 10'.[13] It is from such PAN analytical expressions that *pitu '7', *walu '8' and *Siwa '9' are derived. Specifically, they were derived out of *RaCep-i-tuSa '5+2', *RaCep-a-telu '5+3' and *RaCep-i-Sepat '5+4', shortly after the break-up of PAN, through a process of phonological compression described in great detail in Sagart (2004) and involving procrustean pruning, loss of schwas, reduction of consonant clusters and lenition. The long expressions are preserved as a paradigm by Pazeh, a north-western language: they must therefore have been part of PAN. The numerals for '5' and '10', *lima and *puluq, were derived out of words meaning 'hand' and 'all' respectively.[14] The etymology of *enem 'six' is still unknown.

The distribution of these six numerals in Formosan languages (Table 5.2) is remarkable: as shown in Sagart (2004) there exists between their reflexes an implicational hierarchy such that 'puluq' > 'Siwa' > 'walu' > 'enem' > 'lima' > 'pitu' (where '>' = 'implies'). This implicational hierarchy is reflected in the geography by a pattern of six nested isoglosses bundling on the south-east coast (Figure 5.3).

The hierarchy of implications and the nesting pattern are best explained as the result of successive lexical innovations, forming a compatibility set (on this

Setaria *farmers in East Asia* 147

Table 5.2 The numerals from five to ten in Formosan and PMP

	pitu '7'	lima '5'	enem '6'	walu '8'	Siwa '9'	puluq '10'
Luilang	innai	(na)lup	(na)tsulup	patulunai	satulunai	isit
Saisiat	saivuseaha	rrasu	saivusa	makaspat	ra:ha	ranpon
Pazeh	xasebidusa	xasep	xasebuza	xasebaturu, xasebituru	xasebisupat	isit
Favorlang	naito	achab	nataap	maaspat	tannacho	zchiett
Taokas	yweto	hasap	tahap	mahalpat	tanasu	(ta)isid
Atayal	pitu?	imagal	cziu?	spat	qeru?	lpuu
Sediq	pito	lima	mataro	maspat	maŋali	maxal
Thao	pitu	rima	ka-turu, makalh-turu-turu	kahspat, maka(lh)-shpa-shpat	tanacu	maqcin
Siraya	pĭttu	rima	nəm	kuixpa	matuda	saat kĭttian
Hoanya	pito	Lima	(mi)nun	(mi)alu	(a)sia	(miata)isi
Papora	pitu	nema	(ne)nom	mahal	(me)siya	(me)tsi
Tsou	pítu	eímo	nómə	vóeu	sio	máskə
Saaroa	(k)upito	(k)ulima	(k)ənəmə	(k)ualo	(k)usia	(ku)ma:ɬə
Kanakanabu	pitu	rima	nəm	(h)a:ru	si:ya	ma:nə
Bunun	pitu'	hima'	nuum	vau'	siva'	mas'an
Rukai	pitu	Lima	eneme	vaLu	baŋatə	maŋeale
Paiwan	pitju	lima	enem, unem	alu	siva	puluq
Puyuma	pitu	Lima	nem	waLu	iwa	puLu
Amis	pitu	lima	'enem	falu	siwa	polo
Kavalan	pitu	rima	'nem	waru	siwa	betin
Ketagalan	pitu	tsjima	anəm	wasu	siwa	labatan
PMP	*pitu	*lima	*enem	*walu	*siwa	*puluq

Sources: Amis: Wu (2000); Atayal: Egerod (1980); Bunun: Zeitoun (2000a); Favorlang=Babuza: Ferrell (1969); Hoanya: Ferrell (1969), supplemented with Ino (1998); Kanakanabu: Ogawa and Asai (1935), as cited in Ferrell (1969); Ketagalan-Basai: Tsuchida, Yamada and Moriguchi (1991); Luilang: Ferrell (1969); Paiwan: Ferrell (1982); Papora: Ferrell (1969), supplemented with Ino (1998); Pazeh: Li and Tsuchida (2001); Puyuma: Huang (2000); Rukai: Zeitoun (2000b); Saaroa: Tsuchida, as cited in Ferrell 1969; Saisiat: Ino (1998 for Saitaoyak dialect); Sediq: Pecoraro (1977), Siraya: Ferrell (1969); Taokas: Ferrell (1969), supplemented with Ino (1998); Thao: Blust (2003); Tsou: Tung (1964).

Notes
Shaded cells: reflexes of *lima '5', *enem '6', *pitu '7', *walu '8', *Siwa '9' and *puluq '10'.

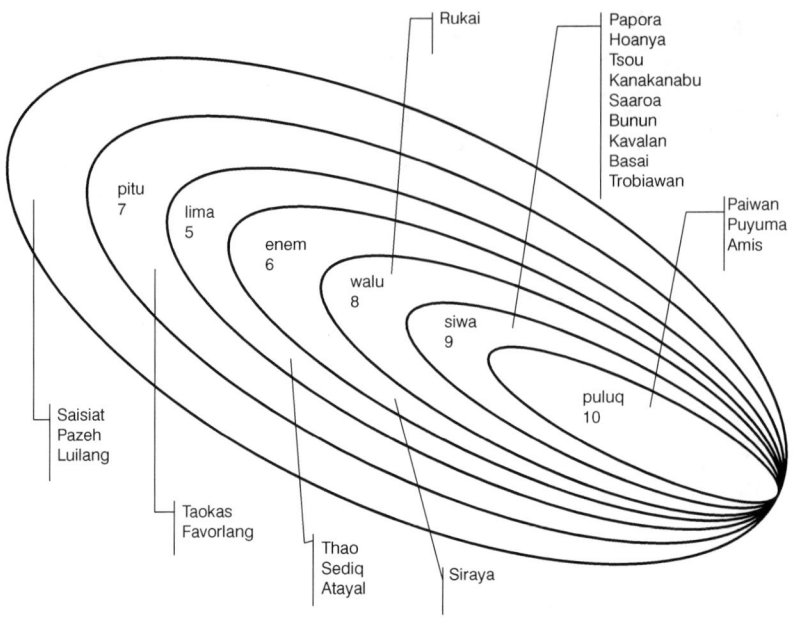

Figure 5.3 Nested isoglosses for the numerals '5' to '10' in Formosan languages.

notion see Meacham and Estabrook 1985), which in turn defines the phylogenetic tree in Figure 5.4.

My theory (Sagart 2004, 2006b) reconstructs the progress of Austronesian colonization of Táiwān primarily from the geography of innovations in the numeral system. It places the Proto-Austronesian homeland in the north-west, precisely in the region where I have argued that the first landing party arrived, because all the Formosan languages which show none of the six innovations, namely Luilang, Pazeh and Saisiat, are (or were, in the case of Luilang and now, sadly, Pazeh) spoken in that region. The geography of innovations argues for a pattern of gradual demic expansion out of the homeland area, in clear contrast to Blust's theory of an instantaneous circling of the island. The decisive factor may have been the presence in Táiwān of hunter-gatherers presenting a threat to isolated settlements.[15] There was safety in staying together.

Because of the geography of Táiwān – a narrow coastal plain circling a 300-km long chain of mountains – and because of the preference for cohesive settlement, demic expansion of the first farming societies in the north-west of the island had to take the shape of a wave of advance along the coast. Movement in a clockwise direction, toward the north and north-east, appears for some reason to have been blocked in the Taipei basin region: so that the advance was in effect unidirectional, first from the north-west along the coast towards the south, then around the southern tip of the island and northwards along the east coast. This mode of expansion has the consequence that innovations taking place on the wave front were always brought forward, while innovations taking place behind the wave front were not. We can explain the bundling of isoglosses on the south-east

Setaria farmers in East Asia 149

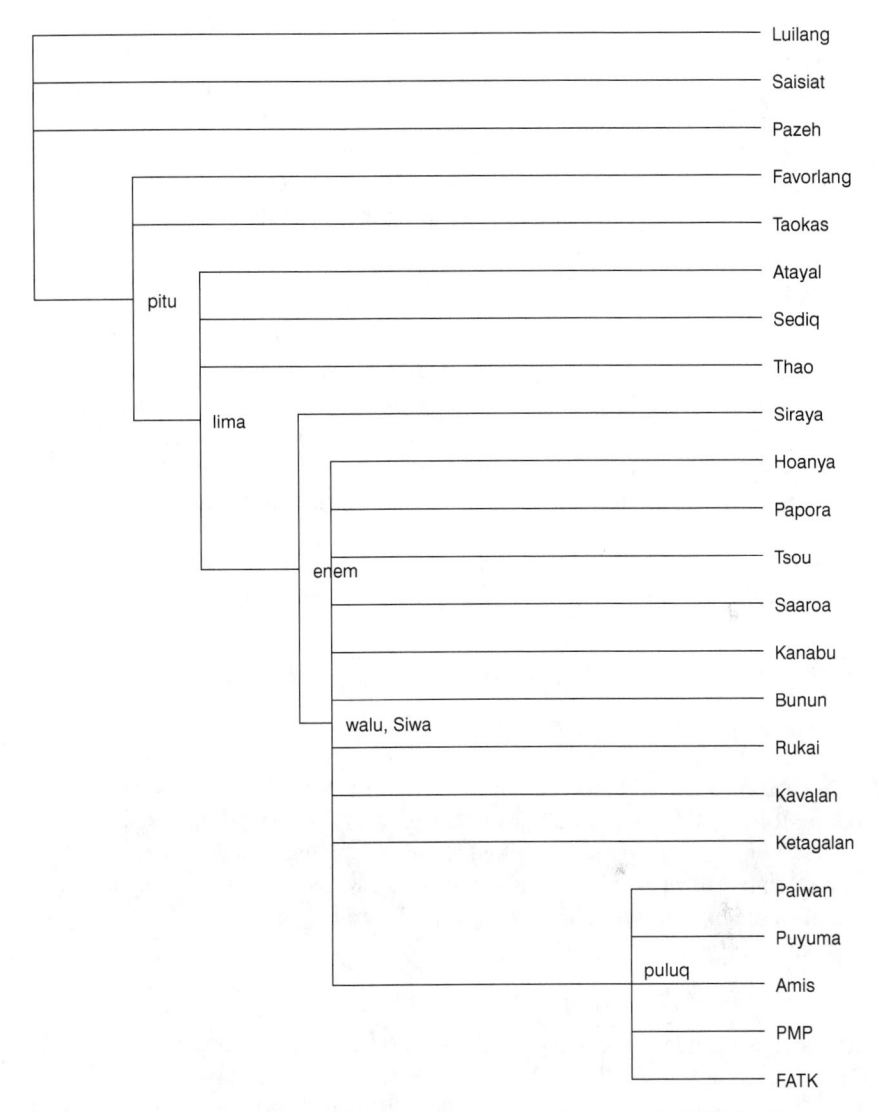

Figure 5.4 Higher AN phylogeny based on numerals from '5' to '10' ('FATK' = 'Formosan Ancestor of Tai-Kadai').

coast by supposing that all six innovations took place on the wave front, except for the last one: *puluq '10', which took place on the south-east coast, when the wave front was already further north on the east coast.

In general, the most plausible geographical locations for the languages in which the innovative forms *pitu, *lima, *enem, *walu, *Siwa and *puluq became fixed, are those where their most direct modern descendants are spoken. By following this principle we arrive at the hypothesis that PAN was located in the north-west of Táiwān; Pituish, the language in which *pitu eliminated all its rivals to become the only word for '7', in the western plains; Limaish and Enemish in western Táiwān; Walu-Siwaish in southern Táiwān; and Puluqish in south-eastern Táiwān (Plate 5.I). Archaeologically the earliest Dàpénkēng sites in north-west Táiwān (including Dàpénkēng itself, 5000 BP or earlier, near Taipei) can be equated with PAN or Pituish, or Limaish; Enemish can be equated with the Nan-kuan-li (Nanguanli) sites near Táinán, cal. 5000–4500 BP. Puluqish may have been the language of the early stratum at Pei-nan in south-eastern Taiwān.

4.6. 4000 BP: out of Táiwān

By the late 3rd millennium BCE, the entire coastal plains around Táiwān would have been settled, hence a need for new agricultural lands. At the same time, the appearance in Walu-Siwaish languages of a word for 'sail', *layaR, and of a new word for 'boat', *baŋka, suggests that sailing technologies were being improved. Improved sea-voyaging capabilities would have allowed the early Austronesians to venture out at sea in search of new lands. Considering that the China coast, from Fújiàn to the Pearl River delta, had already been opened to cultivation by the Austronesians' mainland cousins, the Philippines and the China coast beyond the Pearl River delta, which had not yet been open to cultivation, were prime targets.

4.6.1. To the Philippines: Malayo-Polynesian

4000 BP or slightly later is the time when East-Formosan-like ceramic cultures appear in the Batanes Islands and in the northern Philippines (Bellwood, this volume). It makes excellent sense to equate this movement with the MP migration out of Táiwān. PMP was in all probability spoken in the Philippines. That PMP was a Puluqic language is shown by the fact that it aggregates all six innovative numerals. It follows that its Formosan precursor was also a Puluqic language, and that it was spoken in south or south-eastern Táiwān.

4.6.2 Back to the mainland: Tai-Kadai

It should no longer be controversial that, as Benedict has argued since 1942, TK is genetically related to AN: once the many faulty comparisons presented by him (especially in Benedict 1975) are discarded, a solid core remains in which regularity of sound correspondences excludes an interpretation in terms of accidental resemblances (Sagart 2005a; Ostapirat 2005). Ostapirat (2005) makes significant progress in our understanding of these correspondences; Sagart (2004) shows that while in general TK words have been converted to monosyllables, in Buyang, a TK language recently described by Li Jinfang (1999), a set of disyllables with simplified, but recognizable, first syllables remains.

The words genuinely shared by TK and AN are extremely basic (Benedict 1942). They include the personal pronouns, the numerals, and words of the kind shown in Table 5.3: there is surprisingly little cultural vocabulary among them. Scarcity of cultural vocabulary makes a contact interpretation of the AN–TK

Table 5.3 Disyllabic AN words in Buyang

	Buyang	PAN	MP
die	ma⁰ tɛ54	maCay	matay
eye	ma⁰ ta54	maCa	mata
bird	ma⁰ nuk11	qayam	manuk
eight	ma⁰ ðu312	–	walu
head	qa⁰ ðu11	quluh	quluh
louse	qa⁰ tu54	kuCu	kutu
fart	qa⁰ tut54	qetut	
raw	qa⁰ ʔdip54	qudip	
bear (n.)	ta⁰ mɛ312	Cumay	
cover (v.)	ta⁰ qup11		WMP ta(ŋ)kup

Source: Data from Li Jinfang (1999).

relationship such as Thurgood's (1994) unrealistic. The only explanation left is genetic. But what kind of genetic relationship? Is TK coordinate with Austronesian, as Benedict thought? Or is it a subgroup within Austronesian, as argued in Sagart (2001, 2004, 2005a)?

The evidence that TK is a subgroup within AN, and specifically a member of the Puluqic taxon, is that it has all six innovative numerals (Sagart 2004). The conclusion inescapably follows that, like PMP, Tai-Kadai has its origin in a Puluqic language of south or south-eastern Táiwān. Further, Tai-Kadai shares with PMP a form relatable to the 2sg pronoun *-mu (Sagart 2001), suggesting that TK and PMP belong the same subgroup within Puluqic. A scenario describing the events leading to the formation of PTK might run as follows: in the second half of the 3rd millennium BCE a group of speakers of a Puluqic dialect ('FATK', Formosan Ancestor of Tai-Kadai) left eastern Táiwān by boat in search of new agricultural land. They found it on the coast between the Red River delta in north Vietnam and the Pearl River delta in the present-day Guǎngdōng province of China. In that region they eventually came into intimate contact with, and underwent strong pressure from, a population of mainland farmers speaking a language whose affiliation is difficult to establish,[16] but with possible phylic or macrophylic connections to Austroasiatic. An intense episode of contact resulted in FATK being partially relexified by this donor language, with only the most basic lexical items resisting displacement. PTK was the result of this interaction: it is at the core an AN language, partially relexified by an extinct language.

Criticism of this scenario comes from Ostapirat (2005) who points out that, unlike PMP, TK does not merge *t with *C, *n with *N, and does not change *S to *h: from this he concludes that TK cannot possibly be closely related to PMP. He notes that the merger of *t and *C is characteristic of East Formosan as a whole, and rejects the possibility that TK might be part of an East Formosan clade. His view of the TK–AN relationship is that it is either (a) a contact relationship, (b) a genetic relationship in which TK and AN are coordinate, as Benedict thought, or (c) a genetic relationship in which TK is part of AN, though not part of East Formosan or MP. He appears to favour (b).

The problem raised by Ostapirat can be solved once we realize that the behaviour of regular sound change is best described by the wave model. The choice is whether to base our phylogeny on sound changes or to base it on changes in the basic vocabulary. There is no question in my mind that the basic vocabulary, with its known resistance to borrowing, is a much more reliable index of phylogeny than regular sound change, so prone to transmission across language boundaries. In this case, it is necessary to suppose that *t and *C first merged in one of the east coast languages after the break-up of Puluqish, later spreading to other languages that were in contact with it. At the time of the PMP migration, the merger had affected both Puluqic and non-Puluqic languages: the precursor(s) of Kavalan, Ketagalan and PMP; but it had not reached FATK, Paiwan or Puyuma. The same is true of the merger of *n and *N. As to the change of *S to *h, it is a purely MP innovation which does not help us understand the position of TK *vis-à-vis* MP.

Conclusion

I have presented an account of the formation of the eastern half of the STAN macrophylum and associated Neolithic cultures. Both the linguistic and archaeological processes appear to be different aspects of the expansion of a population of early rice and *Setaria* farmers. Two archaeological markers of the expanding population have been identified: *Setaria italica* and tooth evulsion. It is as yet unclear whether any genetic markers can be identified. A weak point in the model is the scarcity of relevant archaeological sites on the coast of Jiāngsū south of the Yángzi estuary, and in Zhéjiāng. The model argued for here makes the prediction that *Setaria* and tooth evulsion will eventually be found in these regions, whether on the coast or in islands a short distance from the coast, at a time depth of *cal.* 6500–5500 BP.

Acknowledgements

I am grateful to Sander Adelaar, Bill Baxter, Peter Bellwood, Bob Blust, Isabelle Bril, François Dell, George van Driem, Alexandre François, Jeff Marck, Susan McCouch, Estella Poloni, Martha Ratliff, Laurence Reid, Malcolm Ross, Alicia Sanchez-Mazas and other colleagues for useful discussion. None of them necessarily agrees with the contents of this chapter.

Notes

1 See Higham and Lu (1998) for a detailed review of the archaeological evidence for early domesticated rice in the mid-Yángzi area.
2 Due to the lack of a wholly explicit system of reconstruction for TB – let alone ST (Sagart 2006) – the core of the phonological argument is still based on a comparison between reconstructed Old Chinese and PAN.

3 Old Chinese reconstructions follow Sagart (1999).
4 The form cək '*Setaria i.*' was collected in Bhutan by Sjors van Driem, who also identified the plant (pers. comm., June 2004).
5 Matisoff (2003: 516) calls variation between homorganic nasals and stops 'perhaps the most important variational pattern in TB/ST word families'.
6 Chang Kwang-chih (1986: 90) characterized the geographical distribution of the Císhān-Péilǐgāng culture sites thus: 'the lower terraces of the eastern edge of the western highland of north China, facing the marshes and the wetland that separated the western highland from Shantung, and along the Weishui River valley into the western interior at least to Eastern Kansu'.
7 Prof. Yán Wénmíng mentioned to me (pers. comm. 1998) the presence of small quantities of *Setaria* in Jiǎhú; Hu, Ambrose and Wang (2006), based on an isotopic analysis of human bones recovered at Jiǎhú, argue that millet may have been a minor component of the diet in this region.
8 For an early formulation of this concept on exclusively archaeological grounds, see Chang Kwang-chih's 'undifferentiated Sino-Tibetan/Austronesian complex' (Chang 1959), although Chang had in mind a broader definition of the Sino-Tibetan family.
9 But see Wright (2004) for an even earlier site in north Shāndōng, c. 8000 BP.
10 In this connection one should cite the view of Ling Chun-sheng, who considered the Yí and Yuè peoples as ancestral to the present-day Austronesians (Ling 1970: 230): Ling also argued that the spread of the Austronesians in the Pacific was made possible by boat-building skills first developed by the Yí (1970: 234).
11 Tooth evulsion did, however, spread to a small extent to other groups (especially Hmong-Mien) in mainland China.
12 Shortly after the publication of Sagart (2004) I realized that the two main pieces of evidence I had produced in support of my Muish node were problematic. First, the shift of PAN-mu from plural 'you' to singular 'you' did not take place in Trobiawan, as I had thought, misled by Li (1995: 667): 'Trobiawan, a variety of Ketagalan, uses the form *imu* "your (sg)" as in *tama-imu* "your father" … rather than (i)su as in most Formosan languages'; in a later paper (1999: 485), Li silently glossed the same word in the same expression 'your' (pl). Second, I had mistaken the term *manuk* 'bird', exclusively shared by Kavalan, PMP and Tai-Kadai, as an innovation of their most recent common ancestor; however, Martha Ratliff (pers. comm., 2006) has reminded me that a very similar form occurs in proto-Hmong-Mien, throwing doubt on my interpretation. In Sagart (2006b), these characters were not made use of.
13 A possible trace of such a system on the ST side of the STAN macrophylum is the ST word for '7', which is generally regarded as being based on a '5 + 2' prototype (Benedict 1972: 93).
14 Cf. PAN *lima 'hand'; Amis ma-puluq 'all'.
15 Blust's settlement model better applies to large uninhabited islands, like New Zealand at the time of Maori arrival.
16 Because neither its basic vocabulary nor its morphology are known (TK has become isolating under Chinese influence).

References

Bellwood, P. (2001) 'Early agriculturalist population diasporas? Farming, languages and genes', *Annual Review of Anthropology*, 30: 181–207.
Bellwood, P. (2005) 'Examining the farming/language hypothesis in the East Asian context', in L. Sagart, R.M. Blench and A. Sanchez-Mazas (eds) *The Peopling of East Asia: Putting Together Archaeology, Linguistics and Genetics*, pp. 17–30, London: RoutledgeCurzon.

Bellwood, P. and Renfrew, C. (2003) 'Farmers, foragers, languages, genes: the genesis of agricultural societies', in P. Bellwood and C. Renfrew (eds) *Examining the Farming/ Language Dispersal Hypothesis*, pp. 17–28, Cambridge: McDonald Institute for Archaeological Research.

Benedict, P.K. (1942) 'Thai, Kadai and Indonesian: a new alignment in Southeastern Asia', *American Anthropologist*, NS 44: 576–601.

Benedict, P.K. (1975) *Austro-Thai: Language and Culture*, New Haven, CT: HRAF Press.

Benedict, P.K. (1972) *Sino-Tibetan: A Conspectus*, Cambridge: University Printing House.

Blust, R.A. (1977) 'The Proto-Austronesian pronouns and Austronesian subgrouping: a preliminary report', *University of Hawai'i Working Papers in Linguistics*, 9(2): 1–15.

Blust, R.A. (1980) 'Austronesian etymologies', *Oceanic Linguistics*, 19: 1–181.

Blust, R. (1988) 'The Austronesian homeland: a linguistic perspective', *Asian Perspectives XXVI*, 1: 45–67.

Blust, R.A. (1995a) 'An Austronesianist looks at Sino-Austronesian', in W.S.-Y. Wang (ed.) *The Ancestry of the Chinese Language*, *Journal of Chinese Linguistics monograph series*, 8: 283–98.

Blust, R.A. (1995b) 'Sibilant assimilation in Formosan languages and the Proto-Austronesian word for "nine"', *Oceanic Linguistics*, 34: 443–53.

Blust, R.A. (1996) 'The Prehistory of the Austronesian-speaking peoples: a view from language', *Journal of World Prehistory*, 9: 453–510.

Blust, R.A. (1999) 'Notes on Pazeh phonology and morphology', *Oceanic Linguistics*, 38: 321–65.

Blust, R.A. (2003) *Thao Dictionary*, Nankang: Institute of Linguistics (Preparatory Office), Academia Sinica.

Chang Kwang-chih (1986) *The Archaeology of Ancient China*, 4th edn, New Haven, CT and London: Yale University Press.

Chang Kwang-chih (1987) 'Zhōngguó Dōngnán hǎi'ān kǎogǔ yǔ nándǎo yǔzú qǐyuán wèntí' (The archaeology of the southeast coast of China and the question of Austronesian origins), *Nánfāng Mínzú Kǎogǔ*, 1: 1–14.

Chang Kwang-chih (1989) 'Xīn Shíqí shídài de Táiwān Hǎixiá' (The Taiwan Straits in Neolithic times), *Kaogu*, 261: 241–50.

Diffloth, G. (1994) 'The lexical evidence for Austric, so far', *Oceanic Linguistics*, 33(1): 309–22.

Diffloth, G. (2005) 'The contribution of linguistic palaeontology to the homeland of Austroasiatic', in L. Sagart, R.M Blench and A. Sanchez-Mazas (eds) *The Peopling of East Asia: Putting Together Archaeology, Linguistics and Genetics*, pp. 77–89, London: RoutledgeCurzon.

Doré, H. (1926) *Manuel des superstitions chinoises*, Shanghai: Imprimerie de la Mission Catholique à l'orphelinat de T'ou-sè-wè.

Egerod, S. (1980) *Atayal-English Dictionary* (Scandinavian Institute of Asian Studies, monograph 35), London and Malmø: Curzon Press.

Ferrell, R. (1969) *Taiwan Aboriginal Groups: Problems in Cultural and Linguistic Classification* (Institute of Ethnology, Academia Sinica, monograph 17), Nankang: Academia Sinica.

Ferrell, R. (1982) *Paiwan Dictionary*, Canberra: Pacific Linguistics.

Fu Daxiong (2001) 'Xizang Changguogou yizhi xin shiqi shidai nongzuowu yicun de faxian, jianding he yanjiu', (Research on agricultural remains from Changguogu, a neolithic site in Tibet), *Kaogu*, 3: 66–74.

Garris, A.J., Tai, T.H., Coburn, J., Kresovich, S. and McCouch, S. (2005) 'Genetic structure and diversity in *Oryza sativa* L.', *Genetics*, 169(3): 1631–8.

Han, K.X. and Nakahashi, T. (1996) 'A comparative study of ritual tooth ablation in ancient China and Japan', *Anthropological Science*, 104: 43–64.

Harvey, M. (1979) 'Subgroups in Austronesian', BA honours thesis, Canberra, Australian National University.

Harvey, M. (1982) 'Subgroups in Austronesian', in A. Halim, L. Carrington and S.A. Wurm (eds) *Papers from the Third International Conference on Austronesian Linguistics*, vol. 2, *Tracking the Travellers*, pp. 47–99, Canberra: Pacific Linguistics.

Higham, C. (1996) *The Bronze Age of Southeast Asia*, Cambridge: Cambridge University Press.

Higham, C. and Lu, T. (1998) 'The origins and dispersal of rice cultivation', *Antiquity*, 72: 867–77.

Hu, Y., Ambrose, S.H. and Wang, C. (2006) 'Stable isotopic analysis of human bones from Jiahu site, Henan, China: Implications for the transition to agriculture', *Journal of Archaeological Science*, 33(9): 1319–30.

Huáng B. (1992) *Zàng-Miǎn Yǔzú Yǔyán Cíhuì* (A Tibeto-Burman Lexicon), Beijing: Zhōngyāng Mínzú Xuéyuàn Chūbǎnshè.

Huang, Lillian (2000) *Bēinán yǔ cānkǎo yǔfǎ* (A Reference Grammar of Puyuma), Taipei: Yuanliu.

Ino, Y. (1998) 'Xún Tái Rì Chéng' (Journal of a journey in Taiwan), in T. Moriguchi (ed.) *Ino Yoshinori Fānyǔ Diàochá Shǒucè*, Taipei: Southern Materials Center, pp. 13–201.

Jiang, L. and Liu, L. (2006) 'New evidence for the origins of sedentism and rice domestication in the Lower Yangzi River, China', *Antiquity*, 80: 355–61.

Lǐ, J. (1999) *Bùyāng Yǔ Yánjiū* (Researches on the Buyang Language), Beijing: Zhōngyāng Mínzú Dàxué.

Li, P. J-K. (1995) 'Formosan vs. non-Formosan features in some Austronesian Languages in Taiwan', in P.J.-k. Li, D.-a. Ho, Y.-k. Huang, C.-h. Tsang and C.-y. Tseng (eds) *Austronesian Studies Relating to Taiwan* (Symposium series of the Institute of History and Philology, Academia Sinica, no. 3), pp. 651–81, Taipei: Academia Sinica.

Li, P. J-K. (1999) 'Some problems in the Basay Language', *Selected Papers on Formosan Languages*, vol. 1, pp. 479–509, Taipei: Academia Sinica.

Li, P. J-K. (2001) 'Basai yǔ de dìwèi' (The position of Basai), *Language and Linguistics*, 2(2): 155–71.

Li, P. J.-K. and Tsuchida, S. (2001) *Pazih Dictionary*, Nankang: Institute of Linguistics (preparatory office), Academia Sinica.

Ling, C. (1970) *A Study of the Raft, Outrigger, Double and Deck Canoes of Ancient China, the Pacific and the Indian Oceans*, Nankang: Institute of Ethnology, Academia Sinica.

Londo, J.P., Chiang, Y.-C., Hung, K.-H., Chiang, T.-Y. and Schaal, B.A. (2006) 'Phylogeography of Asian wild rice, Oryza rufipogon, reveals multiple independent domestications of cultivated rice, Oryza sativa', *Proceedings of the National Academy of Sciences* (20 June), 103(25): 9578–83.

Lu, T.L.-D. (2005) 'The origin and dispersal of agriculture and human diaspora in East Asia', in L. Sagart, R.M. Blench and A. Sanchez-Mazas (eds) *The Peopling of East Asia: Putting Together Archaeology, Linguistics and Genetics*, London: Routledge Curzon.

Matisoff, J. (2003). *Handbook of Proto-Tibeto-Burman*, Berkeley, CA: University of California Press.

Meacham, C. and Estabrook, G. (1985) 'Compatibility methods in systematics', *Annual Review of Ecology and Systematics*, 16: 431–46.

Norman, J. and Mei, T. (1976) 'The Austroasiatics in ancient south China: some lexical evidence', *Monumenta Serica*, 32: 274–301.

Ogawa, N. and Asai, E. (1935) *The Myths and Traditions of the Formosan Native Tribes*, Taipei.

Ostapirat, W. (2000) 'Proto-Kra', *Linguistics of the Tibeto-Burman Area*, 23: 1.

Ostapirat, W. (2005) 'Kra-Dai and Austronesian: notes on phonological correspondences and vocabulary distribution', in L. Sagart, R.M. Blench and A. Sanchez-Mazas (eds) *The Peopling of East Asia: Putting Together Archaeology, Linguistics and Genetics*, London: RoutledgeCurzon.

Pecoraro, F. (1977) 'Essai de dictionnaire taroko-français', *Cahier d'Archipel*, 7: 1–277.

Reid, L. (1982) 'The demise of Proto-Philippines', in A. Halim, L. Carrington and S.A. Wurm (eds) *Papers from the Third International Conference on Austronesian Linguistics*, vol. 2, *Tracking the Travellers*, pp. 210–16, Canberra: Pacific Linguistics.

Reid, L. (1994) 'Morphological evidence for Austric', *Oceanic Linguistics*, 33: 323–44.

Reid, L. (2005) 'The current status of Austric: a review and evaluation of the lexical and morphosyntactic evidence', in L. Sagart, R.M. Blench and A. Sanchez-Mazas (eds) *The Peopling of East Asia: Putting Together Archaeology, Linguistics and Genetics*, pp. 132–60, London: RoutledgeCurzon.

Renfrew, C. (1996) 'Language families and the spread of farming', in D. Harris (ed.) *The Origins and Spread of Agriculture in Eurasia*, pp. 70–92, London: UCL Press.

Sagart, L. (1994) 'Old Chinese and Proto-Austronesian evidence for Sino-Austronesian', *Oceanic Linguistics*, 33: 271–308.

Sagart, L. (1995) 'Comments from Sagart', in W.S.-Y. Wang (ed.) *The Ancestry of the Chinese Language* (Journal of Chinese Linguistics, monograph series, 8), pp. 337–72.

Sagart, L. (1999) *The Roots of Old Chinese* (Current Issues in Linguistic Theory, 184), Amsterdam: John Benjamins.

Sagart, L. (2001) 'Comment: Malayo-Polynesian features in the AN-related vocabulary in Kadai', paper presented at the workshop 'Perspectives on the Phylogeny of East Asian Languages', 28–31 Aug., Périgueux.

Sagart, L. (2003) 'The vocabulary of cereal cultivation and the phylogeny of East Asian languages', *Bulletin of the Indo-Pacific Prehistory Association*, 23 (Taipei papers), 1: 127–36.

Sagart, L. (2004) 'The higher phylogeny of Austronesian and the position of Tai-Kadai', *Oceanic Linguistics*, 43: 411–44.

Sagart, L. (2005a) 'Tai-Kadai as a subgroup of Austronesian', in L. Sagart, R.M. Blench and A. Sanchez-Mazas (eds) *The Peopling of East Asia: Putting Together Archaeology, Linguistics and Genetics*, pp. 161–76, London: RoutledgeCurzon.

Sagart, L. (2005b) 'Sino-Tibetan-Austronesian: An updated and improved argument', in L. Sagart, R.M. Blench and A. Sanchez-Mazas (eds) *The Peopling of East Asia: Putting Together Archaeology, Linguistics and Genetics*, pp. 177–81, London: RoutledgeCurzon.

Sagart, L. (2006a) 'Review: James A. Matisoff (2003) Handbook of Proto-Tibeto-Burman. System and philosophy of Sino-Tibeto-Burman reconstruction', *Diachronica*, 22: 206–23.

Sagart, L. (2006b) 'The PAN words for "7", "8", "9" and Austronesian subgrouping', Powerpoint presentation for the 10th International Conference on Austronesian Linguistics, Puerto Princesa, Philippines, 17–23 Jan.

Sagart, L., Blench, R.M. and Sanchez-Mazas, A. (2005) 'Introduction', in L. Sagart, R.M. Blench and A. Sanchez-Mazas (eds) *The Peopling of East Asia: Putting Together Archaeology, Linguistics and Genetics*, pp. 1–14, London: RoutledgeCurzon.

Schmidt, W. (1906) *Die Mon-Khmer Völker, ein Bindeglied zwischen Völkern Zentralasiens und Austronesiens*, Brunswick: Friedrich Vieweg & Sohn.

Soothill, W.E. and Hodous, L. (n.d.) *Dictionary of Chinese Buddhist Terms*, digital edition: http://www.hm.tyg.jp/~acmuller/soothill/soothill-hodous.html, accessed 3 Aug. 2004.

Thurgood, G. (1994) 'Tai-Kadai and Austronesian: the nature of the historical relationship', *Oceanic Linguistics*, 33(2): 345–68.

Tsang, C.-h. (2005) 'Recent discoveries at a Tapenkeng culture site in Taiwan: implications for the problem of Austronesian origins', in L. Sagart, R.M. Blench and A. Sanchez-Mazas (eds) *The Peopling of East Asia: Putting Together Archaeology, Linguistics and Genetics*, pp. 63–74, London: RoutledgeCurzon.

Tung, T.H. (1964) *A Descriptive Study of the Tsou Language*, Nankang: Institute of History and Philology, Academia Sinica.

Wright, H.T. (2004) 'New archaeological information on early Holocene communities in central and southeastern China', paper presented to the symposium 'Human Migrations in Continental East Asia and Taiwan: Genetic, Linguistic and Archaeological Evidence', University of Geneva.

Wu, C.-l. (2000) *Aměi yǔ cānkǎo yǔfǎ* (A Reference Grammar of Amis), Taipei: Yuanliu.

Tsuchida, S., Yamada, Y. and Moriguchi, T. (1991) *Linguistic Materials of the Formosan Sinicized Populations*, vol. 1, *Siraya and Basai*, Tokyo: Linguistics Department, University of Tokyo.

Yuasa, H. (2000) *Segawa's Illustrated Ethnography of Indigenous Formosan People/the Tsou*, Taipei: Southern Materials Center.

Zeitoun, E. (2000a) *Lŭkǎi yǔ cānkǎo yǔfǎ* (A Reference Grammar of Rukai), Taipei: Yuanliu.

Zeitoun, E. (2000b) *Bùnóng yǔ cānkǎo yǔfǎ* (A Reference Grammar of Bunun), Taipei: Yuanliu.

Zhang, J. and Wang, X. (1998) 'Notes on the recent discovery of ancient cultivated rice at Jiahu, Henan Province: a new theory concerning the origin of *Oryza Japonica* in China', *Antiquity*, 72: 897–901.

Zhèngzhāng, S. (1991) 'Decipherment of Yuè-Rén-Gē', *Cahiers de Linguistique Asie Orientale*, 20: 159–68.

Part II
Linguistics

6 The integrity of the Austronesian language family

From Taiwan to Oceania

Malcolm Ross

1. Introduction

My purpose in this chapter is to address four questions which relate to the integrity of the Austronesian language family:

1. Are the aboriginal languages of Taiwan and the languages of Oceania related?
2. What is the nature of this relationship? Does it reflect migration?
3. Do these relationships reflect migratory direction?
4. How does a linguist reach these answers?

In the course of answering these questions I will refer to three sets of languages using terms that are well understood by Austronesianist linguists but perhaps rather opaque to other readers. *Formosan* denotes the aboriginal languages of Taiwan, *Malayo-Polynesian* all Austronesian languages outside Taiwan. On the tree in Figure 6.1 the latter are divided into Western Malayo-Polynesian, Central Malayo-Polynesian, South Halmahera/West New Guinea and Oceanic, terms which are discussed in §4 and §7. Today there are 14 Formosan languages (there were perhaps two or three times as many when outsiders reached Taiwan in the 17th century) and perhaps as many as a thousand Malayo-Polynesian languages. The third term, *Oceanic*, denotes a subset of Malayo-Polynesian and includes most of the Malayo-Polynesian languages of New Guinea, Island Melanesia, Polynesia and Micronesia.

2. Are the Formosan and Oceanic languages related?

We may rephrase this question, and ask, 'Are the Formosan and Malayo-Polynesian languages (which include Oceanic) related?' The answer is straightforward. They are all Austronesian, a fact which is self-evident from the vocabulary in Table 6.1, which shows a few common words from Atayal (north Taiwan), Tsou, Rukai and Paiwan (all central/south Taiwan), Tagalog (Luzon, Philippines), Toba Batak (western Sumatra), Uma (central Sulawesi), Manggarai (Flores), Kairiru (off the north coast of New Guinea) and Samoan (Polynesia).

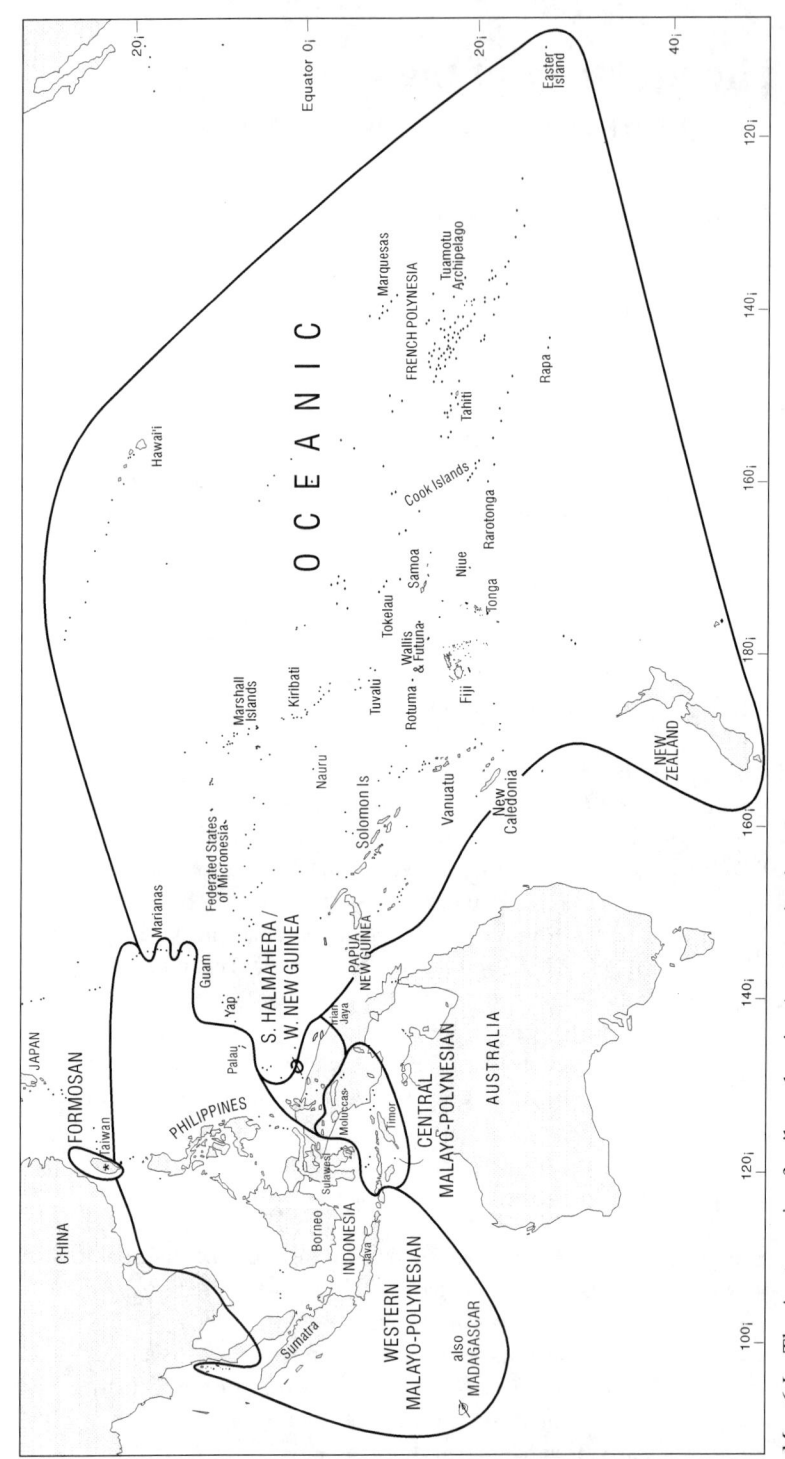

Map 6.1 The Austronesian family and major Austronesian language groups

Table 6.1 Selected words in scattered Austronesian languages

	ear	eye	head louse	three	freshwater eel	seven
Atayal	tʃaŋiaʔ	–	kutʃuʔ	tu-ɤaɬ	tuɤa-qiy	ma-pituʔ
Tsou	–	mtsō	ktsū	turu	tuŋ-roza	pitu
Rukai	tsaḷiŋa	matsa	kotso	toḷo	tola	pito
Paiwan	tsaḷiŋa	matsa	kətsiḷu	tyəḷu	tyulya	pityu
Tagalog	tə̄ŋa	mata	kūto	ta-tlo	–	pito
Toba Batak	–	mata	hutu	tolu	–	pitu
Uma	tiliŋa	mata	kutu	tolo	–	pitu
Manggarai	–	mata	hutu	təlu	tuna	pitu
Kairiru	tiliŋ	mata	qut	tuol	tun	–
Samoan	taliŋa	mata	ʔutu	tolu	tuna	fitu

3. What is the nature of Austronesian relationships?

This question asks about the genesis of new Austronesian-speaking communities. The linguistic evidence suggests that new Austronesian-speaking communities have in most cases been created through the geographical expansion of an old Austronesian-speaking community and its subsequent separation, whether sudden or gradual, into two or more new communities. That is, the relationship among Austronesian languages is usually a genealogical relationship, reflecting continuity across generations.

Important evidence of genealogical continuity occurs in the form of regular correspondences between the sounds of various languages. In Table 6.1, Atayal *tʃ*, for example, corresponds regularly with Tsou, Rukai and Paiwan *ts* and with *t* in all the other languages. This is the result of regular sound changes that have affected speech over time. I return to this below.

A caveat is needed here, however. Some Austronesian-speaking communities have been created through the adoption of an Austronesian language by a community which previously spoke some other language, i.e. by language shift. In general, language shift leaves few linguistic clues, as speakers tend to become highly competent in their new language, but sometimes linguistic clues remain. Speakers may retain items of vocabulary from their former language. Shift probably occurred quite often during the earlier phase of the Austronesian dispersal as agriculturalist Austronesian speakers encountered and (partly) absorbed communities of foragers in the Philippines and the Indo-Malaysian archipelago. Reid (1994) provides evidence of this in the vocabulary of the Austronesian languages of formerly foraging Negrito groups in the Philippines. There have also been shifts as Austronesian speakers have encountered speakers of Papuan languages, also agriculturalists, in New Guinea. Laycock (1973) notes

166   *Malcolm Ross*

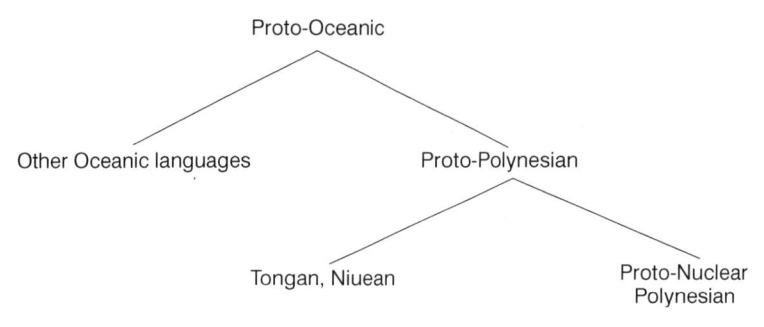

Figure 6.2   A small part of the genealogical tree of Oceanic languages

fourteen Formosan languages form nine primary subgroups of Austronesian, coordinate with each other and with Malayo-Polynesian. This means that there is no ancestor which the Formosan languages share exclusively, as their most immediate shared ancestor is Proto Austronesian, which they also share with Proto Malayo-Polynesian. That is, there is no 'Proto Formosan'. Sagart (2004; this volume) proposes an alternative subgrouping of Formosan languages, but this too recognizes no 'Proto Formosan'.

Similarly, Figure 6.1 shows no 'Proto Western Malayo-Polynesian', as western Malayo-Polynesian groups have no exclusively shared ancestor (Ross 1995). Despite numerous references in the literature to a 'Western Malayo-Polynesian' group, the western Malayo-Polynesian languages consist of some 20–25 groups, each descended from Proto Malayo-Polynesian. A similar comment can be made about the central Malayo-Polynesian languages. I return to these matters in §7.

5. How does a linguist arrive at a genealogical tree?

Various scholars, some of them practitioners of disciplines other than linguistics, have treated Blust's tree as if it were an impressionistic creation which may be easily dismissed (e.g. Meacham 1984; Solheim 1996; Oppenheimer and Richards 2001). For this reason, with apologies to readers who are familiar with the linguistic comparative method, this section is devoted to a rather textbookish discussion of the methodological underpinnings of genealogical (or phylogenetic) trees in historical linguistics.

As I mentioned in relation to Table 6.1, Austronesian languages display largely regular sound correspondences, attesting to largely regular sound changes which reflect generational continuity. Sound correspondences also provide evidence about subgrouping, which allows us to construct a tree (Figure 6.2) which in turn allows us to infer directionality (§4).

We know from historical data that languages undergo change, and that change tends to be regular. Regularity of sound change is attested, for example, by the vowel change in Table 6.2. Wherever Old English (roughly AD 800) had long [u:]

Table 6.2 An English vowel change

Old English	Modern English
hū [huː]	*how* [haʊ]
hūs [huːs]	*house* [haʊs]
mūs [muːs]	*mouse* [maʊs]
ūt [uːt]	*out* [aʊt]
sūð [suːð]	*south* [saʊθ]
būɣan [buːɣan]	*bow* [baʊ]

like the *oo* in modern *moon*, Modern English has [aʊ] as in *how*. That is, Old English [uː] has become Modern English [aʊ].

In the Pacific we usually find ourselves dealing with languages whose earlier stages are undocumented, and so we must reconstruct their earlier stages from their sound correspondences. Table 6.3 shows vocabulary from two closely related languages. The most obvious difference between them is that Minigir *s* corresponds to zero in Tolai. Minigir clearly preserves an earlier stage of the language, whilst *s* has been lost in Tolai. We can, then, reconstruct an earlier stage of the language (here it happens to be identical to Minigir) and infer a sound change in Tolai (loss of *s*). In this case, there is really no alternative analysis, as it is extremely improbable that zero has in unpredictable contexts sporadically become *s*. That is, the sound is unidirectional, and Tolai is the innovating language.

To understand how innovations enable us to detect subgroups and to construct a tree, we need to examine a more complex example. Table 6.4 shows vocabulary from Oceanic languages selected from right across the region. Takia is spoken off the north coast of New Guinea, Tawala in south-east Papua, Motu in central Papua, Bali-Vitu in islands to the north of New Britain and Tolai at the north-eastern end of New Britain. These are representative languages of the Western

Table 6.3 Sound correspondences in two languages of New Britain (Bismarck Archipelago)

Minigir	Tolai	gloss
tasi-	*tai-*	'cross-sibling'
savua-	*avua-*	'widow'
bilausu-	*bilau-*	'nose'
suru	*uru*	'bone'
susu-	*u-*	'breast; suck'
sui	*ui*	'snake'
tasuka	*tauka*	'squid'
mamisa	*mami*	'short yam'
masoso	*mao*	'(banana) ripe'

168 *Malcolm Ross*

Table 6.4 Cognate vocabulary in selected Oceanic languages

	eye	back	father	hand, five	mosquito	ear
Takia	mala-	...	tama-	–	–	–
Tawala	mata-	muli-	ama	nima-	–	taniga-
Motu	mata-	muri-	tama-	ima-	namo	taia
Bali-Vitu	mata-	–	tama-	lima	–	taliŋa-
Tolai	mata	muru-	tama-	lima	–	taliŋa-
Bugotu	mata-	–	tama-	lima-	ñamu	–
Gela	mata-	muri	tama-	lima-	namu	taliŋa
Kwaio	maa-	buri-	maʔa	nima-	namu	ariŋa-
Bauan	mata-	muri	tama-	liŋa-	namu	daliŋa-
Tongan	mata	mui	tamaiª	nima	namu	teliŋa
Samoan	mata	muli	tama	lima	namu	taliŋa
Tahitian	mata	muri	tamaᵇ	rima	namu	tariʔa
Rarotongan	mata	muri	tamaᵇ	rima	namu	tariŋa
Maori	mata	muri	tamaᵇ	rima	namu	tariŋa
Hawaiian	maka	muli	kamaᵇ	lima	–	–

Notes
a Also *tama* 'child'. b 'child'.

Oceanic subgroup. Bugotu, Gela and Kwaio belong to the South-east Solomonic group, Bauan Fijian, Tongan, Samoan, Tahitian, Rarotongan, Maori and Hawaiian to the Central Pacific group. However, to name their subgroups is to anticipate the argument below.

A gap in the table indicates that there is no cognate (i.e. related) word in the language. Footnotes indicate cases where the word which otherwise means 'father' (also) means 'child'. This is an unsurprising change in meaning, as Oceanic kin terms quite often have reciprocal meanings (father/child, grandparent/grandchild). Included in the table are three words that are not strictly cognate with other words in the same column. Tawala *ama* and Kwaio *maʔa* are terms for 'father' which are derived from vocative (address) forms, whereas the other forms in the column (*tama*- etc) reflect the reference form. The vocative and reference forms were systematically related at a much earlier stage of their history. Kwaio *buri*- 'back' occurs where we might expect *muri*-: it reflects an alternative word-form with a complex but explicable relationship to *muri*-, not an irregular sound change (Ross 2003).

The relatedness of the words in Table 6.4 across languages is self-evident. It is also quite obvious that the sounds in these words correspond in a fairly regular manner across languages, and these correspondences are set out in Table 6.5 (a gap – three dots – indicates that the sound is not represented in Table 6.4). Thus the words for 'eye' and 'back' begin with *m*-, except for Kwaio *buri*-, and the words for 'father', 'hand, five' and 'mosquito' all display a medial -*m*-, except Kwaio *maʔa* and Bauan *liŋa*- (which reflects an earlier variant **lim*ʷ*a*). A correspondence involving the *t*- of 'father' and 'ear' and -*t*- of 'eye' is equally obvious. Slightly less transparent is the correspondence involving the *l*- of Tolai 'hand, five' and -*l*- of Tolai 'ear'. Several other correspondences are represented only once in Table 6.4. These involve the -*r*- of Tolai 'back', the *ñ*- of Bugotu 'mosquito' and the -*ŋ*- of Tolai 'ear'. All the correspondences recorded in Table 6.5 occur in other words in these languages, i.e. they are regular correspondences.

On the top row of Table 6.5 are shown the relevant reconstructed consonants of Proto Oceanic, the language ancestral to all Oceanic languages. I will not discuss reconstruction methodology here, but a glance at Table 6.5 shows that, at least in this application, there is nothing particularly esoteric about it.

Now that we have reconstructed Proto Oceanic consonants, we can reconstruct the innovations that have occurred in the various languages. Proto Oceanic *t, for example, has become Kwaio zero, i.e. it has been lost, and Hawaiian *k*.

What is important here is a pattern of innovations displayed by the languages in the five lowest rows of the table, namely Samoan, Tahitian, Rarotongan, Maori and Hawaiian. It is clear from the other languages in the table that Proto Oceanic *l and *r must each be reconstructed. It is also clear that these two sounds have merged in the five languages at the bottom of the table (i.e. both are reflected as *l* in Samoan and Hawaiian and as *r* in Tahitian, Rarotongan and Maori). We can be confident that it is these five languages that have innovated. The alternative would

Table 6.5 Sound correspondences in selected Oceanic languages

Proto Oceanic	*m	*t	*l	*-*r*-	*ñ-	*-*ŋ*-
Takia	m	t-; -l-	...	...	...	...
Tawala	m	t	n	-l-	...	-g-
Motu	m	t	Ø	-r-	n-	-Ø-
Bali-Vitu	m	t	l	...	...	-ŋ-
Tolai	m	t	l	-r-	...	-ŋ-
Bugotu	m	t	l	...	ñ-	...
Gela	m	t	l	-r-	n-	-ŋ-
Kwaio	m	Ø	-l-	-r-	n-	-ŋ-
Bauan	m	t	l	-r-	n-	-ŋ-
Tongan	m	t	-l-	-Ø-	n-	-ŋ-
Samoan	m	t	l	-l-	n-	-ŋ-
Tahitian	m	t	r	-r-	n-	-ʔ-
Rarotongan	m	t	r	-r-	n-	-ŋ-
Maori	m	t	r	-r-	n-	-ŋ-
Hawaiian	m	k	l	-l-	...	...

170 *Malcolm Ross*

be to reconstruct a single consonant in Proto Oceanic, e.g. *l*, and to claim that it had split in the languages from Takia to Tongan. However, this split would be unconditioned, i.e. it would be impossible to predict which of the two outcomes (e.g. Tolai *l* or *r*) would occur in which word. An unconditioned split is a relatively rare phenomenon.

The merger of Proto Oceanic *l* and *r* in these five languages is a *shared innovation*. It happens that these languages (and others) also share other innovations. The most probable explanation of these innovations is *not* that they have occurred in each of the five languages in parallel, but that these five languages (among others) are descended from a single ancestor in which these innovations occurred. Thus shared innovations allow us to identify subgroups, and Samoan, Tahitian, Rarotongan, Maori and Hawaiian are all attributed to the Nuclear Polynesian subgroup of Oceanic. That is, they are descended from a single interstage language, Proto Nuclear Polynesian.

The Nuclear Polynesian languages share a further set of innovations with Tongan and Niuean. These innovations define the Polynesian subgroup of Oceanic (Pawley 1966, 1967; Biggs 1971). Thus we can draw a small part of the genealogical tree of Oceanic languages as in Figure 6.2.

The method that I have briefly outlined here, the comparative method of historical linguistics, was applied by Dempwolff (1937) when he reconstructed *Urmelanesisch*, today known as Proto Oceanic. Further research has slightly modified and has extended Dempwolff's collection of innovations (Lynch *et al.* 2002: ch. 4).

Proto Austronesian

Formosan language groups (nine groups)

Proto Malayo-Polynesian (MP)

Proto Central/Eastern MP

(Proto Eastern MP ??)

Western Malayo-Polynesian language groups (20-25 groups ?)

Central MP linkage

Proto S. Halmahera/ W. New Guinea

Proto Oceanic

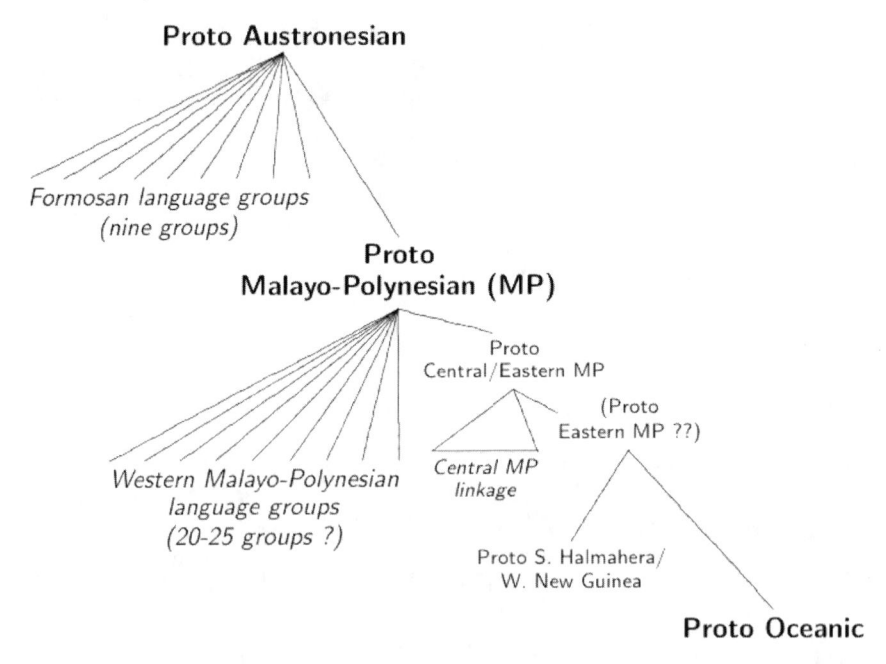

Figure 6.3 An elaborated Austronesian genealogical tree

The same method was used by Dahl (1973) and Blust (1977) to establish the Malayo-Polynesian subgroup of Austronesian, and by Blust (1978, 1982, 1983, 1993) to establish the Central/Eastern Malayo-Polynesian, Central Malayo-Polynesian, Eastern Malayo-Polynesian and South Halmahera/West New Guinea subgroups shown in Figure 6.1.

The method described above is often supplemented by the use of corroboratory evidence from external witnesses. Let us suppose that there were genuine doubt about the direction of the innovation which I have described above as the Proto Nuclear Polynesian merger of Proto Oceanic *l and *r, and that a scholar were seriously entertaining the alternative, that there was just one consonant here, Proto Oceanic *l, which split into two consonants in numerous Oceanic languages. The crucial issue, of course, is whether Proto Oceanic had both *l and *r or just *l. The nodes in the tree above Proto Oceanic in Figure 6.2 are Proto Eastern Malayo-Polynesian, Proto Central/Eastern Malayo-Polynesian and Proto Malayo-Polynesian. If Proto Oceanic inherited both *l and *r from these earlier interstage languages, then we would expect to find these two consonants also separately reflected in languages of other branches of the tree, and indeed we do.[1]

6. The Malayo-Polynesian, Formosan-Philippine and Formosan hypotheses

Clearly, corroboratory evidence from external witnesses cannot be used at the top of the tree. If Proto Austronesian represents the highest known node of the tree, then it must be reconstructed on the basis of evidence from Austronesian languages alone, as there are by definition no external witnesses.

But is this true? Might there be external witnesses? We can be reasonably confident on archaeological grounds (Bellwood, this volume) that the ancestors of Proto Austronesian speakers came to Taiwan from the mainland, but no languages descended from siblings of Proto Austronesian can be identified there with certainty. Three major proposals about the external relationships of Austronesian have appeared in the literature. One, the 'Austric' hypothesis, links it with Austro-Asiatic (Schmidt 1906). Although there are suggestive morphological similarities between certain Austro-Asiatic and Austronesian languages, very little Proto Austric vocabulary has been convincingly reconstructed (Reid 1999, 2005), i.e. there is nothing that can be used as a reliable external witness. Sagart (1994) has suggested that Old Chinese was a close relative of Proto Austronesian, and now proposes that this relationship is due to the fact that both are members of a Sino-Tibetan/Austronesian macrophylum (Sagart 2005b; this volume). He lists possible cognate vocabulary, but it is insufficient to allow Old Chinese to be used as an external witness. The third proposal is that the Tai-Kadai languages are related to Austronesian. Benedict (1942, 1975) proposed a larger 'Austro-Tai' family, but this has been poorly received because of the liberties that Benedict took in his reconstructions. More recently, however, Ostapirat (2005) has shown that there are systematic sound correspondences between the basic vocabularies reconstructed for Proto Tai-Kadai and Proto Austronesian. He takes these as evidence that Tai-Kadai and Austronesian are related, but is agnostic as to whether the two together form an Austro-Tai family or whether Tai-Kadai is a high-order subgroup of Austronesian (Ostapirat shows that it does not reflect the defining innovations of Malayo-Polynesian). Building on Ostapirat's work and his own work on Formosan subgrouping, Sagart (2004, 2005a; this volume) proposes that Tai-Kadai represents a branch of Austronesian that split from the rest of the family at a node perhaps just above Proto Malayo-Polynesian in Figure 6.2. If this is the case, then Tai-Kadai languages are not external witnesses for the purposes of reconstructing Proto Austronesian, although they may provide additional internal evidence.

Hence there are no external witnesses to which appeal can be made in reconstructing Proto Austronesian, and partly for this reason there is more than one hypothesis about the higher-level subgrouping of Austronesian and therefore about where Proto Austronesian was spoken.

Above, I have presented Dahl's (1973) and Blust's (1977) Malayo-Polynesian hypothesis, accepted in its broad outlines by most historical linguists working on Austronesian. However, two linguists, Dyen (1995) and Wolff (1995), have put forward variants of what Pawley (2002) dubs the 'Formosan-Philippine hypothesis',[2] and Peiros (1994; this volume) proposes what I will call a Formosan hypothesis. I shall not discuss alternative hypotheses about the migrations of early Austronesian speakers offered by archaeologists Meacham (1984) and Solheim (1996) or geneticists Oppenheimer and Richards (2001, 2002), as they employ no linguistic evidence.[3]

Under the Malayo-Polynesian hypothesis, a number of innovations are held to define Malayo-Polynesian languages and to have occurred before the dispersal of Proto Malayo-Polynesian speakers. There are three sound-change innovations (Blust 1990):

1   PAn *t and *C merged as PMP *t.
2   PAn *N and *n merged (with some unexplained exceptions) as PMP *n.[4]
3   PAn *S and *h merged as PMP *h.

There is also a number of quite complicated morphological innovations, the details of which are beyond the scope of this chapter. They consist of innovations in pronouns and in verbal affixes. A major set of innovations in pronouns involved a 'politeness shift'. These changes were reconstructed by Blust (1977) and are revised by Ross (2006). Both Proto Austronesian and Proto Malayo-Polynesian had complex and unusual verbal systems, and these systems are largely shared by their modern descendants in Taiwan and the Philippines (these are the similarities noted by the proponents of the Formosan-Philippine hypothesis). The Proto Malayo-Polynesian verbal system, however, underwent innovations that introduced complexities absent from Formosan systems. Among other things, Proto Malayo-Polynesian added the derivational prefixes *paN- 'distributive', *paR- 'durative, reciprocal' and *paka- 'aptative, potential' (Ross 2002).

The Formosan-Philippine hypothesis essentially says that the Formosan and Philippine languages look so similar that they must form a subgroup. The similarities are to be found both in vocabulary and in grammar. This position, however, neglects the methodological point made in §5 that a subgroup is defined by shared innovations. If the Formosan-Philippine hypothesis is to be taken seriously, then it needs to be shown that Formosan and Philippine languages reflect a set of innovations that other Austronesian languages do not share, i.e. that there is evidence for a shared Proto Formosan-Philippine node. Such evidence has not been offered. Instead, it is likely that the similarities among Formosan and Philippine languages are shared retentions of Proto Austronesian features, an inference which causes no difficulty under the Malayo-Polynesian hypothesis. Alternative explanations would also need to be offered for the Malayo-Polynesian innovations noted above, together with an alternative Austronesian subgrouping, but these have not been forthcoming.

Any alternative to the Malayo-Polynesian hypothesis needs to explain away these shared innovations. Of the sound-change innovations, the most important – because of its high token frequency – is (1). It is readily illustrated from Table 6.1, and the relevant sound correspondences are shown in Table 6.6. Under the Malayo-Polynesian hypothesis, Proto Austronesian had two sounds *C (perhaps [ts]) and *t, which are reflected differently in Atayal, Tsou, Rukai and Paiwan, but which merged in Proto Malayo-Polynesian.[5]

An alternative interpretation of the evidence would suggest that only *t occurred in Proto Austronesian, and that it split into two sounds in a language ancestral just to Atayal, Tsou, Rukai, Paiwan and certain other Formosan languages. Peiros (n.d., 1994; this volume) sets out to show that such a split did occur, and that it was regularly conditioned. He uses this as evidence for a Formosan hypothesis, i.e. a hypothesis to the effect that the Formosan languages form a subgroup descended from a 'Proto Formosan' (Peiros, this volume). He accepts the

Table 6.6 Sound correspondences from Table 6.1

Proto Austronesian	*C	*t
Atayal	tʃ	t
Tsou	ts	t
Rukai	ts	t
Paiwan	ts	ty
Proto Malayo-Polynesian	*t	*t
Tagalog	t	t
Toba Batak	t	t
Uma	t	t
Manggarai	t	t
Kairiru	t	t
Samoan	t	t

validity of innovations (2) and (3) above and therefore of the Malayo-Polynesian (his 'non-Formosan') subgroup. This means that, for him, Proto Austronesian underwent a primary split into Proto Formosan and Proto Malayo-Polynesian. If this were so, it seems that the likely homeland of Proto Austronesian, based on the probable homelands of the two daughter-languages, would still be either Taiwan or somewhere in its immediate neighbourhood.

Like the Nuclear Polynesian merger described in §5, the success of a converse hypothesis depends on demonstrating that the split, in this case of *t, occurred under regular conditions. Peiros' account of the putative split of *t into *C and *t is based on data from one Formosan language, Tsou, which, he claims, reflects processes which occurred in Proto Formosan. More specifically, Tsou is said to reflect the placement of stress in Proto Austronesian and Proto Formosan, and *t-split is said to be conditioned by the position in the root of *t, the occurrence in the root of certain other consonants and vowels, and the position of stress. It is probably true that Tsou reflects ancient stress placement, but the conditionings proposed by Peiros are rather implausible (i.e. unlike those commonly occurring in the world's languages), admit of a number of exceptions, and the distribution of *t and *C is more readily accounted for by the operation of Proto Austronesian consonant harmony (Ross 1992).[6] Peiros's study is intriguing and I think that the reconstruction of stress and consonant harmony in early Austronesian needs further investigation, but on balance the present evidence does not support his hypothesis.[7]

This means that there are no convincing innovations supporting either the Formosan-Philippine or Formosan hypotheses, and the Malayo-Polynesian hypothesis stands effectively without a strong challenger.

7. Elaborating the tree

Linguistic inheritance is often more complicated than the model I have outlined so far implies. The divergence of sister-languages is often 'a gradual and untidy affair' (Pawley 2002) which results in innovation-linked subgroups (= linkages) rather than the innovation-defined subgroups discussed in §5 and §6. An innovation-linked subgroup is a group of languages with a network of overlapping innovations. That is, no innovation is shared by all the languages in the subgroup. Instead, for example, languages A, B and C share innovation X, languages B, C, D and E share innovation Y, and languages A, C and E share innovation Z. Innovation-linked subgroups may arise either via a dialect network from gradual diversification within a speech community, or from division within an existing linkage, In this case the new linkage has no discrete protolanguage (Pawley and Ross 1995). Geraghty (1983) shows that such innovation-linked subgroups exist in Fiji.

These observations are relevant to the Austronesian genealogical tree, an elaborated version of which is presented in Figure 6.3. Two of its features are mentioned in §4. The Formosan languages belong, according to Blust (1999), to nine primary Austronesian subgroups, coordinate with each other and with

Malayo-Polynesian. Western Malayo-Polynesian languages belong to 20–25 Malayo-Polynesian groups, coordinate with each other and with Central/Eastern Malayo-Polynesian. A third feature of the elaborated tree is its presentation of the internal structure of Central/Eastern Malayo-Polynesian, which has received rather piecemeal attention in the literature and to which I return below.

The subgrouping of Formosan languages among themselves remains somewhat problematic. Three alternatives to Blust's proposed nine primary Austronesian subgroups are offered in this volume, one by Peiros (in his Table 7.4), a second by Li, and a third by Sagart. However, if Taiwan is indeed the homeland of Austronesian, then it is to be expected that the subgrouping of its Austronesian languages will be hard to disentangle, since (i) the languages are likely to form primary Austronesian subgroups and (ii) contact over the long period that they have been more or less in their present locations is likely to have obscured the boundaries of these subgroups. There is some agreement among the three proposals about the smallest subgroups, but these are outweighed by complex disagreements about larger groupings, and it is clear that this issue needs much more work.

In both the Formosan and Western Malayo-Polynesian branches of Table 6.4, we are confronted by a number of subgroups all descended from a single protolanguage, the relationships between which are murky. However, this murkiness has different causes in each of the two branches, Whereas the problem of sorting out the internal linguistic history of Austronesian in Taiwan is largely a product of a long period of time *in situ* in a contained area, the parallel problem with regard to Western Malayo-Polynesian languages arose (i) because the region was apparently settled rapidly by Austronesian speakers and (ii) because there have been numerous population movements within this region at different times, resulting in a complex linguistic prehistory (Blust 2006). Despite this complexity, there has been some recent progress in sorting out chunks of western Malayo-Polynesian history. Adelaar (2005) proposes a Malayo-Sumbawan subgroup, based on shared lexical and phonological innovations, that includes Malayic, Chamic and the Balinese-Sasak-Sumbawa group in one branch, and Sundanese and Madurese in two other branches. Malayo-Sumbawan does not include Javanese. This is effectively the first progress on this topic since Nothofer (1975). Blust (2006) concludes that the Sama Bajaw language of the so-called 'sea gypsies' has its origins, like Malagasy, among the Barito languages of south-east Borneo.

At the western extreme of the western Malayo-Polynesian area lies Acehnese. It has long been recognized that this is an Austronesian language containing Austroasiatic elements. Thurgood (1999) argued that Acehnese is a member of the Chamic subgroup of Austronesian, and attributes its presence in western Sumatra to a movement of speakers during the late first millennium AD. Recent work by Sidwell (2005) suggests, however, that it has fewer Austroasiatic elements than the Chamic languages and should be regarded as a primary branch of Aceh-Chamic (in opposition to the Chamic languages) because speakers of the language ancestral to Acehnese became relatively isolated from the rest of Aceh-Chamic in their present location by AD 400 as a result of the extension of influence of the

Funan state from the lower Mekong around the Gulf of Thailand to the Isthmus of Kra.

I move now to Central/Eastern Malayo-Polynesian (CEMP) in the eastern part of the Indo-Malaysian archipelago, which is an innovation-defined subgroup, but only just (Blust 1993). The innovation set is less significant than those which define Malayo-Polynesian and Oceanic, indicating that Proto CEMP speakers spent only a short period as a unified speech community. Proto CEMP underwent no innovations in its sound system relative to Proto Malayo-Polynesian, but all known CEMP languages reflect a reduction of heterorganic consonant sequences arising through reduplication, except where the first consonant was a nasal (*m*, *n*, *ŋ*).[8] For example, Proto Malayo-Polynesian *bukbuk 'wood weevil' became Proto CEMP *bubuk, i.e. the heterorganic Proto Malayo-Polynesian sequence *kb was reduced to Proto CEMP *b. There were also a number of irregular changes to single words. For example, Proto Malayo-Polynesian *maRi 'come' became Proto CEMP *mai. As a result of crossing the Wallace Line, Proto CEMP speakers acquired words for marsupials (Blust 1982). CEMP languages also underwent quite radical grammatical changes, but these are more readily attributed to widespread metatypy due to contact with now lost non-Austronesian languages than to changes which occurred in Proto CEMP (this is an area which needs more research).

Central Malayo-Polynesian languages form an innovation-linked group, i.e. there was never a Proto Central Malayo-Polynesian (Blust 1993). Instead, they are simply what was left of the CEMP group after the communities ancestral to Proto South Halmahera/West New Guinea (SHWNG) and Proto Oceanic had separated from it.

If there was ever a Proto Eastern Malayo-Polynesian speaking speech community, its existence was even more fleeting than that of Proto CEMP. Evidence for the Eastern Malayo-Polynesian grouping consists of putative innovations in vocabulary (Blust 1978 gives 56), but some of these may prove to be inherited words.

The two putative daughters of Proto Eastern Malayo-Polynesian, which may actually have been daughters of Proto CEMP, were Proto SHWNG and Proto Oceanic. Each is a subgroup defined by a clear set of sound changes (for SHWNG, see Ross 1995) and in the case of Oceanic by other kinds of innovation too. Oceanic is the most clearly defined of all Austronesian subgroups, first established by Dempwolff (1937). The innovation set has since undergone modifications and additions which have strengthened it. Summaries are given by Ross (1995, 1998) and Lynch *et al.* (2002: ch. 4).

What is the point of elaborating Blust's tree in Figure 6.1 in this way? First, because Figure 6.3 is in various respects a more accurate presentation of the dispersal of Austronesian speakers. Second, because it tells us something about the speed of the Austronesian dispersal. We may infer that where a subgroup is well defined by innovations, its speakers spent a period of time as a unified speech community, during which the innovations in their speech occurred. This is true of Proto Malayo-Polynesian, Proto SHWNG and Proto Oceanic (further east it is also true of Proto Polynesian and Proto Nuclear Polynesian). The CEMP and Eastern Malayo-Polynesian nodes in Blust's tree are much less well defined, however, suggesting that the putative Proto CEMP and Proto Eastern Malayo-Polynesian speech communities each remained a unity only for a short time (and the latter perhaps not at all).

These findings accord with the archaeological record, which indicates that Malayo-Polynesian speakers dispersed at some speed from the northern Philippines southwards into the Indo-Malaysian archipelago and eastwards to New Guinea and the Bismarck Archipelago. According to Bellwood and Hiscock (2005), they settled this region in about nine centuries, between 2300 and 1400 BC. The speed of settlement is attested by the fact that CEMP and Eastern Malayo-Polynesian are tiny blips in the rapid eastward progress of Austronesian speakers. No significant lengths of time were spent in one place by speakers ancestral to the CEMP languages until they reached New Guinea, where the excellent definition of the Oceanic subgroup indicates that the Proto Oceanic speech community remained integrated for some time, a fact which correlates with the efflorescence of the Lapita Culture in north-west Melanesia from about 1400 BC (Kirch 1997; Ross et al. 1998, 2002).

Notes

1 We need to be assiduous in this task. It happens that the languages of the South Halmahera/West New Guinea group, the 'sibling' of Oceanic, also exhibit a merger of the consonants ancestral to Proto Oceanic *l and *r.
2 Wolff (2006) indicates that he now accepts the Malayo-Polynesian hypothesis and has abandoned the Formosan-Philippine hypothesis.
3 Interestingly, Hurles (2002) offers an alternative explanation of the genetic data used by Oppenheimer and Richards. The alternative account accords well with the Malayo-Polynesian hypothesis.
4 *N is written as *L by some scholars.
5 They have also merged in certain Formosan languages (Blust 1999), but these languages do not share in the other Malayo-Polynesian innovations, and so it is inferred that the merger occurred separately in these languages and in Proto Malayo-Polynesian.
6 Ross (1992) includes a critique of Peiros (n.d.) which also applies to Peiros (1994).
7 Peiros (this volume) also offers a lexicostatistical classification supporting a Formosan subgroup. I have strong methodological objections to lexicostatistics, but these lie beyond the scope of this chapter. Setting these aside, however, it should be noted that Peiros does not clarify the position of non-Formosan languages in relation to his Formosan subgroup, i.e. he does not show that they form a separate lexicostatistically documented subgroup. Thus his lexicostatistics do not support a hypothesis different from Blust's or Sagart's.
8 'Heterorganic' means 'articulated at different points in the mouth'. For example, p, b and m are labial, t, d, n and r are apical (pronounced with the point of the tongue), k, g and $ŋ$ are velar (pronounced with the back of the tongue).

References

Adelaar, A. (2005) 'Malayo-Sumbawan', *Oceanic Linguistics*, 44: 357–88.
Bakker, P., and Mous, M. (eds) (1994) *Mixed Languages: Fifteen Case Studies in Language Intertwining* (Studies in Language and Language Use, 13), Amsterdam: Institute for Functional Research into Language and Language Use (IFOTT).
Bellwood, P. and Hiscock, P. (2005) 'Australia and the Austronesians', in C. Scarre (ed.) *The Human Past*, London: Thames & Hudson, pp. 264–305.
Benedict, P.K. (1942) 'Thai, Kadai and Indonesian: a new alignment in southeastern Asia', *American Anthropologist*, 44: 576–601.
Benedict, P.K. (1975) *Austro-Thai Language and Culture: With a Glossary of Roots*, New Haven, CT: HRAF Press.
Biggs, B.G. (1971) 'The languages of Polynesia', in T.A. Sebeok (ed.) *Current Trends in Linguistics*, vol. 8, pp. 466–505, The Hague: Mouton.
Blust, R.A. (1977) 'The Proto-Austronesian pronouns and Austronesian subgrouping: a preliminary report', *University of Hawaii Working Papers in Linguistics*, 9(2): 1–15.
Blust, R.A. (1978) 'Eastern Malayo-Polynesian: Aa subgrouping argument', in S.A. Wurm and L. Carrington (eds) *Second International Conference on Austronesian Linguistics: Proceedings*, pp. 181–234, Canberra: Pacific Linguistics.
Blust, R.A. (1982) 'The linguistic value of the Wallace line', *Bijdragen tot de Taal-, Land- en Volkenkunde*, 138: 231–50.
Blust, R.A. (1983) 'More on the position of the languages of eastern Indonesia', *Oceanic Linguistics*, 22–23: 1–28.
Blust, R.A. (1990) 'Patterns of sound change in the Austronesian languages', in P. Baldi (ed.) *Linguistic Change and Reconstruction Methodology*, pp. 231–63, Berlin: Mouton de Gruyter.
Blust, R.A. (1993) 'Central and Central-Eastern Malayo-Polynesian', *Oceanic Linguistics*, 32: 241–93.
Blust, R.A. (1999) 'Subgrouping, circularity and extinction: Some issues in Austronesian comparative linguistics', in E. Zeitoun and P.J.-K. Li (eds) *Selected Papers from the Eighth International Conference on Austronesian Linguistics* (Symposium Series of the Institute of Linguistics (Preparatory Office), Academia Sinica, 1), pp. 31–94, Taipei: Academia Sinica.
Blust, R.A. (2006) 'The linguistic macrohistory of the Philippines: some speculations', in H.-c. Liao and C.R. Galvez Rubino (eds) *Current Issues in Philippine Linguistics and Anthropology: Parangal kay Lawrence A. Reid*, pp. 31–68, Manila: Linguistic Society of the Philippines and SIL Philippines.
Capell, A. (1943) *The Linguistic Position of South-Eastern Papua*, Sydney: Australasian Medical Publishing Co.
Dahl, O.C. (1973) *Proto-Austronesian*, Oslo: Studentlitteratur.
Dempwolff, O. (1937) *Vergleichende Lautlehre des Austronesischen Wortschatzes* (Beihefte zur Zeitschrift für Eingeborenen-Sprachen, 2), Berlin: Dietrich Reimer.
Dixon, R.M.W. (1997) *The Rise and Fall of Languages*, Cambridge: Cambridge University Press.
Dyen, I. (1995) 'Borrowing and inheritance in Austronesianistics', in P.J.-K. Li, D.-A. Ho, Y.-K. Huang, C.-H. Tsang and C.-Y. Tseng (eds) *Austronesian Studies Relating to Taiwan* (Symposium Series of the Institute of Linguistics (Preparatory Office), Academia Sinica, 4), pp. 455–519, Taipei: Institute of History and Philology, Academia Sinica.

Geraghty, P. (1983) *The History of the Fijian Languages* (Oceanic Linguistics special publication), Honolulu, HI: University of Hawaii Press.

Hurles, M. (2002) 'Can the hypothesis of language/agriculture co-dispersal be tested with archaeogenetics?', in P. Bellwood and C. Renfrew (eds) *Examining the Farming/ Language Dispersal Hypothesis*, pp. 299–310, Cambridge: McDonald Institute of Archaeological Research.

Kirch, P.V. (1997) *The Lapita Peoples: Ancestors of the Oceanic World*, Oxford: Blackwell.

Laycock, D.C. (1973) 'Sissano, Warapu, and Melanesian pidginization', *Oceanic Linguistics*, 12: 245–78.

Lynch, J., Ross, M.D. and Crowley, T. (2002) *The Oceanic Languages*, Richmond: Curzon Press.

Meacham, W. (1984) 'On the improbability of Austronesian origins in South China', *Asian Perspectives*, 26: 89–106.

Nothofer, B. (1975), *The Reconstruction of Proto-Malayo-Javanic*, The Hague: Martinus Nijhoff.

Oppenheimer, S.J. and Richards, M. (2001) 'Slow boat to Melanesia?', *Nature*, 410: 166–7.

Oppenheimer, S.J. and Richards, M. (2002) 'Polynesians: devolved Taiwanese rice farmers or Wallacean maritime traders with fishing, foraging and horticultural skills?', in P. Bellwood and C. Renfrew (eds) *Examining the Farming/Language Dispersal Hypothesis*, pp. 287–97, Cambridge: McDonald Institute of Archaeological Research.

Ostapirat, W. (2005) 'Kra-Dai and Austronesian: Notes on phonological correspondences and vocabulary distrubution', in L. Sagart, R.M. Blench and A. Sanchez-Mazas (eds) *The Peopling of East Asia: Putting Together Archaeology, Linguistics and Genetics*, pp. 107–31, London: RoutledgeCurzon.

Pawley, A.K. (1966) 'Polynesian languages: a subgrouping based on shared innovations in morphology', *Journal of the Polynesian Society*, 75: 39–64.

Pawley, A.K. (1967) 'The relationships of Polynesian outlier languages', *Journal of the Polynesian Society*, 76: 259–96.

Pawley, A.K. (2002) 'The Austronesian dispersal: languages, technologies and people', in P. Bellwood and R. Renfrew (eds) *Examining the Farming/Language Dispersal Hypothesis*, pp. 251–73, Cambridge: MacDonald Institute for Archaeological Research, University of Cambridge.

Pawley, A.K. and Ross, M.D. (1995) 'The prehistory of Oceanic languages: a current view', in P.S. Bellwood, J.J., Fox. and D.T. Tryon (eds) *The Austronesians: Historical and Comparative Perspectives*, pp. 39–74, Canberra: Department of Anthropology, Research School of Pacific and Asian Studies, Australian National University.

Peiros, I. (n.d.) 'Nekotorye osobennosti cousskich jazykov Taivanja', unpublished typescript.

Peiros, I. (1994) 'Some problems of Austronesian accent and *t~*C (notes of an outsider)', *Oceanic Linguistics*, 33: 105–26.

Reid, L.A. (1994) 'Unravelling the linguistic histories of Philippine negritos', in T. Dutton and D.T. Tryon (eds) *Language Contact and Change in the Austronesian World*, pp. 443–75, Berlin: Mouton de Gruyter.

Reid, L.A. (1999) 'New linguistic evidence for the Austric hypothesis', in E. Zeitoun and P.J.-K. Li (eds) *Selected Papers from the Eighth International Conference on Austronesian Linguistics* (Symposium Series of the Institute of Linguistics (Preparatory Office), Academia Sinica, 1), pp. 1–30, Taipei: Academia Sinica.

Reid, L.A. (2005) 'The current status of Austric: a review and evaluation of the lexical and morphosyntactic evidence', in L. Sagart, R.M. Blench and A. Sanchez-Mazas (eds) *The Peopling of East Asia: Putting Together Archaeology, Linguistics and Genetics*, pp. 132–60, London: RoutledgeCurzon.

Ross, M.D. (1992) 'The sound of Proto-Austronesian: an outsider's view of the Formosan evidence', *Oceanic Linguistics*, 31: 23-64.

Ross, M.D. (1994) 'Areal phonological features in north central New Ireland', in T. Dutton and D.T. Tryon (eds) *Language Contact and Change in the Austronesian World*, pp. 551–72, Berlin: Mouton de Gruyter.

Ross, M.D. (1995) 'Some current issues in Austronesian linguistics', in D.T. Tryon (ed.) *Comparative Austronesian Dictionary*, vol. 1, pp. 45–120, Berlin: Mouton de Gruyter.

Ross, M.D. (1996) 'Contact-induced change and the comparative method: cases from Papua New Guinea', in M. Durie and M.D. Ross (eds) *The Comparative Method Reviewed: Regularity and Irregularity in Language Change*, pp. 180–217, New York, NY: Oxford University Press.

Ross, M.D. (1998) 'Proto-Oceanic phonology and morphology', in M.D. Ross, A.K. Pawley and M. Osmond (eds) *The Lexicon of Proto Oceanic*, vol. 1, *The Culture and Environment of Ancestral Oceanic Society*, pp. 15–35, Canberra: Pacific Linguistics.

Ross, M.D. (2002) 'The history and transitivity of western Austronesian voice and voice-marking', in F. Wouk and M.D. Ross (eds) *The History and Typology of Western Austronesian Voice Systems*, pp. 17–62, Canberra: Pacific Linguistics.

Ross, M.D. (2003) 'Talking about space: terms of location and direction', in M.D. Ross, A.K. Pawley and M. Osmond (eds) *The Lexicon of Proto Oceanic: The Culture and Environment of Ancestral Oceanic Society*, vol. 2, *The Physical World*, pp. 221–84, Canberra: Pacific Linguistics.

Ross, M.D. (2006) 'Reconstructing the case-marking and personal pronoun systems of Proto Austronesian', in H.Y.-L. Chang, L.M. Huang and D.-A. Ho (eds) *Streams Converging into an Ocean: Festschrift in Honor of Professor Paul Jen-Kuei Li on his 70th Birthday*, pp. 521-564, Taipei: Institute of Linguistics, Academia Sinica.

Ross, M.D., Pawley, A.K. and Osmond, M. (eds) (1998) *The Lexicon of Proto Oceanic*, vol. 1, *The Culture and Environment of Ancestral Oceanic Society*, Canberra: Pacific Linguistics.

Ross, M.D., Pawley, A.K. and Osmond, M. (eds) (2003) *The Lexicon of Proto Oceanic: The Culture and Environment of Ancestral Oceanic Society*, vol. 2, *The Physical World*, Canberra: Pacific Linguistics.

Sagart, L. (1994) 'Old Chinese and Proto-Austronesian evidence for Sino-Austronesian', *Oceanic Linguistics*, 33: 271–308.

Sagart, L. (2004) 'The higher phylogeny of Austronesian and the position of Tai-Kadai', *Oceanic Linguistics*, 43: 411–44.

Sagart, L. (2005a) 'Tai-Kadai as a subgroup of Austronesian', in L. Sagart, R.M. Blench and A. Sanchez-Mazas (eds) *The Peopling of East Asia: Putting Together Archaeology, Linguistics and Genetics*, pp. 161–76, London: RoutledgeCurzon.

Sagart, L. (2005b) 'Sino-Tibetan-Austronesian: an updated and improved argument', in L. Sagart, R.M. Blench and A. Sanchez-Mazas (eds) *The Peopling of East Asia: Putting Together Archaeology, Linguistics and Genetics*, London: RoutledgeCurzon.

Schmidt, W. (1906) *Die Mon-Khmer-Völker: Ein Bindeglied zwischen Völkern Zentralasiens und Austronesiens*, Brunswick: F. Vieweg/Anthropos Institut.

Sidwell, P. (2005) 'Acehnese and the Aceh-Chamic Language Family', in A. Grant and P. Sidwell (eds) *Chamic and Beyond: Studies in Mainland Austronesian Languages*, pp. 211–46, Canberra: Pacific Linguistics.

Solheim II, W. (1996) 'The Nusantao and north–south dispersals', in P. Bellwood (ed.) *The Chiang Mai Papers*, vol. 2, *Bulletin of the Indo-Pacific Prehistory Association*, 15: 101–9.

Thurgood, G. (1999) *From Ancient Cham to Modern Dialects: Two Thousand Years of Language Contact and Change* (Oceanic Linguistics Special Publication, 28), Honolulu, HI: University of Hawai'i Press.

Wolff, J.U. (1995) 'The position of the Austronesian languages of Taiwan within the Austronesian group', in P.J.-K. Li, D.-A. Ho, Y.-K. Huang, C.-H. Tsang and C.-Y. Tseng (eds) *Austronesian Studies Relating to Taiwan* (Symposium Series of the Institute of Linguistics (Preparatory Office), Academia Sinica, 1), pp. 521–83, Taipei: Institute of History and Philology, Academia Sinica.

Wolff, J.U. (2006) 'Are the Malayo-Polynesian languages a subgroup?', paper presented to the 10th International Conference on Austronesian Linguistics, Puerto Princesa City, Philippines.

7 The Formosan language family

Ilia Peiros

It is difficult to overestimate either the role of the Aboriginal languages of Taiwan in Austronesian linguistics or their impact on various models of prehistoric movements in Southeast Asia. Therefore in this paper I will concentrate on two issues:

- whether the Formosan languages form a single genetic subgroup within the Austronesian family or whether they constitute several primary branches of Austronesian;
- whether Taiwan and its languages play a special role in ancient migrations of early Austronesian speakers.

In the literature we find two competing opinions on the first issue. Dyen (1963)[1] suggested that Formosan languages form one group. This view is shared by Tsuchida (1976). A different view is defended by Blust who claims that: 'on the bases of unambiguous evidence of exclusively shared innovations the Formosan languages appear to belong to no fewer than nine primary branches of the Austronesian family' (Blust 1999b: 31).

The exclusive role of Taiwan in ancient Austronesian migrations appears in most modern models proposed both by linguistics and archaeologists (see e.g. Bellwood 1997).

Let us first address the issue of genetic relations between the languages of Taiwan. There are fourteen Formosan languages still spoken on the island. Several of them are nearly extinct, while others are quite vigorous. About the same number of languages is already dead, but preserved to some extent in various records. The spoken languages are as follows.

(1) Atayal and (2) Seediq: a reconstruction of their common proto-language is based on the analysis of five Atayal and four Seediq dialects which was undertaken by Li (1981).

This system (Figure 7.1) is practically identical to the one proposed by Li. The main difference is how we identify the phonetic value of *č, *ǯ and *š. Li has reconstructed them as *c, *g' and *s. Their reflexes in the Atayal dialects have merged basically into š, so it seems reasonable to preserve their palatal feature in the reconstructions.

The Formosan language family   183

*p	*b	*m	*w	
*t	*d	*n	*l	*r
*č	*ǯ		*y	*š
*k	*g	*ŋ		*x
*q				
*ʔ				*h

Figure 7.1 The consonants of Proto-Atayal.

Both languages are represented by good-sized dictionaries (e.g. Egerod 1980/99; Liao 2003; Pecoraro 1977).

(3) A Pazeh dictionary has been recently published by Li and Tsuchida (2001). Major features of Pazeh historical phonology have been investigated by Blust (1999a). This allows us to discuss Pazeh etymologies with more confidence than previously.

(4) Two Saisiyat dialects have been compared by Li (1978). With minor modifications to Li's reconstruction, the Proto-Saisiyat consonant system can be represented as in Figure 7.2.

*p	*b	*m	*w		
*t	*ð	*n	*l	*ϑ	
			*ḷ		
			*y	*š	*ŕ
*k		*ŋ			
*ʔ				*h	

Figure 7.2 The Proto-Saisiyat consonant system.

Li gives about 900 Proto-Saisiyat etymologies, but there is still no dictionary of this language or any of its dialects.

(5) Thao is represented by a good-sized dictionary and a grammar (Blust 2003). An overview of its historical phonology originally published by Blust (1996) is also included in the dictionary, together with a list of Thao words which have Austronesian etymologies.

(6) Five Bunun dialects have been compared by Li (1988). With some minor changes made to specify the phonetic value of the phonemes, the proto-language consonant system is shown in Figure 7.3.

Nearly a thousand Bunun etymologies are listed by Li. There are several Bunun dictionaries (Cheng 1971, Nihira 1983, etc.) containing many additional words.

The well established Tsouic group consists of three languages: (7) Saaroa, (8) Kanakanabu and (9) Tsou. Tsuchida (1976) has identified 30 phonological correspondences between the Tsouic languages and thus 30 proto-phonemes have been reconstructed. Not all of those correspondences seem to be regular (see Table 7.1).

184   Ilia Peiros

*p	*ʔb	*m	*v
*t	*ʔd	*n	*l
			*δ	*š
*k		*ŋ	
*q			
*ʔ			*h
*Ø			

Figure 7.3   The proto-language consonant system of Bunun.

Table 7.1   Some correspondences in the Tsouic group

Tsou	Kanakanabu	Saaroa	
t	c	c	reconstructed as *c1
r	ʔ	r	reconstructed as *l1
Ø	Ø	ʔ	reconstructed as *ʔ4

Each of these reconstructed phonemes is found only in a few examples.

Some other correspondences can be explained away as being environmentally caused (Peiros 1994).

A re-examination of Tsuchida's data has provided me with 20 regular phonological correspondences leading to the reconstruction of Proto-Tsouic consonant system, as in Figure 7.4.

*p	*b	*m	*w	
*t		*n	*r	
*c			*z	*s
	*ʒ́	*ń	*ĺ	*y
*k	*g	*ŋ		
*ʔ				
*Ø				

Figure 7.4   A reconstruction of the Proto-Tsouic consonant system (based on Tsuchida's data). All palatal phonemes have the same reflex as ʒ in Saaroa.

This reconstruction is based on the set of regular correspondences extracted from Tsuchida's book. They are found in Table 7.2. Apart from forms given in Tsuchida (1976), not much is known about Kanakanabu and Saaroa (see, however, Ferrell 1969, Tsuchida 2003). Additional information on Tsou may be found in Tsuchida's contribution to Tryon (1995), as well as in some other publications, but so far, there is no published dictionary of this language.

(10) An analysis of internal relationships of five Rukai dialects by Li (1977) provides us with the reconstruction of Proto-Rukai consonants in Figure 7.5.

Table 7.2 Proto-Tsou consonantal correspondences

Pr.TS	Tsou	Kana	Saa	Tsuchida	Pr.TS	Tsou	Kana	Saa	Tsuchida
*p	p	p	p	*p	*c	c	ć	c, š	*c, *č
*b	f	v	v	*v	*s	s	š, #	š, #	*s, *S, *ϑ
*m	m	m	m	*m	*ʒ́	∅	r	ł	*z
*w	v	∅	∅	*w	*ń	x-x-n	ŋ	ł/n	*ń
*t	t	t	t	*t	*ĺ	k/x	n	ł	*ł
*n	n	n	n	*n	*y	ź/-y	ř/-y	ł/-y	*ž, *y
*k	ʔ	k	k, ∅	*k, *kl	*r	r	r	r	*l
*g	k	k	k	*K	*ř	r	ř	ř	*r
*ŋ	ŋ	ŋ	ŋ	*ŋ	*z	r	c	š	*ř
*ʔ	ʔ, ∅	ʔ	ʔ, ∅	*ʔ1, *ʔ2, *ʔ3	*∅	∅	∅	∅	*∅

*p	*b	*m	*w			
*t	*d	*n	*l	*r	*ϑ	*s
	*ḍ		*ḷ			
*c			*y			
*k	*g	*ŋ				
*ʔ						

Figure 7.5 A reconstruction of Proto-Rukai consonants.

This reconstruction is based on more than 600 lexical comparisons; about 1200 words of the Budai dialect (however, without the stress being marked) are given in Li (1995).

(11) The only source of Kavalan lexicon available to me is the list of forms given by Ferrell (1969).

(12) The primary source for Amis remains the dictionary by Fey (1986). According to the map given in the dictionary, there are four main dialects of this language, but systematic information about their differences is missing.

(13) Six closely related Puyuma dialects have been compared by Ting (1978). The correspondences which connect consonants of these dialects are quite simple, allowing the reconstruction of seventeen proto-consonants.

*p	*b	*m	*v		
*t	*d	*n		*l	*s
*ṭ	*ḍ		*r	*ḷ	
				*y	
*k	*g	*ŋ			

Figure 7.6 The reconstruction of 17 proto-consonants for Puyuma.

186 *Ilia Peiros*

This reconstruction is supported by 700 etymologies listed in Ting's study. Additional information on Puyuma lexicon can be found in a wordlist by Tsuchida (1983) and in the dictionary by Cauquelin (1991).

(14) According to Ferrell (1982: 4) speakers of the various Paiwan dialects easily communicate among themselves. Nevertheless we have a detailed comparison of five dialects supported by approximately 700 etymologies (Ho 1978). Accordingly, the Proto-Paiwan consonantal system is as shown in Figure 7.7.

*p	*b	*m	*v	*w
*t	*d	*n		
	*ḍ		*ḷ	*r
*t́	*d́		*í	
*c			*z	*s
*k	*g	*ŋ		
*q				
*ʔ				

Figure 7.7 The Proto-Paiwan consonantal system.

Two dictionaries of Paiwan (Ferrell 1982; Egli 2002) provide additional information about the lexicon of this language.

Major correspondences between the Formosan systems have been well established (see e.g. Blust 1999b: 43). In slightly modified form they are given in Table 7.3, which is used in a reconstruction of proto-consonants. The reconstruction is given in Table 7.4.

According to Blust, the poorly known Kavalan language preserves the Proto-Austronesian distinction between *l and *r, while in other Formosan languages it is lost. Until more information is available, I prefer to ignore this distinction and reconstruct only *l.

Now let us discuss what has just been reconstructed. Two main interpretations are possible:

(i) This is a modification of the well-known Proto-Austronesian consonant system.
(ii) This is the consonant system of the Proto-Formosan language, i.e. the Formosan languages form a group within the Austronesian family.

According to the comparative method, languages are genetically related if they share the same ancestor, which may be either recorded or reconstructed. All languages with the same ancestor form a language family. The ancestral language of such a family is called its 'proto-language'. The only way to prove that languages are genetically related is to present their common ancestor. This general issue, however, is not a problem for our case, as all Aboriginal languages of Taiwan can be eventually traced back to Proto-Austronesian.

Table 7.3 Phonetic correspondences between the Formosan languages

Proto	*p	*b	*m	*w	*t	*c	*ḍ	*d	*ʒ	*s	*š
Pr. Tsou	*p	*b	*m	*w	*t	*c	*c	*c	*ʒ́	*s	s
Pr. Atayal	*p	*b	*m	*w	*t	*č	*d	*d	*ǯ	*h, *x	*š
Pazeh	p	b	m	w	t̲	s	d	d	ʒ/-t	ʒ	s
Saisiyat	p	b	m	w	t	ɵ	r̓	r̓	δ	h	š
Thao	p	f	m	w	t	ɵ/ɬ	s	s	δ	t	š, #
Pr. Rukai	*p	*b	*m	*v / *a#i	*t	*c	*d	*d	*g/#	*ϑ	*s
Pr. Bunun	*p	*ʔb	*m	*v	*t	*t	*ʔd	*?d	#	*š	*š
Pr. Puyuma	*p	*b	*m	*w	*t	*ṭ	*ḍ, *d	*ḍ, *ḍ	*d, *ḍ	*s	#
Pr. Paiwan	*p	*v	*m	*w	*t́	*c	*ḍ́, *z, *ḍ	*ḍ́, *z, *ḍ	*d	*t	*s

Proto	*l̥	*r	*l	*ń	*n	*k	*g	*ŋ	*q	*h	*y
Pr. Tsou	*r	*r	*y	*ń	*n	*k	*g	*ŋ	*ʔ?	*h	*y
Pr. Atayal	*r	*g	*l	*l	*n	*k		*ŋ	#	#	*z
Pazeh	r	x	l	l	n̲	k	k	*ŋ	*q	*h	*y
Saisiyat	l	ļ.	l	l	n	k		ŋ	#	x	y
Thao	r	ɬ, (h)	δ	δ	n	k		ŋ	?	h	y
Pr. Rukai	*l	*r, *ʔ	*l	*l	*n	*k	*g	*ŋ	q	ʔ (?)	y
Pr. Bunun	#	*l	*n	*n	*n	*k	*k	*ŋ	#	#	*y-*δ-*y
Pr. Puyuma	*l	*r	*l	*l	*n	*k	*g	*ŋ	*q	#	*δ
Pr. Paiwan	*ḷ	*r	*ĺ	*ĺ	*n	*k	*g	*ŋ	*q	(*h)	*y

188   Ilia Peiros

Table 7.4 Reconstructed consonants

*p	*b	*m	*w		
*t	*d	*n	*l		*s
	*ḍ		*ḷ	*r	
*c	*ʒ	*ñ	*y		*š
*k	*g	*ŋ			
*q					
*ʔ					(*h)[a]

Note
a I'm not convinced that it is absolutely necessary to reconstruct *h which is supposed to be the source of h in Saisiyat and x in Pazeh.

It is much more difficult to demonstrate that related languages should be grouped together within a larger family. In some cases we can reconstruct a common ancestor which is not identical to the proto-language of the whole family. Both English and German, for example, are traced back to the reconstructed Proto-Germanic language, which is different from its ancestor, Proto-Indo-European. In other cases linguists tend to justify their groupings using the method of 'shared innovations'. However, I am not aware of any well-proven classification built exclusively on innovations used for better known language families (Indo-European, Altaic, Semitic, etc.).

Table 7.4 (of reconstructed consonants) suggests that using only data from the Formosan languages we can reconstruct a consonant system practically identical to Proto-Austronesian, as reconstructed by Blust (1999b: 34) like in Table 7.5.

Three Proto-Austronesian phonemes, *C, *N and *S, are reconstructed solely on the Formosan evidence. This well-known fact allows us to distinguish two major groups of Austronesian languages: Formosan and non-Formosan with different systems of consonants.

Formosan *l and *š may be traced back to the PAN *N and *S, while the status of *c requires additional discussion. In 1994 I published an article demonstrating that the difference between *t and *c in Tsou is caused by the position of stress (Peiros 1994). After a decade the basic statement remains intact: in Proto-Tsou *t and *c were in a complementary distribution. The choice was conditioned by the stress, reconstructed for this proto-language. Table 7.3 shows that Proto-Tsouic *t and *c have different correspondences in most other Formosan languages. Therefore one may reconstruct both phonemes for the proto-language, where they

Table 7.5 Using Formosan languages to reconstruct a consonant system

Pr.Austronesian	*p	*b	*m	*w	*t	*C	*d	*z	*j	*s	*S
Pr.Formosan	*p	*b	*m	*w	*t	*c	*ḍ	*d	*ʒ	*s	*š

Pr.Austronesian	*l, *r	*R	*N	*ñ	*n	*y	*k	*g	*ŋ	*q	??
Pr.Formosan	*l	*r	*l	*ñ	*n	*y	*k	*g	*ŋ	*q	*ʔ

also should be in complementary distribution, under the conditions similar to those in Proto-Tsou. Thus the split of PAN *t into *t and *C can be seen as a Proto-Formosan innovation. On the other hand, Bunun and Amis have only *t, which may be explained as a later loss of the older distinction. However, another option cannot be ruled out, namely that the *t/*c split has spread across the languages as a local non-genetic feature. In any case, the split of *t and *c took place after the separation of Proto-Formosan from Proto-Austronesian. If this split could be attributed to the proto-language, Proto-Formosan would have its own unique phonological innovation.

The non-Formosan group has two innovations: the losses of *N and *S. These phonemes have been also lost in some Formosan languages: Proto-Tsou doesn't distinguish *s and *S, while Bunun merges *N and *n), but these phonemes definitely should be reconstructed for Proto-Formosan.

Summarizing the phonological discussion, I can say that the existing evidence permits us to divide the Austronesian family into two groups: Formosan and Non-Formosan. The latter has at least two specific innovations, while the former might have none or one, depending on the interpretation of the *t/*c distinction. It is important to emphasize, however, that there are no phonological reasons preventing us from grouping the languages of Taiwan into a single Formosan family.

Can we find such reasons in grammar or lexicon? The general answer is 'no', simply because linguists still do not have a Proto-Austronesian grammar or etymological dictionary representing the whole diversity of the family.

An important piece of evidence in support of the reality of Proto-Formosan comes from lexicostatistics. However, here some general comments have to be made.

Let us take three related languages, A, B and C, with A and B (but not C) belonging to the same sub-family. This means that A and B will have common etymologies inherited either from Proto-ABC or from its daughter-language Proto-AB. Due to permanent changes in the histories of all human languages, Proto-ABC and Proto-AB will not be identical. Since C can share etymologies with A (or B), which can be inherited only from Proto-ABC, the amount of these etymologies is always smaller than that shared by A and B.[2]

A similar statement may be made when we are dealing with the 100-item lexicostatistical Swadesh list. Namely: 'if we know histories of A, B and C, the amount of non-borrowed words with the same etymologies is always higher between A and B'.

Both observations seem to be universal. At last, no contradictory examples can be found in better known language families.

The statement made about the 100-item list is a basic axiom of lexicostatistics, a method not generally accepted in Austronesian studies. Two considerations are used to justify this negative attitude:

(a) the totally unconvincing Austronesian lexicostatistical classification by Dyen (1965) and
(b) Blust's theory of 'various retention rates' in the Austronesian languages.

190   *Ilia Peiros*

An unsuccessful application of the lexicostatistical method by Dyen by no means proves that the method itself is erroneous. It shows only that linguists have to know the linguistic histories used in their lexicostatistical study. Due to the lack of comparative studies, Dyen had to base his etymological decisions on intuition rather than on the solid results of historical phonology. In Dyen's classification one group includes all the languages with better understood histories. The remaining 39 groups are formed by languages without known histories or transparent phonologies. The history of most of those languages still remains unknown.[3] Under such circumstances even the best intuition would generate wrong etymologies leading to a wrong classification. Dyen's etymologies have never been published, so it is impossible to evaluate them.

Two general remarks must be made:

(i) any lexicostatistical study should be based on the results of comparative phonology and etymological studies;
(ii) etymological identifications used for calculations should always be published together with the results of a lexicostatistical analysis.

The second set of arguments against lexicostatistics is provided by Blust, who for a long time has argued that the rates of retention of Proto-Austronesian vocabulary differ considerably among modern Austronesian languages. To demonstrate this statement the author compares 200-item lists of various languages with the lists reconstructed by him for Proto-Austronesian, Proto-Malayo-Polynesian and Proto-Oceanic. Wordlists of individual languages have been compared with those reconstructions and ranked according to their retention rates (Blust 2000: 329). Malay and closely related Iban are the most stable languages (58.0 and 54.3 per cent of retentions), while Asumboa and Kaulong are the least stable (7.2 and 5.2 per cent).

Now, an interesting topic to explore is why there is a correlation between languages listed by Blust as less conservative and major groups in Dyen's lexicostatistical classification. Languages present in both studies are shown in Table 7.6. Could this be a coincidence or is there is a correlation reflecting a deeper similarity between the results?

Table 7.6 Correlation between Blust's less conservative languages and major groups in Dyen's lexicostatistical classification

Language	retention (in %)	Dyen's group
Dehu	9.8	Loyalty (n.25)
Nengone	7.7	Loyalty (n.25)
Zabana	9.9	Zabana (n.39)
Tomoip	10.2	Tomoip (n.31)
Varisi	11.7	Choiseul (n.25)
Ririo	7.5	Choiseul (n.25)

The phenomenon of various retention rates observed by Blust could potentially undermine the whole method of lexicostatistics, so it needs to be thoroughly discussed. Three main questions can be asked:

(i) Have the lists of modern languages been compiled properly?
(ii) Can proto-language lists be used in lexicostatistics?
(iii) Is there any other explanation of the facts noticed by Blust?

It is well-known that the wordlists collected for a lexicostatistical classification (diagnostic lists) have to meet certain requirements. Each diagnostic list must be homogeneous, that is, it must consist of one regional dialect, rather than a combination of forms taken from different dialects. It must also reflect a language spoken in a given period of time. Words in a diagnostic list should always be the main unmarked forms of everyday usage, rather than taboo terms, archaic forms, etc. The words included in diagnostic lists are expected to be the most precise representations of the meanings selected for lexicostatistical analysis. If these requirements are not met, the results of the analysis may be misleading.

Given Blust's extensive experience I have no doubts that the diagnostic lists for modern languages are properly compiled. There is also no doubt that the proto-lists do contain forms which can be reconstructed for the corresponding chronological levels. But how can one demonstrate that these proto-lists are the diagnostic lists required for lexicostatistics? How can one prove that the reconstructed words are 'the main unmarked forms' of a proto-language? How can this be done, when, for example, at least a half of the Oceanic languages are still poorly known?

By comparing proto-lists with diagnostic lists from modern languages we learn only about the role played by modern languages in etymological analysis. Better known languages are used in etymological studies more often than poorly recorded languages or languages with obscure phonological histories. Therefore, it is not surprising that Malay is represented in 58.0 per cent of a reconstructed lexicon, Kaulong only 5.2 per cent.

Table 7.7 Lexicostatistical matrix for Formosan languages

	ATA	PAZ	SAI	THA	BUD	BUN	PUY	PAY	TSO
Atayal	x	37	37	33	25	28	29	30	28
Pazeh	37	x	41	43	27	32	32	35	35
Saisiyat	37	41	x	45	28	35	39	39	36
Thao	33	43	45	x	31	43	42	38	35
Budai	25	27	28	31	x	38	36	41	28
Bunun	28	32	35	43	38	x	38	38	31
Puyuma	29	32	39	42	36	38	x	45	38
Paiwan	30	35	39	38	41	38	45	x	34
Tsou	28	35	35	35	28	31	38	34	x

Lexicostatistical calculations and classification[4] of the Formosan group is shown in Table 7.7 and Plate 7.I.[5] The diagnostic lists of modern languages and the results of their etymological analyses are presented in Appendix I.

Several observations can be made:

(1) The Formosan family is divided into three main branches:[6]
    - Northern: Atayal, Pazeh, Saisiyat and Thao.
    - Central: Tsou
    - Southern: Bunun, Paiwan, Puyuma and Budai.

    This branching clearly reflects modern geographic location of the languages, which, however, may not be the reason for the classification. In my view, it is more likely that closely related languages are still located not far from each other.
(2) No phonological innovations support the branching.
(3) The Formosan family seems to be not very old: it consists of languages which share not less than 29 per cent of common words in a 100-item wordlist. This gives us 4500 BP.

Roughly the same age has been suggested for several well-known families as shown in Table 7.8.[7] It is only 400 years older than Proto-Central Pacific (around 4160 BP, Gell-Mann et al. n.d.) and is roughly contemporary to the split between Proto-Batanic and the rest of the Philippine family (around 4300 BP, Peiros n.d.). At the same time, the Formosan family is significantly younger than Proto-Austronesian, which began to disintegrate not earlier than 7000 years ago.

Table 7.8 Ages suggested for several well-known families

Family	Date
Finno-Ugric	4230 BP
Indo-Iranian	4300 BP
Katu-Bahnaric	4290 BP

The existence of the Formosan family changes major points in the scenario of ancient Austronesian-speaking migrations, which I can describe as follows.

1 About 7000 years ago Proto-Austronesian was spoken somewhere in the coastal areas of modern China. Two sets of arguments support this proposal. (i) The Austronesian languages belong to the Austric macro-family, which includes also Tai-Kadai, Austroasiatic and Miao-Yao families. The homeland of Austric was presumably located somewhere in modern China; this indicates that at least in the earliest period of its development Proto-Austronesian must be spoken on the mainland. (ii) Proto-Austronesian and Proto-Chinese reveal a significant number of common roots which indicate linguistic contacts. These contacts took place on the mainland, as there are no reasons to look for the Proto-Chinese homeland somewhere else. Well-

known lexical reconstructions support the coastal subtropical localization of the Austronesian homeland (see the discussion in Peiros 1998).
2   About 4500 thousand years ago a single group of Austronesians, who spoke Proto-Formosan began to populate Taiwan. Later this proto-language gave rise to all aboriginal languages of the island.
3   That migration to Taiwan had nothing to do with the movements from mainland Southeast Asia to the rest of the Austronesian world.

Notes

1   In a contradiction to his own lexicostatistical classification (1965) which separates Atayal and Eastern Formosan languages.
2   Dealing with borrowings one can expect other situations,
3   Language group A can be called 'known' from historical point of view if:
    (i)   there is a phonological reconstruction of its proto-language describing also histories of individual daughter-languages;
    (ii) means to identify borrowings into its daughter-languages;
    (iii) there is an etymological dictionary of the proto-language. No doubt, information about historical morphology or syntax is also very valuable, but the mentioned conditions are crucial. From this point of view, only a few Austronesian groups can be called 'known'.
4   All calculations are made using STARLING, a software package for comparative linguistics designed by Starostin.
5   Tsuchida gives different results (1976: 7) but without diagnostic lists and etymological identifications.
6   Due to the lack of reliable comparative data Amis and Kavalan are not yet classified.
7   Datings are taken from various databases published in starling.rinet.ru. About modified glottochronology see Starostin 2000

References

Adelaar, A. (2005) 'Austronesian languages of Asia and Madagascar: a historical perspective', in A. Adelaar and N. Himmelmann (eds) *The Austronesian Languages of Asia and Madagascar*, pp. 1–42, London and New York, NY: Routledge.

Bellwood, P. (1997) 'Taiwan and the prehistory of the Austronesian-speaking peoples', *Review of Archaeology*, 18(2): 39–48.

Bender, B., Goodenough, W., Jackson, F., Marck, J., Rehg, K., Sohn, Ho-min, Trussel, S. and Wang, J. (2003) 'Proto-Micronesian reconstructions', *Oceanic Linguistics*, 42(1): 2–110; 42(2): 271–328.

Blust, R. (1995) 'The position of the Formosan languages: methods and theory in Austronesian comparative linguistics', in P. Jen-kuei Li, Ho Dah-an, Huang Ying-kuei, Tsang Cheng-hwa and Tseng Chiu-yu (eds) *Austronesian Studies Relating to Taiwan* (Symposium Series of the Institute of History and Philology, Academia Sinica, 4), pp. 585–650, Taipei: Academia Sinica.

Blust, R. (1996) 'Some remarks on the linguistic position of Thao', *Oceanic Linguistics*, 35(2): 272–94.

Blust, R. (1999a) 'Notes on Pazeh phonology and morphology', *Oceanic Linguistics*, 38(2): 321–65.

Blust, R. (1999b) 'Subgrouping, circularity and extinction: some issues in Austronesian comparative linguistics', in E. Zeitoun and P. Li (eds) *Selected Papers from the Eighth International Conference of Austronesian Linguistics* (Symposium Series of the Institute of Linguistics Prepatory Office), Academia Sinica, 1), pp. 31–94, Taipei: Academia Sinica.

Blust, R. (2000) 'Why lexicostatistics doesn't work: The "universal constant" hypothesis and the Austronesian languages', in C. Renfrew, A. McMahon and L. Trask (eds) *Time Depth in Historical Linguistics*, vol. 2, pp. 311–32, Cambridge: McDonald Institute for Archaeological Research.

Blust, R. (2003) *Thao Ddictionary*, Taipei: Academia Sinica, Institute of Linguistics (Preparatory Office).

Cauquelin, J. (1991) *Dictionnaire Puyuma–Français*, Paris and Jakarta: École Française d'Extrême-Orient.

Cheng, Heng-hsiung (1971) *A Bunun–English Dictionary*, Taipei: no publ.

Dyen, I. (1963) 'The position of the Malayo-Polynesian languages of Formosa', *Asian Perspectives*, 7(1–2): 261–71.

Dyen, I. (1965) *A Lexicostatistical Classification of the Austronesian Languages*, Supplement to *International Journal of American Linguistics*, 31(1), Baltimore, MD: Waverly Press.

Egerod, S. (1980) *Atayal–English Dictionary*, London: Curzon Press (2nd edn 1999).

Egli, H. (2002) *Paiwan Wörterbuch*, Wiesbaden: Harrassowitz Verlag.

Ferrell, R. (1969) *Taiwan Aboriginal Groups: Problems in Cultural and Linguistic Classification* (Institute of Ethnology, Academia Sinica, 17), Taipei: Academia Sinica.

Ferrell, R. (1982) *Paiwan Dictionary*, Canberra: Pacific Linguistics, C-73.

Fey, V. (1986) *Amis Dictionary*, Taipei: Evangelical Alliance Mission.

Gell-Mann, M., Starostin, S. and Peiros I. (n.d.) 'Lexicostatistics compared with shared innovations: the Polynesian case', MS.

Ho, Dah-an (1978) 'A preliminary comparative study of five Paiwan dialects', *Bulletin of the Institute of History and Philology*, 49(4): 565–681.

Li, Paul Jen-kuei (1977) 'The internal relationship of Rukai', *Bulletin of the Institute of History and Philology*, 48(1): 1–92.

Li, Paul Jen-kuei (1978) 'A comparative vocabulary of Saisiyat dialects', *Bulletin of the Institute of History and Philology*, 49(2): 133–99.

Li, Paul Jen-kuei (1981) 'Reconstruction of Proto-Atayalic phonology', *Bulletin of the Institute of History and Philology*, 52(2): 235–301.

Li, Paul Jen-kuei (1988) 'A comparative study of Bunun dialects', *Bulletin of the Institute of History and Philology*, 59(2): 479–508.

Li, Paul Jen-kuei (1995) 'Rukai list', in Tryon *et al*. (eds).

Li, Paul Jen-kuei, and Tsuchida, S. (2001) *Pazih Dictionary*, Taipei: Academia Sinica, Institute of Linguistics (Preparatory Office).

Liao, Yingzhu (2003) *Atayal–English Dictionary*, 2 vols, Nantou Shi: Liao Yingzhu.

Nihira, Y. (1983) *A Bunun Dictionary*, Private publication.

Pecoraro, F. (1977) *Essai de dictionnaire taroko-frangçais*, Paris: SECMI.

Peiros, I. (1994) 'Some problems of Austronesian accent and *t~*C (notes of an outsider)', *Oceanic Linguistics*, 33(1): 105–26.

Perios, I. (1998) *Comparative Linguistics in Southeast Asia*, Canberra: Pacific Linguistics, Series C-142.

Peiros, I. (2000) 'Family diversity and time depth', in C. Renfrew, A. McMahon and L. Trask (eds) *Time Depth in Historical Linguistics*, vol. 1, pp. 75–108, Cambridge: McDonald Institute for Archaeological Research.

Peiros, I. (n.d.) 'Lexicostatistical classification of Philippines and beyond', MS.

Starostin, S. (2000) 'Comparative-historical linguistics and lexicostatistics', in C. Renfrew, A. McMahon and L. Trask (eds) *Time Depth in Historical Linguistics*, vol. 2, pp. 223–59, Cambridge: McDonald Institute for Archaeological Research.

Ting, Pang-hsin (1978) 'Reconstruction of Proto-Puyuma phonology', *Bulletin of the Institute of History and Philology*, 49(3): 321–92.

Tryon, D. (ed.) (1995) *Comparative Austronesian Dictionary: An Introduction to Austronesian Studies*, 5 vols, Berlin: Mouton de Gruyter.

Tsuchida, S. (1976) *Reconstruction of Proto-Tsouic Phonology* (Study of Languages and Cultures of Asia and Africa Monograph Series, 5), Tokyo: Institute for the Study of Languages and Cultures of Asia and Africa.

Tsuchida, S. (1983) 'Puyuma-English Index (Austronesian languages of Taiwan)', *Working Papers in Linguistics*, Tokyo: Department of Linguistics, University of Tokyo.

Tsuchida, S. (1995) 'Tsou', in Tryon (ed.) *Comparative Austronesian Dictionary: An Introduction to Austronesian Studies*, 5 vols, Berlin: Mouton de Gruyter.

Tsuchida, S. (2003) *Kanakanavu Texts (Austronesian Formsan)*, Osaka: Endangered Languages of the Pacific Rim.

Zeitoun, E., and Li, P. (eds) (1999) *Selected Papers from the Eighth International Conference of Austronesian Linguistics* (Symposium Series of the Institute of History and Philology, Academia Sinica, 33), Taipei: Academia Sinica.

Appendix I

Lexicostatistical lists for Formosan languages

Note: Etymological identifications are marked by identical numbers; borrowed items are marked by negative numbers; missing items are marked as --.

1 all

Atayal : --;
Pazeh : dadua (3);
Saisiyat : sabəh (427);
Thao : ʔaz=ʔaz (2);
Rukai : dəmə-dəmə (1);
Bunun : mal=toos (4);
Tsou : --;
Puyuma : pəniya (450);
Paiwan : pənulat (426).

2 ashes

Atayal : qabu-łiʔ (5);
Pazeh : abu (5);
Saisiyat : ʔäboʔ (5);
Thao : qafu (5);
Rukai : abo (5);
Bunun : qabu (5);
Tsou : fuu (5);
Puyuma : ʔabu (5);
Paiwan : qavu (5).
<> 5: *qabu.

3 bark

Atayal : qałiʔ (6);
Pazeh : rapay (427);
Saisiyat : toḷak (428);
Thao : --;
Rukai : bakoro (8);
Bunun : kal=kal (508);
Tsou : raptɨ (9);
Puyuma : kuliṭ (738);
Paiwan : qaḷic (6).
<> 6: *qalic.

4 belly

Atayal : na-buwas (45);
Pazeh : tian (10);
Saisiyat : tial (10);
Thao : ti:yaδ (10);
Rukai : baraŋə (430);
Bunun : tian (10);
Tsou : cfuo (499);
Puyuma : tial (10);
Paiwan : tial (10).
<> 10: *ti[]al.

5 big

Atayal : rahuwał (547);
Pazeh : ma-taru (15);
Saisiyat : θobaḷöh (431);
Thao : ma-ra'in (-1);
Rukai : ma:-ḍaw (201);
Bunun : ma-daiŋ (16);
Tsou : mro-isi (12);
Puyuma : maʔiḍaŋ (16);
Paiwan : kuḍaḷ (11).
<> Thao < Bunun (Blust 1996, 292).

6 bird

Atayal : kaBah-niq (17);
Pazeh : ayam (18);
Saisiyat : kab=kabähäḷ (17);
Thao : rumfaz (19);
Rukai : aδa-δamə (18);
Bunun : qazam (18);
Tsou : zomɨ (18);
Puyuma : ʔayam (18);
Paiwan : qaya-qayam (18).
<> 17: *kabas; 18: *qayam.

7 bite
Atayal : k-um-aat (20);
Pazeh : mu-ŋazip (23);
Saisiyat : k<om>ala ϑ (20);
Thao : q-m-irqir (21);
Rukai : wa-kaacə (20);
Bunun : kalat (20);
Tsou : b-orci̵ (20);
Puyuma : k<əm>araṭ (20);
Paiwan : k-əm-ac (20).
<> 20: *karac.

8 black
Atayal : ma-ɣaɫawaʔ (24);
Pazeh : terehen, terehel (28);
Saisiyat : ʔəlŋih-an (432);
Thao : ma-qusum (27);
Rukai : ma-icə̣lə̣ŋə (26);
Bunun : ma-taqduŋ (29);
Tsou : kuaʔoŋ-a (25);
Puyuma : ʔudədəm (27);
Paiwan : kə-cəŋə-cəŋəḷ (26).
<> 26: *təŋəl; 27: *-dəm.

9 blood
Atayal : ramu:x (30);
Pazeh : damu (30);
Saisiyat : ramoʔ (30);
Thao : taɫum (30);
Rukai : əray (31);
Bunun : qaidaŋ (33);
Tsou : xmuru (30);
Puyuma : ḍamuk (30);
Paiwan : ḍamuq (30).
<> 30: *damu-; Blust (1995: 595ff) treats this word as a borrowing.

10 bone
Atayal : baqniʔ (37);
Pazeh : bul (37);
Saisiyat : bəʔəl (37);
Thao : puqu (36);
Rukai : coolalə (35);
Bunun : tuqunaz (35);
Tsou : ci̵rxi̵ (35);
Puyuma : ukak (433);
Paiwan : cuqəḷaḷ (35).
<> 37: *bəqəN / *baqən; 433: *ʔukak.

11 breast
Atayal : xuxuʔ (39);
Pazeh : nunuh (40);
Saisiyat : höhöʔ (39);
Thao : tutu (39);
Rukai : ϑuϑu (39);
Bunun : susu (39);
Tsou : nunʔu (40);
Puyuma : susu (39);
Paiwan : tutu (39).
<> 39: *su-su; 40: *nuq-nuq.

12 burn tr.
Atayal : ši-čuɫiŋ (41);
Pazeh : anat- (46);
Saisiyat : ϑ<om>ähöʔ (486);
Thao : šu-naraʔ (745);
Rukai : wa-laobo (43);
Bunun : pis-taba (38);
Tsou : max- (42);
Puyuma : purḅu (434);
Paiwan : muḍək (44).
<> 745: *nala.

13 claw (nail)
Atayal : ka-kamiɫ (55);
Pazeh : kalikux (49);
Saisiyat : kakloköh (49);
Thao : kuku (49);
Rukai : k=al=əsəkəs=anə (49);
Bunun : kus=kus (49);
Tsou : xuʔo (937);
Puyuma : skiʔ (49);
Paiwan : kalusəkusan (49).
<> 49: *kuš / *kus.

14 cloud

Atayal : hamhum (51);
Pazeh : buruŋ (54);
Saisiyat : ḷəm=ḷəm (51);
Thao : urum (51);
Rukai : əmə:=mə (51);
Bunun : luhum (51);
Tsou : --;
Puyuma : kuṭəm (435);
Paiwan : qərəpus (52).
<> 51: *-rəm / *-ləm (Atayal etymology is not quite reliable).

15 cold

Atayal : tlaʔ=tuʔ (56);
Pazeh : peŋet (57);
Saisiyat : ʔiyäḷaðaw (58);
Thao : ma-šimzaw (58);
Rukai : maŋaŋərəcə (921);
Bunun : kanqav (58);
Tsou : --;
Puyuma : taliŋ=tiŋ (436);
Paiwan : vəcəḷəl (48).
<> 58: *-ʒaw.

16 come

Atayal : mwah (59);
Pazeh : puzah- (64);
Saisiyat : waḷiʔ (59);
Thao : mu-nay (63);
Rukai : wa-kəla (923);
Bunun : mun-iti (63);
Tsou : uso (60);
Puyuma : alamu (63);
Paiwan : idu (62).
<> 59: *wa-; 60: *kuša; 63: *mu-.

17 die

Atayal : minuqiɬ (67);
Pazeh : puriahat, purihat (69);
Saisiyat : maϑay (68);
Thao : m-acay (68);
Rukai : wa-pacay (68);
Bunun : m-ataz (68);
Tsou : mcoi (68);
Puyuma : m<in>aṭay (68);
Paiwan : macay (68).
<> 68: *-acay.

18 dog

Atayal : xuyiɬ (73);
Pazeh : wazu < *wasu (73);
Saisiyat : ʔähöʔ (73);
Thao : atu < *(w)asu (73);
Rukai : tawpuŋo (72);
Bunun : asu (73);
Tsou : avʔu (71);
Puyuma : suan (73);
Paiwan : vatu (73).
<> 73: *wasu / *ʔasu.

19 drink

Atayal : m-nubu-a-ɣ (74);
Pazeh : daux- (79);
Saisiyat : ž<om>äʔöḷ (79);
Thao : mi-qiɬa (78);
Rukai : wa-oŋolo (76);
Bunun : qod; qud (79);
Tsou : m-imo (75);
Puyuma : ṭ<əm>kəḷ (-77);
Paiwan : t-əm-əkəḷ (77).
<> 75: *ʔima-; 79: *daquR / *ruqud; Puyuma for is a Paiwan borrowing (Blust 1999).

20 dry

Atayal : ma-rŋuʔ (81);
Pazeh : ma-katit (83);
Saisiyat : ʔäḷ=ʔäḷiw (84);
Thao : qaɬiw (84);
Rukai : ma-məalə (82);
Bunun : qazav (84);
Tsou : ormiʔmi (80);
Puyuma : marum (80);
Paiwan : mətad (83).
<> 80: *ʔarəm; 83: *-taʒ / *tiʒ; 84: *qariw / *qayaw.

21 ear
Atayal : čaŋia? (87);
Pazeh : saŋira (87);
Saisiyat : ϑali?il̥ (87);
Thao : ł̣arina (87);
Rukai : cal̥iŋ (87);
Bunun : taiŋa (87);
Tsou : koru (22);
Puyuma : ṭaŋil̥a (87);
Paiwan : cal̥iŋa (87).
<> 87: *caliŋa.

22 earth
Atayal : rauq (88);
Pazeh : daxe (88);
Saisiyat : žal̥i? (88);
Thao : pruq (90);
Rukai : daə (88);
Bunun : dalaq (88);
Tsou : croa (88);
Puyuma : darə? (88);
Paiwan : qipo (89).
<> 88: *darəq.

23 eat
Atayal : m=an=iq (91);
Pazeh : ken (91);
Saisiyat : ϑ<om>i?əl (440);
Thao : k-m-an (91);
Rukai : wa-kanə (91);
Bunun : ka?un (91);
Tsou : b-onə (91);
Puyuma : məkan (91);
Paiwan : k-əm-an (91).
<> 91: *kan / *ka[]ən.

24 egg
Atayal : batu? (355);
Pazeh : batu (355);
Saisiyat : ?öϑiδol̥ (93);
Thao : qaricuy (93);
Rukai : batoko (355);

Bunun : laobun (425);
Tsou : fcuru (93);
Puyuma : biṭunun (93);
Paiwan : qəcil̥u (93).
<> 93:*qacəl̥u-.

25 eye
Atayal : rawiq (94);
Pazeh : daurik (-94);
Saisiyat : maϑa? (95);
Thao : maca (95);
Rukai : máca (95);
Bunun : mata (95);
Tsou : mco: (95);
Puyuma : maṭa (95);
Paiwan : maca (95).
<> 95: *maca; Pazeh form is an Atayal borrowing (Blust 1995: 337).

26 fat n.
Atayal : qnu? (98);
Pazeh : selem (97);
Saisiyat : šimal̥ (97);
Thao : ł̣imaš (97);
Rukai : simaa (97);
Bunun : simal (97);
Tsou : simro (97);
Puyuma : --;
Paiwan : qal̥um (47).
<> *šimar

27 feather
Atayal : pał̇i? (100);
Pazeh : bekes (143);
Saisiyat : ?öl̥oböh (443);
Thao : kupur (103);
Rukai : l̥omo (102);
Bunun : --;
Tsou : ropŋu (101);
Puyuma : guṃul (442);
Paiwan : pal̥al (924).

28 fire

Atayal : hapuniq, hapuy (106);
Pazeh : hapuy (106);
Saisiyat : hapoy (106);
Thao : apuy (106);
Rukai : apoy (106);
Bunun : sapuz (106);
Tsou : puzu (106);
Puyuma : apuy (106);
Paiwan : sapoi (106).
<> 106: *šapuy / *hapuy

29 fish

Atayal : quɬih (107);
Pazeh : alaw (407);
Saisiyat : ʔälaw (407);
Thao : ruṣaw (925);
Rukai : káaŋ (109);
Bunun : iskan (112);
Tsou : roskɨ (108);
Puyuma : kuraw (926);
Paiwan : ciqaw (110).
<> 407: *ʔalaw; 110: *ciqaw

30 fly v.

Atayal : man-bahaɣ (113);
Pazeh : bahar- (-113);
Saisiyat : l<om>ayap (116);
Thao : marfaẓ (113);
Rukai : ŋi-a-palay (116);
Bunun : kusbat (117);
Tsou : tor-soso (114);
Puyuma : mubiʔi (444);
Paiwan : miŋ-layap (116).
<> 116: *layap; Pazeh form is a borrowing from Atayal (Blust 1999).

31 foot

Atayal : kukuy (118);
Pazeh : karaw (120);
Saisiyat : žapal (119);
Thao : kuskuṣ (121);
Rukai : ḍapalə (119);
Bunun : bantas (122);
Tsou : capxə (119);
Puyuma : dapal (119);
Paiwan : kuḷa (120).
<> 119: *ḍapaN; 120: *kula / *kalaw.

32 full

Atayal : ma-tŋiʔ (123);
Pazeh : bini- (128);
Saisiyat : mayhaʔ=haʔ (247);
Thao : puniš (127);
Rukai : so-a-ətə (125);
Bunun : tmuz (445);
Tsou : ŋaŋcɨ=cŋɨ (124);
Puyuma : matəmuy (445);
Paiwan : ma-pəluq (126).
<> 445: *təmuy / *tuməš.

33 give

Atayal : muay (129);
Pazeh : mu-baxa (129);
Saisiyat : bəlay (129);
Thao : anạ (131);
Rukai : baay (129);
Bunun : suno (105);
Tsou : mo-fi (129);
Puyuma : bəray (129);
Paiwan : pa-vai (129).
<> 129: *bəray.

34 good

Atayal : baɬa-iq (132);
Pazeh : riak (137);
Saisiyat : kayðäh (447);
Thao : qitan (136);
Rukai : ma-ϑarili (134);
Bunun : sihal (392);
Tsou : ɨmnɨ (133);
Puyuma : ʔinaba (446);
Paiwan : na-ŋuaq (135).

35 green
Atayal : ma-wašiq (138);
Pazeh : turulix (142);
Saisiyat : ləϑʔiδ (448);
Thao : δišlum (141);
Rukai : saləəsəsə (916);
Bunun : ma-saŋlav (139);
Tsou : reŋxov-a (139);
Puyuma : --;
Paiwan : qə-ĺəŋə-ĺəŋəq (139).
<> 139: *ŋVlaw.

36 hair
Atayal : ʔaBaɣ (181);
Pazeh : bekes (143);
Saisiyat : bokəš (143);
Thao : fukish (143);
Rukai : isiw (14);
Bunun : qulbu (146);
Tsou : fʔisɨ (143);
Puyuma : ʔarbu (146);
Paiwan : ŋis=ŋis (145).
<> 143: *bukəš; 146: *-rVbu.

37 hand
Atayal : qabaʔ (148);
Pazeh : rima (147);
Saisiyat : ḷima (147);
Thao : rima (147);
Rukai : aḷima (147);
Bunun : ima (147);
Tsou : mucu (149);
Puyuma : ḷimaʔ (147);
Paiwan : ḷima (147).
<> 147: *ḷima; 149: *ramuc.

38 head
Atayal : tunux (151);
Pazeh : punu (153);
Saisiyat : taʔölöh (927);
Thao : puṇuq (153);
Rukai : aoḷo (152);
Bunun : buŋu (150);
Tsou : fŋu: (150);
Puyuma : taŋuruʔ (449);
Paiwan : quḷu (152).
<> 150: *buŋuh; 152: *qulu-; 153: *punu-; 449: *taŋur / *taŋar.

39 hear
Atayal : muŋ (154);
Pazeh : tumala (158);
Saisiyat : bažäʔ (179);
Thao : t-in-maδa (158);
Rukai : ki-laḷa (156);
Bunun : taʔaza (-158);
Tsou : --;
Puyuma : kilŋaw (157);
Paiwan : ki-ḷaŋ=da (-157).
<> Bunun form is a borrowing from Thao (Blust 1996); Paiwan form is a borrowing from Puyuma (Blust 1999a).

40 heart
Atayal : qaqariyat (159);
Pazeh : babu (639);
Saisiyat : ʔäḷoʔ (453);
Thao : šnaw̩ (185);
Rukai : avaava (928);
Bunun : qumun (509);
Tsou : tʔuxu (160);
Puyuma : mardudu (452);
Paiwan : qavuvuŋ (162).

41 horn
Atayal : taŋuqiy (165);
Pazeh : uxuŋ (165);
Saisiyat : kähʔöŋ (165);
Thao : --;
Rukai : laoŋo (165);
Bunun : vaqa (510);
Tsou : suŋu (165);
Puyuma : suʔaŋ (165);
Paiwan : təquŋ (165).
<> 165: *səquŋ /*qəsuŋ.

42 I

Atayal : ʔi-kuiŋ (167);
Pazeh : aku (167);
Saisiyat : yako (167);
Thao : yaku < *i-aku (167);
Rukai : ko-akó (167);
Bunun : sak (167);
Tsou : aʔo (167);
Puyuma : ku (167);
Paiwan : tiakən (167).
<> 167: *i-aku.

43 kill

Atayal : t-um-utiŋ (169);
Pazeh : tahay (68);
Saisiyat : t<om>bok (248);
Thao : ka-m-p-acay (68);
Rukai : paa-pacay (68);
Bunun : ma-pataz (68);
Tsou : opcoi (68);
Puyuma : p<in>aṭay (68);
Paiwan : q<əm>ci (68).
<> 68 = 'die'.

44 knee

Atayal : tariʔ (65);
Pazeh : ilas (174);
Saisiyat : pöʔöʔ (455);
Thao : qaruf (173);
Rukai : pacoḷo (171);
Bunun : --;
Tsou : kaʔli (170);
Puyuma : suŋaḷ (-172);
Paiwan : cuŋaḷ (172).
<> Puyuma form is a borrowing from Paiwan (Blust 1999a).

45 know

Atayal : Baq-un (179);
Pazeh : baza- (179);
Saisiyat : žaḷam (456);
Thao : faðaq (179);
Rukai : ϑiŋalə (177);
Bunun : makan-siap (180);
Tsou : bo-cxio (176);
Puyuma : malaḍam (456);
Paiwan : k<əm>əlaŋ (313).
<> 179: *baʒaq / *badaq ; 456: *-ḷam.

46 leaf

Atayal : ʔabaɣ (184);
Pazeh : rabax (-184);
Saisiyat : biḷäʔ (184);
Thao : fiɬaq (184);
Rukai : vasaw (183);
Bunun : lisav (183);
Tsou : xəŋə (182);
Puyuma : biraʔ (184);
Paiwan : asaw (183).
<> 183: *wašaw / *-asaw; 184: *biRaq; Pazeh form is a borrowing from Atayal (Blust 1999a).

47 lie

Atayal : mataɣa=ɣaɣ (186);
Pazeh : --;
Saisiyat : --;
Thao : pan-taqnar (190);
Rukai : saro-takaŋa (191);
Bunun : mal-takðaŋ (191);
Tsou : o-rvoi (187);
Puyuma : --;
Paiwan : ki-taŋəz (189).
<> 189: *taŋəd / rVŋət; 191: *takaŋa / *takVyaŋ.

48 liver

Atayal : šayik (199);
Pazeh : asay (199);
Saisiyat : žäʔäl (458);
Thao : riši (200);
Rukai : aϑay (199);
Bunun : qataz (199);
Tsou : xʔonɨ (198);
Puyuma : rami (457);
Paiwan : qacay (199).
<> 199: *qacay.

49 long

Atayal : qanaru:x (201);
Pazeh : lupas- (204);
Saisiyat : ʔinažoʔ (201);
Thao : ma-kuliuš (938);
Rukai : --;
Bunun : ma-duqpus (204);
Tsou : tacvohʔi (202);
Puyuma : baḷakas (144);
Paiwan : ḷaḍuq (201).
◇ 201: *-aduq; 204: *-paš / *-puš.

50 louse

Atayal : kučuʔ (205);
Pazeh : kusu (205);
Saisiyat : koϑoʔ (205);
Thao : kucu (205);
Rukai : koco (205);
Bunun : kutu (205);
Tsou : kcu: (205);
Puyuma : kuṭu (205);
Paiwan : kucu (205).
◇ 205: *kucu.

51 man

Atayal : mamałiku (211);
Pazeh : mamaleŋ (211);
Saisiyat : kamamanžaḷan (211);
Thao : ayuδi (210);
Rukai : saovalay (209);
Bunun : banan=az (212);
Tsou : xaxocŋi (208);
Puyuma : maʔinayan (209);
Paiwan : uqalai (209).
◇ 209: *qalay; 211: the reconstruction is quite reliable.

52 many

Atayal : payux (217);
Pazeh : dahu (222);
Saisiyat : ʔakoy (461);
Thao : ma-naša (221);
Rukai : maakaḷa (219);
Bunun : ma-diʔa (511);
Tsou : manʔi (218);
Puyuma : saḍu (460);
Paiwan : ḷiaw (220).

53 meat

Atayal : hiʔ (223);
Pazeh : rumut (228);
Saisiyat : božiḷ (226);
Thao : bunłaδ (-227);
Rukai : bwatə (225);
Bunun : titi (223);
Tsou : braxci (224);
Puyuma : --;
Paiwan : vucul (226).
◇ 223: *ʔisiʔ; 224: *-cul / *-lic; Thao form is a borrowing, as is suggested by a voiced stop.

54 moon

Atayal : bua-tiŋ (230);
Pazeh : ilas (232);
Saisiyat : ilaš (232);
Thao : fuṟaδ (230);
Rukai : ḍamarə (231);
Bunun : buan (230);
Tsou : froxɨ (230);
Puyuma : buḷan (230);
Paiwan : qilas (232).
◇ *230: buḷal; 232: *qilaš.

55 mountain

Atayal : raɣiyax (233);
Pazeh : binayu (236);
Saisiyat : koḷ=koḷol (424);
Thao : hudun (512);
Rukai : ləgə=ləgə (877);
Bunun : lu(t)dun (512);
Tsou : furŋu (234);
Puyuma : ḍənan (462);
Paiwan : gadu (235).
◇ Thao form is a Bunun borrowing (Blust 1996).

56 mouth

Atayal : ŋaquaq (237);
Pazeh : rahal, rahan (241);
Saisiyat : ŋabaϑ (237);
Thao : ruðic (240);
Rukai : ŋódoy (285);
Bunun : ŋulus (285);
Tsou : ŋaro (237);
Puyuma : ʔiṇdan (239);
Paiwan : aŋal (237).
◇ 237: *ŋa-; 285: *ŋu[]u[š].

57 name

Atayal : raɬuʔ (242);
Pazeh : laŋat (245);
Saisiyat : žažoḷoʔ (242);
Thao : ɬanaδ (245);
Rukai : naganə (245);
Bunun : ŋalan (245);
Tsou : oŋko (245);
Puyuma : ŋaḷad (245);
Paiwan : ŋadan (245).
◇ 242: *ḍaluʔ; 245: *ŋaʒa- / *-aŋaʒ.

58 neck

Atayal : wariyuŋ (249);
Pazeh : hahur (92);
Saisiyat : važəŋ (929);
Thao : buqtur (-252);
Rukai : ḷəə (251);
Bunun : mudan (253);
Tsou : sɨnɨ (250);
Puyuma : niʔən (463);
Paiwan : ḷiqu (251).
◇ 251: * ḷiʔə-; Thao form is a borrowing, as is indicated by a voiced stop.

59 new

Atayal : ʔiqaš (254);
Pazeh : xias (254);
Saisiyat : šašoʔ (256);
Thao : faqɬu (255);
Rukai : báavanə (255);
Bunun : baqlu (255);
Tsou : farva (255);
Puyuma : bəkaḷ (255);
Paiwan : vaqu-an (255).
◇ 255: *baqru-.

60 night

Atayal : mhatan (257);
Pazeh : ahu-an (262);
Saisiyat : haḷoan (465);
Thao : tanɬuan (465);
Rukai : maóŋo (259);
Bunun : i-qumut (260);
Tsou : friŋna (258);
Puyuma : karaub (464);
Paiwan : qə-zəmə-zəmət (260).
◇ 260: *-əmət; 465: *rəw=an.

61 nose

Atayal : ŋuhuɣ (265);
Pazeh : muziŋ (266);
Saisiyat : kaŋoϑəlan (265);
Thao : muðin (266);
Rukai : ŋo=ŋoanə (265);
Bunun : ŋutus (265);
Tsou : ŋicɨ (265);
Puyuma : tiŋran (466);
Paiwan : ŋuḍus (265).
◇ 265: *ŋu-; 266: *muʒiŋ.

62 not

Atayal : ʔiniʔ (269);
Pazeh : ini < *ini (269);
Saisiyat : ʔiðiʔ (467);
Thao : ani < *ani (269);
Rukai : ini (269);
Bunun : ni (269);
Tsou : ʔoa (268);
Puyuma : --;
Paiwan : ini (269).
◇ 269: *-iniʔ.

63 one

Atayal : qutux (270);
Pazeh : adaŋ (273);
Saisiyat : ʔähäʔ (272);
Thao : tata < *esa (272);
Rukai : ísa (272);
Bunun : tasa (272);
Tsou : coni (271);
Puyuma : sa (272);
Paiwan : ita (272).
<> 272: *(-)sa(-).

64 person

Atayal : čuquɬ-iq (214);
Pazeh : sau (214);
Saisiyat : mäʔiḷäh (468);
Thao : caw (214);
Rukai : oma-ómasə (215);
Bunun : bunun (216);
Tsou : cou (214);
Puyuma : ṭau (214);
Paiwan : caw-caw (214).
<> 214: *caw (// *ca[]u).

65 rain

Atayal : quaɬax (277);
Pazeh : udal (277);
Saisiyat : ʔö-ʔöžal (277);
Thao : qusað (277);
Rukai : ódalə (277);
Bunun : qudan (277);
Tsou : tnɨrɨ (276);
Puyuma : ʔuḍal (277);
Paiwan : quḍál (277).
<> 277: *quḍal.

66 red

Atayal : ma-tanah (278);
Pazeh : lubahi (283);
Saisiyat : a il h=an (469);
Thao : ma-quɬa (282);
Rukai : dirərə lə (280);
Bunun : ma-da qas (284);
Tsou : fɨxŋor-a (279);
Puyuma : midaraŋ (485);
Paiwan : qu-didíl (281).

67 road

Atayal : raniq (286);
Pazeh : daran (286);
Saisiyat : žaḷan (286);
Thao : saran (286);
Rukai : ka-daḷan-anə (286);
Bunun : --;
Tsou : cronɨ (286);
Puyuma : daḷan (286);
Paiwan : ḍaḷan (286).
<> 286: *daḷan.

68 root

Atayal : ɣamiɬ (930);
Pazeh : xames (287);
Saisiyat : ḷaməϑ (287);
Thao : ɬamic (287);
Rukai : balacə (288);
Bunun : lamis (-287);
Tsou : rmisi (287);
Puyuma : rami (287);
Paiwan : kapaz (289).
<> 287: *ramək / *ramiš; the Bunun form is a borrowing from Thao (Blust 1996).

69 round

Atayal : m-tumurul (291);
Pazeh : rumux- (291);
Saisiyat : --;
Thao : ma-buðuq (-295);
Rukai : liməmətəkə (293);
Bunun : mai-lalo (512);
Tsou : taucunu (292);
Puyuma : --;
Paiwan : ḷiŋúl (294).
<> 291: *rumuR / *rumur; the Thao form is a borrowing, as is indicated by a voiced stop.

70 sand

Atayal : bunaqiy (297);
Pazeh : bunat (297);
Saisiyat : bonað (297);
Thao : bunað (-297);
Rukai : ənay (299);
Bunun : bunuk (301);
Tsou : furfuʔu (301);
Puyuma : buṭək (301);
Paiwan : vudas (300).
<> 297: *bunaʒ; 301: *-buk; the Thao form is a borrowing, as is indicated by a voiced stop.

71 say

Atayal : k-um-a:ɬ (302);
Pazeh : kawas-, kuas- (307);
Saisiyat : maʔyakaḷiʔ (471);
Thao : k-m-uða (306);
Rukai : kawariva (307);
Bunun : tu-pa (308);
Tsou : ao-motɨʔɨ (303);
Puyuma : marŋay (470);
Paiwan : c-əm-umal (305).
<> 307: *kawa-.

72 see

Atayal : k-um-ita-aɬ (310);
Pazeh : kita- (310);
Saisiyat : k<om>itaʔ (310);
Thao : m-riqað (314);
Rukai : wa-də:lə (312);
Bunun : sa-du (316);
Tsou : b-aito (310);
Puyuma : mənaʔu (472);
Paiwan : ḻ<əm>əŋ=ləŋ (313).
<> 310: *kita.

73 seed

Atayal : ga-ghap (130);
Pazeh : buxu=an (317);
Saisiyat : pi=piϑ (474);
Thao : puqu (36);
Rukai : cápə (140);
Bunun : toos (96);
Tsou : --;
Puyuma : ukak (433);
Paiwan : --.
<> 36: see 'bone'.

74 sit

Atayal : ma-thawnak (318);
Pazeh : tuku- (323);
Saisiyat : š<om>aḻəŋ (931);
Thao : ɬuŋqu (-319);
Rukai : wa-nənə (320);
Bunun : is-a-noqo (514);
Tsou : ru-suxŋu (319);
Puyuma : katəŋaḍau (475);
Paiwan : q<əm>iḻad (321).
<> the Thao for is a borrowing from Bunun ma-luŋqu (Blust 1996,289).

75 skin

Atayal : kuahiɬ (324);
Pazeh : --;
Saisiyat : baŋəš (429);
Thao : šapạ (327);
Rukai : ikidi (326);
Bunun : kahuŋ (328);
Tsou : snɨfɨ (325);
Puyuma : ḻubiṭ (7);
Paiwan : qalic (6).
<> 6: *qalic; 429: *baŋəš.

76 sleep

Atayal : ma-qiɬa:p (141);
Pazeh : idem- (195);
Saisiyat : mäʔžəm (195);
Thao : kaɬus (194);
Rukai : áapəcə (188);
Bunun : ma-sabaq (196);
Tsou : o-rŋitɨ (189);
Puyuma : alupəʔ (141);
Paiwan : taqəd (193).
<> 141: *ʔalupəq / *qilap-aʔ; 195: *qidəm.

77 small

Atayal : tikay (329);
Pazeh : pusirit (333);
Saisiyat : ʔol=ʔolaʔan (477);
Thao : laŋqisusay (332);
Rukai : tiki-anə (329);
Bunun : atikis (329);
Tsou : oko-si (477);
Puyuma : makitəŋ (476);
Paiwan : kədi (331).
<> 329: *tikay / *tiki-; 477: *qula- / *qala.

78 smoke

Atayal : ɣuhiɬuq (340);
Pazeh : busu=bus (104);
Saisiyat : kaϑbol (932);
Thao : qumbu (516);
Rukai : əbə̣lə (341);
Bunun : qusʔul, pusʔul (516);
Tsou : fru=fru (341);
Puyuma : ʔasban (932);
Paiwan : cəvúl (932).
<> 341: *qəbəl; 932: *cəbul (the etymology of Puyuma is not quite reliable).

79 stand

Atayal : -čaʔrux, čaqruɣ (343);
Pazeh : kizex- (347);
Saisiyat : miẓili̧ʔ (345);
Thao : mi-ɬiɬi (345);
Rukai : idii (345);
Bunun : min-daŋkaδ (348);
Tsou : racʔɨ (344);
Puyuma : --;
Paiwan : mi-gacál (346).
<> 345: *diri-.

80 star

Atayal : buliq, buɬuq (349);
Pazeh : bintul (352);
Saisiyat : bintöʔän (352);
Thao : kiɬpuδ (354);
Rukai : tariaw (351);
Bunun : bintuq-an (352);
Tsou : coŋroxa (350);
Puyuma : tiʔur (478);
Paiwan : vituqan (352).
<> *bituq-en / *bintuq-en;

81 stone

Atayal : batu-nux (355);
Pazeh : batu (355);
Saisiyat : batoʔ (355);
Thao : fatu (355);
Rukai : ḷənəgə (356);
Bunun : batu (355);
Tsou : fatu (355);
Puyuma : barạsaʔ (335);
Paiwan : qacilay (357).
<> 355: *batu.

82 sun

Atayal : waɣiʔ (358);
Pazeh : ridax, rizah (361);
Saisiyat : hähilaḷ (359);
Thao : --;
Rukai : vai (358);
Bunun : vali (358);
Tsou : xire (359);
Puyuma : kadaw (360);
Paiwan : qadaw (360).
<> 358: *wari; 359: *silaḷ; 360: *-aʒaw

83 swim

Atayal : ɬ-um-aŋuy (362);
Pazeh : laŋuy- (362);
Saisiyat : l<om>aŋoy (362);
Thao : rauδ (363);
Rukai : laŋoy (362);
Bunun : soŋ-a-haul (364);
Tsou : ru:-xŋuzu (362);
Puyuma : mu-laŋuy (362);
Paiwan : l<əm>aŋuy (362).
<> 362: *laŋuy.

84 tail
Atayal : ŋaʔŋuʔ (365);
Pazeh : dulut (370);
Saisiyat : kikol̥ (368);
Thao : wawiš=wiš (369);
Rukai : taoϑo (367);
Bunun : ikul (368);
Tsou : civci (366);
Puyuma : ikur (368);
Paiwan : iku (368).
<> 368: *ʔikur.

85 that
Atayal : --;
Pazeh : sia (389);
Saisiyat : h=ao (479);
Thao : haya / huya (371);
Rukai : --;
Bunun : ipa (373);
Tsou : --;
Puyuma : idi=yu (479);
Paiwan : azua (376).
<> 371: *šiya; 376: *-də-; 479: *-ʔu.

86 this
Atayal : ha-ni (375);
Pazeh : im=ini (375);
Saisiyat : h=iniʔ (375);
Thao : i-pruq (374);
Rukai : kay (53);
Bunun : deʔe (376);
Tsou : eni (375);
Puyuma : id=ini (375);
Paiwan : aicu (916).
<> 375: *-ni-.

87 thou
Atayal : ʔi-šuʔ (377);
Pazeh : siw (377);
Saisiyat : šoʔo (377);
Thao : ihu (377);
Rukai : ko-so (377);
Bunun : asu (377);
Tsou : si (377);
Puyuma : kanu (480);
Paiwan : ti-su=n (377).
<> 377: *šuʔ.

88 tongue
Atayal : hmaʔ (378);
Pazeh : dahama (378);
Saisiyat : kähmaʔ (378);
Thao : ðama (378);
Rukai : l̥idamə (822);
Bunun : mʔama (378);
Tsou : umo (378);
Puyuma : smaʔ (378);
Paiwan : səma (378).
<> 378: *-əmaʔ (the Puyuma form may be a borrowing from Amis).

89 tooth
Atayal : γipun (382);
Pazeh : lepeŋ (382);
Saisiyat : nəpən (382);
Thao : nipin (382);
Rukai : valisi (380);
Bunun : nipun (382);
Tsou : xisi (380);
Puyuma : wal̥i (380);
Paiwan : alis (380).
<> 380: *-ališ; 382: *-ipən.

90 tree
Atayal : kahuniq, kahuy (383);
Pazeh : kahuy (383);
Saisiyat : kähöy (383);
Thao : kawi (383);
Rukai : aŋato (384);
Bunun : lukis (784);
Tsou : evi (383);
Puyuma : kawi (383);
Paiwan : kasiw (383).
<> 383: *kahuy / *kawis.

91 two
Atayal : ʔuša-iŋ (385);
Pazeh : dusa (385);
Saisiyat : žošaʔ (385);
Thao : tuša (385);
Rukai : ḍosa (385);
Bunun : dusa (385);
Tsou : ruso (385);
Puyuma : ḍua (385);
Paiwan : ḍusa (385).
<> 385: *ḍuša.

92 walk (go)
Atayal : h-um-akay (386);
Pazeh : zakay (386);
Saisiyat : žimaʔ (933);
Thao : ma-qitan (390);
Rukai : mwa (59);
Bunun : mun-ivaq (63);
Tsou : cor-corni (286);
Puyuma : wa (59);
Paiwan : vaik (59).
<> 59 'come'; 386: *sakay.

93 warm (as water)
Atayal : --;
Pazeh : lalap- (393);
Saisiyat : --;
Thao : --;
Rukai : --;
Bunun : is-naqat (517);
Rukai : --;
Puyuma : --;
Paiwan : səmaḷaəlan (50).

94 water
Atayal : qušiyaʔ (394);
Pazeh : dalum (395);
Saisiyat : žalom (395);
Thao : sazum (395);
Rukai : acilay (396);
Bunun : danum (395);
Tsou : cxumu (395);

The Formosan language family 209

Puyuma : ʔənay (481);
Paiwan : zalum (395).
<> 395: *dalum.

95 we
Atayal : ʔi-čami (398);
Pazeh : ami (398);
Saisiyat : yami (398);
Thao : yamin (398);
Rukai : ko-nai (399);
Bunun : saam (398);
Tsou : aʔmi (398);
Puyuma : mimi (398);
Paiwan : ti=amən (398).
<> 398: *i-ami.

96 what
Atayal : namu-an (400), (934);
Pazeh : asay (403);
Saisiyat : kanoʔ (934);
Thao : numa (400), (934);
Rukai : manə=manə (400), (934);
Bunun : maʔaq (934);
Tsou : cuma (934);
Puyuma : a=manay (934);
Paiwan : a-nə=ma (400), (934).
<> 400 *nə-; 934: *ma.

97 white
Atayal : ma-ʔubaʔ (405);
Pazeh : risilaw (410);
Saisiyat : bolalaϑ-an (936);
Thao : ma-puδi (409);
Rukai : po-poli (409);
Bunun : ma-duqlas (411);
Tsou : firciʔz-a (935);
Puyuma : burnan (406);
Paiwan : vu-təqi-təqil (408).
<> 409: *puli.

98 who
Atayal : ʔimaʔ (412), (934);
Pazeh : ima (412), (934);

Saisiyat : hia? (412);
Thao : tima (412), (934);
Rukai : anə=anə (400);
Bunun : simaq (412), (934);
Tsou : sia (412);
Puyuma : ʔi=manay (412), (934);
Paiwan : ti=ma (412), (934).
<> 412: *ʔi- / *si-; 934: *ma.

99 woman

Atayal : kanayrił (918);
Pazeh : mamis (414);
Saisiyat : min=kožiŋ=an (482);
Thao : binanau'az (-416);
Rukai : a-ba-bay (415);
Bunun : binanauʔ=az (416);
Tsou : mamespiɲi (414);
Puyuma : babay=an (415);
Paiwan : va-vai-an (415).
<> 414: *mamiš; 415: *bay / *bahi.

100 yellow

Atayal : ma-turakiš (417);
Pazeh : barak- (418);
Saisiyat : labial-an (315);
Thao : šadunan (421);
Rukai : bo-bolavanə (419);
Bunun : ma-sinhay (423);
Tsou : xofʔor-a (418);
Puyuma : malulu? (483);
Paiwan : qu-lizа-lizal (420).
<> 418: *balak / *bikal;.

Plate 1.1 Red-slipped bowl sherds decorated with friezes of circle-stamped meanders, from Sunget (left hand example is 5.3 cm wide)

Plate 1.II A selection of Taiwan nephrite artifacts recovered in 2005 from Anaro. Top row: debitage connected mainly with the manufacture of ear ornaments. Bottom row: two nephrite adzes at left, plus various cut blanks.

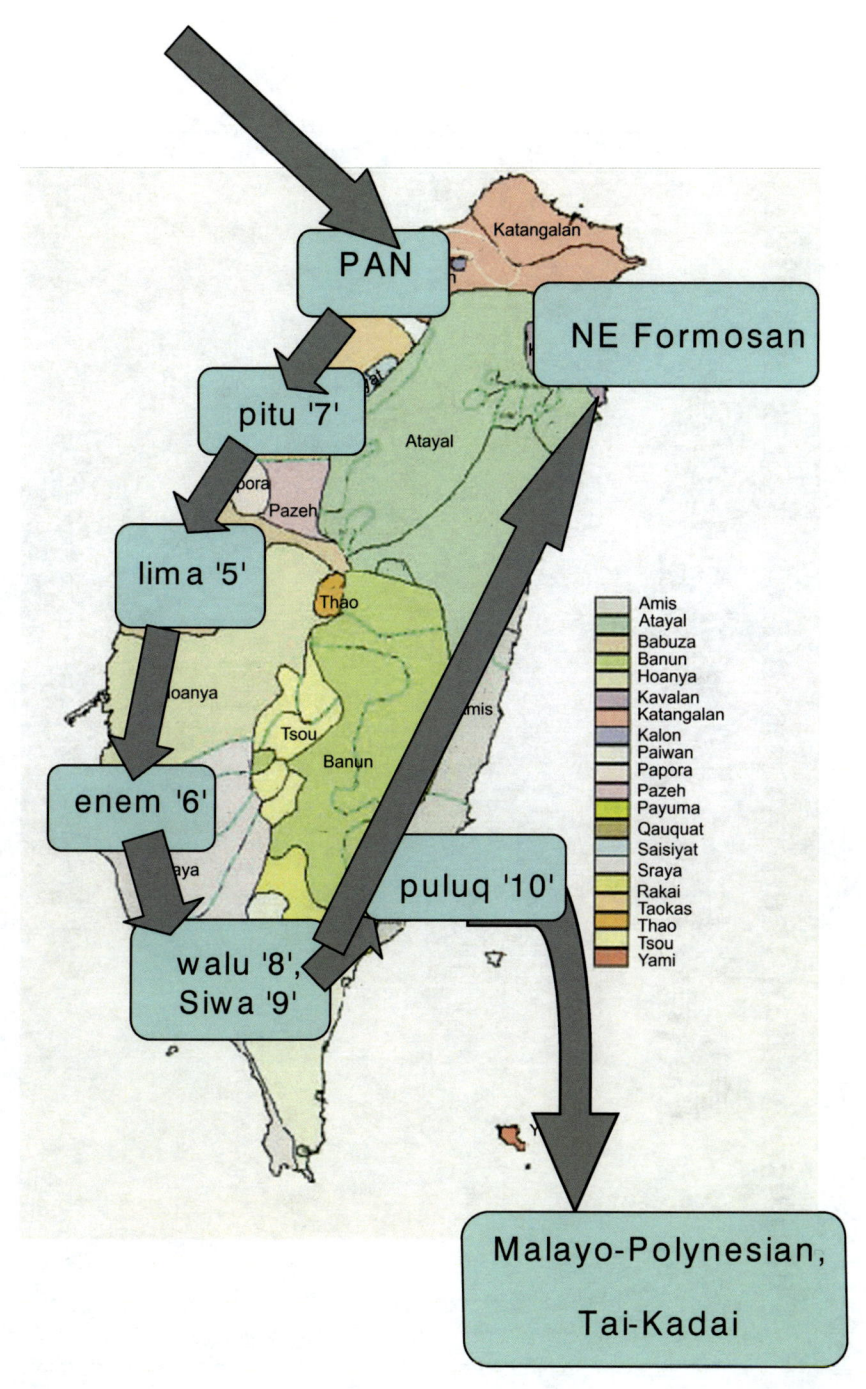

Plate 5.1 The AN settlement of Taiwan with the Malayo-Polynesian and Tai-Kadai migrations

The Dispersal of the Formosan Aborigines in Taiwan
臺灣南島民族遷移圖

Thao Village and District Names around 1850
十九世紀中葉部族部落分布圖

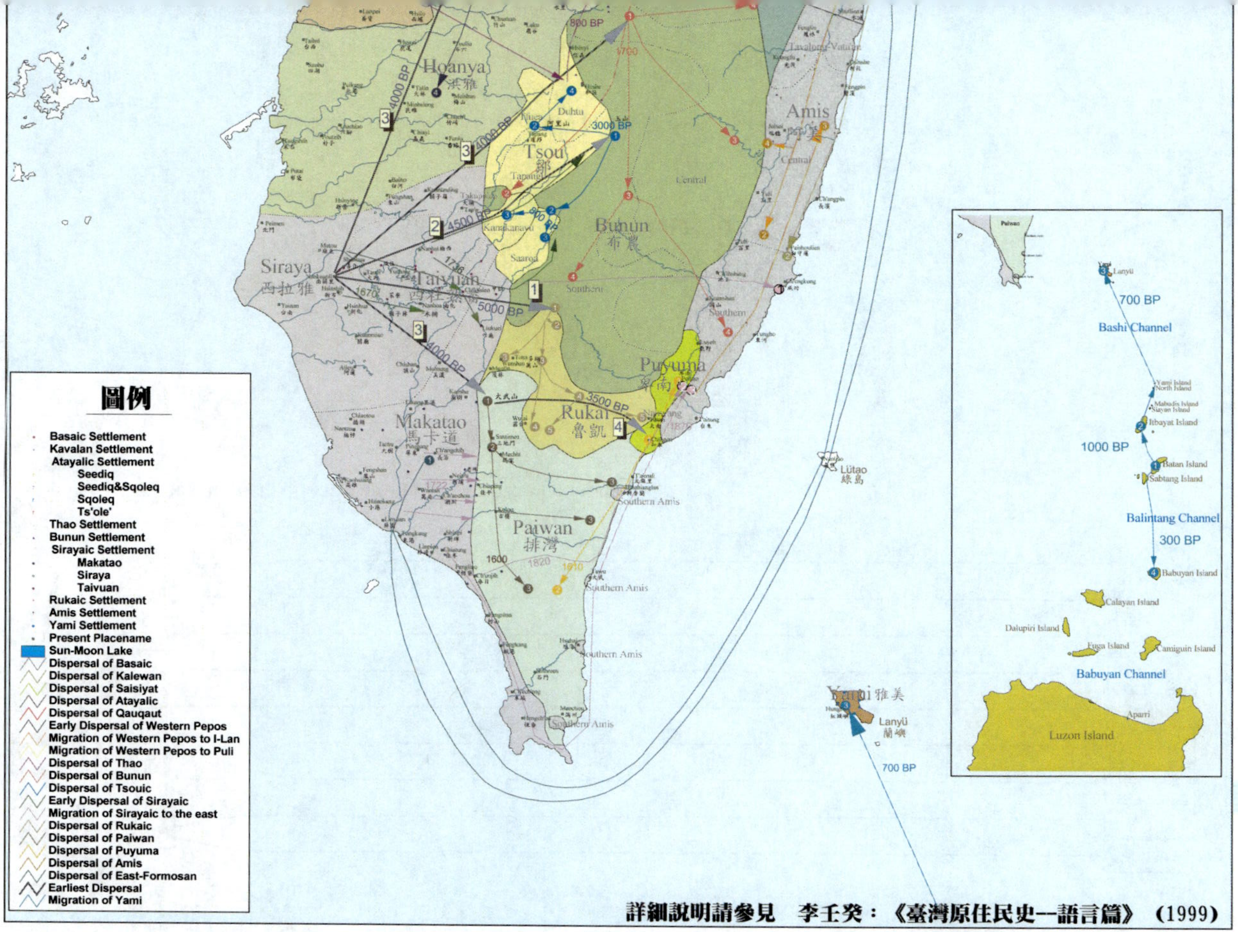

Plate 8.1 The dispersal of the Formosan Aborigines in Taiwan

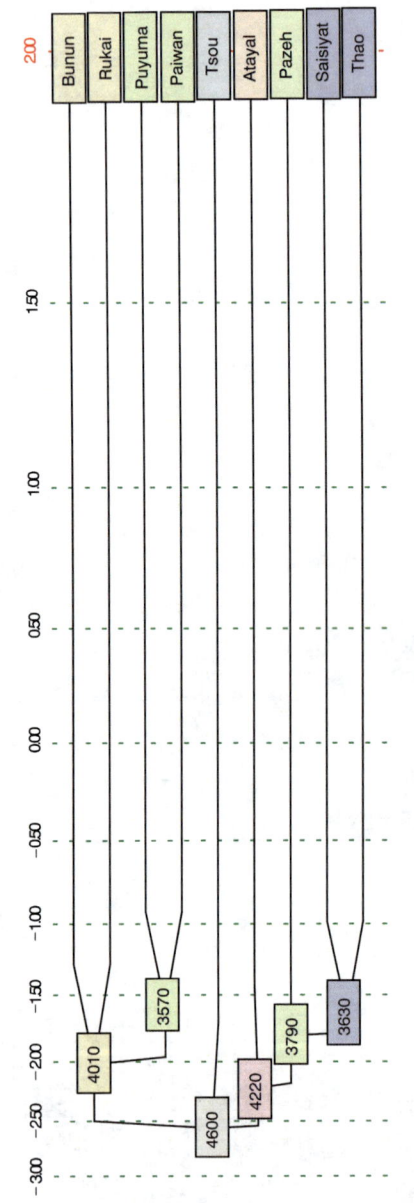

Plate 7.1 Lexicostatistical classification of Formosan languages

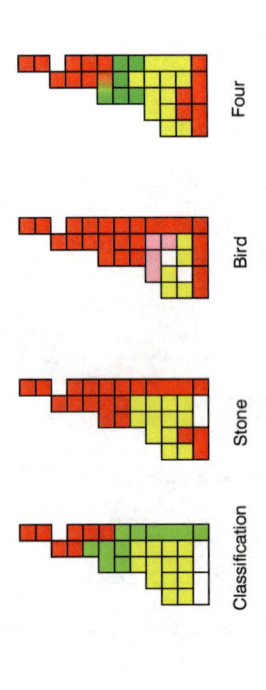

Plate 12.1 Schematic representations of language groupings

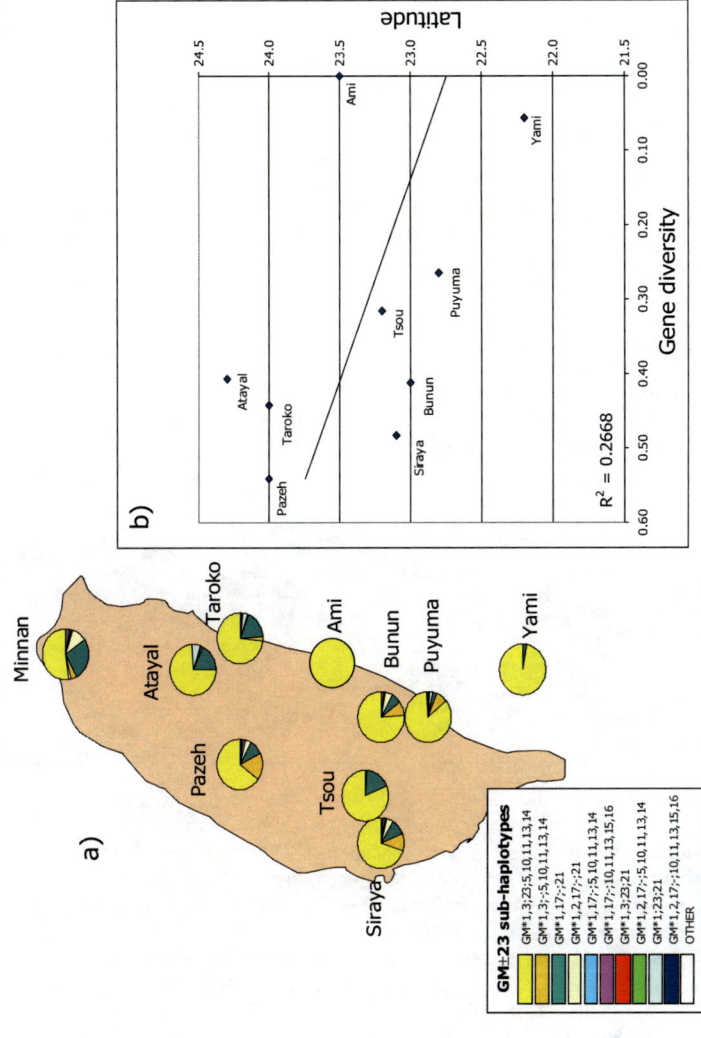

Plate 13.1 a) Map of Taiwan showing GM haplotype frequencies (pies) for all Taiwanese populations tested in this study. The Minnan have been placed at the top of the map for the sake of clarity; b) Plot of the gene diversity (estimated by the expected heterozygosity) in each Aboriginal population from Taiwan against latitude

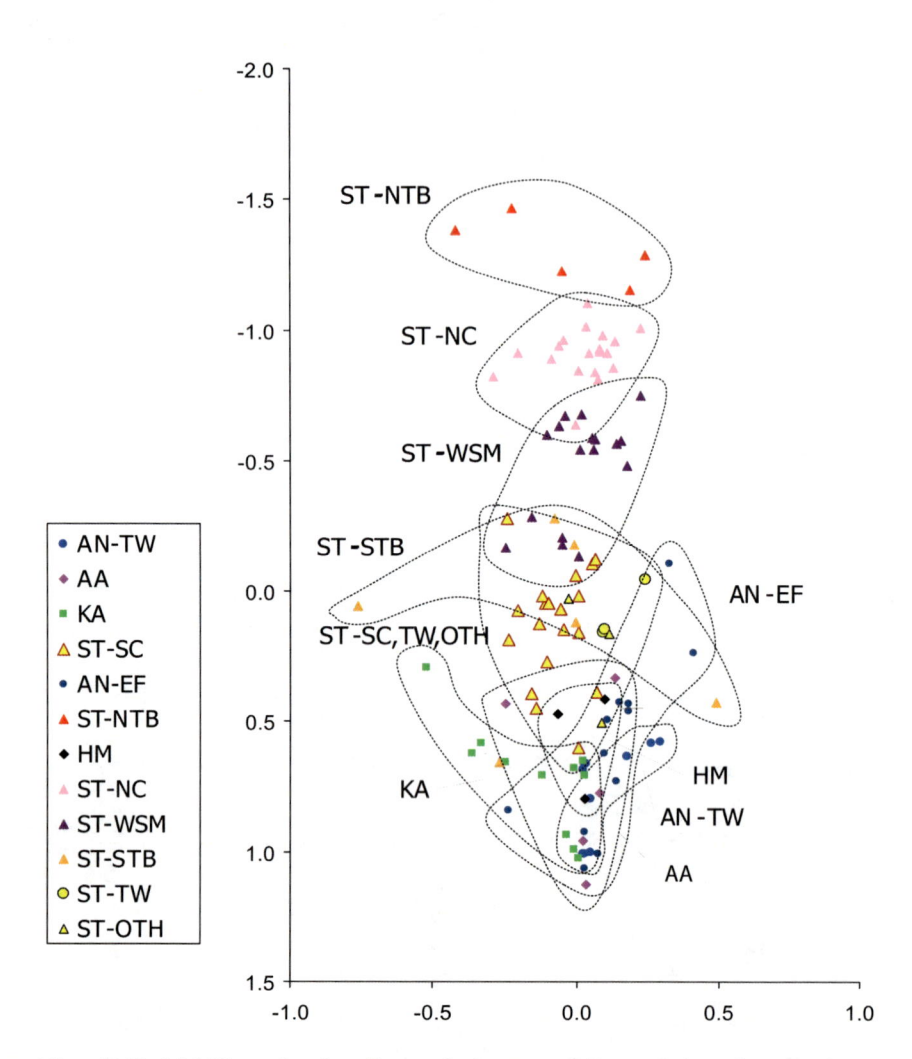

Plate 13.II Multidimensional scaling analysis among 113 populations from Southeast Asia based on the frequencies of GM broad haplotypes. Prevosti's et al. (1975) distances have been used. Populations speaking languages belonging to the same linguistic (sub-) family have been clustered. Final stress = 0.085 (good).
ST-NTB: Sino-Tibetan, Northern Tibeto-Burman; ST-NC: Sino-Tibetan, Northern Chinese (all Mandarin but Southeastern); ST-WSM: Sino-Tibetan, Wu and Southeastern Mandarin; ST-STB: Sino-Tibetan, other Tibeto-Burman; ST-SC: Sino-Tibetan, Southern Chinese (Min, Xiang, Gan, Hakka, Yue); ST-TW: Sino-Tibetan from Taiwan; ST-OTH: other Sino-Tibetan; KA: Tai-Kadai; AN-EF: Extra-Formosan Austronesian; HM: Hmong-Mien; AN-TW: Autronesian from Taiwan; AA: Austroasiatic.

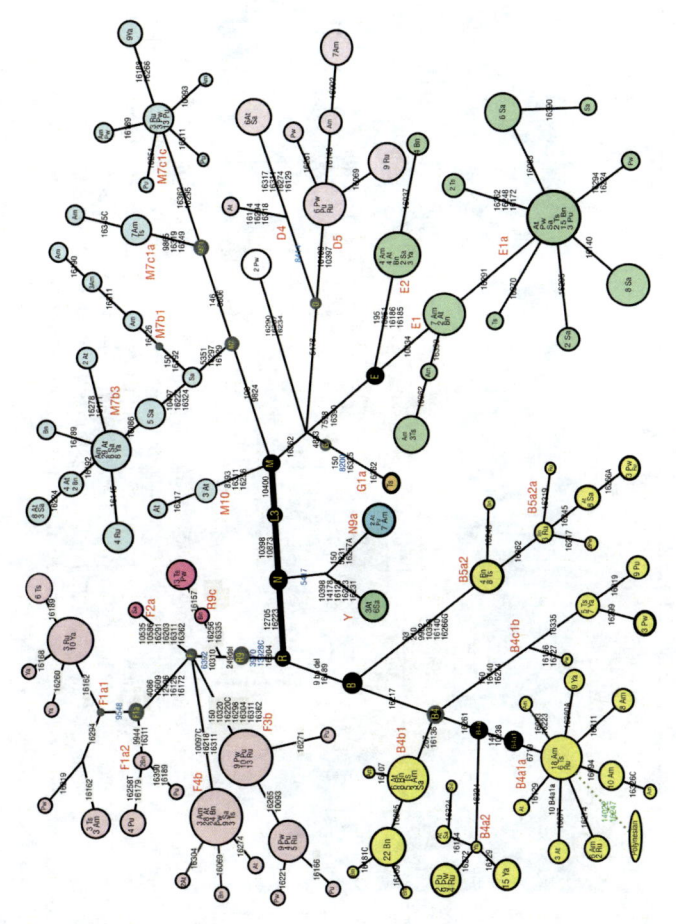

Plate 14.1 Tree drawn from a median-joining network of 96 mtDNA haplotypes observed in nine indigenous Taiwanese populations. The tree is based on sequences of HVS-I (16,024-16,390) and a coding region stretch covering 9,793 to 10,899 bps. Haplogroups defining HVS-II mutations were manually added after the generation of the network. Additional coding region mutations, ascertained through sequencing of an individual of each subclade of the haplogroup defined by the mutation, were used to generate the network and are shown in blue. All nucleotide positions are numbered according to reference sequence (Andrews et al. 1999). Mutations in italic indicate back conversions. Nucleotide change is specified only for transversions. Node areas are proportional to haplotype frequencies of the pooled nine tribes. The population codes are as follows: At – Atayal, Bn – Bunun, Am – Ami, Pw – Paiwan, Ru – Rukai, Sa – Saisiat, Pu – Puyuma, Ts – Tsou, Ya – Yami.

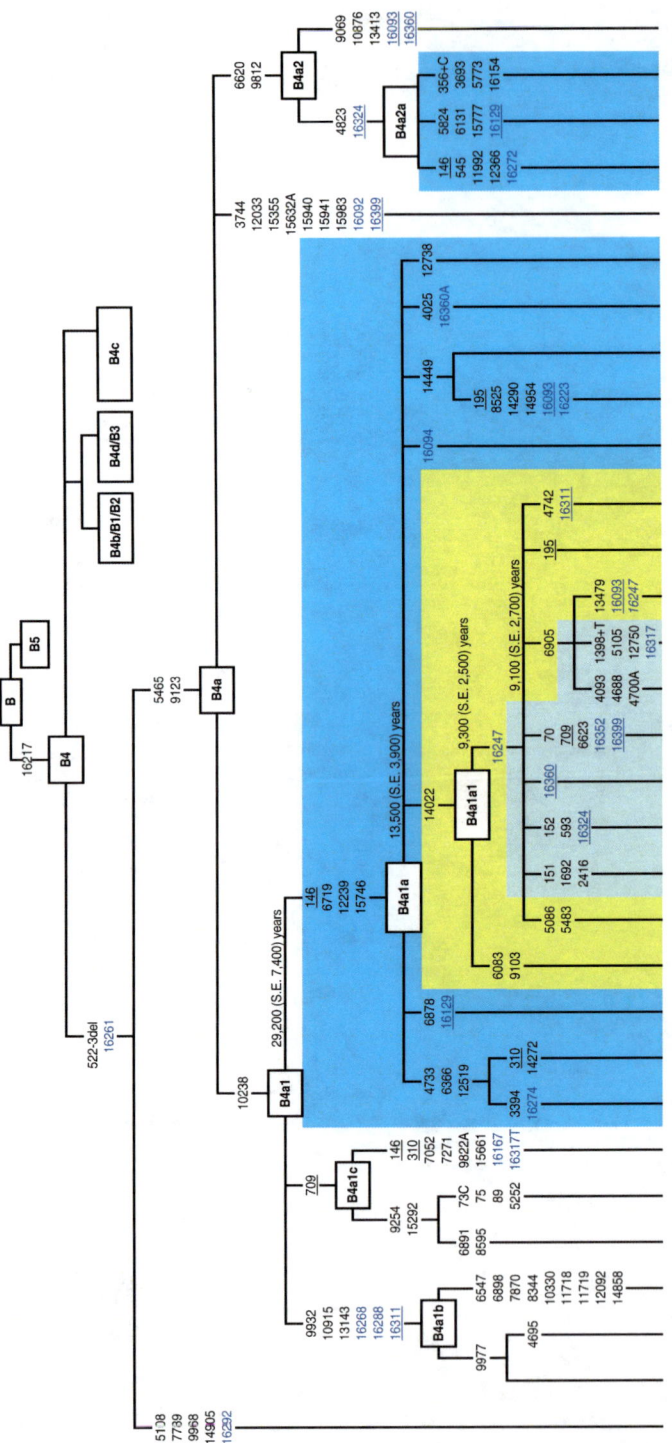

Plate 14.II Most parsimonious tree reconstruction relating Taiwanese Aboriginal, Asian and Oceanian complete mtDNA sequences of haplogroup B4a. Variable positions are shown along branches. Recurrent mutations are underlined. Nucleotide change is specified only for transversions. Coalescence times are shown beside nodes. The following complete mtDNA sequences of haplogroup B4a affiliation were taken from published sources: GD7812 (Kong et al. 2003); HN153 and JD 73 (Tanaka et al. 2004); P3 (Yoneda et al. 1990; Ozawa 1995); AF346993 and AF347007 (Ingman et al. 2000); AY195770, AY289076, AY289080, AY289068, AY289102, AY289094, AY289069, AY289093, AY289083 and AY289077 (Ingman and Gyllensten 2003). The complete sequences determined for Taiwanese aboriginal samples in this study are as follow: EMBL (http://www.ebi.ac.uk/) mtDNA complete sequence data accession numbers AJ842744-AJ842751.

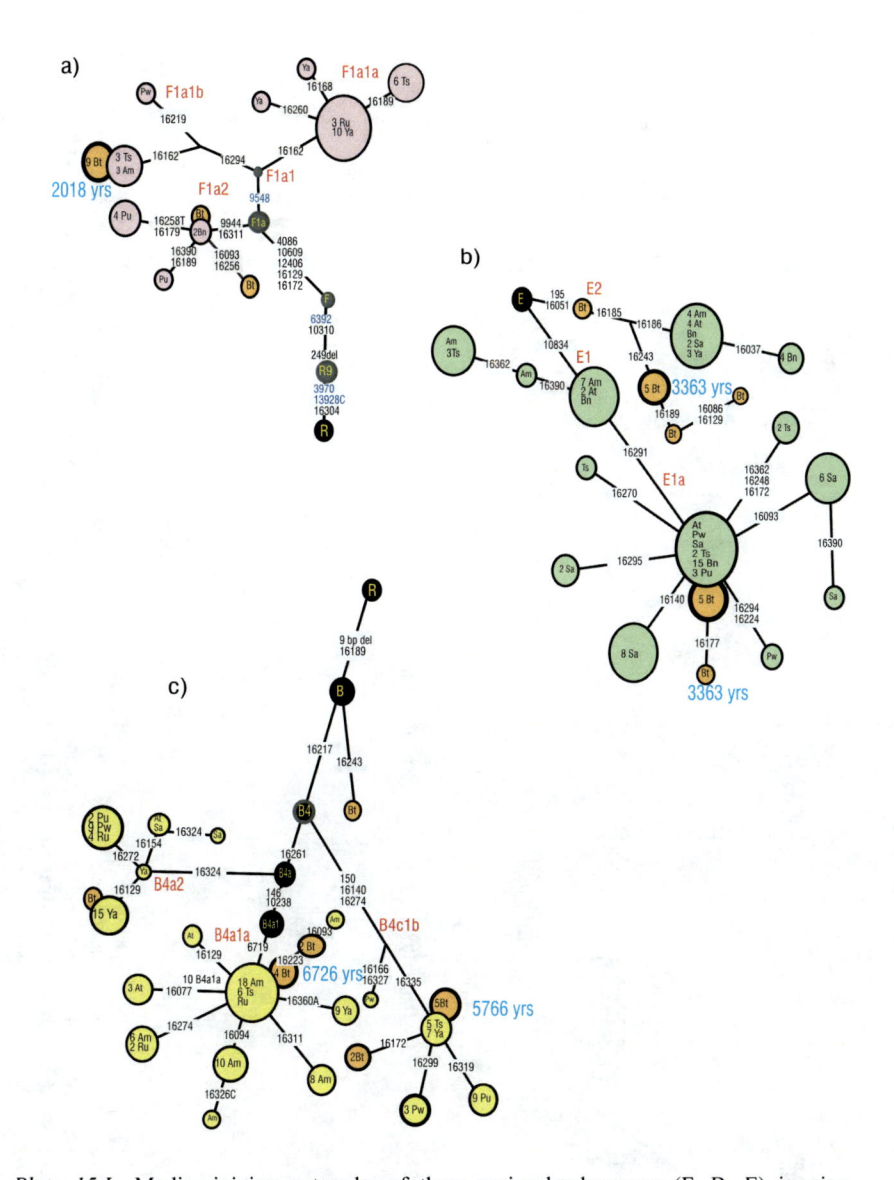

Plate 15.1 Median-joining networks of three major haplogroups (F, B, E) in nine indigenous Taiwanese populations and Batanes from the Philippines. The tree is based on sequences of HVS-I (16,024- 16,390) and a coding region segment covering 9,793 to 10,899 bps. Haplogroup defining HVS-II mutations were manually added after the generation of the network. Additional coding region mutations, ascertained through complete mtDNA sequencing of one individual in each subclade of the haplogroup defined by the mutation, were used to generate the network and are shown in blue. All nps are numbered according to the mtDNA reference sequence (Andrews et al. 1999). Mutations in italics indicate back conversions. Nucleotide change is specified for transversions. Node areas are proportional to haplotype frequencies in the nine ethnic groups pooled together. Population codes are as follows: At, Atayal; Bn, Bunun; Am, Amis; Pw, Paiwan; Ru, Rukai; Sa, Saisiat; Pu, Puyuma; Ts, Tsou; Ya, Tao; and Bd, Batan. Coalescence time estimations are indicated only for Batan clusters where standard errors were generally close to the estimated values.

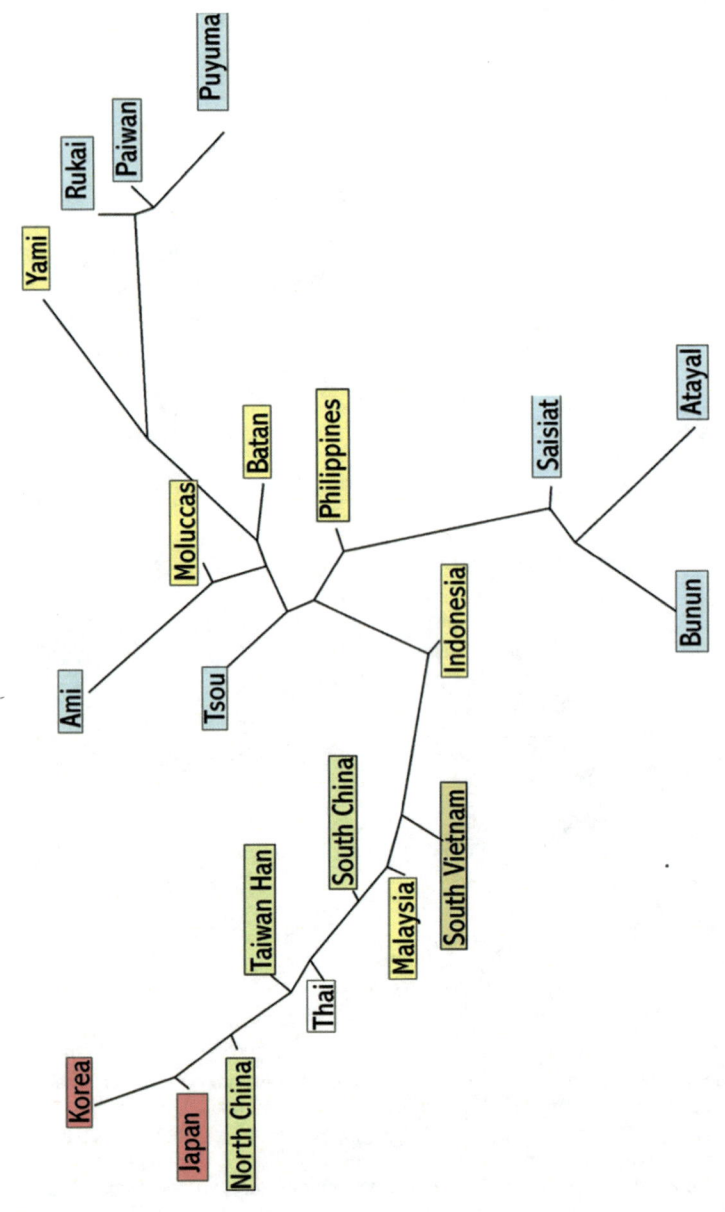

Plate 15.II Phylogenetic tree of nine indigenous Taiwanese Populations, Batan and other populations of Asia. The tree is obtained from a matrix of mtDNA haplogroup frequencies in nine Taiwan indigenous tribes, northern and southern Chinese, Taiwan urban populations (Minan and Hakka), Japan, Korea, Moluccas, Indonesia, Ryukyu, Malaysia, South Vietnam, Thai, Philippines and Batan. Different colours were used for different linguistic phyla: blue: Austronesian from Taiwan; yellow: Malayo-Polynesian; red: Koreo-Japonic; green: Sino-Tibetan ; brown: Austro-Asiatic.

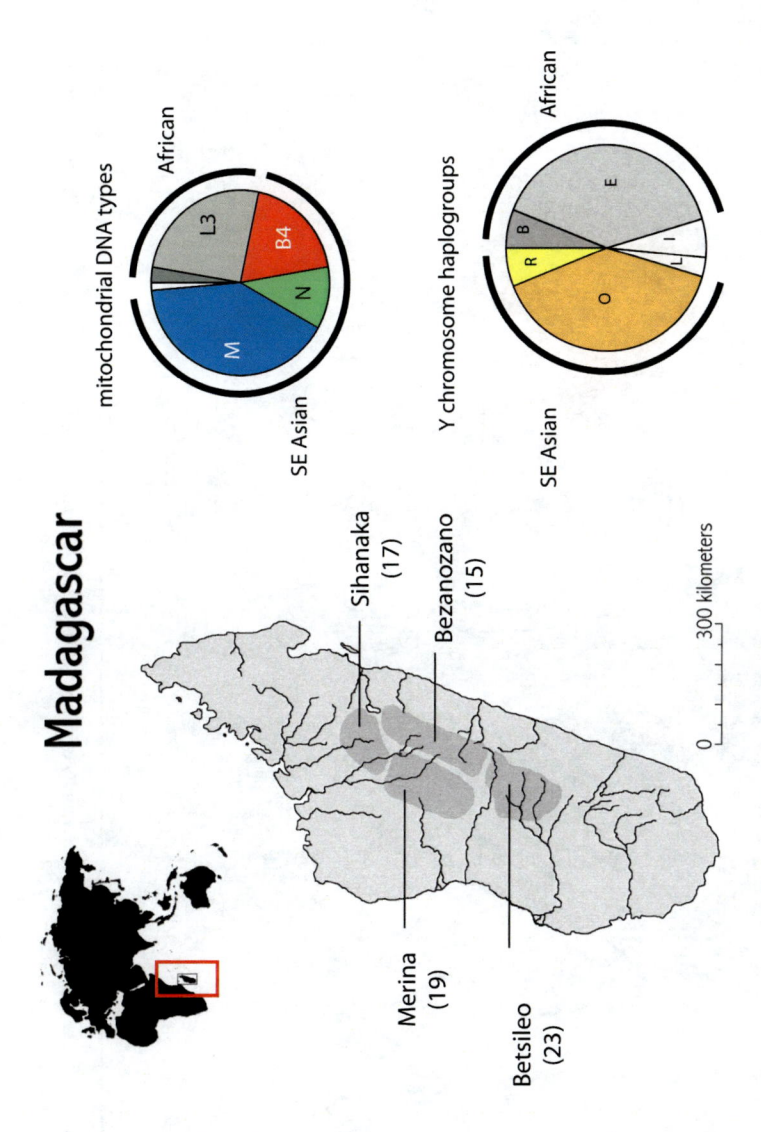

Plate 16.1 Map of Madagascar showing the ethnic groups included in our study, and the composition of maternal (mtDNA) and paternal (Y chromosome) types. The numbers in parentheses indicate the sample size of each population.

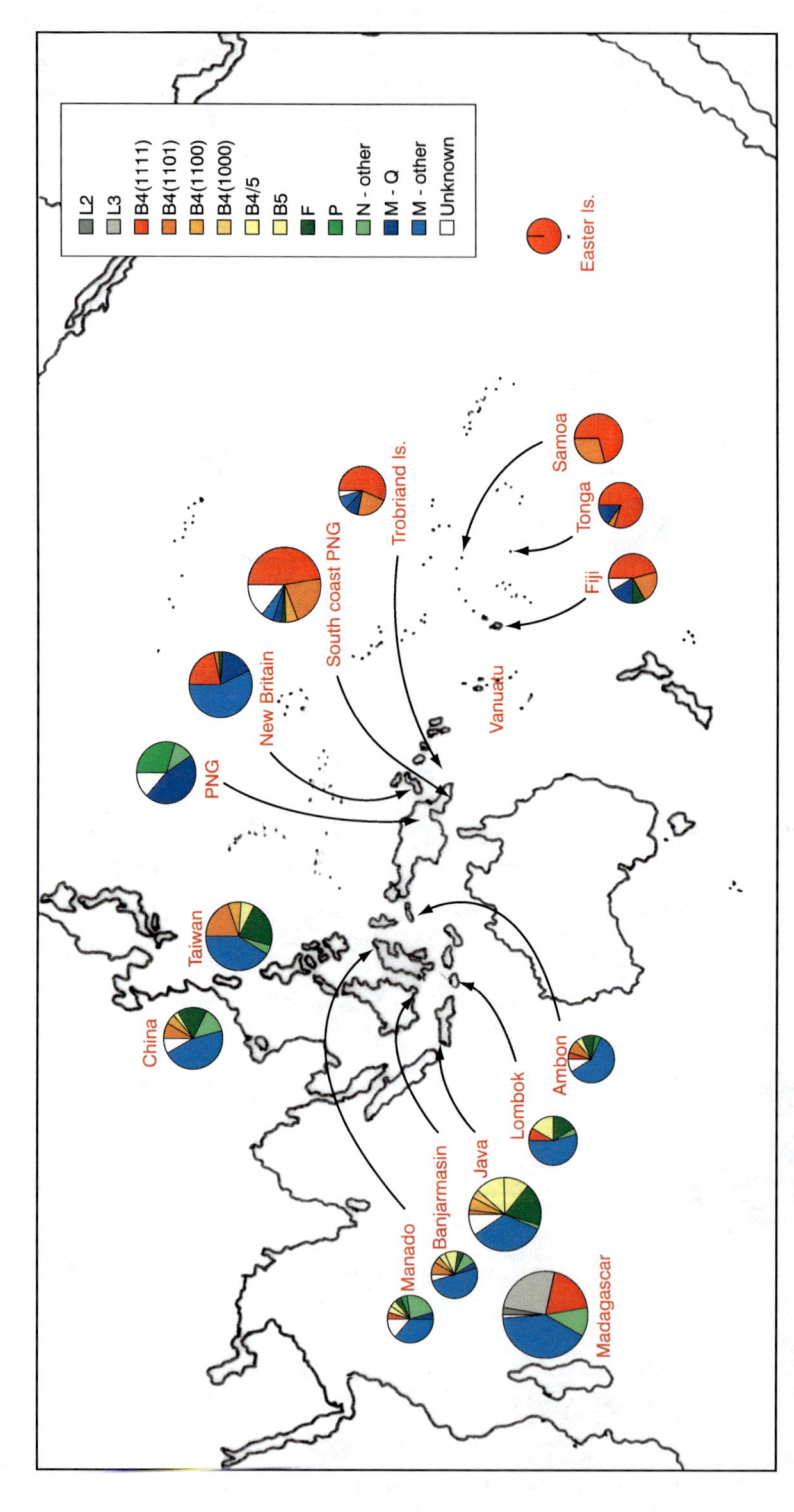

Plate 16.II Map of the Pacific showing the frequency of mitochondrial DNA haplogroups in the locations including in our study. The size of the circles reflects the sample size, shown in Table 16.1.

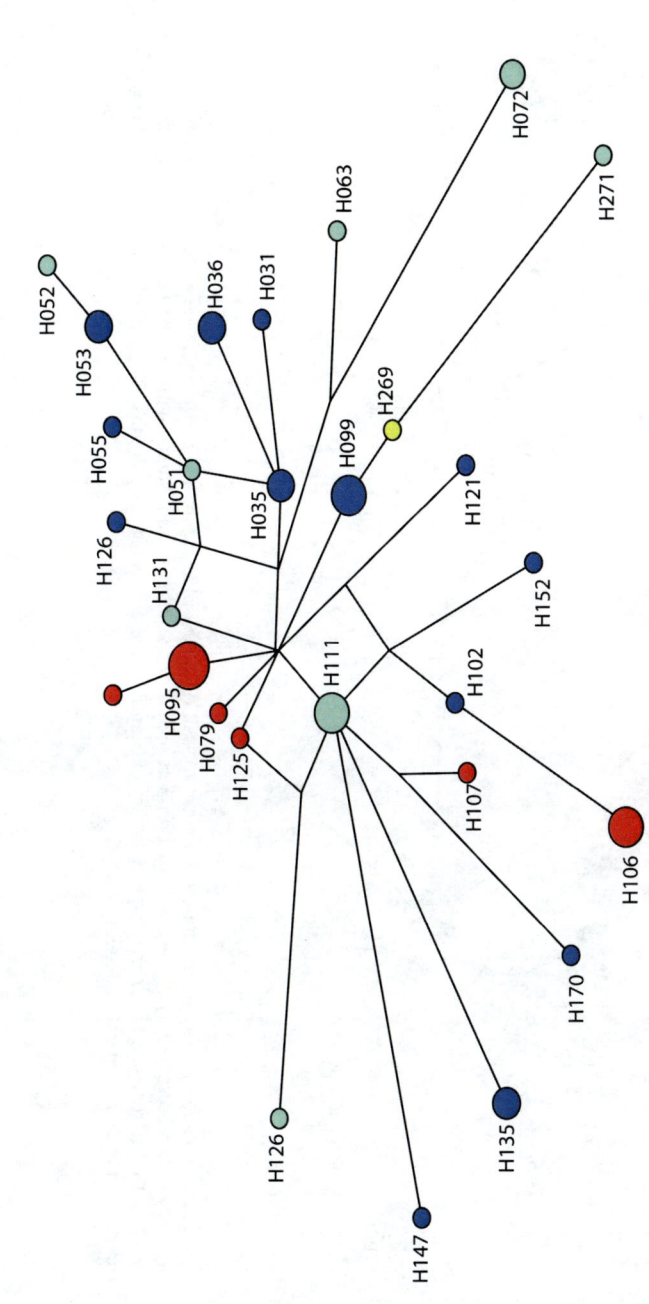

Plate 17.1a Median-joining microsatellite networks for haplogroup O-M95 in Gunung Kawi in older subaks. Microsatellite haplotypes are represented by circles with area proportional to the number of individuals with that haplotype. Colors indicate affiliation to different subaks. Shared haplotypes are indicated by pie charts. Branch lengths are proportional to the number of one-repeat mutations separating haplotypes

Plate 17.1b Median-joining microsatellite networks for haplogroup O-M95 in Gunung Kawi in younger subaks. Microsatellite haplotypes are represented by circles with area proportional to the number of individuals with that haplotype. Colors indicate affiliation to different subaks. Shared haplotypes are indicated by pie charts. Branch lengths are proportional to the number of one-repeat mutations separating haplotypes

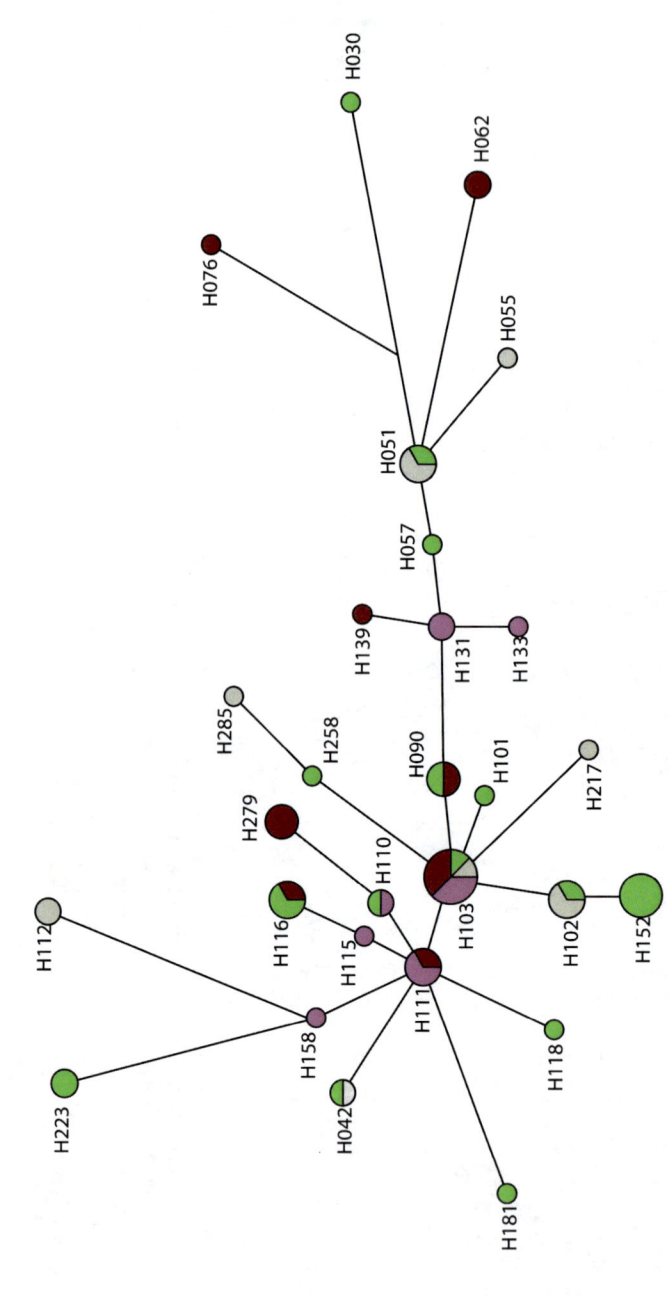

8 Time perspective of Formosan Aborigines

Paul Jen-kuei Li

Introduction

All the aboriginal peoples in Taiwan speak languages belonging to the Austronesian family. The linguistic evidence indicates that their ancestors arrived in Taiwan at the same time, cal. 6500 BP.[1] The Formosan languages they speak are generally believed to be more diverse than the Austronesian languages of any other area outside Taiwan. They must have started to split into different ethnic groups at a great time depth. Since there was no written document for any of the Formosan languages until the 17th century, we have to rely on linguistic methods to reconstruct the early stages of the dispersal of Formosan aborigines. We can only give approximate dates or a relative chronology at this stage of knowledge, and these are summarized in Plate 8.I.

Written documents have been available ever since the Dutch period (1624–62). We are able to give specific or more precise dates for the more recent dispersal of some ethnic groups, including the mountain tribes: Paiwan (1600), Bunun (1700) and Atayal (1750), as based on Mabuchi's (1953–4) anthropological study, and for the plains tribes: the dispersal of the south-western tribes of Siraya to the interior in 1670, of Makatao also to the interior in 1722, of Taivoan to mountain areas in 1736, the collective migration of the five western plains tribes (Taokas, Papora, Babuza, Hoanya and Pazih) to the north-east coast of Taiwan in 1804 and eastward to the interior to Puli in 1823, and that of Kavalan people southward to the east coast in 1840, as based on Chinese written documents (Y. Chang 1951).

However, we can only give approximate dates or a relative chronology for dispersal at much earlier time depths. For instance, Rukai must have started to disperse southward perhaps more than a thousand years ago, splitting into Mantauran and the ancestor of the non-Mantauran dialects; Matauran is the most divergent dialect both phonologically and syntactically (Li 1996, 2001). The split of the non-Mantauran ancestor into Maga-Tona and Budai-Labuan-Taromak may have occurred about 1000 BP (Li 2001). The subsequent split of the latter into Budai and Labuan-Taromak probably took place only a few hundred years ago because these dialects are all very closely related and their oral traditions indicate that they were separated only recently.

Another example is the East Formosan group (Blust 1999; Li 2004a), which may have started to disperse to the east coast from the south-western coast of Taiwan between 3000 and 4000 BP. This subgroup further split into Basay and Kavalan. The former migrated to the northern coast of Taiwan around 1800 BP while the latter migrated to the northeast coast around 1300 BP, as based on carbon-14 dating. The second wave of dispersal of the East Formosan group to the east coast, later known as Amis, may have taken place *cal.* 3000 BP.

Still another example is the successive stages of the splits and dispersal of the western plains tribes, which were much more complex and less certain. Linguistically it is clear that Taokas, Babuza, Papora and Hoanya are all very closely related (Tsuchida 1982: 9) and they may have started to split off less than a thousand years ago. The common ancestor of these four has a closer genetic relationship with Thao (Blust 1996), which may have split off from it around 2000 BP. Their relationship with Pazih and Saisiyat is less clear. If it can be firmly established, then Pazih and Saisiyat may have split off from the other western plains tribes 3000 BP or even earlier.

How do we determine those dates without any written documents or carbon-14 dating information? The dates in the paragraphs above are inferred from linguistic subgrouping and relative linguistic chronology, and an estimated date is assigned to each successive split. Some help is provided by archaeological dating (see below, especially Figure 8.3). Otherwise we have to rely on 'informed guesswork'.

Origin of Formosan aborigines

What was the origin of the Formosan aborigines before they came to Taiwan? The answer to the question largely depends on which language family or families Austronesian is genetically related to. Different hypotheses have been proposed regarding the possible genetic relationship between various of the language families in South-east Asia. I suggest that we compare sets of cognates as identified and reconstructed by world-recognized scholars to see if there is sufficient linguistic evidence to establish genetic relationships among these language families. We should compare and examine basic vocabulary, and avoid cultural items that are apt to be borrowed. Examples of comparison include pairs of semantically related cognates, numerals and personal pronouns. A whole set of numerals can be borrowed from one language to another belonging to a different language family, such as the well-known Japanese borrowing of Chinese numerals. A systematic comparison of the personal pronouns reconstructed for different language families will show that it is extremely unlikely that a set of personal pronouns can be borrowed from one language to another. I concluded in my recent study that the genetic relationship between Chinese and Tibeto-Burman is well established, whereas there is little evidence for Austro-Tai, Sino-Tai or Sino-Austronesian (Li 2004c). However, there is plenty of linguistic evidence that indicates that there was much language contact between Tai-Kadai and Austronesian (Thurgood 1994) in the early period of history. The lexical evidence 'between Austronesian and Austroasiatic is not impressive, but nevertheless exists' (Diffloth 1994). It is, therefore, almost certain that the origin of pre-Austronesian is in continental South-east Asia. Archaeological and genetic evidence points to the same area.

Early dispersal of the Formosan aborigines

It is generally believed that Taiwan is the most likely Proto-Austronesian (PAN) homeland and that Proto-Austronesian speakers started to disperse outside Taiwan from the homeland about 4000 BP (Bellwood, this volume). The correct hypothesis about the centre of dispersal largely depends on a reasonable subgrouping hypothesis. Different hypotheses have been proposed for PAN subgrouping: two primary subgroups according to Starosta (1995; see Figure 8.1), but ten (including the Malayo-Polynesian subgroup) according to Blust (1999; see Figure 8.2). It would be almost impossible to pinpoint the centre of dispersal if there were ten primary subgroups. It is much more feasible to work with Starosta's binary splitting hypothesis: the first offshoot is Rukai, the second Tsou[2] and so on. Since both Rukai and Tsou are situated in southern Taiwan, it is natural to postulate the south-western plain, Tainan, as the center of dispersal, as Starosta (pers. comm.) has done. Hence I shall use Starosta's theory as a working hypothesis and starting point in this chapter. The main difference between Blust's subgrouping hypothesis and Starosta's is that the former is based on phonological evidence alone while the latter is based on morphosyntactic evidence. I do not see why one should take only one type of linguistic evidence into consideration. However, Starosta did not cover all Formosan languages and I do not agree with all of his subgrouping, so I make several inferences based on my own studies. Further to adopting Starosta's hypothesis treating Rukai as the first split and Tsou (or more accurately Tsouic) as the second, my own classification of Formosan languages includes the following:

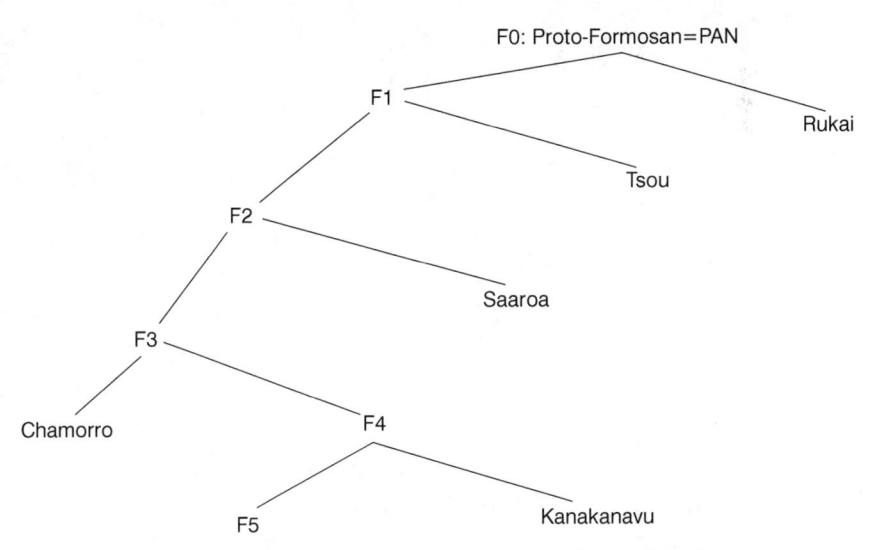

Figure 8.1 Proto-Austronesian subgrouping according to Starosta (1995).

214 *Paul Jen-kuei Li*

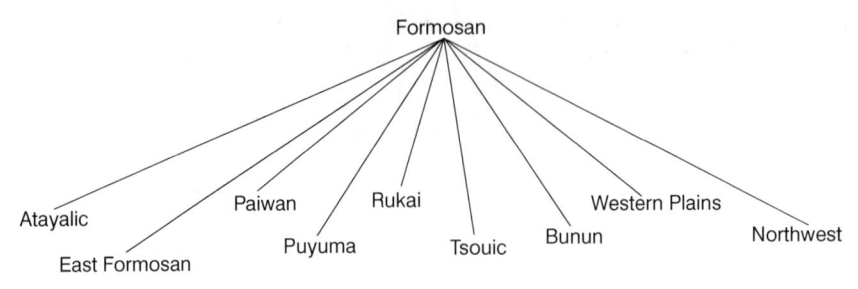

Figure 8.2 Proto-Austronesian subgrouping according to Blust (1999).

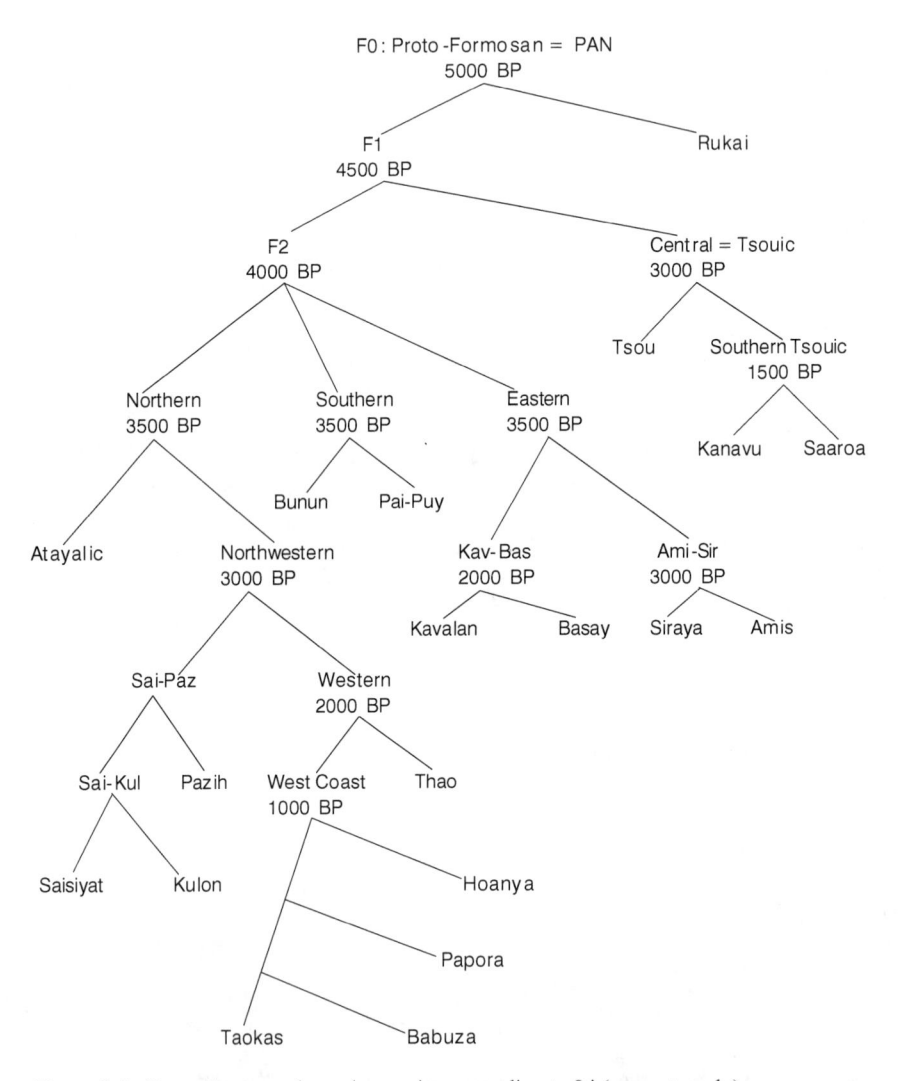

Figure 8.3 Proto-Austronesian subgrouping according to Li (present study).

(1) Northern, including Atayalic and Northwestern (Li 1985, 2003), (2) Southern, including Bunun, Paiwan and Puyuma, and (3) Eastern, including Kavalan, Basay, Amis and Siraya (Blust 1999; Li 2004a); see Figure 8.3.

There are nonetheless unresolved problems with this subgrouping. Most problematic is the Southern group, which is mainly based on lexicostatistical rather than phonological evidence. There is no phonological evidence for a close relationship among Bunun, Paiwan and Puyuma. There is also little morphological evidence for a close relationship between Paiwan and Puyuma, as based on most recent studies. The position of Rukai is the most controversial: Tsuchida (1976: 15) treats it as more closely related to Tsouic languages, based on lexicostatistic evidence, while Ho (1983) believes it to be one of the Paiwanic languages, i.e. part of my Southern group, as based on a comparison of fourteen grammatical features. In fact, Japanese anthropologists did not distinguish between Rukai, Paiwan and Puyuma in the early stage of their studies. In addition to the grammatical evidence presented by Starosta, Rukai is unique among all Formosan languages: (1) unlike all other Formosan languages, it has no focus system at all, and (2) while most Formosan languages distinguish between human and nonhuman numerals, Rukai, especially the Tanan dialect, makes an animate and inanimate distinction instead. Hence I shall follow Starosta in treating Rukai as the first offshoot of the proto-language in this chapter.

There is less problem with the Northern, Central and Eastern subgroups. A unique phonological innovation, i.e. the merger of PAN *n and *j, clearly defines the Eastern group and sets it apart from all the other Austronesian languages. Both phonological and lexical evidence for the Eastern group seems to be fairly solid (Li 2004a).

The Central (Tsouic) group has the following phonological innovations: (1) PAN *C, *d > c, (2) PAN *y > Proto-Tsouic *z (z in Tsou, l in Kanakanavu, and $ɬ$ in Saaroa), and (3) PAN *R > r. However, (2) and (3) are not exclusively shared by the Tsouic group: PAN *y > ð in Bunun and *ð (only in medial-position) in Proto-Rukaic; PAN *R > r also in Puyuma. It is extremely unlikely that the Tsouic languages would be more closely related to Bunun or Puyuma. It is more likely that independent and parallel changes have taken in these languages. The Tsouic subgroup is based on Tsuchida's (1976) work, and his evidence is mainly lexical rather than phonological. H. Chang (2006) has recently suggested that Tsou and the so-called 'Southern Tsouic' languages may not constitute a subgroup.

In the Northern group, PAN *S_2 and *H_1 merged as h (Dahl 1981). In the Atayalic languages and Saisiyat, PAN *s also merged with *S_2 and H_1 as h, but this has not happened in Pazih, Thao or the four Western Plains languages. Again phonological evidence is not so strong as lexical for the Northern group (Li 1985).

Recently a large number of Tapenkeng Culture remains, including artifacts, ecofacts and human skeletons, were excavated from the sites of Nan-kuan-li and Nan-kuan-li East in the Tainan Science-based Industrial Park, which will provide valuable information for the problem of Austronesian origin and dispersal. The oldest carbon-14 dating from the sites to date is around 5000 BP (Cheng-hwa Tsang, pers.comm.).

The following successive dispersal and migration scenario can thus be reconstructed. (1) The first group of PAN speakers to split off, Rukai, dispersed to the east about 5000 years ago. (2) The second group to split off was the Tsouic group, which dispersed to the north-east *cal.* 4500 BP, and subsequently split into Tsou and Southern Tsouic *cal.* 3000 BP. (3) The third split may have resulted in the Northern group (Atayalic and Northwestern), the Southern group (Paiwan, Puyuma, and Bunun), and the East Formosan group *cal.* 4000 BP. Among the Southern group, the Paiwan-Puyuma group dispersed to the south-east while Bunun dispersed to the north-east *cal.* 3500 BP. Paiwan and Puyuma are believed to be more closely related to each other, as based on lexicostatistical evidence (Dyen 1963, 1971). Puyuma may have split from Paiwan and dispersed to the east coast of Taiwan *cal.* 3000 BP. However, there is no phonological or morphological evidence to show a closer relationship between them, or between Bunun and any other Formosan language (Blust 1999). The Northern group, including Atayalic and Northwestern, split off and dispersed to the north *cal.* 4000 BP. The subsequent split of the group into the Atayalic and Northwestern was *cal.* 3500 BP, and then the Northwestern group split into Saisiyat/Pazih and the West Plains group (Thao, Taokas, Babuza, Papora and Hoanya) *cal.* 3000 BP. (4) The fourth group, Eastern (Blust's 1999 'East Formosan'), simply stayed on in the homeland site, Tainan, until its subsequent split into Siraya, Amis and Kavalan/Basay about 500 years later: The Kavalan/Basay group dispersed to the east coast of Taiwan *cal.* 3500 BP, and then the Amis group also to the east coast about 500 years later, i.e. 3000 BP, both by sea.[3] The Basay group migrated to the northern coast of Taiwan *cal.* 1800 BP, and the Kavalan migrated to the north-east coast *cal.* 1300 BP, both based on recent carbon-14 dating (Tsang 2007).

More recent dispersal of the Formosan aborigines

Written documents in Dutch, Spanish and Chinese have been available since the 17th century. Precise dates were recorded or nearly precise dates can be inferred for the migration of the plains tribes, including the Western Plains tribes, Siraya and Kavalan, especially in the past two centuries (Y. Chang 1951). If precise dates are unavailable, approximate dates will be given or inferred whenever possible.

I have discussed the more recent dispersal of various Formosan ethnic groups in some detail in an earlier paper (Li 2001), and interested readers are referred to it.

Notes

1   All Formosan languages except Puyuma retain PAn *S, which has become h or lost in all extra-Formosan languages. Although Saaroa has mostly lost *S, it exhibits s for *S6 (Tsuchida 1976: 159), and it is retained in the closely related language, Kanakanavu.

The oldest carbon-14 dating for Tapenkeng archaeological sites in Taiwan is cal. 6500 bp (Tsang 2007).
2 Tsou is unique among all Formosan languages in several aspects. For one thing, its focus system is very different from the others, namely -i, -a and -eni instead of -en, -an and si- or sa-, as commonly found in most other Formosan languages. For another, Tsou has a very elaborate auxiliary system, and every clause requires an auxiliary. See H. Chang (2006) for other unique features of Tsou.
3 Amis, Kavalan and Basay have the similar oral tradition that their ancestors came from an island named Sinasay, which is generally interpreted as the Green Island off the southeast coast of Taiwan. According to Mabuchi (1953–4), there is evidence that Basay settled in north Hualian before they moved on to northern Taiwan.

References

Bellwood, P. (1991) 'The Austronesian dispersal and the origin of languages', *Scientific American*, 265(1): 88–92.
Blust, R. (1985) 'The Austronesian homeland: A linguistic perspective', *Asian Perspectives*, 26(1): 45–67.
Blust, R. (1996) 'Some remarks on the linguistic position of Thao', *Oceanic Linguistics*, 35(2): 272–94.
Blust, R. (1999) 'Subgrouping, circularity and extinction: Some issues in Austronesian comparative linguistics', in E. Zeitoun and P. Li (eds) *Selected Papers from the Eighth International Conference on Austronesian Linguistics* (Symposium Series of the Institute of Linguistics (Preparatory Office), 1), pp. 31–94, Taipei: Academia Sinica.
Chang, H.Y. (2006) 'Rethinking the Tsouic subgroup hypothesis: A morphosyntactic perspective', in H. Chang, L. Huang and D. Ho (eds) *Streams Converging into an Ocean: Festschrift in Honor of Professor Paul Jen-kuei Li on his 70th Birthday*, pp. 565–83, Taipei: Institute of Linguistics, Academia Sinica.
Chang, Y.C. (1951) 'A comparative name-list of the plain tribe villages through the historical ages', *Wenshien Zhuankan* (Taipei), 2(1/2): 1–84 (in Chinese).
Dahl, O. (1981) *Early Phonetic and Phonemic Changes in Austronesian*, Oslo: Institute for Comparative Research in Human Culture.
Diffloth, G. (1994) 'The lexical evidence for Austric, so far', *Oceanic Linguistics*, 33(2): 309–21.
Dyen, I. (1963) 'The position of the Malayopolynesian languages of Formosa', *Asian Perspectives*, 7(1/2): 261–71.
Dyen, I. (1971) 'The Austronesian languages of Formosa', *Current Trends in Linguistics*, 8: 168–99.
Ho, D.A. (1983) 'The position of Rukai in the Formosan languages', *Bulletin of the Institute of History and Philology, Academia Sinica*, 54(1): 121–68 (in Chinese).
Li, P. (1977) 'The internal relationships of Rukai', *Bulletin of the Institute of History and Philology, Academia Sinica*, 48(1): 1–92.
Li, P. (1985) 'The position of Atayal in the Austronesian family', in A. Pawley and L. Carrington (eds) *Austronesian Linguistics at the 15th Pacific Science Congress, Pacific Linguistics*, C-88: 257–80.
Li, P. (1996) 'The pronominal systems in Rukai', in B. Nothofer (ed.) *Reconstruction, Classification, Description: Festschrift in Honour of Isidore Dyen*, pp. 209–30, Hamburg: Abera Verlag.
Li, P. (2001) 'The dispersal of the Formosan aborigines in Taiwan', *Language and Linguistics*, 2(1): 271–8.

Li, P. (2003) 'The internal relationships of six western plains languages', *Bulletin of the Department of Anthropology*, 61: 39–51.
Li, P. (2004a) 'Origins of the East Formosan peoples: Basay, Kavalan, Amis and Siraya', *Language and Linguistics*, 5(2): 363–76.
Li, P. (2004b) *Selected Papers on Formosan Languages*, 2 vols (Language and Linguistics Monograph Series, C3), Taipei: Institute of Linguistics, Academia Sinica.
Li, P. (2004c) 'Establishing genetic relationship between language families in Southeast Asia', *Studies on Sino-Tibetan Languages: Papers in Honor of Professor Hwang-cherng Gong on his Seventieth Birthday*, pp. 11–42, Taipei: Institute of Linguistics, Academia Sinica.
Mabuchi, T. (1953–4) 'Migration and distribution of the Formosan aborigines', *Anthropological Studies* (Tokyo), 18(1/2): 123–54; 18(4): 23–72 (in Japanese).
Starosta, S (1995) 'A grammatical subgrouping of Formosan languages', in P. Li, Cheng-hwa Tsang, Ying-kuei Huang, Dah-an Ho, and Chiu-yu Tseng (eds) *Austronesian Studies Relating to Taiwan*, pp. 683–726, Taipei: Institute of History and Philology, Academia Sinica.
Thurgood, G. (1994) 'Tai-Kadai and Austronesian: The nature of the historical relationship', *Oceanic Linguistics*, 33(2): 345–68.
Tsang, C. (2007) 'Taiwan as viewed from archaeology', *Eleven Lectures on Taiwan History*, 1–34, Taipei: National Museum of History (in Chinese).
Tsuchida, S. (1976) *Reconstruction of Proto-Tsouic Phonology* (Study of Languages and Cultures of Asia and Africa, Monograph Series, 5), Tokyo: University of Foreign Studies.
Tsuchida, S. (1982) *A Comparative Vocabulary of Austronesian Languages of Sinicized Ethnic Groups in Taiwan*, part I, *West Taiwan* (Memoirs of the Faculty of Letters, 7), Tokyo: University of Tokyo.

9 To which language family does Chinese belong, or what's in a name?

George van Driem

There are at least five competing theories about the linguistic prehistory of Chinese. Two of them, Tibeto-Burman and Sino-Tibetan, originated in the beginning of the 19th century. Sino-Caucasian and Sino-Austronesian are products of the second half of the 20th century, and East Asian is an intriguing model presented in 2001. These terms designate distinct models of language relationship with divergent implications for the peopling of East Asia. What are the substantive differences between the models? How do the paradigms differently inform the direction of linguistic investigation and differently shape the formulation of research topics? What empirical evidence can compel us to decide between the theories? Which of the theories is the default hypothesis, and why? How can terminology be used in a judicious manner to avoid unwittingly presupposing the veracity of improbable or, at best, unsupported propositions?

1. The default hypothesis: Tibeto-Burman

The first rigorous polyphyletic exposition of Asian linguistic stocks was presented in Paris by the German scholar Julius Heinrich von Klaproth in 1823.[1] His *Asia Polyglotta* was more comprehensive, extended beyond the confines of the Russian Empire and included major languages of East Asia, Southeast Asia and Polar America. Based on a systematic comparison of lexical roots, Klaproth identified and distinguished twenty-three Asian linguistic stocks, which he knew did not represent an exhaustive inventory. Yet he argued for a smaller number of phyla because he recognized the genetic affinity between certain of these stocks and the distinct nature of others. One of the major linguistic phyla identified by Klaproth was the language family which comprised Burmese, Tibetan and Chinese and all languages which could be demonstrated to be genetically related to these three.

Klaproth explicitly excluded languages known today to be members of the Daic or Kra-Dai family, e.g. Thai, or members of the Austroasiatic family, e.g. Vietnamese and Mon (1823a: 363–5). Yet Klaproth did not devise labels for each of the many distinct language phyla which he identified in Asia. From 1852 onwards, John Logan became one of the first to use the term 'Tibeto-Burman' in print for the language family identified by Klaproth, and to which Logan added Karen and other related languages.

```
                    Tibeto-Burman
        ┌───────────────┼───────────────┐── ── ──
     Tibetan         Chinese         Burmese
```
...and all languages which can be demonstrated to be genetically related to these three

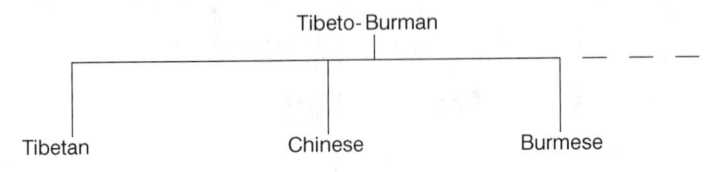

Figure 9.1 One of the language families identified by Julius Heinrich von Klaproth in his polyphyletic view of Asian linguistic stocks (1823a, 1823b). He explicitly excluded languages today known to be Daic, e.g. Thai, or Austroasiatic, e.g. Mon, Vietnamese.

Yet Logan, like many other scholars of his day in the British Isles, was an adherent of the Turanian theory dreamt up by Friedrich Max Müller in Oxford. So he treated Tibeto-Burman as an ingredient in this hypothetical Turanian family, which supposedly encompassed all languages of the world other than the Indo-European and Afroasiatic languages. Logan later also coined the label 'Chino-Tibetan' for a subset of ancient Tibeto-Burman tribes between East and Central Asia (1856: 16).[2] Subsequently, Charles Forbes observed:

> The term 'Tibeto-Burman' has latterly crept into use as the convenient designation of a very large family of languages which appear more or less to approximate to each other. (1878: 210)

Scholars such Bernard Houghton, who worked on languages in Burma, followed Klaproth in recognizing Chinese to be a member of this Tibeto-Burman family. Houghton observed that in Tibeto-Burman far-reaching phonological change had altered the appearance of many shared roots, particularly in the 'tonic languages' which had 'suffered much from phonetic decay'. False cognates that look alike ought not to be confused with genuine shared Tibeto-Burman roots:

> If many such exist in Burmese, where phonetic decay is comparatively moderate, how much more must it be the case in extreme cases like Chinese (even the re-construction of the old sounds in this language barely brings it to the same stage as modern Burmese) and Sgaw-Karen, in which latter every final consonant, even nasals, has been elided. (Houghton 1896: 28)

Robert Cust likewise followed Klaproth in treating 'Tibeto-Burman', including Karen, as a family distinct from the 'Tai' and the 'Mon-Anam' families (1878).

Epistemologically, Klaproth's model makes the fewest assumptions and thus continues to represent the most agnostic theory about the genetic relationship of Chinese. The Tibeto-Burman theory asserts that Tibetan, Burmese and Chinese are genetically related. Furthermore, the theory assumes that there is a family of languages that can be demonstrated to be genetically related to these three languages, and that, at this reconstructible level of relationship, Tibeto-Burman excludes both the Daic or Kra-Dai languages and the Austroasiatic languages. No new nomenclature is proposed. Tibeto-Burman is used in its original sense to denote the family tree recognized by Julius von Klaproth and accepted by scholars such as Forbes, Houghton and Cust. The Tibeto-Burman theory makes no explicit assertions about the internal subgrouping of the family. So, what is the evidence for the Tibeto-Burman theory?

A vast body of data and comparative work has come to fill the literature on Tibeto-Burman ever since Nicolaes Witsen published the first Tibetan word list and first specimens of Tibetan script in the West in 1692. Most of this literature is cited in the bibliography of my handbook (van Driem 2001), and a number of outstanding contributions have appeared since, e.g. Burling (2004), Coupe (2003), Genetti (2003), Haller (2004), Hari and Chhegu (2004), Hildebrandt (2003), Jacques (2004), Lahaussois (2002), Opgenort (2004, 2005), Plaisier (2005), Strahm and Maibaum (2005), Turin (2005), Wāng (2004), Watters (2002, 2004). All early and recent descriptions of Tibeto-Burman languages support the Tibeto-Burman theory. Comparative historical studies, reconstructions of Proto-Tibeto-Burman and of Tibeto-Burman subgroups such as Old Chinese, all bear out Klaproth's original model, even when some of the scholars who have marshalled this evidence entertained different, less agnostic theories of language relationship, e.g. Shafer (1963, 1966, 1967, 1968, 1974), Benedict (1972, 1976), Matisoff (2003).[3]

As the most agnostic and best supported theory about the genetic affinity of Chinese, the Tibeto-Burman theory constitutes the default hypothesis. No additional evidence need be adduced to bolster the case of Tibeto-Burman. Rather, the burden of proof lies on proponents of theories that make a greater number of assertions about the genetic relationship of Chinese. We shall now turn to four of these other theories and assess the weight of evidence in their favour.

2. Tibeto-Burman proper vs. pinioned 'Tibeto-Burman'

Both monophyletic models, Indo-Chinese or Turanian, lumped most Asiatic languages into a single grand stock and obscured the genetic position of Chinese. Adherents of either Indo-Chinese or Turanian remained confused about Chinese and undertook to treat Sinitic as something outside of Tibeto-Burman. Müller's Turanian was mentioned above. Indo-Chinese was the invention of the Scottish travelling scholar John Leyden (1806, 1808), whose hypothetical language family encompassed all faraway tongues of Eurasia and Oceania. The anomalous treatment meted out to Chinese within both monophyletic conceptions was due to various causes.

Race and language used to be confused by many laymen and even by some linguists. Much was made of the fact that the Chinese appeared to be racially different from the Burmese, for example; though linguists such as Klaproth and Müller stressed the absolute distinction in principle between race and language, many remained deaf to their explanations.[4]

222 George van Driem

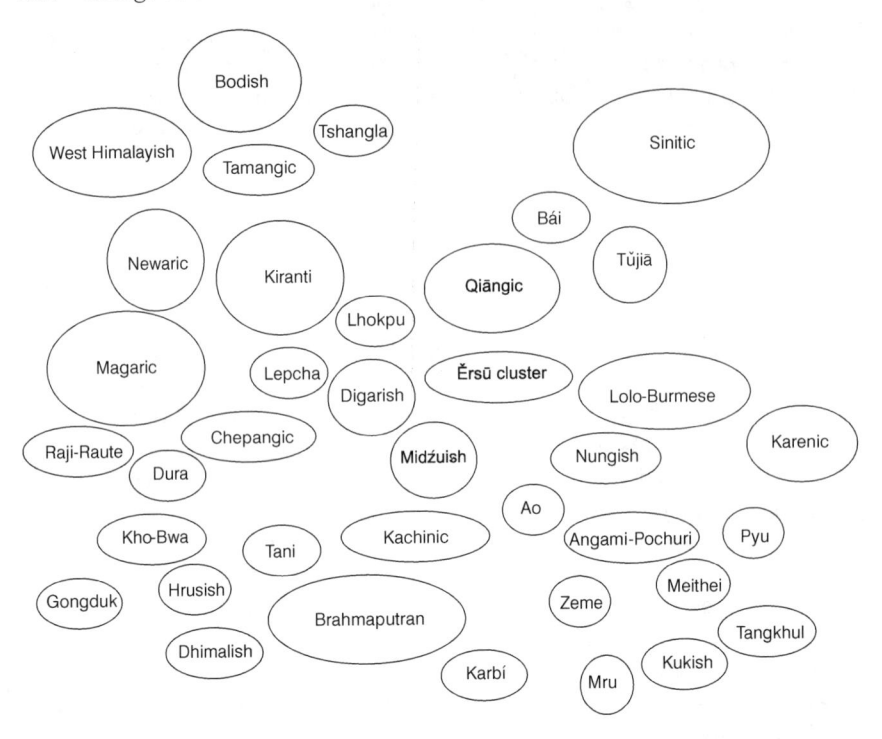

[Figure showing ovals with Tibeto-Burman subgroup names: Bodish, Tshangla, Sinitic, West Himalayish, Tamangic, Bái, Newaric, Kiranti, Qiāngic, Tǔjiā, Lhokpu, Magaric, Lepcha, Ěrsū cluster, Digarish, Lolo-Burmese, Karenic, Raji-Raute, Chepangic, Midźuish, Nungish, Dura, Ao, Kho-Bwa, Kachinic, Angami-Pochuri, Pyu, Tani, Gongduk, Hrusish, Zeme, Meithei, Brahmaputran, Tangkhul, Dhimalish, Karbí, Mru, Kukish]

Figure 9.2   Tibeto-Burman subgroups identified since Julius von Klaproth. Brahmaputran may include Kachinic and Dhimalish. Various other subgrouping proposals are discussed in my handbook (van Driem 2001).[5]

A second source of confusion was language typology. In 1782, Rüdiger proposed that structural differences between languages were the result of differences in the stage of development attained by various language communities. Language types therefore reflected a hierarchy of thought. The morphological simplicity of Chinese puzzled typologists who wondered how a people speaking a language at the bottom of the ladder in terms of structural complexity could have produced a great civilization.

In 1854, Arthur de Gobineau attempted to resolve this quandary by speculating that Chinese, whilst a primitive tongue, had been successful because the language was male. Half of the world's languages, he reasoned, were male, and half were female. Male languages are naturally endowed with greater precision than female languages, which are replete with vague notions and emotive terms. Other linguists like Ernest Renan resolved the apparent contradiction in their minds by ascribing a 'sècheresse d'esprit et de cœur' and all sorts of other nasty attributes to the Chinese. Wilhelm von Humboldt and August Friedrich Pott were amongst the linguists who challenged racist notions propagated by the language typologists.

Scholars in Germany working in the tradition of Klaproth had sound intuitions about historical phonology and lucid insights into its implications for historical grammar. Carl Richard Lepsius insisted that Chinese tones were phonological and could not be equated with either musical tones or intonation. In comparing Tibetan and Southern Chinese dialects with Mandarin, Lepsius recognized that 'die Chinesischen Tonaccente' had arisen from the loss of syllable finals and the loss of distinctions between older syllable initials. Therefore, Lepsius argued both against the diachronic implication of the ladder of language evolution invented by the typologists and against the independent genetic status accorded to Chinese by the monophyleticists. In terms of their historical phonology, Chinese dialects did not represent 'embryonische unentwickelte Ursprachen'. Rather, Chinese dialects were much evolved languages whose apparent 'Einsilbigkeit' was the result of sound changes which had obscured their genetic proximity to their closest cousins.

These diachronic developments had not only reduced phonological distinctions in the roots, but had in the process also partially or wholly obliterated smaller flexional elements that differentiated words which had at one time been morphologically articulate (Lepsius 1861: 472, 492–6). Based on lexical comparison with other Tibeto-Burman languages such as Lepcha, Kuki-Chin and Tibetan, Wilhelm Grube arrived at the same conclusion (1881: 19–20). A century later, Søren Egerod eloquently reiterated this sinological view:

> Quand le chinois apparaissait comme une langue écrite sur les bronzes ou dans de vieilles œuvres comme le *Shū Jīng*, nous n'avions plus de doute que nous ayons devant nous une langue dont la morphologie était développée, mais dont l'écriture était de telle nature que cette morphologie se cachait assez largement. On a continué d'écrire pendant très longtemps des expressions morphologiques différentes d'une racine avec un caractère unique. Ainsi, quand on lisait un texte, on suppléait la lecture par une interprétation de la langue écrite. (1972 [1967]: 101)[6]

Wilhelm Schott, another adherent of Klaproth's polyphyletic model, argued against both Turanian and Indo-Chinese. In a wonderfully worded letter now kept at the Royal Asiatic Society in London, Schott tried to persuade Brian Houghton to abandon Müller's Turanian theory. Likewise, in the proceedings of the Royal Academy in Berlin, Schott complained that the term *indo-chinesisch* was '*eine unpassende Benennung*' because the three best known languages of Southeast Asia, Burmese, Vietnamese and Thai, were known to belong to three separate language families (1856: 161–2). Schott used the term 'Siam-sprachen' for the Daic or Kra-Dai languages, but he invented no term for the other two language families identified by Klaproth. Rather, somewhat diffidently, Schott resigned himself to the fact that people might go on using the term *indo-chinesisch*, but cautioned that those using the label ought not to adopt the uninformed monophyletic model that it represented.

Here history teaches us an important lesson. The English term 'Indo-Chinese', adopted in German as *indochinesisch*, with or without a hyphen, remained popular, and inexorably along with the catchy name came the model of genetic relationship that it denoted. As a consequence, much subsequent scholarship either uncritically accepted the family tree or attacked the language family from within, only to end up belatedly with the same set of language families at the end of the 20th century that Klaproth had identified for this part of the world at the beginning of the 19th century.

Unfettered by the Indo-Chinese paradigm, Francis Mason recognized the Mon-Khmer-Kolarian or Austroasiatic family when he established the genetic relationship between the Munda languages of the Indian subcontinent and the Mon-Khmer languages of Southeast Asia (1854, 1860). By contrast, working within the monophyletic paradigm, Ernst Kuhn had to extricate Austroasiatic from Indo-Chinese to get 'zwei Hauptgruppen von Sprachen', one of which encompassed 'die Sprachen von Annam, Kambodscha und Pegu', whereas the other group lumped together 'die Sprachen von Tibet, Barma, Siam und China' (1883, 1889), to which Kuhn also added Karen and the languages of the Himalayas.

Subsequently, several tendencies conspired to take Chinese out of Tibeto-Burman and assign it to the wrong language family. Ignorance of Chinese historical phonology and widespread preconceptions about race led scholars like American philologist John Avery[7] to treat Chinese as something outside of Tibeto-Burman (1885). At the same time, scholars of Indo-Chinese, unlike scholars who followed Klaproth, proved unable to distinguish between inherited and borrowed vocabulary in Thai. Konow and Grierson criticized the Indo-Chinese and Turanian views but adopted a cardinal legacy of its proponents by putting Chinese together with Daic or Kra-Dai into a 'Siamese-Chinese' family, distinct from 'Tibeto-Burman' (Grierson 1904, 1909). This bifurcation into a western and an eastern branch, which Kurt Wulff (1934) called 'das Tibeto-Barmanische' and 'das Siamesisch-Chinesische', became the hallmark of the Indo-Chinese model, shown in Figure 9.3. As long as the name Indo-Chinese remained in use, those who employed the term adopted the model it designated, e.g. Georg von der Gabelentz (1881), Emile Forchhammer (1882), August Conrady (1896), Berthold Laufer (1916).

Indo-Chinese was renamed 'sino-tibétain' by Jean Przyluski in 1924, and the new name gradually caught on. Finally, in the 1930s, Robert Shafer decided to take Daic out of Indo-Chinese, but on a pilgrimage to Paris he was convinced by

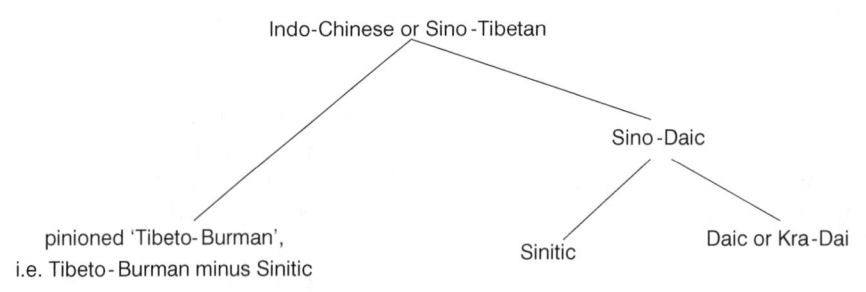

Figure 9.3 The Indo-Chinese or Sino-Tibetan theory: Daic or Kra-Dai has been excluded since the Second World War.

Maspero to leave Daic inside Sino-Tibetan (Shafer 1955: 97–8). So Paul Benedict was able to scoop Shafer by removing Daic in 1942 after he too had joined Kroeber's Berkeley project. Shafer patently rejected a bifurcation of the language family into 'Tibeto-Burman' and 'Siamese-Chinese'. Therefore, aside from Daic, which Shafer retained against his better intuitions, his Sino-Tibetan consisted of five divisions, i.e. Sinitic, Bodic, Burmic, Baric and Karenic. Benedict, however, stuck with the Indo-Chinese model which had been passed down from generation to generation, and after the excision of Daic the resultant tree effectively brought back the family to Klaproth's original Tibeto-Burman with one salient difference. The postulation of a reduced 'Tibeto-Burman' subgroup, from which Sinitic has been excised and which is coordinate with Sinitic under the top node, remains the sole defining trait of the Sino-Tibetan model.[8]

Sino-Tibetan, therefore, is essentially a subgrouping hypothesis that posits a pinioned 'Tibeto-Burman' taxon, as opposed to the originally conceived Tibeto-Burman family which I shall continue to call Tibeto-Burman proper. The 'Tibeto-Burman' of the Sino-Tibetanists encompasses all languages of the family other than Sinitic. Since these languages have never been shown to share any common innovation that would set them off collectively as a subgroup against and on par with Sinitic, the Sino-Tibetan hypothesis remains unsupported by evidence to date. Matisoff has continued to reproduce the Sino-Tibetan family tree as an article of faith (2000, 2003), but, when challenged to defend this subgrouping hypothesis, he has failed to adduce any shared innovation or compelling lexical evidence for pinioned 'Tibeto-Burman'.

Some subgrouping proposals are ambivalent with regard to a choice between Tibeto-Burman proper or Indo-Chinese, e.g. Shafer's Bodic or Burmic, in that these proposals could be subgroups within either model. This cannot be said for either Sino-Bodic or pinioned 'Tibeto-Burman'. Sino-Bodic essentially dates back to Klaproth's own observation that Tibetan appeared to be genetically closer to Chinese than either was to Burmese (1823a: 346, 356, 365). Additional evidence in support of the Sino-Bodic hypothesis was presented by Simon (1927–9), Shafer (1955, 1966, 1967, 1968, 1974), Bodman (1980) and myself (van Driem 1997). My coinage 'Sino-Bodic' reflects Shafer's view that the alleged affinity is between Sinitic and the nebulously delineated Bodic, not just between Sinitic and Bodish.[9] Moreover, a complex relationship of borrowing may have existed between Chinese and languages such as Tibetan at various stages of their history, and this process may have been further complicated by a contact phenomenon described by Ferlus as 'hypercorrection by affected imitation', masking a layer of borrowings which has hitherto not been clearly identified in historical comparative studies (2003: 274).

Matisoff was able to eliminate only 12 of the 39 specific Sino-Bodic correspondences, namely 40, 48, 49, 56, 58, 60, 61, 64, 66, 69, 74 and 77 in Matisoff's numbering.[10] A few more correspondences were unconvincingly challenged. For example, the alternative cognate set which Matisoff proposes for correspondence 75 is contestable, and his alternative explanation for correspondence 46 makes less semantic sense. Given the speciousness of some of Matisoff's etymologies (e.g. 1992, cf. Sagart 1994b), his semantic sensibilities, as diagrammed in his 'metastatic flow charts' (e.g. 1978), are not always to be trusted. In addition to Sino-Bodic lexical isoglosses, my article presented Tibeto-Burman correspondences for which the phonological match with Sinitic is generally better for Bodic than for cognate forms from other branches of Tibeto-Burman.[11] In addition to leaving most of the Sino-Bodic evidence unassailed, Matisoff failed to address relevant evidence adduced by Shafer and Bodman.

So, in contradistinction to Sino-Tibetan, for which no evidence has ever been presented, lexical and morphological evidence warrants entertaining Sino-Bodic as a viable working hypothesis about the closest relatives of Sinitic within Tibeto-Burman. Stanley Starosta accepted Sino-Bodic and incorporated the hypothesis in his East Asian phylogeny, discussed below. Matisoff rails that the evidence for Sino-Bodic might be 'turning all our ideas about ST/TB subgrouping upside down' (2000: 366). Matisoff's histrionic reaction and strident tone must be seen as a sally not against Sino-Bodic *per se*, but against the threat which Sino-Bodic poses to Sino-Tibetan, the subgrouping hypothesis about pinioned 'Tibeto-Burman' that he inherited from his mentor Paul Benedict in 1968.

It has been suggested that perhaps the distinction between what is reconstructed as *a vs. *ə (or *ā vs. *a) in current versions of Proto-Sinitic might conceivably represent an ancient 'Sino-Tibetan' distinction lost in a merger which affected all 'Tibeto-Burman' languages, but this idea has not been pursued. Not all branches of Tibeto-Burman have been scrutinized in this regard, and ultimately such a conjecture cannot be sustained on the basis of an unwarranted limitation of the available evidence. A tentative cursory study by Jean Robert Opgenort has shown that whereas Old Chinese *a (or *ā) appears most often to correspond to an /a/ in modern Kiranti languages, the Tibeto-Burman vowel reflected by Old Chinese *ə (or *a) appears to have engendered a more complex pattern of vocalism in Kiranti (pers. comm., July 2005).

More importantly, even if the Old Chinese distinction were shown not to be reflected outside of Sinitic, then there is yet no way of knowing, given the present state of the art, whether the Sinitic distinction does not represent one of many innovations which define Sinitic as a branch of Tibeto-Burman. In light of correspondences between Kulung and Old Chinese long vowels, Tolsma previously raised the question whether Old Chinese long vowels are a Tibeto-Burman retention 'or that a sound change which yielded long vowels took place as early as the Old Chinese period' (1999: 497). Persistent misunderstandings about diachronic developments in Slavic accentuation are especially instructive in this regard (Kortlandt 2003). Czech vowels show a phonological length contrast, but the ontogeny of the distinction is complex. At the present state of our knowledge, even if the distinction were not to be shared with Kiranti, the most parsimonious explanation would be that the Old Chinese distinction between *a vs. *ə represents a split in Sinitic rather than a merger shared by all other Tibeto-Burman languages.

Another last straw for a drowning hypothesis to grasp at is held out by the idea that pinioned 'Tibeto-Burman' shares some lexical items not found in Sinitic.

However, each and every branch of Tibeto-Burman, including Sinitic, lacks reflexes of some common Tibeto-Burman roots. Gongduk, for example, resembles Chinese in lacking a reflex of the ubiquitous Tibeto-Burman root for 'pig', the most recently postulated reconstruction of which is still *p^{w}ak (Benedict 1972: 217; Matisoff 2003: 662). Yet pork plays an important role in Gongduk culture just as it always has in Chinese cuisine. The diversity in vocabulary and grammar in Tibeto-Burman may not be as great as in Indo-European or Afroasiatic. Yet the Tibeto-Burman language family is not at all as cohesive a group as was once assumed.

Old Chinese represents an older stage of Sinitic, a phonologically innovative branch. So it is to be expected that the reconstructible Old Chinese syllabary should, because of its time depth, resemble other Tibeto-Burman languages more closely than do modern Sinitic languages. Yet the recent improved reconstructions by Baxter and Sagart differ dramatically from Karlgren's pioneering work and now make Old Chinese look like a very run-of-the-mill Tibeto-Burman language from the Himalayan perspective. The Sino-Tibetan view of Chinese as the odd man out is not just sustained by a lack of familiarity with recent breakthroughs in Sinitic reconstruction. More typically, this view is nourished by a lack of familiarity with languages of other branches of the family such as Gongduk, Hrusish or the Kho-Bwa cluster, all spoken in the Tibeto-Burman heartland closer to the language family's centre of gravity and all just as divergent from 'mainstream' Tibeto-Burman as are the modern Sinitic languages.[12]

It is natural to assume that the linguistic ancestors of Sinitic might have lost some of their original Tibeto-Burman lexicon on their long trek from the greater Himalayan region to the North China plain. Lured as they were by the riches of the advanced Neolithic civilizations along the Yellow River, it would also have been natural for them to adopt new vocabulary from the affluent pre-Tibeto-Burman resident populations of the North China plain. This migration may have taken place at the dawn of the Shāng dynasty, when common Tibeto-Burman had probably already broken up into the major branches attested today. At present, there is no evidence that the rest of the language family was still a unity at the time that Sinitic split off. Sino-Tibetan designates the abidingly incorrect Indo-Chinese construct in its most recent incarnation. The fact that there is no evidence for Sino-Tibetan does not diminish the fact that the hypothesis represents an intrinsically interesting proposition. Yet the theory which makes the least assumptions and is best supported by evidence is the default, and after nearly two centuries Klaproth's Tibeto-Burman is still the default hypothesis.

3. Grand monophyletic views: Sino-Austronesian

The old monophyletic views failed to correctly appraise the genetic position of Chinese. Turanian had generally been abandoned by the end of the 19th century, whereas Indo-Chinese still survives though it has been whittled down and renamed Sino-Tibetan. A twist in the history of linguistics is that new grand monophyletic models have been developed to genetically unite many of the languages of eastern

Eurasia and in the process define the genetic position of Chinese. Here three theories will be examined, i.e. Sino-Austronesian, Sino-Caucasian and East Asian. All three theories are fascinating and will no doubt continue to influence our conjectures about prehistory, as the evidence is accumulated, sifted and tested.

Sino-Austronesian is a new theory first presented at a conference in Texas in 1990. The Sino-Austronesian theory is an ongoing story which continues to unfold in fascinating and unexpected ways. In the first version of Sino-Austronesian, Sagart (1990, 1991, 1993) held that the evidence warranted entertaining the view that Sinitic is genetically related to Austronesian rather than, or more so than, to 'Tibeto-Burman'. The claim of a family comprising just 'Chinese plus Austronesian' was generally rejected, e.g. Blust (1995), Li (1995), Pulleyblank (1995) and Starostin (1995a, 1995b), but some, including myself, gave the intriguing evidence adduced by Sagart a fair hearing.

At the time, I speculated that the correspondences adduced by Sagart might be the residue of a contact situation between ancient Northern Tibeto-Burmans, i.e. Sinitic or Sino-Bodic peoples, and ancient Austronesians (van Driem 1998). I proposed that proto-Austronesians were the behind littoral cultures which lay south of the Yangtze delta such as the Hémǔdù culture on Hángzhōu Bay in Zhèjiāng, the Dàpènkēng of Formosa, the Fùguódūn of Quemoy and related Neolithic cultures of Fukien of the 5th and early 4th millennia BC. The contact situation between Proto-Austronesian and an ancient variety of Tibeto-Burman which accounted for Sagart's correspondences ensued upon the northward expansion of Proto-Austronesians from south of the Yangtze delta, giving rise to the Lóngshān interaction sphere which emerged in the 4th and 3rd millennia BC and connected coastal cultures from north to south, such as the Dàwènkǒu assemblage in Shāndōng, the Qīngliángǎng culture of northern Jiāngsū, and the Mǎjiābāng culture of the Yangtze delta.

The second version of Sino-Austronesian came to encompass 'Chinese plus Tibeto-Burman plus Austronesian' after a number of 'direct Proto-Austronesian-Proto-Tibeto-Burman comparisons not involving Old Chinese, or with better semantic agreement between Proto-Austronesian and Proto-Tibeto-Burman' led Sagart to concede that the facts now 'render less likely the possibility that the material shared by Old Chinese and Tibeto-Burman reflects a contact situation. They suggest that Tibeto-Burman languages may stand closer to Chinese (and to Proto-Austronesian) than I had originally assessed' (1994a: 303). In addition to reintroducing Tibeto-Burman into the equation, Sagart had improved his comparisons by replacing Otto Dempwolff's reconstruction of *Uraustronesisch*, taxonomically comparable to Malayo-Polynesian, with Robert Blust's proto-Austronesian reconstructions. Sagart also addressed relevant methodological issues (1995a, 1995b, 1995c).

The third and most recent incarnation of Sino-Austronesian (Sagart 2005a) is the most interesting and methodologically most rigorous. Li Fang-kuei's reconstruction of Old Chinese has been replaced with Sagart's own 1999 reconstruction. The comparanda now feature only Proto-Austronesian reconstructions in the accepted system of sound correspondences, and Sagart's comparisons rigorously distinguish between etyma reflected at the Proto-Austronesian and the Malayo-Polynesian levels. In the process, the evidence in support of Sino-Austronesian has grown rather than diminished.

Sagart's Sino-Austronesian theory is now based on 75 lexical comparisons, 61 involving 'basic vocabulary' and 14 items of 'cultural vocabulary'. The Austronesian comparanda are taken from the Proto-Austronesian level or involve reconstructed 'Proto-East-Coast-Linkage'. The latter used to be something of a taxon within Austronesian, although the group has recently been abolished by Sagart's own 2004 revision of Austronesian phylogeny. Sagart's new Austronesian phylogeny, based on arguments advanced by Haudricourt (1956) and new insights into the time depth of Kra-Dai or Daic as a taxon (Ostapirat 2005), has both solved the 'Austro-Thai' problem and incorporated Kra-Dai into the Sino-Austronesian equation (Sagart 2002, 2004, 2005a, 2005b). For 69 out of the 75 correspondences, the Tibeto-Burman comparanda are reconstructed Old Chinese forms. For 45 of these 69 comparisons Sagart is able to adduce an additional cognate from another language, usually Tibetan or Burmese. In three instances, a Tibeto-Burman reconstruction by Peiros and Starostin (1996) is used, and in several cases the comparanda are taken from a modern language, e.g. Chepang, Lushai or Lepcha. Only six of the 75 comparisons involve a non-Sinitic form only, for which Sagart found no Old Chinese cognate.

Fourteen of the 75 items are cultural vocabulary and include items relating to cereal cultivation. Their special significance lies in the fact that two salient items relating to rice cultivation are uniquely shared by Tibeto-Burman and Austronesian, whilst Austronesian and Austroasiatic do not share this vocabulary (Sagart 2003a, 2005a). One of these correspondences, Austronesian *beRas 'husked rice' vs. Tibetan ḥbras 'rice', was first pointed out by Hendrik Kern (1889: 5). Whereas Kern believed that this correspondence reflected an early borrowing which indicated whence the ancestors of the Tibetans had first acquired rice, Sagart adduces the correspondence in support of a Sino-Austronesian phylum and adds the Old Chinese cognate 糲 ᵇmə-rat-s. A second rice term is Austronesian *Sumay 'rice as food' vs. Old Chinese 米 ᵃmijʔ 'grain of cereal' and Garo *may* 'paddy'. Sagart also presents correspondences between Austronesian *beCeng '*Setaria*' vs. Old Chinese 稷 ᵇtsïk and Austronesian *Numay '*Panicum*' vs. Old Chinese 麻 and 黍 ᵃmaj.

The Sino-Austronesian roots adduced to date reflect the proto-meanings: body hair, bone, brain, elbow, female breast, foot, head, palm of the hand, pus, mother, egg, horn or antler, leech, snake, worm, cloud or cloudy, earth, moon, salt, sunlight, water, wind, cave or hole, year, carry, chew, close or shut, come or go, short or cut off, dig, drown or disappear, fall, flow or water or river, follow, grasp or embrace, hold something in one's fist or hold something in one's mouth, lick, meet, open, put together, ruin or damage, scrape I, scrape II, sink, sleep, speak or say, think, vomit or spit, wash, gird, bent or crooked, broad, bent, ear, far, high or tall, hot, old or grown-up, sharp, thick, this, *Setaria*, *Panicum*, husked rice, paddy, chicken, cage or enclosure, net, broom, stopper or plug, to bury or tomb, loincloth or robe, plait or braid, shoot, hunt.

Sagart's thinking about genetic relationships has by no means remained static. He describes himself as 'one of the last doubters' that Chinese was even genetically related to Tibeto-Burman. So, when he finally accepted this genetic relationship, it was naturally Sino-Tibetan that he adopted, for this model maintained a safe distance between Sinitic and all its closest relatives. However, recently, Sagart has come to question the Sino-Tibetan paradigm espoused principally by Matisoff. Tibeto-Burman has most recently come to mean non-Sinitic for Sagart, who stresses that his 'use of the term should not' be construed to imply that he is 'presently convinced that it is a valid grouping' (2006). I submit that it is less misleading then to simply say 'non-Sinitic', since 'Tibeto-Burman' is used by believers in Sino-Tibetan to denote non-Sinitic languages as if they together formed a valid taxon. In all his previous work, Sagart too used the term 'Tibeto-Burman' explicitly in this meaning. Sagart's present non-acceptance of pinioned 'Tibeto-Burman' is an implicit disavowal of the Sino-Tibetan hypothesis that may indicate that he is well on the way to accepting the original Tibeto-Burman theory first propounded in Paris some 128 years before Sagart himself was born there. By the same token, Sagart's original name 'Sino-Austronesian' is to be preferred above the newer and unwieldy 'Sino-Tibetan-Austronesian', which incorporates the name of a hypothesis from which he has dissociated himself.[13]

At the same time, Sagart is uniting several of Klaproth's language families in ways that must be catching most scholars by surprise. Sagart's new Austronesian phylogeny, with his identification of Kra-Dai as a lower-level offshoot of a Muish

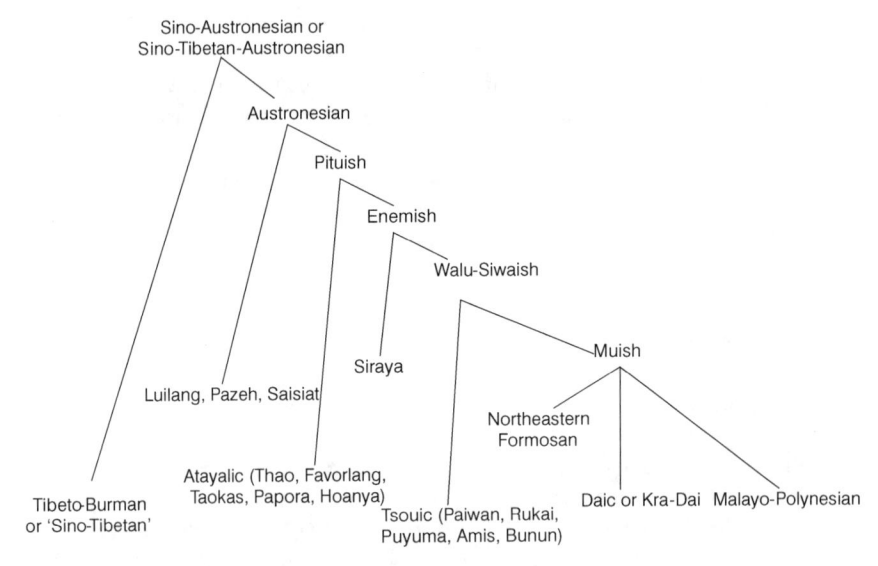

Figure 9.4 Sagart's Sino-Austronesian theory (2005), incorporating Sagart's major revision of Austronesian phylogeny (2004). Northeastern Formosan comprises Kavalan and Ketagalan. Under the Muish node, Northeastern Formosan is coordinate with the Formosan ancestor languages which gave rise to Kra-Dai and Malayo-Polynesian respectively.

ancestor language on Formosa, not only solves the Austro-Thai enigma, but also points the way towards a fundamental revision of the Austric problem.

Wilhelm Schmidt was the first to propose an Austric language family consisting of Austroasiatic and Austronesian, a later version of which even included Japanese (1906, 1930). Additional evidence in support of Austric was adduced by Kuiper (1948) and Reid (1994, 1999, 2005). August Conrady (1916, 1922) and Kurt Wulff (1934, 1942) proposed a mega-Austric superfamily consisting of Austroasiatic, Austronesian and Indo-Chinese, i.e. Kra-Dai and Tibeto-Burman. Another expanded Austric theory, Greater Austric, united Austroasiatic, Austronesian, Kra-Dai and Hmong-Mien (Blust 1996; cf. van Driem 2001: 298–302). Reid (2005: 150) is right to assess that:

> With the accumulation of evidence presented by Sagart ... the concept of 'Austric' as a language family may eventually need to be abandoned in favour of a wider language family which can be shown to include both Austronesian and Austroasiatic languages but not necessarily as sisters of a common ancestor.

4. Grand monophyletic views: Sino-Caucasian

Whereas Sino-Austronesian is a new theory, Sino-Caucasian emerged from a long tradition of scholarship which sought genetic links between language isolates such as Basque and Burushaski, distant languages such as Chinese and Tibetan, and isolated families such as Yeniseian and the languages of the Caucasus, e.g. Trombetti (1905, 1925), Bleichsteiner (1930), Bouda (1936, 1950, 1954, 1964). The chief current proponent of Sino-Caucasian is the late Russian linguist Sergei Starostin, Sagart's junior by five years.[14] The four main branches of Sino-Caucasian are North Caucasian, Sino-Tibetan, Yeniseian and Burushaski.

Even North Caucasian is itself not a universally accepted theory, but a genetic relationship proposed by Nikolai Trubetzkoy (1922) between West Caucasian, or Abkhazo-Adyghean, and East Caucasian. Evidence was adduced for this relationship by Georges Dumézil and later by various Soviet scholars. Most recently, Nikolaev and Starostin published a dictionary of reconstructed North Caucasian (1994). Two of the most interesting ingredients of the North Caucasian theory are the inclusion of the extinct Hattic language into West Caucasian, a hypothesis proposed at the beginning of the 20th century, and the inclusion of the extinct languages Hurrian and Urartaean into East Caucasian, a theory proposed by Forrer (1919: 1040). Both hypotheses have been discussed elsewhere (van Driem 2001: 1057–60). Orël and Starostin have recently even added Etruscan to East Caucasian (1990).

Sino-Caucasian has undergone continual expansion, and the arguments in favour of the phylum are scattered throughout the literature, e.g. Starostin (1982, 1984, 1991, 1995a, 1995b, 2002), Nikolaev and Starostin (1984, 1994). Sino-Caucasian is just one leg of a phylogenetic centipede which unites all languages of the world within a single genetic phylum. The next higher node, Dene-Caucasian,

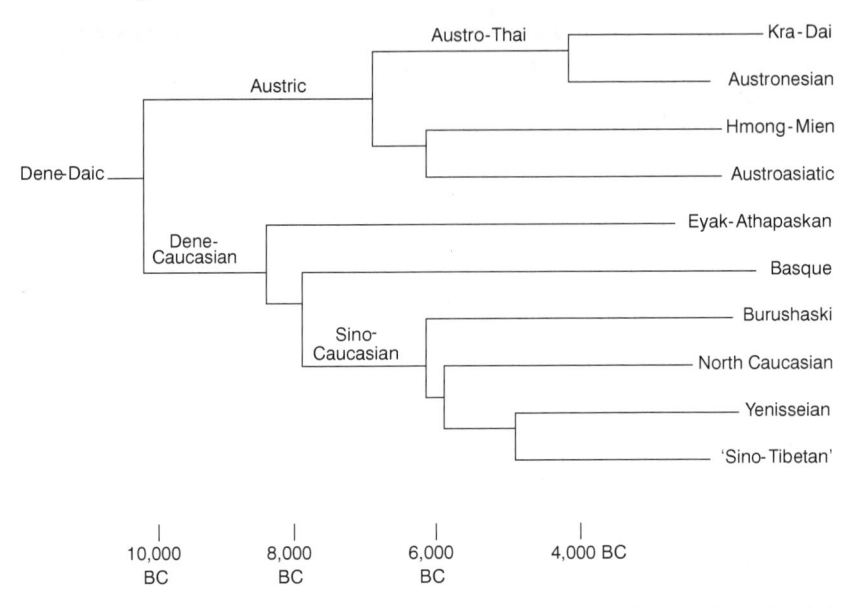

Figure 9.5 Starostin's Sino-Caucasian and Dene-Daic theories (2005). North Caucasian consists of West Caucasian, including Hattic, and East Caucasian, is taken to include Hurro-Urartaean and Etruscan. The extinct languages Sumerian Iberian and Pelasgian are also part of the equation. Starostin used the Chinese name Miáo-Yáo for Hmong-Mien.

comprises Basque and the Na-Dene languages (Starostin 1984, 1995a; Ruhlen and Starostin 1994). The treatment of the Basque material has been criticised by Trask (1994, 1995a, 1995b). Dene-Caucasian has been expanded to include extinct languages of the Iberian peninsula, about which hardly anything is known, as well as Sumerian and Pelasgian (Nikolaev 1991; Bengtson 1991).

The current state of the art in Sino-Caucasian comparative linguistics is posted on Starostin's webpage <ehl.santafe.edu>, as it appeared during the summer of 2005, where 1358 Sino-Caucasian etymologies were listed. Sino-Caucasian reconstructions are based on Starostin's reconstructed roots for North Caucasian, 'Sino-Tibetan', Yenisseian and Burushaski. The Sino-Tibetan reconstructions correspond largely to those given in Peiros and Starostin (1996), which are based on five strategically chosen Tibeto-Burman languages, i.e. Old Chinese, Tibetan, Burmese, Jinghpaw and Lushai. Starostin's website has been strengthened by the inclusion of a Kulung dictionary provided by Gerard Tolsma, a Yamphu dictionary by Roland Rutgers and Limbu and Dumi dictionaries by myself.

In most cases, the Sino-Tibetan reconstructions in Peiros and Starostin are not reflected in all five languages, and in many cases they are supported by reflexes in only two of the five chosen languages. The same applies *mutatis mutandis* to the reconstructions posted on the website. This *modus operandi* is similar in principle to the assumption made at the Indo-European Etymological Dictionary (IED) in Leiden, whereby a form is judged to be reconstructible as a common

Indo-European root or process if the etymon in question is well reflected in any two out of twelve branches of Indo-European. The difference, of course, is that Indo-European is a language family with a well-understood history. Moreover, a modern Lushai form is not a reconstructed Mizo-Kuki-Chin etymon. So Peiros and Starostin's 'Sino-Tibetan' is somewhat analogous to a reconstruction of Indo-European based on Kurdish, French, English, Ardhamāgadhī and Norse runes.

Whenever a 'Sino-Tibetan' root is based just on reflexes in languages which according to a subgrouping hypothesis could belong to a single branch of Tibeto-Burman, such as Old Chinese, Tibetan and Kiranti as members of the hypothetical Sino-Bodic, the correspondences in question may not legitimate the reconstruction of a root at the Tibeto-Burman or 'Sino-Tibetan' level. The best analogue at present to the twelve branches of Indo-European is the model of the fallen leaves of the Tibeto-Burman tree depicted in Figure 9.2. Although a reconstruction of Proto-Kiranti consonants, for example, is available (Opgenort 2005), no reconstructions are available for most branches of Tibeto-Burman.

On the face of things, Starostin's 1358 reconstructions for Sino-Caucasian would seem to outweigh the 75 correspondences adduced for Sino-Austronesian by Sagart. However, only 130 of the 1358 Sino-Caucasian reconstructions are supported by reconstructions from all four putative member families, and only 847 additional correspondences involve reconstructed 'Sino-Tibetan' roots at all. Sino-Caucasian is not an established and generally accepted language family like Indo-European. Rather, the plausibility of Sino-Caucasian has yet to be demonstrated. So decisive evidence for Sino-Caucasian cannot be based on reconstructed etyma from only two or three of the purported constituent groups. What are we to make of the 64 Sino-Caucasian reconstructions supported only by a North-Caucasian reconstruction, the five Sino-Caucasian etyma supported by only a reconstructed 'Sino-Tibetan' root, the one postulated Sino-Caucasian root supported only by a common Yenisseian reconstruction, and the one Sino-Caucasian root reflected only by Burushaski? Are these Sino-Caucasian roots posited merely to furnish comparanda at yet higher putative nodes such as Dene-Caucasian or Dene-Daic?

Some Sino-Caucasian correspondences are intriguing, such as the reconstruction *xGwV 'thou', synthesized from North Caucasian *ʁwV̄, Sino-Tibetan *Kʷa-, Yenisseian *kV-/*ʔVk- ~ *gV-/*ʔVg- and Burushaski *gu-/go- (record 241). An etymon, perhaps very much like Starostin's 'Sino-Tibetan' reconstruction *Kʷa- 'thou', is reflected both as an independent pronoun and in verbal agreement prefixes in different branches of Tibeto-Burman. For this reconstructed root, Starostin's 'etymological database' on the web gives only the purported Tibetan and Burmese reflexes, whereas the reconstruction would appear to be based on more than just Burmese and Tibetan. A problem with Starostin's etymological databases on the web is that they do not in fact render explicit either the empirical basis for the proposed reconstructions nor the process by which he arrives at them.

Another intriguing etymon Sino-Caucasian *=í-xGĂr- 'dry' is constructed on the basis of North Caucasian =iG̣wĂr, Sino-Tibetan *kār, Yenisseian *qɔ(ʔ)r$_1$- ~ qɔ(ʔ)l- and Burushaski *qhar- (record 320). To this Sino-Caucasian etymon it is interesting to juxtapose Sagart's Sino-Austronesian reconstruction *kaR 'dry', based on Sagart's reconstructed Proto-Austronesian root *-kaR 'dry', Old Chinese 乾 ᵃkar 'dry' and Burmese *khân* 'dry up, evaporate, be exhausted (of a liquid)' (Sagart, pers. comm. 30 July 2005), whereby the Burmese final -n reflects an earlier final *-r (Matisoff 2003: 388). So, are both Sino-Caucasian and Sino-Austronesian reconstructions just disjointed parts of a bigger puzzle? Whatever the case may be, the sound laws connecting the Sino-Caucasian forms are not made explicit on the website, but some are detailed in earlier published work, e.g. Starostin (1984, 1991). Yet many Sino-Caucasian correspondences do not obey even these laws, and Starostin has invoked unspecified 'accentual factors' in the past to discount the frequent exceptions (1995a, 1995b).

Several examples taken at random are typical. Sino-Caucasian *HɨrxkV̄, glossed as 'male deer or goat', is extrapolated from the reconstructed North Caucasian root *whīrx̱V 'mountain goat', Sino-Tibetan *rjōk ~ *rjūk 'a kind of deer', Yenisseian *ʔɨʔx̱(V) 'male deer or billy goat' and Burushaski *har 'bull, ox' (record 66). This Sino-Caucasian root for 'deer' exists alongside four other Sino-Caucasian proto-forms for 'deer' (records 175, 472, 696 and 697) and yet another Sino-Caucasian root for 'goat', viz. *kwɨʔnɨ, supported solely by the North Caucasian reconstruction *kwɨʔnɨ ~ kwɨʔnǯ ~ kwɨʔă (record no. 1299). Equally unfathomable is the Sino-Caucasian reconstruction *=VʔwV́ŋ 'go, travel', derived from North Caucasian *=VʔwVn, Sino-Tibetan *ʔʷă (s-, -ŋ), Yenisseian *hejVŋ and Burushaski *né- (record 200).

More often than not,[15] a Sino-Caucasian reconstruction is based on one or two reconstructed reflexes from the four proposed member families. Sino-Caucasian *HVlV, glossed as 'moon; burn(?)', is based solely on Sino-Tibetan *x̱ʷelH, which in turn is supported by Old Chinese 煨 *x̱ʷejʔ 'blazing fire' and a Proto-Kiranti root *wăl[16] (records 1338, 2656). Yet another Sino-Caucasian reconstruction *HVrV, likewise signifying 'burn', is based solely on Sino-Tibetan *rĕw(H) (rec. 1252). Generally, Sino-Caucasian proto-forms rely most heavily on the North Caucasian reconstructions, which contain the most reconstructed segments to play with. In addition, proto-forms at various levels of reconstruction show much variation. Sino-Caucasian *=HixqwV́, 'to bear, be born' is based on North Caucasian *=HiqwĀ(n), Sino-Tibetan *Ki(j) ~ Ke(j), Yenisseian *kej- ~ *qej- ~ *gej- and Burushaski *-ˊk 'children' (record 217). Sino-Caucasian *= HVǯV̄ 'clear (of weather)' is based on North Caucasian *=Huǯ_Vn, Sino-Tibetan *Čōj ~ *Čōl, Yenisseian *ʔēǯ- and Burushaski *čāŋ ~ *čān, ~ *ǯāŋ (record 42). Sino-Caucasian *xVx̱ɨHé 'hand, sleeve' is based on North Caucasian *x̱ĕlHe ~ *x̱ĕlHa 'sleeve' and Yenisseian *xɨre 'arm', with the added caveat 'A very complicated picture: confusion of *kwīlʔɨ, *xq(w)ɨʔi, *xqwV́ɨʔV̆ and *x̱V̆lHe' (record 980).

Semantics at the Sino-Caucasian level can often get a trifle vague. For example, there are seven etyma denoting 'a kind of tree', viz. record numbers 68, 252, 634, 983, 1155, 1306, 1315. There are eighteen Sino-Caucasian proto-forms signifying 'hair', viz. record numbers 130, 258, 263, 360, 554, 575, 603, 988, 1023, 1024, 1060, 1141, 1144, 1201, 1257, 1259, 1290, 1329. One of these is based solely upon, and is isomorphic with, the North Caucasian *ćhwāró 'hair' (record 1290), whereas Sino-Caucasian *burV 'hair' is based solely on Burushaski *bur (record

1259). Out of the four Sino-Caucasian proto-forms denoting 'a kind of relative' (viz. records 108, 277, 284, 1027), Sino-Caucasian *q̇V̄r[H]V̇ is synthesized from North Caucasian *q̇ar[H]V 'cousin', Sino-Tibetan *Kʷrij ~ *Kruj 'child-in-law', Yenisseian *qär₁- ~ *xär₁- 'grandchild' and Burushaski *-rék 'sibling-in-law' (record 284).

There are five Sino-Caucasian roots denoting 'pus' (viz. records 95, 162, 760, 761, 907). The only one of these reflected in all four purported branches of Sino-Caucasian is the unwieldy *něwxq̇wV̌, extrapolated from North Caucasian *něwq̇ǔ, Sino-Tibetan *(s-)nuāk ~ *(s-)nuāŋ, Yenisseian dɔ(ʔ)kŋ and Burushaski *nagéi ~ *magéi 'boil, sore' (record 162). Sino-Caucasian *[b]VjV, glossed as 'an internal organ', appears to have been constructed on the basis of Sino-Tibetan *phe 'spleen' and Yenisseian *b[a]jbVl 'kidney' (record 103). Three more Sino-Caucasian proto-forms denote 'an internal organ', viz. record numbers 354, 419, 1236. There are five reconstructed Sino-Caucasian roots meaning 'to laugh' (viz. records 16, 477, 880, 903, 957), and none are reflected in more than two of the four member families of this widespread family.

The time frame of the domestication of various cereals is called into question by two Sino-Caucasian agricultural terms, both glossed ambiguously as 'millet, rice'. Sino-Caucasian *λwɨʔwV̇ has been constructed on the basis of the irregular North Caucasian root *λwɨʔwV 'millet' and the shaky Sino-Tibetan *lɨwH ~ *λɨwH denoting some type of grain (record 590), whereas Sino-Caucasian *bŏlćwɨ is constructed from North Caucasian root *bŏlćwɨ ~ *bŏnćwɨ 'millet', Sino-Tibetan *phrē(s) 'rice' and Burushaski *baẏ 'millet' (record 733).

The notational intricacy of the ensemble of Starostin's reconstructions raises the question as to how much phonological complexity may plausibly be imputed to any putative proto-language. At the same time, some forms would appear to be attributable to a widespread tendency towards sound symbolism, a phenomenon recognized ever since Court de Gébelin (1774). For example, Sino-Caucasian *[p]ūHV̌ 'blow' is extrapolated from North Caucasian *pūHV, Sino-Tibetan *bǔ(-t), Yenisseian *pV(j) and Burushaski *phu (record 280).

Grammatical etyma are at best vaguely supported. A Sino-Caucasian 'interrogative stem' *mV is based on a reconstructed North Caucasian interrogative stem *mV, an assumed but not really reconstructed Sino-Tibetan root *mV, an interrogative root *wi- ~ *we gleaned from Yenisseian pronominal forms, and Burushaski *me- 'who' (record 426), but what are these comparanda precisely? The best reflected out of three Sino-Caucasian negative particle is *bV, ostensibly reflected in the reconstructions North Caucasian -bV, Old Chinese 不 *pə, Yenisseian *-pun 'without, -less' and Burushaski *be 'not' (record 1187). There are two more, even shakier reconstructed Sino-Caucasian negative particles, viz. record numbers 1073, 1187. Some comparanda do not have much substance. The Sino-Caucasian verb 'to be', *ʔa, is based on a reconstructed North Caucasian auxiliary *=a ~ *=i, a poorly supported Sino-Tibetan locative or object marker *ʔă* ~ *ɣ̌ă, an unexplained Yenisseian reconstruction *ʔa and the Burushaski reconstruction *b-a- 'to be' (record 861).

5. Sino-Austronesian vs. Sino-Caucasian

How do Sino-Austronesian and Sino-Caucasian compare? The first difference involves the many degrees of freedom in Starostin's reconstructions as compared with Sagart's Sino-Austronesian. The comparanda in long-range comparisons are themselves reconstructions, and an element of subjectivity enters into the choice of reconstructions, which, at various levels, are usually Starostin's own. Given his stated aim of building a genealogical tree of all of the world's languages and the reduction of the number of nodes to common ancestors of particular language families, this multiple leeway in the choice of reconstructions cannot but afford ample room for the harmonization of phonological shape and meaning of constructed proto-forms, whether or not such a process is a conscious one. In the Sino-Austronesian comparison, by contrast, Sagart utilizes Blust's reconstructions for Austronesian along with just a few of his own. The semantics of Old Chinese forms is arguably as attested in the texts. Sagart's 1999 reconstruction of Old Chinese is largely corroborated by Baxter's reconstruction (1992, 1995), particularly where the rimes are concerned. Moreover, Sagart's reconstruction takes into account earlier reconstructions such as that of Jaxontov (1965), Lǐ Fānggui (1971, 1974, 1976, 1983), Pulleyblank (1984, 1991), Zhèngzhāng Shàngfāng (1987) and Starostin (1989).

Starostin (1995a) once claimed to have found thirteen semantically precise Sino-Caucasian matches on Jaxontov's 33-word list. By contrast, Sagart's Sino-Austronesian material contains only seven semantically close matches on the Jaxontov list, i.e. including the numeral 'one' (Sagart 2005a). However, an average of between one and two phonological segments match per lexical comparison in Starostin's thirteen best correspondences, whereas an average of about three segments match phonologically in Sagart's seven correspondences. Calculations of this type involve a number of arbitrary decisions. Whereas an average of between three and four phonological segments per lexical comparison match in Sagart's overall list, the score is lower on the short list, simply because two of the seven items, viz. 'one' and 'this', consist of only two segments. More generally, however, this discrepancy in the number of phonological matches per adduced lexical comparison characterizes the entire corpus of correspondences adduced by Starostin <ehl.santafe.edu> and Sagart (2005a). Often enough, as in many of the examples extracted above from Starostin's website, only one phonological segment seems to match in a comparison. At present, therefore, Sagart's Sino-Austronesian would appear to come somewhat closer to attaining the rigour of the first sound laws formulated by Lambert ten Kate in 1710 and 1723 than does Starostin's Sino-Caucasian.

Another difference between the two theories of distant relationship is that several morphological processes have been found to be shared by Tibeto-Burman and Austronesian. No Sino-Caucasian shared morphology is in evidence, and most Sino-Caucasian grammatical morphemes are shaky. By contrast, the Tibeto-Burman nominalizing suffix *<-n>, intransitive prefix *<m-> and valency-increasing prefix *<s-> appear to be related to the Proto-Austronesian nominalizing and goal focus marker *<-ən>, actor focus marker *<m- ~ -m-> and instrumental or beneficiary focus prefix *<Si-> respectively, all three morphemes being processes 'which form the backbone of Austronesian verbal morphology' (Sagart 2005a: 168–71). Sagart also proposes that the distributive marker *<-ar-> might be a morphological process shared by both families.

The Sino-Tibetan problem explained in the first half of this article presents a serious impediment to both Sino-Austronesian and Sino-Caucasian comparison, since both implicitly incorporate the Sino-Tibetan hypothesis and are thus built upon an unsupported assumption about the genetic position of Sinitic with respect to its closest relatives. The assumed veracity of the Sino-Tibetan paradigm compromises the validity of any long-range comparison involving Tibeto-Burman proper, but this problem can easily be remedied, at least in principle. Meanwhile, Sino-Tibetan continues to shape the reconstructions and the identity of correspondences and so compromise the evidence adduced for Sino-Austronesian and Sino-Caucasian. This affects both theories of distant relationship, but the problem is compounded in the case of Sino-Caucasian by the reliance on lexicostatistics.

The nodes in Starostin's genealogical tree of languages are dated by glottochronology as determined by lexicostatistics, based on the assumption of a fixed rate of change in core vocabulary over time, whereby lexical divergence is calculated by a neighbour-joining algorithm. Popular in Russia today, lexicostatistics was invented by Constantine Samuel Rafinesque (1831) in order to win a gold medal worth 1,000 francs in a competition held by the Société de Géographie in Paris[17] to determine the origin of Asiatic negritos.

Yet for Tibeto-Burman linguistics the question as to whether Old Chinese was a pidgin or creole which arose when the linguistic ancestors of the Chinese first came to the Yellow River Valley at the dawn of the Shāng period will continue to haunt us. Whatever the prehistory of Sinitic may be, no shared feature has yet been shown to unite the rest of Tibeto-Burman as opposed to Sinitic. Moreover, lexicostatistical studies that once were meant to show Sinitic to be the first branch to split off characteristically ignored most branches of Tibeto-Burman shown in Figure 9.2. By contrast, Jaxontov's 1996 Tibeto-Burman phylogeny based on lexicostatistics, reproduced by van Driem (2003: 112–113), resembles Shafer's family tree in that Sinitic is just one of several branches of the language family. There is no bifurcation of the family into Sinitic and some truncated 'Tibeto-Burman' construct.

At the same time, Starostin stressed the importance of the hierarchical principle, which he attributed to Vladislav Markovič Illič-Svityč, who, in reconstructing Nostratic, compared entities taken to have existed at the same time depth. Illič-Svityč compared Proto-Altaic with Proto-Uralic, for example, and did not draw comparanda from disparate levels, such as an ancient tongue and a modern language. Yet the presumption of an unsupported and probably false hierarchy is the hallmark of the 'Sino-Tibetan' model. Reconstructions within this paradigm accord as much weight to reconstructed Old Chinese as to all other language data from the entire language family. Furthermore, Peiros and Starostin's 'Sino-Tibetan' reconstruction violates the hierarchical principle in basing itself entirely on the comparison of Old Chinese, written Tibetan, written Burmese and modern Jinghpaw and Lushai. By the same token, if Sagart's new Austronesian phylogeny is correct, comparisons between 'Austro-Thai' and Austroasiatic violate the hierarchical principle as well. At the same time, Starostin's reconstructed Austroasiatic comparanda are not taken seriously by leading specialists in Austroasiatic and do not respect the accepted hierarchy of Austroasiatic phylogeny (cf. Diffloth 2005).

In this context, it is relevant to keep in mind that Old Chinese is not the 'oldest language' in the family. Old Chinese is not an entity comparable to, say, Latin, Greek and other extinct languages written in an alphabetic script. Old Chinese was written in an ideogrammatic script, in which symbols represented words and morphemes. Because of the antiquity of the written tradition, however, Old Chinese is also something more than just a reconstruction analogous to Proto-Romance. Scholars who conduct the useful exercise of reconstructing Proto-Romance on the basis of the attested modern tongues arrive at a system reminiscent of Latin, but the resultant construct is not Latin by any stretch of the imagination and lacks much of the morphology which is known to have characterized the common ancestral tongue (Mazzola 1976; Hall 1984). On the basis of Proto-Romance it would be difficult even to ascertain whether Latin was closer to Faliscan or to Oscan and Umbrian. Epistemologically, Old Chinese is not as much as a Tibeto-Burman analogue of Latin, nor is Old Chinese as little as a Tibeto-Burman analogue of Proto-Romance.

Old Chinese is a linguistic edifice founded upon reconstructed Middle Chinese and built with the rimes of the *Shī Jīng* 'Book of Odes', dating from between the 8th and 5th centuries BC, and the phonetic components in Chinese characters that were devised in the Shāng and Zhōu period, buttressed by refined philological arguments. Much phonological information on Old Chinese was lost, albeit not all of it irretrievably, when the script was unified during the Qín dynasty in the 3rd century BC. Much has yet to be learnt from original specimens of writing antedating this period.

Middle Chinese, the foundation upon which Old Chinese is built, is reconstructed on the basis of the comparison of modern Sinitic languages, traditionally known as 'Chinese dialects', Chinese loanwords which entered Vietnamese, Korean and Japanese, and the *Qièyùn*, a Táng dynasty dictionary published in 601 containing *fǎnqiè* spellings that specify the pronunciation of a character by two other ideograms, one representing the *zìmǔ* 'initial' and the other specifying the *yùnmǔ* 'rime'.

Coblin (2003) has soberingly reviewed the epistemological underpinnings of reconstructing older stages of Sinitic. Old Chinese is not the language spoken by the ancient Chinese, but a reconstructible syllabary. Yet the language spoken at the time was no doubt more than just a syllabary, as Lepsius mooted in 1861. Whichever recently reconstructed syllabary one prefers, Old Chinese now looks like a reconstruction of a Tibeto-Burman language and gives the lie to the Sino-Tibetan hypothesis.

Starostin's comparisons assume etymological identity, and he excludes look-alikes such as Sino-Tibetan *miǝŋ 'name' and Proto-Indo-European *(e)nomen- 'name', between which no system of correspondence obtains despite phonetic similarity. Yet the sound laws which unite 'Sino-Tibetan' and Sino-Caucasian as well as entities such as Dene-Daic are not made explicit. How are we then to know that the comparanda adduced in Sino-Caucasian comparisons are real, much less that the correct cognates have been identified in the purportedly related language families? How much of this construction is science, and how much of it is arcane? Much can be improved by making the sound laws and presumed regularities explicit, testable or open to scrutiny.

Long rangers often see scholars working in individual recognized language families as conservative and as hoarding their data. Yet scholars with greater and more detailed knowledge of individual languages and language groups are particular about getting the data correctly analysed and accurately represented. So the perceived difference in subcultures is more than just a sociological phenomenon but a question of methodological rigour. Taking the language family as a whole more seriously would inevitably lead to the removal of the 'Sino-Tibetan' bias and result in more credible reconstructions. In summary, the evidence for Sino-Caucasian appears tenuous, especially due to the shaky nature of some of the reconstructed 'Sino-Tibetan' comparanda. At the same time, it is significant, though not strictly a linguistic issue, that the Sino-Caucasian theory makes little sense of the archaeology or of the findings of population genetics to date.

The overall size of the empirical base in support of either Sino-Austronesian or Sino-Caucasian is not overwhelmingly vast. None the less, for reasons explained above, Sagart's 75 comparisons look more compelling than Starostin's 1358. Even so, Sagart's comparison notably excludes personal pronouns and numerals, which do not compare well, a fact which Sagart thinks is explicable in terms of 'far-reaching paradigmatic changes (analogy, politeness shifts involving deictics)' (2005a: 165). Sceptics may therefore still dismiss the selection of purported cognates as representing look-alikes or borrowings. Indeed, Starostin is inclined to dismiss Sagart's Sino-Austronesian correspondences as loans or to attribute them to a new Dene-Daic or Sino-Austric node at an even greater time depth. My first and present inclination has been to attribute Sagart's data to an ancient contact situation which I have already described above. If in future the evidence involving shared morphology is borne out by more rigorous studies of Tibeto-Burman historical grammar, however, then a deep genetic relationship becomes more likely than an ancient contact situation.

Just as in the case of *indochinesisch*, after Schott in 1856 diffidently resigned himself to the fact that other scholars would continue using the term, so too today scholars who continue to use the term 'Sino-Tibetan' likewise continue to adhere to the theory of genetic relationship which the term designates. That is, they continue to speak of Tibeto-Burman in the pinioned rather than the proper sense, in contexts which presume the veracity of this catch-all subgroup as a genetic construct coordinate with Sinitic. Since there is no evidence for a unitary truncated

'Tibeto-Burman' subgroup coordinate with Sinitic, the term 'Sino-Tibetan' must be abandoned along with the phylogenetic model which it designates.

6. East Asian and future prospects

Finally, I shall turn to a theory which Stan Starosta proposed a year before he died in July 2002. The theory, called East Asian, proposes an ancient phylum encompassing Kra-Dai, Austronesian, Tibeto-Burman, Hmong-Mien and Austroasiatic. The ancient morphological processes shared by the families of this phylum are ostensibly an agentive prefix *<m->, a patient suffix *<-n>, an instrumental prefix <s-> and a perfective prefix *<n->. The East Asian word was disyllabic and exhibited a canonical structure CVCVC. The proto-homeland of the East Asian proto-language or Proto-East-Asian dialect continuum ('linkage') lay in the region laced by the Hàn, the Wèi and the central portion of the Yellow River in the period from 6500 to 6000 BC. Indeed, Starosta identified the Péilígǎng and Císhān neolithic with Proto-East-Asian.

Starosta envisaged the linguistic ancestors of the Austronesians as the first group to have split off of East Asian. This family spread to the coast and then down the eastern seaboard to establish the Hémǔdù and Dàwènkǒu Neolithic cultures of 5000 BC, ultimately to cross over to Formosa. Much later, emerging from Formosa, one migration gave rise to the Malayo-Polynesian expansion to insular Southeast Asia, Oceania and parts of peninsular Southeast Asia, whereas another migration led back to the South China mainland, where it gave rise to Kra-Dai or Daic.

Back on the North China Plain, a second group split off and left the East Asian homeland to move south and settle along the Yangtze, where they shifted from millet to rice agriculture. These 'Yangtzeans' in turn later split up into the first Austroasiatic language communities, whom Starosta envisaged behind the Kūnmíng Neolithic of 4000 BC, and the Hmong-Mien, who later, according to Pulleyblank (1983), first burst into history in what is now Húběi and northern Húnán as the Chǔ polity (770–223 BC) which challenged the Eastern Zhōu.

Back in the central Yellow River basin, a third descendant group of East Asian remained. This third family was Tibeto-Burman. Starosta accepted the Sino-Bodic hypothesis and so rejected Sino-Tibetan.[18] Tibeto-Burman in Starosta's conception split into Sino-Bodic, which he associated with the Yǎngsháo Neolithic of 5800 BC, and a branch which he called Himalayo-Burman, which he associated with the Dàdìwān Neolithic in Gānsù 6500 BC. Sino-Bodic split up into Sinitic and Bodic. Starosta appears to have relabelled Bodic 'Tangut-Bodish' because he mistakenly supposed Tangut to be more closely related to Bodish rather than to Qiāngic. Starosta's Himalayo-Burman split up into Qiāngic, Kāmarūpan and Southern Himalayo-Burman. Qiāngic is a recognized subgroup, which possibly includes Tangut. Southern Himalayo-Burman may presumably be taken to include groups such as Karen, Lolo-Burmese, Mizo-Kuki-Chin and perhaps Pyu. Kāmarūpan is a misleading 'hypothesis' introduced by Matisoff which groups together languages known not to constitute a genetic taxon (Burling 1999; van Driem 2001: 405–7).

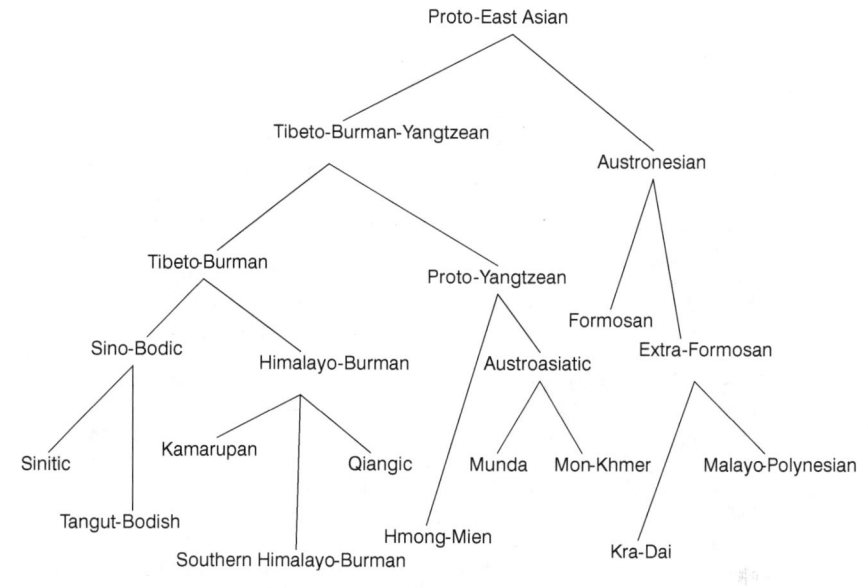

To which language family does Chinese belong? 241

Figure 9.6 Starosta's Proto-East-Asian. This diagram faithfully represents Starosta's proposed East Asian phylogeny and corrects editorial errors which crept into his posthumously published tree diagram (2005: 183). The hypercorrect spelling 'Yangzi' has likewise been restored to the traditional English name 'Yangtze'.[18]

Starosta's theory basically proposes an agricultural dispersal of the type envisaged by Peter Bellwood and Colin Renfrew. The farming dispersal model is not problematic in straightforward cases such as the Polynesian colonization of hitherto uninhabited lands. However, this simplistic model is deficient for reconstructing linguistic intrusions and dispersals on continents, where population prehistory has been far more complex than the spread of agriculture reflected in the archaeological record. My qualified criticisms of the unqualified use of this hypothesis to argue the location of linguistic homelands can be consulted elsewhere (van Driem 2001: 423–6, 1004–21, 1051–65; esp. 2002: 238–9).

Although I do not currently subscribe to the East Asian theory any more than I do to Sino-Austronesian or Sino-Caucasian, I have attempted here to give both Sino-Austronesian or Sino-Caucasian a fair and sympathetic hearing. This final section sets the record straight about Starosta's intrinsically interesting hypothetical reconstruction of linguistic prehistory, particularly with regard to Tibeto-Burman and Sino-Bodic, since Starosta's theory somehow came out garbled in the posthumously published version. Starosta modestly concluded that the scenario which he sketched 'is almost certainly wrong in a number of points', but that 'its potential utility' lay 'in helping to focus scholars' efforts on particular specific questions, resulting in the replacement of parts of this hypothesis with better supported arguments' (2005: 194). It should come as no surprise if a good

242 *George van Driem*

number of Starosta's novel and insightful hunches were to be borne out by future research.

Notes

1. A polyphyletic view of linguistic stocks and language families arguably dates as far back as 1647. A fuller historical account of the rise of polyphyletic historical linguistic comparison has been provided elsewhere (van Driem 2001: 1039–51; 2005: 285–91).
2. In his quixotic attempts to reconcile the diversity which he observed with the monophyletic Turanian vision, Logan devised numerous *ad hoc* terms for real or imagined genetic ties between larger groups, e.g. 'Malagaso-Asonesian', 'Draviro-Asonesian', 'Tibeto-Ultraindian', 'Himalayo-Asonesian', 'Chino-Himalaic', 'Dravido-Australian', 'Ultra-Indo-Gangetic', 'Gangeto-Ultraindian'. None of these coinages was to be so enduring as Tibeto-Burman.
3. These first attempts at reconstruction inevitably suffered from major shortcomings and oversights and do not yet constitute reconstructions in the conventional historical linguistic sense, cf. Miller (1968, 1974), Sagart (2006).
4. Müller's writings on the topic are copious. I shall draw just one example from Klaproth on the distinction between ethnic and linguistic relationship: 'Es ist richtig zu sagen, die deutsche Sprache stammt von denselben Wurzeln ab als das *Sanskrit*, aber unsinnig darum das *Deutsche Volk* von den Hindu abzuleiten' (1823a: 43). Some scholars such as Huot agreed: 'L'opinion de M. Klaproth ne fait, selon nous, que confirmer notre opinion qui est celle de tous qui étudient la nature: que les langues ne peuvent que fournir des caractères incertains pour la classification des *espèces* ou des *races* d'hommes' (Malte-Brun 1832: 1. 521), but this essential distinction was to be lost on many people.
5. In Figure 9.2, the Ěrsū cluster is another name for 'Southern Qiāngic', and may in fact consist of several subclusters. Qiāngic is 'Northern Qiāngic', which is currently supposed to include the rGyal-rongic group recognised by Jackson Sun (Sūn Tiānxīn) and Huáng Bùfán. In fact, the precise phylogenetic relationships between the diverse rGyal-rong languages, Ěrgōng, Qiāng, Mi-ñag (Mù yǎ), Tangut, Ěrsū, Lǔsū, Tosu (Duōsū), Nà mùyì, Shǐ xīng, Guì qióng, Choyo (Quèyù), Zhābà and Prinmi (Pǔmǐ) have yet to be demonstrated. Whether or not the Qiāngic group which features prominently in Chinese scholarly literature is a valid clade has yet to be convincingly demonstrated, and there is a lot of work left to be done in Sìchuān and Yúnnán provinces.
6. By contrast, Matisoff's 'view from the Sinosphere' does not correspond to the insights of Sinologists but represents his self-confessed predilection to envisage the proto-language as endowed with Benedict's two proto-tones and structurally similar to Lahu, a language for which he professes great fondness (2000: 367)
7. Benedict's unusual treatment of Karen between 1972 and 1976, based mainly just on word order typology, may have been influenced by the view propounded by Avery at New Haven, Connecticut, that 'the position of the Karen dialects of British Burma is not yet settled, since they present features of both the isolating and agglutinating languages' (1885: xviii).
8. Well into the 1970s, Sino-Tibetanists still classified Daic or Kra-Dai as part of the Sino-Daic branch of Sino-Tibetan, e.g. Milner and Henderson (1965). General linguists still often continue to present Sino-Tibetan as a family comprising 'le chinois, le thaï, le tibétain et le birman', e.g. Malherbe (2001: 35).
9. Shafer pointed out: 'Bodish is genetically closer to Chinese than it is to Burmese. To anyone not led by the exotic appearance of Chinese characters to regard the language as a thing apart, this conclusion should not come as a surprise in view of geography

To which language family does Chinese belong? 243

and history' (1955: 97). His later discussion of the divisions extended the observation to Bodic as a whole.

10 The exhilaratingly productive search for Sino-Bodic evidence in Kiranti languages was abruptly curtailed when the member of the Himalayan Languages Project with whom I had undertaken to pursue this work fell chronically ill.

11 My article explicitly stated that the latter set of roots is reflected outside of Bodic, particularly in Brahmaputran, and Matisoff acknowledged that I stated this to be so, yet in the same article he insinuates that the latter cognate set too was adduced as representing exclusive Sino-Bodic isoglosses.

12 Just like British scholars in the 19th century, Jaxontov proposed a homeland in Sìchuān (1977). Subsequently, so did I (van Driem 1998). In their archaeological discussion of the Sìchuān homeland hypotheses, Aldenderfer and Zhang 'agree with van Driem that Sichuan is a likely source for a Neolithic package' which gave rise to cultures on the Yellow River (2004: 39). Yet Aldenderfer and Zhang (2004: 37) appear to think that I do not include the mKhar-ro site near Chab-mdo or any other Tibetan archaeological sites in my model. The Tibetan archaeological site mKhar-ro or mKhar-chu, which I discuss at length (van Driem 2001: 430–1), is sinicized in the Chinese archaeological literature with characters that are correctly romanized as Kǎruò, and which Aldenderfer and Zhang incorrectly transcribe as 'Karou'. Sites should be named properly in accordance with archaeological convention. Their misunderstanding again provides the context for my assertion that: 'Numerous artificial problems in Tibetan toponymy and cartography currently result from the practice of listing only the sinified version of Tibetan place names in Hànyǔ Pīnyīn romanisation without providing the real place names' (loc.cit.). Incorrect Hànyǔ Pīnyīn transcriptions merely exacerbate the problem. Aldenderfer and Zhang identify mKhar-ro or Kǎruò as a colonial exponent of the Mǎjiāyáo neolithic in Gānsù, but their cursory familiarity with the literature leads them to think that they are the first to do so. In fact, a good number of Chinese archaeologists (e.g. Xīzàng etc. 1979; Ān 1992) had already identified mKhar-ro or Kǎruò as a colonial exponent of the Mǎjiāyáo neolithic, and my model followed this consensus. Aldenderfer and Zhang do not differentiate between language spread by demic diffusion and language intrusion by colonial migration, and they inexplicably attempt to interpret 'Karou' as the result of demic diffusion from Sìchuān. Purely on linguistic grounds, Peiros's lexicostatistical classification based on the highest diversity of primary taxa purportedly indicates 'a possible location of the homeland in the territories south of the Himalayas', whereas the location of Sinitic could be 'easily explained as the result of later migration' (1998: 217). In Dec. 2004, at the 10th Himalayan Languages Symposium in Thimphu, I presented other arguments for a possible Himalayan homeland for Tibeto-Burman.

13 No doubt the acronym STAN will lead some to speculate that Sagart adopted the new name to commemorate the late Stanley Starosta, just as some have speculated that I named Sino-Bodic after the late Nicholas Cleaveland Bodman, who was one of its proponents before me. In fact, I only spoke with Bodman once in Lund in 1987, and Bodic is Shafer's old term for a hypothetical superordinate branch within the language family. Both the terms 'Bodish' and 'Bodic' contain the Tibetan word *Bod* 'Tibet'.

14 Sergei Starostin sadly passed away in Moscow at the age of 52 on 30 September 2005, just after this article had first been submitted for publication, several months after he had been awarded an honorary doctorate at Leiden.

15 In total, 331 Sino-Caucasian reconstructions are based only on North Caucasian and Sino-Tibetan reconstructions, 197 Sino-Caucasian reconstructions on correspondences between North Caucasian, Sino-Tibetan and Yenisseian reconstructions, 163 Sino-Caucasian reconstructions on North Caucasian, Sino-Tibetan and Burushaski correspondences, 134 Sino-Caucasian reconstructed roots on North Causasian and Yenisseian correspondences, 110 Sino-Caucasian roots on North Causasian and Burushaski correspondences, 86 Sino-Caucasian roots on Sino-Tibetan and Yenissieian

correspondences, 57 Sino-Caucasian roots on North Causasian, Yenissiean and Burushaski correspondences, 44 Sino-Caucasian reconstructions on Sino-Tibetan and Burushaski correspondences, 26 Sino-Caucasian reconstructions on Sino-Tibetan, Yenisseian and Burushaski correspondences, and 9 Sino-Caucasian reconstructions on correspondences between Yenisseian and Burushaski reconstructions.

16 Based on forms in Kiranti languages the names of which are misspelt as 'Kaling' (*recte* Khaling) and 'Tulung' (*recte* Thulung).
17 For a fuller historical account of the origin of lexicostatistics and the original mathematical models employed, see the relevant section in my paper for the Linguistic Society of Nepal (van Driem 2005).
18 However, the term 'Sino-Tibetan' appears in the posthumously published version of Starosta's article. Likewise, the tree diagram which was drawn up for Starosta posthumously misrepresents his proposed East Asian phylogeny for Tibeto-Burman or 'Sino-Tibetan'. The corrected tree diagram is given here as Figure 9.6.
19 The Mandarin Chinese for the Yangtze is Cháng Jiāng. The English name Yangtze derives from an older designation of a branch of the river in the Yangtze delta in Jiāngsū province downstream from Yángzhōu. This former branch of the river was named after a strategic ford Yángzǐ, the site of which no longer lies on the present course of the Yangtze.

References

Aldenderfer, M. and Zhang, Y. (2004) 'The prehistory of the Tibetan Plateau to the seventh century A.D.: Perspectives from China and the West since 1950, *Journal of World Prehistory*, 18(1): 1–55.

Ān Zhìmǐn (1992) 'Neolithic communities in eastern parts of Central Asia', in A.H. Dani and V.M. Masson (eds) *History of Civilizations of Central Asia*, vol. 1, *The Dawn of Civilization: Earliest Times to 700 BC*, pp. 153–89, Paris: United Nations Educational Scientific and Cultural Organization.

Avery, J. (1885) 'The Tibeto-Burman group of languages', *Transactions of the American Philological Association*, 16, appendix, Morning Session, Wednesday, July 8, 1885, pp. xvii–xix, New Haven, CT.

Baxter III, W.H. (1992) *A Handbook of Old Chinese Phonology*, Berlin: Mouton de Gruyter.

Baxter III, W.H. (1995) 'Ongoing Research: Old Chinese Version 1.1', paper presented at the Old Chinese Seminar held at Leiden University on 14 and 17 July 1995.

Belyi, V.V. (1997) 'Rafinesque's linguistic activity', *Anthropological Linguistics*, 39(1): 60–73.

Benedict, P.K. (1942) 'Thai, Kadai and Indonesian: A new alignment in southeastern Asia', *American Anthropologist*, 44: 576–601.

Benedict, P.K. (1972) *Sino-Tibetan: A Conspectus*, Cambridge: Cambridge University Press.

Benedict, P.K. (1976) 'Sino-Tibetan: another look', *Journal of the American Oriental Society*, 96 (2): 167–97.

Bengtson, J.D. (1991) 'Notes on Sino-Caucasian ... Some Macro-Caucasian etymologies', in V. Sheveroshkin (ed.) *Dene-Sino-Caucasian*, pp. 67–172, Bochum: Universitätsverlag Dr N. Brockmeyer.

Bleichsteiner, R. (1930) ,Die werschikisch-buruschkische Sprache im Pamirgebiet und ihre Stellung zu den Japhetitensprache des Kaukasus', *Wiener Beiträge zur Kulturgeschichte*

und Linguistik, Veröffentlichungen des Institutes für Völkerkunde an der Universität Wien, 1: 289–331.
Blench, R.M. and Spriggs, M. (1998) 'General introduction', in R.M. Blench and M. Spriggs (eds) *Archaeology and Language II: Correlating Archaeological and Linguistic Hypotheses*, pp. 1–19, London: Routledge.
Blust, R.A. (1995) 'An Austronesianist looks at Sino-Austronesian', in W.S.-Y. Wang (ed.) *The Ancestry of the Chinese Language* (Journal of Chinese Linguistics Monograph Series, 8), pp. 283–98, Berkeley, CA: University of California Press.
Blust, R.A. (1996) 'Beyond the Austronesian homeland: the Austric hypothesis and its implications for archaeology', in W.H. Goodenough (ed.) *Prehistoric Settlement of the Pacific*, pp. 117–140, Philadelphia, PA: American Philosophical Society.
Bodman, N.C. (1980) 'Proto-Chinese and Sino-Tibetan: Data towards establishing the nature of the relationship', in F. van Coetsem and L.R. Waugh (eds) *Contributions to Historical Linguistics: Issues and Materials*l, pp. 34–199, Leiden: E.J. Bril.
Bouda, K. (1936) 'Jeniseisch-tibetische Wortgleichungen', *Zeitung der Deutschen Morgenländischen Gesellschaft*, 90: 149–59.
Bouda, K. (1950) 'Die Sprache der Buruscho', *Eusko-Jakintza, Revue d'Études Basques*, 4: 37–50.
Bouda, K. (1954) 'Burushaski Etymologien', *Orbis, Bulletin International de Documentation Linguistique*, 3(1): 228–30.
Bouda, K. (1964) 'Burushaski Etymologien II', *Orbis, Bulletin International de Documentation Linguistique*, 13(2): 604–9.
Burling, R. (1999) 'On "Kamarupan"', *Linguistics of the Tibeto-Burman Area*, 22(2): 169–71.
Burling, R. (2004) *The Languages of the Modhpur Mandi (Garo)*, vol. 1, *Grammar*, New Delhi: Bibliophile South Asia.
Coblin, W.S. (2003) 'The *Chiehyunn* and the current state of Chinese historical phonology', *Journal of the American Oriental Society*, 123(2): 377–83.
Conrady, A. (1896) *Eine indochinesische Causativ-Denominativ-Bildung und ihr Zusammenhang mit den Tonaccenten: Ein Beitrag zur vergleichenden Grammatik der indochinesischen Sprachen, insonderheit des Tibetischen, Barmanischen, Siamesischen und Chinesischen*, Leipzig: Otto Harrassowitz.
Conrady, A. (1916) 'Eine merkwürdige Beziehung zwischen den austrischen und den indochinesischen Sprachen', in *Aufsätze zur Kultur- und Sprachgeschichte vornehmlich des Orients: Ernst Kuhn zum 70. Geburtstage am 7. Februar 1916 gewidmet von Freunden und Schülern*, pp. 475–504, Munich: Verlag von M. & H. Marcus.
Conrady, A. (1922) 'Neue austrisch-indochinesische Parallelen', in *Asia Major: Hirth Anniversary Volume*, pp. 23–66, London: Robsthan and Company.
Coupe, A.R. (2003) *A Phonetic and Phonological Description of Ao: A Tibeto-Burman Language of Nagaland, Northeast India*, Canberra: Pacific Linguistics, Australian National University.
Court de Gébelin, A. (1774) *Monde Primitif, analysé et comparé avec le monde moderne, considéré dans l'Histoire Naturelle de la Parole; ou Grammaire universelle et comparative*, Paris: chez l'auteur, Boudet, Valleyre, Veuve Duchesne, Saugrain & Ruault.
Cust, R.N. (1877) *Languages of the Indo-Chinese Peninsula and the Indian Archipelago*, London: Trübner for the Philological Society.
Cust, R.N. (1878) *A Sketch of the Modern Languages of East India*, London: Trübner & Co.

Diffloth, G. (2005) 'The contribution of linguistic palaeontology and Austroasiatic', in L. Sagart, R.M. Blench and A. Sanchez-Mazas (eds) *The Peopling of East Asia: Putting Together Archaeology, Linguistics and Genetics*, pp. 77–80, London: Routledge Curzon.

Driem, G. van (1997) 'Sino-Bodic', *Bulletin of the School of Oriental and African Studies*, 60(3): 455–88.

Driem, G. van (1998) 'Neolithic correlates of ancient Tibeto-Burman migrations', in R.M. Blench and M. Spriggs (eds) *Archaeology and Language II*, pp. 67–102, London: Routledge.

Driem, G. van (2001) *Languages of the Himalayas: An Ethnolinguistic Handbook of the Greater Himalayan Region, containing an Introduction to the Symbiotic Theory of Language*, 2 vols, Leiden: Brill.

Driem, G. van (2002) 'Tibeto-Burman phylogeny and prehistory: Languages, material culture and genes', in P. Bellwood and C. Renfrew (eds) *Examining the Farming/ Language Dispersal Hypothesis*, pp. 233–49, Cambridge: McDonald Institute for Archaeological Research.

Driem, G. van (2003) 'Tibeto-Burman vs. Sino-Tibetan', in B. Bauer and G.-J. Pinault, (eds) *Language in Time and Space: A Festschrift for Werner Winter on the Occasion of his 80th Birthday*, pp. 101–19, Berlin: Mouton de Gruyter.

Driem, G. van (2005) 'Sino-Austronesian vs. Sino-Caucasian, Sino-Bodic vs. Sino-Tibetan, and Tibeto-Burman as default theory', in Y.P.Yadava, G. Bhattarai, R.R. Lohani, B. Prasain and K. Parajuli (eds) *Contemporary Issues in Nepalese Linguistics*, pp. 285–338, Kathmandu: Linguistic Society of Nepal.

Egerod, S. (1972) 'Les particularités de la grammaire chinoise', in J.M.C. Thomas and L. Bernot (eds) *Langues et techniques, nature et société: Études offertes en hommage à André Georges Haudricourt*, vol. 1, *Approche linguistique*, pp. 101–9, Paris: Éditions Klincksieck.

Ferlus, M. (2003) 'On borrowing from Middle Chinese into Proto-Tibetan: A new look at the problem of the relationship between Chinese and Tibetan', in D. Bradley, R. LaPolla, B. Michailovsky and G. Thurgood (eds) *Language Variation: Papers on Variation and Change in the Sinosphere and in the Indosphere in Honour of James A. Matisoff*, pp. 263–75, Canberra: Pacific Linguistics, Australian National University.

Forbes, C.J.F.S. (1878) 'On Tibeto-Burman languages', *Journal of the Royal Asiatic Society of Great Britain and Ireland*, NS 10: 210–27.

Forchhammer, E. (1882) 'Indo-Chinese languages', *Indian Antiquary*, 11: 177–89.

Forrer, Emil (1919) 'Die acht Sprachen der Boghazköi-Inschriften', *Sitzungsberichte der Preussischen Akademie der Wissenschaften*, LIII: 1029–41.

Gabelentz, H.G.C. von der (1881) *Chinesische Grammatik mit Ausschluss des niederen Stiles und der heutigen Umgangssprache*, Leipzig: T.O. Weigel.

Genetti, C.E. (2003) *Tibeto-Burman Languages of Nepal: Manange and Sherpa*, Canberra: Pacific Linguistics, Australian National University.

Grierson, G.A. (ed.) (1904) *Linguistic Survey of India*, vol. 2, *Mōn-Khmēr and Siamese-Chinese Families (Including Khassi and Tai)*, Calcutta: Superintendent of Government Printing, India.

Grierson, G.A. (ed.) (1909) *Linguistic Survey of India*, vol. 3, part I, *Tibeto-Burman Family: Tibetan Dialects, the Himalayan Dialects and the North Assam Group*, Calcutta: Superintendent of Government Printing, India.

Grube, W. (1881) *Die sprachgeschichtliche Stellung des Chinesischen*, Leipzig: T.O. Weigel.

Hall, R.A. Jr. (1984) *Proto-Romance Morphology*, Amsterdam: John Benjamins.
Haller, F. (2004) *Dialekt und Erzählungen von Themchen* (Beiträge zur tibetischen Erzählforschung, 14), Bonn: Vereinigung für Geschichtswissenschaft Hochasiens Wissenschaftsverlag.
Hari, A.M. and Chhegu L. (2004) *Hyolmo-Nepālī-A☐grejī Śabdakoś Yohlmo-Nepali–English Dictionary*, Kathmandu: Central Department of Linguistics, Tribhuvan University.
Haudricourt, A.-G. (1956) 'De la restitution des initiales dans les languages monosyllabiques: le problème du thai commun', *Bulletin de la Société de Linguistique de Paris*, 52: 307–22.
Hildebrandt, K.A. (2003) 'Manange Tone: Scenarios of Retention and Loss in Two Communities', doctoral dissertation: University of California at Santa Barbara.
Houghton, B. (1896) 'Outlines of Tibeto-Burman linguistic palæontology', *Journal of the Royal Asiatic Society*, 1896: 23–55.
Jacques, G. (2004) 'Phonologie et morphologie du japhug (rGyalrong)', thèse en vue de l'obtention du doctorat de linguistique, Université Paris VII – Denis Diderot, 9 Sept.
Jaxontov, S.E. (1965) *Drevnekitajskij jazyk,* Moscow: Jazyki narodov Azii i Afriki.
Jaxontov, S.E. (1977) 'Jazyki vostočnoj i jugovostočnoj Azii v pervom tysjačiletii do našej èry', in N.N. Čeboksarov, M.V. Krjukov and M.V. Sofronov (eds) *Rannjaja ètničeskaja istorija i narody vostočnoj Azii,* Moscow: Nauka, pp. 98–108.
Kate, Lambert Hermanszoon ten (1710) *Gemeenschap tussen de Gottische Spraeke en de Nederduytsche vertoont*, vol. 1, *By eenen Brief nopende deze Stoffe*; vol. 2, *By eene Lyste der Gottische Woorden, gelykluydig met de onze, getrokken uyt het Gothicum Evangelium*; vol. 3, *By de Voorbeelden der Gottische* Declinatien *en* Conjugatien*, nieulyks in haere Classes onderscheyden. Alles gericht tot Opheldering van den Ouden Grond van 't Belgisch*, Amsterdam: Jan Rieuwertsz.
Kate, Lambert Hermanszoon ten (1723) *Aenleiding tot de Kennisse van het Verhevene Deel der Nederduitsche Sprake waer in Hare zekerste Grondslag, edelste Kragt, nuttelijkste Onderscheiding, en geregeldste Afleiding overwogen en nagespoort, en tegen het Allervoornaemste der Verouderde en Nog-levende Taelverwanten, als 't Oude Moeso-Gotthisch, Frank-Duitsch, en Angel-Saxisch, beneffens het Hedendaegsche Hoog-Duitsch en Yslandsch, vergeleken word*, 2 vols, Amsterdam: Rudolph & Gerard Wetstein.
Kern, H. (1889) 'Het stamland der Maleisch-Polynesische volken', *Tijdschrift voor Nederlandsch-Indië*, 18(2): 1–9.
Klaproth, J.H. von (1823a) *Asia Polyglotta*, Paris: A. Schubart.
Klaproth, J.H. von (1823b) *Asia Polyglotta: Sprachatlas*, Paris: A. Schubart.
Klaproth, J.H. von (1826) *Mémoires relatifs à l'Asie, contenant des recherches historiques, géographiques et philologiques*, 2 vols, Paris: Société Asiatique de Paris.
Konow, Sten: See Grierson (1904, 1909).
Kortlandt, F.H.H. (2003) 'Bad theory, wrong conclusions: M. Halle on Slavic accentuation', in J. Schaeken, P. Houtzagers and J. Kalsbeek (eds) *Dutch Contributions to the Thirteenth Annual Congress of Slavists, Ljubljana, August 15–21, 2003: Linguistics* (Studies in Slavic and General Linguistics, 30), pp. 237–40, Amsterdam and New York: Rodopi.
Kuhn, E. (1883) *Ueber Herkunft und Sprache der transgangetischen Völker: Festrede zur Vorfeier des Allerhöchsten Geburts- und Namensfestes Seiner Majestät des Königs Ludwig II., gehalten in der öffentlichen Sitzung der Königlichen Akademie*

der Wissenschaften zu München am 25. Juli 1881, Munich: Verlag der Königlichen Bayerischen Akademie.

Kuhn, E. (1889) 'Beiträge zur Sprachenkunde Hinterindiens (Sitzung vom 2. März 1889)', *Sitzungsberichte der Königlichen Bayerischen Akademie der Wissenschaften* (Munich), Philosophisch-philologische Classe, 2: 189–236.

Kuiper, F.B.J. (1948) 'Munda and Indonesian', in *Orientalia Neerlandica: A Volume of Oriental Studies, published under Auspices of the Netherlands' Oriental Society (Oostersch Genootschap in Nederland) on the Occasion of the Twenty-Fifth Anniversary of Its Foundation, May 8th, 1945*, pp. 372–401, Leiden: A.W. Sijthoffs Uitgeversmaatschappij.

Lahaussois, A. (2002) 'Aspects of the Grammar of Thulung Rai, an Endangered Himalayan Language', doctoral dissertation, University of California at Berkeley.

Laufer, B. (1916) 'The Si-hia language, a study in Indo-Chinese philology', *T'oung Pao*, 17: 1–126.

Lepsius, C.R. (1861) 'Über die Umschrift und Lautverhältnisse einiger hinterasiatischer Sprachen, namentlich der Chinesischen und der Tibetischen', *Abhandlungen der Königlichen Akademie der Wissenschaften zu Berlin* (for 1860): 449–96.

Leyden, J.C. (1806) 'Plan for the Investigation of the Language, Literature, History and Antiquities of the Indo-Chinese Nations', 69-page manuscript held by the British Library, ADD. MSS 26,564; later published with changes as Leyden (1808).

Leyden, John Casper (1808) 'On the languages and literature of the Indo-Chinese nations', *Asiatic Researches*, 10: 158–289.

Li Fang Kuei (= Lǐ Fānggui) (1971) 'Shànggǔ yīn yánjiū', *Tsing Hua Journal of Chinese Studies*, 9: 1–61.

Li Fang Kuei (1974) 'Studies on Archaic Chinese' (trans. G.L. Mattos), *Monumenta Serica*, 31 (1974–5): 219–87.

Li Fang Kuei (1976) 'Jǐge shànggǔ shēngmǔ wèntí', in *Zǒngtǒng Jiǎng Gōng Shìshì Zhōunián Lùnwén Jí*, pp. 1143–50, Taipei: Academia Sinica.

Li Fang Kuei (1983) 'Archaic Chinese', in David N. Keightley (ed.) *The Origins of Chinese Civilization*, pp. 393–408, Berkeley, CA: University of California Press.

Li, P.J. (1995) 'Is Chinese genetically related to Austronesian?', in W.S.-Y. Wang (ed.) *The Ancestry of the Chinese Language* (Journal of Chinese Linguistics Monograph Series, 8), pp. 93–112, Berkeley, CA: University of California Press.

Logan, J.R. (1852, 1853, 1854, 1855, 1857) 'Ethnology of the Indo-Pacific islands', *Journal of the Indian Archipelago and Eastern Asia* (Singapore), 6: 57–82, 653–88; 7: 20–63, 105–37, 186–224, 301–24; 8: 28–79, 200–61, 421–504; 9: 1–52, 162–272, 359–441, NS 1(2): 1–150.

Logan, J.R. (1856) 'The Maruwi of the Baniak Islands', *Journal of the Indian Archipelago and Eastern Asia* (Singapore), NS 1(1): 1–42.

Logan, J.R. (1858) 'The West-Himalaic or Tibetan tribes of Asam, Burma and Pegu', *Journal of the Indian Archipelago and Eastern Asia* (Singapore), NS 2(1): 68–114.

Logan, J.R. (1859) 'Ethnology of the Indo-Pacific islands: The affiliation of the Tibeto-Burman, Mon-Anam, Papuanesian and Malayo-Polynesian pronouns and definitives, as varieties of the ancient Himalayo-Polynesian system; and the relation of that system to the Draviro-Australian', *Journal of the Indian Archipelago and Eastern Asia* (Singapore), 3(1): 65–98.

Malherbe, M. (2001) 'La planète des langues', *Science et Avenir*, special issue, 'Quelle langue parlait-on il y a 100 000 ans? La langue d'Homo erectus' (Dec. 2000–Jan. 2001), 28–35.

Malte-Brun, C. (1832) *Précis de la géographie universelle, ou description de toutes les parties du monde sur un plan nouveau, d'après les grandes divisions naturelles du globe: Nouvelle édition, revue, corrigée, mise dans un nouvel ordre et augmentée de toutes les nouvelles découvertes par J.J.N. Huot*, 6 vols, Brussels: Th. Lejeune (posthumous).

Mason, F. (1854) 'The Talaing language', *Journal of the American Oriental Society*, 4: 277–89.

Mason, F. (1860) *Burmah, its people and Natural Productions, or Notes on the Nations, Fauna, Flora and Minerals of Tenasserim, Pegu and Burmah*, Rangoon: Thomas Stowe Ranney.

Matisoff, J.A. (1978) *Variational Semantics in Tibeto-Burman: The 'Organic' Approach to Linguistic Comparison*, (Occasional Papers of the Wolfenden Society on Tibeto-Burman Linguistics, 6), Philadelphia: Institute for the Study of Human Issues.

Matisoff, J.A. (1992) 'A key etymology', *Linguistics of the Tibeto-Burman Area*, 15(1): 139–43.

Matisoff, J.A. (2000) 'On "Sino-Bodic" and other symptoms of neosubgroupitis', *Bulletin of the School of Oriental and African Studies*, 63(3): 356–69.

Matisoff, J.A. (2003) *Handbook of Proto-Tibeto-Burman: System and Philosophy of Sino-Tibeto-Burman Reconstruction*, Berkeley, CA: University of California Press.

Mazzola, M.L. (1976) *Proto-Romance and Sicilian*, Amsterdam: John Benjamins.

Miller, R.A. (1968) 'Review of Robert Shafer, *Introduction to Sino-Tibetan*, Parts I and II', *Monumenta Serica*, 27: 398–435.

Miller, R.A. (1974) 'Sino-Tibetan: Inspection of a Conspectus', *Journal of the American Oriental Society*, 94(2): 195–209.

Milner, G.B. and E.J.A. Henderson (eds) (1965) *Indo-Pacific Linguistic Studies*, 2 vols, Amsterdam: North-Holland Publishing Co.

Müller, F.M. (1855) *Languages of the Seat of War in the East, with a Survey of the Three Families of Language, Semitic, Arian, and Turanian* (frontispiece title: *Max Müller's Survey of Languages*, 2nd edn), London: Williams & Norgate.

Nikolaev, S.L. (1991) 'Sino-Caucasian languages in America', in V. Sheveroshkin (ed.) *Dene-Sino-Caucasian*, pp. 42–66. Bochum: Universitätsverlag Dr. N. Brockmeyer.

Nikolaev, S.L. and Starostin, S.A. (1984) 'Severnokavkazskie jazyki i ix mesto sredi drugix jazykovyx semej Perednej Azii', in *Lingvističeskaja rekonstrukcija i drevnejsaja istorija vostoka*, vol. 3, *Jazykovaja situacija v Perednej Azii v X-IV tysjačeletijax do našej ery*, pp. 26–34, Moscow: Nauka, Glavnaja Redakcija Vostočnoj Literatury.

Nikolaev, S.L. and Starostin, S.A. (1994) *A North Caucasian Etymological Dictionary*, Moscow: Asterisk Publishers.

Opgenort, J.R. (2004) *A Grammar of Wambule: Grammar, Lexicon, Texts and Cultural Survey of a Kiranti Tribe of Eastern Nepal*, Leiden: Brill.

Opgenort, J.R. (2005) *A Grammar of Jero, with a Historical Comparative Study of the Kiranti Languages*, Leiden: Brill.

Orël, V.È. and Starostin, S.A. (1990) 'Etruscan as an East Caucasian language', in V. Sheveroshkin (ed.) *Proto-Languages and Proto-Cultures: Materials from the First International Interdisciplinary Symposium on Language and Prehistory, Ann Arbor, Michigan, November 1988*, pp. 60–8, Bochum: Universitätsverlag Dr. N. Brockmeyer.

Ostapirat, W. (2005) 'Kra-Dai and Austronesian: Notes on phonological correspondences and vocabulary distribution', in L. Sagart, R.M. Blench and A. Sanchez-Mazas (eds) *The Peopling of East Asia: Putting Together Archaeology, Linguistics and Genetics*, pp. 107–31, London: RoutledgeCurzon.

Pallas, P.S. (1786, 1789) *Linguarum Totius Orbis Vocabularia Comparativa Augustissimae cura collecta: Sravnitel'nye Slovari Vsěx Jazykov" i Narěčij sobrannye Desniceju Vsevysočajšej Osoby*, 2 vols, St Petersburg: Johannes Carolus Schnoor.

Peiros, I. (1998) *Comparative Linguistics in Southeast Asia*, Canberra: Pacific Linguistics.

Peiros, I. and Starostin, S.A. (1996) *A Comparative Vocabulary of Five Sino-Tibetan Languages*, 6 fascicles, Parkville: University of Melbourne, Department of Linguistics and Applied Linguistics.

Plaisier, H. (2005) *A Grammar of Lepcha*, Leiden University: doctoral dissertation.

Pott, August Friedrich (1833, 1836) *Etymologische Forschungen auf dem Gebiete der Indo-Germanischen Sprachen, mit besonderem Bezug auf die Lautumwandlung im Sanskrit, Griechischen, Lateinischen, Littauischen und Gothischen*, 2 vols, Lemgo: Meyersche Hof-Buchhandlung.

Przyluski, J. (1924) 'Le sino-tibétain', in A. Meillet and M. Cohen (eds) *Les Langues du Monde*, pp. 361–84, Paris: Librairie Ancienne Édouard Champion.

Pulleyblank, E.G. (1983) 'The Chinese and their neighbours in prehistoric and early historic times', in D.N. Keightley (ed.) *The Origins of Chinese Civilization*, pp. 411–66, Berkeley, CA: University of California Press.

Pulleyblank, E.G. (1984) *Middle Chinese: A Study in Historical Phonology*, Vancouver: University of British Columbia Press.

Pulleyblank, E.G. (1991) *Lexicon of Reconstructed Pronunciation in Early Middle Chinese, Late Middle Chinese, and Early Mandarin*, Vancouver: University of British Columbia Press.

Pulleyblank, E.G. (1995) 'Comments from Pulleyblank', in W.S-Y. Wang (ed.) *The Ancestry of the Chinese Language* (Journal of Chinese Linguistics Monograph Series, 8), pp. 325–35 Berkeley, CA: University of California Press.

Rafinesque, Constantine Samuel (1831) 'Mémoires sur l'origine des nations nègres, ou Introduction à l'histoire des nègres indigènes d'Asie, d'Afrique Polynésie, Amérique et Europe par C.S. Rafinesque, professeur des Sciences historiques et naturelles à Philadelphie', manuscript kept at the American Philosophical Society in Philadelphia [cited by Belyi 1997].

Reid, L.A. (1994) 'Morphological evidence for Austric', *Oceanic Linguistics*, 33(2): 323–44.

Reid, LA. (1999) 'New linguistic evidence for the Austric hypothesis', in E. Zeitoun and P. Jen-kuei Li (eds) *Selected Papers from the Eighth International Conference on Austronesian Linguistics*, pp.1–30, Taipei: Academia Sinica.

Reid, L.A. (2005) 'The current status of Austric: a review and evaluation of the lexical and morphosyntactic evidence', in L. Sagart, R. Blench and A. Sanchez-Mazas (eds) *The Peopling of East Asia: Putting together Archaeology, Linguistics and Genetics*, pp. x–y, London: RoutledgeCurzon.

Ruhlen, M. and Starostin, S.A. (1994) 'Proto-Yenisseian reconstructions, with extra-Yenisseian comparisons', in M. Ruhlen (ed.) *On the Origins of Languages: Studies in Linguistic Taxonomy*, pp. 70–92, Stanford, CA: Stanford University Press.

Sagart, L. (1990) 'Chinese and Austronesian are genetically related', paper presented at the 23rd International Conference on Sino-Tibetan Languages and Linguistics, 5–7 Oct., University of Texas at Arlington.

Sagart, L. (1991) 'Chinese tones from Austronesian final consonants', in M. Ratliff and E. Schiller (eds) *Papers from the First Annual Meeting of the Southeast Asian Linguistics Society*, pp. 367–79, Tempe, AZ: Arizona State University.

Sagart, L. (1993) 'Chinese and Austronesian: Evidence for a genetic relationship', *Journal of Chinese Linguistics*, 21(1): 1–62.
Sagart, L. (1994a) 'Proto-Austronesian and Old Chinese evidence for Sino-Austronesian', *Oceanic Linguistics*, 33(2): 271–308.
Sagart, L. (1994b) 'Discussion note: A reply to J. A. Matisoff's 'a key etymology', *Linguistics of the Tibeto-Burman Area*, 17(1): 167–8 [published 1996].
Sagart, L. (1995a) 'Some remarks on the ancestry of Chinese', in W.S-Y. Wang (ed.) *The Ancestry of the Chinese Language* (Journal of Chinese Linguistics Monograph Series, 8), pp. 195–223, Berkeley, CA: University of California Press.
Sagart, L. (1995b) 'Comments from Sagart', in W.S-Y. Wang (ed.) *The Ancestry of the Chinese Language* (Journal of Chinese Linguistics Monograph Series, 8), pp. 337–7, Berkeley, CA: University of California Press.
Sagart, L. (1995c) 'Questions of method in Chinese-Tibeto-Burman comparison', *Cahiers de Linguistique, Asie Orientale*, 24(2): 245–55.
Sagart, L. (1999) *The Roots of Old Chinese*, Amsterdam: John Benjamins.
Sagart, L. (2002) 'Sino-Tibeto-Austronesian: an updated and improved argument', Paper presented at the 9th International Conference on Austronesian Linguistics at Australian National University, Canberra, 11 January 2002.
Sagart, L. (2003a) 'The vocabulary of cereal cultivation and the phylogeny of East Asian languages', *Bulletin of the Indo-Pacific Prehistory Association*, 23 (Taipei Papers, vol. 1): 127–36.
Sagart, L. (2003b) 'Sources of Middle Chinese manner types: Old Chinese prenasalized initials in Hmong-Mien and Sino-Tibetan perspective', *Language and Linguistics*, 4(4): 757–68.
Sagart, L. (2004) 'The higher phylogeny of Austronesian and the position of Tai-Kadai', *Oceanic Linguistics*, 43(2): 411–44.
Sagart, L. (2005a) 'Sino-Tibetan-Austronesian: an updated and improved argument', in L. Sagart, R.M. Blench and A. Sanchez-Mazas (eds) *The Peopling of East Asia: Putting Together Archaeology, Linguistics and Genetics*, pp. 161–76, London: RoutledgeCurzon.
Sagart, L. (2005b) 'Tai-Kadai as a subgroup of Austronesian', in L. Sagart, R.M. Blench and A. Sanchez-Mazas (eds) *The Peopling of East Asia: Putting Together Archaeology, Linguistics and Genetics*, pp. 177–81, London: RoutledgeCurzon.
Sagart, L. (2006) 'Review of Matisoff (2003)', *Diachronica*, 23(1): 206–23.
Schmidt, W. (1906) 'Die Mon-Khmer Völker, ein Bindeglied zwischen Völkern Zentral-Asiens und Austronesiens', *Archiv für Anthropologie, Neue Folge*, V: 59–109.
Schmidt, W. (1930) 'Die Beziehungen der austrischen Sprachen zum Japanischen', *Wiener Beiträge zur Kulturgeschichte und Linguistik, Veröffentlichungen des Institutes für Völkerkunde an der Universität Wien*, I: 239–51.
Schott, Wilhelm (1856) 'Über die sogenannten indo-chinesischen Sprachen insonderheit das Siamische', *Abhandlungen der Königlichen Akademie der Wissenschaften zu Berlin aus dem Jahre 1856*, Philosophisch-historische Klasse: 161–79.
Shafer, R. (1955) 'Classification of the Sino-Tibetan languages', *Word, Journal of the Linguistic Circle of New York*, 11: 94–111.
Shafer, R. (1966, 1967, 1968, 1974) *Introduction to Sino-Tibetan*, parts I, II, III and IV, Wiesbaden: Otto Harrassowitz.
Simon, W. (1927–9) 'Zur Rekonstruktion der altchinesischen Endkonsonanten', *Mitteilungen des Seminars für Orientalische Sprachen an der Friedrich-Wilhelms-Universität zu Berlin*, 30(1): 147–67, 175–204; 32(1): 157–228.

Starosta, S. (2005) 'Proto-East-Asian and the origin and dispersal of languages of East and Southeast Asia and the Pacific', in L. Sagart, R.M. Blench and A. Sanchez-Mazas (eds) *The Peopling of East Asia: Putting Together Archaeology, Linguistics and Genetics*, pp. 182–97, London: RoutledgeCurzon.

Starostin, S.A. (1982) 'Praenisejskaja rekonstrukcija i vnešnie svjazi enisejskix jazykov: Opyt rekonstrukcii praenisejskoj zvukovoj sistemy', in E.A. Alekseenko, I.I. Goxman, V.V. Ivanov and V.N. Toporov (eds) *Ketskij sbornik: Antropologija, ètnografija, mifologija, lingvistika*, pp. 144–237, Leningrad: Nauka.

Starostin, S.A. (1984) 'Gipoteza o genetičeskix svjazjax sinotibetskix jazykov s enisejskimi i severnokavkazskimi jazykami', in *Lingvističeskaja rekonstrukcija i drevnešjaja istorija vostoka: Tezisy i doklady konferencii*, vol. 4, *Drevnejšaja jazykovaja situacija v vostočnoj Azii*, pp. 19–38, Moscow: Izdatel'stvo 'Nauka'.

Starostin, S.A. (1989) *Rekonstrukcija drevnekitajskoj fonologičeskoj sistemy*. Moscow: Izdatel'stvo 'Nauka'.

Starostin, S.A. (1991) 'On the hypothesis of a genetic connection between the Sino-Tibetan languages and the Yenisseian and North Caucasian languages', in V. Sheveroshkin (ed.) *Dene-Sino-Caucasian*, pp. 12–42, Bochum: Universitätsverlag Dr N. Brockmeyer.

Starostin, S.A. (1994) 'The reconstruction of Proto-Kiranti', paper presented at the 27ème Congrès International sur les Langues et la Linguistique Sino-Tibétaines, Centre International d'Études Pédagogiques à Sèvres, 14 Oct.

Starostin, S.A. (1995a) 'Old Chinese vocabulary: A historical perspective', in W.S-Y. Wang (ed.) *The Ancestry of the Chinese Language* (Journal of Chinese Linguistics Monograph Series, 8), pp. 225–51, Berkeley, CA: University of California Press.

Starostin, S.A. (1995b) 'Comments from Starostin', in W.S-Y. Wang (ed.) *The Ancestry of the Chinese Language* (Journal of Chinese Linguistics Monograph Series, 8), pp. 393–404, Berkeley, CA: University of California Press.

Starostin, S.A. (1995c) 'Sravnitel'nyj slovar' enisejskix jazykov', in S.A. Starostin (ed.) *Ketskij sbornik: Lingvistika*, pp. 176–315, Moscow: Izdatel'skaja Firma 'Vostočnaja Literatura' Rossijskoj Akademii Nauk.

Starostin, S.A. (1996) 'Word-final resonants in Sino-Caucasian', *Journal of Chinese Linguistics*, 24(2): 281–311.

Starostin, S.A. (1998) 'Hurro-Caucasica', in T.M. Nikolaeva (ed.) *Politropon: k 70-letiju Vladimira Nikolaeviča Toporova*, pp. 90–9, Moscow: Izdatel'stvo 'Indrik'.

Starostin, S.A. (1999a) 'Comparative-historical linguistics and lexicostatistics', in V. Shevoroshkin and P.J. Sidwell (eds) *Historical Linguistics and Lexicostatistics*, pp. 3–50, Melbourne: Association for the History of Language.

Starostin, S.A. (1999b) 'Methodology of long-range comparison', in V. Shevoroshkin and P.J. Sidwell (eds) *Historical Linguistics and Lexicostatistics*, pp. 61–6, Melbourne: Association for the History of Language.

Starostin, S.A. (2002) 'A response to Alexander Vovin's criticism of the Sino-Caucasian theory', *Journal of Chinese Linguistics*, 30(1): 142–53.

Starostin, S.A. (2005) 'Current state of long-range linguistic taxonomy', paper presented on 9 June at Leiden University on the occasion of the conferral of an honorary doctorate upon him.

Strahm, E. and Maibaum, A. (2005) *Jirel-Nepālī-A☐grejī Śabdakoś Jirel-Nepali–English Dictionary*, Kathmandu: Centre for Nepal and Asian Studies, Tribhuvan University.

Tolsma, G. (1999) 'Internal reconstruction and comparative evidence of the long vowels in Kulung', in Y.P. Yadava and W.W. Glover (eds) *Topics in Nepalese Linguistics*, pp. 495–7, Kathmandu: Royal Nepal Academy.

Trask, R.L. (1994) 'Basque: The search for relatives', *Dhumbadji!*, 2(1): 3–54.
Trask, R.L. (1995a) 'Basque: The search for relatives (part 2)', *Dhumbadji!*, 2(2): 3–18.
Trask, R.L. (1995b) 'Basque and Dene-Caucasian', *Mother Tongue*, 1: 3–82, 172–201.
Trombetti, A. (1905) *L'unità d'origine del linguaggio*, Bologna: Libreria Treves di Luigi Beltrami.
Trombetti, A. (1925) *Le origini della lingua basca* (Memoria presentata alla Reale Accademia delle Scienze dell'Istituto di Bologna nella Sessione del 24 Novembre (1923) Bologna: Cooperativa Tipografica Azzoguidi.
Trubetzkoy (i.e. Trubeckoj), N.S. (1922) 'Les consonnes latérales des langues caucasiennes septentrionales', *Bulletin de la Société Linguistique de Paris*, 23(3): 184–204.
Turin, M. (2005) *A Grammar of Thangmi*, Leiden University: doctoral dissertation.
Wáng Fēng (2004) 'Language contact and language comparison: The case of Bái', doctoral dissertation, City University of Hong Kong.
Watters, D.E (2002) *A Grammar of Kham*, Cambridge: Cambridge University Press.
Watters, D.E. (2004) *A Dictionary of Kham: Taka Dialect (A Tibeto-Burman Language of Nepal)*, Kirtipur: Central Department of Linguistics, Tribhuvan University.
Witsen, N. (1692) *Noord en Oost Tartarye, ofte Bondig Ontwerp van eenige dier Landen en Volken, welke voormaels bekent zijn geweest, beneffens verscheide tot noch toe onbekende, en meest nooit voorheen beschreven Tartersche en Nabuurige Gewesten, Landstreeken, Steden, Rivieren, en Plaetzen, in de Noorder en Oostelykste Gedeelten van Asia en Europa*, 2 vols, Amsterdam: François Halma (2nd impr, 1705).
Wulff, K. (1934) *Chinesisch und Tai: Sprachvergleichende Untersuchungen* (Det Kongelige Danske Videnskabernes Selskab, Historisk-filologiske Meddelelser, 20/3), Copenhagen: Levin & Munksgaard.
Wulff, K. (1942) [posthumous] *Über das Verhältnis des Malay-Polynesischen zum Indochinesischen*, Copenhagen: Munksgaard.
Xīzàng Zìzhìqū Wénwù Guánlǐ Wěiyuán Huì [Managing Committee for Cultural Affairs of the Autonomous Region of Tibet] (1979) 'Xīzàng Chāngdū Kǎruò yízhǐ shíjué jiǎn bào' (Brief report of an initial excavations of the site at mKhar-ro, Chab-mdo, Tibet), *Wénwù*, 1979(9): 22–8.
Zhēngzhāng Shàngfāng (1987) 'Shànggǔ yùnmǔ xìtǒng hé sìděng jièyīn shēngdiào de fāyuán wèntí', *Wēnzhōu Shīyuàn Xuébào (Shèhuì kēxué bǎn)*, 4: 67–90.

10 Altaic loans in Old Chinese

Sergei A. Starostin, with an introduction by Ilia Peiros

1. The tip of the iceberg: an introduction (Ilia Peiros)

This is one of the last papers prepared by Sergei Starostin before his tragic death on 30 September 2005. The paper is written in Sergei's typical style with an emphasis on new data while the interpretation is only given in a few words. This makes reading Sergei's papers difficult for inexperienced readers not accustomed to 'data-heavy' publications. As this book is aimed at a broader audience, some comments need to be made to facilitate reading the paper.

The following statements have been made by Sergei:

1. A number of similar words are found in Old Chinese and Proto-Altaic, the common ancestor of Turkic, Mongolian, Tungus-Manchu and Korean-Japanese languages.
2. The Chinese forms, although known from the earliest written sources, are not inherited from Proto-Sino-Tibetan, the common ancestor of hundreds of languages spoken mainly in China, India, Nepal and Burma.
3. The Altaic forms in question are always found in Korean and Japanese, which have inherited them from their proto-language.
4. Old Chinese must have borrowed the words from a Korean-Japanese language: ancient varieties of Korean, Japanese or another language of this group.
5. The semantics of these borrowings indicates cultural contacts in a far-from-peaceful environment.

All the above statements are based on comparative work conducted by Sergei. Let us briefly discuss the related aspects of his research.

The first significant result obtained by Sergei was his reconstruction of Old Chinese phonology (1979, 1989a), which allowed him to obtain a more reliable reading of ancient characters. The Chinese book (734 pages long) contained however only a part of the scholar's results. His Old Chinese Dictionary and a statistical study of rhymes and initials remain unpublished. All Old Chinese forms used in this article are reconstructed along the lines proposed in Sergei's book (1989a), which should be consulted for necessary explanations.

Research in Chinese historical phonology led Sergei to a broader field of Sino-Tibetan studies. Our joint work in this area began when Sergei was still a university student and lasted till the end of his life. Two major results have been achieved. A comparative dictionary of Proto-Sino-Tibetan consisting of more than 2,800 entries (Peiros and Starostin 1996) has been compiled followed by a lexicostatistical classification of the family. According to our classification, the Sino-Tibetan family is formed by several major branches, such as Chinese, Bodo-Kachin, Karen, Tibeto-Burman and a few others. Disintegration of the proto-language began about six thousand years ago. Most of the etymologies were proposed by the authors, but all reliable suggestions found in the literature are also included. The statement that the Chinese forms in this chapter do not have Sino-Tibetan etymologies is backed by this research.

The Japanese language, its history and origins were also among Sergei's interests. As an undergraduate student he published several articles on various aspects of Japanese historical phonology (Starostin 1972, 1975). Lexicostatistical analysis of the Altaic origins of Japanese was presented in his 1991 monograph. The study of the Japanese language later evolved into full-scale research into the Altaic language family culminating in an Altaic Etymological Dictionary prepared by Sergei Starostin together with Anna Dybo and Oleg Mudrak (Starostin *et al.* 2003). The dictionary is based on a detailed comparative phonology and a thorough investigation of all available sources, including reconstructions of Proto-Turkic, Proto-Mongolian and Proto-Tungus-Manchu languages. A comparison of these three proto-languages with Korean and Japanese has produced more than three thousand etymologies, thus providing solid proof for the Altaic family. The major conclusions were as follows:

> Proto-Altaic split into three branches, viz. Turko-Mongolian, Tungus-Manchu and Korean-Japanese, around the 6th millennium B.C. Tungus-Manchu must have occupied a central dialectal position, which explains it shared isoglosses both with Turko-Mongolian and Korean-Japanese.
>
> Two subbranches – Turko-Mongolian and Korean-Japanese – in their turn, has split rather early, around the 4th millennium B.C. ... There is still some doubt about the existence of common Korean-Japanese: the specific similarities between these two subbranches might be due to secondary dialectal interaction.
>
> The next splits occurred already closer to our era: first the split of Tungus-Manchu, next split of Turkic, Japanese and Korean dialects.
>
> (Starostin *et al.* 2003: 236)

One of our joint unfinished projects was the completion of a Chinese etymological dictionary, to include all Chinese words with known Sino-Tibetan etymologies along with words borrowed from unrelated languages. Until recently we knew only about linguistic contacts between Old Chinese and Austronesian (Benedict 1975; Peiros and Starostin 1984). In this chapter, Sergei presents proposals for Old Chinese borrowings from a Korean-Japanese language.

How does one interpret this observation and its implications? Sergei discussed these problems with his friends and colleagues and I present the following hypotheses based on our conversations:

- It is possible to localize the Altaic homeland in Northern China and to propose an association with the Yangshao Neolithic culture that existed along the central Yellow River from around 5000 to 2000 BCE. The cultural lexicon of Proto-Altaic reveals a much better correlation with Yangshao than that of Sino-Tibetan. The east–west distribution of Altaic (proto-)languages is in good agreement with this proposal, with the original centre now occupied by Chinese speakers.
- There is no reason to localize the Sino-Tibetan homeland in Northern China. It is more likely that the proto-language was spoken somewhere else, say, in the sub-Himalayan region, as proposed some time ago (Peiros 1998). Speakers of Proto-Sinitic began their migration to Northern China after the disintegration of Proto-Sino-Tibetan no earlier than the 3rd millennium BCE. During this migration they came in contact with speakers of local languages, including ancient Austronesian and Korean-Japanese languages.
- Their contacts with Proto-Austronesian were bilateral, each language borrowing from the other (Peiros and Starostin 1984).
- Ancient contacts between Chinese and Altaic languages were of a different nature, with only Chinese being a recipient of borrowings. This may have begun when the ancient Chinese speakers reached the Yellow River valley.
- There are some lexical comparisons between Japanese and Austronesian, but so far we do not know whether the Austronesian languages were in contact with Korean. This possibility is yet to be investigated.

2. Altaic loans in Old Chinese (Sergei Starostin)

Loanwords from Chinese are certainly well known in quite a number of Altaic languages, starting with Korean and Japanese that have huge Chinese layers in their vocabulary, and ending with Turkic that can be shown to have borrowed several important lexemes from Chinese as early as the Proto-Turkic level. This is of course due to China's great political and cultural influence in historical times.

However, not all Chinese-Altaic lexical matches can be explained by borrowings from Chinese. With the publication of Benedict (1972), Shafer (1974), Schuessler (1987), Baxter (1992), Starostin (1989b), Peiros and Starostin (1996), we now possess a much better knowledge of Chinese and Sino-Tibetan historical phonology and Sino-Tibetan subclassification. It has become possible to identify inherited Sino-Tibetan vocabulary in Chinese and separate it from a large layer of words having no Sino-Tibetan etymology. We also have much more information about adjacent language families, such as Altaic, Austro-Asiatic and Austronesian.

In this paper I shall not discuss lexical contacts between Chinese (Sino-Tibetan) and its southern neighbours. But I want to draw attention to a large group of lexical matches between Chinese and Altaic that are characterized by the following features:

1   The Old Chinese words are usually attested starting with Early Zhou at the earliest (only a few of them are attested later than 6th century BCE).
2   For none of these words have any Sino-Tibetan parallels been proposed.
3   On the Altaic side, the words are particularly well represented in the Eastern area (Korean, Japanese and Tungus-Manchu).

These matches are presented below. The Old Chinese forms follow the reconstruction in Starostin (1989a); Proto-Altaic, Korean, Japanese, Turkic and Tungus-Manchu forms are cited from Starosin *et al.* (2003). I omit much of the etymological discussion provided in that work.

On the whole, the most plausible explanation of these matches seems to be to suggest a layer of early Altaic loanwords in Old Chinese, indicating rather early lexical contacts, not later than the 2nd millennium BCE. At least some of these matches (including those in Japanese) have already been published, but were usually treated as early Chinese borrowings into Japanese (e.g. OJ *karasi* 'mustard', *mugji* 'wheat', *kuni* 'country', *koromo* 'clothes'; see for example Miller 1972: 203, 235). A more detailed etymological analysis now allows us to propose a reversal of the direction of borrowing.

This analysis has a number of important implications for untangling the extremely difficult prehistoric situation in China and East Asia. Cf. the following cases in Table 10.1.

Table 10.1 Lexical matches between Chinese and Altaic

Old Chinese	Proto-Altaic	Korean	Japanese	Turkic	Mongolian	Tungus-Manchu
爪 ćrū? 'claw'	*čìuru (~ -a) 'to scratch, claw' (EDAL 402)	*čūr 'file'		*dïr-ŋa- 'scratch, claw'		*ǯuri- 'scratch, draw'
李 rhə? 'plum'	*èri 'plum, fruit' (EDAL 517–18)	*irim 'clematis berries, akebi seed'	*ìtápi 'Japanese fig'	*erük 'plum, apricot'	*türil 'plum'	
兔 thā(k)s 'rabbit, hare'	*tʰógsu 'hare' (EDAL 1451)	*thóskí 'hare'			*togsi- 'run away jumping'	*tuksa- 'run; hare'
姑 kā 'father's sister, aunt, mother-in-law'	*ēkʻà 'elder sister; mother' (EDAL 499–500)	*kjə- 'woman'	*kaka 'mother'	*eke 'elder sister'	*eke 'mother'	*eke 'woman; elder sister'
芥 krēts 'mustard' [LZ]	*kabro(-čʻV) 'a k. of ferment' (EDAL 626)	*kòr-ăči 'wine fungus'	*kara- 'bitter'; *karasi 'mustard'	*Kor- 'ferment; bitter'	*kowr 'poison'	
客 khrāk 'guest'	*kàra(-kʻV) (~kʻ-) 'opposite, enemy' (EDAL 647–8)		*kàtà-ki 'enemy'	*Kar- 'opposite'; *Karak 'bandit'	*kar- 'foreign, alien'	
盆 bhə̄n 'tub'	*pòjnV (~ pʻ-) 'vessel; boat' (EDAL 1103)	*pāi 'boat'	*pùnà-i 'boat, vessel'		*haji- 'ship'	
軌 kru? 'wheel-axle ends'	*kịuru 'wheeled vehicle' (EDAL 708)		*kurumá 'vehicle'		*kür-dün 'wheel'	
凍 tōŋs 'to freeze up' [LZ]	*tuŋa 'cold, frost' (EDAL 1385–6)		tumeta- 'cold'	*doŋ 'cold, freeze'	*dayara- 'freeze'	*doŋota 'cold, frost, freeze'
祖 cā? 'deceased grandfather, ancestor'	*ăčV 'elder relative, ancestor' (EDAL 271–2)	*ačă- 'aunt, uncle'		*ăčaj / *ēčej 'elder relative'		

continued...

Table 10.1 continued

Old Chinese	Proto-Altaic	Korean	Japanese	Turkic	Mongolian	Tungus-Manchu
貢 kōŋ-s (< *kōm-s?) 'tribute, present'	*kʻōmu 'offering, respect' (EDAL 838)	*kōmá 'respect'	*kuma 'offering to gods'	*Kom- 'inheritance, legacy'		*uma-kta 'brier, cornel'
梅 mə̄ 'Japanese apricot, plum'	*i̯umu 'a k. of fruit or berry' (EDAL 618)		*úmái 'plum'	OT imiti 'hawthorn'		
粒 rəp 'cereals, grain as food'	*àrpʻá 'barley, millet' (EDAL 312–13)		*àpá 'millet'	*arpa 'barley'	*arbaj 'barley'	Man. arfa 'barley'
麥 mrə̄k 'wheat, barley'	*mi̯urgu 'wheat' (EDAL 935)	*mírh 'wheat'	*mùinki 'wheat, barley'			*murgi 'barley'
惑 wə̄k 'to deceive, err'	*ukʻe 'stupid' (EDAL 1489–90)		OJ wokwo 'stupid'		*(h)ŭki 'stupid'	Man. uxu-ken 'stupid'
棣 lhāj-s 'wild plum'	*ṓjle (~ -i) 'small fruit' (EDAL 1044)	*òìjə́s 'plum'			*ōlir 'wild apple'	*ulīn-(kta) 'wild apple'
琴 ghəm 'a musical instrument with 7 strings'	*kúma 'a musical instrument' (EDAL 737)	*kə̀mìnkó 'a Korean harp of 7 strings'		*Komuŕ 'musical instrument'		*kumu-n 'music'
罩 trākʷ-s 'basket for covering and thus catching fish'	*tʻóbru(-kʻV) 'net' (EDAL 1449)	*tàrà̄čhí 'basket'	*túr- 'fishing'	*tor 'net'	*towr 'net'	*turka- to get caught (in a trap, net)
農 nūŋ 'agriculture; peasant, farmer'	*ni̯àpu / *ɲi̯àpu 'field' (EDAL 988)	*nôn 'rice field'	*nùa 'field'	*(i)apïŕ 'stubble-field'	*nuntug 'grazing place'	*ɲaŋi / *ɲoŋi 'place of hunting'
過 kʷāj-s 'to pass beyond, pass over'	*kèi̯u 'to pass beyond' (EDAL 658)		*kúaja-	Chuv. kaj- 'go away'		*kḗj-
賓 pin 'visitor, guest'	*pʻi̯ùŋi 'other, foreign' (EDAL 1162)		*pina 'province, barbarians'	*ȫŋi 'other'		*puŋie 'other, someone else's'

Old Chinese	Proto-Altaic	Korean	Japanese	Turkic	Mongolian	Tungus-Manchu
劍 kam-s 'sword'	*kʻemá 'sharp, sharp tool' (EDAL 775)		*kámá 'sickle'			*xemer 'sharp'
敵 dhēk 'enemy; enmity'	*dàgì 'enemy' (EDAL 457)	*tōi 'barbarian'	*(d)íkù-sà 'war, warrior'	*jagï 'enemy, war'	*dajin 'war'	*dagu-r 'friend'
稷 cək 'non-glutinous variety of broom-corn millet (Panicum miliaceum effusum); by some identified as Setaria italica'	*žiugi 'millet' (EDAL 1547–8)	*čòh 'millet'		*jügür- 'millet'		*žija- / *žije- (~-g-) 'millet'
縣 gʷēn-s 'district' [LZ]	*kiune 'people, country' (EDAL 705–6)		*kúní 'country'	*Kün 'people'	*küyün 'person'	*kün- 'clan (name)'
轂 k(l)ōk 'nave of wheel'	*kòlbèk'V 'wheel hub' (EDAL 716)		*kə̀ʿsiki 'wheel hub'	*Kŏĺ-luk 'arrow hub'	*kolkibči 'hub'	Evk. kulbukā 'hub'
鵲 shiak 'magpie'	*sako-sako id. (EDAL 1202)		*kàsàsáki	*sagïsgan	*siyaǯigaj	*saksa(ki)
麒麟 g(h)ə-r(h)ən 'unicorn' [cf. also 麋 krun 'waterdeer']	*gúri(-nV) 'deer; game' (EDAL 574)	*kòrámí 'deer, elk'			*gȫrüγe- 'antelope, game'	*gurna- 'ermine; squirrel (?)'
茇 bhə-lə́ʔ 'plantain'	*biola 'a k. of bush' (EDAL 349)	*pùrò 'salad, Lactuca'	*bàrà(m)pí 'fern'	*baḷgïn 'viburnum'	*bal- 'heracleum, angelica'	*boloka 'spiraea'
旆 b(h)āt-s 'streamer'	*pádà 'flag, standard' (EDAL 1071)		*pátà 'flag, banner'	*bAd-rak 'banner, flag'	*bad- 'flag, standard'	
豻 ŋ(h)ān-s 'wild dog'	*ŋ̀indó 'dog' (EDAL 1029)		*ìní	*ït / *ït		*ǯinda-

continued...

Table 10.1 continued

Old Chinese	Proto-Altaic	Korean	Japanese	Turkic	Mongolian	Tungus-Manchu
筥 kraʔ 'round basket'	*kʼure 'basket' (EDAL 854)	*kóří	*kuà	*Küri-		*xurid- 'vessel for berries'
葚 d(h)əmʔ 'berry (of mulberry tree)'	*čamu (~ tí-) 'a k. of tree, mulberry' (EDAL 392)		*tum(u)i 'mulberry'		*dom 'lime-tree'	*žamu 'brier'
緄 kūnʔ 'cord, string'	*kʼjuńi 'thread, cloth' (EDAL 821–2)	*kính 'string, tassel'	*kínú 'silk, cloth'	*köjŋe-lek 'shirt'	*kejeŋ 'edge of cloth'	
緱 kàdù 'horse-bit'	*kádü 'bridle' (EDAL 629)	*kùr-ə́i	*kátúwá		*kada-	*kadala / *kadara
獮 snharʔ 'autumnal hunt'	*sònu 'dog hunt' (EDAL 1309)	*sànhàiŋ 'hunting'	*sùná-tər- 'to fish' (< *'hunt')	*sonar 'dog hunting'		*suna 'dog rope'
馘 kʷrə̄k 'cut-off ears of slain enemies, ear-tokens'	*kʼüjlu(-kʼV) 'ear' (EDAL 847)	*kúi 'ear'	*ká-k- 'hear'	*Kul-kak 'ear'	*kulki 'ear-wax; middle ear'	*xūl- 'to sound'
劓 ŋ(h)rets 'to cut off the nose'	*ŋiakča 'nose' (EDAL 1030)	*nǎčh 'face'			*nagčar-kai 'back of nose'	*ŋiaksa 'nose'
刎 m(h)ənʔ 'cut the throat'	*mōjno 'neck' (EDAL 939)	*mjə-k 'neck, throat'	*nəmpV 'neck'	*bōjn 'neck'	*mundaya 'crest, withers'	*mori- 'neck'
襟 krəm 'overlap of a robe'	*kúro(mV) 'a k. of clothes' (EDAL 746)	*korom 'clothes string, lace'	*kə́rə́mə́ 'clothes'	*Kur 'belt'	*kormaj 'lap, skirt'	*kurumV 'a k. of upper clothes'

Notes

a Jap. tumeta- is attributed in EDAL to Proto-Altaic *tumu 'cold, snot'; phonetically, however, it is ambiguous and may well reflect Proto-Altaic *tupa (cf. especially Tungus-Manchu *dopota with similar suffixation).

b Only the reconstruction *čamu is given in EDAL; however, *tjamu is not excluded given the absence of crucial in this case Korean reflex.

References

Baxter, W. (1992) *A Handbook of Old Chinese Phonology*, Berlin: Mouton de Gruyter.

Benedict, P.K. (1972) *Sino-Tibetan: A Conspectus*, Cambridge: Cambridge University Press.

Benedict, P. (1975) *Austro-Tai: Languages and Culture, with a Glossary of Roots*, New Haven, CT: HRAF Press.

Benedict, P. (1990) *Japanese/ Austro-Tai,* Ann Arbor, MI: Karoma Publishers.

Kawamoto, T. (1977) 'Toward a comparative Japanese-Austronesian. I', *Bulletin of Nara University of Education*, 26(1).

Kawamoto, T. (1981) 'Proto-Oceanic Paradigms and Japanese', *Bulletin of Kyoto Sangyo University*, 2(4): 139–55.

Miller, R.A. (1972) *Nihongo*, Tokyo (Japanese edn). Originally published as *The Japanese Language*, Chicago, IL: University of Chicago Press, 1967.

Peiros, I. (1998) *Comparative Linguistics in Southeast Asia*, Canberra: Pacific Linguistics, Series C-142.

Peiros, I. and Starostin, S. (1984) 'Sino-Tibetan and Austro-Thai', *Computational Analyses of Asian and African languages*, 22.

Peiros, I. and Starostin, S. (1996) *A Comparative Vocabulary of Five Sino-Tibetan Languages*, 6 vols, Melbourne: Department of Linguistics, University of Melbourne.

Pokorny, J. (1959) *Indogermanisches etymologisches Wörterbuch*, Berne: Francke.

Sagart, L. (1995) 'Some Remarks on the Ancestry of Chinese', *Journal of Chinese Linguistics, Monograph Series*, 8: 195–223.

Schuessler, A. (1987) *A Dictionary of Early Zhou Chinese*, Honolulu: University of Hawaii Press.

Shafer, R. (1974) *Introduction to Sino-Tibetan*, Wiesbaden: Harrassowitz.

Starostin, S. (1972) 'К проблеме реконструкции праяпонской фонологической системы', *Конференция по сравнительно-исторической грамматике индоевропейских языков (12–14 декабря)*, pp. 72–75, Moscow: Nauka.

Starostin, S. (1975) 'К вопросу о реконструкции праяпонской фонологической системы', *Очерки по фонологии восточных языков*, pp. 271–280, Moscow: Nauka.

Starostin, S. (1979) *Проблемы реконструкции древнекитайской фонологической системы*, PhD thesis, Moscow: Institute of Oriental Studies.

Starostin, S. (1989a) *Реконструкция древнекитайской фонологической системы*, Moscow: Nauka.

Starostin, S. (1989b) 'Сравнительно-историческое языкознание и лексикостатистика', *Лингвистическая реконструкция и древнейшая история Востока*, vol. 1, pp. 3–39, Moscow: Nauka.

Starostin, S. (1991) *Алтайская проблема и происхождение японского языка*, Moscow: Nauka.

Starostin, S. (2000) 'Comparative-historical linguistics and lexicostatistics', in C. Renfrew, A. McMahon and L. Trask (eds) *Time Depth in Historical Linguistics*, vol. 1, pp. 223–59, Cambridge: McDonald Institute for Archaeological Research.

Starostin S. (1995) 'Response to L. Sagart's "Some remarks on the ancestry of Chinese"', *Journal of Chinese Linguistics, Monograph Series*, 8: 393–404.

Starostin, S., Dybo, A., and Mudrak, O. (2003) *Etymological Dictionary of the Altaic Languages*, Leiden and Boston, MA: Brill.

11 Comparing Japanese and Korean

Roy Andrew Miller

Until recently, and in particular until the long-awaited publication of Starostin, Dybo and Mundrak's *Etymological Dictionary of the Altaic Languages* (2003; hereafter *EDAL*), any survey of the existing literature concerned with the historical-linguistic comparison of Japanese and Korean must necessarily have come to the conclusion that, whatever the nature, if any, of a historical connection, if any, between these two languages might have been, that connection nevertheless has remained, for some reason or another, beyond the grasp of the traditional comparative method of the neo-grammarians. Now with the three volumes of the *EDAL* at last in hand, we have available a full-scale exhibition of the linguistic evidence relating both these languages to an original Altaic linguistic unity. The *EDAL*'s clarification of the Japanese and Korean members of this linguistic stock may well, in the long run, prove to be one of the major contributions of that publication to the historical-linguistic literature.

Meanwhile, it may still be of value to inspect some of the earlier comparative literature concerning these two languages, even though most of it is now rendered obsolete by the *EDAL*, in order to see what it has to teach us about how this particularly parochial branch of comparative linguistics happened to wander astray over the decades preceding its publication.

Such an inspection of the record is also important because the view that 'nothing of scientific value is known or may ever be discovered about the genetic affiliation(s) of Japanese to other languages' has long been – and today mostly continues to be – the accepted, indeed the orthodox and canonical, position of virtually all contemporary Japanese scholarship on the history of the Japanese language. Despite its early roots in the linguistic-philological traditions of the German universities, modern Japanese scholarship, particularly as a consequence of its wholesale Americanization following the defeat of Japan in World War II, has done little except to repeat over and over the now politically correct position that 'no historical relation or connection between the language of Our Country and any other human language has ever been proven, or ever can be' – an *a priori* position that apparently serves the national interest of the country's educated elite as well in these 'post-war' years as it did in the days of the Greater East Asia Co-Prosperity Sphere.

Modern Korean scholarship has generally approached the history of the Korean language from a different perspective. Following the publication of Ramstedt (1950), it became commonplace in Korea to classify Korean as 'Altaic', at least until the virulent anti-Altaic polemic firestorm – first unleashed in German universities some 30 years ago, and thereafter practically removing the postulation of an 'Altaic' language family from serious scholarly consideration in Western European circles – reached the peninsula via Japanese contacts.

Ramstedt (1950) did not come into existence out of a scholarly vacuum. During the Finnish scholar's residence in Japan on diplomatic service from March 1920 through November 1923 he became acquainted with Japan's leading scholar of Korean, Shiratori Kurakichi (1865–1942). Between June 1914 and May 1916 Shiratori had published a long study of possible lexical evidence relating Korean to 'Ural-Altaic' in the *Tōyō Gahukō*. Then as now, it was out of the question for a responsible 'university professor' to suggest that Japanese might be related to other languages in the world, but of course – and indeed fortunately – this intellectual firewall did not protect the language of an occupied colonial subject-state such as Korea. More than one of the 502 *lemmata* studied by Shiratori found their way into the pages of Ramstedt (1950); many have also continued to turn up, most often without citation of source, in a wide variety of contemporary Korean publications down to the present day; and many too have survived the etymological winnowing of Starostin and his collaborators to appear in the pages of the *EDAL*.

In order properly to understand the long-term influence that Shiratori's 'Ural-Altaic' etymological study of Korean has continued to have on the development of the field, it is necessary to point out two important facets of his work that might otherwise escape notice.

First, there is virtually no mention of Japanese or of Japanese historical linguistics anywhere in the 502 often lengthy *lemmata* that Shiratori assembled and that Ramstedt studied. Whenever possible Shiratori cites Uralic and/or Altaic forms for his Korean *Stichwörter*, but in the process he virtually goes out of his way to avoid directing attention to even the possibility of Japanese cognates. It goes without saying that this approach did much to influence later Japanese scholarship on Japanese. Shiratori elaborately demonstrated, by example if not *expressis verbis*, his conviction – and the conviction of his academic peers – that while the language of a country like Korea was one that could be shown to have historical connections with other human languages on the planet, that of Japan of course by definition was not.

Second, and particularly in order to understand his selection of Turkic lexical materials, Shiratori's contribution must constantly be referred to the years of its publication, and its etymological suggestions evaluated in the light of the situation in the field of Turkic-Altaic studies as it obtained *c*.1914–16.

Only a few years later, Ramstedt (1922) would himself for the first time formulate the basic hypothesis that Chuvash and Mongol *r* and *l* were linguistically older than Turkic *z* and *š*. In the years that followed this brilliant insight into one of the most fascinating but at the same time most perplexing etymological constellations in the entire field of Altaic historical linguistics, Ramstedt continued to collect lexical data that appeared to point in the direction of a genetic connection between Korean and what eventually became his reconstruction of the Altaic proto-language. But here we confront what can only be termed an unfortunate but virtually fatal accident in the timing of publications. In his etymological study of Korean, Shiratori of course knew nothing of the hypothesis that from 1922 on would eventually clarify the historical connection of a large number of Turkic-Altaic cognates. This meant that he necessarily passed in silence over a significant portion of the Korean evidence for 'common inherited vocabulary' that required this hypothesis for its clarification, while Ramstedt, in his turn, unfortunately followed Shiratori in this as well. Even more unfortunately, Ramstedt, in his astonishingly diligent work in comparative Altaic linguistics carried on over many subsequent years and despite many difficult personal circumstances, in the end never did come to grips with the Korean (much less the Japanese) evidence for what we must now recognize as the key elements pointing in the direction of the essential Altaic connection that Ramstedt himself had been the first to recognize, viz., the correspondences for the four original Altaic liquids, i.e., the four contrasting phonemes of the original language now generally written in the literature with the convenient if still controversial symbols $*l$ $*l^2$, $*r$, $*r^2$.

Independently, but in a certain sense also coincidentally, much the same was true of the principal post-Ramstedt contribution to the genetic history of Korean, the important study of 320 cases of probable lexical-evidence apparently relating Korean to Japanese published by S.E. Martin (1966). This extensive, indeed pioneering, collection of lexical 'lookalikes', particularly in view of the large number of *lemmata* that it registered, might well have been expected to provide not only a more or less definitive answer to the question of the linguistic-historical relationship, if any, between Korean and Japanese, but also, in the long run, an answer to the question of possible further linguistic connections involving both languages with other, and larger, language families and stocks. That it did not accomplish these much-desired ends was due to several self-imposed limitations on the part of its author; these unfortunately conspired together effectively to hamstring his contribution's historical-explanatory potential.

Chief among three unfortunate limitations was Martin's decision to ignore what even in 1966 was widely known concerning the historical phonology of Japanese. In particular he overlooked the meticulous and elaborate if often somewhat exasperating phonogram evidence of the extensive corpus of Old Japanese texts that has long been available to linguistic science. These texts show that at the earliest period for which we have the evidence of written records for Japanese, the language had eight significantly contrasting vocalic entities. These eight are, for a variety of complicated reasons that are fully explained in the literature and so need not be elaborated here, generally (and almost surely correctly) understood as *a* and *u* plus two varieties each of *e*, *o*, and *i*. But further consideration of the distribution patterns for these eight vowels, that are distinguished as such by the phonograms employed in the written records of Old Japanese, also leads to the conclusion that, in the language behind these texts generally, we have also to deal not only with these eight vowel phonemes, which we may note as /a, u, e^1, e^2, o^1, o², i¹, i² /, but also with three vocalic archiphonemes of neutralization {e, o, i}. Further, each of these archiphonemes of neutralization, in certain specific, well-defined linear contexts, subsumed the contrastive properties of the two similarly transcribed phonemes; in other words, {e} < / e¹, e² /, etc.

Admittedly, this system of the Old Japanese vocalization is in more than one sense cumbersome for the modern linguist. It is always difficult to explain to those unfamiliar with the Old Japanese phonogram texts and their orthographic conventions, and it obviously presents substantial problems for the comparativist. But these considerations, real though they be, hardly justify simply ignoring everything that is known about Old Japanese and turning instead to the simple five-vowel system of the modern language of Tokyo, as Martin did in 1966. By the very reason of its intricacy the vowel system of Old Japanese, phonemes and archiphonemes alike, obviously has much to contribute to any discussion of the possible genetic connection between Japanese and other languages, particularly when, as was the case with Martin, the problem is approached almost entirely on the level of lexical comparison.

Under these special circumstances, it was unfortunate in 1966 (and indeed even today remains somewhat astonishing) that in comparing Korean and Japanese lexical data, Martin had recourse to the evidence of Middle Korean written records at the same time that he totally ignored the materials available in Old Japanese phonogram texts concerning the early vocalization of that language. Needless to say, this variety of comparison was, by the very nature of its self-imposed philological limitations, unable to generate convincing evidence for historical relationships.

What is most curious about all this is that, at the same time that Martin resolutely refused even to consider earlier documentary evidence for the Japanese vocalization, he nevertheless confronted his Japanese lexical forms – entirely modern so far as their vowels were concerned, but decked out with a few 'antique' touches in the consonants – with Korean transliterations that, by and large, attempted to reproduce a stage of Korean phonology considerably earlier than that of the modern language of Seoul.

These earlier Korean forms are uniformly designated 'Middle Korean' in Martin (1966), although in actual fact many of them range over a fairly extensive time-span of written records. Some do indeed go back to the time of the so-called 'invention' of the Korean script (more precisely, its adaptation and refinement of the Mongolian hPhags-pa alphabet in the first decades of the 15th century), while many others are attested much later, some in almost modern times. In either case – but particularly in the case of the former – Martin neglected the all-important step of first studying the Middle Korean vowels as a system. Instead he merely transcribed each Middle Korean vowel symbol and in turn treated each as a separate unit unrelated to any larger structure. Naturally this only added to the problems of his comparisons, not to mention his reconstructions, for in its own way his treatment of the earlier Korean vocalization was, if anything, even more flawed methodologically than was his replacement of the earlier eight-vowel system of the Old Japanese written records by the modern five Tokyo vowels.

At least the modern Tokyo vowels as they appear in Martin's 1966 comparisons represent an actual and documented linguistic reality, whereas the 'Middle Korean' vocalization with which he confronted them is in a number of important details of its phonological structure little more than a transcriptional fiction.

Central to this problem is the fact, too often overlooked in modern Western studies of the early linguistic evidence preserved for us in all hPhags-pa-related writing systems (such as that devised for Korean), that the hPhags-pa alphabet itself was never a system for identifying and 'writing' individual phonemic (or even, archiphonemic) entities, but instead a phonetic script, pure if not always simple. It was invented for the purpose of writing a considerable number of different languages, in particular the diverse languages of the Mongol Empire; and its employment for writing Middle Korean was entirely in keeping with this, its original goal. It was, in a word, an early 'international phonetic alphabet', with the emphasis on 'phonetic'. The scribes who adapted it to this or that language naturally focused their attention upon phones, not phonemes, devising additional symbols when necessary in order to 'write' acoustic features that they found striking, without consideration of their structural role or relevance in the language involved.

In this connection, specific problems on the comparative level arise, for example, in the case of at least two of the Middle Korean orthographic vowel entities, those generally transcribed as ă and ŭ. It is clear from several varieties of evidence, not the least of which is to be detected in the very structure of the letters that were devised for these entities in the hPhags-pa-derived Korean script, that in these two vowels we have to deal, in turn, with some pronunciation-variety of reduced [a] on the one hand, and of reduced [u] on the other. This does not mean that Middle Korean, at least in its earliest documented varieties, did not possess two contrasting phonemes that were realized more or less along these same lines; or that these phonemes may not with reason be searched for, and possibly even their history traced, in cognate languages (including Japanese) by means of lexical comparisons. But at the same time this must not be allowed to obscure the evidence that in many other occurrences the reduced ă of the Middle Korean orthography was precisely that, i.e. structurally it was an allophone of / a / (cf. MK .*pal* 'foot', but with the reduced vowel in the denominal verb :*pălp-* 'walk'). Similarly, the reduced ŭ was, to be sure, on occasion the orthographic recognition of a phonemic element in the language, but also in many instances no more than an impressionistic rendering of a pronunciation-variant of original / u /, or sometimes of original / i / (cf. Miller 1994: 87–90). Needless to say, lexical comparisons between Korean and Japanese, no matter of what period, must take notice of these facts of the earlier stages of the language as they are reflected in the script in which the Middle Korean lexical sources have been transmitted. Despite their frequently bewildering mingling of phonetic, phonemic, and archiphonemic-neutralization data, the Middle Korean records are quite as central to the problems of historical-linguistic comparison between these two languages as is the phonogram evidence of the earliest Japanese texts for the Old Japanese vocalization. Martin (1966) ignored both varieties of evidence, with the result that his extensive lexical comparisons in the end do little to inform us further about the nature, not to mention the details, of the historical connection between these two languages. Nor of course do they throw much light upon the historical connection(s), if any, of either (or both) with any other linguistic family or stock, including those with Altaic.

In his 1966 contribution Martin sporadically cited lexical 'lookalikes' for many of his Korean–Japanese comparative *lemmata* from a wide variety of other languages, including (but by no means limited to) the languages generally designated as 'Altaic'. But he did not attempt to bring order into the data provided by these citations, much less to employ them in order to substantiate a scenario of larger historical relations; nor in fact did he ever clarify the overall purpose of these citations. In subsequent publications, however, he has made it more than clear that he finds little or nothing in the so-called 'Altaic hypothesis' in general, and even less in attempts to relate Japanese and Korean to an earlier Altaic linguistic unity. In view of this, it is difficult to escape the conclusion that in 1966 Martin's goal in citing the occasional Turkic, or Hungarian, or Ainu lexical item in connection with one or the other of his Korean–Japanese comparisons was primarily to discredit the hypothesis of a genetic relationship among the Altaic languages as then generally understood, and in the process ultimately to render moot any attempts by others to relate Korean and Japanese to Altaic.

If that indeed was the case, the result has ultimately proven to be somewhat ironic, to say the least, because without wishing to do so – and for that matter probably without realizing what was happening – Martin (1966) actually assembled a fairly impressive body of lexical-comparative evidence that strikingly supports the most extensively discussed, and in certain circles still the most elaborately debated, artifact of the classical Ramstedt–Poppe reconstruction of Proto-Altaic, namely their evidence for the early existence sometime in the history of the original unity of a set of contrastive 'lateral and vibrant' phonemes, the four phonemes that we have already alluded to above as $*r$, $*r^2$, $*l$, $*l^2$.

In the original formulation of the lexical correspondences for this set of phonemes, Ramstedt (and later Poppe 1960, by and large following him) dealt only with evidence from Turkic, Mongol, and Tungus. The two last-named language families appeared not to preserve evidence for two varieties of $*r$ along with two varieties of $*l$; that evidence was only to be identified (or so Ramstedt and Poppe believed) in non-Chuvash Turkic. And even though, particularly near the end of his life, Ramstedt devoted a considerable amount of effort to locating and documenting Korean cognates for his Tukic-Mongol-Tungus-centered Altaic reconstructions, he did not in the course of that work identify any significant evidence to contradict the assumption that Korean, like Mongol and Tungus, did not know, i.e. did not preserve, comparative evidence for the earlier existence of $*r^2$ and $*l^2$ in Proto-Altaic. Moreover, despite his period of residence in Japan, Ramstedt seldom if ever availed himself of Japanese lexical materials. Shiratori's Korean–'Ural-Altaic' comparisons were, as we have seen, carried out too early to have recognized this important facet of the reconstructed Altaic proto-language. Poppe relied entirely upon Ramstedt for the (relatively few) citations of Korean to be found in his own later work on the phonology of Proto-Altaic; and the net result of this series of historical accidents was that it was not until fairly recently that the Korean, as well as the Japanese, evidence that impressively supports the earlier four-lateral system has been available in the literature. Now the details of that evidence may conveniently be consulted in the hundreds of *lemmata* in the *EDAL* that bear upon this question; these leave no room for doubt that the much-discussed and still-much mooted *r, *r^2, *l, *l^2 of the Ramstedt–Poppe reconstructions are reflected by and substantiated in both Korean and Japanese.

This means that in fact Martin (1966) unwitting overlooked significant patterns of sound-correspondences between Japanese and Korean that, in their turn, point directly to each of these two languages having, in its turn, inherited these same features from Proto-Altaic, moreover from a Proto-Altaic that must have corresponded in impressive detail to the classical Ramstedt–Poppe reconstruction of a system with four contrasting laterals. Virtually unnoticed in the decades since its publication in 1966, this entirely independent, if at the same time entirely covert, evidence for the essential validity of the Ramstedt–Poppe reconstruction, as well as for the Altaic inheritances of both Korean and Japanese, is to say the least striking in the extreme, all the more so because it entirely passed notice by Martin himself.

This evidence may conveniently be summarized under five headings, as follows.

1. Evidence for the Ramstedt–Poppe Proto-Altaic *l^2

For his correspondence of Kor. *l* :: Jap. *s* , Martin reconstructed Proto-Korean-Japanese *$š$. But in a significant number of his examples, the lexical items involved are obvious cognates for Altaic etyma otherwise and independently reconstructed with *l^2. Since the comparisons in Martin (1966) are arranged alphabetically by English tags, it is sufficient here to identify his materials by citing his glosses; key-words in this category include 'stone', 'flesh', and 'measure', among many that might be cited. Most of these now appear with correct documentation of their Altaic originals, and evidence for their original *l^2, in *EDAL*, s.vv.

2. Evidence for *r^2

This is to be found in Martin's correspondence of Kor. *l* :: Jap. *t*. For this Martin reconstructed *l; but in a very large number of his examples (even more numerous than those to be found under category 1 above) it is clear that we have here to deal with Korean and Japanese reflexes of forms with the Ramstedt–Poppe *r^2; key-words in this category include 'summer', 'inside', and 'dirt'. Although there is no question that Martin's *l is to be understood as Ramstedt–Poppe's *r^2, it is nevertheless necessary to go further afield in order convincingly to identify the considerable number of lexical items for which this phoneme is attested. Fortunately this may now conveniently be accomplished thanks to the resources of the *EDAL*, *q.v., s.vv.* 'rise; up' (1065), 'know' (1219/20), 'old' (622), 'bee' (1136), 'flag' (1071/2).

3. Martin's reconstruction of **r* for correspondence of Kor. *l* :: Jap. *r*

Rather less complicated but equally important for understanding the relationship between Korean and Japanese in terms of their individual and separate inheritances from Proto-Altaic is Martin's reconstruction of **r* for the correspondence of Kor. *l* :: Jap. *r*. This coincides with the Ramstedt–Poppe **r* in such forms as 'enter'; so also in 'rise; fly' (*EDAL* 974) and 'be in a row' (*EDAL* 999).

4. Other sets of correspondences between Kor *l*. :: Jap. *r*

Somewhat more involved are still other sets of correspondences between Kor *l*. :: Jap. *r*, also ignored by Martin, where further comparison with other languages, in particular with Tungus and Mongol, show that the original phoneme at issue must be reconstructed as the Ramstedt–Poppe **l* ; examples include 'room' (*EDAL* 900), 'rub, plaster' (*EDAL* 1088), and 'sick, weak' (*EDAL* 941/2).

The pros and cons of the reconstruction of these four Altaic laterals has been the focus of much of the intense debate that has distinguished the study of the history of the Altaic languages over the past several decades. For some, this set of four contrasting phonemes, obviously necessary to reconstruct in order to account for the reflexes in the various later languages, has been one of the 'main pillars of the Altaic hypothesis'; for others it has been, and apparently still remains, no more than evidence of 'a fundamental misunderstanding of the basic elements of Turkic linguistic history'. The further study of the question of the history of these phonemes on the basis of Korean and Japanese comparative evidence will now be greatly facilitated by the rich materials collected in the *EDAL*; and even though of course not all the forms cited there, or the comparisons proposed, will eventually be accepted by everyone, nevertheless there is no question that the *EDAL* will soon make it possible finally to advance the consideration of this too-long disputed facet of Altaic historical phonology beyond the boundaries of the Turkic domain, where unfortunately it has more or less stagnated ever since the early part of the last century.

5. Jap. *r* corresponds to null in Korean

Finally, there is a small but historically important set of correspondences, similarly obscured by their treatment in Martin (1966), in which Jap. *r* corresponds to null in Korean. Representative examples include 'melon' (*EDAL* 1448) and 'mountain' (*EDAL* 956); further comparisons with forms in other languages ('bird of prey', *EDAL* 949; 'spring, source', *EDAL* 1200/1) make it possible to identify this with the Ramstedt–Poppe **r*, in these forms too inherited from Altaic as in (3) above and preserved as such in Japanese, but by the time of Middle Korean at the latest reduced to null in Korean when originally found between a back and front vowel. This was a phonological process in all probability not unrelated to the loss of certain cases of inherited -*r*- in Tungus, the so-called '-*r*- *Verschleiss*' (Menges 1968: 132, 157, 205, 236).

In this fashion, then, Martin's 1966 collection of Korean–Japanese 'lookalikes' unwittingly pointed in the direction of an ultimate genetic relationship of both languages, in one manner or another, to the original Altaic linguistic unity reconstructed by Ramstedt and Poppe. In fact, since as we have seen Martin's materials provide specific lexical evidence for the existence of four original contrasting laterals in that same proto-language – evidence that both Ramstedt and Poppe believed was only to be detected in Turkic – these same Korean–Japanese comparisons turn out to provide important independent substantiation for the classical Altaic hypothesis, as well as for the canonical reconstructions of the two great pioneers in these studies, particularly for the details of their much-disputed 'four lateral' system for the proto-language.

But useful, indeed essential, though it will be in this work that is still ahead of us, the *EDAL* will, like any reference tool, require caution and considerable philological acumen on the part of all who consult it if its wealth of comparative evidence is to be evaluated in a manner that ultimately enhances our understanding of the relationship of Korean and Japanese to the original Altaic language. Certain of the problems that we may confidently expect to encounter along the way while engaged in this task deserve exploration here, if necessarily only in brief, as an indication of the overall nature of many of the questions that still lie ahead of all of us who continue to be interested in these matters. These problems may conveniently be approached through inspection of two *lemmata* in Martin (1966), here selected more or less at random but nevertheless representative of the difficulties that stem from this source, difficulties that have persisted in one way or another now into the pages of the *EDAL*.

First, Martin (1966: 232) s.v. FOG, compared Jap. *kiri* 'fog, mist' with Kor. *hŭli*- 'be cloudy', further adding to this comparison 'Cf... Tk. *kıragi* "frost, dew", Hungarian *köd* "fog" ...'. To begin with Martin's two key lexical citations, his Japanese form is modern Tokyo. The Old Japanese texts have *ki²ri* for this word; the vowel in the first syllable of that form contrasts with the vowel in *ki¹ri* 'awl', which also yielded New Jap. *kiri*. (Both words had the archiphoneme of neutralization OJap.{ -*i* } in their second syllable. Moreover, though the point is not entirely relevant to the problem of comparison here being discussed, both these Old Japanese nouns are deverbal formations in -*i* onto, respectively, the verb *ki²r*- 'to cloud up, be misty' and the verb *ki¹r*- 'to cut'.) In 1966 Martin lumped these two etyma together under the same New Japanese vowel *i* (thus, his p. 229), effectively obscuring the phonemic contrast registered for all the relevant forms in the Old Japanese texts. In subsequent publications he belatedly took notice of the phonological data of those texts, but he has consistently avoided treating these two vowels (and by the same token, similar parallel vowel sets) as contrasting phonemes. Instead he evolved a transcription that appeared to point in the general direction of the distinction, but in actual fact runs directly contrary to what we know about Old Japanese phonetics as well as Old Japanese phonology, transcribing the i^2 vowel as a simple unitary vowel, but rendering the i^1 vowel as *ji*, a combination of glide + vowel.

This transcription is misleading in two different ways. It is clear from the compound-noun morphology of Old Japanese that if either of these vowels was pronounced with a glide fore-or-aft it was not the vowel that Martin so transcribes but rather the one that we mark as i^2. It is also well established that the glide in this case came after, not before, the nuclear vowel, as Martin's revisionist transcription would have it.

Unfortunately the *EDAL* has now followed Martin throughout in his misinterpretation of Old Japanese phonology, e.g. writing *kjiri* 'awl' for ki^1ri (*EDAL* 791), and *kiri* 'mist' for ki^2ri (*EDAL* 816). If indeed there eventually proves to be an etymological connection between the Old Japanese word that Martin compares in this *lemma* and the Turkic form that he adds to his etymological speculation (mistranscribed; read instead *kıragı*, and misglossed; read instead 'hoar frost'; both correctly registered in *EDAL* 212, where only the Old Japanese data are incorrect), which for that matter is highly likely, that relationship is *ab initio* rendered needlessly obscure both in Martin (1966) and now also in *EDAL* thanks to Martin's revisionist transcription of the Old Japanese vowel in the first syllable of this word, a transcription (and phonological misinterpretation) that deftly obscures what here otherwise appears to be a striking (and probably historically significant) one-on-one correspondence between OJap. i^2 and Trk. *ı* < Proto-Altaic *i. Similar misinterpretations of the vowels unfortunately obscure virtually every citation of Old Japanese throughout the *EDAL*, with the result that almost every citation of Japanese in these volumes must now be reworked, along with the historical-comparative conclusions to which they relate. Further, Kor. *hŭli-* that Martin proposes as a cognate for this *lemma* is glossed incorrectly; MKor. *hŭli-* is 'to be dirty, soiled, besmirched' (correctly at *EDAL* 1270), which further lessens the utility of the etymology as a whole. Finally, the problem of what Martin intended by the citation of Hng. *köd* 'fog' must be left for others to solve.

Second, in a significant number of cases, uncritical reliance by the *EDAL* on Martin (1966) has led its authors to overlook important Korean–Japanese comparisons that provide evidence for Altaic connections of considerable time-depth. This is especially striking in the case of forms that, while adequately attested in the Middle Korean sources, have not survived into the modern language, an accident that probably explains why they have been generally neglected by the comparativist literature.

A representative example is provided by Tokyo *sigure* 'inclement, stormy weather, particularly at sea', attested in Early Middle Japanese generally as 'drizzling rain in autumn or early winter'. The *EDAL* (1242/3) correctly relates this form to Tungus and Mongol cognates, but registers no Korean member of the etymology, probably because the term is missing from Martin (1966). In fact, not only does a Korean cognate exist, but it happens to illustrate two specific historical-phonological details that throw important light upon the nature of the

Altaic relationships not only of the Korean but also of the Japanese member of this etymology.

The form at issue is MKor. *si.Gui* 'a flood', attested as early as the Chinese–Korean bilingual lexicon of 1527 (= A3a, p. 31; A6a, p. 161 in the two earliest prints reproduced in the 1971 Tankuk University facsimile edition), a source that appears to have drawn in its turn upon a 1517 bilingual source to which we have no direct access.

Two phonological details of this form are of importance, both for the larger Altaic comparison in the *EDAL*, and also for its comparison with Jap. *sigure*:

1   The hPhags-pa-based orthography of the Middle Korean texts that register this form overtly write a voiced velar or laryngeal consonant as the initial of the second syllable of the form, here transcribed by our -*G*-. This is an obvious Korean reflex for the intervocalic voiced velars of the Japanese, Tungus and Written Mongol forms in the *EDAL* etymology. Since the Korean form in question has been ignored by the *EDAL*, it is not possible to guess how it would there have been transcribed, i.e. interpreted historically. But elsewhere in this source parallel Middle Korean writings have been misunderstood and their overt orthographic evidence for this same -*G*- obscured by writing no more than -'- (e.g. *EDAL* 1302, *s.v.* 'wine'). But here and in many parallel forms, this MKor. -*G*- did not simply 'drop', nor in the early texts was it by any means merely 'a writing for hiatus', as the -'- transcription of the *EDAL* apparently seeks to indicate. Rather, on the evidence of still earlier, non-hPhags-pa-based writings, particularly a significant number in Chinese transcription, this Middle Korean phoneme corresponds to earlier -*b*-, and thus finds its proper place in the category of sound correspondences involving sets of -*b*- :: -*g*- forms long ago explained by Poppe in terms of the position of original Altaic suprasegmentals (see now Miller (2003: 201–36)).

2   Equally critical for identifying the Altaic as well as the Japanese historical connections of this neglected Middle Korean form is its terminal vocalic sequence -*ui*. By means of confrontation with the Altaic forms cited in *EDAL*, *loc. cit.*, and now additionally taking notice of the -*r*- in Jap. *sigure*, we are able to identify this as another secure example of the operation, early in the history of Korean (but not in the history of Japanese!) of a sound-change completely parallel to (if not actually part of) the Tungus '-*r*- *Verschleiss*' already noted above.

In this fashion, the addition of this single Middle Korean form, long available in the lexical sources but strangely overlooked in the literature for all that, proves to document two important Altaic sound-changes. The first, *-*b*- :: *-*g*-, was operative both in early Korean and in early Japanese, both of which inherited it intact from Altaic; the second, by reason of the preservation of an intervocalic *-*r*- in Japanese but its loss in Korean, points to early isolation of proto-Japanese from proto-Korean, despite their ultimate common origins in Altaic.

Curiously enough, shortcomings in method and materials of the variety pointed out here appear to have played little if any part in the generally negative reception accorded to Martin (1966) in the decades following its publication. The scholarly community concerned with such matters was and continues to be almost entirely hostile to his work, but for reasons that are in most cases not entirely clear, and are at any rate seldom if ever based upon direct arguments against specific points.

Typical is the wholesale rejection of Martin's work by Bowring and Kornicki (1993: 114), who allege that in the comparison of Korean and Japanese 'it is extremely difficult to identify words with a common root that could not at the same time simply be loanwords from Korean into Japanese'. An encyclopaedia is, of course, a genre of scholarly discourse that easily lends itself to far-reaching generalizations; but surely it was irresponsible of the Cambridge editors to entrust this particular broadside to two authors whose special fields (literature; bibliography) do not in any manner engage linguistic science.

Even more critical has been the view of Juha Janhunen, who in contrast to Bowring and Kornicki is of course familiar with the problems and materials of this variety of historical-linguistic comparison. Nevertheless, Janhunen is even more negative than the two Cambridge dons; and his rhetoric is by that same token both more colorful and more devastating. For him, the entire Altaic hypothesis is no more than an 'illusion of genetic relationship', growing out of a 'methodological error' that, simply because it is so gravely in error, has tempted certain misguided persons to 'extend the Altaic hypothesis to Korean and Japanese' (1996a: 209). Janhunen's views carry weight, if only by reason of his tenure of a distinguished post at the University of Helsinki; he is in this sense the successor of G.J. Ramstedt – who, if we follow Janhunen, was not the founder of Altaic linguistics and the pioneer of Korean comparative studies, but only someone misguided enough to propagate illusion and methodological error. Janhunen's judgments are clear enough; but based as they are, in this representative contribution, solely on invective ('illusion', 'error') rather than on the critical examination of specific data, they are also all but impossible to refute.

Mutatis mutandis, the same holds true of a second contribution, setting forth his position in the same tenor but far more elaborately, that Janhunen published in the same year (1996b). Still characteristically castigating the 'phantom reconstructions' of Ramstedt and the other Altaicists, and along with them any suggestion that Jap. *isi* 'stone' might possibly have etymological roots elsewhere in Asia (1996b: 240–1), Janhunen this time around actually cites four Korean–Japanese lexical comparisons from Martin (1966) ('island', 'blowfish', '(garden) field', 'blade'), but he does this only to dismiss them all out of hand – again without discussion or critical examination, but solely on the basis of their meanings and without reference to any early Japanese or Korean documentation (which in at least three of the four is extensive). With these (and by implication all of Martin's total of 320 *lemmata*) ruled out of court, he then suddenly and curiously changes the direction of his attack, claiming himself to have identified two important pre- (or at least very early) Japanese forms in the first Chinese account of Japan. The forms in question are in fact well-known to every student of early Japan; but Janhunen's glosses for both ('prince', 'priestess queen') are unsupported by the easily available documentary evidence, as is his allegation that both are compounds with a form related to OJap. *Fi¹* 'sun'. Once more, if we are to believe Janhunen, there is nothing in the hundreds of proposed comparisons in Martin (1966), or in any of the other literature on this question prior to 1996, that is not mere 'illusion' and 'methodological error'. That may very well be so; but Janhunen's rhetoric does not explain why or how he arrived at the position he so colorfully sets forth, nor do his erroneous glosses reassure us that he too, unlike those his criticizes, may never on occasion fall victim to 'illusion' and even downright 'error'.

Moreover, as we study Janhunen's two 1996 contributions, we cannot but be struck by a serious internal contradiction that distinguishes both studies, particularly the first cited above. There he argues in particular that the 'illusion' that in his view continues to entrap the Altaicists is 'largely due to the non-binary approach applied in conventional Altaic comparisons', and further that '[a]ny serious suggestions of genetic relationship between [Turkic, Mongol, Tungus, Korean, Japanese] should be based on strictly binary comparison, preferably between adjacent entities' (1996a: 209). But a 'strictly binary comparison ... between adjacent entities' is precisely what Martin carried out in 1966; and we have seen above that, unbeknown to Martin or any of his critics, including Janhunen, that same 'strictly binary comparison' actually produced a set of correspondences that runs precisely parallel to one of the most important (and most mooted) phonological artifacts of the classical Ramstedt–Poppe reconstruction of Altaic – including, one must add, a phoneme in that very word for 'stone' to whose reconstruction Janhunen takes particular exception. Under these circumstances, one can only ask in turn what it is that the 'strictly binary comparison' so highly prized and so greatly desired by Janhunen might be expected to reveal that has not already been made clear.

Of course, not all the literature concerned with the comparison of Korean and Japanese following the publication of Martin (1966) has been negative, or even critical. Particularly supportive both of Martin's reconstructions and of his 'strictly binary comparison' appears to have been John Whitman's 1985 Harvard doctoral dissertation. Unfortunately this dissertation remains unpublished and its details are not accessible to the field at large. All that we have is a segment published as Whitman (1990), which does not incline one toward the view that Whitman's further exploration of Martin's 'strictly binary comparison', even though precisely the sort of thing favoured by Janhunen, very greatly advanced our understanding of the historical connections between Korean and Japanese; it also suggests that the well-known Harvard University ban, unique among American universities, on publishing doctoral dissertations may indeed from time to time have much to be said in its favor.

In the published fragment at least, the words that Whitman cites from both languages are in most cases incorrect either in their forms or in their meanings, most often in both. The semantics of his comparisons are frequently incomprehensible: Korean 'head' is alleged to correspond to Japanese 'eye', and 'leg, limb' to 'arm, hand'; the Middle Korean term for a perennial herb is glossed 'lizard tail (*similax*)', in apparent confusion with the trade-name of a popular American laxative preparation; and the Middle Korean reflex of an Old Korean posthumous royal title generally reconstructed as **marip(kan)* is compared with Jap. *mara* 'penis' (this last a particularly astonishing lexical confrontation, about which one can say little except to point out its surely unintentional echo of Martial's bawdy epigram (9. 33) on 'Maro in the Bath'; can anyone imagine that Old Korean posthumous royal titles incorporated overt references to the late rulers' genital endowments?).

Of the eight *lemmata* that Whitman cites (1990: 527–8) to illustrate MKor. -*l*- following a long vowel, not a single one stands up under careful inspection, every example failing either in form or meaning or in both; of the ten he cites (p. 529) to illustrate his proposed Japanese loss of an -*l*- reflected in Korean only a single example ('field', cf. *EDAL* 1120) is even possibly valid, while in all the others the -*l*- is absent in Korean but present in Japanese; etc., etc. In a word, not much can be made of any of this.

Nevertheless, those fortunate enough to have inspected the unpublished dissertation from which Baldi's fragment was extracted have been unstinting in their appreciation and even praise of Whitman's work. Martin believes that 'Whitman's conclusions are sound, and his productive approach opens up an exciting era of more rigorous and realistic comparison and reconstruction that promises to lift research in the genetic relationship of [Korean and Japanese] above the level of mere speculation' (in Baldi 1990: 274–5). Similarly laudatory has been A. Vovin, who not once but twice, using the same words, has hailed Whitman's work as 'a major breakthrough in recent years in Japanese-Korean comparative linguistics' (1994a: 370; 1994b: 98).

Hence it comes as little or no surprise to find, even more recently, Whitman's theories, whatever they may be, concerning the conditions for the loss or retention of *-*l*- (or *-*r*- ?) in Japanese and/or Korean cited in support of developments that may be documented entirely from within Japanese of forms for which no Koran cognates are ever cited. J. R. Bentley (2001: 57) now seeks to explain the relationship of Jap. *yoru* 'evening' to Jap. *yo* 'id' on the basis of the loss of an original *-*r*- following an original long vowel; but where, and/or in what language, attested or reconstructed, these 'original' consonants and long vowels were found is never made clear. No relevant forms are (or can be) cited from Korean, or indeed from any other language. Bentley himself can only suggest a Tungus form with -*l*-, but again there is no long vowel in the record. Instead of that Janhunen desideratum, a 'strictly binary comparison', what we have in Bentley is a 'strictly unitary comparison'. But will this tell us anything that we do not already know?

Further, we are told in the same place not only that '[t]his rule is known as Whitman's Law', but also that '[t]he term was coined by Alexander Vovin' (Bentley 2001: 57 n. 29). Unlike the Indo-Europeanists, whose work teems with 'laws' named for various individuals, Altaicists have been generally cautious about naming anything in honor of anybody. This has probably been because so few of us can agree on any single statement concerning the history of the languages with which we work, no matter who first published it – or for that matter, about almost anything else concerning these languages.

At any rate, we have all got along very well for decades without reference to a Ramstedt's Law or a Poppe's Law, though in both cases more than one important historical statement concerning the history of and the relationships between various Altaic languages surely could have been thus named without injustice to the individuals concerned, or violence either to the history of scholarship or to the scientific process. But now, and quite without warning, it appears not only that an authority exists who is in a position to designate such honors, in the person of A. Vovin of the University of Hawaii, but that such designations may, in the field of the Altaic languages, be bestowed upon statements and historical-linguistic scenarios known only to a select few, while their details (if any there be) remain concealed in the decent obscurity of the pages of unpublished Harvard dissertations.

If on the other hand the field of Altaic historical linguistics is actually in need of newly named 'laws' that identify significant discoveries by honoring specific individuals, Vovin could hardly do better at his next awards ceremony than to reawaken interest in a long-neglected hypothesis first proposed by Omeljan Pritsak (1964). In that contribution Pritsak suggested that somewhere behind, i.e. somewhere prior in history to, the much disputed four-lateral inventory of the classical Ramstedt–Poppe reconstruction of Altaic there may very well have existed a simpler two-lateral ($*r$, $*l$) system, and that there are indications in forms that may be cited from the later languages that the notorious $*r^2$, $*l^2$ additions to that system were the result of 'fusions', i.e. assimilations in close juncture, of consonant + consonant combinations with $*r$, $*l$ in the prior position.

Pritsak's concern was solely with the evidence of Turkic, Mongol, and Tungus, the so-called 'inner languages' of Altaic; he made no mention of Korean or Japanese materials in evolving his hypothesis. Hence it is hardly surprising that his penetrating if perhaps all-too succinct 1964 analysis of the problem has virtually escaped subsequent notice, even by those most interested in the history of Korean and Japanese, the so-called 'outer languages'. Martin provided a singular exception, having made a single reference to the possibility of identifying somewhere in these languages evidence for 'the mystery morpheme postulated by Pritsak' (in Baldi 1990). But Pritsak did not suggest the existence of a 'mystery morpheme', and apart from this one laconic aside Martin apparently never returned to the problems and proposed solutions set forth in Pritsak (1964), which at any rate he cannot, to judge from this remark, have read very carefully.

In actual fact, in much the same way that the entirely binary comparisons of Martin (1966) unwittingly adumbrated much of the classical Ramstedt–Poppe reconstruction of Altaic, particularly the details of their four-way lateral contrast system, so also does the Pritsak hypothesis, when viewed in the light of additional Korean and Japanese lexical evidence that played no part in his argumentation, provide exciting clues to the historical relationships of these two additional languages. Moreover, in the process it also supplies us with evidence that further strengthens the arguments for the independent descent of each of these two 'outer languages' from the Altaic proto-language.

Unfortunately, neither the Pritsak hypothesis nor the light that it is able to throw upon details of the earliest stages of the original Altaic linguistic unity has found a place anywhere in the *EDAL*; indeed, no mention of Pritsak (1964) is even to be found in this work's otherwise exemplary 'Bibliography' (pp. 241–65). Nevertheless, one of the most valuable services that the *EDAL* will be able to offer to the field of comparative Altaic linguistics in future surely may be the relatively easy access it now provides (thanks to its remarkable 'Indices' volume) to comparative data embracing the entire range of Altaic, 'outer' as well as 'inner'. When, as now awaits future scholarship, its latent resources in this connection are fully explored and exploited, we will surely be in a much more secure position to speak with authority concerning many of the historical-linguistic issues that involve Korean and Japanese, and as a result find ourselves considerably advanced toward the solution of many of the questions that still arise when Korean and Japanese are compared.

For the moment, and without even attempting here to enter upon the proper exploitation of these rich resources, we may give some idea of what awaits our field in this connection by references to page-numbers and semantic keys (generally abbreviated) to *lemmata* in the *EDAL*. There one may find comparative data that, on the one hand, relate Korean and Japanese forms to Altaic originals reconstructed with $*r^2 *l^2$, while on the other hand at the same time they convincingly explain those phonemes, at least in the forms at issue, as historically later innovations that arose, early in the history of Altaic, through Pritsak's 'fusion' or 'collisions' of still earlier $*r$ or $*l$ with an immediately following consonant:

1   *EDAL* 1065 'rise, up' || Trk. *z*, Jap. *r*, Kor. *l*, but WMo. *rg*
2   *EDAL* 1423/4 'dirt' || Trk. *z*, Jap. *t*, Kor. *l*, but Tg. *rg*
3   *EDAL* 1089 'be overripe' || Trk. *š*, Jap. *s*, Kor. *l*, but Tg. *lb*, WMo. *lj*
4   *DAL* 836 'couple' || Trk. *š*, Jap. *s*, but Kor. *lp*, Tg. *lb*, WMo. *lb*
5   *EDAL* 1133/4 'walk, run' || Trk. *š*, Jap. *s*, Tg. *l*, but Kor. *lp*, WMo. *ld*
6   *EDAL* 848 'reed' || Trk. *lg*, Tg. *lg*, but MKor.*l* < OKor. *š*

Note that in all these transcriptions of Korean cognates the symbol *l* has uniformly been employed throughout not as a phonetic (or phonemic) transcription but simply as a transliteration of the single grapheme that in New Korean orthography renders a morphophoneme that is variously realized as phonetic [l] or [r] according to its environment, and that furthermore presumably served the same function in writing Middle Korean. The *EDAL*, it must be noted in this connection, is frequently misleading, rendering this single entity sometimes as *l*, but at other times as *r*, for no linguistically significant reason. Note also that no matter what transcription we may wish to employ for this entity, the original sources of this morphophoneme in pre-Korean may be established by comparative evidence, and only by comparative evidence, as above.

In this all-too brief summation of the evidence, it is clear that in (1) and (2) we have to deal with $*r^2$ (here the differences in the Japanese reflexes are, as usual with this Altaic phoneme, conditioned by the quantity of the preceding vowel), while in (3), (4), (5) we have *l^2, as also in (6), where Japanese evidence is lacking but where a rare Old Koguryŏ form (attested in texts in Chinese phonograms) has š, showing in turn that here the Middle Korean form in *l* necessarily represents a later development from a different variety of Old Korean, a language for which at least three distinct varieties are attested, even though piecemeal, in our texts. A wealth of similarly significant *lemmata* awaits discovery and exploitation in the pages of the *EDAL*. When all of them have been properly categorized and carefully studied we will without question be in a far more satisfactory situation with respect to our understanding of the relationships of Korean and Japanese to Altaic, as well as to one another.

But even with the above all-too-abbreviated summary of representative examples from the evidence, it is clear that Pritsak's hypothesis is capable of serving as an overall guide for eventually sketching a rather more detailed, not to mention a far more comprehensive, internal history of the Altaic linguistic unity than has previously been achieved. It is also clear that Korean and Japanese individually, as well as taken together as a 'working entity' of comparison, will play significant roles in establishing the numerous historical stages that, to judge from this evidence, must now be reckoned with in our reconstructions of Altaic. After all, historical linguistics is, as the term implies, a study of history; and proto-languages must have had their own histories, which we must also study, just as did (and do) the attested languages upon which we base our recovery ('reconstruction') of those proto-languages.

Above I have already pointed out that one important clue to the relationship between Korean and Japanese, as well as to their mutual (if independent) relationships to Altaic, has been obscured in the literature by secondary sources and studies that carelessly overlook the overt orthographic evidence of the hPhags-pa-based Middle Korean writing system. This is particularly true of its provision of multiple graphemes for writing velar-spirant and laryngeal phonemes. In more than one case, when the evidence for the existence of these elements that functioned in the earliest fully documented stages of Korean is properly recognized, we shall discover data of considerable importance for understanding the historical developments that resulted in the later, more familiar but linguistically less significant forms of the modern language.

Thus, the etymological relationship between OJap. *aF-* 'join, meet' and MKor. *aGo-r-* 'unite' is needlessly obscured by the *EDAL* 488 transcription *a'or-* for the Korean member of the etymology; so also for the *EDAL* 1286/7 transcription *si'ur* for MKor. *siGur* 'edge', to be compared with OJap. *suwe* 'extremity'. This *lapsus* is all the more serious because both these etyma, in view of their respective cognates in Tg. *-b-*, WMo. *-g-*, and Trk. *-b-* (details in *EDAL*, *loci cit.*), impressively illustrate a phonological relationship precisely parallel to the suprasegmental-related velar-labial 'sound law' long ago described by Poppe, and subsequently almost uniformly either ignored or maligned by most scholars in the field, even though it convincingly connects a large number of forms in all these languages.

In still other forms, e.g. MKor. *sul Gui* 'carriage' (mistranscribed as MKor. *sur'ui* at *EDAL* 1299), when confronted with their cognates in Tg. *r*, Jap. *r*, and Trk. *z* (*EDAL loc. cit.*), precisely illustrate Pritsak's hypothesis for the ultimate source of at least many of the cases for which we must reconstruct Altaic *$*r^2$*, namely (as here) in the 'collision' or 'fusion' of a still earlier **r* with a non-vibrant/lateral consonant originally following it in close-juncture, here the consonant in question being the velar or laryngeal indicated in the Middle Korean orthography by the hPhags-pa-based symbol here rendered as -*G*-. In like fashion, MKor. *pol.Goi* 'worm, insect', when correctly transcribed (and *contra EDAL* 1151), documents the ultimate origin of the Altaic *$*l^2$ otherwise evident in its Japanese cognate *musi* 'id.' Further, for this etymon we have modern Korean forms in -*ll*-, such as *polloi* (Martin *et al.*, *Kor.–Eng. Dict*, 766a); these also testify to the historical-phonological reality of the Middle Korean -*G*-, since they show that the same variety of 'collision' or 'fusion' proposed by Pritsak on the one hand resulted in *-*l*+*G* > *$*l^2$ > Jap. *s*, but on the other in NKor. -*ll*-.

Of course, in exploiting the important historical-linguistic information at hand in the hPhags-pa-based Middle Korean script, we must always use due discretion concerning the sources and dating of the forms we investigate. Not everything written in later texts that employ this orthography necessarily reflects the language of the early 15th century, any more than e.g. does contemporary English spelling – this would appear to be a common-sense proposition that does not require elaboration, but such is not always the case. In later centuries (and for that matter in the modern period) certain of the original hPhags-pa-based velar and laryngal consonant symbols were (and are) employed simply as orthographic devices for indicating vocalic onset; to attempt to equate their employment in such cases with their earlier phonological roles is to wander too far afield from phonetic (not to mention) phonological reality. A particularly instructive example may be cited from the *EDAL* 1045. This compares a form that it cites as 'MKor. *o'ai-* "sailors' song"', and attempts to compare it with 'OJap. *ukep-* "to pray to gods"'. At first glance we might think that the *EDAL*'s writing '*o'a*' might mask an old intervocalic -*G*- , particularly in view of the proposed Japanese cognate with its intervocalic -*k*-. But a search for the source of the Korean form (aided, to be sure, by a useful dictionary citation in the *EDAL, loc. cit.*) reveals that it is attested no earlier than a collection of lyric poetry (*sičo*) published in 1728; at this date the graph in question was surely no longer writing -*G*- but merely serving to link one vowel to another. Moreover, in that same unique text it is clear that the form does not mean 'sailors' song', but is instead a sound-imitative formation characteristic of the *sičo* genre, reproducing a rowers'chantey (something like 'yo, heave ho!'); additionally, the Old Japanese form (with its incorrect second vowel copied from Martin) is also glossed misleadingly (see Miller and Naumann 1994: 122–34, for this important early Japanese shamanistic term). In a word, here the forms are incorrect, their meanings are false, and as a consequence none of the words cited in the *lemma* have anything to do with one another.

Throughout several decades, the Altaic hypothesis, including the possibility of relating Korean and Japanese to the 'inner languages', has frequently been subjected to sheer verbal abuse (e.g. Janhunen's views above), at other times to serious methodological criticisms (e.g. Gerard Clauson, Gerhard Doerfer and others). The former approach, though colorful, of course need not detain us long; but the latter calls for some comment, especially as it relates to the comparison of Korean and Japanese.

The single point that most of the critics of the comparative grammars and reconstructions of Ramstedt–Poppe make time and time again has been that forms in the various languages that the pioneers of these studies considered to be later, changed forms of a now-lost original form in a proto-language (i.e. 'cognates', in the historical-linguistic sense of that term) are instead no more than borrowings from one language into another. Some have argued that everything that Ramstedt and Poppe mistakenly believed to be 'Altaic' was simply borrowed by the Mongols from Turks; others see the loans in the reverse direction; and most of these critics agree that the Tungus must have borrowed everything in their languages from somebody else, most likely from the Mongols. As we have seen above (e.g. Bowring and Kornicki), it is still popular to use this argument in discrediting any hypothesis of a genetic link between Korean and Japanese, or between either of these languages and an Altaic proto-language. Critics who argue along these lines are still pretty well evenly divided in their opinions about who borrowed from whom: some find everything to be original on the peninsula, others in the islands. Most simply evade the question of the direction of these presumed borrowings; instead they argue that since borrowing is always possible, therefore it must always have taken place, and as a consequence it does not matter in which direction it happened.

Of course, it was the general lack of early written records for the majority of the Altaic 'inner languages' that encouraged this free-wheeling guess-work, particularly when it began to be applied to semantic and formal 'lookalikes' in the Turkic and Mongol lexicons. But it is time to stop playing this 'tennis match without a net' in the case of both Korean and Japanese. For Japanese we have important early records, as early as anything we possess from Turkic (and coincidentally at the other geographical extremity of the Altaic domain); and even for Korean we have a large body of written documents, beginning with a still mostly unexploited treasure trove of early lexical evidence in Chinese transcription, dealing in particular with three almost equally antique Old Korean languages, then followed from the early decades of the 15th century on by the meticulous records in hPhags-pa-based phonetic orthography that we generally call 'Middle Korean'. And fortunately also, for both languages we have the assistance of reliable secondary lexicological sources that provide us with information about earliest attestations and the dates of most of the texts in which the forms appear; all this of course is of obvious value in weighing arguments for or against specific loanword hypotheses. Elsewhere in Altaic, decisions concerning loanword possibilities have almost entirely been made without any documentary evidence; but that need not be the case in the study of Korean and Japanese as representative Altaic languages.

In view of this aspect of the problem, it is particularly unfortunate that the *EDAL* has now gone in a direction directly opposite to that familiar to us from the well-known and largely accepted work of Doerfer and Clauson. We find its authors arguing against the identification of loanwords time and time again – and this, most remarkably, even in certain cases where there is abundant evidence in early written records documenting the precise route of this or that borrowing (e.g. 'falcon', *EDAL* 670; 'fortress', *EDAL* 703). Sometimes this wholesale antipathy of the *EDAL* toward loanwords even goes so far as to set up paper-tigers merely in order to demolish them (e.g. 'sable', *EDAL* 326/7). Without question, Doerfer and Clauson frequently went too far in 'recognizing' loanwords, particularly between Mongol and Turkic, and frequently in Tungus as well. But now the *EDAL* goes too far in the other direction, especially where Korean and Japanese are concerned.

The greatest problem in all this is that, thus far in the Altaic comparative literature, no clear-cut criteria have ever generally been applied to the question of whether two 'lookalike' forms are loanwords or cognates. Phonology has mainly been ignored, while most often judgment has been made on the basis of 'common sense': words that look 'too much alike' must be loans in one direction or another; words that refer to technological innovations must have followed such introductions of techniques, etc. Only rarely have these criteria (not all of which are by any means trivial) been supported by datable data from documents, for the obvious reason that, in the case of Mongol and Tungus in particular, and to a certain extent in Turkic as well, such data are lacking. But now with Japanese and Korean, this becomes possible in many cases. Since, as I have already remarked, the *EDAL* is remarkably if understandably reluctant to categorize any of its Korean and Japanese *lemmata* as loanwords, its resources may not be exploited in this connection without constant caution. But once reasonable philological control is exercised upon the data that it does record, there is, as we might expect, much to be learned in this connection from this massive new research tool.

For example, one of the most frequently cited Korean–Japanese 'lookalikes' is the pair NKor. *hŏli*, Jap. *kosi* 'small of the back'. The forms look much alike, and they mean the same thing. But it is difficult to understand why, if the Japanese is a borrowing from the Korean, it has -*s*- for an original -*l*-, and so also, but in reverse, if we are to assume a borrowing into Korean from Japanese. The intervocalic *l* :: *s* correspondence of course fits in well with our received Altaic paradigms of phonological reconstruction, but the initials (*h* :: *k*) do not. Starostin had earlier (1991: 76, 289) tried to account for this correspondence in the initials by an unconvincing *ad hoc* phonological rule; now the *EDAL* (773/4) goes instead to an even less convincing morphological gambit that does no more than sidestep the phonological problems of the forms.

Unfortunately in this case our Japanese and Korean text-resources record nothing that will throw light upon this problem. However, texts are not the only artifacts that may supply evidence concerning linguistic loans; language operates in a wide cultural spectrum, many segments of which may also be placed under contribution in studying the possibility of loanword identifications. Given the important role of the sacroiliac (the body part to which both forms have specific reference) in traditional Asian medical praxis involving acupuncture, it is not only tempting but, as such things go, fairly safe to assume that the Japanese form is a medical term early borrowed from the continent, as we know acupuncture itself was. But that borrowing obviously did not involve any of the Middle or New Korean forms that we have documented; rather we must assume that it exploited some otherwise unrecorded pre- or Old Korean – or other Altaic! – form with -*s*- for *-*l*²- (cf. in *EDAL*, *loc. cit.*, citations of Tungus forms in -*lg*- and Trk. -*š*-, again, we confront evidence for Pritsak's hypothesis). This in turn would also provide some explanation for the still troublesome initial correspondences to which Starostin had reference in 1991. Similarly involved with medical history would appear to be NKor. *pŭl* 'scrotum; testicle(s)'. Martin (1966: 250) cites MKor. *pŭl* for this word and compares it with Jap. *huguri* 'scrotum', proposing an unattested earlier Korean form *puhul to account for the internal velar in the Japanese word. But no disyllabic Korean form is attested; and Martin's so-called 'Middle Korean' form is scarcely that. Its four earliest citations are to be found only in texts as late as 1613, 1690, 1748, and 1724–76; interestingly enough, the form is also used for 'testicle(s)' in a text of 1623–49 with specific reference to equine veterinary praxis. Given the extensive lexical influence of Mongol horsemanship and equine medicine in early Korea, particularly during the Mongol occupation of the peninsula, it is by no means out of the question to identify in Kor. *pŭl* a loanword related to such Mongol forms as Khal., Dag. *bör*, WMo. *bögere* 'kidney, testicle(s)' (Poppe 1955: 72). What might otherwise perhaps appear to be the somewhat curious gloss of Mongol 'kidney, testicle(s)' is in fact a semantic constellation also documented in and probably original with the vocabulary of traditional Chinese medicine; it eventually derives from early anatomical observation of the manner in which the testes originate in the lower body cavity near the kidneys, migrating ('descending') to their position within the scrotum in about the seventh or eighth month of the development of the embryo. The attempt of the *EDAL* (1102) to account for the absence of an intervocalic velar in the Korean form cited there as cognate with Tungus, Turkic, and Mongol passes in dignified silence over Martin's entirely teleological postulation of an intermediate 'Middle Korean' form in *-*h*- to account for the Jap. -*g*- (this last further obscured by his baseless reconstruction of earlier Jap. *-*nk*-). When, as with Martin, one *ad hoc* form after another is first summoned up to supply a single phonological 'explanation' and then immediately discarded, one can only, particularly in the semantic context of these forms, recollect that perhaps the ancients were not far wrong after all when they argued that *testis unus testis nullus*.

In other words, there are of course, as we would naturally expect, plenty of loanwords that complicate the comparison of Korean and Japanese. Unfortunately too many of them have now been either passed over in silence or deleted from the record by the *EDAL*. This treatment is almost as misleading as that of our Cambridge critics who flatly maintained that it is impossible ever to distinguish between inherited cognates and 'loanwords from Korean into Japanese', and methodologically equally as flawed as was the approach of Clauson and Doerfer – both always over-eager to assume that forms in different languages at all similar in shape and sense were somehow borrowed, one from the other, even in the total absence of documentary evidence, and frequently also despite phonological constraints that make such borrowing highly unlikely, or at times even impossible.

Much if not most of the interest in this question of comparing Korean and Japanese has arisen because of extra-linguistic considerations, in particular the geographic propinquity of the two nations, and especially their recent political history. Until very recently little if any attention has been focused on the larger issues of the possible relation of each of these languages to some larger linguistic entity, in particular, to Altaic. *Mutatis mutandis*, this has been very much akin to 'comparing English and French' without knowing anything of Indo-European, or of Germanic, or of Romance, and at the same time ignoring all available documentation for the flood of loanwords into the British islands after '1066 and all that'. Now, thanks to the long-awaited publication of the *EDAL*, and above all thanks to the years of unremitting scholarly effort on the part of our colleague S.A. Starostin and his several faithful collaborators, we have a comprehensive tool that will place all of us in a position to attack this problem anew, and this time from a solid historical-linguistic position. Like any reference source – indeed, like any text in the larger sense – the *EDAL* must be used with cautious discrimination. But here to call attention, as I have done, to some of the major problems of its rich repertory of materials is not by any means intended to underestimate its enormous potential for all Altaic historical research, including the study of Korean and Japanese, two important languages that now for the first time find their proper place as Altaic comparative evidence alongside Turkic, Mongol, and Tungus in the pages of the *EDAL*.

Of course, this evaluation of the *EDAL* is itself predicated upon a generally unverbalized assumption, but one that in view of certain allegations in the recent literature apparently needs to be set forth in plain terms. Many of us in this field, no doubt as a consequence of our early training in the comparative method of the Indo-European neo-grammarians, have long worked on the assumption that in historical linguistics it is the words and their histories that are always at issue. Now it appears that this too has been questioned by newcomers to the field. Whitman now alleges that 'the real interest in a linguistic phenomenon – a language or the genesis of a vowel system – is in the rules that govern it rather than the identity of its elements' (in Baldi 1990: 541). Astonishing though this claim may appear to many of us, it can hardly be ignored, and at least it has the benefit of consistency. It certainly explains why Whitman is not concerned that so many of the Japanese and Korean forms he compares are incorrect either in form or in meaning, or frequently in both. For him, 'the identity' of a language's elements, i.e. its words and their meanings, do not matter when we study historical linguistics. Others of us will remain of a different opinion.

Four decades ago, writing of Ramstedt's Mongol–Korean comparisons, Kara (1965) remarked, 'la première chose à faire, ici est de vérifier les étymologies proposées par Ramstedt' (1965: 25). Much the same must be said today with respect to the *EDAL*. This verification must begin with attention to forms and their meanings: *pace* Whitman, the 'identity of the elements' in a language – and in languages generally – does matter in historical linguistics. This in turn means that there can be no better way to advance our study of the linguistic histories of Korean and Japanese than carefully first to inspect, then to winnow out, and finally to refine the many etymologies both new and old for both languages now conveniently at hand in the *EDAL*, by the publication of which Sergei Starostin, Anna Dybo, and Oleg Mudrak have placed us all in their debt.

References

Baldi, P. (ed.) (1990) *Linguistic Change and Reconstruction Methodology*, Berlin: Mouton de Gruyter.

Bentley, J.R. (2001), *A Descriptive Grammar of Early Old Japanese*, Leiden: Brill.

Bowring, R. and Kornicki, A. (eds) (1993) *The Cambridge Encyclopaedia of Japan,* New York, NY: Cambridge University Press.

Janhunen, J. (1996a) 'Prolegomena to a comparative analysis of Mongolic and Tungusic', in G. Stary (ed.) *Proceedings of the 38th Permanent International Altaistic Conference (PIAC)*, Kawasaki, Japan, August 7–12, 1995, Wiesbaden: Harrassowitz.

Janhunen, J. (1996b) *Manchuria: An Ethnic History* (Mémoires de la Société Finno-Ougrienne, 222), Helsinki: Finno-Ugrian Society.

Kara, G. (1965) 'Le dictionnaire étymologique et la langue mongole', *Acta Orientalia (Hungary)*, 18: 1–32.

Martin, S.E. (1966) 'Lexical evidence relating Korean to Japanese', *Language*, 42: 185–251.

Menges, K.H. (1968) 'Die tungusischen Sprachen', in B. Spuler (ed.) *Altaistik* (*Handbuch der Orientalistik*, 1/5, *Nahe und der Mittlere Osten*), Leiden: Brill.

Miller, R.A. (1994) 'Review of Starostin (1991)', *Ural-Altaische Jahrbücher*, NS, 13: 68–107.

Miller, R.A. (2003) 'The Middle Mongolian vocalic hiatus', *Acta Orientalia (Hungary)*, 55: 179–205.

Miller, R.A. and Naumann, N. (1994) *Altaische schamanistische termini im Japanischen,* Hamburg: Gesellschaft für Natur- und Völkerkunde Ostasiens.

Poppe, N.N. (1955) *Introduction to Mongolian Comparative Studies* (Suomalais-ugrilaisen Seuran toimituksia, 110), Helsinki: Suomalais-ugrilainen seura.

Poppe, N.N. (1960) *Vergleichende Grammatik der altaischen Sprachen*, part 1, Wiesbaden: Harrassowitz.

Pritsak, O. (1964) 'Der "Rhotazismus" und "Lambdaizmus"', *Ural-Altaische Jahrbücher*, 35: 337–49.

Ramstedt, G.J. (1922) 'Zur Frage nach der Stellung des Tschuvassischen', *Journal de la Société Finno-Ougrienne*, 38(1).

Ramstedt, G.J. (1950) *Studies in Korean Etymology* (Suomalais-ugrilaisen Seuran toimituksia, 95), Helsinki: Suomalais-ugrilainen seura.

Shiratori Kurakichi (1970) (reprint) 'Chōsengo to Ural-Altai.go to no hikaku kenkyū'. In: *Shiratori Kurakichi zenshū*, vol. 3, 1-280, Tokyo Iwanami Shoten (= *Tōyō Gakuhō* 4.2 [June 1914] – 6.3 [October 1916]).

Starostin, S.A. (1991) *Altaiskaia problema i proiskhozhdenie iaponskogo iazyka*, Moscow: Izdatel'stvo 'Nauka'.

Starostin, S.A., Dybo, A. and Mudrak, O. (2003) *Etymological Dictionary of the Altaic Languages*, 3 vols, Leiden: Brill.

Vovin, A. (1994a) 'Is Japanese Related to Austronesian?', *Oceanic Linguistics*, 33: 369–89.

Vovin, A. (1994b) 'Long-distance relationships, reconstruction methodology, and the origins of Japanese', *Diachronica*, 11: 95–114.

Whitman, J.B. (1985) 'The phonological basis for the comparison of Japanese and Korean', Ph.D. dissertation, Harvard University.

Whitman, J.B. (1990) 'A Rule of Medial *-r- Loss in Pre-Old Japanese', in P. Baldi (ed.) *Linguistic Change and Reconstruction Methodology*, Berlin: Mouton de Gruyter.

12 The speed of language change, typology and history

Languages, speakers and demography in North-East India

François Jacquesson

This chapter will study the demography of wet-rice plains in traditional Assam (India) and in the slash-and-burn hills around, and will relate these observations to two sets of linguistic data that provide an interesting contrast: the Tani-speaking people of the eastern Himalayas and the Naga people on the other side of the Brahmaputra river, facing Burma. I will describe the extent to which the speed of language change is dependent upon a number of integrated factors, among them population density.

Populations of North-East India: density and history

North-eastern India is subdivided into 'states' or provinces (see Map 12.I); the main one is Assam, which corresponds to the course of the Brahmaputra river after it emerges from the eastern Himalayas and before it reaches Bengal. Assam is mainly lowland and has long been inhabited by people (whatever their languages) whose staple food is rice. They use the well-known system of 'nurseries' from which young plants are transferred to paddy-fields. It is monsoon country and when all goes well one can live satisfactorily. All around Assam, in the six other states, the landscape is far more hilly, and most of the time wet-rice cultivation is not possible: the people use 'jhum', the local name for slash-and-burn. Of the two systems, wet-rice allows the larger population.

The British census

In order to demonstrate how population density can bear upon communication and upon linguistic change, I will use the last British census of 1931. It has the double advantage of being reasonably reliable and describing a situation which, although not without colonial distortions, gives a good image of the contrasts between the valley and the hills, and between different parts of both.

Wet paddy-fields in the hills are rare, except in the Angami country (in Nagaland) where local people had been engaged in terrace cultivation for a long time when the British discovered them, and in the wet fields of the Apatani (Arunachal, Subansiri district), a secluded valley among the first higher slopes of the Himalayas.

288 François Jacquesson

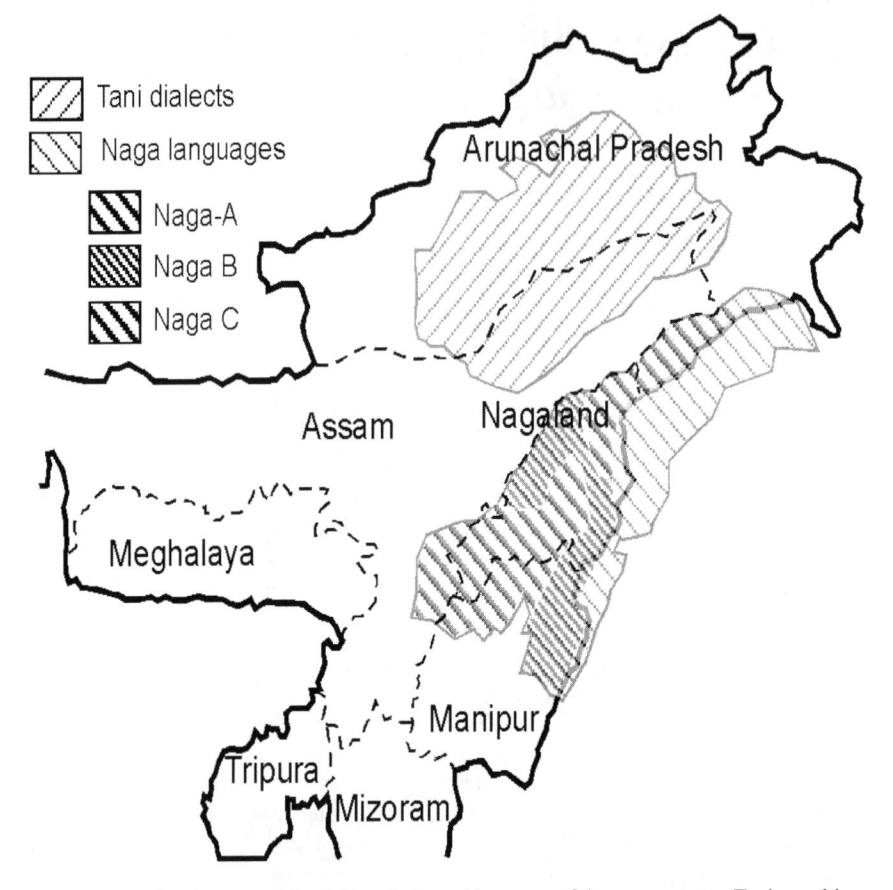

Map 12.1 Sketch map of North-East India, with names of the seven states, Tani-speaking and 'Naga'-speaking areas (Naga A is for 7 languages, Naga B for 8 languages, Naga C for 12 languages; Naga that are neither A, B, nor C live in Burma).

Table 12.1 is a slightly simplified version of a summary table in the 1931 census. The arrangement in the first column on the left is into three sections: (a) the Surma Valley is the total of the five lines that follow, all of them concerned with regions south of Assam proper; (b) the Assam valley is likewise the total of the seven districts that follow, most of them still in Assam, the exception being Garo Hills, now in Meghalaya; (c) the four lines at the end are the two Frontier Tracts (F. T.), and the two then independent states – which happily were also censused. Areas are in square miles. Then follow columns for the number of towns and villages, for occupied houses, and for people. A clever distinction is made between towns (population more than 5,000), where most foreigners live, and villages.

Table 12.1 The 1931 British Census: Assam and its surroundings

	Area	Towns	Villages	Occupied houses			Persons		
				Total	Town	Village	Total	Town	Village
Surma valley	24,170	10	15,299	76,3397	18687	749710	3,708047	72,017	3,636,030
Cachar	3,862	2	1,607	122,963	2,962	120,001	570,531	15,071	555,460
Sylhet	5,478	5	11,717	548,541	8,036	540,505	2,724,342	44,343	2,679,999
Khasi-Jaintia	2,445	2	954	22,061	1,929	20,132	109,926	9,844	100,082
Naga hills	4,293	1	481	47,598	760	46,838	178,844	2,759	178,085
Lushai hills	8,092		540	22,234	–	22,234	124,404	–	124,404
Assam valley	27,084	18	17,169	996,193	26,086	967,207	4,855,711	137,034	4,718,677
Goalpara	3,965	3	3,188	157,961	4,292	153,669	882,748	21,442	861,306
Kamrup	? 3,044	3	2,738	189,035	8,127	180,908	976,746	39,028	937,718
Darrang	2,842	2	1,978	129,182	2,520	126,662	584,817	11,964	572,853
Nowgong	3,896	2	2,323	104,185	3,133	101,052	562,581	13,511	549,070
Sibsagar	5,181	4	2,284	204,036	4,948	199,088	933,326	23,175	910,151
Lakhimpur	4,234	4	2,498	172,229	5,968	166,263	724,582	27,914	696,668
Garo Hills	3,152	–	2,160	39,565	–	39,565	190,911	–	190,911
Sadiya F.T.	3,200	1	373	10,397	973	9,724	53,345	4,370	48,975
Balipara F.T.	560	–	38	1,008	–	1,008	5,148		5,148
Manipur State	8,620	1	1,372	89,151	17,463	71,688	445,606	85,804	359,802
Khasi States	3,700	–	1,475	38,288	3,380	34,908	180,000	16,692	163,308

Density and paddy

I first extract (a) population densities in persons per km² (p/km²), after converting square miles into km², then (b) the average territory of a village, then (c) the average number of inhabitants per village – three types of data which help us to assess regional differences (see Table 12.2).

A neat classification emerges from the perusal of densities:

(1) Very low densities, less than 10 p/km²: the two Frontier Tracts and the Lushai Hills (resp. present Arunachal and Mizoram). In Figure 12.1: Bal(ipara), Lus(hai), Sad(iya).
(2) Low densities, about 20 p/km²: Khasi and Jaintia (Kha) plus the Khasi States (KhaS) and the Garo Hills (Gar) (the complete present-day Meghalaya), the Naga Hills (Nag) and Manipur State (Man).

290 François Jacquesson

Table 12.2 Population densities in 1931 Assam

	km²	Villages	Persons (rural)	Persons/ km²	km²/ village	Persons/ village
				a	b	c
Surma valley	62,600	15,299	3,636,030	59.2		
Cachar	10,003	1,607	555,460	57.0	6.2	
Sylhet	14,188	11,717	2,679,999	192.0	1.2	228.7
Khasi & Jaintia	6,333	954	100,082	17.4	6.6	104.9
Naga hills	11,119	481	178,085	16.1	23.1	370.2
Lushai hills	20,958	540	124,404	5.9	38.8	230.4
Assam valley	70,148	17,169	4,718,677	69.2		
Goalpara	10,269	3,188	861,306	86.0	3.2	270.2
Kamrup	7,884	2,738	937,718	123.9	2.9	342.5
Darrang	7,361	1,978	572,853	79.4	3.7	289.6
Nowgong	10,091	2,323	549,070	55.8	4.3	236.4
Sibsagar	13,419	2,284	910,151	69.6	5.9	398.5
Lakhimpur	10,966	2,498	696,668	66.1	4.4	278.9
Garo Hills	8,164	2,160	190,911	23.4	3.8	88.4
Sadiya F.T.	8,288	373	48,975	6.4	22.2	131.3
Balipara F.T.	1,450	38	5,148	3.7	38.2	135.5
Manipur State	22,326	1,372	359,802	20.0	16.3	262.2
Khasi States	9,583	1,475	163,308	18.8	6.5	110.7

(3) Higher densities, more than 50 p/km²: all other places, with two peaks, one in Kamrup (where Gauhati, the main city of Assam, is located) with 124 p/km², and Sylhet district (in present-day Bangladesh) with 192 p/km². The population pressure from Bengal is not new, nor is the influx of Bengali people into Assam. For this last category, Figure 12.1 skips Kamrup and Sylhet.

The gap between the (very) low densities and the higher ones is striking, and corresponds to the gap between slash-and-burn and wet rice. It also partly corresponds to the difference between 'tribal' and 'non-tribal' population; partly only, because all low density populations live on dry rice and are tribal, but there are also several tribal populations down in the valley – nearly all of them speaking Boro-Garo languages, a sub-group of Tibeto-Burmese languages (see Map 12.II, letter F).

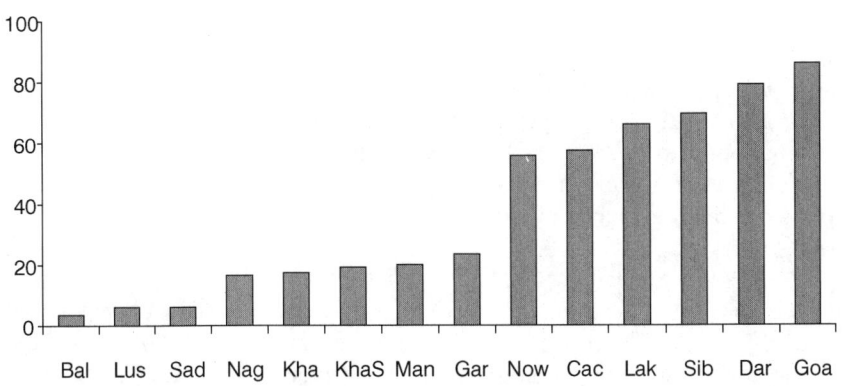

Figure 12.1 Population densities by district, Assam 1931.

Importance of history

Although higher densities largely result from more crops, we have to take into account two more factors that tend to blur into each other in the census. Especially in Sibsagar and Lakhimpur districts, a very significant part of the population is made up of immigrants, the labour force for the tea gardens. The space allotted to the tea gardens, incidentally, is not negligible, even if they often occupy gentle slopes and do not necessarily displace rice cultivation. This more or less forced immigration was described in the 1909 *Gazetteer*:

> The population of the [Lakhimpur] District at the last four enumerations was
>
> 1872   121,267
> 1881   179,893
> 1891   254,053
> 1901   371,396
>
> Within 29 years the population has more than trebled, this enormous increase being partly due to the fact that Lakhimpur, unlike Lower and Central Assam, has been healthy, so that the indigenous inhabitants increased in numbers, but still more to the importation of thousands of coolies required for the tea gardens and other industries of the district.
>
> (Allen 1909: 593)

Of the 371,000 people in Lakhimpur district in 1901, 174,000 are reported as 'tribal'. Of these, 48,000 are Munda or Santal, i.e. labour imported from the Munda-speaking provinces of Orissa or Western Bengal, making up 13 per cent of the district population. In Sibsagar district on the south bank, 'in 1904 there were 159 gardens, with 79,251 acres [c.320 km²] under cultivation' (Allen 1909: 576).

Although the district was then slightly smaller [12,989 km²] than in 1931, and we may estimate the tea surface as very minor, the labour population was not: it amounted to 36,000 people.

Another immigration is perhaps still more interesting. The Mishing people (often called Miri in Assamese) are a Tani tribe, with a language very close to other Tani tribal groups in Arunachal. The census gives the growing numbers of these people, compared in Table 12.3 with another tribal people living in the valley, the Boros.

The increase between 1891 and 1931 is 142 per cent for Boros, but 215 per cent for Mishings. This points to a Mishing immigration, confirmed by old reports. In his report for the 1901 census, B.C. Allen wrote under the title *Miri Hills* that 'large numbers of the tribe have now settled on the Assam plains' (Allen 1909: 149). Nearly fifty years before, in his 1853 report, Moffatt Mills wrote about Lakhimpur district:

> The exactions of these [revenue] agents and the misrule of Poorunder Sing (who continued the same revenue system) and the aggressions of the frontier tribes, added to the ravage of the Burmese, combined to make this District almost a wilderness, from which it will take years to recover.
>
> (Moffatt Mills 1853: 645)

E.T. Dalton, the future author the *Descriptive Ethnology of Bengal* (1872), is quoted in the same document with regard to the corresponding south bank, and he adds another reason for this 'wilderness':

> The population have decreased in numbers since our occupation [1839] of their territory, owing to migration to Lower Muttock and Saikwah [further east] of many who found they would not have so much to pay in the *mehals* where they were assessed according to the quantity of land they had under cultivation. The population that remains is now nothing, as compared with the extensive tract that is called after them.[1]

The estimated area of this district was about 5000 square miles, with a population of 85,296 (Moffatt Mills 1853: 649), which puts the density at c.6.6 p/km²—very similar to tribal mountainous tracts.

Wars and taxation were likely reasons for a near 'wilderness', but this wilderness soon looked attractive to newcomers. Peaceful Mishings came pouring

Table 12.3 Mishing immigration

	Mishing	Boro
1881	25,636	?
1891	37,530	198,705
1901	47,720	239,458
1931	80,831	282,582

from the mountains where they had problems with better armed Tani cousins, and they liked their new locations. British agents came and found the place perfect for tea gardens. Since the local labor force was next to nil or looked unreliable, they imported one.

This bit of history of Lakhimpur district helps to nuance the seemingly straightforward interpretation of the 1931 densities. Who would imagine the wilderness of the previous century? It also helps us to understand how quickly a demographic disaster, in this case following the murderous Burmese wars, can be surmounted – when the ecological conditions allow it.

The fact that the same district passed, in less than one century, from a density of 6.6 to a density of 66 is not explained by (a) 'progress': other districts in Lower Assam did not experience the same change; (b) simple cultural shift: populations fled, others came from various places, either willingly or not, but certainly it is not a matter of one homogeneous population being replaced by another homogeneous population with different agricultural experience. It was war, and then a complex mixture of people coming back to a devastated home and profiteers organizing trade and labour, as well as immigration from the hills.

Village network

There are at least two parameters for explaining the contrastive densities of peacetime. A higher density reflects many big villages, a lower density sparse small villages. But a medium density reflects either a few bigger villages or numerous hamlets. Several facts bear on the four possible variants, and we can examine them *live* because – and this is one reason why North-Eastern India provides a good case study – all four of them are attested there.

If we focus on the 1931 low and very low densities, we find the results shown in Table 12.4. Comparing columns (a) and (b), giving population density and

Table 12.4 Rural population (lower densities)

	km^2	villages	persons (rural)	persons/ km^2	km^2/ village	persons/ village
				a	b	c
Balipara F. T.	1,450	38	5,148	3.7	38.2	135.5
Lushai hills	20,958	540	124,404	5.9	38.8	230.4
Sadiya F.T.	8,288	373	48,975	6.4	22.2	131.3
Naga hills	11,119	481	178,085	16.1	23.1	370.2
Khasi & Jaintia	6,333	954	100,082	17.4	6.6	104.9
Khasi States	9,583	1,475	163,308	18.8	6.5	110.7
Manipur State	22,326	1,372	359,802	20.0	16.3	262.2
Garo Hills	8,164	2,160	190,911	23.4	3.8	88.4

294 François Jacquesson

village territory, we see that, when the density grows, village territory becomes less. Nothing surprising here except that (putting aside the Manipur special case) the growth of the first parameter and the decrease of the second do not follow the same rate, as Figure 12.2 shows.

Khasi and Jaintia (under direct British administration) and the Khasi States (indirectly administered) are the same people and the same territory, and statistics confirm this. The Garo Hills are an extension of this territory (now Meghalaya) and the same configuration, but with a difference: villages are slightly smaller (88 persons instead of 105~110) but more numerous (territory about 4 km² instead of 6.5), with a net result of higher density (23 p/km² instead of 17~19 p/km²). I combine this territory in Table 12.5 under its present-day name of Meghalaya.

If we label the 38~39 km² category 'bigger territory' and the 22~23 km² category 'smaller territory' (omitting Meghalaya for the moment), and if we label the 370 Naga average village size and the 230 Lushai average village size 'bigger village' and the 99~135 village size 'smaller village', we obtain the four theoretical variants described earlier (see Figure 12.3).

There is an expected corollary: while the Naga Hills have a comparatively high density (16.1) and Balipara F.T. a comparatively low density (3.7), Sadiya F.T.,

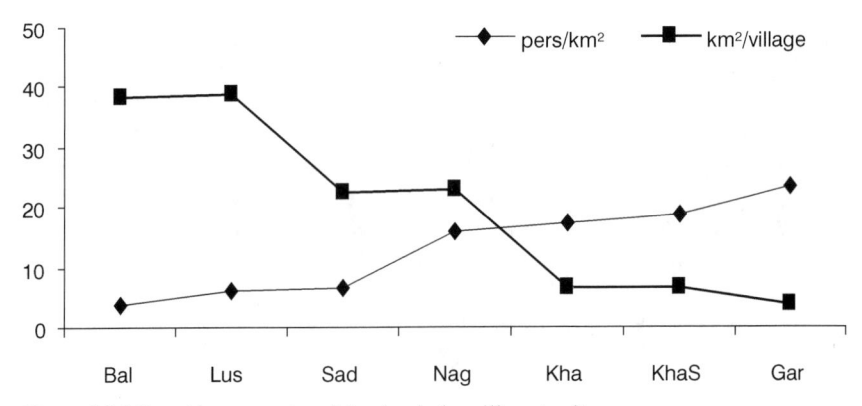

Figure 12.2 Densities are not explained only by village territory.

Table 12.5 Low-density rural population, grouped

	km²	villages	persons (rural)	persons/ km²	km²/ village	persons/ village
				a	b	c
Balipara F.T.	1,450	38	5,148	3.7	38.2	135.5
Lushai hills	20,958	540	124,404	5.9	38.8	230.4
Sadiya F.T.	8,288	373	48,975	6.4	22.2	131.3
Naga hills	11,119	481	178,085	16.1	23.1	370.2
Meghalaya	24,080	4,589	45,4301	18.9	5.25	99.0

		Village	
		Small	Big
Territory	Big	Balipara F.T.	Lushai Hills
	Small	Sadiya F.T.	Naga Hills

Figure 12.3 The four variants in North-Eastern India

where the Mishmi live, and Lushai Hills have similar densities (6.4 and 5.9) but for opposite reasons.

Hills and plains

This descriptive and structural scheme works well because, although the four regions are different in many important ways, all have a comparable background: no 'kingdom' with concentrated power (this is the difference from Manipur and, in some measure, Khasi–Jaintia people), slash-and-burn everywhere, and a more or less mountainous ecological setting.

The Meghalaya context is similar to the hill people in that it belongs to the 'small village' category, but these villages are much more numerous than the most numerous mountain areas, with the obvious consequence of a still higher density than in the Naga Hills. Meghalaya in various ways forms an eco-demographic category transitional between mountain and plain.

The plains in 1931 looked like a different world from the previous century. Densities has risen abruptly to about 60 p/km² and higher, as Table 12.6 shows. The villages are not critically bigger than those we met in our previous 'big village' category: Nowgong villages, right in the center of Assam (236), are not much different from the average Lushai village (at 230) in this respect (but in other respects, Nowgong is different), and Naga villages (at 370) are bigger than most villages on the plains, except in the old semi-urbanized country of Sibsagar. What is critically different is the social network. Villages on the plains have very small territories, incredibly so for visitors born in the hills; you have hardly walked out of one village than you enter another. The rich crops allow this closely set pattern. But even with carefully tended wet rice, there is a limit and when a village lives on hardly more than 1 km², as is the case in 1931 Bangladesh (Sylhet in Table 12.6), the smallest perturbation ends in disaster.

Languages, settlement pattern and density

The Brahmaputra corridor and Assamese

The plains of Assam are not uniform as far as language is concerned. Yet these valleys were in 1931, and had been for several centuries, the terrain of one major language, Assamese, an Indo-Aryan language closely related to Bengali.

296 François Jacquesson

Table 12.6 Rural population (higher densities)

	km²	villages	persons (rural)	persons/ km²	km²/ village	persons/ village
				a	b	c
Nowgong	10,091	2,323	549,070	55.8	4.3	236.4
Cachar	10,003	1,607	555,460	57.0	6.2	
Lakhimpur	10,966	2,498	696,668	66.1	4.4	278.9
Sibsagar	13,419	2,284	910,151	69.6	5.9	398.5
Darrang	7,361	1,978	572,853	79.4	3.7	289.6
Goalpara	10,269	3,188	861,306	86.0	3.2	270.2
Kamrup	7,884	2,738	937,718	123.9	2.9	342.5
Sylhet	14,188	11,717	2,679,999	192.0	1.2	228.7

Before deforestation (still going on but not in the valleys, now nearly bare of trees except for those that are useful around the villages), the river banks were dangerous: elephants, tigers, leeches, gadflies and mosquitoes. Rivers were the main arteries for trade and travel: virtually all traffic was by boat, and the Brahmaputra was covered with craft of every description. The railroad was the first newcomer, originally installed to serve the coal mines, petrol and gas production in Upper Assam, and tea production. Then came the lorries and the metalled roads, and later the bridges across the Brahmaputra. Today the big river is nearly empty, ferry boats are rare and fishermen are few. It is difficult to imagine what the river was like in the past.

Conquerors, both peaceful and aggressive, would follow the river.[2] When the Boro and Koch chiefs of lower Assam, sensitive to the beauties of India, began admitting Brahmin families and craftsmen to their domains, the eastern Indo-Aryan dialects brought by these people went up river. In many places, people became bilingual, and some of them still are. After a period of bilingualism, many eventually shifted to Assamese for good, and this is the situation we have now. To this have been added new immigrants, most importantly people from present-day Bangladesh (some Bengali dialects are very close to Assamese), who are probably close to outnumbering the Assamese. These immigrants live on wet rice. They could not survive in the hills. And in peaceful times their population density has sometimes risen rather rapidly.

Tibeto-Burmese language groups

The fact that we still find 'tribals', speaking 'tribal' languages, in wet rice country is remarkable. And still more interesting is the fact that all the languages spoken there, apart from Assamese, Mishing and other recent intruders, belong to one sub-group: the Boro-Garo languages. Boro-Garo languages belong to the Tibeto-Burmese group. Nearly all languages spoken by tribal groups in the hills and mountains surrounding Assam are Tibeto-Burmese, but they belong to a variety of subgroups, among them (see Map 12.II):

A. Isolated languages in Himachal Pradesh (to the west of Nepal), e.g. Kanauri.
B. Tibetoid group (technically called *Bodish*) in Tibet and around (Balti and Ladaki in Kashmir, Sherpa in Nepal), in northern Nepal (Gurung, Tamang), Sikkim and Bhutan.
C. Kiranti languages in Eastern Nepal and Sikkim.
D. Tani dialects in Arunanchal Pradesh, India.
E. Mishmi languages in the Himalaya/Burma nexus.
F. Boro-Garo:[3] the main group in North-Eastern India (Assam, Meghalaya, Tripura).
G. Northern Naga: links with Bodo-Garo and Jingpho have been proposed by Burling.
H. Naga languages: hardly a connected group, a possible continuum with Kuki.
I. Kuki-Chin. The Mizo language became the only 'Tribal' language with official status in India, when Mizoram (earlier 'Chin Hills') became a state within the Indian Union.
J. Meitei.

The consistency of the Boro-Garo sub-group on the plains obviously antedates the influx of Indo-Aryan speakers from India proper. This must be so because, had

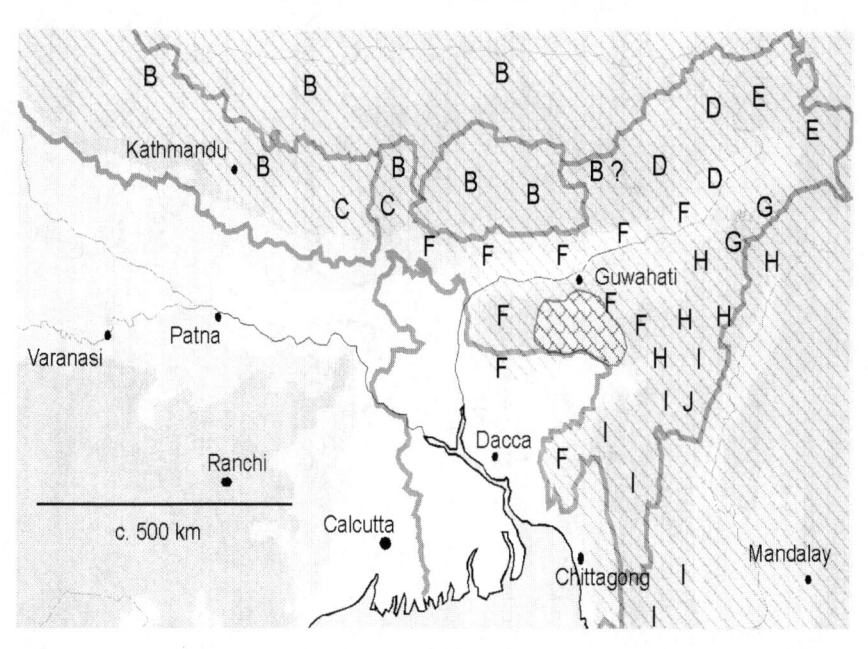

Map 12.II East and North-East India: Tibeto-Burmese language sub-groups (the brick-patterned patch in the Meghalaya hills NE of Dacca represents Khasi (Mon-Khmer) languages).

298 *François Jacquesson*

a majority of Assamese speakers already been settled in the valley, there would have been no opportunity for Tibeto-Burman newcomers to develop a uniform dialect group, 'ancestral' to a closely set group of languages (Boro-Garo). The fact that most river names in Assam are still now of Boro-Garo origin (see Map 12.III) shows that Boro-Garo speakers had been living in the valley for some time when Indo-Aryan influence began to be felt.

Hill tribes, their languages and the difficulty of calculating language difference

We saw how tribal groups living on dry rice in the hilly regions around the valley, usually have a much lower population density. We also saw how more precise information can be derived from the older census and that among the hill people we can discern several distinct reticulation[4] patterns, combining village size and village network: two important criteria for explaining population density gradation. These have the characteristics shown in Figure 12.4.

Can we correlate these population findings regarding with language geography? Can we measure the density of languages? This is a difficult question, because it is hardly possible to *measure* languages at all. When we compare things using a specific measure, we must be sure the things in question can be measured in the

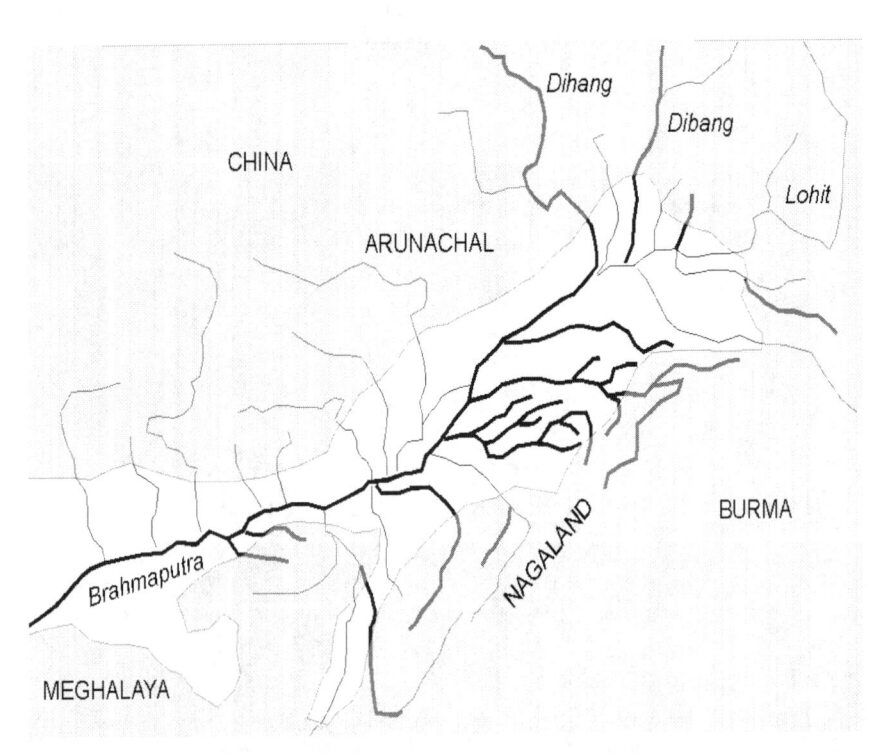

Map 12.III Rivers with a Boro-Garo name are depicted with a thick line.

Tani	Mishmi

The Plains of Assam

Lushai	Naga

Density 4 Small villages Big territories	Density 6 Small villages Small territories

The Plains of Assam

Density 6 Big villages Big territories	Density 16 Big villages Small territories

Figure 12.4 Distinct reticulation patterns.

same way: we compare number of inhabitants with number of inhabitants, or surfaces with surfaces when reduced to the same scale. But there is no scale to measure languages because (a) they are multi-dimensional,[5] (b) the relationships between the several dimensions vary from language to language, and (c) there is no reliable norm for a language[6] because languages are manifested in people's speech.

The Tani dialect chain

In 1931, the Balipara Frontier Tract at 1,450 km² was not large. It would fit ten times into Limousin. International difficulties prompted British authorities to ascertain borders, and it became the 'North East Frontier Area' (NEFA) which also included the Sadiya Frontier Tract. This large border area between India and China, now labelled Arunachal Pradesh, is often more than 100 km wide and is divided into six successive large units corresponding to river basins. Table 12.7 shows them from west to east (see also Map 12.IV).

The Tani dialect chain has 600,000 speakers spread over 40,000 km² according to Sun (2003). People understand their neighbours' dialects but less so the next dialect away. Dialects at the two ends of the chain are mutually unintelligible, but

Table 12.7 Some tribes in Arunachal Pradesh (Tani tribes are in upper case)

	1	2	3	4	5	6
Region	Kameng	Subansiri	Siang	Dibang	Lohit	Tirap
River	Kameng	Subansiri	Dihang =Siang	Dibang	Lohit =Tellu	N. Dihing =Diyum
Tribes	Dhammai Bugun Hruso-Aka Sherdukpen	Sulung BANGNI NISHI APATANI	BOKAR GALONG ADI	Idu Digaru	Meyor Miju Khamti	Singpho Tangsa Nocte Wancho

300 *François Jacquesson*

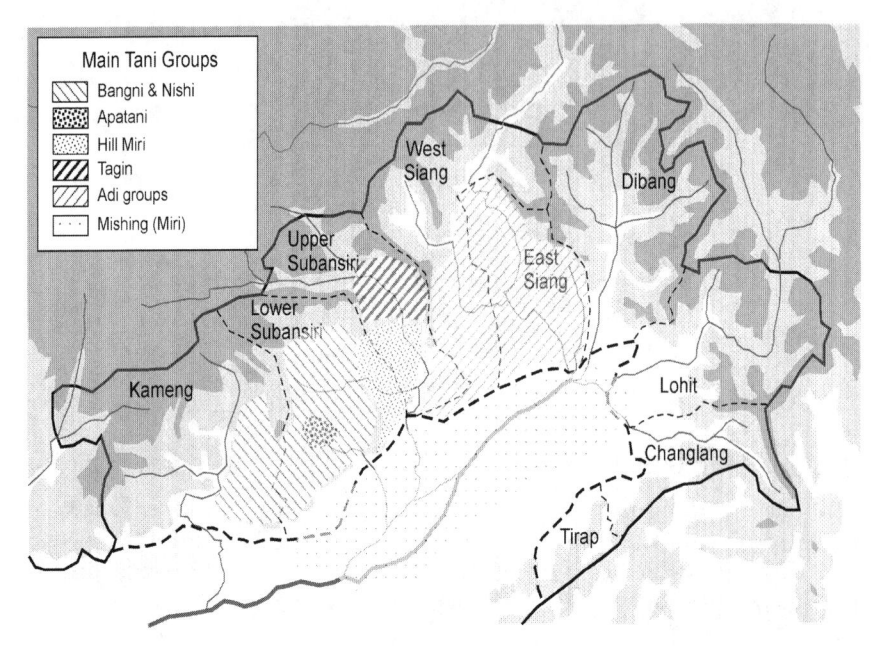

Map 12.IV Arunachal Pradesh now, with the main district limits (the most numerous Tani-speaking sub-groups are indicated (for scale see Map12.V).

people who travelled slowly enough to learn on the road would progress from dialect to dialect without a noticeable gap. Consequently, it is very difficult to posit unequivocal borders. Looking at the local forms (collected mainly by Indian district officers) for 'stone', 'bird' and 'four' in Table 12.8 gives a fair idea of how close these dialects are.[7]

This situation is 'normal', insofar as it is not confused by one dialect imposing itself as the common language – a common enough event on the plains, where communication is easier and quicker. Since, generally speaking, most languages investigated by linguists thrive on plains and have become the medium of communication of powerful institutions, the resulting 'abnormal' situation seems more common than that of undisturbed dialects. The result is that dialect chains look strange to people like the modern British or French, who find it 'normal' to use one and only one standard national language.

Compared with its neighbours, the Tani dialect group is remarkable in being spread over a relatively large area. We might have thought that deep gorges and high peaks, difficult paths and harsh climate would imply a scattering of small isolated groups. The groups are indeed small and scattered, but not isolated: they communicate with each other precisely because they are too small for a viable social unit. This is why their dialects are mutually comprehensible over a wide area, notwithstanding the climate and the terrain.

Table 12.8 Three words in Tani dialects

	District	Speakers	Stone	Bird	Four[a]
Nishi	Low Sub	139,856	éli	petta, péta	é-pi
Nishi (FJ 97, Yazhali)	Low Sub		ïllï		ï-phyi
Nishing-1 (Papum Pare)	Low Sub		eli	peta	e-pi
Nishing-2 (Kolo Riang)	E Kam		ellang	peta	a-pi
Nishing-3	E Kam		elang	pata	a-pi
Apatani	Low Sub	11,000	yalang	?	pi-lyi, -pe
Nah	Up Sub	105,46 [91]	éleng	pétta	ap-pi
Tagin	Up Sub	20,000	éling	péta	a-pi'
Hill Miri	Up Sub		eli, elyi	peta	e-pi
Bori (Adi)	W Siang	1,852 [71]	eling	pétang	ap-pi
Bokar (Adi)	W Siang	3,052	éling	péttang	ap-pi
Pailibo (Adi)	W Siang	1,382 [81]	i'li	petta	ap-pi
Karko (Adi)	E Siang	1,795 [81]	éling	péttang	ap-pyi
Milang (Adi)	Siang	2,595	dabu	?	-pe
Padam (Adi)	E Siang		dabu, eli'ng	pettang	ap-pi
Galong (W Siang)			?	pïtta	a-ppi
Padam (Bor Abor)	E Siang		e-ling, da-bu	pet-tang	a-pi
Mishing (Dibrugarh)	Assam		ülüng	püttang	ap-pi

Notes
Column 1 gives the name of the dialect according to author or informant. Column 2 gives the district. Column 3 gives the population number or estimate, when known; the date of the census is given in square brackets, e.g. [81] for 1981. Nishi (FJ 97), Galong and Mishing data are from my fieldnotes. Published sources are for Nishi, Tayeng (1990); Nishing-1, -2, -3, Goswami (1995); Apatani, Sai (1993); Nah, Pertin (1994); Tagin, Das Gupta (1983); Hill Miri, Chutia (2003); Bori, Megu (1988); Bokar, Megu (1990); Pailibo, Badu (1994); Karko, Megu (1993); Milang, Tayeng (1976); Padam, Tayeng (1983); Padam, Lorrain (1903) who calls them 'Bor Abor'a; see Jacquesson (1998).
a On the insertion of the hyphen see Jacquesson (2004).

Naga culture: the school of distinction

The contrast with the Naga situation is complete. 'Naga tribes' are widespread not only in Nagaland, but also in the northern half of Manipur (Map 12.V). Its southern half is settled by Kuki-speaking people. If we add Nagaland's surface (16,527 km²) to half of Manipur's (22,327), we get a rough total of 27,000 km² (about the same as Brittany, less than Belgium), far less than the Tani dialect chain area, but occupied by at least 30 languages. If we added the Naga languages in Burma, the area would grow but so would the number of languages.

Map 12.V Sketch map of 'Naga' languages, on both sides of the international border (thick line); dotted lines indicate Nagaland, Manipur and Assam state borders; thin lines show approximate language areas, with the language name (map adapted from Stirn and van Ham 2003: 31).

The rich and diversified array of languages among the Nagas was striking to the first British administrators or explorers.[8] Butler wrote in 1873 that 'Of all the tribes inhabiting that enormous tract of mountainous country hemming in Assam on the south, the "Nagas" are one of the most numerous' and Mackenzie, who quotes him, spoke of them in these terms:

> ... a group of tribes inhabiting part of the great mountain system which lies to the south of Assam valley – tribes many in number and differing in characteristics – but which extend under the generic name of Naga.
> (1884: 77)

In his 1905 *Gazetteer*, B.C. Allen described the average Naga village:

> The Naga villages are very different from the straggling groves of plantain, palms, and bamboos, to which, on the plains, this name is generally applied. They are generally built along the tops of hills, and in the old days of intertribal feuds were strongly fortified and entered through a village gate. On the plains of Assam, it is often hard to say where one village ends and the next begins; but there is none of this uncertainty in the Naga Hills. The village is like a little town which often stands out sharp against the sky line, and it possesses distinct and definite village lands which are cultivated by its inhabitants, or are sometimes let to their fortunate neighbours.
> (Allen 1905: 81)

This short description captures important points. Nagas love borders and do not like trespassers. The feeling of belonging to a close community begets their tribal spirit, with its love for specific features and its parochialism as a way of life. It also implies an utter skepticism regarding the tastes and movements of foreigners, and head-hunting was constant. The plains were constantly raided. In 1874–5, Angamis from Khonoma and Mozema plundered six villages and killed 334 people (Allen 1905: 21). The British lost many sepoys in those hills, and officers were occasionally killed too. Many Naga people died also, and many Naga villages were burnt in reprisal. But for the Naga the war against the British intruder was simply an extension of either the plundering of the plains with its profit in slaves, or of the warfare against neighbours in the hills. It was not new: the Tai-Ahom annals make many allusions to such behaviour at the beginning of the 13th century, although they sometimes claim to 'tame the Nagas'.

The language mosaic was one result of this parochial spirit. Let us take three examples from Geoffrey Marrison's *The Classification of the Naga Languages of North-East India* (1967), a work made by compiling older data and adding new. Marrison's book includes a kind of comparative dictionary of about 900 lexicon items for 31 languages. I have chosen 'stone', 'bird' and 'four' because they make an easy comparison with the Tani dialects in Table 12.9. The column on the left (A-1 etc.) gives Marrison's classification, based not only on lexical but also on morphological and syntactic criteria: three major groups A, B and C, each with its own subgroups. Twenty-seven of the languages are shown in Table 12.9, and four non-Naga are added (again according to Marrison).

Marrison's ordering from A-1 to C-2 happens to be roughly geographical as well. This is shown on Map 12.II and in Plate 12.I in the distribution of languages by classification shown on the left: the dark colour in the upper part represents A languages, the medium colour in the middle and on the right edge represents B languages, and the light colour represents C languages. The disposition of the little squares is a fair approximation of geography. The two rectangles at the bottom are Lushai (on the left) and Meitei (in the middle).

In the (very simple) distribution of words for 'stone' the dark colour indicates languages that use the root *lung* or an obvious modification of it, or a combination of it with something else; the light colour indicates forms of the root *to/tau/tso/ tsu* etc. The case of 'stone' is simple because only two roots contrast, and the second one makes a block consisting of all C languages except for the Puiron speakers, who borrowed their word from their Lushai neighbours. It is also a good opportunity to note that 'Naga' languages are not the island they pretend to be. In fact, as far as languages are concerned, many Naga forms sound very much like those in the Kuki languages, also Tibeto-Burmese, and here represented by Lushai.

The distribution of words for 'bird' is slightly more complicated. The dark colour marks languages that use some variant of *vu/wo/wa* or *ao*. This root is also found in Lushai, and incidentally in Meitei. Only eight languages clearly show two other roots: *ra* (Angami, Chokri, Mao) and *roi/rui*, which may be descended from a single form, but this is another question. The distribution of words for 'four' confirms certain patterns, notably the fact that the non-Naga languages in the south (Kuki-Lushai, Meitei, and the Naga languages they locally influenced) may sound quite similar to Naga languages to the north, although intervening languages of the C group sometimes disrupt that continuity. The case of 'four' shows up something of Marrison's B group, where some languages (medium colour) have a *zü/zhü/zyü* form, while the dark-coloured languages have a *le/lai/ li* form and the light-coloured a *dai/dei* form. Here again, it is likely that the three basic forms had a common source, but the goal of comparative linguistics is not only to identify what is identical behind variation: it is also to understand the role of variation itself.

These 30 or so languages are spread over less than 300 km from north to south and about 100 km from east to west. When we compare the numerous and conflicting discontinuities we observe in the Naga languages (Map 12.V) with the clean and easy continuum (for the same meanings) among the Tani dialects, the contrast is bewildering. I described above the largely cultural aspects of this contrast. It now remains to link it with demography.

Conclusions

The 1931 census showed the demographic difference between plains and hills. A diversity of situations was observed, which I described in terms of different

Table 12.9 Three words in 27 'Naga' languages

		Stone	Bird	Four
A-1	Tangsa Yogli	lung	wu	bülai
A-1	Tangsa Moshang	lung	vu	bali
A-1	Nocte	long	vo	beli
A-1	Wancho	long	ao	li
A-2	Konyak	yong	aoha	peli
A-2	Phom	yong	outhü	ali
A-2	Chang	lang	ao	lei
B-1	Yacham	lung-mango	uso	phale
B-1	Ao	lung	waya, ozü	phüli
B-2	Lotha	olung, onung	woro	mezü
B-2	Yimchunger	lung	wununü	phiyi
B-2	Ntenyi	alung, anong	aowa	mezhü
B-1	Sangtam	long	uza	müzyü
B-3	Tangkhul	lunggui	vanao	mati
B-3	Maring	talung	wa(cha)	phili
C-1	Sema	athu	ao	bidhi
C-1	Angami	katsie	pera	die
C-1	Chokri	kütsü	müra	da
C-1	Mao	otsu	raho	padei
C-2	Rengma	tso	tegü	pezi
C-2	Zeme	tingchu	nruine	medai
C-2	Mzieme	tangtsu	mruine	madai
C-2	Liangmai	tatu	thingna	madai
C-2	Maram	ato	saramrui	madai
C-2	Nruangmei	ntau	nruaina	padei
C-2	Khoirao	ntau	(ram)roi	malhi
C-2	Puiron	lung	basa, masa	mali
Kuki	Lushai	lung	sava	pali
	Meitei	nung	uchek	mari
	Kachin	nlong	u, wu	mali
BoroG	Dimasa	longthai	dao	biri

reticulation patterns: village populations and village land areas contributed to these in different ways. Within this patterning, two extreme situations can be described: small widely scattered villages (the Arunachal situation) giving very low population density, and not so rare big villages (the Naga situation) giving high population density. We can call them 'sparse' and 'dense'.

It would be difficult and probably circular to try and decide whether the proud behaviour of the Naga ('proud' is intended to be complimentary) is the cause or the consequence of their rather distinct demography, itself perhaps partly dependent on land resources. Instead of assuming with Hegel that the soul of a nation (*Volkgeist*) is the cause for its behavior and its fate, or conversely with Marx that economic setting and production explain the soul of the people, it seems reasonable (1) to admit that these phenomena may indeed be correlated in some measure, (2) to remark that the correlation does not imply a one-way-only mechanism, but rather reflects people battling their way through the circumstances that continue to envelop them.

The traditional unwillingness to see phenomena in this way comes from the fact that languages are commonly supposed to change by themselves, like clocks beating their own rhythm. It is then difficult to look at languages as patterns of speakers' usage. However, languages do not change at the same pace all the time (this is the reason why glottochronology is wrong). Using a consistent framework, we have found a web of reasons why the pace is different. Some of those reasons are right out of the speakers' control: one cannot, for example, grow wet rice up in the Dibang valley. Some of them are well within their control. As in the case of the Tani, one can maintain relationships with distant neighbours, which implies that one's children will not be allowed to impose their personal slang on the household. But if, as in the Naga case, intruders are not welcome (and the only neighbours with whom one relates are within whistling distance), then one will probably meet these neighbours often, and any innovation in costume or language will be considered with interest since it may provide a new password for the community. Human initiative and control bears heavily on language use, and consequently on language change.

Demography is one possible approach to such a correlation. It is not a mechanical approach, as it admits numbers and scales. This is an unusual way of thinking about language change, for reasons which were alluded to earlier. It is not mechanical because one has to consider context. The super-high population densities of wet-rice people form a different system altogether from the Nagas. They form a different world, and this is one of the reasons why the Nagas could only

Table 12.10 'Sparse' and 'dense' extremes

	'Sparse'	*'Dense'*
Population	sparse	dense
Differentiation	slow	quick
Languages	continuum	sharp distinction

imagine a predatory relationship with the plains. But the relatively low population densities of the hill dwellers form an understandable and comprehensive pattern when one realizes how village weight and village territory complement each other. At one extreme, widely scattered people have to cover long distances in order to maintain a viable society. At the other extreme, a dense population must remain concentrated in their small valley in order to maintain another viable societal type. An expression of this contrast is that innovations will be slowed down in the first case, and encouraged in the second, which means that low density languages will change slowly, while high density languages will change far more quickly. The result is that the Tani dialects remain a dialect chain, whereas the Naga dialects have broken down into sharply differentiated languages.

Notes

1 After this Dalton develops a plan for stopping these bad migrating habits, which make taxation difficult.
2 About the history of Assam, see Gait (1926), Baruah (1985), Jacquesson (1999).
3 Often spelled 'Bodo-Garo'.
4 Reticulation combines, in a net-like pattern, the size of the mesh (here the size of village territory, or the number of villages per surface unit) and the size of the knit or knot (here the importance of the village in number of inhabitants).
5 A language description is typically composed of phonology (the sounds of the language), morphology (how sounds are combined into words), syntax (how these words are combined into phrases, sentences, texts), lexicon. Complete information about one level cannot be derived from another. Units at each level must be described independently: for instance within morphology nouns cannot provide complete information about verbs.
6 'Language' is a convenient but deceptive cover term for a number of closely related dialects. These dialects may be dispersed along geographical clines (regional dialects), or along social clines because suburbs and/or fashionable circles tend to develop identity markers, or in many other ways.
7 Most divergent in this list is Apatani, with a very dense population. The Apatani country and way of life in the 1940s is described by Bower (1953: see the second photo after p. 84 of a densely packed Apatani village). See also Fürer-Haimendorf (1946).
8 The best introduction to the British literature on Nagas and Nagaland is Elwin (1969).

References

Allen, B.C. (1905) *Gazetteer of the Naga Hills and Manipur*, repr. by Mittal Publications, Delhi, 2002.
Allen, B.C. (1909) *Gazetteer of India: Eastern Bengal and Assam*, repr. by Mittal Publications, Delhi, 1979.
Baruah, S.L. (1985) *A Comprehensive History of Assam*, New Delhi: Munshiram Manoharlal Publishers.
Bower, U.G. (1953) *The Hidden Land*, London: John Murray; repr. by Allied Publishers, Delhi, 1978.

Elwin, V. (1959) *India's North-East Frontier in the Nineteenth Century*, Delhi: Oxford University Press.
Elwin, V. (1969) *The Nagas in the Nineteeth Century*, Delhi: Oxford University Press.
Formoso, B. (2004) 'A l'unisson des tambours: Note sur l'ordre social et la chasse aux têtes parmi les Wa de Chine', *Anthropos*, 99: 353–63.
Fürer-Haimendorf, C. von (1946) 'Agriculture and land-tenure among the Apa-Tanis', *Man in India*, 26: 20–49.
Gait, Sir E. (1926) *A History of Assam*, 2nd edn, Guwahati: Lawyer's Book Stall.
Jacquesson, François (1998) 'L'évolution et la stratification du lexique: contribution à une théorie de l'évolution linguistique', *Bulletin de la Société de Linguistique de Paris*, 93: 77–136.
Jacquesson, F. (1999) 'Abrégé d'histoire de l'Assam jusqu'à l'installation anglaise', *Journal Asiatique*, 287: 191–284.
Jacquesson, F. (2004) 'Gallong et en angami (Tibéto-birman)', in P.J.L. Arnaud (ed.) *Le Nom composé: Données sur 16 langues*, Lyon: Presses Universitaires de Lyon.
Mackenzie, A. (1884) *History of the Relations of the Government with the Hill Tribes of the North-East Frontier of Bengal*, reprinted as *The North-East Frontier of India*, Delhi: Mittal Publications.
Mitra, A. (ed.) (1961a) *Census of India*, vol. 1, *India*, part II-A (i), *General Population Tables*, New Delhi: Office of the Registrar General.
Mitra, A. (ed.) (1961b) *Census of India*, vol. 1, *India*, part IV-A (iii), *Report on House Types and Village Settlement Patterns in India*, New Delhi: Office of the Registrar General.
Moffatt Mills, A.J. (1853) *Report on the Province of Assam*, repr. by the Publication Board of Assam, Guwahati, 1984.
Stirn, A. and van Ham, P. (2003) *The Hidden World of the Naga: Living Traditions in Northeast India and Burma*, Munich: Prestel.
Sun, J.T.-S. (2003) 'Tani Languages', in G. Thurgood and R. LaPolla (eds) *The Sino-Tibetan Languages*, pp. 456–66, London: Routledge.
Thurgood, G. and LaPolla, R. (eds) (2003) *The Sino-Tibetan Languages*, London: Routledge.

Tibeto-Burmese language sources (see Notes of Table 12.8)

Badu, T. (1994) *Pailibo Language Guide*, Itanagar: Directorate of Research, Government of Arunachal Pradesh.
Chutia, R. (2003) *The Hill Miris of Arunachal Pradesh: A Descriptive Study of a Himalayan Tribe*, New Delhi: Spectrum.
Das Gupta, K. (1995) *An Outline on Tagin Language*, Shillong: North-East Frontier Agency.
Goswami, S.N. (ed.) (1995) *Nishing (Bangni) Language Guide*, Itanagar: Director of Information and Public Relations, Arunachal Pradesh.
Lorrain, J.H. (1907) *A Dictionary of the Abor-Miri Language*, Shillong: Director of Information and Public Relations, Arunachal Pradesh.
Marrison, G. (1967) 'The Classification of the Naga Languages of North-East India', PhD thesis, School of Oriental and African Studies, University of London.
Megu, A. (1988) *Bori Phrase Book*, Itanagar: Directorate of Research, Government of Arunachal Pradesh.

Megu, A. (1990) *Bokar Language Guide*, Itanagar: Directorate of Research, Government of Arunachal Pradesh.

Megu, A. (1993) *The Karkos and their Language*, Itanagar: Directorate of Research, Government of Arunachal Pradesh.

Pertin, K. (1994) *Nah Language Guide*, Itanagar: Directorate of Research, Government of Arunachal Pradesh.

Sai, T. (1993) *A Guide to Apatani Language*, Shillong: Director of Information and Public Relations, Arunachal Pradesh.

Tayeng, A. (1983) *A Phrase Book in Padam*, Shillong: Director of Information and Public Relations, Arunachal Pradesh.

Tayeng, A. (1976) *Milang Phrase Book*, Shillong: Director of Information and Public Relations, Arunachal Pradesh.

Tayeng, A. (1990) *Nishi Phrase Book*, Itanagar: Director of Information and Public Relations, Arunachal Pradesh.

Part III
Genetics

13 The GM genetic polymorphism in Taiwan aborigines

New data revealing remarkable differentiation patterns

Alicia Sanchez-Mazas, Ludmilla Osipova, Jean-Michel Dugoujon, Laurent Sagart, and Estella S. Poloni

Introduction

Taiwan (ex-Formosa), a large island of about 36,000 square kilometres located off the south-eastern coast of China, has aroused great interest among scientists from different disciplines whose study focuses on the history of settlement of East Asia and Oceania. The population of Taiwan was 22 million people in 2004, distributed among a large variety of populations. Among them, the Chinese, who for the most part migrated to the island in the 17th century after short-term occupations by the Portuguese (1544–82), Dutch (1624–62) and Spanish (1626–42), currently represent almost 98 per cent of its inhabitants. The main Chinese groups in Taiwan speak southeast Chinese dialects: the Minnan dialect (about 70 per cent) and the Hakka dialect (about 15 per cent). A further 12 per cent correspond to Han people who migrated from the mainland after World War II and are typically speakers of Mandarin, although most other Chinese dialects are also represented. Besides the Chinese, the island is also inhabited by aboriginal peoples who now represent about 2 per cent of the population. Twelve 'tribes', speaking distinctive Austronesian languages, some subdivided into dialects, are officially recognized (Map 13.I): the Ami, Atayal, Bunun, Kavalan, Paiwan, Puyuma, Rukai, Saisiat, Thao, Tsou and Sedik (including the Taroko), plus the Yami in Lan-Yu ('Orchid') Island. The Yami are not linguistically Formosan, but speak an Austronesian language within Batanic, a Northern Philippine group. Geographically, these populations are located on the east coast and in the mountains in the centre of the island. Twelve additional Formosan languages: Babuza, Basay, Hoanya, Ketagalan, Kulon, Luilang, Pazeh, Papora, Qauqaut, Siraya, Taokas and Trobiawan are extinct or on the verge of extinction (Pazeh). Most were spoken on the western and northern coasts of the island, the focal points of Chinese settlement.

The Austronesian phylum is the second largest in the world after Niger-Congo in terms of the number of different languages spoken (1268 according to the Ethnologue).[1] Taiwan represents its northernmost geographic boundary. Linguists are generally agreed that all the non-Taiwanese Austronesian languages (spoken in

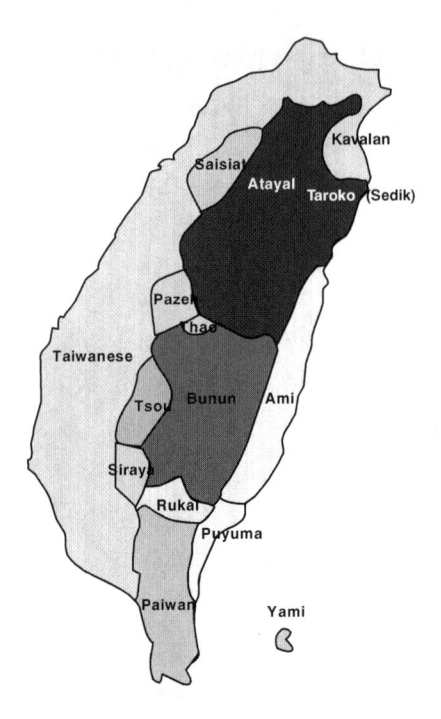

Map 13.1 Map of Taiwan showing the areas settled by the aboriginal populations (Austronesian) and the Taiwanese (Chinese).

the Philippines, Indonesia, Island and Coastal Melanesia, Micronesia, Polynesia, part of continental Southeast Asia, and Madagascar) belong to only one subgroup, 'Malayo-Polynesian' (Blust 1977), while opinions differ on whether Malayo-Polynesian is a primary branch of Austronesian (Blust 1999), or part of a branch also including some Formosan members such as Ami (Harvey 1979; Reid 1982; and many others). The number of primary Austronesian branches represented in Taiwan varies between two (Starosta 1995) and nine (Blust 1999). This makes Taiwan the most diverse area in the entire Austronesian area, and therefore, by Sapir's principle (Sapir 1916), the most likely candidate for the Austronesian homeland. The Formosan languages are also archaic in various respects, which fits well with the idea of a Taiwanese homeland. Blust (1988) has given a highly plausible picture of the cultural and environmental changes involved in the Malayo-Polynesian migration, as reflected in the Austronesian lexicon. Finally, Gray and Jordan (2000), using lexical information and parsimony analysis, have produced a phylogeny for 77 languages of the Austronesian family that places Formosan languages at the top of the tree.

The thesis of a Formosan homeland is also supported by archaeological data. Since the 1970s, Peter Bellwood has argued for a close relationship between the geographical spread of Austronesian-speakers and the likely diffusion of farming societies identified by a sequence of Neolithic sites throughout the Austronesian area, with Taiwan representing the most ancient settlements (Bellwood 1978, 1997; Bellwood and Dizon, Chapter 1, this volume). In turn, the earliest Austronesian settlers are viewed as originating on the East Asia mainland: Chang Kwang-chih (1969) has identified ceramic sites on the mainland side of the Taiwan straits that are contemporary with, and culturally similar to, the earliest ceramic sites on Taiwan, pointing to the mainland as the origin of the Austronesian peopling of Taiwan (see also Blench, Chapter 4, this volume).

Those ideas gave rise to the so-called 'express-train to Polynesia' hypothesis (Diamond 1988) that has more recently been revisited by Peter Bellwood himself; indeed, this author considers that the train was not so express, since it took at least 1000 and perhaps 1500 years for Taiwanese people to migrate out of Taiwan since their first settlement in the island (Bellwood and Dizon, Chapter 1, this volume). His main argument is that, among other archaeological evidence, recent findings of carbonized grains at Nanguanli (south Taiwan) indicate rice and foxtail millet cultivation around 5,000 years ago in the island (Tsang 2005), and the likely earliest date for Taiwan Neolithic could then be around 3500 BCE. By contrast, although archaeological material found in the neighbouring Batan archipelago and the north of Philippines indicates a close cultural relationship with Taiwan, no Neolithic cultures appear to have moved from Taiwan until around 2500 BCE, or later (Bellwood and Dizon, Chapter 1, this volume); hence a temporal gap of at least 1000 years.

Several scenarios have been proposed for the initial differentiation of Austronesian languages on Taiwan. Starosta (1995) examined morphological innovations and presented a tree-like phylogeny taking the southwest coast of Taiwan to be the Austronesian homeland. In a study of the main sound changes in the Formosan languages, Blust (1999) could not detect a tree-like signal, and distinguished no less than 10 primary Austronesian branches, nine in Taiwan and a tenth – Malayo-Polynesian – outside of Taiwan. Another proposal, mostly based on lexical innovations in the numerals system, was proposed by Sagart (2005; and Chapter 5, this volume). It implies a geographic expansion of Formosan populations out of the northwest coast of Taiwan, where the first settlers arrived from China, southwards along the west coast to the south and southeast, from where migrations out of the island took place. This model has been integrated by Sagart (Chapter 5, this volume) into a larger scenario of Neolithic population movements in eastern China. According to his model, the Austronesian languages are a sister language to Sino-Tibetan ('STAN' hypothesis); Sagart also regards the Tai-Kadai languages of mainland Southeast Asia as a subgroup within Austronesian and a sister clade to Malayo-Polynesian.

Taiwan has been studied intensively from a genetic point of view. Most data come from field studies undertaken by Marie Lin's team to sample aboriginal populations, leading to the analysis of numerous genetic systems, among which blood groups and proteins, HLA, microsatellites and mtDNA (Lin and Broadberry 1998; Lin et al. 2000, 2005; Chu et al. 2001; Lee et al. 2002; Trejaut et al. 2005; Trejaut et al., Chapter 14, this volume). Some samples were also studied in other laboratories for mtDNA (Tajima et al. 2003), Y chromosome markers (Su et al.

2000; Capelli et al. 2001) and serum proteins (Matsumoto et al. 1972; Schanfield et al. 2002). All those studies reveal both a high level of genetic heterogeneity among Taiwanese aboriginal populations and some remarkable genetic features that differentiate them from mainland East Asian populations. The patterns of genetic variation among Taiwanese and between Taiwanese and other East Asian and Oceanic populations seem to be quite complex, and their relationship to the history of the peopling of this island still remains to be clarified.

The present study is a new contribution to the genetic history of Taiwan. Within the framework of a collaborative study, partly sponsored by the CNRS (OHLL programme), between the Mackay Memorial Hospital in Taipei (Marie Lin), the Siberian Branch of the Russian Academy of Sciences in Novosibirsk (L.O.), the CRLAO in Paris (L.S.), the Centre of Anthropology in Toulouse (J.-M.D.), and the AGP and LGB laboratories in Geneva (A.S.M. and E.S.P.), we investigated the GM polymorphism of human immunoglobulins in several aboriginal and non-aboriginal populations of Taiwan as well as in two non-Taiwanese populations from the Philippines and Thailand. Although many 'classical' genetic systems have already been studied in Taiwanese aborigines, the pattern of genetic variation within Taiwan has not yet been explored in detail for the GM polymorphism; moreover, these new data will help complement our extensive work on GM genetic variation in East Asia (Poloni et al. 2005).

The GM polymorphism

The GM polymorphism is characterized by a series of 'allotypes' detected by serological techniques on human antibodies (IgG immunoglobulins) circulating in the blood serum. Each individual is normally tested for the whole set of GM allotypes, which makes it possible to determine the GM phenotypic distribution in a given population sample and to estimate GM haplotype frequencies in the corresponding population. One particularity of the GM polymorphism is its high level of genetic heterogeneity among continental population groups at the world scale. By subdividing the world into 10 continental or subcontinental regions, Dugoujon et al. (2004) found a proportion of genetic diversity due to genetic differences among groups, or F_{CT}, of 39.15 per cent. This value is much higher than inter-population diversity components obtained among human continental groups for protein polymorphisms (Lewontin 1972), the human major histocompatibility complex HLA (Sanchez-Mazas 2007) or DNA markers (Barbujani et al. 1997; Excoffier and Hamilton 2003): it is of the order of 10 to 15 per cent for most of them. This difference may be due to the fact that the GM polymorphism is tested by serological typing, thereby providing only a broad description of its molecular variation. As a consequence, the frequencies of the most common haplotypes in each geographic area are probably overestimated, leading to an increased estimation of intergroup variation. However, GM haplotypes, like chromosome Y haplogroups (Underhill et al. 2000), are groups of phylogenetically related haplotypes which provide clear genetic information on worldwide and continental genetic differentiation, while more detailed molecular information is often more difficult to interpret. Using GM haplotypes, previous studies have shown that population genetic differentiations can be correlated to geography on a global scale (Sanchez-Mazas and Langaney 1988; Dugoujon et al. 2004; Sanchez-Mazas and Polini 2008), and to linguistic differentiation in some continental areas, like sub-Saharan Africa (Excoffier et al. 1987, 1991; Sanchez-Mazas and Poloni 2008). GM is thus likely to reveal relevant information for human peopling history studies.

Populations tested and methods used

In this study, we contribute original GM data for eight aboriginal populations from Taiwan: the Siraya, Pazeh, Taroko (a group within Sedik), Atayal, Tsou, Bunun, Puyuma, and Yami. We also typed a Chinese population from Taiwan (the Minnan), an extra-Formosan population from Batan Islands located between Taiwan and the Philippines, the Ivatan, whose language is closely related to that of the Yami, and a 'hill tribe' from Northern Thailand, the Ahka (Sino-Tibetan). All samples were collected by Marie Lin and tested by a hemagglutination-inhibition technique for allotypes $G_1M(1, 2, 3, 17)$, $G_2M(23)$ and $G_3M(5, 6, 13, 15, 16, 21)$ by L.O. in Novosibirsk. Data on the Ami were already available in the literature (Schanfield 1971; Schanfield et al. 2002). However, as no test for $G_2M(23)$ was performed by these authors, we decided to collect an additional sample of 28 Ami individuals to check the presence of this allotype. Typings done by J.M.D. in Toulouse revealed that all individuals were $G_2M(23)$ positive.

We estimated GM haplotype frequencies from complex phenotypes by a standard maximum-likelihood procedure, using the computer program GENEF. Consistent hypotheses on GM haplotype distributions were obtained for all populations except Ivatan (Table 13.1). For this population, however, satisfactory results were obtained when we estimated the frequencies of the GM broad haplotypes, i.e. not discriminated by the presence/absence of allotype $G_2M(23)$ (see below). The hypothesis of Hardy–Weinberg equilibrium (HWE) was tested by chi-square. P-values were above 1 per cent (i.e. non significant) for all populations except Ahka and Ivatan (Table 13.1). However, in these populations, the high chi-square value obtained for HWE test is due to two phenotypes with expected values lower than five individuals,[2] and the null hypothesis of HWE cannot be rejected on this basis. We can thus regard all populations tested as in HWE equilibrium.

We compared the new Taiwanese samples to data published in the literature: first to other Taiwanese, and second to a large database of East Asian populations tested for GM (*GeneVA* database maintained by A.S.M.). As many populations were not typed for the allotype $G_2M(23)$, we performed our analyses according to two different levels of genotypic resolution: a 'high resolution level', by including the information brought by $G_2M(23)$, for a small set of populations (15), and a 'low resolution level', by ignoring the information contributed by this allotype, for a large set of populations (113). The Ivatan sample, for which $G_2M(23)$ typing appeared to be problematic, was only used in the latter analyses. For the sake of clarity, we will talk of *GM broad haplotypes*, when we do not consider the information brought by $G_2M(23)$ typings, and of *GM±23 sub-haplotypes*, when we consider that information.

Table 13.1 GM frequencies in Aborigines and some other populations of East Asia

	Ahka	Minnan	Pazeh	Siraya	Taroko	Atayal	Bunun	Tsou	Puyuma	Ami	Yami	Ivatan*
N	41	50	74	52	56	60	49	50	52	28	69	48
1,3;23;5*	0.406	0.5231	0.6492	0.7045	0.7267	0.75	0.7592	0.81	0.8553	1	0.971	0.8959
1,3;-;5*	0.1672	0.0367	0.1683	0.1128	0.0323	0	0.0875	0	0.0774	0	0	
1,3;23;5	0	0.0202	0	0	0	0	0	0	0	0	0	
1,17;-;21	0.1737	0.2668	0.1002	0.1019	0.1786	0.175	0.0714	0.18	0.026	0	0.029	0.0625
1,17;23;21	0	0	0	0	0	0	0	0	0	0	0	
1,2,17;-;21	0.1046	0.1032	0.0417	0.052	0.0089	0.0083	0.0507	0	0.0221	0	0	0.0104
1,17;-;5*	0	0.01	0	0	0	0	0	0.01	0.0096	0	0	0.0208
1,17;23;5*	0	0	0	0	0	0	0	0	0	0	0	
1,2,17;-;5*	0	0.01	0.0203	0.0096	0	0	0.0105	0	0.0096	0	0	0.0104
1,17;-;10,11,13,15,16	0.0915	0.03	0.0203	0.0192	0	0	0	0	0	0	0	
1,2,17;-;10,11,13,15,16	0	0	0	0	0	0.0083	0	0	0	0	0	
1,23;21	0	0	0	0	0.0297	0.0584	0	0	0	0	0	
1,2;-;15,16,21	0	0	0	0	0.0089	0	0	0	0	0	0	
1,17;-;	0.0448	0	0	0	0	0	0	0	0	0	0	
1,17;-;16	0	0	0.0135	0	0	0	0	0	0	0	0	
1,3;23;21	0.0122	0	0.0068	0	0.0149	0	0.0207	0	0	0	0	
Number of haplotypes	7	8	7	6	7	5	6	3	6	1	2	5
HW-chi-2	42.82	6.86	9.29	22.08	25.02	4.11	5.83	2.75	14.91	n.a.	0.06	52.04
df	14	19	17	12	14	8	10	3	10	n.a.	1	6
P-value	0.0001	0.9949	0.9307	0.0366	0.0344	0.8471	0.8293	0.4318	0.1354	n.a.	0.8065	0.0000
Gene diversity (h)	0.765	0.648	0.541	0.482	0.442	0.407	0.412	0.315	0.264	0.000	0.057	0.195

* Tests for GM(23) are not taken into account (see text); N: sample size; 5* stands for 5,10,11,13,14; n.a.: not available.

Genetic structure of Taiwanese populations

GM frequencies

Previous global and continental surveys of the GM polymorphism (Steinberg and Cook 1981; Blanc et al. 1990; Dugoujon et al. 2004; Poloni et al. 2005) as well as statistics based on more than 450 population samples collected in our GM database indicate that four GM broad haplotypes are common in East Asia: GM*1,3;;5*, mostly observed in Southeast Asia and the Pacific, where it can reach frequencies of about 90 per cent; GM*1,17;;21 and GM*1,2,17;;21, commonly found in all continents, but more frequent in Northeast Asia, and even more so in Amerindians; and Gm*1,17;;10,11,13,15,16, which reaches its highest frequencies, of the order of 30 per cent, in Northeast Asia. Based on a subset of 96 population samples tested for $G_2M(23)$, we also know that, among GM±23 sub-haplotypes, GM*1,3;23;5* is generally much more frequent than GM*1,3;-;5*, although both sub-haplotypes are commonly observed in East Asia and the Pacific; on the other hand, GM*1,17;23;21 and GM*1,2,17;23;21 are rare compared to GM*1,17;-;21 and GM*1,2,17;-;21, respectively, and GM*1,17;23;10,11,13,15,16 has never been observed.

The present study provides the first description of GM±23 sub-haplotypes in Taiwan and Lan-Yu. Their frequencies are shown in Plate 13.Ia[3] for 10 populations. GM*1,3;23;5* is the most frequent, as in the majority of East Asian and Pacific populations studied so far. The frequency of this haplotype is much higher in Taiwan aborigines than in the Minnan population (0.523). However, it also varies greatly among the former, from 0.649 in the Pazeh, to 0.855, in the Puyuma, and it is even higher in Yami from Lan-Yu (0.971). The new Ami sample tested by us was found to be monomorphic for GM*1,3;23;5*. However, as only 28 individuals were typed in this population, GM*1,3;23;5* frequency is probably closer to 0.95, as estimated for the broad GM haplotype GM*1,3;;5* in the two Ami samples tested by Schanfield (1971; Schanfield et al. 2002). GM*1,3;-;5* also exhibits heterogeneous frequencies among Taiwanese: it reaches 0.168 in the Pazeh, while it is not observed in Atayal, Tsou and Yami, and has a low frequency in Minnan (0.037). The third common sub-haplotype is GM*1,17;-;21, with the highest frequency in Tsou (0.180) and the lowest in Puyuma (0.026), while GM*1,2,17;-;21 is always observed at low frequencies (< 5 per cent) in Taiwan Aborigines. These two latter sub-haplotypes are much more frequent in the Minnan (0.267 and 0.103, respectively).

Taiwanese populations also exhibit many uncommon sub-haplotypes: GM*1,17;-;5* (≤ 1 per cent), in Puyuma and Tsou; GM*1,17;-;10,11,13,15,16, in Siraya and Pazeh (≤ 2 per cent); GM*1,3;23;21 (≤ 2 per cent), in Pazeh, Taroko, and Bunun, GM*1,2,17;-;5* (≤ 1 per cent), in Puyuma, Siraya, and Bunun; and GM*1,2,17;-;10,11,13,15,16 (≤ 1 per cent), in Atayal. Very unusual variants have also been considered to explain some rare phenotypes: GM*1;23;21, in Taroko and Atayal; GM*1,17;−;16 in Pazeh, and GM*1,2;−;15,16,21 in Taroko. The frequency of these variants are below 2 per cent, except for GM*1;23;21

(3 per cent in Taroko and 6 per cent in Atayal). An unusual variant is also observed in Minnan (GM*1,3;23;5).

Gene diversity

As indicated in Table 13.1, Taiwanese aborigines exhibit heterogeneous but generally low levels of gene diversity (here estimated by the expected heterozygosity h). The lowest h values are found in the Ami (0 when estimated in our Ami sample of 28 individuals, but 0.091–0.094 when estimated in the Ami samples tested by Schanfield and co-workers) and the Yami from Lan-Yu (0.057). Gene diversity is also rather low in other southern populations, like the Puyuma (0.264). We thus note a general decrease in heterozygosity from north to south when we plot this statistic against latitude (Plate 13.Ib), although the estimated correlation coefficients ($r = 0.517$, when we include the Yami, and $r = 0.268$, when we do not include them) are not significant. Actually, gene diversity is highest on the west coast (Pazeh, Siraya), and lowest on the south-east coast (Puyuma, Ami) and Lan-Yu (Yami), decreasing along a northwest to southeast direction. It corresponds to a gradual increase of the frequency of one haplotype, GM*1,3;23;5,10,11,13,14, to the detriment of the less frequent ones, meaning that all genetic profiles may be derived continuously from one another. However, we do not have samples from populations of the northeast coast such as the Kavalan. We are therefore not claiming that the pattern of decreasing diversity from north to south is found among populations of the Formosan east coast.

Genetic distance analyses

We performed a multidimensional-scaling analysis (or MDS) among the 10 Taiwanese populations tested in this study (including the Yami) on the basis of GM±23 sub-haplotypes frequencies (the highest level of resolution). To investigate the genetic relationships between Formosan aborigines and Chinese, we also included five mainland Han populations which had been tested for $G_2M(23)$ (Figure 13.1). Links were drawn between some populations to indicate the cases where genetic differentiation between them is not sustained statistically (at the 5 per cent level). We used two different tests, an exact test and a permutation test on pairwise FSTs. The exact test is more powerful; i.e. in the present case, its power to detect genetic differentiation when such differentiation is true is higher; on the other hand, there is also a higher risk of erroneous detection of a differentiation. The permutation test is more conservative; i.e. in the present case, it will detect genetic differentiation only when the statistical result is clearly unambiguous; on the other hand, there is also a higher risk of missing true cases of genetic differentiation. Therefore, the solid lines drawn on the graph between some populations indicate the cases where populations are considered as undifferentiated genetically according to both tests, while the dotted lines have to be treated more cautiously as they represent cases where genetic differentiation can be concluded from the exact test, but not the permutation test.

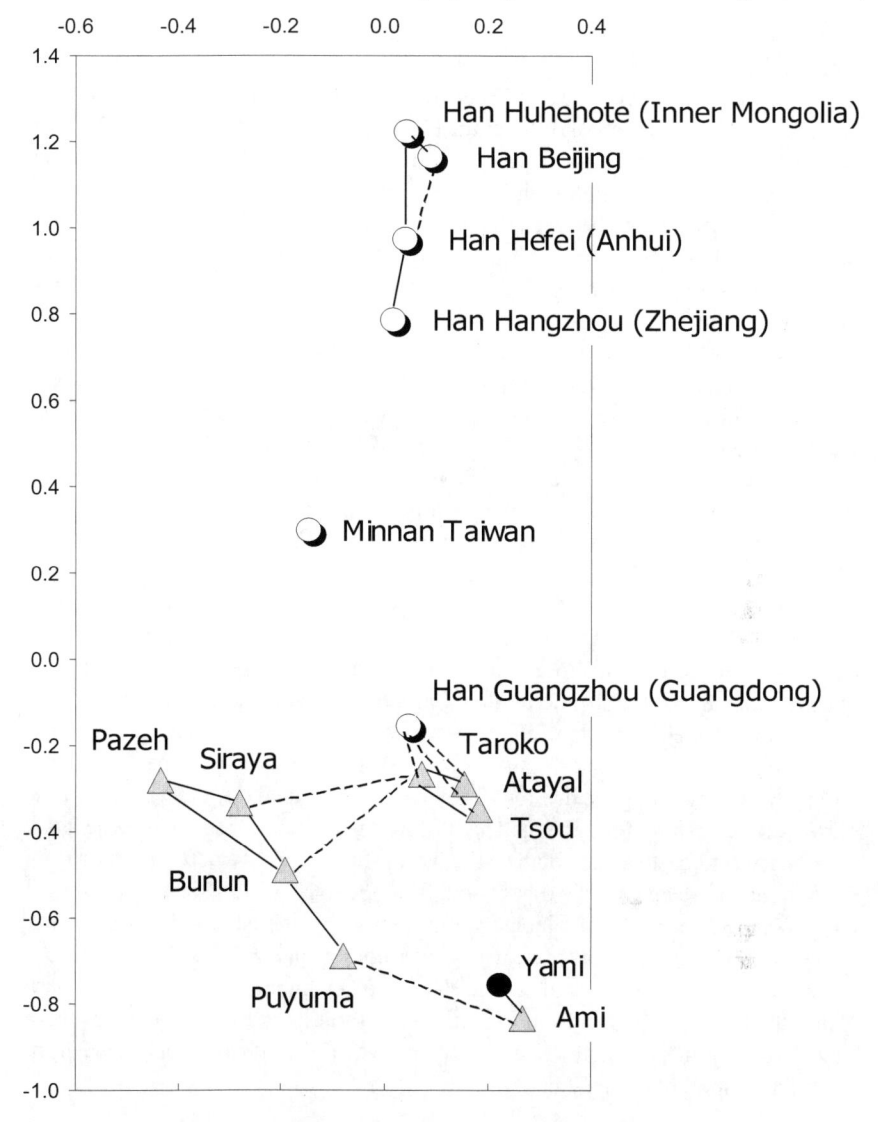

Figure 13.1 Multidimensional scaling analysis among 15 populations from Taiwan and China based on the frequencies of GM ± 23 sub-haplotypes. Prevosti's *et al.* (1975) distances have been used. Solid lines link populations that are undifferentiated at the 5% level according to an exact test of population differentiation. Dotted lines link populations that are undifferentiated at the 5% level according to a permutation test on pairwise Fst's, but not to the exact test. Final stress = 0.041 (excellent). White circles: Sino-Tibetans; triangles: Austronesians from Taiwan; black circle: Extra-Formosan Austronesians.

The MDS (characterized by a very good stress value of 0.041) segregates four Northern and Central Han populations at the top, the Minnan from Taiwan in a central position, and the Southern Han from Guangzhou, the eight Austronesian populations from Taiwan and the extra-Formosan Yami at the bottom. The four Northern and Central Han populations are genetically linked to each other according to a pattern recalling their relative geographic position. The Minnan are genetically intermediate between the Northern and the Southern Han but are very distant from both groups and significantly differentiated from all populations. Within the last group, we observe three clusters of genetically related populations: the Atayal, Taroko and Tsou; the Pazeh, Siraya, Bunun and Puyuma; and the Ami and Yami. In addition, we find that the Southern Han from Guangzhou are genetically very close to the Taroko, Atayal and Tsou, from whom they are not differentiated significantly according to the permutation statistical test (dotted lines). Genetic relationships are also suggested between the Taroko and both the Siraya and Bunun, and between the Puyuma and the Ami according both to the permutation test and to their relative position in the MDS.

The results of this analysis indicate a genetic continuity from the populations of the west coast of Taiwan (Pazeh, Siraya) to those of the southeast coast (Puyuma), the South-Central Bunun being in between. This pattern further extends to the Ami, located on the east coast, and to the extra-Formosan Yami on Lan-Yu. It corresponds to a marked decrease in gene diversity (Plate 13.Ib). On the other hand, the northern Atayal and Taroko and the south-central Tsou form a homogeneous cluster, relatively separated from the former, again with a decreasing level of genetic diversity from the Atayal and Taroko to the Tsou (Plate 13.Ib). A reduction in gene diversity is generally explained by genetic drift. These observations, then, suggest that genetic differentiations occurred, on the one hand, from the west coast to the southeast coast of Taiwan via a south-central region (Bunun location), and, on the other hand, from the north of Taiwan southwards (to Tsou location) in the mountainous central regions of the island (but see another interpretation below). Moreover, it is worth noting that the northern Taiwanese group is much closer genetically to the Han from Guangdong Province in southern China than to the Minnan from Taiwan. Actually, this is true for all Taiwanese tribes, suggesting a genetic relationship between aboriginal populations from Taiwan and southeastern Chinese.

Comparison to other East Asian populations

We pursued our study by comparing the Taiwanese populations to other populations from East and Southeast Asia. Those data were gathered from the literature and were already used in our previous work (Poloni *et al*. 2005). We excluded all populations located in the northern part of East Asia to keep only those speaking languages belonging to the Sino-Tibetan, Tai-Kadai, Austroasiatic, Hmong-Mien and Austronesian linguistic families. A total of 113 populations representing 15,904 individuals were compared. Unfortunately, these comparisons were only done by using the frequencies of broad GM haplotypes (thus with a lower level of resolution than for the analysis presented in Figure 13.1) because $G_2M(23)$ was most often not tested in those populations.

We performed a first MDS (Plate 13.II) including the whole set 113 populations (a good stress of 0.085 is obtained). The graph is basically similar to the MDS among 102 populations presented in our former work (Poloni *et al.* 2005: figure 15.3), except that it also incorporates the 11 populations tested in the present study (all new samples but the Ami, due to its low sample size),[4] and that it uses a different genetic distance. Indeed, we computed the distances of Prevosti *et al.* (1975) rather than Reynolds *et al.* (1983), because the former generally discriminates the populations better than the latter, while both of them produce a similar differentiation pattern (personal results). Using Prevosti's distance is thus more useful when numerous populations are genetically very close, like here.

As observed by Poloni *et al.* (2005), many populations tend to group together according to their linguistic affiliation (Northern Tibeto-Burman; Northern Chinese; Wu and Southeastern Mandarin; and other Tibeto-Burman), although without any discontinuity between them; on the other hand, substantial overlapping is observed for the other groups.

We thus performed a second MDS by keeping only those 63 populations speaking Southern Chinese dialects, Austroasiatic, Tai-Kadai, Hmong-Mien and Austronesian languages (Figure 13.2). Despite a general overlapping of most groups (a less good but still acceptable stress of 0.135 is here obtained), some results are worthy of mention: first, all Southern Chinese are displayed at the top of the plot, all Tai-Kadai at the bottom-left, and all Austronesians (including both Taiwanese and Extra-Formosan) at the bottom right with a few exceptions corresponding to very isolated populations (one of the Aetas and the Mamanwas) who have probably undergone rapid genetic drift. Those three groups are thus relatively well discriminated from each other, despite their very different levels of genetic heterogeneity. This is harder to say for the Hmong-Mien, only represented by three populations, and the Austroasiatic-speakers, which are very dispersed due to their high level of inter-population diversity (Poloni *et al.* 2005). Secondly, among the Chinese populations, those located in the Guangdong province (except in one case) are closer genetically to the Southeast Asian groups (Tai-Kadai, Austronesian, Hmong-Mien and Austroasiatic) than those from other regions. On the other hand, the Chinese from Taiwan (here represented by several populations) are genetically closer to populations from regions further inland in China, such as Fujian, Jiangxi and Hunan, and, to a lesser extent, Sichuan. Finally, Taiwan aborigines share distinct relationships with non-Taiwanese populations: in particular, this confirms the general pattern in Figure 13.1 where the Ami (here represented by two samples) and Puyuma are the most distant from the southern Chinese. The Saisiat, who were not tested for $G_2M(23)$ and thus not represented in Figure 13.1, cluster with the Siraya and Pazeh. Also, the Ami and the Puyuma are very close to the Extra-Formosan Austronesians from Lan-Yu (Yami), the Philippines (Ivatan) and Borneo (Kadazan).

In Figure 13.3, we also represented the average genetic distance between each aboriginal population from Taiwan and the populations belonging to

324 *Alicia Sanchez-Mazas* et al.

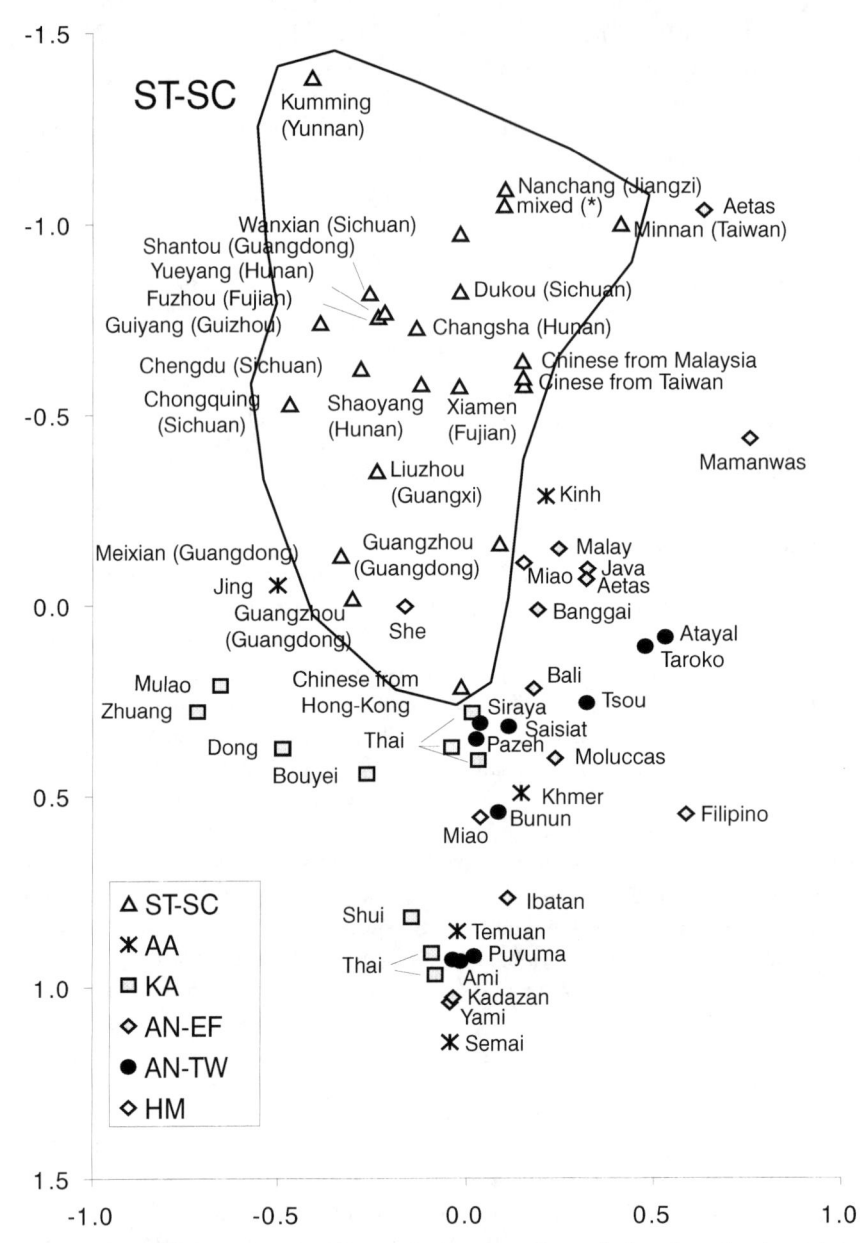

Figure 13.2 Multidimensional scaling analysis among 63 populations from Southeast Asia excluding all Sino-Tibetans but the Southern Chinese (grouped). Prevosti's *et al.* (1975) genetic distances have been computed from the frequencies of GM broad haplotypes. Final stress = 0.135 (fair). The 'mixed' sample is composed of individuals from Fujian, Zhejiang, Jiangxi, and Hunan. ST-SC: Sino-Tibetan, Southern Chinese (Min, Xiang, Gan, Hakka, Yue); AA: Austroasiatic; KA: Tai-Kadai; AN-EF: Extra-Formosan Austronesian; AN-TW: Autronesian from Taiwan; HM: Hmong-Mien.

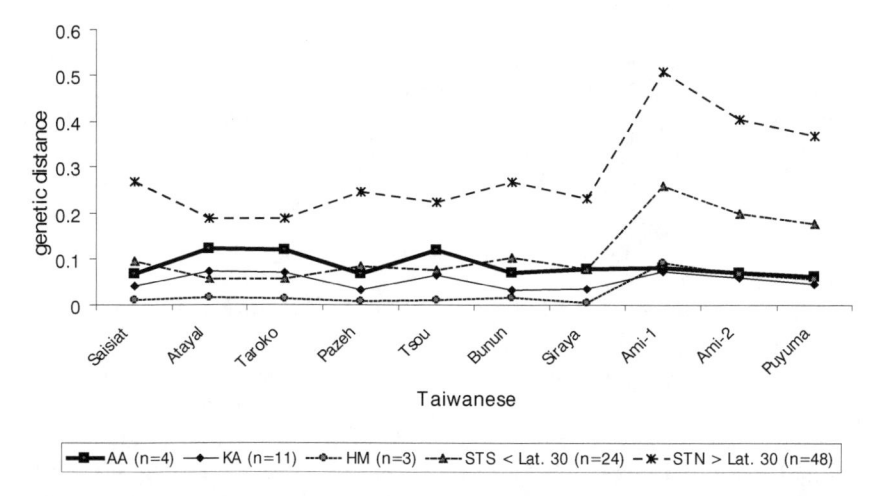

Figure 13.3 Average Reynold's *et al.* (1983) genetic distances between each aboriginal population from Taiwan tested in this study (except Ami-1, Ami-2 and Saisiat typed by Schanfield *et al.* 1971, 2002), and the populations belonging to different linguistically defined groups of Southeast Asia (with their number given in parentheses). The Taiwanese populations are ordered according to their latitude. AA: Austroasiatic; KA: Tai-Kadai; HM: Hmong-Mien; STS: Southern Sino-Tibetan, located below latitude 30°N; NTS: Northern Sino-Tibetan, located above latitude 30°N.

different linguistically defined groups of Southeast Asia (Austroasiatic, Tai-Kadai, Hmong-Mien, Southern Sino-Tibetan (populations located below latitude 30°N) and Northern Sino-Tibetan (populations located above latitude 30°N). This graph confirms that Taiwanese aboriginals are closer to southern than to northern Chinese and that Ami and Puyuma are the most distant from both of them. In addition, we note that, on average, Ami and Puyuma are at equal distance from all other groups, i.e. Austroasiatic, Tai-Kadai and Hmong-Mien, while all other Taiwanese are slightly closer to Hmong-Mien than to Austroasiatic, the Tai-Kadai (and, often, the southern Chinese) lying in between. However, such differences may not be significant.

Discussion

The present study provides a new and appreciable examination of the genetic diversity of Taiwanese populations thanks to the complete analysis of the GM polymorphism, only partially tested before on some populations of that island. The results reveal an important heterogeneity among its aboriginal populations: there are marked differences in their internal gene diversity, in their genetic distances from each other, and in their genetic relationships to other East Asian populations.

First, in agreement with studies of other genetic markers (Lin and Broadberry 1998; Schanfield *et al.* 2002; Sewerin *et al.* 2002; Sanchez-Mazas *et al.* 2005), the Ami are very unusual for GM, as they are almost monomorphic for the predominant haplotype in East Asians, GM*1,3;23;5*. This implies that the Ami, while being today the largest aboriginal group with about 140,000 people (Chu 1997), underwent an extreme bottleneck, losing their genetic diversity from an original gene pool where GM*1,3;23;5* was already very frequent. Such a loss of diversity is compatible with observations in a previous HLA study (Sanchez-Mazas et al. 2005) where we emphasized that only seven HLA-DRB1 alleles were detected in that population compared to an average of 20.6 in 48 other East Asian populations.

The uniqueness of the Ami has been discussed by other authors in relation to either natural selection or affinities to other, more distant, population groups. The idea that GM*1,3;;5* would be advantageous in an environment endemic to malaria has been invoked to explain the high frequency of this haplotype in lowland areas like the east coast of Taiwan (Schanfield et al. 2002). In relation to another region of the world, i.e. Sardinia, a similar explanation was formerly given for allotype $G_2M(23)$, which was then considered to be selectively advantageous (Piazza et al. 1976). However, no other evidence has ever corroborated these hypotheses. On the contrary, many counter-examples can be given where such a correlation is not verified. For example, other plains tribes of Taiwan, like the Pazeh and Siraya, have lower frequencies of GM*1,3;23;5*; we also know that $G_2M(23)$ is very rare in sub-Saharan Africa (Blanc et al. 1990), where malaria is endemic. Therefore, we do not have enough evidence to accept the hypothesis of this type of selection acting on the GM system.

Nor does our knowledge of the GM system support the idea that the Ami are related to more distant population groups. Although some HLA alleles and haplotypes shared by the Ami and Australian Aborigines or Papuans could be taken as a possible evidence of a remote relationship between Taiwanese and an ancient peopling of Sundaland (Lin et al. 2005), Australians, Melanesians as well as Amerindians are characterized by completely different GM genetic profiles, where GM*1,12;21 or GM*1,17;5* or GM*1,2,17;21 are the most frequent haplotypes, and GM*1,3;5* is rare or not observed (Steinberg and Cook 1981; Sanchez-Mazas and Pellegrini 1990; Dugoujon et al. 2004). Therefore, the genetic profile observed in the Ami is undeniably an extreme differentiation of a Southeast Asian genetic pool. Moreover, the results shown in Plates 13.I and 13.II and Figure 13.1 reveal a correlation between genetic and geographic proximity: the Ami are genetically related to the Puyuma, a geographically close population located in the south of Taiwan, the Yami, just situated off the southeast coast of Taiwan, the Ivatan, living a little bit further south in the Philippines, and the Kadazan from Borneo. Interestingly, the Puyuma, while being in genetic continuity with the Ami, exhibit many rare haplotypes in addition to their very high GM*1,3;23;5 frequency. The Ami thus probably underwent a extreme bottleneck either when they reached the southeast of Taiwan or later, a hypothesis already proposed in a previous work based on an analysis of the HLA-DRB1 polymorphism (Sanchez-Mazas et al. 2005).

As opposed to the Ami, two groups of Taiwanese populations are characterized by a high level of gene diversity, but distinct genetic profiles. On one hand, the Pazeh, Siraya and Bunun (plus Saisiat, when only broad GM haplotypes are considered) exhibit several haplotypes with middling frequencies, i.e. GM*1,3;-;5*, GM*1,2,17;21, and GM*1,17;10,11,13,15,16. We observe a genetic continuity between these populations and the Puyuma and Ami, with a loss of diversity in the latter. On the other hand, the Atayal, Taroko and Tsou show GM*1,2,17;21 at a relatively high frequency, in addition to GM*1,3;23;5*. Atayal and Taroko populations also share a rare haplotype, GM*1;23;21, while the Tsou, with only two haplotypes, exhibit a much lower genetic diversity (Plate 13.Ib).

The two groups of populations described above could represent the descendents of an initial split of Austronesian populations into two primary branches: Atayal-Tsouic versus the rest of Austronesian. However the chances that the similarity we observe between speakers of Atayalic languages (Atayal and Taroko) and the Tsou are due to independent parallel developments are significant, because the Tsou basically have only two haplotypes, which are also present, albeit at lower frequencies, among the Siraya and other populations. The location of the Tsou in the midst of Taiwan's central mountain range is conducive to genetic drift, which could also account for the simplification of a Siraya-type profile into a Tsou-type profile (see below).

It is often argued (Lee *et al.* 2002) that the 'plains tribes' of Taiwan, i.e. those living in the west coast (Pazeh, Siraya), have been 'sinicized', that is, underwent high levels of gene flow from neighbouring Chinese people, this explaining their greater proximity to the latter ('gene flow hypothesis'). However, our study does not show any peculiar genetic relationship between the 'plains tribes' and the local Chinese, who began settling the island more than three centuries ago. First, the Minnan are only distantly related to the Taiwanese aborigines, whether from the plains or the mountains (Figures 13.1 and 13.2). Second, although Siraya and Pazeh (i.e. 'plains tribes') lie closer to some populations from South China (Hong Kong) according to our low-resolution analysis (Figure 13.2), this is not true when we consider GM typings at high resolution (which includes G_2M23 typings), where Taroko and Atayal (i.e. 'mountain tribes') are closer than the 'plains tribes' to the southern Chinese from Guangdong Province (Figure 13.1). Moreover, the level of genetic diversity is not different in the 'plains' and 'mountain tribes' mentioned above (Plate 13.Ib), while one would expect the 'plains tribes' to be more diversified under an admixture hypothesis. Different levels of gene flow from the Chinese do not explain the observed GM diversity.

Having excluded natural selection and significant Chinese gene flow, the only explanation left is that the GM genetic patterns observed in Taiwan are mainly the signal of its ancient peopling history. Two questions may then be asked: first, is it possible to define a geographic origin for the Taiwanese Austronesians? And, second, what have we learnt about Taiwanese differentiation?

Based on our analyses at a continental scale, we have shown that Taiwanese are on average almost equally distant from the Hmong-Mien, Tai-Kadai, south Chinese and even Austroasiatic population groups (except the Ami and Puyuma who are genetically far from the Chinese) and that most Southeast Asian groups overlap (Figures 13.3 and 13.2, respectively). Therefore, due to the low resolution of our data, we cannot answer the first question. However, the MDS presented in Figure 13.2 indicates that all Southeast Asian populations, including Austronesians from Taiwan and most Extra-Formosans, appear to be closer to Chinese populations from Hong Kong, located near the Pearl River delta in southerly Guangdong Province, while the Minnan (and other ethnically undefined Chinese from Taiwan) share a similar genetic profile with Chinese populations from Fujian (across from Taiwan on the mainland) and provinces further inland like Jiangxi, Hunan and even Sichuan. Thus, if we accept, like most scholars today, the theory of an origin of the Austronesians in the mainland Chinese, the general proximity of Formosans to Hong Kong Chinese could support an origin of Formosan populations in the Pearl River delta region, as argued by Tsang (2005) on the basis of similarity in pottery types; but it is also compatible with an origin on the coast of Fujian (Chang 1969) assuming that the present-day population of Fujian reflects Chinese expansion in the 1st millennium BCE (incorporating a high level of genetic diversity through gene flow with populations from other regions and/or linguistic groups), while the present-day population of Guangdong more faithfully reflects the genetic make-up of the early southeast China coast at the time of the Austronesian movement to Taiwan. A passage from Fujian to northwestern Taiwan is advocated by Sagart (Chapter 5, this volume) on the grounds that (a) the sea crossing is shortest there; (b) Taiwan is visible from the Fujian side; (c) the Austronesian languages of Northwestern Taiwan are the most diverse and show none of the post-Proto-Austronesian innovations in the numeral system. In our study, that the populations of northwestern Taiwan are the most diverse in the island fits better with a northwestern passage than with a southwestern, which Tsang's hypothesis of a Pearl River delta origin implies.

As mentioned above, the first peopling of Taiwan was eventually followed by an early differentiation into two main groups: a northern group from whom Taroko and Atayal (and maybe Tsou) differentiated, and a western group including the other populations (Pazeh, Siraya, Bunun, Puyuma and Ami). An attractive explanation to account for the variability observed in the western group is that populations differentiated from northwestern to south and southeastern regions, losing their genetic diversity as they moved gradually along the west, south and east coasts, and/or partly through central regions (where the Bunun currently live). Such a scenario is in agreement with the linguistic theory proposed by Sagart (2005; and Chapter 5, this volume), although in Sagart's thesis Tsou is a southern language whose sisters are Bunun, Rukai and Kavalan, without any particular proximity to Atayalic. However, we propose that the Tsou underwent rapid genetic drift due to their isolation in the central mountains of Taiwan; their genetic closeness to Atayal and Taroko would then be an accidental convergence due to an increase of the GM*1,17;-;21 haplotype frequency (the second most frequent after GM+1,3;23;5,10,11,13,14) and the loss of all rarer haplotypes through genetic drift from any southern genetic pool. Indeed, other 'classical' and HLA polymorphisms do not reveal such a relationship (Lin *et al.* 2005, and personal results not shown) and results based on DNA data indicate an intense bottleneck for the Tsou (Chen et al. 2001) and/or the Atayal (Chen et al. 2001; Shepard et al. 2005).

Finally, our approach does not allow us to propose any time depth for the peopling of Taiwan. Based on mtDNA lineages, Trejaut et al. (2005; and Chapter 14, this volume) support the idea that 'the prevalence of the gene pool of aboriginal Taiwanese initiated from late Pleistocene settlers'. Genetic evidence for ancient settlement is also sustained by Hill et al. (2007) from mtDNA analyses, although the two research groups do not agree on the role of Taiwan in the spread of Austronesians towards the Pacific. According to Trejaut et al. (Chapter 14, this volume), the origin of the Austronesian migration can be traced back to Taiwan (or to a wider region encompassing Taiwan, the Philippines and Borneo), while Hill et al. (2007) claim that a mid-Holocene migration from that region is demographically minor. It is worth recalling, here, besides the caution to consider when using molecular dating (see Blench, Ross and Sanchez-Mazas, Introduction, this volume), that mtDNA is maternally transmitted; therefore, those studies reconstruct the phylogeny of female lineages only, and the demographic history of men may have been quite different than that of women.

To our view, there is no reason to exclude *a priori* a contribution of Palaeolithic populations to the present Taiwanese genetic diversity, as archaeological excavations indicate that Taiwan was settled by modern humans at least 15,000 years ago and probably as early as 30,000 years ago based on the remains of the Changpin culture (Sung 1978). A possible introgression of ancient mtDNA lineages to the Taiwanese genetic pool, with an eventual origin in Island Southeast Asia, as suggested by some mtDNA shallow lineages (Trejaut et al., Chapter 14, this volume), does not contradict the hypothesis that most of the GM variability currently observed in Taiwan was shaped during the Neolithic. A similar situation occurs in Europe, where demic diffusion of Neolithic farmers explains a high percentage of the variability observed for classical and DNA genetic markers in Europe, where early settlements by modern humans in the Palaeolithic are well-documented (Ammerman and Cavalli-Sforza 1984; Cavalli-Sforza et al. 1994; Chikhi et al. 1998, 2002), despite some debate on that subject (Barbujani and Chikhi 2006). Likewise, our results fit the model of an Austronesian expansion from Taiwan to the Philippines and Indonesia in relatively recent times, as the progressive loss of genetic diversity towards the south would be more difficult to reconcile with the main thrust of peopling coming from the south, as advocated by some geneticists (Oppenheimer and Richards 2002; Hill et al. 2007).

Acknowledgements

This work was supported by grant # 3100A0-112651 of the Swiss National Foundation (FNS) to A.S.M. and by the French CNRS OHLL (Origine de l'Homme, du Langage et des Langues) Action to E.S.P. and L.S. We express our warmest thanks to Professor Marie Lin for providing aboriginal Taiwanese,

Minnan, Ivatan and Ahka samples, and to Professor An-Vu-Trieu for providing Khmer samples from Viet Nam.

Notes

1 http://www.ethnologue.com.
2 The maximum-likelihood procedure did not converge for this population, meaning that no satisfactory GM haplotype frequency distribution was obtained.
3 To simplify, we represented the Minnan at the top of the island, but in reality, the Minnan occupy a very large area (see Map 13.1).
4 In the present analysis, the same samples as in Poloni *et al.* (2005) have been considered, except that we have added the 11 populations tested for GM in the present study, plus one Khmer sample from Viet Nam provided by An-Vu-Trieu and tested for GM by J.M.D, plus two Taiwanese samples (Ami and Saisiat) tested by Schanfield *et al.* (2002) and that we have excluded three Taiwanese samples tested by Matsumoto *et al.* (1972) due to very low resolution typing.

References

Ammerman, A.J. and Cavalli-Sforza, L.L. (1984) *The Neolithic Transition and the Genetics of Populations in Europe*, Princeton, NJ: Princeton University Press.
Barbujani, G. and Chikhi, L. (2006) 'DNAs from the European Neolithic', *Heredity*, 97: 84–5.
Barbujani, G., Magagni, A., Minch, E. and Cavalli-Sforza, L.L. (1997) 'An appointment of human DNA diversity', *Proceedings of the National Academy of Science USA*, 94: 4516–19.
Bellwood, P. (1978) *Man's Conquest of the Pacific: The Prehistory of Southeast Asia and Oceania*, Oxford: Oxford University Press.
Bellwood, P. (1997) *Prehistory of the Indo-Malaysian Archipelago*, Honolulu, HI: University of Hawaii Press.
Bellwood, P. (2005) 'Examining the farming/language dispersal hypothesis in the East Asian context', in L. Sagart, R. Blench and A. Sanchez-Mazas (eds) *The Peopling of East Asia: Putting Together Archaeology, Linguistics and Genetics*, pp. 17–30, London and New York, NY: RoutledgeCurzon.
Blanc, M., Sanchez-Mazas, A., Hubert van Blyenburgh, N., Sevin, A., Pison, G. and Langaney, A. (1990) 'Inter-ethnic genetic differentiation: Gm polymorphism in Eastern Senegal', *American Journal of Human Genetics*, 46: 383–92.
Blust, R. (1977) 'The Proto-Austronesian pronouns and Austronesian subgrouping: a preliminary report', *University of Hawai'i Working Papers in Linguistics*, 9(2): 1–15.
Blust, R. (1988) 'The Austronesian homeland: a linguistic perspective', *Asian Perspectives*, 26(1): 45–67.
Blust, R. (1999) 'Subgrouping, circularity and extinction: some issues in Austronesian comparative linguistics', in E. Zeitoun and P.J.-K. Li (eds) *Selected Papers from the Eighth International Conference on Austronesian Linguistics* (Symposium Series of the Institute of Linguistics (Preparatory Office), Academia Sinica, 1), Taipei: Academia Sinica.
Capelli, C., Wilson, J.F., Richards, M., Stumpf, M.P., Gratrix, F., Oppenheimer, S., Underhill, P., Pascali, V.L., Ko, T.M. and Goldstein, D.B. (2001) 'A predominantly indigenous paternal heritage for the Austronesian-speaking peoples of insular Southeast Asia and Oceania', *American Journal of Human Genetics*, 68: 432–43.

Cavalli-Sforza, L.L., Menozzi, P. and Piazza, A. (1994) *The History and Geography of Human Genes*, Princeton, NJ: Princeton University Press.

Chang, K.-c. (1969) *Fengpitou, Tapenkeng and the Prehistory of Taiwan*, New Haven, CT: Yale University Press.

Chen, Y.-F., Chen, S.-J., Chen, C.-H., Chu, C.L., Hsu, M., Yeh, J.-I. and Wang, L.Y. (2001) 'A study of microsatellite loci on Y chromosome of Taiwan aborigines', International Symposium on Austronesian Cultures: Issues Relating to Taiwan.

Chikhi, L., Destro-Bisol, G., Bertorelle, G., Pascali, V. and Barbujani, G. (1998) 'Clines of nuclear DNA markers suggest a largely neolithic ancestry of the European gene pool', *Proceedings of the National Academy of Science USA*, 95: 9053–8.

Chikhi, L., Nichols, R.A., Barbujani, G. and Beaumont, M.A. (2002) 'Y genetic data support the Neolithic demic diffusion model', *Proceedings of the National Academy of Science USA*, 99: 11008–13.

Chu, C.C., Lin, M., Nakajima, F., Lee, H.L., Chang, S.L., Juji, T. and Tokunaga, K. (2001) 'Diversity of HLA among Taiwan's indigenous tribes and the Ivatans in the Philippines', *Tissue Antigens*, 58: 9–18.

Chu, H.L. (1997) *An Introduction to the Indigenous Culture of Taiwan*, Taipei: Charity Printing Industrial Co.

Diamond, J.M. (1988) 'Express train to Polynesia', *Nature*, 336: 307–8.

Dugoujon, J.-M., Hazout, S., Loirat, F., Mourrieras, B., Crouau-Roy, B. and Sanchez-Mazas, A. (2004) 'The GM haplotype diversity of 82 populations over the world suggests a centrifugal model of human migrations', *American Journal of Physical Anthropology*, 125: 175–92.

Excoffier, L. and Hamilton, G. (2003) 'Comment on "Genetic structure of human populations"', *Science*, 300: 1877.

Excoffier, L., Harding, R., Sokal, R.R., Pellegrini, B. and Sanchez-Mazas, A. (1991) 'Spatial differentiation of RH and GM haplotype frequencies in Sub-Saharan Africa and its relation to linguistic affinities', *Human Biology*, 63: 273–97.

Excoffier, L., Pellegrini, P., Sanchez-Mazas, A., Simon, C. and Langaney, A. (1987) 'Genetics and history of Sub-Saharan Africa', *Yearbook of Physical Anthropology*, 30: 151–94.

Gray, R.D. and Jordan, F.M. (2000) 'Language trees support the express-train sequence of Austronesian expansion', *Nature*, 405: 1052–5.

Harvey, M. (1979) *Subgroups in Austronesian*, Canberra: Australian National University.

Hill, C., Soares, P., Mormina, M., Macaulay, V., Clarke, D., Blumbach, P.B., Vizuete-Forster, M., Forster, P., Bulbeck, D., Oppenheimer, S. and Richards, M. (2007) 'A mitochondrial stratigraphy for island southeast Asia', *American Journal of Human Genetics*, 80: 29–43. Epub 16 Nov. 2006.

Lee, J.C.-I., Lin, M., Tsai, L.-C., Hsu, C.-M., Hsieh, H.-M., Huang, N.-E., Shih, R.T.-P., Wun, J.-H., Chang, J.-G., Ko, Y.-C., Tzeng, C.-H. and Linacre, A. (2002) 'Population study of polymorphic microsatellite DNA in Taiwan', *Forensic Science Journal*, 1: 31–7.

Lewontin, R.C. (1972) 'The apportionment of human diversity', in T. Dobzhansky, M.K. Hecht and W.C. Steere (eds) *Evolutionary Biology 6*, New York: Appleton-Century-Crofts.

Lin, M. and Broadberry, R.E. (1998) 'Immunohematology in Taiwan', *Transfusion Medicine Reviews*, 12: 56–72.

Lin, M., Chu, C.C., Broadberry, R.E., Yu, L.C., Loo, J.H. and Trejaut, J.A. (2005) 'Genetic diversity of Taiwan's indigenous peoples: possible relationship with insular Southeast

Asia', in L. Sagart, R. Blench and A. Sanchez-Mazas (eds) *The Peopling of East Asia: Putting Together Archaeology, Linguistics and Genetics*, pp. 230–47, London and New York: RoutledgeCurzon.

Lin, M., Chu, C.C., Lee, H.L., Chang, S.L., Ohashi, J., Tokunaga, K., Akaza, T. and Juji, T. (2000) 'Heterogeneity of Taiwan's indigenous population: possible relation to prehistoric Mongoloid dispersals', *Tissue Antigens*, 55: 1–9.

Matsumoto, H., Miyazaki, T., Fong, J.M. and Mabuchi, Y. (1972) 'Gm and Inv allotypes of the Takasago tribes in Taiwan', *Japanese Journal of Human Genetics*, 17: 27–37.

Oppenheimer, S. and Richards, M. (2002) 'Polynesians: devolved Taiwanese rice farmers or Wallacean maritime traders with fishing, foraging, and horticultural skills?', in P. Bellwood and C. Renfrew (eds) *Examining the Farming/Language Dispersal Hypothesis*, pp. 287–97, Cambridge: McDonald Institute for Archaeological Research.

Piazza, A., Loghem, E. van, Lange, G. de, Curtoni, E.S., Ulizzi, L. and Terrenato, L. (1976) 'Immunoglobulin allotypes in Sardinia', *American Journal of Human Genetics*, 28: 77–86.

Poloni, E.S., Sanchez-Mazas, A., Jacques, G. and Sagart, L. (2005) 'Comparing linguistic and genetic relationships among East Asian populations: a study of the RH and GM polymorphisms', in L. Sagart, R. Blench and A. Sanchez-Mazas (eds) *The Peopling of East Asia: Putting Together Archaeology, Linguistics and Genetics*, pp. 252–72, London and New York: RoutledgeCurzon.

Prevosti, A., Ocaña, J. and Alonso, G. (1975) 'Distances between populations of Drosophila subobscura based on chromosome arrangement frequencies', *Theoretical and Applied Genetics*, 45: 231–41.

Reid, L. (1982) 'The demise of Proto-Philippines', in A. Halim, L. Carrington and S.A. Wurm (eds) *Papers from the Third International Conference on Austronesian Linguistics*, vol. 2, *Tracking the Travellers*, pp. 201–16, Canberra: Pacific Linguistics.

Reynolds, J., Weir, B.S. and Cockerham, C.C. (1983) 'Estimation for the coancestry coefficient: basis for a short-term genetic distance', *Genetics*, 105: 767–79.

Sagart, L. (2005) 'Sino-Tibetan-Austronesian: an updated and improved argument', in L. Sagart, R. Blench and A. Sanchez-Mazas (eds) *The Peopling of East Asia: Putting Together Archaeology, Linguistics and Genetics*, pp. 161–76, London and New York: RoutledgeCurzon.

Sanchez-Mazas, A. (2007) 'An apportionment of human HLA diversity', *Tissue Antigens*, 69, suppl.1: 198–202.

Sanchez-Mazas, A. and Langaney, A. (1988) 'Common genetic pools between human populations', *American Journal of Human Genetics*, 78: 161–6.

Sanchez-Mazas, A. and Pellegrini, B. (1990) 'Polymorphismes Rhésus, Gm et HLA et histoire de l'Homme moderne', *Bulletins et Mémoires de la Société d'Anthropologie de Paris*, NS, 2: 57–76.

Sanchez-Mazas, A., Poloni, E.S. (2008) 'Genetic diversity in Africa', in *Encyclopedia of Life Science* (ELS), Chichester: John Wiley & Sons.

Sanchez-Mazas, A., Poloni, E.S., Jacques, G. and Sagart, L. (2005) 'HLA genetic diversity and linguistic variation in East Asia', in L. Sagart, R. Blench and A. Sanchez-Mazas (eds) *The Peopling of East Asia: Putting Together Archaeology, Linguistics and Genetics*, pp. 273–96, London and New York: RoutledgeCurzon.

Sapir, E. (1916) 'Time perspective in aboriginal American culture: a study in method', in D.G. Mandelbaum (eds) *Selected Writings of Edward Sapir*, Berkeley and Los Angeles, CA: University of California Press.

Schanfield, M.S. (1971) 'Population Studies on the Gm and Inv antigens in Asia and Oceania', PhD thesis, University of Michigan, Ann Arbor.

Schanfield, M.S., Ohkura, K., Lin, M., Shyu, R. and Gershowitz, H. (2002) 'Immunoglobulin allotypes among Taiwan aborigines: evidence of malarial selection could affect studies of population affinity', *Human Biology*, 74: 363–79.

Sewerin, B., Cuza, F.J., Szmulewicz, M.N., Rowold, D.J., Bertrand-Garcia, R.L. and Herrera, R.J. (2002) 'On the genetic uniqueness of the Ami aborigines of Formosa', *American Journal of Physical Anthropology*, 119: 240–8.

Shepard, E.M., Chow, R.A., Suafo'a, E., Addison, D., Perez-Miranda, A.M., Garcia-Bertrand, R.L. and Herrera, R.J. (2005) 'Autosomal STR variation in five Austronesian populations', *Human Biology*, 77: 825–51.

Starosta, S. (1995) 'A grammatical subgrouping of Formosan languages', in P.J.-k. Li, D.-a. Ho, Y.-k. Huang, C.-h. Tsang and C.-y. Tseng (eds) *Austronesian Studies Relating to Taiwan* (Symposium Series of the Institute of History and Philology), Taipei: Academia Sinica.

Steinberg, A.G. and Cook, C.E. (1981) *The Distribution of the Human Immunoglobulin Allotypes*, Oxford: Oxford University Press.

Su, B., Jin, L., Underhill, P., Martinson, J., Saha, N., McGarvey, S.T., Shriver, M.D., Chu, J., Oefner, P., Chakraborty, R. and Deka, R. (2000) 'Polynesian origins: insights from the Y chromosome', *Proceedings of the National Academy of Science USA*, 97: 8225–8.

Sung, W.H. (1978) 'Prehistoric Taiwan', Proceedings of Taiwan Historical Research Society, Taipei.

Tajima, A., Sun, C.S., Pan, I.H., Ishida, T., Saitou, N. and Horai, S. (2003) 'Mitochondrial DNA polymorphisms in nine aboriginal groups of Taiwan: implications for the population history of aboriginal Taiwanese', *Human Genetics*, 113: 24–33.

Trejaut, J.A., Kivisild, T., Loo, J.H., Lee, C.L., He, C.L., Hsu, C.J., Lee, Z.Y. and Lin, M. (2005) 'Traces of archaic mitochondrial lineages persist in Austronesian-speaking Formosan populations', *Public Library of Science (PLoS) Biology*, 3: e247. Epub 5 July 2005.

Tsang, C.-h. (2005) 'Recent discoveries at the Tapenkeng culture sites in Taiwan: implications for the problem of Austronesian origins', in L. Sagart, R. Blench and A. Sanchez-Mazas (eds) *The Peopling of East Asia: Putting Together Archaeology, Linguistics and Genetics*, pp. 63–73, London and New York: RoutledgeCurzon.

Underhill, P.A., Shen, P., Lin, A.A., Jin, L., Passarino, G., Yang, W.H., Kauffman, E., Bonne-Tamir, B., Bertranpetit, J., Francalacci, P., Ibrahim, M., Jenkins, T., Kidd, J.R., Mehdi, S.Q., Seielstad, M.T., Wells, R.S., Piazza, A., Davis, R.W., Feldman, M.W., Cavalli-Sforza, L.L. and Oefner, P.J. (2000) 'Y chromosome sequence variation and the history of human populations', *Nature Genetics*, 26: 358–61.

14 Maternal lineage ancestry of Taiwan Aborigines shared with the Polynesians

*Jean A. Trejaut, Toomas Kivisild,
Jun Hun Loo, Chien Liang Lee,
Chun Lin He, Chen Chung Chu,
Hui Lin Lee, and Marie Lin*

Introduction

Austronesian is the world's largest and most widely distributed language phylum with nine of its ten subfamilies (Puyuma, Paiwan, Ami, Bunun, Saisiat, Atayal, Rukai, Tsou and Malayo-Polynesian) found in Taiwanese aboriginal populations (Blust 1999). It is possible that the expansion of the tenth family in Asia-Oceania is associated with the spread of agriculture during the 4th to 6th millennia BC (Diamond and Bellwood 2003). Previous studies based on mitochondrial DNA (mtDNA) and Y chromosome have failed to demonstrate equally direct evidence for genetic continuity of aboriginal Taiwanese maternal and paternal lineages in populations of Near and Remote Oceania (Kayser *et al.* 2000; Oppenheimer and Richards 2001; Underhill *et al.* 2001). Although the mtDNA D-loop precursor haplotype (nps 16,189–16,217–16,261) of the Polynesian motif (nps 16,189–16,217–16,261–16,247) in haplogroup B4 has been found in Taiwanese, it is likely of very ancient origin. The equal presence of B4 in island and mainland Asian populations has not allowed a definite phylogenetic inference that maternal Polynesian ancestry can be related specifically back to Taiwanese aboriginals (Oppenheimer and Richards 2001). The presence in Polynesians of genetic lineages specific to Melanesian populations that are absent in Taiwan has become the basis for the 'slow boat' model according to which the Polynesian migration could be explained as an expansion from Melanesia without any direct thread leading back to Taiwan (Hurles *et al.* 2003).

An overwhelming majority of mainland East Asian mtDNA lineages are nested within haplogroups A-G, M, N9, and R9 (Torroni *et al.* 1994; Kivisild *et al.* 2002; Yao *et al.* 2002, 2003; Yao and Zhang 2002; Tanaka *et al.* 2004). Here we attempt to define the distribution of these haplogroups in nine Taiwan indigenous tribes (Ami, Atayal, Bunun, Paiwan, Puyuma, Rukai, Saisiat, Tao (= Yami), and Tsou) and examine the hypothesis that the distinctive mtDNA variations and genetic structure in present-day Taiwan mountain tribes might be the result of a long separation from common ancestors of the modern Chinese (see also Loo *et al.* Chapter 15, this volume). In addition, to see if Taiwanese B4a lineages have a closer genetic link to Polynesians, we determined the complete sequence for eight different B4a lineages from Taiwanese aborigines.

Material and methods

Populations

In this study, the mtDNA sequence variation of the mtDNA D-loop HVS-I region (nps 16,006–16,397) was characterized for 640 samples drawn from nine Taiwan indigenous mountain peoples representative of most of the languages, cultures, and geographical settlements on the island over the last four centuries. The following tribes were selected: in the north of Taiwan the Atayal (N=109) and the Saisiat (N=63), in the central mountain ranges the Tsou (N=60) and the Bunun (N=89), in the east the Ami (N=98) and the Tao (or Yami, N=64), and in the south the Rukai (N=50), the Paiwan (N=55) and the Puyuma (N=52). All indigenous people had both parents belonging to the same tribe, and gave consent to participation in this study.

In addition to the D-loop HVS-I region, the coding region (CR) nps 9,959–10,917 was sequenced and the mtDNA 9-bp deletion in the COII/tRNA^{LYS} was determined. Finally, significant restriction fragment length polymorphisms (RFLPs) were used to remove unavoidable errors in haplogroup designation.

DNA extraction

Blood samples were collected in ACD tubes and treated at the Transfusion Medicine Research Laboratory of the Mackay Memorial Hospital in Taipei. Genomic DNA was extracted from 500 µl of buffy coat using the QIAmp DNA kit (QIAml blood kit, Qiagen inc. Chatsworth CA 91311 USA) with minor modifications to the procedure recommended by the manufacturer.

DNA sequence analysis

Using primers L15997-H16401 and L048-H408 (Wilson *et al.* 1995), two segments of 404 and 401 nucleotides from the D-loop HVS-I and HVS-II of the mtDNA control region were obtained, respectively. Primer pairs 5, 7, 8, 11–14, 19 and 24 F&R described by Rieder *et al.* (1998) were used for typing informative RFLP sites using the following restriction enzymes: *Alu*I (nps 5,176 and 13,262), *Bspe*I (np 4,710), *Hae*III (np 663, nps 3,391 and 8,391), *Hha*I (nps 4,830, 7,598 and 9,053), *Hinf*I (np 9,820), *Hpa*I (np 12,405), *Mbo*II (np 12,704), *Nla*III (np 6,719) and *Tsp*509I (np 5,416) (Forster *et al.* 2001; Yao *et al.* 2002; Trejaut *et al.* 2005). Primers 15F (Rieder *et al.* 1998) and H10917 (5' gAACAgCTAAATAggTTg 3') were used to amplify a 959 nucleotide segment used for sequencing both CR strands (nps 9,959 to 10,917). Length variation in the COII/tRNA^{LYS} (9 bps-del.) region was assayed by PCR-SSP method, using primer pair L8215/H3274 (Yao *et al.* 2002). PCR was performed in 20 µl reactions and carried out for 36 cycles using the following final conditions: 20 mM Tris-HCl (pH 8.4), 50mM KCL, 0.2 mM deoxyribonucleotide triphosphate each, 2 mM $MgCl_2$, 0.25 U recombinant Taq DNA polymerase (Life Technologies Taiwan), 5 per cent glycerol, cresol red 0.075 mg/ml, 0.2 mM of each primer and 30–100 ng of DNA sample. Thermal cycling conditions were 1 min at 95° followed by 36 cycles of 95° for 10 s, 60° for 30 s, and 72° for 30 s. Following the thermal cycling, the samples were maintained at 75° for 10 min. Prior to sequencing, the amplified products were separated from excess dNTP and primers by first pre-treating with shrimp alkaline phosphatase (Sap) and Exo I enzymes (USB Product number US 70995 pre-sequencing Kit, Pharmacia Taiwan) following the conditions recommended by the manufacturer (37° for 30 min and 85° for 15 min). For each individual, sequencing of nps 16,006 to 16,397 was performed on both strands using the Perkin-Elmer/Applied Biosystems Division (ABI Taiwan) DyeDeoxy™ Terminator Cycle Sequencing Kit (Foster City, CA, USA) according to the recommendations of the manufacturer. Purification on a G50 sephadex column was performed before the final run on an automated DNA sequencer (ABI Model 377). In our inter-population analysis with other studies, the region including nps 16,182 to 16,183 was excluded as an upstream adenosine homo-polymeric region may cause poor sequencing. Consequently, substitutions at nps 16,182 and 16,183 were not indicated in Plates 14.I and 14.II.

Data analysis

Indices of molecular variance were calculated by using the ARLEQUIN package 2.0 (Schneider et al. 2000). A principal component (PCA) map constructed with the ADE-4 package (Thioulouse et al. 1997) using an HVS-I matrix of haplotype frequencies was obtained for the nine indigenous tribes of Taiwan and other regions of Asia. Coalescence times were calculated using ρ statistic and HVS-I mutation rate of one transition per 20,180 years in bps 16,090–16,365 (Forster et al. 1996; Saillard et al. 2000). For complete coding region sequences, a mutation rate of 1.7×10^{-8} substitutions per site per million years was used assuming five million years for the split between human and chimpanzee lineages (Ingman et al. 2000). A more conservative rate calibration of 1.26×10^{-8} (Mishmar et al. 2003), assuming a split of humans and chimpanzees 6.5 million years ago, would imply that all the coalescence times based on complete sequence data discussed in the text would be approximately 1.4 times older still.

A three-dimensional principal component analysis was performed using optimally adjusted frequencies from the nine Taiwanese tribes, islanders from Itbayat, a village of the Batan group of islands and province of the Philippines (Loo et al., Chapter 15, this volume), the Philippines, Malaysia, South Vietnam (Tajima et al. 2004), Indonesia, Ryukyu (Horai et al. 1996), Thai (Fucharoen et al. 2001; Oota et al. 2001), east-coast Chinese from Fujian (unpublished data), Taiwanese Han (Tsai et al. 2001), northern and southern Chinese (Yao et al. 2002), Japan (Seo et al. 1998), and Korea (Lee et al. 1997). The three-dimensional solution was calculated and plotted using ADE 4 (Thioulouse et al. 1997).

Results

We have assessed mitochondrial DNA variation in 640 individuals from nine indigenous tribes of the central mountain ranges and east-coast regions of Taiwan. Major differences were observed in the frequency distribution of individual haplogroups among the tribes (Table 14.1). In Taiwan, more than 98 per cent of the Han-speaking population is Minnan and Hakka who immigrated there four centuries ago from the southeast coast of China, and other Chinese from other regions who immigrated after World War II. In contrast to Han-speaking populations, Taiwan indigenous tribes (less than 2 per cent) showed a low frequency of haplogroups D4 and G and the absence of haplogroups A, C, Z, M8 and M9. Instead, more than 80 per cent of the maternal lineages of indigenous Taiwanese were nested within haplogroups B, R9, and M7 that are characteristic to Austronesian populations of Oceania but also occur at significantly lower proportions in continental China (39 per cent; Table 14.1). Another 12 per cent of Taiwanese aboriginal haplotypes belong to haplogroup E, which has rarely been seen in continental Chinese populations.

Principal component analysis

Principal component analysis (PCA) (Figure 14.1) using haplogroup frequencies revealed a high level of differentiation between Taiwanese aborigines compared to other Asian populations. Most particularly, Taiwanese aboriginals appeared closer to Island Southeast Asian populations (Luzon, Philippines, Moluccas and Indonesia) than to those from, China, Japan, Korea and mainland East Asia (South Vietnam, Malaysia and Thailand). The three southernmost populations of Taiwan group with the Yami from Tao Island. This cluster is clearly separated from the northern and central populations of the island, among whom the Bunun appear as an outlier. Although the Ami cluster closely together with northern and central tribes in the first two dimensions of the PCA, their haplogroup structure and relatively high frequency of B4a, D5, and M7c clades shows at the same time their close relationship with the southern tribes of Taiwan.

To permit a comparison between genetic and linguistic relationships, we mark the linguistic affiliation of each population. Austronesian-speaking populations (Figure 14.1) are well separated from Sino-Tibetan (clear stars), Austro-Asiatic (8-point black stars), Tai-Kadai (black diamonds) and Koreo-Japonic (black stars). The linguistic and the genetic distributions correlate well with each other. For example, northern Formosan speakers (Atayal and Saisiat) are clustered toward the top of the PCA map, and the three southern populations (Puyuma, Paiwan and Rukai) are well grouped at the bottom left. Nonetheless, Ami (eastern Formosan) are closer to the Malayo-Polynesian populations (Moluccas and Philippines) than the Yami, or Bunun who stand very far from the southern Formosan speakers, although they belong to the same linguistic group.

Table 14.1 Mitochondrial haplogroup frequencies among Taiwan Aborigines, Northern and Southern Han populations

Haplogroups	All Tribes %	Northern mountain range Atayal (n=109)	Northern mountain range Saisiat (n=63)	Central mountain range Tsou (n=60)	Central mountain range Bunun (n=89)	Southern mountain range Paiwan (n=55)	Southern mountain range Rukai (n=50)	East coast Puyuma (n=52)	East coast Ami (n=98)	East coast Tao (n=64)	Southeast Asia Luzon (n=37)	Southeast Asia Philippines (n=59)	Southeast Asia Indonesia (n=54)	Southeast Asia Moluccas (n=62)	Indo-China South Vietnam (n=35)	Indo-China Malaysia (n=51)	Indo-China Thai (n=33)	South Asia Taiwanese (n=155)	South Asia South China (n=142)	South Asia North China (n=189)	North Asia Japan (n=62)	North Asia Korea (n=320)	North Asia Ryukyu (n=48)
A	8.74	3.67	-	10.00	-	-	6.00	-	-	-	-	-	-	-	-	1.96	-	6.45	1.41	8.99	6.45	8.44	-
B*	6.37	0.92	-	-	-	-	8.00	3.85	44.90	14.06	-	-	-	3.23	2.86	-	3.03	0.65	1.41	1.06	-	-	-
B4*	-	-	3.17	-	-	16.36	-	-	-	25.00	-	1.69	-	-	-	-	-	1.29	2.11	1.59	6.45	0.94	-
B4a*	6.04	5.50	1.58	8.33	34.83	-	-	17.30	4.08	10.90	-	15.25	9.26	24.19	11.43	3.92	-	7.74	10.56	3.70	-	1.56	2.08
B4a1*	-	-	-	-	-	7.30	10.00	-	-	-	-	1.69	-	-	-	-	-	-	-	-	-	-	-
B4a2	4.87	-	-	8.33	-	-	-	-	-	-	-	10.17	-	-	-	-	-	-	-	-	-	-	-
B4b	5.86	0.90	12.70	13.33	6.70	9.10	-	-	-	13.51	2.70	6.78	3.70	6.45	5.71	1.96	12.12	3.87	4.93	3.17	3.23	0.63	2.08
B4c1*	4.76	-	-	-	-	-	-	-	-	-	-	5.08	7.41	4.84	2.86	7.84	6.06	3.23	3.52	0.53	3.52	0.63	-
B5	10.86	-	-	-	-	12.70	20.00	1.90	8.20	-	-	-	1.85	-	5.71	5.88	-	2.82	2.82	4.23	8.06	2.81	-
M8a (C/Z/M8a)	6.06	6.40	31.74	13.33	23.59	3.63	-	5.76	13.26	-	-	20.34	11.11	9.68	-	5.88	15.15	7.10	3.52	12.17	4.84	6.56	-
D5	0.21	-	-	15.00	2.25	1.82	6.00	7.69	3.06	18.75	8.11	5.08	16.67	24.19	11.43	5.88	6.06	1.94	0.70	1.59	-	-	2.08
E (E*/1a/1b)	-	-	-	-	-	-	-	1.92	-	-	13.51	-	-	-	-	-	-	5.81	2.65	2.12	1.61	-	-
F1a	-	-	-	-	-	-	-	-	-	-	-	-	-	-	-	-	-	0.65	0.70	1.06	-	-	-
F1b	-	-	-	-	-	-	-	-	-	-	-	-	-	-	-	-	-	2.58	2.82	-	-	0.31	-
F1c	11.44	-	-	1.66	-	34.55	36.00	30.76	-	-	2.70	1.69	-	-	-	1.96	-	-	1.41	-	-	-	-
F2	8.97	28.44	14.29	5.00	28.09	1.82	-	-	3.06	-	-	-	1.85	1.61	-	-	-	-	-	-	-	-	-
F3	2.91	-	1.58	21.66	1.12	1.81	8.00	-	-	-	5.41	3.39	5.56	1.61	17.14	7.84	6.06	5.81	3.52	3.17	3.23	2.81	12.50
R	8.97	39.44	23.80	-	3.40	7.30	6.00	28.85	6.12	26.60	8.11	8.47	7.41	1.61	14.29	5.88	15.15	7.10	10.56	5.29	11.29	6.88	33.33
M7(a/b)	8.97	-	-	1.70	-	-	-	-	10.24	-	21.62	6.78	-	0.00	0.00	3.92	0.00	1.94	1.41	2.65	3.23	2.81	-
M7c (all)	0.41	3.70	-	-	-	-	-	-	-	-	-	-	1.85	-	-	-	3.03	1.29	0.70	3.17	-	1.88	2.08
M9	1.20	1.80	-	-	-	-	-	1.92	7.10	-	-	1.69	-	-	2.86	-	-	7.10	4.23	2.12	-	0.31	-
M10/M4	-	-	-	-	-	-	-	-	-	-	-	-	3.70	-	5.71	-	-	1.29	0.70	3.70	1.61	2.81	-
N9a	-	-	-	-	-	-	-	-	-	-	-	3.39	1.85	9.68	-	3.92	-	-	-	0.53	-	-	-
N(other)	-	-	-	-	-	-	-	-	-	-	-	-	-	-	-	-	-	-	-	-	-	-	-
P	-	-	-	-	-	-	-	-	-	-	-	-	-	-	-	-	-	-	-	-	-	-	-
Q	1.37	2.80	9.50	-	-	-	-	-	-	-	2.70	3.39	3.70	3.23	-	-	-	1.29	-	1.59	-	2.19	-
Y	1.48	6.40	1.60	1.70	-	3.60	-	-	-	-	16.22	5.08	22.22	6.45	14.29	33.33	33.33	24.52	24.65	30.16	45.16	56.88	45.83
M (all)	-	-	-	-	-	-	-	-	-	-	-	-	-	-	2.86	-	-	-	-	-	-	-	-
U2	-	-	-	-	-	-	-	-	-	-	-	-	-	-	-	-	-	-	-	0.53	-	-	-
T1	-	-	-	-	-	-	-	-	-	-	-	-	-	-	-	-	-	-	-	-	-	-	-
Gene diversity ± SD	0.853 ± 0.022	0.922 ± 0.012	0.906 ± 0.018	0.838 ± 0.021	0.881 ± 0.026	0.91 ± 0.018	0.868 ± 0.025	0.924 ± 0.013	0.864 ± 0.016	0.92 ± 0.018	0.985 ± 0.006	0.936 ± 0.008	0.997 ± 0.005	0.997 ± 0.008	0.984 ± 0.008	0.986 ± 0.003	0.996 ± 0.001	0.996 ± 0.002	0.997 ± 0.001	0.998 ± 0.006	0.992 ± 0.002	0.989 ± 0.008
Nucleotide diversity ± SD	nd	0.015 ± 0.008	0.018 ± 0.009	0.015 ± 0.008	0.015 ± 0.008	0.014 ± 0.008	0.016 ± 0.009	0.017 ± 0.009	0.014 ± 0.009	0.017 ± 0.009	0.014 ± 0.008	0.018 ± 0.009	0.021 ± 0.011	0.022 ± 0.010	0.018 ± 0.009	0.019 ± 0.01	0.018 ± 0.009	0.019 ± 0.01	0.018 ± 0.009	0.017 ± 0.009	0.015 ± 0.008	0.011 ± 0.006

Population references are described in the text; N= Number of individuals; -= not seen; *= all other subtypes; all = compound frequency; nd= not determined; SD=standard deviation.

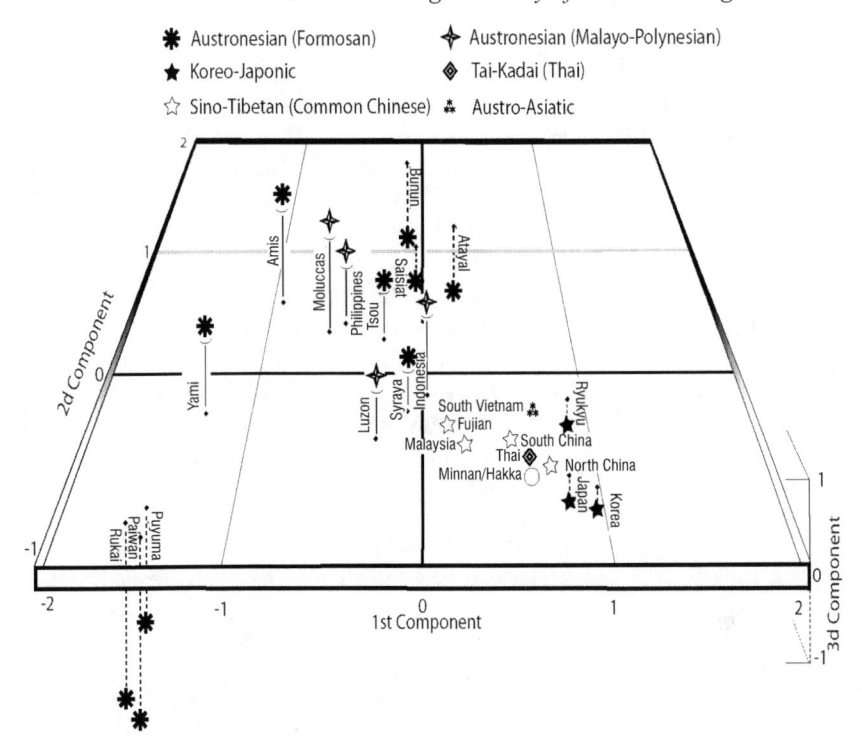

Figure 14.1 Principal component analysis map obtained from a matrix of haplogroup frequencies in nine Taiwan indigenous tribes (Table 14.1), northern and southern Chinese (Yao *et al.* 2002), Taiwan urban population (Tsai *et al.* 2001), Japan (Seo *et al.* 1998), Korea (Lee *et al.* 1997), Luzon (Sykes *et al.* 1995), Moluccas (Redd *et al.* 1995), Indonesia and Philippines (Tajima *et al.* 2004). Austronesian-speaking populations are represented by 4- or 8-point black stars.

Haplogroup structure

R9 and F haplogroups

Except for haplogroup R9c seen mostly in the Tsou, all subclades of R9, defined by a deletion at np 249 (249del) and a transition at np 16,304, belong to haplogroup F. Over one quarter of the Taiwanese from Northern and Central Mountain regions (Atayal, Saisiat and Bunun) belong to a novel subclade, F4b, distinctive by its D-loop motif 249del-16,218–16,304–16,311 and five additional substitutions (at nps 6,653, 8,020, 8,575, 8,603, and 10,097) (Ingman and Gyllensten 2003) in the coding region (Plate 14.I). In contrast, F4b frequency in other indigenous populations of Taiwan is significantly lower (8/377). Yet, considering available mtDNA datasets for Southeast Asia, haplogroup F4 shows a marginally low frequency (< 1 per cent) in mainland China (Kivisild *et al.* 2002; Yao *et al.* 2002) and is not found among 519 Thai samples (Fucharoen *et al.* 2001; Oota *et al.*

2001), where the overall haplogroup F frequency is one of the highest in Asia (22 per cent).

Haplogroup F3b, previously labeled as R9a, has been encountered at low frequencies in south and west China (Kivisild et al. 2002; Yao et al. 2002; Kong et al. 2003). High frequencies of this clade were observed specifically among the three southernmost populations (Puyuma, Paiwan and Rukai), whereas among other tribes F3b was virtually absent, consistent with the distribution of the respective HVS-I cluster C2 in the study of Tajima et al. (2003). Interestingly, the HVS-I motif of all Taiwanese F3b samples is different from the motif commonly observed among the Chinese. Namely, the Taiwanese F3b samples are characterized by a transversion at np 16,220 and lack a transition at np 16,355. This 16,220C variant of haplogroup F3 has been observed previously in two Bai samples from Yunnan and in one Japanese sample from Honshu (Horai et al. 1996; Yao et al. 2002). In both cases, however, the difference with the closest Taiwanese HVS-I haplotype was two or more HVS-I substitutions and a transition at coding region np 9,947 and 10,320 (Kong et al. 2003).

Finally, the highest frequencies of haplogroup F1a were seen in the Tsou and Yami populations. Interestingly, among the Yami, only the F1a1 subclade defined by a HVS-I motif 16,129–16,162–16,172–16,304 was detected, though other haplogroup F subclades (F3b and F4b) occur at high frequencies throughout other populations of Taiwan.

M7 haplogroups

The M7 haplogroup, genetically determined using coding region mutations nps 9,924, 10,398 and 10,400, revealed two distinct M7c subclades and two distinct M7b subclades. M7c1a (nps 9,865, 16,249 and 16,319) prevailed uniquely among Ami and Tsou, and subclade M7c1c (nps 16,295 and 16,362) was seen principally in Puyuma, Paiwan, Yami, the Philippines and at lower frequencies in other regions of southern Asia. Three complete mtDNA sequences (reported by Herrnstadt et al. 2002; Kong et al. 2003) allow an estimation of the time to the most recent common ancestor (TMRCA) of these M7c haplotypes at around 17,000 ± 1350 years. Haplogroup M7b3, was restricted to Saisiat, Atayal, Yami, Rukai and was also seen in the Philippines and Yunnan (Ingman and Gyllensten 2003). M7b3 is a sister clade of M7b1 which was seen only in Ami and the Philippines, and of M7b2 seen uniquely in Japan (Ryukyu) (Tanaka et al. 2004). Complete sequencing data (Ingman and Gyllensten 2003; Tanaka et al. 2004; and Trejaut et al. unpublished data) indicated a TMRCA for the two sister clades M7b1 and M7b2 of 20,556 ± 1245 years. The third sister clade, M7b3, appears to have been only in insular Southeast Asia for a much longer time (~50,000 ± 900 years) and supports a southern origin for the M7 haplogroup.

E haplogroups

Haplogroup E (nps 16,362 and 16,390), a subset of haplogroup M9, is nearly unseen in continental Asia. Again, a southern origin of Taiwanese Aborigines is suggested by the unique distribution of haplogroup E in Indonesia, Malaysia, Thailand, Vietnam and the Philippines (Table 14.1). Two specific subclades, E1 and E2, cover the vast majority of its lineages in Taiwan. The rare type of E2 (characterized by np 16,051) shows virtually no downstream mutations and has been observed in PNG and the Philippines (Ingman and Gyllensten 2003). In contrast, haplogroup E1 (characterized by np 10,834) is relatively more divergent, specifically in the Saisiat population, and is frequent in the Philippines (Pedro Soares, pers. comm.).

B haplogroups

B5a Two subclades of haplogroup B5a were defined here for the first time based on our data, available RFLP and HVS-I information from Southeast Asia (Ballinger *et al.* 1992; Lee *et al.* 1997; Nishimaki *et al.* 1999; Kivisild *et al.* 2002; Yao *et al.* 2002). The loss of a *Hae*III site at np 6,957 in association with 16,266A allele defines the major sub-clade B5a1 spread in southwest China, Thailand and Vietnam, while among Taiwan aborigines, the presence of +11,146 *Dde*I site at np 11,146 defines a B5a2 clade that is predominantly in association with 16,266G allele. Within the B5a2 clade, available D-loop information allows us to postulate the presence of two further branches that are highly region-specific in Southeast and East Asia: HVS-I motif 16,140–16,189–16,266G–16,362 (B5a2a), which has been observed so far exclusively in Taiwan (Melton *et al.* 1998; Tajima *et al.* 2003), and another motif, 16,140–16,187–16,189–16,266A/G, which characterizes all B5a variants observed so far in Korean, Japan and Han lineages from northeast China (Horai *et al.* 1996; Lee *et al.* 1997; Nishimaki *et al.* 1999; Yao *et al.* 2002). In Taiwanese aborigines, B5a2 lineages are found all over the island while their frequency, probably due to drift, is highest in north–central regions, among the Tsou and Saisiat.

B4b Highly homogeneous haplogroup B4b1 lineages are concentrated to the northern and central regions of Taiwan, probably involving a founder effect in Bunun. This clade is frequent in southern Chinese who include exact matches for the dominant B4b1 haplotype observed among the Taiwanese (Kivisild *et al.* 2002). Based on matches from mainland China, haplogroups B4b1, Y, and D4, observed only in the northern–central parts of Taiwan, in Atayal and Saisiat, and Bunun, could represent a recent admixture of Han Chinese, mediated through the urban populations.

B4c All 25 Taiwanese B4c lineages with the exception of one Tsou occur only in the southernmost populations (Puyuma, Paiwan, and Yami) and, except one Paiwan lineage, belong to a specific sub-clade B4c1b, defined by a D-loop motif 16,140–16,189–16,217–16,274–16,335. This subclade, with a coalescent time of 10,000 ± 8000 years in Taiwanese, is absent elsewhere in Oceania and has been previously detected at low frequency only in two southern provinces of China: Guangdong and Yunnan (Qian *et al.* 2001; Kivisild *et al.* 2002).

342 *Jean A. Trejaut et al.*

B4a Finally, two distinct subgroups of B4a were characterized by specific variation in Taiwanese aboriginals. The first variation, B4a1a, was distinguished by the presence of +6,719 *Nla* III due to a substitution at np 6,719 (Plates 14.I and 14.II) that occurred frequently among the Ami and Yami, and the second, B4a2, was distinguished by a HVS-I transition at np 16,324 that was common in Paiwan and, again, most frequent among the Yami.

We determined the complete mtDNA sequence of eight members of haplogroup B4a1a in aboriginal Taiwanese and assayed the phylogenetically informative sites revealed in the rest of the Han from China and Taiwan, and aboriginal samples. Interestingly, the majority of B4a lineages that account on average for 15 per cent of the mtDNA sequences in Taiwanese aborigines were found to be associated with three coding region substitutions, defining a new subclade B4a1a that occurred at its highest frequency (45 per cent) among the Ami population (Plates 14.I and 14.II, and Table 14.1). To test whether B4a1a could have been imported recently to Taiwan from the mainland, we also genotyped the defining markers of this clade (nps 6,719 and 10,238) in 47 Vietnamese and 79 Han speakers from Fujian, the closest province of China to Taiwan, and from 127 Minnan and 53 Hakka (data not shown). We did not observe any carriers of haplogroup B4a1a. Consequently, assuming a split of five million years for humans and chimpanzees, the coalescence times of B4a1a were estimated to $13,169 \pm 3841$ years in Taiwan, and $9,300 \pm 2500$ years in Papuans and Polynesians (Ingman and Gyllensten 2003).

Coalescence times

A number of mtDNA haplogroups in Taiwan showed limited haplotype and nucleotide diversity. Consequently, according to control sequence information, sequences belonging to haplogroups B4b, D4, E2, F4b, N9a, Y and possibly R9c (when ignoring the unique Bunun specimen) coalesced within the last 2000 years (Table 14.2). These short coalescence times may be due either to drift or to bottlenecks affecting locally evolving lineages, or they may be due to founder effects following admixture with recent immigrants from outside the island. The presence or the absence of matching sequence types elsewhere, as detailed above, can be considered as the best possible way to evaluate these two scenarios. The nearly complete absence of haplogroup E in China makes it unlikely that the shallow time depth of E2 lineages in Taiwan could be explained by a migration from China. However, both E1 and E2 have been observed in many populations from Island Southeast Asia (ISEA) with diversities greater to equal the ones seen in Taiwan, and this strongly suggests that these lineages derive from a migration from ISEA.

More than half of Taiwanese mtDNA lineages fall into clades B4a1a, B4c1b, E1a, F1a1, F1a2, F3b, M7c1c, and M7b3 that show, with a broad range of standard errors, average coalescence times between 7700 and 16,100 years. The dates for clades M7c1c and M7b3 are similar to those of M7b1 and M7b2 previously reported in ISEA. It is likely that these four M7b daughter clades, together with other subclades of haplogroups B4, E, and F3b, began to diversify following the rise in sea levels after the end of the Younger Dryas cold spell approximately 11,000 years ago in distinct islands close to mainland Southeast Asia.

Discussion

Most mtDNA lineages observed in Taiwanese aboriginal populations are only distantly related to those found in China and Taiwan Minnan and Hakka populations. On the other hand, these Taiwanese aboriginal lineages were all closely related to those lineages observed in the Philippines and other regions of ISEA. This suggests that the prevalence of the gene pool of aboriginal Taiwanese

Table 14.2 Coalescence dates for haplogroups

Haplogroup nodes	N	$\rho \pm \sigma$	Age ± SE (years × 1000)
E2[a]	18	0.0 to 0.06[a]	0 to 1.1[a]
N9a[a]	10	0.0 to 0.10[a]	0 to 2.0[a]
Y*[a]	9	0.0 to 0.11[a]	0 to 2.2[a]
D4[a]	7	0.0 to 0.14[a]	0 to 2.9[a]
B4b	47	0.04 ± 0.03	0.8 ± 0.6
F4b	72	0.04 ± 0.03	0.9 ± 0.6
R9c[b]	15	0.07 ± 0.07[b]	1.3 ± 1.3[b]
F1a1	21	0.38 ± 0.29	7.7 ± 5.9
B4a1a	66	0.47 ± 0.23	12.2 ± 4.7
B4c1b	24	0.50 ± 0.4	10.1 ± 8.0
M7b3	73	0.51 ± 0.23	10.3 ± 4.5
E1a	44	0.59 ± 0.26	11.91 ± 5.2
D5	26	0.61 ± 0.38	12.3 ± 7.7
M7c1c	33	0.70 ± 0.4	14.1 ± 8.1
F1a2	7	0.71 ± 0.59	14.4 ± 11.9
F3b	54	0.79 ± 0.22	16.1 ± 4.5
R9c	15	0.93 ± 0.87	18.8 ± 17.6
B4a2	34	1.00 ± 0.63	20.2 ± 12.7
M7b1	5	1.00 ± 0.66	20.2 ± 13.4
B5a2	33	1.12 ± 0.57	22.6 ± 11.7
E1	59	1.25 ± 0.47	25.2 ± 9.7

Notes

N = number of lineages observed in the specified haplogroup; ρ and σ = estimator for the age of the specified haplogroup root and its standard error (Saillard *et al*. 2000); Age = Coalescence expressed as the product of ρ by 20180 years; SE= standard error on Age expressed as the product of σ by 20180 years.

(a) When haplogroups have no descendent associated lineage, one step mutation is introduced in the estimation of the ρ statistic and Age.

(b) Possible alternative calculation where np 16,157 is treated as a reverse conversion in a unique R9c Bunun lineage.

began with late Pleistocene settlers. The incidence of haplogroup E among the tribes (~12 per cent), for example, cannot be traced back to an origin in southeast China, unless implying scenarios of almost total replacement of the Neolithic population of southern China by a later migration from elsewhere. Extensive genetic differences between Taiwanese populations (Table 14.1) parallel their linguistic diversity (Diamond and Bellwood 2003) and suggest long-term cultural and biological isolation on the island. In particular, this isolation is well shown in the principal components analysis where Austronesian languages segregate clearly from the Sino-Tibetan, Austro-Asiatic, Tai-Kadai and Koreo-Japonic families. In addition, the isolation within Taiwan is also demonstrated. Most noticeably, the northern tribes (Atayal, Saisiat) are well separated from the three southern tribes (Puyuma, Rukai and Paiwan) and the eastern tribes (Ami and Tao). However, some contradictions between genetic and linguistic relationships are present, as shown by the unexpectedly distant relation of the Bunun to the southern tribes, and the closeness of the Ami to Malayo-Polynesian populations. While both languages and genes are passed onto the next generations, they follow unpredictable and unrelated random processes that make their differences much more noticeable within a restricted region than across a large geographic area. Interestingly, the phylogeny of B4a1a genome resembles the linguistic reconstruction of Austronesian languages, with nine of its primary branches restricted to Taiwan and the tenth branch spread all over Oceania.

By defining a new haplogroup B4a1a from complete sequence information and showing its combined high frequency and diversity in Taiwan, particularly among Ami, we provide the first direct phylogenetic evidence that Polynesians shared an ancestry likely within or south of Taiwan 13,000 years ago. A later maturation of B4a1a and interaction phase somewhere in East Indonesia or Melanesia contributed to the development among Polynesians of B4a1a1p (i.e. coding and control region mutations of the 'Polynesian Motif'), and of haplogroups not specific to Taiwanese Aborigines. The time window between coalescence times of B4a1a lineages in Taiwan (13,200 ± 3800 years) and of B4a1a1p in Melanesia and Polynesia (9100 ± 2700 years) indicates the possibility that these variants were co-spread with farmers in the Pacific. (More recent evaluations of these coalescence times, using the synonymous clock, now give an estimate that appears more compatible with archeological C^{14} dating: 7900 ± 1700 years for B4a1a and 6200 ± 1800 years for B4a1ap (Friedlaender *et al.* 2007)). Considering the deficiency of specific Y chromosomal elements commonly shared by the Taiwanese aboriginals and Polynesians, the mtDNA evidence provided here is also consistent with the assumption that proto-Oceanic societies were matrilocal (Hage and Marck 2003; Hurles *et al.* 2003).

Conclusion

Taiwanese aboriginal populations share their maternal ancestry with populations of mainland East Asia with mtDNA haplogroups B, R9, and M7 as their main genetic components. At the same time, the haplogroup structure at a finer phylogenetic resolution suggests the relatively long-term isolation of Taiwan aborigines from the mainland populations. The coalescent dates of B4a1a, F3, F4, R9c, M7c1c lineages in Taiwan point to local founder effects ranging from recent (0–2000 years) to more ancient times (7000–20,000 years). These results most likely reflect the drift in small endogamous populations of the island that became isolated by the rising sea levels after the last ice age.

The phylogenetic reconstruction of B4a1a complete mtDNA sequences (13,200 ± 3800 years or 7900 ± 1700 years by the synonymous clock) requires that we adopt a model according to which the origin of Austronesian migration can be traced back to Taiwan, or to a wider region of similar genetic profile embracing Taiwan, the Philippines and Borneo, followed by an interaction period eastward in Southeast Asia or Melanesia where the complete motif specific to Polynesian B4a1a1p sequences was acquired.

Acknowledgements

We are grateful to all Taiwan indigenous people for joining this project. The project was supported by grant no 92-2314-B-195-019 from the National Science Council of Taiwan. T. K. received support from Estonian Science Foundation grant 5574.

References

Andrews, R.M., Kubacka, I., Chinnery, P., Lightowlers, R. and Turnbull, D. (1999) 'Reanalysis and revision of the Cambridge Reference Sequence for human mitochondrial DNA', *Nature Genetics*, 23: 147.

Ballinger, S.W., Schurr, T.G., Torroni, A., Gan, Y.Y., Hodge, J.A., Hassan, K., Chen, K.H. and Wallace, D.C. (1992) 'Southeast Asian mitochondrial DNA analysis reveals genetic continuity of ancient mongoloid migrations', *Genetics*, 130: 139–52.

Blust, R. (1999) 'Subgrouping, circularity and extinction: some issues in Austronesian comparative linguistics', in E. Zeitoun and J.K. Li (eds) *Selected Papers from the Eighth International Conference on Austronesian Linguistics*, pp. 31–94, Taipei: Institute of Linguistics (Preparatory Office), Academia Sinica.

Diamond, J., and Bellwood, P. (2003) 'Farmers and their languages: the first expansions', *Science*, 300: 597–603.

Forster, P., Harding, R., Torroni, A. and Bandelt, H.-J. (1996) 'Origin and evolution of Native American mtDNA variation: a reappraisal', *American Journal of Human Genetics*, 59: 935–45.

Forster, P., Torroni A., Renfrew, C. and Rohl, A. (2001) 'Phylogenetic star contraction applied to Asian and Papuan mtDNA evolution', *Molecular Biology and Evolution*, 18: 1864–81.

Friedlaender, J.S., Friedlaender, F.R., Hodgson, J.A., Stoltz, M., Koki, G., Horvat, G., Zhadanov, S., Schurr, T.G. and Merriwether, D.A. (2007) 'Melanesian mtDNA complexity', *Public Library of Science (PLoS) ONE*, www.plosone.org.e248.

Fucharoen, G., Fucharoen, S., and Horai, S. (2001) 'Mitochondrial DNA polymorphisms in Thailand', *Journal of Human Genetics*, 46: 115–25.

Hage, P. and Marck, J. (2003) 'Matrilineality and the Melanesian origin of Polynesian Y chromosomes', *Current Anthropology*, 44: S121–7.

Herrnstadt, C., Elson, J.L., Fahy, E., Preston, G., Turnbull, D.M., Anderson, C., Ghosh, S.S., Olefsky, J.M., Beal, M.F., Davis, R.E. and Howell, N. (2002) 'Reduced-median-network analysis of complete mitochondrial DNA coding-region sequences for the major African, Asian, and European haplogroups', *American Journal of Human Genetics*, 70: 1152–71.

Horai, S., Murayama, K., Hayasaka, K., Matsubayashi, S., Hattori, Y., Fucharoen, G., Harihara, S., Park, K.S., Omoto, K. and Pan, I.H. (1996) 'mtDNA polymorphism in East Asian populations, with special reference to the peopling of Japan', *American Journal of Human Genetics*, 59: 579–90.

Hurles, M.E., Matisoo-Smith, L., Gray, R.D. and Penny, D. (2003) 'Untangling Oceanic settlement: the edge of the knowable', *Trends in Ecology and Evolution*, 18: 531–40.

Ingman, M. and Gyllensten, U. (2003) 'Mitochondrial genome variation and evolutionary history of Australian and New Guinean aborigines', *Genome Research*, 13: 1600–6.

Ingman, M., Kaessmann, H., Pääbo, S. and Gyllensten, U. (2000) 'Mitochondrial genome variation and the origin of modern humans', *Nature*, 408: 708–13.

Kayser, M., Brauer, S., Weiss, G., Underhill, P.A., Roewer, L., Schiefenhovel, W. and Stoneking, M. (2000) 'Melanesian origin of Polynesian Y chromosomes', *Current Biology*, 10: 1237–46.

Kivisild, T., Tolk, H.V., Parik, J., Wang, Y., Papiha, S.S., Bandelt, H.J. and Villems, R. (2002) 'The emerging limbs and twigs of the East Asian mtDNA tree', *Molecular Biology and Evolution*, 19: 1737–51.

Kong, Q.P., Bandelt, H.-J., Sun, C., Yao, Y.-G., Salas, A., Achilli, A., Wang, C.-Y., Zhong, L., Zhu, C.-L., Wu, S.-F., Torroni, A. and Zhang, Y.-P. (2003) 'Phylogeny of East Asian mitochondrial DNA lineages inferred from complete sequences', *American Journal of Human Genetics*, 73: 671–6.

Lee, S., Shin, C., Kim, K., Lee, K., and Lee, J. (1997) 'Sequence variation of mitochondrial DNA control region in Koreans', *Forensic Science International*, 87: 99–116.

Li, H., Pan, W.Y., Wen, B., Yang, N.N., Jin, J.Z., Jin, L. and Lu, D.R. (2003) 'Origin of Hakka and Hakkanese: a genetics analysi's', *Yi Chuan Xue Bao*, 30: 873–80.

Melton, T., Clifford, S., Martinson, J., Batzer, M. and Stoneking, M. (1998) 'Genetic evidence for the proto-Austronesian homeland in Asia: mtDNA and nuclear DNA variation in Taiwanese aboriginal tribes', *American Journal of Human Genetics*, 63: 1807–23.

Mishmar, D., Ruiz-Pesini, E., Golik, P., Macaulay, V., Clark, A., Hosseini, S., Brandon, M., Easley, K., Chen, E., Brown, M., Sukernik, R., Olckers, A. and Wallace, D. (2003) 'Natural selection shaped regional mtDNA variation in humans', *Proceedings of the National Academy of Science USA*, 100: 171–6.

Nishimaki, Y., Sato, K., Fang, L., Ma, M., Hasekura, H. and Boettcher, B. (1999) 'Sequence polymorphism in the mtDNA HV1 region in Japanese and Chinese', *Legal Medicine*, 1: 238–49.

Oota, H., Settheetham-Ishida, W., Tiwawech, D., Ishida, T. and Stoneking, M. (2001) 'Human mtDNA and Y-chromosome variation is correlated with matrilocal versus patrilocal residence', *Nature Genetics*, 29: 20–1.

Oppenheimer, S.J. and Richards, M. (2001) 'Polynesian origins: slow boat to Melanesia?', *Nature*, 410: 166–7.

Ozawa, T. (1995) 'Mechanism of somatic mitochondrial DNA mutations associated with age and diseases', *Biochimica et biophysica acta*, 1271: 177–89.

Qian, Y.P., Chu, J.Y., Chu, Z.T., Wei, C.D., Dai, Q. and Horai, S. (2001) 'Genetic relationship among four Yunnan populations revealed by sequence of mtDNA D-loop', *Yi Chuan Xue Bao*, 28: 291–300.

Redd, A.J., Takezaki, N., Sherry, S.T., McGarvey, S.T., Sofro, A.S. and Stoneking, M. (1995) 'Evolutionary history of the COII/tRNALys intergenic 9 base pair deletion in human mitochondrial DNAs from the Pacific', *Molecular Biology and Evolution*, 12: 604–15.

Rieder, M.J., Taylor, S.L., Tobe, V.O. and Nickerson, D.A. (1998) 'Automating the identification of DNA variations using quality-based fluorescence re-sequencing: Analysis of the human mitochondrial genome', *Nucleic Acids Research*, 26: 967–73.

Saillard, J., Forster, P., Lynnerup, N., Bandelt, H.-J. and Nørby, S. (2000) 'mtDNA variation among Greenland Eskimos: the edge of the Beringian expansion', *American Journal of Human Genetics*, 67: 718–26.

Schneider, S., Roessli, D., and Excoffier, L. (2000) *Arlequin version 2.000: A Software for Population Genetics Data Analysis*, Geneva: University of Geneva, Genetics and Biometry Laboratory.

Seo, Y., Stradmann-Bellinghausen, B., Rittner, C., Takahama, K. and Schneider, P. (1998) 'Sequence polymorphism of mitochondrial DNA control region in Japanese', *Forensic Science International*, 97: 155–64.

Sykes, B., Leiboff, A., Low-Beer, J., Tetzner, S. and Richards, M. (1995) 'The origins of the Polynesians: an interpretation from mitochondrial lineage analysis', *American Journal of Human Genetics*, 57: 1463–75.

Tajima, A., Hayami, M., Tokunaga, K., Juji, T., Matsuo, M., Marzuki, S., Omoto, K. and Horai, S. (2004) 'Genetic origins of the Ainu inferred from combined DNA analyses of maternal and paternal lineages', *Journal of Human Genetics*, 49: 187–93.

Tajima, A., Sun, C.S., Pan, I.H., Ishida, T., Saitou, N. and Horai, S. (2003) 'Mitochondrial DNA polymorphisms in nine aboriginal groups of Taiwan: implications for the population history of aboriginal Taiwanese', *Human Genetics*, 113: 24–33.

Tanaka, M., Cabrera, V.M., Gonzalez, A.M., Larruga, J.M., Takeyasu, T., Fuku, N., Guo, L.J., Hirose, R., Fujita, Y., Kurata, M., Shinoda, K., Umetsu, K., Yamada, Y., Oshida, Y., Sato, Y., Hattori, N., Mizuno, Y., Arai, Y., Hirose, N., Ohta, S., Ogawa, O., Tanaka, Y., Kawamori, R., Shamoto-Nagai, M., Maruyama, W., Shimokata, H., Suzuki, R. and Shimodaira, H. (2004) 'Mitochondrial genome variation in eastern Asia and the peopling of Japan', *Genome Research*, 14: 1832–50.

Thioulouse, J., Chessel, D., Doledec, S. and Olivier, J.M. (1997) 'ADE-4: a multivariate analysis and graphical display software', *Statistics and Computing*, 7: 75–83.

Torroni, A., Miller, J.A., Moore, L.G., Zamudio, S., Zhuang, J., Droma, T. and Wallace, D.C. (1994) 'Mitochondrial DNA analysis in Tibet: implications for the origin of the Tibetan population and its adaptation to high altitude', *American Journal of Physical Anthropology*, 93: 189–99.

Trejaut, J.T., Kivisild, T., Loo, J.H., Lee, C.L., He, C.L., Hsu, C.J., Li, Z.Y. and Lin, M. (2005) 'Traces of Archaic mitochondrial lineages persist in Austronesian-speaking Formosan populations', *Public Library of Science (PLoS) Biology*, 3(8): e247.

Tsai, L.C., Lin, C.Y., Lee, J.C., Chang, J.G., Linacre, A. and Goodwin, W. (2001) 'Sequence polymorphism of mitochondrial D-loop DNA in the Taiwanese Han population', *Forensic Science International*, 119: 239–47.

Underhill, P.A., Passarino, G., Lin, A.A., Marzuki, S., Oefner, P.J., Cavalli-Sforza, L.L. and Chambers, G.K. (2001) 'Maori origins, Y-chromosome haplotypes and implications for human history in the Pacific', *Human Mutation*, 17: 271–80.

Wilson, M.R., Butler, J., Dizinno, J.A., Replogle, J. and Budowle, B. (1995) 'Extraction, PCR amplification and sequencing of mitochondrial DNA from human hair shafts', *Biotechniques*, 18: 662–9.

Yao, Y.G. and Zhang, Y.P. (2002) 'Phylogeographic analysis of mtDNA variation in four ethnic populations from Yunnan Province: new data and a reappraisal', *Journal of Human Genetics*, 47: 311–18.

Yao, Y.G., Kong, Q.P., Bandelt, H.J., Kivisild, T. and Zhang, Y.P. (2002) 'Phylogeographic differentiation of mitochondrial DNA in Han Chinese', *American Journal of Human Genetics*, 70: 635–51.

Yao, Y.G., Kong, Q.P., Man, X.Y., Bandelt, H.J. and Zhang, Y.P. (2003) 'Reconstructing the evolutionary history of China: a caveat about inferences drawn from ancient DNA', *Molecular Biology and Evolution*, 20: 214–19.

Yoneda, M., Tanno, Y., Horai, S., Ozawa, T., Miyatake, T. and Tsuji, S. (1990) 'A common mitochondrial DNA mutation in the t-RNA(Lys) of patients with myoclonus epilepsy associated with ragged-red fibers', *Biochemistry International*, 21: 789–96.

15 Mitochondrial DNA diversity of Tao-Yami and Batan islanders

Relationships with other Taiwanese aborigines

Jun Hun Loo, Jean Trejaut, Chen-chung Chu, and Marie Lin

Introduction

Languages spoken by populations of Taiwan and Island Southeast Asia, the Pacific islands including New Zealand and Easter Island, and Madagascar are Austronesian (Blundell 2000). Taiwan, with nine subgroups of Austronesian (the Formosan languages), possesses the greatest diversity, while all languages spoken outside Taiwan including Yami (or Tao) from Lanyu (Orchid Island) and Batan from the Batanes Islands, belong to the Malayo-Polynesian branch with more than 1200 languages (Li 2000). According to oral tradition, the Yami and Batanes islanders have been continuously interacting since prehistoric times. Nowadays, the Batanes group of islands belongs politically to the Philippines and Orchid Island belongs to Taiwan (Chen 2001). The Batan archipelago comprises ten small islands of which only Batan, Itbayat and Sabtang are inhabited. The central position of the Batan group, 500 km north of Manila, and 128 km south of Orchid Island, made the archipelago a much frequented area by Austronesian speakers, but also by sailors at all times and epochs. Four hundred years ago, 40-seater sailing ships were regularly travelling back and forth between Orchid Island and Batan. During the Spanish dominion in the 18th century, communication between Orchid Island and Batan ceased. Since 1986, when an Ivatan woman married into a Yami family, sailing between Ivatan and Yami restarted. More recently, Christian missionaries went to Batan, and used a Yami Bible translation, as Yami is understood by both Batan and Yami islanders.

In June 1999, a group of Yami people, believing that Batan was their original homeland, arranged a trip to Batan in search for traces of their heritage. As part of this endeavour, the Mackay Memorial Hospital of Taipei collected blood samples from Batanes people for genetic analysis.

Between 2002 to 2004, Peter Bellwood's group went to the Batanes Islands to conduct archaeological excavations (Bellwood *et al.* 2003, this volume). Using C^{14} dating, the group described three phases of occupation: the Sunget Phase (1200 to 800 BC), the Naidi Phase (800 BC to the 1st millennium AD), and the Rakwaydi Phase (AD 1000 to the present). Cultural deposits from the Sunget Phase revealed strong relationship to Neolithic cultures from Taiwan.

In this study, we analyse:

1 the relationship between Taiwanese aborigines and Batan islanders;
2 the genetic organisation of Batan islanders and Yami; and
3 their relationships with other Southeast Asians.

Methods

Population samples

We examined a total of 48 unrelated individuals from Batan in Batanes province of the Philippines for mtDNA.[1] In addition, we included a total of 1887 samples from 21 other Asian populations classified as Taiwan indigenous (109 Atayal, 63 Saisiat, 60 Tsou, 89 Bunun, 55 Paiwan, 50 Rukai, 52 Puyuma, 98 Ami and 64 Yami: see Table 14.1 of Trejaut *et al.*, this volume). Other populations included 59 individuals from the Philippines, 51 Malaysian, 35 South Vietnamese (Tajima *et al.* 2004), 54 Indonesians and 48 Ryukyuans (Horai *et al.* 1996), 62 Indonesians from Moluccas (Redd *et al.* 1995), 33 Thai (Fucharoen *et al.* 2001; Oota *et al.* 2001), Taiwanese Han (Tsai 2001), 189 northern and 142 southern Chinese (Yao *et al.* 2002), 62 Japanese (Seo *et al.* 1998), and 320 Koreans (Lee *et al.* 2001).

mtDNA sequence analysis

The sequence variation of the mtDNA D-loop hypervariable segments I and II (HVS-I and HVS-II) was characterized in 48 samples drawn from the Batan islanders. In addition, the coding region (CR) nps 9,959–10,917 was sequenced and the mtDNA 9-bp deletion in the COII/tRNA^{LYS} was screened by sequence specific polymorphism (SSP) with primer pair L8215/H8297 (Yao et al. 2002). Finally, significant restriction fragment length polymorphisms (RFLPs) were used to remove unavoidable errors in haplogroup designation. All methods used in this analysis have previously been described (Yao *et al.* 2002; Trejaut *et al.* 2005).

Data analysis

Indices of molecular variance were calculated with ARLEQUIN package 2.0 (Schneider et al. 2000). Genetic distance (Nei 1987) from mtDNA haplogroup frequencies of nine indigenous tribes of Taiwan and other regions of Asia (Table 14.1 in Trejaut *et al.* this volume) was estimated by the expression

$$D = -\ln\left(\sum_m \sum_i p_{1mi} p_{2mi}\right) / \left(\sum_m \sum_i p_{1mi^2}\right)^{1/2} \left(\sum_m \sum_i p_{2mi^2}\right)^{1/2}$$

where *m* is summed over loci, *i* over alleles at the *m*-th locus, and where p_{1mi} is the frequency of the *i*-th allele at the *m*-th locus in population 1. A neighbor-joining tree (Saitou and Nei 1987) was constructed from the distance matrix using

PHYLIP package (Felsenstein 2002). Coalescent times were calculated using ρ statistic and HVS-I mutation rate of one transition per 20,180 years in bps 16,090–16,365 (Saillard et al. 2000).

Results

MtDNA haplogroup distribution in Yami and Batan and their relationships to Taiwanese aborigines

We analysed the pattern of genetic variation of the HVS-I, HVS-II, sequencing of CR nps 9,959–10,917, and CR relevant RFLPs from Batan. In the Batan islanders' gene pool, four groups of genes can be distinguished (Plate 15.I, and Plate 14.I from Trejaut et al., this volume).

The first group, otherwise restricted to the Paiwan (Pw), Puyuma (Pu) and Rukai (Ru) peoples in the south of Taiwan, involves three haplogroups: M7c1c, D5 and F3b (Plate 14.I of Trejaut et al., this volume). The presence of those genes in a restricted geographic location may indicate that they have been conserved via genetic drift or founding events. Interestingly, these genes belong to the southern tribes of Taiwan (Pw, Pu, and Ru) and to the Philippines (data not shown). Only one haplogroup (M7c1c) contributes to the genome of Yami or Batan. One step descendent of the major node of M7c1c is unique to Batan, and one two step descendent with a transition and a transversion is unique to Yami (Ya) (Plate 14.I of Trejaut et al., this volume) and may point to a longer period of isolation among the Yami.

The second group includes five haplogroups (M7c1a, M7b1 (Plate 14.I of Trejaut et al. this volume), B4a1a, F1a1b and E1 (Plate 15.I)). In this group, except for haplogroup E1 and M7b1, the Ami genes are always seen together with the Tsou and support archaeological views that Ami and Tsou may have cohabited in the past (Yi-Chang Liu, pers. comm.). Interestingly, F1a1b lineage is seen in Batanes (18 per cent) (Plates 15.Ic and 15.Ia, respectively) but not in Yami, indicating a clear population difference between these two islands. Also, the core lineage of haplogroup B4a1a is shared between Taiwan (Am, TS and Ru), the Philippines (Tajima et al. 2004), and Batan (8.3 per cent), but not Yami, showing possibly loss of B4a1a core haplotype in Yami through drift or sampling. Furthermore, indication of a movement from the Philippines toward Taiwan may be indicated by the successive stages of mutations seen in B4a1a lineages (1) Philippines to Batan: np 16223, (2) Batan to Ami: np 16093. B4a1a has also been shown to be a precursor of the Polynesian motif (PM) (Trejaut et al. 2005), its descendent lineages are seen in other Southeast Asian regions but have not been detected in continental Asia (Yao et al. 2002). The absence of the PM (np 16,247) in Batanes islanders and in the Philippines supports the hypothesis of an emergence of PM in a region much further south of the Batanes and the Philippines, possibly east in Indonesia or PNG (Melton et al. 1995). Lastly, nine Batan individuals share haplogroup F1a1b with 3 Ami and 3 Tsou (Plate 15.Ia). F1a1b has also been observed in the Philippines, Thailand and south China (Fucharoen et al.

2001; Yao et al. 2002; Tajima et al. 2003, 2004). The sharing of the same F1a1b lineage between Batan, Tsou and Ami indicates recent migration on Batan Island but cannot designate a clearly exclusive genetic contribution from either Taiwan or the Philippines.

The third set of haplogroups, seen in the Ami (Am), Atayal (At), Bunun (Bn) and Saisiat (Sa) peoples on Taiwan comprises haplogroups E2, E1a, F4b and B4b1. This set is homogeneously distributed among these tribes, most particularly among At, Bn and Sa. Haplogroup E (Plate 15.Ib) has rarely been seen in continental Asia. Here, E1a is observed among Taiwanese indigenous populations (6.9 per cent), Batanes (12.5 per cent) and the Philippines (11 per cent). It is therefore difficult to define whether its presence in Batan indicates migration from Taiwan or Island Southeast Asia (ISEA). Interestingly, a subclade of E2 with a transition at np 16,243 is specific to the Batanes and the Philippines. Its deeper branching position on the network and its absence in Taiwan supports a close and ancient relationship between Batan and the Philippines. The widespread distribution of E1a and the southern origin of the E2 (np16, 243) subclade may well indicate overall an origin of E in ISEA.

The fourth group (M7b3, F1a1, and B4c1b) reflects well the relationships of the Yami with Rukai and Tsou peoples. Also observed to a lesser extent with B4a1a, this relationship is well emphasized by the presence of F1a1a in the three tribes (Ya, Ru and Ts in Plate 15.Ia). A similar pattern is observed with B4c1b (Plate 15.1c). Nonetheless, the Yami, Rukai and Tsou are genetically well differentiated from each other, as indicated in Plate 15.II. Seven Batan haplotypes belong to haplogroup B4c1b, among them, five correspond to the B4c1b founding node, and two differ from it by one transition at np 16,172 (Plate 15.Ic). The equal sharing of B4c1b between Yami and Batan shows inter-island exchanges, but the presence of B4c1b also among South and Southeast Asians, Filipinos, and Tsou makes it difficult to ascertain a definite origin for Batan or Yami coming from Taiwan or ISEA.

Coalescence times estimated for Batan haplotypes are indicated in Plate 15.I. The coalescence times of haplogroups E1a, B4c1b, B4a1a in Taiwan range from 10,100 to 12,200 years before present (BP). The time obtained for the same haplogroups in the Batanes ranges from 3360 to 6600 years BP. These periods between Taiwan and Batan are well within the range with those obtained from C^{14} dating of material from recent archaeological excavation (Bellwood et al. 2003).

Finally, six major haplotypes (M7b3, M7c1c (Plate 14.I from Trejaut et al., this volume), F1a1, B4a1a, B4a2 and B4c1b (Plate 15.I)), with frequencies varying from 10 to 23 per cent, represent more than 90 per cent of the Yami genome. Only lineages of haplogroups B4a2 and B4c1b are shared between Yami and Batan. No movement of migration may be inferred from B4c1b, which is seen throughout Southeast Asia, Taiwan and ISEA. B4a2, seen in Batan, is absent from the Philippines and suggests Yami influence.

On the contrary, all Yami haplogroups are also seen in Taiwan. However, despite this apparent close relationship, for four haplogroups (M7b3, F1a1a, B4c1b and

E2), Taiwan aborigines and Yami only share founding haplotypes. On the other hand, all three high frequency haplogroups B4a2, B4a1a and M7c1c seen in Yami have a one step mutation from the founding node, thereby indicating a recent founding event and/or isolation of the Yami.

A phylogenetic tree constructed using haplogroup frequencies of Taiwanese aboriginal and neighboring populations of South, East, and Southeast Asia (Table 14.1 of Trejaut *et al.* this volume) is shown in Plate 15.II. In this tree, Yami are isolated, but show a closer relationship to other Austronesian speakers (in blue and yellow in Plate 15.II) than to non-AN-speaking populations. Actually, the complexity of the tree does not allow a clear delineation of the genetic relationship between Batan or Yami with either the Philippines or Taiwan and calls for further studies using more sequencing of complete mtDNA or the use of other genetic systems such as the non-recombining region of the Y chromosome or the HLA system.

Discussion

In this study, mtDNA sequences of 48 unrelated Batanes individuals were analysed and compared to Yami on Orchid Island. The two peoples are speakers of Western Malayo-Polynesian (Proto-Philippines) branch and practice cultural exchanges, trading, and, recently, intermarriages (Chen 2001; Sanchez-Mazas *et al.* 2005).

Most Batanes lineages belonged to haplogroups also seen among Taiwanese aborigines and the Philippines. It was therefore not possible, using only HVS-I analysis, to decide whether the matrilineal relationship of the Batanes inclined more towards the Philippines or Taiwan aboriginal peoples. However, at the haplotype level, and using a more extended mtDNA analysis (HVS-I, HVS-II, and relevant coding region markers, RFLPs and nps 9,959–10,917 sequencing), we showed that only seven out of twenty Batanes haplotypes were shared with Taiwanese aborigines, and only two were seen in Yami. Most other subhaplogroups could be traced back to the Philippines gene pool. Moreover, phylogenetic analysis showed that Batan clustered with the Austronesian populations (Plate 15.II). This was well supported by the fact that very few subhaplogroups, seen among Batanes or Taiwan aborigines, were also in mainland Asia. Only two subhaplogroups, B4a2 and B4c1b, were shared between Batan and Yami. This limited genetic relationship contrasts with their close linguistic and cultural relationships. This is even more unexpected since previous researches in our laboratory on HLA and on a rare MNS blood group type, MiIII (data not shown), showed a closer genetic relationship than uncovered by this mtDNA study:

1. HLA alleles A2407, B1502, DR 1502, and HLA haplotypes A*0201-B75 and A*2402-B38 are shared between Batan and Yami.
2. To a lesser extend, presence of MiIII, in Batan (2 per cent) and in Yami (34 per cent) may indicate a remote relationship between the two islands or a migration of Ami who have a high frequency of MiIII (88 per cent).

Similar to Batan, the Yami appear as equally related genetically to Taiwanese aborigines as to Filipinos, and only have one haplogroup subtype (F1a1a_tw) is seen only in Taiwan (data not shown). Other haplogroups (not haplotypes) seen in Yami were also detected in Batan and were shared preferentially with Taiwan aboriginal peoples, the Paiwan, Puyuma, Rukai, Ami and Tsou. Both high frequency (>10 per cent) of six out of ten haplotypes and low genetic diversity of the Yami indicate population isolation. Nonetheless, Chen (2001), using archaeological data, described two periods of possible contact between Yami and other populations: an earlier period characterized by relationships between Yami and Taiwan, and a later period characterized by relationships between Yami, the Batanes and the Philippines. While the first period is supported by genetics, the evidence for the later period is only linguistic and cultural and may have been too recent to allow detection of any significant genetic traces in the present-day Yami gene pool.

Acknowledgements

The project was supported by grant No 92-2314-B-195-019 from the National Science Council of Taiwan.

Note

1 This study was approved by the ethics committee of the Mackay Memorial Hospital in Taipei (Taiwan) and all Batan individuals gave informed consent to participate in this analysis.

References

Andrews, R., Kubacka, I., Chinnery, P.F., Lightowlers, R.N., Turnbull, D.M. and Howell, N (1999) 'Reanalysis and revision of the Cambridge reference sequence for human mitochondrial DNA', *Nature Genetics*, 23: 147.

Bellwood, P., Stevenson, J., Anderson, A. and Dizon, E. (2003) 'Archeological and Palaeoenvironmental research in Batanes and Ilocos Norte provinces, northern Philippines', *Indo-Pacific Prehistory Association Bulletin*, 23: 141–61.

Blundell, D. (2000) *Austronesian Taiwan: Linguistics, History, Ethnology, Prehistory: Language Connecting the World*, Berkeley, CA: Phoebe A. Hearst Museum, University of California.

Chen, Y.-M. (2001) 'Tai'Tong county history, Yami tribe section', Tai'Tong County Government Taiwan (in Chinese).

Felsenstein, J. (2002) *Phylip; Phylogeny Inference Package Release*, version 3.6 (alpha3), Seattle, WA.

Fucharoen, G., Fucharoen, S. and Horai, S. (2001) 'Mitochondrial DNA polymorphisms in Thailand', *Journal of Human Genetics*, 46: 115–25.

Horai, S., Murayama, K., Hayasaka, K., Matsubayashi, S., Hattori, Y., Fucharoen, G., Hariharan, S., Park, K.S., Omoto, K. and Pan, I.H. (1996) 'mtDNA polymorphism in East Asian Populations, with special reference to the peopling of Japan', *American Journal of Human Genetics*, 59: 579–90.

Lee, W.J., Lee, H.W. Palmer, J.P., Park, K.S., Lee, H.K., Park, J.Y., Hong, S.K. and Lee, K.U. (2001) 'Islet cell autoimmunity and mitochondrial DNA mutation in Korean subjects with typical and atypical Type I diabetes', *Diabetologia*, 44: 2187–91.

Li, P.J.-k. (2000) 'Formosan languages: the state of the art', in D. Blundell (ed.) *Austronesian Taiwan: Linguistics, History, Ethnology, Prehistory*, Berkeley, CA, and Taipei: Phoebe A. Hearst Museum of Anthropology and Shung Ye Museum of Formosan Aborigines Publishing.

Melton, T., Peterson, R., Redd, A.J., Saha, N., Sofro, A.S., Martinson, J. and Stoneking, M. (1995) 'Polynesian genetic affinities with Southeast Asian populations as identified by mtDNA analysis', *American Journal of Human Genetics*, 57: 403–14.

Nei, M. (1987) *Molecular Evolutionary Genetics*, New York: Columbia University Press.

Oota, H., Settheetham-Ishida, W., Tiwawech, D., Ishida, T. and Stoneking, M. (2001) 'Human mtDNA and Y-chromosome variation is correlated with matrilocal versus patrilocal residence', *Nature Genetics*, 29: 20–1.

Redd, A.J., Takezaki, N., Sherry, S.T., McGarvey, S.T., Sofro, A.S. and Stoneking, M. (1995) 'Evolutionary history of the COII/tRNALys intergenic 9 base pair deletion in human mitochondrial DNAs from the Pacific', *Molecular Biology and Evolution*, 12: 604–15.

Saitou, N. and Nei, M. (1987) 'The neighbor-joining method: a new method for reconstructing phylogenetic trees', *Molecular Biology Evolution*, 4: 406–25.

Saillard, J., Forster, P., Lynnerup, N., Bandelt, H.-J. and Nørby, S. (2000) 'mtDNA variation among Greenland Eskimos: the edge of the Beringian expansion', *American Journal of Human Genetics*, 67: 718–26.

Sanchez-Mazas, A., Poloni, E.S., Jacques, G. and Sagart, L. (2005) 'HLA genetic diversity and linguistic variation in East Asia', in L. Sagart, R. Blench and A. Sanchez-Mazas (eds) *The Peopling of East Asia Putting Together Archaeology, Linguistics and Genetics*, London: RoutledgeCurzon.

Schneider, S., Roessli, D. and Excoffier, L. (2000) *Arlequin Version 2.000: A Software for Population Genetics Data Analysis*, Geneva: University of Geneva, Genetics and Biometry Laboratory.

Seo, Y., Stradmann-Bellinghausen, B., Rittner, C., Takahama, K. and Schneider, P. (1998) 'Sequence polymorphism of mitochondrial DNA control region in Japanese', *Forensic Science International*, 97: 155–64.

Tajima, A., Hayami, M., Tokunaga, K., Juji, T., Matsuo, M., Marzuki, S., Omoto, K. and Horai, S. (2004) 'Genetic origins of the Ainu inferred from combined DNA analyses of maternal and paternal lineages', *Journal of Human Genetics*, 49: 187–93.

Tajima, A., Sun, C.S., Pan, I.H., Ishida, T., Saitou, N. and Horai, S. (2003) 'Mitochondrial DNA polymorphisms in nine aboriginal groups of Taiwan: implications for the population history of aboriginal Taiwanese', *Human Genetics*, 113: 24–33.

Trejaut, J.A., Kivisild, T., Loo, J.H., Lee, C.L., He, C.L., Hsu, C.J., Li, Z.Y. and Lin, M. (2005) 'Traces of archaic mitochondrial lineages persist in Austronesian speaking Formosan populations', *Public Library of Science (PLoS) Biology*, 3(8): e247.

Tsai, L.C., Lin, C.Y., Lee, J.C., Chang, J.G., Linacre, A. and Goodwin, W. (2001) 'Sequence polymorphism of mitochondrial D-loop DNA in the Taiwanese Han population', *Forensic Science International*, 119: 239–47.

Yao, Y.G., Kong, Q.P., Bandelt, H.J., Kivisild, T. and Zhang, Y.P. (2002) 'Phylogeographic differentiation of mitochondrial DNA in Han Chinese', *American Journal of Human Genetics*, 70: 635–51.

16 A genetic perspective on the origins and dispersal of the Austronesians

Mitochondrial DNA variation from Madagascar to Easter Island

Erika Hagelberg, Murray Cox,
Wulf Schiefenhövel, and Ian Frame

Introduction

This chapter describes the study of one genetic system, mitochondrial DNA (mtDNA), within the Austronesian-speaking world, and discusses whether the patterns of genetic variation at this genetic locus are consistent with the principal models of the settlement and linguistic diversity in this vast geographical region. Mitochondria are the seat of cellular metabolism and have their own complement of DNA. MtDNA is a tiny proportion of the genetic makeup of a human being, and has both advantages and disadvantages in population studies. It is inherited maternally, in contrast with the nuclear chromosomal DNA inherited from both parents. (Note: the mitochondria of the spermatozoon are eliminated from the egg soon after fertilization, so offspring do not inherit paternal mtDNA, although there are exceptions to this rule, as shown by Schwartz and Vissing 2002.) The maternal mode of inheritance permits the study of female lineages through time.

Despite the small size of the mitochondrial genome, each mitochondrion has many thousands of copies of mtDNA, and there are many mitochondria in each cell. The abundance of mtDNA in cells has been exploited in anthropological research on ancient, rare or degraded biological samples, including archaeological bones, old hair samples, or dried blood (Hagelberg 1994). MtDNA accumulates mutations at a relatively fast rate, and so is useful for the investigation of recent evolutionary events. These features have made mtDNA an excellent marker for geneticists interested in human evolutionary history (see Wallace 1995 for review).

Advances in molecular genetics, stimulated by genome sequencing projects, biotechnology and biomedical research, have increased the wealth of available data. There is now a huge amount of mtDNA sequence information on human populations worldwide, used to make inferences about recent human evolution, including migrations and expansions. Researchers claim to have a definitive family tree of human mitochondrial genomes (e.g. Macaulay *et al.* 1999; Herrnstadt *et al.* 2002). Unfortunately, the ease of data acquisition and high public and scientific interest of human evolutionary studies pressure scientists to publish fast, and generate unnecessary duplications, and conclusions that are sometimes facile or indeed exaggerated. Small sample sizes or inappropriate samples can bias research, and the results of phylogenetic analyses are often presented with insufficient caveats. Moreover, researchers interested in human evolution sometimes forget that mitochondria are not solely provided for the convenience of molecular anthropologists, but are structures of vital importance for the metabolic function of cells, and involved in complex biological processes, as well as in disease and ageing. Most mtDNA studies assume that the patterns of variation in human populations are the result of migration alone, and disregard possible effects of biological selection (Elson *et al.* 2004; Ruiz-Pesini *et al.* 2004). Likewise, paternal mtDNA inheritance and recombination with maternal mtDNA (even if rare phenomena) may have profound consequences for the interpretation of phylogenetic and evolutionary studies, but are generally disregarded by population geneticists (Hagelberg 2003).

Genetic studies often appear convincing, and may fail to be challenged appropriately by archaeologists and linguists, especially if the latter are discouraged by complicated computer analyses or specialist jargon. Conversely, geneticists sometimes lack sophisticated knowledge of the history, culture and subsistence patterns of past human populations. Models drawn from genetic data are frequently bolstered by selective linguistic or archaeological data, rather than interpreted independently, resulting in circular arguments. Genetic data can yield rich insights about human prehistory if interpreted thoughtfully, and this does not necessarily require complicated statistics and computer analysis methods. Fortunately, scholars in different fields are endeavouring to improve mutual intelligibility, as shown by conferences like the one which has led to this book.

The origin of the Austronesian languages

In the present study, we analyzed mtDNA markers in population samples spanning most of the Austronesian world to shed light on the origins and expansion of the Austronesians. Geneticists frequently refer to Austronesian people, or Austronesian genes. But who are the Austronesians, and is there such a thing as an Austronesian gene? The Austronesian language family is perhaps the largest in the world. It comprises about 1000–1200 distinct languages spoken by some 270 million indigenous people distributed more than halfway around the earth, from Madagascar to Easter Island, and from Taiwan to New Zealand. Austronesian languages can be divided into a number of major subgroups, all except one of which are confined to Taiwan, where Austronesian languages are thought to have developed more than five millennia ago. One subgroup of Austronesian languages, Malayo-Polynesian, includes the languages spoken throughout most of Malaysia and Indonesia, parts of Vietnam, some parts of coastal Papua New Guinea (PNG), much of island Melanesia, and Micronesia and Polynesia (Blust 1977, 1999). Although Austronesian language speakers are very diverse culturally and biologically, it is believed that they constitute a family of related peoples. This is consistent with the view that the Austronesian languages were not acquired by pre-existing static populations, but were spread mainly by colonizers *who shared a common origin*. The dispersal of the Austronesian languages is thought to have been driven by the spread of agriculture from a homeland in southern China, leading eventually to the development of long-range maritime economies in Island Southeast Asia and the Pacific. Scholars believe that while the descendents of the colonizers diversified and adapted to specific local conditions, they retained enough common features to remain a coherent people, often named 'The Austronesians' (Bellwood 1995; Bellwood et al. 1995).

Linguistic evidence suggests that there was one single expansion of Austronesian speakers into Oceania (the vast area of the Pacific east of a line drawn through Micronesia and Irian Jaya), where the so-called Oceanic subgroup of the Austronesian language is spoken. The Oceanic subgroup includes all the Austronesian languages of Melanesia (except the very west of New Guinea), most of Micronesia, and all of Polynesia. The only non-Austronesian languages spoken in Oceania, other than the languages introduced after European contact, are the Papuan languages spoken in many parts of New Guinea and island Melanesia. These non-Austronesian or Papuan languages are hugely diverse and number more than 700.

The spread of the Oceanic language speakers has been the subject of intensive study by geneticists using both classical and molecular genetic markers. Genetic research has focused largely on the question of the settlement of Polynesia and generally involves rather simplistic classifications of Oceanic peoples into the three major groups, Polynesian, Micronesian and Melanesian. The main conclusion of these studies is that the so-called Melanesian peoples are genetically diverse, whereas Polynesians are relatively homogeneous. Genetic studies have concluded that the greater genetic diversity in Melanesia, compared to Polynesia, reflects the depth of occupation of the two respective areas (see e.g. Hill and Serjeantson 1989; Cavalli-Sforza et al. 1994 for reviews). In this model, New Guinea and island Melanesia are areas where genetic and linguistic diversity are thought to have accumulated gradually by mutation and drift since the time of first settlement, about 50,000 years before the present (Groube et al. 1983; Wickler and Spriggs 1988). In contrast, the islands within the Polynesian triangle are believed to be culturally, linguistically, and biologically homogeneous because there was less time for mutations (whether linguistic or genetic) to accumulate since the expansion of a small group of founders. The first human settlement only occurred relatively recently, about 3000 years ago in the case of western Polynesia, and was only concluded with the colonization of New Zealand in the 12th century AD (Anderson 1991).

Scholars have postulated different models for the origin of Oceanic populations, with labels such as the 'express train' (Diamond 1988), the 'entangled bank' (Terrell et al. 2001), and alternatives such as the 'slow boat' hypothesis (Oppenheimer and Richards 2001a). The term 'express train' was coined by Diamond to explain the rapid spread of Austronesian languages and the Lapita culture to the central Pacific (Fiji, Tonga, and Samoa). In this model, the Austronesian-speaking, Lapita pottery-making horticulturalists with developed navigational skills presumably originated in Taiwan, and their eastward expansion into the Pacific was driven ultimately by the emergence of agriculture in southern China (Bellwood 1991). The 'express train' model assumes that the expansion of the proto-Polynesians/ Austronesians was rapid and there was little genetic admixture between the recent immigrants and the earlier Melanesian/Papuan settlers of the western Pacific.

Mitochondrial DNA diversity in the Pacific

Genetic studies by Clegg and colleagues, based on globin gene polymorphisms inherited from both parents (Hill *et al.* 1989; O'Shaughnessy *et al.* 1990), indicated that the proto-Polynesians had moved into the eastern Pacific after considerable admixture with Papuan language speakers in Melanesia. These researchers observed that certain globin types causing thalassaemia (an inherited blood disorder), thought to be associated with resistance to malaria in people in malarial regions of coastal and island Melanesia, were also carried at remarkably elevated frequencies by Polynesians (including Tahitians and Maori) from islands where malaria never existed. This finding suggested that the proto-Polynesian immigrants had 'picked up' the thalassaemia genes during their sojourn in Melanesia *en route* to the eastern Pacific. This conclusion was confirmed by more recent studies, based on the male Y chromosome, that indicated that a high proportion of Y chromosomes in Polynesia (Cook Islands and Samoa) appeared to derive from Y chromosomes in coastal New Guinea and island Melanesia (Kayser *et al.* 2000). Both these studies supported an 'entangled bank' model of Pacific settlement.

In contrast, the earliest studies based on mtDNA markers provided strong evidence of the 'express train' scenario. The first mtDNA marker that was useful for research on Pacific peoples was the so-called 9-base-pair (9-bp) deletion, a harmless deletion of one of two copies of a 9-bp tandem repeat, first observed in a proportion of present-day peoples of Asian origin (Wrischnik *et al.* 1987). Hertzberg *et al.* (1989) analyzed present-day human DNA samples from various locations in the Pacific, and observed no instances of the mutation in New Guinea highlanders, while it was found at moderate frequency in peoples of coastal PNG, and at fixation levels (100 per cent frequency) in Polynesians. The 9-bp deletion appeared to be a truly Polynesian genetic marker that linked Polynesians to mainland and Southeast Asia, but not to Papuan speakers.

Shortly after this observation, one of us (E.H.) performed an analysis of mtDNA in human skeletal remains from archaeological sites in the Pacific. Thirty-eight bone samples, including some of the oldest human remains from the Pacific, were surveyed, and 21 yielded results for the 9-bp deletion locus. All the skeletal samples from Polynesian prehistoric sites had the 'Polynesian' 9-bp deletion, while the older samples, from Lapita, post-Lapita, or related sites in the western Pacific, did not have the deletion. Several of the bone samples yielded additional DNA sequence information for a highly informative part of the mitochondrial genome, called the first hypervariable region (Figure 16.1). Prehistoric bone samples from

360 *Erika Hagelberg* et al.

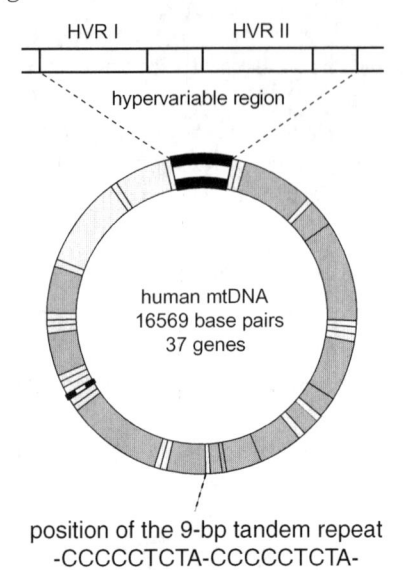

Figure 16.1 Diagram of human mitochondrial DNA, showing the position of the informative 9-base-pair (9-bp) deletion, a deletion of one of two copies of a 9-bp motif (CCCCCTCTA) observed frequently in people of Asian origin. The highly variable non-coding region contains most of the sequence variability in the mitochondrial genome.

the Chatham Islands and Hawaii carried nucleotide substitutions that were different to those in previously sequenced DNA of living Europeans and other peoples, at positions 16,217, 16,247, and 16,261 of the reference mtDNA sequence (Anderson *et al.* 1981). These specific substitutions were also observed in four unrelated present-day Tahitians analyzed for comparison. Two other prehistoric individuals, from the Society Islands and Hawaii, had a similar pattern of mutations, with the exception of that at position 16,247. These results confirmed that prehistoric people within the Polynesian triangle had a homogeneous genetic heritage. The same 'Polynesian' mtDNA markers were also detected in 12 prehistoric skeletons from two archaeological sites in Easter Island, supporting the view that the island was settled originally by Polynesian navigators, and not Amerindians (Hagelberg *et al.* 1994).

In contrast, the lack of the 9-bp deletion in bone DNA of prehistoric people associated with presumably 'Austronesian' sites in the western Pacific indicated that they were genetically 'Melanesian' and not 'Polynesian'. While generally supporting the express train scenario, we suggested (with many caveats) that Papuan-language speakers had expanded to the central Pacific before the arrival of the Polynesians. This conclusion uncoupled the Polynesian expansion from the Lapita Cultural Complex (Hagelberg and Clegg 1993). Our subsequent research on present-day Pacific islanders, discussed in this chapter, has tended to confirm the view that the Polynesians do not derive directly from the so-called Lapita people.

These studies on archaeological bone samples may appear trivial compared with the vast number of sequences on modern DNA that can be generated today. However, they represent the earliest application of bone DNA typing to a question of prehistory and, with the study by Rebecca Cann and colleagues on DNA of present-day Pacific islanders, identified for the first time a unique mtDNA sequence type associated with a geographically distinct population group (Lum et al. 1994).

This Polynesian mtDNA type, which later became known as the 'Polynesian motif', was characterized by a suite of mtDNA mutations observed in Polynesians, namely the 9-bp deletion, and the substitutions at positions 16,217, 16,247, and 16,261. Interestingly, Redd, Stoneking and colleagues detected the 9-bp deletion, a marker previously considered to be characteristically Asian, in DNA samples of sub-Saharan Africans, and they advised caution in the interpretation of data based on just one mtDNA locus (Redd et al. 1995). The 9-bp deletion observed in Africans occurred together with mtDNA sequence types quite distinct from the 'Polynesian motif', suggesting that the deletion had occurred independently in Africa and in Asia. The 'Asian' type of 9-bp deletion was always associated with the Polynesian motif, or with mtDNA variants that had a subset of the nucleotide substitutions of the motif. These Asian variants included the type without the 16,247 mutation observed earlier in Polynesian bone DNA (Hagelberg and Clegg 1993), a third type, with the 16,217 mutation and the 9-bp deletion (identical to a mtDNA variant found in haplogroup B, one of the four mitochondrial lineages A, B, C, and D, previously identified in the Americas by Ballinger et al. 1992), and, lastly, a mtDNA variant with a substitution at position 16,189 (Melton et al. 1995; Redd et al. 1995). The Polynesian motif and related mtDNA types were subsequently observed in present-day individuals in additional locations throughout the Pacific and Southeast Asia (Sykes et al. 1995). The studies on mtDNA variation in living Pacific islanders supported an 'express train' mode of settlement, beginning somewhere in Asia and characterized by a rapid eastwards expansion of Austronesian, 9-bp deletion-carrying peoples to reach all corners of the Polynesian triangle.

Redd, Stoneking and colleagues (Melton et al. 1995; Redd et al. 1995) proposed that the four 'Asian' mtDNA types, variants, or lineages had developed sequentially from an ancestral form, in the following sequence (the number refers to the mtDNA position where an informative mutation is observed):

1 9-bp deletion + 16,189
2 9-bp deletion + 16,189 + 16,217 (present also in the Americas)
3 9-bp deletion + 16,189 + 16,217 + 16,261
4 9-bp deletion + 16,189 + 16,217 + 16,247 + 16,261 (Polynesian motif)

These four types can also be identified using a binomial notation, to indicate the presence (1) or absence (0) of each of the four nucleotide substitutions, on the 9-bp deletion background (identified as haplogroup B):

1   B – 1000
2   B – 1100
3   B – 1101
4   B – 1111 (Polynesian motif)

Polynesian origins in eastern Indonesia?

Based on the estimated rate of mutation of mtDNA and statistical analysis of sequence data, Melton et al. (1995) and Redd et al. (1995) proposed that the 9-bp deletion had originated in mainland Asia about 58,000 years ago (95 per cent confidence interval, CI = 12,000–104,000). An expansion out of Asia was thought to have occurred 27,000 years ago (95 per cent CI = 17,000–65,000) probably through Taiwan, reaching Indonesia but not further east. Lastly, they proposed that the mutation at 16,247 that characterized the full Polynesian motif probably happened in Indonesia about 17,000 years ago, and the early Polynesians expanded out of Indonesia about 5500 years ago (95 per cent CI = 1300–9600) and moved east to colonize the rest of the Pacific. The huge confidence intervals of these calculations make them almost meaningless, and the expansion times of peoples between Taiwan and Indonesia (sometime about 30,000 years ago according to the mtDNA data calculations) seem very large when compared with the linguistic and archaeological evidence of the time of settlement of Taiwan and the expansion of Austronesian languages in island Southeast Asia, thought to have been about 6000 years ago.

The full Polynesian motif mtDNA variant (1111), observed throughout Polynesia in present-day peoples (and in prehistoric remains as far apart as Hawaii, Chatham Islands, and Easter Island), was also detected in the Malagasy (Soodyall et al. 1995). Melton et al. (1995) observed the motif at high frequency in coastal PNG, and in a small number of Malays, as well as east Indonesian individuals, from the Moluccas and Nusa Tengaras. In east Indonesia, the motif was found in 6 of a total of 55 individuals analyzed, and it is among these 6 individuals that the genetic diversity was highest, suggesting the Polynesian motif was the oldest there. These data were seized by Richards et al. (1998), who revised them using a different statistic. They calculated the mean divergence time of the Polynesian motif in the following places: eastern Indonesia (number of subjects, n = 6), coastal PNG (n = 22), Samoa (n = 38), and Cook Islands (n = 48). The divergence times for the Polynesian motif were estimated to have been 17,000 years ago in east Indonesia, 5000 years in coastal PNG, 3000 years in Samoa, and 1000 years in the Cook Islands. While the ages for the expansion of the Polynesian motif in PNG and Polynesia are within the realms of possibility, the date of 17,000 years ago for eastern Indonesia is hard to reconcile with any inferred proto-Polynesian expansion event in that or any other region. Nevertheless, these authors argue strongly for the origin of the Polynesian expansion in the Indonesian archipelago (Oppenheimer and Richards 2001a, 2001b). The conclusion that the proto-Polynesians did not originate in Taiwan or China but in tropical Southeast Asia, most probably east Indonesia, is founded ultimately on genetic data from six individuals, and must be regarded with caution.

Genetic links between Taiwan and Polynesia

As part of an ongoing collaborative research project on genetic variation in the circum-Pacific region, we performed a comparison between the results obtained from analyses of mtDNA, the male Y chromosome, and nuclear HLA (human leukocyte antigens) loci (Hagelberg *et al*. 1999a). We examined these genetic systems in samples of human DNA from China, Taiwan, Java, PNG highlands, PNG south coast, Trobriand Islands, New Britain, and Western Samoa. The Y chromosome analyses involved microsatellites, or short tandem repeats (Y-STRs), and preceded the development of many of the so-called biallelic markers that have been shown to be highly informative in the Pacific. However, one of the Y-STRs (a deletion at the DYS390 locus) was shown to be characteristic of Polynesian male lineages, and was found in the Samoans (70 per cent), and at lower frequencies in coastal PNG (17 per cent), the Trobriands (9 per cent), and New Britain (19 per cent), but not in China, Taiwan, Java, or PNG highlanders. This result undoubtedly linked Melanesian and Polynesian Y chromosomes, and was later confirmed by Kayser *et al*. (2000) using additional Y chromosome markers.

The mtDNA and HLA analyses also showed a link between Polynesia and coastal and island Melanesia. In the case of the HLA analyses, the results were dramatic. A previously described HLA variant, DPB1 0501, known to occur in Asian populations, was found at high frequencies in the Han Chinese (47 per cent), aboriginal Taiwanese (70 per cent), in south PNG (71 per cent), Samoa (70 per cent), and in a staggering 98 per cent of the Trobriand Islanders. The allele was observed in only 13 per cent of PNG highlanders and 14 per cent of Javanese (and is virtually absent in Europeans and Africans) (Zimdahl *et al*. 1999). The HLA analysis showed a connection between China and Taiwan, and coastal PNG, island Melanesia, and Polynesia. Very similar results were obtained from the mtDNA analyses: the coastal and island Melanesians and the Samoans had a very elevated frequency of the mtDNA Polynesian motif (1111), whereas this type was absent in Java and the PNG highlands. The mtDNAs ancestral to the Polynesian motif could be traced back to Taiwan (the 1101 and 1100 types) and ultimately mainland Asia (the 1100 type). Both mtDNA and HLA data showed a link between Taiwan and Polynesia, to the exclusion of Java and PNG highlands, a result consistent with an express train from Taiwan model of settlement.

Mitochondrial DNA variation in the Indonesian archipelago

We extended our mtDNA survey of the Austronesian world by increasing the sample of Han Chinese, and adding new sequence information from other regions, including Tonga, Fiji, several locations in Indonesia, and Madagascar, listed in Table 16.1. All these samples were from present-day individuals, with the exception of Easter Island, where we used previously published ancient DNA sequences,

Table 16.1 List of the population samples of this study, with the number of individuals and observed mitochondrial haplogroups.

Population	n	L2	L3	B4 1111	B4 1101	B4 1100	B4 1000	B5	F	P	N-other	M-Q	M-other	Not assigned
Easter Island	12			12										
Samoa	24			17	7									
Tonga	20			16	1							3		
Fiji	24			11	5					2		4		2
Trobriand Is.	55			26	12	3				1		2	3	8
New Britain	42			9	1					1		7	24	
PNG south coast	23			13	5							2	2	1
PNG highlands	37									11	4	17		5
Ambon	22			1	2			1	2	1			13	2
Lombok	24			2				4	4		1		13	
Manado	22			1				2	1	1	5	1	8	3
Java	53				1	3	2	13	10		1		18	5
Banjarmasin	22				2	1		3	1		2		11	1
Taiwan	46				9	3		3	10		2	1	19	
China	38				3	2		1	6		5		17	4
Madagascar	74	2	19	14							8		30	1
Total	538	2	19	122	48	12	2	27	34	17	28	37	158	32

These data are represented graphically in Map 16.1.

still the only published molecular genetic data on Easter Island (Hagelberg et al. 1994). A total of 538 individuals were included in this analysis.

All subjects were surveyed for the mtDNA 9-bp deletion and hypervariable region. With the exception of the previously published Easter Island sequences, the first hypervariable segment of mtDNA (HVRI) was sequenced as described earlier (Hagelberg et al. 1999a, 1999b). Typically, fragments of 400 base pairs of HVRI were obtained for both DNA strands, between position 16,000 and 16,400 of the mitochondrial genome. A subset of the individuals was tested for three different informative restriction fragment length polymorphisms (RFLPs), at positions 3,594, 10,398, and 10,400, and for a base substitution at position 16,390, to help assign them to known world mtDNA haplogroups (Quintana-Murci et al. 1999). The results are summarized in Tables 16.1 and 16.2 and shown graphically in Plate16.II.

The population samples of Fiji, Tonga, and Samoa were characterized by a high frequency of the Polynesian mtDNA types 1111 and 1101 (known in the literature as B4 or B4a). A small proportion of individuals, both in Fiji and in Tonga, had mtDNA type Q (part of the major world haplogroup M), a previously described 'Papuan' mtDNA type. One of the Fijians had an unknown mtDNA sequence, identical to that observed in six Trobriand Islanders (n = 55). The Asian mtDNA type F was also detected in two Fijians (n = 24). Asian type F is abundant in China, Taiwan, and Indonesia (particularly Java and Lombok). Polynesian mtDNA types (1111 and 1101) were present at low frequencies throughout the Indonesian archipelago but, in agreement with previous studies, the full Polynesian motif was only found in east Indonesia (Ambon, Lombok, and Manado).

We detected a mtDNA type characterized by the 9-bp deletion and a substitution at mtDNA position 16,140 (sometimes accompanied by 16,217) in all our Indonesian samples. This mtDNA type, known sometimes as B5, was abundant in Java and Lombok, and observed in Borneo, Manado, and Ambon, as well as in Taiwan and China (confusingly, some authors, like Kivisild et al. 1999, and Jin et al. 2005, call it B4, as the Polynesian motif, although it appears to be quite a different haplogroup, and restricted to East Asia and Island Southeast Asia, not the Pacific). This B5 type (shown in yellow in Plate 16.II) might be a signature of the Austronesian expansion southwards from Taiwan to the Indonesian archipelago.

The mtDNA diversity in present-day Taiwanese aboriginals was low, just 24 different mtDNA sequence types in a sample of 46 individuals of 4 tribal groups, suggesting that these people were relatively isolated or endogamous in recent history. The view that Taiwanese have been isolated from other Asian populations is supported by other studies of mtDNA and nuclear DNA variation (Melton et al. 1998). Nevertheless, we observed a relatively high degree of similarity, indeed overlap, between the mtDNA types of Taiwan and the Indonesian archipelago.

The Asian M, F, and B5 types are distributed all the way from China and Taiwan to Indonesia. Indonesia has also a small proportion of the 'Papuan' Q (M) and P (N) mtDNA types in the east, as well as the Polynesian types, but the predominant haplogroups throughout the archipelago are the various subgroups of the major group M, and to a lesser extent the N subgroups F and B5, found also in Taiwan,

Table 16.2 Summary of the population statistics calculated in each population on mtDNA sequences between positions 16,081 and 16,380

	n	9-bp %	No. of haplotypes	Haplotype diversity	SD	Mean pairwise difference	SD	Nucleotide diversity	SD	Tajima D
Easter Island	12	100	3	0.44	0.16	0.48	0.45	0.002	0.002	−0.85
Samoa	24	100	4	0.59	0.08	0.70	0.55	0.002	0.002	−0.41
Tonga	20	85	7	0.52	0.13	4.24	2.20	0.014	0.008	−1.20
Fiji	24	67	12	0.85	0.06	5.95	2.94	0.020	0.011	−0.53
Trobriand Is.	55	75	15	0.82	0.05	4.36	2.19	0.015	0.008	−1.07
New Britain	42	24	16	0.81	0.05	7.11	3.40	0.024	0.013	0.04
PNG south coast	23	78	7	0.65	0.10	4.92	2.49	0.016	0.009	−0.64
PNG highlands	37	0	28	0.98	0.01	10.95	5.09	0.037	0.019	−0.82
Indonesia – Ambon	22	14	17	0.94	0.05	7.23	3.52	0.024	0.013	−1.51
Indonesia – Lombok	24	25	19	0.97	0.02	7.45	3.61	0.025	0.013	−1.05
Indonesia – Manado	21	14	18	0.99	0.02	8.93	4.29	0.030	0.016	−1.40
Indonesia – Java	53	36	38	0.99	0.01	9.06	4.23	0.030	0.016	−1.27
Indonesia – Banjarmasin	22	27	21	1.00	0.02	8.36	4.03	0.028	0.015	−1.21
Taiwan	46	33	24	0.94	0.02	7.57	3.60	0.025	0.013	−0.81
China	38	16	35	1.00	0.01	9.02	4.25	0.030	0.016	−1.45
Madagascar	75	21	16	0.90	0.01	6.65	3.18	0.022	0.012	−0.11
Andamans	85	0	7	0.68	0.03	2.83	1.51	0.009	0.006	0.27

Notes
The Arlequin program (Schneider *et al.* 2000) was used; SD: standard deviation; the haplotype diversity gives an estimate of the variation in each population, taking into account the sample size and the number of different haplotypes observed in the sample. The mean pairwise difference between sequences was calculated using the Tamura and Nei substitution model, assuming a gamma distribution alpha = 0.4.

reflecting millennia of human interaction within Island Southeast Asia, and the wide distribution of Austronesian languages within the region. Only haplotype B4 1101, observed in 15 per cent of our Taiwanese sample, provides a clear-cut link between the mitochondrial types in Taiwan and Polynesia (not forgetting the previously typed HLA-DPB1 type 0501, which also connects Taiwan and Polynesia), consistent with an origin of the proto-Polynesians in Taiwan, and not east Indonesia, as suggested by others (Richards *et al.* 1998; Oppenheimer and Richards 2001a, 2001b).

Interestingly, our previously published genetic data on the Andaman Islanders of the Bay of Bengal, peoples who speak languages that have no relation to the Austronesian languages or other known languages of mainland and Southeast Asia, showed that these people carried mtDNA types solely belonging to a subtype of M haplogroup distinct to the types seen in the Austronesian world, and no N types, including F or B (Thangaraj et *al.* 2003).

Table 16.2 shows some simple population statistics for our samples, calculated using the Arlequin computer program (Schneider *et al.* 2000). The haplotype diversity is an estimate of the variation of a population and takes into account the sample size and the frequency of each haplotype. It is lowest in Easter Island, followed by the rest of Polynesia and our PNG south coast sample (and the Andaman Islands). The nucleotide diversity is also lowest in these locations, and highest in the PNG highlanders, followed by Han Chinese and Indonesians, reflecting the greater time depth of these populations. The Tajima D statistic is a rough measure of population growth and is negative in growing populations, and positive or near zero in static or contracting populations, like the Andamanese. The errors of these estimates are high due to the small size of our samples.

Mitochondrial DNA variation in Madagascar

We analyzed 74 individuals from Madagascar, from the groups Merina, Betsileo, Sihanaka, and Bezanozano. Madagascar is of particular interest to Austronesian scholars because the first permanent settlements appear to be associated with incursions from Southeast Asia 5th–7th century (Dewar 1994) or at least in the 2nd century AD (Burney 1993; Burney *et al.* 2004). Malagasy belongs to the Austronesian family, and is claimed to be closest to the South Barito group of languages spoken in Borneo (Dahl 1991), although more recent research links it to another Austronesian dialect, to Sama-Bajaw (Blust 2005).

Previous studies have shown that present-day Malagasy people derive from both Southeast Asian and African ancestors (Buettner-Janusch *et al.* 1973; Hewitt *et al.* 1996; Migot *et al.* 1995). Soodyall and colleagues showed that the 9-bp deletion was present in a high frequency of Malagasy in association with the Polynesian motif (Soodyall *et al.* 1995, 1996). A study by Hurles *et al.* (2005) indicated that the mtDNA and Y chromosome lineages in Malagasy groups show affinities to Southeast Asia and Africa. Their study included just 33 individuals of precisely the same sample collection as our study.

We detected 16 different mtDNA sequences among our 74 Malagasy, a relatively low genetic diversity (Table 16.2). In common with Hurles et al. (2005), we detected both African and Southeast Asian mtDNA lineages. Slightly less than a third of the maternal lineages were African types L2 and L3, and the rest were of Asian origin, while approximately half of the male lineages were African, and half Asian (Plate 16.I). A total of 14 (19 per cent) individuals carried the full Polynesian motif (1111), but none had the ancestral B4 types or B5 types with the 9-bp deletion, or the F type, observed throughout Southeast Asia. The other N or M Asian types were similar to other sequences found in Southeast Asia, but only one haplotype, found in 8 of the Malagasy, matched precisely a mtDNA type (M/D) found at low frequency in Java, Lombok, Manado, and Taiwan samples. Our results confirm that Malagasy have both Southeast Asian and African biological influences, but the high frequency of the Polynesian motif is intriguing, as this mtDNA type is not frequent in Indonesians, the presumed Southeast Asian source population of the Malagasy. We believe that this finding, together with the observation of high frequencies of the full Polynesian motif in parts of coastal New Guinea and island Melanesia, merits serious consideration.

Polynesian outliers in coastal and island Melanesia

The vast majority of the mtDNA types we observed in the Trobriand Islands and southern PNG were Polynesian (1111 and 1101), and identical to the types found by us and others throughout the Pacific triangle, as far as New Zealand (Murray-McIntosh et al. 1998). The presence of the Polynesian motif in island and coastal Melanesia might be compatible with an entangled web scenario of settlement, with Austronesian newcomers with the Polynesian motif (from a presumed homeland in east Indonesia) intermingling with resident Melanesians, followed by a genetic bottleneck in Melanesia (Melton et al. 1998; Oppenheimer and Richards 2001a, 2001b). However, we find this conclusion unlikely. We previously suggested that the Polynesian mtDNA type might have been carried from east Polynesia westwards towards island and coastal Melanesia. The low levels of genetic diversity observed at both the mtDNA and HLA loci in island and coastal Melanesia argue for a recent expansion of people into these areas (Hagelberg et al. 1999a). Looking at the genetic data alone, there is a strong argument for a relatively recent influx of Polynesians (not proto-Polynesians), and the question remains whether there is sufficient archaeological or linguistic evidence, or other genetic evidence, to support the contention of a recent east to west expansion.

An extensive study of mtDNA diversity in the Solomon Islands revealed relatively high frequencies of the Polynesian motif in both Austronesian and in many of non-Austronesian-language-speaking parts of island Melanesia, with the exception of the most remote non-Austronesian-speaking areas. The study concluded that Austronesians arriving *from the west* about 3500 years ago had carried the 9-bp deletion into Bougainville and New Britain (Merriwether et al. 1999; Friedlaender et al. 2002). When we surveyed ten different islands in Vanuatu, we also found the Polynesian motif in most of that Melanesian archipelago (Hagelberg *et al.* 1999b; Hagelberg unpublished observations). However, the Polynesian component of the population of these islands appeared evolutionarily younger than would be expected if derived from an Austronesian/ Lapita expansion 3500 years ago. Rather than relics of a west to east settlement of early Austronesian seafarers, many parts of island and coastal Melanesia appear to be 'Polynesian outliers', or pockets of Polynesia in Melanesia. As mentioned previously (Hagelberg *et al.* 1999a), the presence of the Polynesian *kava* (a Pacific shrub, *Piper methysticum*, used to make an intoxicating beverage known by the same name) as far west as Fly River, suggests that contacts with Polynesia extend considerably westwards along the PNG coast.

The question of Polynesian outliers in Melanesia is not new. As early as 1938, Peter Buck commented on the existence of Polynesian-looking people with a Polynesian culture and Polynesian dialects on many small Melanesian islands. He wrote: 'the "Polynesian outliers" are not stopping places on the route from New Guinea to Fiji but rather colonies which have been established by movements from the east and the north' (Buck 1938: 45). Buck argued for a northern trajectory of Polynesian settlement through Micronesia, with subsequent interactions between Polynesia, Micronesia and small Melanesian islands. As pointed out by Irwin (1992), the pattern of winds and currents supports this proposition, and archaeological evidence suggests multiple contacts throughout these islands. Irwin suggests that Polynesian inroads in many Melanesian islands were highly probable, but that local differences in population size and degree of isolation must have determined the degree of cultural or biological replacement and whether the Polynesian settlements lasted. He refers to Terrell (1986), who believed that, rather than being marginal phenomena, the kind of interactions that produced these apparent outliers were characteristic of Pacific prehistory.

East to west navigation in the Pacific is extremely efficient (Horridge 1995), as demonstrated by Lieutenant Bligh and other survivors of the *Bounty* mutiny, who sailed in an open boat from the central Pacific directly through the Torres Strait to Timor in east Indonesia. If Europeans could achieve this in the 18th century, why not Polynesian seafarers? Moreover, if sailing through the Torres Strait towards Indonesia was feasible, it is likely that the Polynesians would have done so. This could explain why the Polynesian motif is found in east Indonesia, but not in the west of the Indonesian archipelago, areas more inaccessible from the eastern Pacific.

This conclusion raises important questions. What proportion of the Austronesian genetic signature in coastal and island Melanesia is due to recent back-migrations? If the Polynesian mtDNA motif did not originate in east Indonesia but was taken there in recent centuries by Polynesians, where did it originate? If the ancestors of the Polynesians indeed expanded out of Taiwan, which route did they take into the Pacific? Is it possible that proto-Polynesian navigators might have taken a northern route, via Micronesia (as favoured by earlier ethnographers, discussed by Buck 1938)? These questions will not be answered by molecular genetics, however powerful its techniques, but will require the combined efforts of archaeologists, linguists, and biologists.

Conclusions

The vast majority of the maternal lineages of the inhabitants of the Polynesian triangle east of Samoa are of one single type, characterized by the so-called Polynesian mtDNA motif. The diversity of the DNA sequences is very low, suggesting a recent evolutionary history. This agrees with archaeological evidence of a recent settlement of Polynesia, and the homogeneity of the languages within Polynesia. The Polynesian mtDNA motif derives from mitochondrial types that are present in Asia. There is a clear link between the Polynesian motif and an ancestral but closely related type found in Taiwanese aboriginals (15 per cent). The full Polynesian motif and ancestral type are rare in Indonesia, being mostly confined to east Indonesia. However, these types are found at remarkably high frequencies in island and coastal PNG, accounting for 70 per cent of the mtDNA types in the Trobriand Islands, and 78 per cent in the south coast of PNG. We suggest that these sequences are not relics of the Austronesian settlement of the Pacific, but were carried in recent centuries by Polynesians into island Melanesia and coastal PNG, and as far as east Indonesia, to make these essentially Polynesian outliers.

In highland PNG there are two major mtDNA lineages, M (Q) and N (P). These lineages are ancient, and split from each other before the settlement of New Guinea. They form very distinct clusters in a phylogenetic tree of Southeast Asia and the Pacific, suggesting comparative isolation from the Indonesian archipelago. Mitochondrial types related to these 'Papuan' lineages are found in the Pacific throughout the Solomons and Vanuatu and as east as Fiji, and also westwards in Indonesia. The M and N types in Southeast Asia are related to the types found in PNG, notwithstanding the ancient split, and are found in areas where Austronesian languages are spoken today.

In Madagascar, about a third of the maternal lineages derive from Africa, and the rest from Southeast Asia. Many of the Southeast Asian mtDNA types in Madagascar are similar to those found in Indonesia. About 20 per cent of Malagasy carry the full Polynesian motif, found only at low frequencies in east Indonesia, and absent in the presumed Austronesian source population in Borneo. We suggest that the Malagasy Polynesian motif is indeed ultimately of Polynesian origin, and was carried to Madagascar not by Polynesians, but by the Malay settlers, who presumably acquired the motif through intermarriage with the descendants of the Polynesians in east Indonesia and coastal PNG. The very high proportion of the motif is tantalizing, and should not be dismissed as a genetic curiosity, but taken as possible evidence of long-range trade incursions, possibly associated with slave raids, from the Indonesian archipelago into coastal New Guinea.

The distribution of the Asian mtDNA F, and B5 haplotypes and some of the M types suggest the expansion of peoples from East Asia to Taiwan and Indonesia, with an active network of interactions that contrasts with the comparative isolation of New Guinea, which only has two principal, although ancient, mtDNA lineages.

The Polynesian motif seems to be derived from an ancestral type in Taiwan, and its exact time of entry into the Pacific is unclear, but the genetic evidence is consistent with a route of migration through the Philippines and Micronesia. The Polynesian expansion seems considerably more recent than the Lapita complex. We suggest the Polynesians continued their expansion westwards, replacing many maternal lineages in island Melanesia and the east and south coast of PNG, and reaching as far as east Indonesia. The picture suggested by mtDNA data is one of high mobility and complex interactions in the Pacific and Indian Ocean, including trade networks that continued until they were disrupted by competing Portuguese, Dutch, English, and French trading interests.

Acknowledgments

We are grateful to John Clegg and Chris-Tyler Smith for their generosity in providing DNA samples.

References

Anderson, A. (1991) 'The chronology of colonization in New Zealand', *Antiquity*, 65: 767–95.
Anderson, S., Bankier, A.T., Barrell, B.G., de Bruijn, M.H.L., Coulson, A.R., Drouin, J., Eperon, I.C., Nierlich, D.P., Roe, B.A., Sanger, F., Schreier, P.H., Smith, A.J.H., Staden, R. and Young, I.G. (1981) 'Sequence and organization of the human mitochondrial genome', *Nature*, 290: 457–65.
Ballinger, S.W., Schurr, T.G., Torroni, A., Gan, Y.Y., Hodge, J.A., Hassan, K., Chen, K.-H. and Wallace, D.C. (1992) 'Southeast Asian mitochondrial DNA analysis reveals genetic continuity of ancient mongoloid migrations', *Genetics*, 130: 139–52.
Bellwood, P. (1991) 'The Austronesian dispersal and the origin of languages', *Scientific American*, 265: 88–93.
Bellwood, P. (1995) 'Austronesian prehistory in southeast Asia: Homeland, expansion and transformation', in P. Bellwood, J.J. Fox and D. Tryon (eds) *The Austronesians: Historical and Comparative Perspectives*, Canberra: Australian National University.
Bellwood, P., Fox, J.J. and Tryon, D. (eds) (1995) *The Austronesians: Historical and Comparative Perspectives*, Canberra: Australian National University.
Blust, R.A. (1977) 'The Proto-Austronesian pronouns and Austronesian subgrouping: a preliminary report', *Working Papers in Linguistics*, Honolulu, HI: University of Hawai'i Department of Linguistics.
Blust, R.A. (1999) 'Subgrouping, circularity and extinction: some issues in Austronesian comparative linguistics', in E. Zeitoun and P.J.-k. Li (eds) *Selected Papers from the Eighth International Conference on Austronesian Linguistics*, pp. 31–94, Taipei: Institute of Linguistocs (Preparatoty Office), Academia Sinica.
Blust, R.A. (2005) 'The linguistic history of the Philippines: some speculations', in Hsiu-chuan Liao and C.R.G. Rubino (eds) *Current Issues in Philippines Linguistics and Anthropology: Parangal kay Lawrence A. Reid*, Manila: Linguistic Society of the Philippines and Summer Institute of Linguistics.
Buck, P.H. (1938) *Vikings of the Sunrise*, Philadelphia, PA: J.B. Lippincott Co.

Buettner-Janusch, J., Reisman, R., Coppenhaver, D., Mason, G. and Buettner-Janusch, V. (1973) 'Transferrins, haptoglobins and ceruplasmins among tribal groups of Madagascar', *American Journal of Physical Anthropology*, 38: 661–71.

Burney, D. (1993) 'Late Holocene environmental changes in arid southwestern Madagascar', *Quaternary Research*, 40: 98–106.

Burney, D.A., Burney, L.P., Godfrey, L.R., Jungers, W.L., Goodman, S.M., Wright, H.T. and Jull, A.J. (2004) 'A chronology for late prehistoric Madagascar', *Journal of Human Evolution*, 47: 25–63.

Cavalli-Sforza, L.L., Menozzi, P. and Piazza, A. (1994) *The History and Geography of Human Genes*, Princeton, NJ: Princeton University Press.

Dahl, O.C. (1991) *Migration from Kalimantan to Madagascar* (Institute for Comparative Research in Human Culture), Oslo: Norwegian University Press.

Dewar, R.E. (1994) 'The archaeology of the early settlement of Madagascar', in J. Reade (ed.) *The Indian Ocean in Antiquity*, pp. 471–86, London and New York: Kegan Paul and British Museum.

Diamond, J.M. (1988) 'Express train to Polynesia', *Nature*, 336: 307–8.

Elson, J.L., Turnbull, D.M. and Howell, N. (2004) 'Comparative genomics and the evolution of human mitochondrial DNA: assessing the effects of selection', *American Journal of Human Genetics*, 74: 229–38.

Friedlaender, J.S., Gentz, F., Green, K. and Merriwether, D.A. (2002) 'A cautionary tale on ancient migration detection: mitochondrial DNA variation in Santa Cruz Islands, Solomon Islands', *Human Biology*, 74: 453–71.

Groube, L., Chappell, J., Muke, J. and Price, D. (1983) 'A 40,000 year-old occupation site at Huon Peninsula', *Nature*, 324: 453–5.

Hagelberg, E. (1994) 'Ancient DNA studies', *Evolutionary Anthropology*, 2: 199–207.

Hagelberg, E. (2003) 'Recombination or mutation rate heterogeneity? Implications for Mitochondrial Eve', *Trends in Genetics*, 19: 84–90.

Hagelberg, E. and Clegg, J.B. (1993) 'Genetic polymorphisms in prehistoric Pacific islanders determined by analysis of ancient bone DNA', *Proceedings of the Royal Society of London*, Series B, *Biological Sciences*, 252: 163–70.

Hagelberg, E., Goldman, N., Lió, P., Whelan, S., Schiefenhövel, W., Clegg, J.B. and Bowden, D.K. (1999b) 'Evidence for mitochondrial DNA recombination in a human population of island Melanesia', *Proceedings of the Royal Society of London*, Series B, *Biological Sciences*, 266: 485–92.

Hagelberg, E., Kayser, M., Nagy, M., Roewer, L., Zimdahl, H., Krawczak, M., Lió, P. and Schiefenhövel, W. (1999a) 'Molecular genetic evidence for the human settlement of the Pacific: analysis of mitochondrial DNA, Y chromosome and HLA markers', *Philosophical Transactions of the Royal Society of London*, Series B, *Biological Sciences*, 354: 141–52.

Hagelberg, E., Quevedo, S., Turbon, D. and Clegg, J.B. (1994) 'DNA from ancient Easter Islanders', *Nature*, 369: 25–6.

Herrnstadt, C., Elson, J.L., Fahy, E., Preston, G., Turnbull, D.M., Anderson, C., Ghosh, S.S., Olefsky, J.M., Beal, M.F., Davis, R.E. and Howell, N. (2002) 'Reduced-median-network analysis of complete mitochondrial DNA coding-region sequences for the major African, Asian, and European haplogroups', *American Journal of Human Genetics*, 70: 1152–71.

Hertzberg, M., Mickleson, K.N., Serjeantson, S.W., Prior, J.F. and Trent, R.J. (1989) 'An Asian-specific 9-bp deletion of mitochondrial DNA is frequently found in Polynesians', *American Journal of Human Genetics*, 44: 504–10.

Hewitt, R., Krause, A., Goldman, A., Campbell, G. and Jenkins, T. (1996) 'ß-globin haplotype analysis suggests that a major source of Malagasy ancestry is derived from Bantu-speaking Negroids', *American Journal of Human Genetics*, 58: 1303–8.

Hill, A.V.S. and Serjeantson, S.W. (eds) (1989) *The Colonization of the Pacific: A Genetic Trail*, Oxford: Clarendon Press.

Hill, A.V.S., O'Shaughnessy, D.F. and Clegg, J.B. (1989) 'Haemoglobin and globin gene variants in the Pacific', in A.V.S. Hill and S.W. Serjeantson (eds) *The Colonization of the Pacific: A Genetic Trail*, pp. 246–85, Oxford: Oxford University Press.

Horridge, A. (1995) 'The Austronesian conquest of the sea – upwind', in P. Bellwood, J.J. Fox and D. Tryon (eds) *The Austronesians: Historical and Comparative Perspectives*, pp. 134–51, Canberra: Australian National University.

Hurles, M.E., Sykes, B.C., Jobling, M.A. and Forster, P. (2005) 'The dual origin of the Malagasy in Island Southeast Asia and East Africa: evidence from maternal and paternal lineages', *American Journal of Human Genetics*, 76: 894–901.

Irwin, G. (1992) *The Prehistoric Exploration and Colonisation of the Pacific*, Cambridge: Cambridge University Press.

Jin, H.J., Kwak, K.D., Hong, S.B., Shin, D.J., Han, M.S., Tyler-Smith, C. and Kim, W. (2005) 'Forensic genetic analysis of mitochondrial DNA hypervariable region I/II sequences: an expanded Korean population database', *Forensic Science International*, 158/125: 30.

Kayser, M., Brauer, S., Weiss, G., Underhill, P.A., Roewer, L., Schiefenhövel, W. and Stoneking, M. (2000) 'Melanesian origin of Polynesian Y chromosomes', *Current Biology*, 10: 1237–46.

Kivisild, T., Bamshad, M.J., Kaldma, K., Metspalu, M., Metspalu, E., Reidla, M., Laos, S., Parik, J., Watkins, W.S., Dixon, M.E., Papiha, S.S., Mastana, S.S., Mir, M.R., Ferak, V. and Villems, R. (1999) 'Deep common ancestry of Indian and western-Eurasian mitochondrial DNA lineages', *Current Biology*, 9: 1331–4.

Lum, J.K., Rickards, O., Ching, C., and Cann, R.L. (1994) 'Polynesian mitochondrial DNAs reveal three deep maternal lineage clusters', *Human Biology*, 66: 567–90.

Macaulay, V., Richards, M., Hickey, E., Vega, E., Cruciani, F., Guida, V., Scozzari, R., Bonné-Tamir, B., Sykes, B. and Torroni, A. (1999) 'The emerging tree of West Eurasian mtDNAs: a synthesis of control-region sequences and RFLPs', *American Journal of Human Genetics*, 64: 232–49.

Melton, T., Clifford, S., Martinson, J., Batzer, M. and Stoneking, M. (1998) 'Genetic evidence for the proto-Austronesian homeland in Asia: mtDNA and nuclear DNA variation in Taiwanese aboriginal tribes', *American Journal of Human Genetics*, 63: 1807–23.

Melton, T., Peterson, R., Redd, A.J., Saha, N., Sofro, A.S.M., Martinson, J. and Stoneking, M. (1995) 'Polynesian genetic affinities with Southeast Asian populations as identified by mtDNA analysis', *American Journal of Human Genetics*, 57: 403–14.

Merriwether, D.A., Friedlaender, J.S., Mediavilla, J., Mgone, C., Gentz, F. and Ferrell, R.E. (1999) 'Mitochondrial DNA variation is an indicator of Austronesian influence in Island Melanesia', *American Journal of Physical Anthropology*, 110: 243–70.

Migot, F., Perichon, B., Danze, P.-M., Raharimalala, L., Lepers, J.-P., Deloron, P. and Krishnamoorthy, R. (1995) 'HLA class II haplotype studies bring molecular evidence for population affinity between Madagascans and Javanese', *Tissue Antigens*, 46: 131–5.

Murray-McIntosh, R.P., Scrimshaw, B.J., Hatfield, P.J. and Penny, D. (1998) 'Testing migration patterns and estimating founding population size in Polynesia by using human mtDNA sequences', *Proceedings of the National Academy of Sciences USA*, 95: 9047–52.

O'Shaughnessy, D.F., Hill, A.V., Bowden, D.K., Weatherall, D.J. and Clegg, J.B. (1990) 'Globin genes in Micronesia: origins and affinities of Pacific island peoples', *American Journal of Human Genetics*, 46: 144–55.

Oppenheimer, S. and Richards, M. (2001a) 'Fast trains, slow boats, and the ancestry of the Polynesian islanders', *Science Progress*, 84: 157–81.

Oppenheimer, S.J. and Richards, M. (2001b) 'Polynesian origins: slow boat to Melanesia?', *Nature*, 410: 166–7.

Quintana-Murci, L., Semino, O., Bandelt, H.-J., Passarino, G., McElreavey, K. and Santachiara-Benerecetti, A.S. (1999) 'Genetic evidence of an early exit of Homo sapiens sapiens from Africa through eastern Africa', *Nature Genetics*, 23: 437–41.

Redd, A.J., Takezaki, N., Sherry, S.T., McGarvey, S.T., Sofro, A.S.M. and Stoneking, M. (1995) 'Evolutionary history of the COII/tRNALys intergenic 9 base pair deletion in human mitochondrial DNAs from the Pacific', *Molecular Biology and Evolution*, 12: 604–15.

Richards, M., Oppenheimer, S. and Sykes, B. (1998) 'mtDNA suggests Polynesian origins in eastern Indonesia', *American Journal of Human Genetics*, 63: 1234–6.

Ruiz-Pesini, E., Mishmar, D., Brandon, M., Procaccio, V. and Wallace, D.C. (2004) 'Effects of purifying and adaptive selection on regional variation in human mtDNA', *Science*, 303: 223–6.

Schneider, S., Roessli, D. and Excoffier, L. (2000) *Arlequin Version 2.000: A Software for Population Genetics Data Analysis*, Geneva: University of Geneva, Genetics and Biometry Laboratory.

Schwartz, M. and Vissing, J. (2002) 'Paternal inheritance of mitochondrial DNA', *New England Journal of Medicine*, 347: 576–80.

Soodyall, H., Jenkins, T., Hewitt, R., Krause, A. and Stoneking, M. (1996) 'The peopling of Madagascar', in A.J. Boyce and C.G.N. Mascie-Taylor (eds) *Molecular Biology and Human Diversity*, pp. 156–70, Cambridge: Cambridge University Press.

Soodyall, H., Jenkins, T. and Stoneking, M. (1995) '"Polynesian" mtDNA in the Malagasy', *Nature Genetics*, 10: 377–8.

Sykes, B., Leiboff, A., Low-Beer, J., Tetzner, S. and Richards, M. (1995) 'The origins of the Polynesians: an interpretation from mitochondrial lineage analysis', *American Journal of Human Genetics*, 57: 1463–75.

Terrell, J. (1986) *Prehistory in the Pacific Islands*, Cambridge: Cambridge University Press.

Terrell, J., Kelly, K.M. and Rainbird, P (2001) 'Foregone conclusions? In search of "Papuans" and "Austronesians"', *Current Anthropology*, 42: 97–124.

Thangaraj, K., Singh, L., Reddy, A.G., Rao, V.R., Sehgal, S.C., Underhill, P.A., Pierson, M., Frame, I.G. and Hagelberg, E. (2003) 'Genetic affinities of the Andaman Islanders, a vanishing human population', *Current Biology*, 13: 86–93.

Wallace, D.C. (1995) 'Mitochondrial DNA variation in human evolution, degenerative disease, and aging', *American Journal of Human Genetics*, 57: 201–23.

Wickler, S. and Spriggs, M. (1988) 'Pleistocene human occupation of the Solomon Islands, Melanesia', *Antiquity*, 62: 703–6.

Wrischnik, L.A., Higuchi, R.G., Stoneking, M., Erlich, H.A., Arnheim, N. and Wilson, A.C. (1987) 'Length mutations in human mitochondrial DNA: direct sequencing of enzymatically amplified DNA', *Nucleic Acids Research*, 15: 529–42.

Zimdahl, H., Schiefenhövel, W., Kayser, M., Roewer, L. and Nagy, M. (1999) 'Towards understanding the origin and dispersal of Austronesians in the Solomon Sea: HLA class II polymorphism in eight distinct populations of Asia-Oceania', *European Journal of Immunogenetics*, 26: 405–16.

17 A DNA signature for the expansion of irrigation in Bali?

*J. Stephen Lansing, Tatiana M. Karafet,
John Schoenfelder, and Michael F. Hammer*

Introduction

Archaeologists infer changes in social structure indirectly from the distribution of artifacts in space. But the chain of assumptions required for such inferences can sometimes become tenuous. Genetic markers offer a more direct approach to tracing not only the movement of populations on the landscape, but also patterns of genetic relatedness within communities. Here we utilize non-coding regions of DNA with rapid mutation rates to analyze changes in social structure associated with the historical development of wet-rice farming on the Indonesian island of Bali. We begin by reviewing current debates about irrigation in Bali. Subsequently, we present a model to explain the origins and spread of irrigation systems on Balinese volcanoes. We then test some of the model's predictions by means of a comparative analysis of genetic relatedness in 21 villages and nine regions of Bali.

The puzzle of Balinese irrigation

Anthropologists and historians have long debated the respective roles of princes and villagers in the creation and management of irrigation systems in Bali (Hauser-Schaüblin 2003). Elsewhere in Southeast Asia, the spread of irrigated rice agriculture was usually linked with the expansion of pre-colonial kingdoms. Typically, the earliest irrigation systems were constructed by particular villages, and then later consolidated and expanded by their rulers (Kulke 1986). But because of Bali's steep volcanic topography, 'the spatial distribution of Balinese irrigation canals, which by their nature cross community boundaries, made it impossible for irrigation to be handled at a purely community level' (Christie 1992). Thus even the earliest Balinese irrigation systems required a system of management that could extend beyond the boundaries of villages. The problem was solved by a new institution called *subak*, which begins to appear in 11th-century royal inscriptions. *Subak* were associations of farmers who shared water from a common source, such as a spring or irrigation canal. Typical ancient irrigation systems included multiple *subaks*, strung like melons on a vine to take advantage of water flowing through irrigation tunnels, aqueducts, and canals. For example, an inscription dated AD 1072 refers to a single *subak* comprising fields located in 27 named hamlets (Atmodjo 1986).

But while Balinese volcanoes gradually became honeycombed with irrigation tunnels, canals, and aqueducts, the spread of irrigation in Bali was largely unrecorded because Balinese kingdoms never entered an imperial phase, and stopped issuing inscriptions altogether by the middle of the 14th century. Half a millennium later, in 1811, Sir Stamford Raffles visited Bali and recorded his surprise that the rajahs of Bali were merely one group of landowners among many others; 'The sovereign [that is, the Raja of Buleleng] is not here considered the universal landlord; on the contrary, the soil is almost invariably considered as the private property of the subject, in whatever manner it is cultivated or divided' (Raffles 1817). The marginal role of Balinese kings in irrigation, also noted by later colonial observers (Geertz 1980), prompted a question that has been debated for nearly a century: does Bali provide an exception to the thesis that irrigation encourages the centralization of power? Some scholars envision a slow process of irrigation expansion driven by the needs of villagers, while others argue that the key role was played by the rajahs, with the *subaks* serving as merely a reservoir of manpower (Hauser-Schaüblin 2003; Lansing 2005). In the absence of definitive written records, the evidence needed to resolve this dispute must come from archaeology and, as we shall show, population genetics.

Archaeology of irrigation in Bali

The earliest Balinese irrigation systems were probably simple canals channeling water from natural springs into adjacent valleys. A few systems of this type are still functioning today, and in 1997 we undertook an archaeological study of one of them: the Gunung Kawi irrigation system, which is located near the upper reaches of one of Bali's major rivers, the Petanu (Map 17.I).

The temple of Gunung Kawi encloses two natural springs located in a deep natural depression, just south of the village of Sebatu. Closest to the springheads are fountains where water can be collected for ritual purifications. Below them the water is led into pools for bathing, and then into a fishpond. The spring water then enters a short tunnel and emerges a few hundred meters downstream, where it irrigates 0.89 hectares of rice terraces. From there the unused water enters a canal that continues for 4 km before emerging atop a terraced hill where it is used to irrigate 31 hectares of paddies near the village of Dlod Blungbang (Figure 17.1). This system of irrigation canals includes five tunnels, the longest of which is 1.5 km long. We speculated that, long before the start of irrigation in Bali, farmers would have been drawn to this site as an ideal place to grow typical Austronesian crops such as coconuts, taro, bananas, and possibly rice. Later, with the appearance of irrigation technology, the site would have become even more desirable. Water from the spring could easily be channeled into the depression downstream. Digging the short surface canal needed for this purpose would have been much easier than carving irrigation tunnels through the

378   J. Stephen Lansing et al.

Map 17.1   Map of Bali showing locations of Gunung Kawi (Gianyar) and Tabanan *subaks*, site of archaeological study (Sebatu), and boundaries of the nine regions from which DNA samples were taken.

volcanic rock, so this site would likely have been one of the first to be exploited by early farmers.

We mapped the temple, the irrigation canals that flow out of it, and the fields that depend on this flow (Figure 17.2). We also sank 18 soil cores to a depth of up to 5 meters and carried out analyses of sediment, pollen, and phytoliths on the samples thus extracted. We found that, as predicted, before the advent of irrigated rice cultivation, the valley bottom was a swampy forest dominated by palms and bananas. Taro was probably also grown but because it does not produce pollen, this could not be directly confirmed. Later, irrigated rice was grown in the small concave depression immediately downstream from the water temple. Sedimentology indicated a very rapid buildup of sediments after the appearance of irrigation systems. For example, a radiocarbon date from a core extracted from a currently unutilized terrace surface north of the temple showed that nearly 3 meters of soil had been deposited at this location in the past 500 years. Local farmers showed us how the predictable buildup of sediments could be managed to contour the landscape, enlarging the area suitable for terracing and facilitating the flow of water in small canals. The little basin located south of the temple widened as a result of sediment buildup, but even today it is much too small to use more than a small fraction of the water that flows from the springs. So at some point, the farmers began to construct a series of small tunnels, aqueducts, and canals, which now transport most of the flow 4 km downstream to the *subak* of Dlod Blungbang. Three of our 16 cores struck

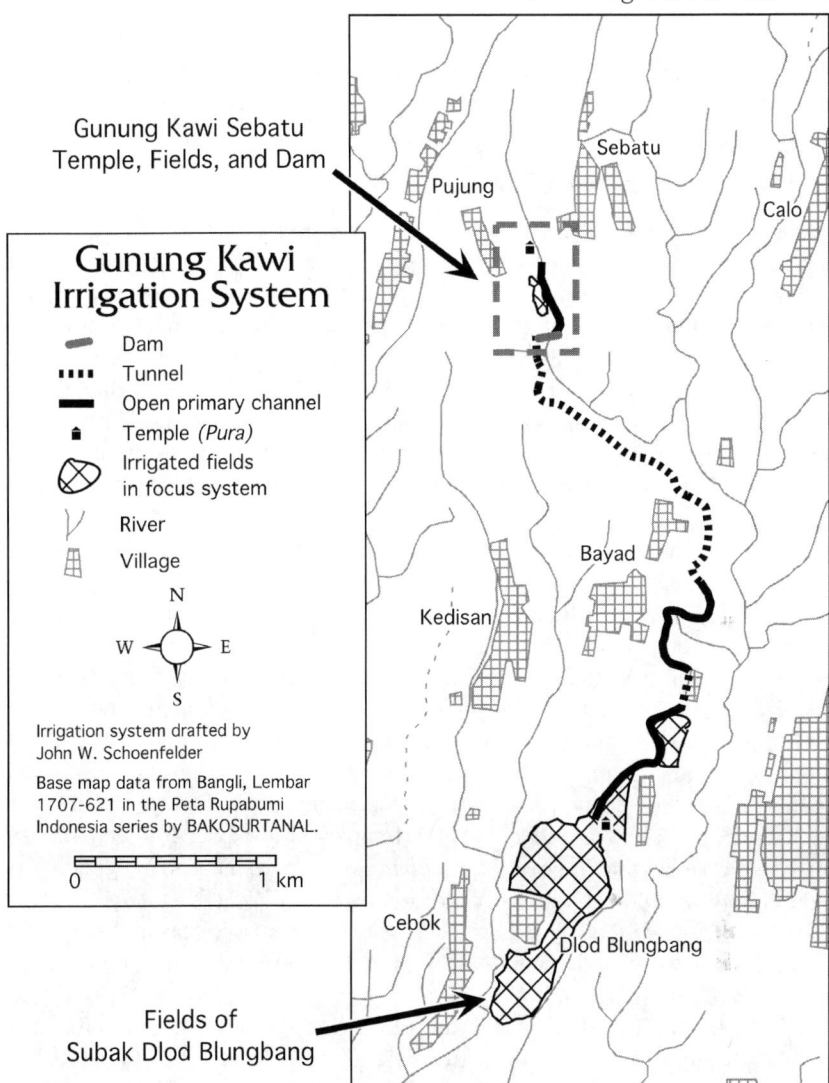

Figure 17.1 Irrigation systems originating from springs at Gunung Kawi Sebatu, the site of our archaeological investigation.

defunct irrigation tunnels, evidence for the frequency with which landscape changes, including the accumulation of sediment, compelled the farmers to modify their irrigation systems. We spoke with older farmers who recalled participating in the demolition of a weir and construction of new tunnels and canals leading out of the topmost fields about 40 years before. Altogether, these results suggested that, over a period of centuries, small teams of farmers were continuously engaged in skilled micro-engineering to maintain control of the flows of water and sediment. There was no evidence for the mobilization of large teams of laborers, or the use of more sophisticated technology than that available to the villagers (Scarborough *et al.* 1999, 2000).

The problem of cooperation

The results of the Gunung Kawi study are consistent with a slow, accretive expansion of irrigation systems organized and executed by local farmers. There is no obvious technical need for a higher authority to carry out the construction of these irrigation works. But irrigation water is often in short supply during the dry season. Consequently there is a need for some mechanism or authority to safeguard the water rights of downstream communities such as Dlod Blungbang. A solution to this problem must have been found centuries ago; otherwise the kilometers-long irrigation systems linking multiple *subaks* would be pointless, and the total area of terraced fields on the island could never have reached its historic extent.

To find out how the problem of water sharing is solved by farmers today, we undertook ethnographic studies of the *subaks* located in the vicinity of our archaeological investigations at Gunung Kawi. In general, every *subak* collectively manages its irrigation system and flows as a form of common property. Monthly meetings provide a venue for *subak* members to make plans, organize work teams, and assess fines or other penalties on members who do not fulfill their obligations. In addition, all of the *subaks* located near the site of our excavations belong to the congregation of a nearby water temple, Pamos Apuh. Each *subak* elects a leader to represent them at monthly meetings of the 'Greater Subak of the Pamos Apuh Temple', a group of fourteen *subaks* that has the right to adjudicate inter-*subak* issues pertaining to irrigation. To find out how well this system works, or in other words whether *subaks* located downstream receive their fair share of irrigation water, we measured the flows to eleven *subaks* during the month of July in 1997 and 1998, at the height of the dry season (Table 17.1).

Sebatu, Jasan, Timbul, and Calo, the *subaks* located furthest upstream, have a slight advantage over their downstream neighbors. However, this is probably a consequence of the way that flows are measured, not a deliberate attempt to cheat. Water rights are based on proportional division (*tektek*) at the points where the flow is divided. This method does not take into account downstream losses from percolation and evaporation. Consequently it is to be expected that downstream *subaks* will receive slightly less water. It is also apparent that the *subaks* furthest downstream (Kebon, Kedisan Kelod, and Pakudui) are only slightly disadvantaged. A survey of 150 farmers from ten *subaks* supports this conclusion. In answer to the question, 'Is the division of water by the Pamos Water Temple equitable?', all said yes.

A DNA signature in Bali 381

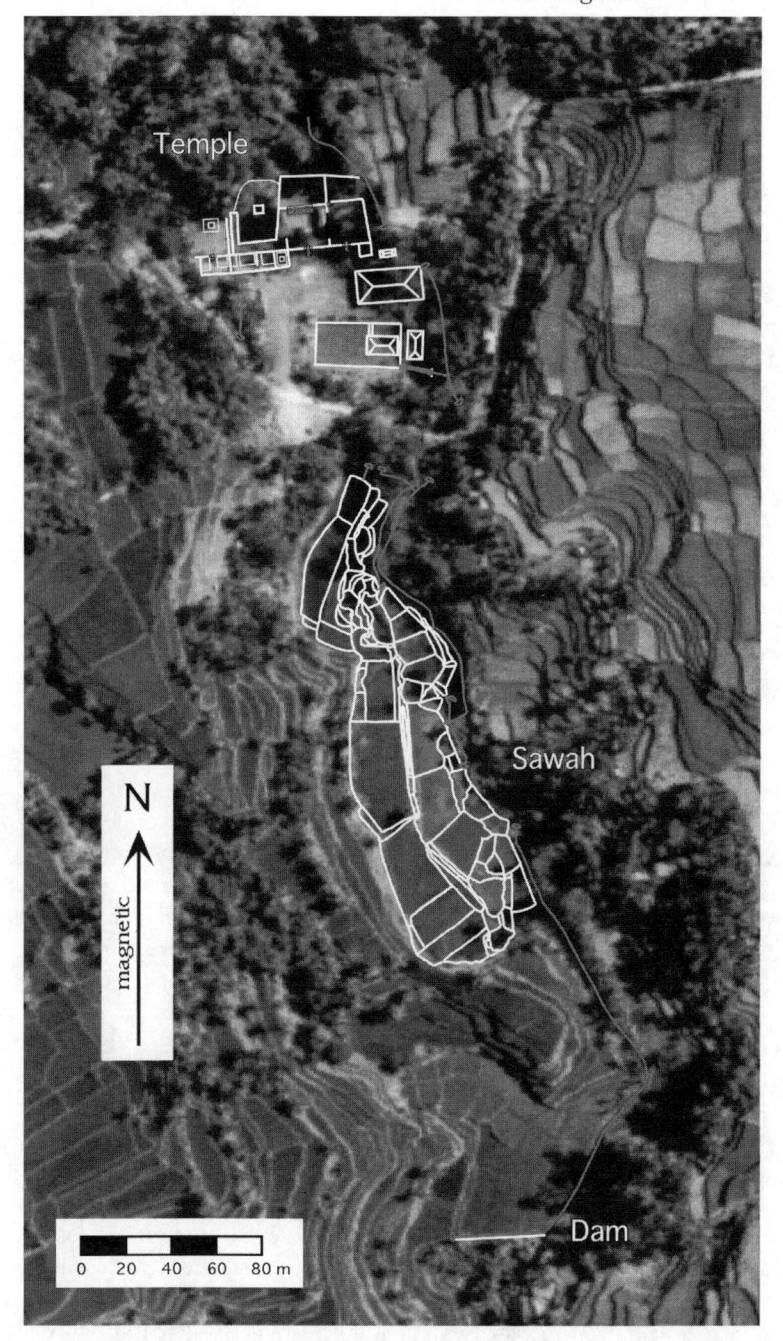

Figure 17.2 Aerial photograph with outline of the Gunung Kawi water temple and adjacent rice paddies superimposed. The small area of irrigated rice paddies (sawah) shown in outline lies at a slightly lower elevation than the temple with its springs.

Table 17.1 Comparison of average measured irrigation flows (in liters per second) and water rights for 11 *subaks* in the vicinity of Gunung Kawi (Gianyar) during the dry season, July 1997 and July 1998

Subaks	Average flow (liters/sec)	% of flow	Water rights in tektek	% of tekteks
Jasan, Sebatu	368	19.42	16.0	17.02
Timbul, Calo	460	24.27	21.0	22.34
Pujung kaja	207	10.92	11.5	12.23
Kedisan kaja, Kedisan kelod	214	11.29	16.0	17.02
Bayad	198	10.45	7.0	7.45
Pujung kelod	111	5.86	5.5	5.85
Kebon, Kedisan kelod, Pakudui	337	17.78	17.0	18.09
Total	1895	100.00	94.0	100.00

Water rights are measured in proportional shares of the total flow (tektek).

Mechanisms to promote cooperation

Both our flow measurements and the survey results support the conclusion that farmers in downstream *subaks* can rely on a steady supply of irrigation water reaching their fields after it passes through, beneath, or alongside the terraced fields of their upstream neighbors. Although it would be easy for the upstream farmers to take more than their agreed-upon share of water, in our surveys most farmers reported only mild anxiety with regard to the danger of water theft. There was a single exception: in one *subak*, weak leadership triggered a need for the farmers to organize teams to police the irrigation works several times a day during the dry season of 1997 (Lansing 2006). But this was the exception that proved the rule: ordinarily there appears to a very high level of cooperation within and between *subaks*. How is such cooperation sustained? We identified two relevant mechanisms. One has its roots in the ecology of the rice paddies, and the other in marital alliances. We begin with the ecological mechanism.

Rice is vulnerable to a variety of pests, including rodents, insects, and bacterial and viral diseases spread by insects. But Balinese farmers are able to reduce pest populations by synchronizing fallow periods in large contiguous blocks of rice terraces. After harvest, the fields are flooded, depriving pests of their habitat and thus causing their numbers to dwindle. The need to minimize losses from pests provides a strong motivation for farmers to cooperate with their neighbors in synchronous planting schedules. This gives downstream farmers a bargaining lever in negotiations over water with their upstream neighbors: if the downstream farmers don't receive enough water to synchronize their planting schedule with upstream farmers, then there will be no widespread fallow interval, and rice pests may migrate upstream. Pest control is an important consideration for the farmers:

after a few seasons of unsynchronized cropping schedules, losses from pest outbreaks can approach 100 per cent.

To test whether this logic reflects the thinking of the farmers, in the summer of 1998 we carried out a survey of farmers in ten *subaks* that belong to the congregation of the Pamos water temple. In each of the ten *subaks*, we chose a random sample of fifteen farmers. Of these fifteen, five were selected whose fields are located in the upstream part of their *subak*; five more from the middle of the *subak*, and the last five from the downstream section of the *subak*. We asked 'Which problem is worse, damage from pests or irrigation water shortages?' The results, shown in Figure 17.3, show that upstream farmers worry more about pests, while downstream farmers are more concerned with water shortages.

The same dynamics can occur at the next level up (Figure 17.4). Not only individual farmers, but whole *subaks* must decide whether or not to cooperate. In our sample, six of the ten *subaks* were situated in upstream/downstream pairs, where the downstream *subak* obtains most of its water from its upstream neighbor. Thus it was also possible to compare the aggregate response of all the farmers in each downstream *subak* to the response of their upstream neighbors.

Here also, upstream farmers are more concerned with potential damage from pests than from water shortages, and so have a reason to cooperate with downstream neighbors. By adjusting their own irrigation flows the upstream *subaks* have the power to promote a solution that is beneficial for everyone. In a recent publication, we presented a formal model showing that cooperation is the predicted outcome for farmers faced with this tradeoff between water sharing and pest control, for a wide range of field conditions (Lansing and Miller 2005).

The observed pattern of marriages by the farmers suggests a second mechanism sustaining cooperation. If cooperation is vital to the success of the *subak* as an egalitarian institution managing a vital common resource (water), then marital

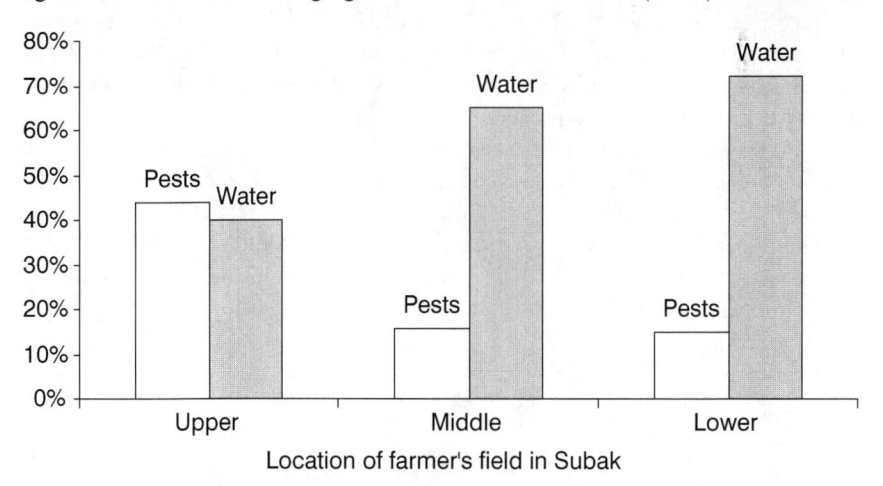

Figure 17.3 Relationship of the location of a farmer's fields to his views on the relative importance of losses from pests or water shortages, based on a sample survey of 150 farmers in ten *subaks* in the Gunung Kawi Sebatu region.

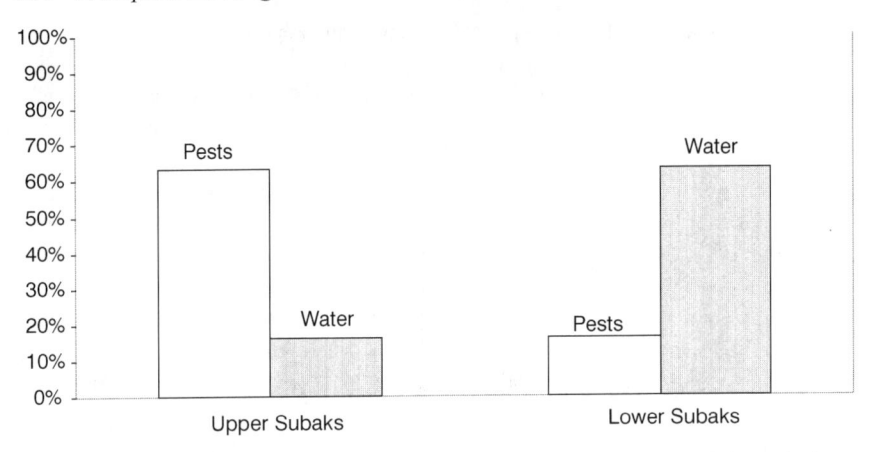

Figure 17.4 Aggregate responses of 90 farmers in three upstream *subaks* and three downstream *subaks*.

alliances provide a way to create bonds between farm families. We asked about twenty married men in each of thirteen *subaks*, a total of 252 individuals, whom they had married: 84 per cent had chosen a wife from among the daughters of men belonging to their own *subak*. Interestingly, a survey of marriage preferences in two highland villages (where *subaks* do not exist) showed that these men are much less likely to marry within their communities; the rate of endogamous marriages falls to 34 per cent. A fuller analysis of these mechanisms is presented by Lansing (2006).

Insights from genetics on the history of the *subaks*

Results from our archaeological studies are consistent with a model of expansion of wet-rice irrigation carried out by villagers rather than the state: demographic pressure provided an incentive for villages to gradually bud off daughter settlements downstream as the island's population grew. This is similar to Peter Bellwood and James Fox's Austronesian expansion model, in which some younger siblings become pioneers who create new communities. Bellwood suggests that 'junior founders ... could establish senior lines, aggrandize their resources, and attempt to ensure methods of genealogical inheritance which would retain privileges for their descendants' (Bellwood 1996: 19). Kinship bonds would provide a motive for cooperation with daughter settlements in the first phase of this process. Later on, cooperation could be sustained by the joint need to control rice pests. Consequently, there would be little need for an external coercive authority (e.g. the state) to enforce water rights for downstream *subaks* in large multi-*subak* irrigation systems.

In the absence of historical documents for the relevant period (14th–19th centuries), how could this model be tested? Conventional archaeological methods (such as those we used at Gunung Kawi) provide insights into the historical development of irrigation technology but permit only indirect inferences about the social management of irrigation. However, in the last decade, geneticists have developed tools to assess variation in non-coding regions of the human genome that are subject to very rapid rates of mutation. Using these markers it is possible to trace micro-migrations and changing patterns of relatedness within small communities in the recent past. The amount of genetic variation observed in populations is deeply influenced by demography and thus can shed light on settlement patterns (Hurles *et al.* 2005).

We can construct two alternative scenarios for the expansion of irrigation and rice cultivation, which would produce contrasting signals in the genetic structure of farming villages. If the expansion of irrigation was accomplished by the farmers rather than their rulers, then population movement of males (patrilineages) would occur only as a result of demographic pressure leading to the formation of new daughter settlements close to the parent villages. This budding model would predict the formation of small communities located along irrigation systems, with the oldest settlements located at the irrigation outtakes located closest to the most ancient weirs or springs. Small population size and reproductive isolation would produce high rates of genetic drift; the older the community, the more evidence of drift. On the other hand, the younger *subaks* would undergo a substantial founder effect, in particular for the male part of the population. Patrilineages should exhibit less evidence of movement on the landscape than matrilineages, because only males inherit rights to farmland. But matrilineages should also be very localized because of the preference for marriage within one's own *subak*. Thus a budding model of irrigation expansion by the *subaks* would predict a clear pattern of population structure for both patrilineal and matrilineal inheritance in the rice-growing regions of Bali.

In the alternative scenario in which the expansion of irrigation was managed by the state, none of these constraints would be in evidence. Instead, the population would serve as a reservoir of labor, which could be relocated by the rulers to build and service new irrigation systems. Overall, this scenario would predict a more fluid population structure with less nucleation of settlements and less genetic drift within settlements, compared with the budding model. In 2001, we began to gather the genetic data needed to test these hypotheses.

A genetic test of the budding model

DNA samples

We analyzed a total of 507 Balinese males. One group consisted of 287 farmers from 13 *subaks* belonging to the Pamos Apuh water temple, in the vicinity of Gunung Kawi as described above. These 13 *subaks* are located in the region where most of the earliest Balinese kingdoms appeared. Irrigated rice cultivation is frequently mentioned in royal inscriptions addressed to villages in this region in the 10th through the 13th centuries (Ardika 1986, 1994; Goris 1954; van Stein Callenfels 1926). Although they obtain irrigation water from numerous sources, including three weirs and the springs described above, these *subaks* are all located in a relatively small cluster (with average geographic distances among *subaks* only 3.2 km), and are of similar size, averaging 63 hectares.

The second group consists of 120 farmers belonging to eight *subaks* located along the Sungi river in the regency of Tabanan (Map 17.I). These *subaks* were included in the study to provide a contrast with the Gunung Kawi *subaks*. The absence of archaeological evidence for early kingdoms in Tabanan suggests that rice cultivation began later there than in the Gunung Kawi region; consequently the Tabanan *subaks* should be younger. The Tabanan *subaks* were also chosen to shed light on the relative permanence of farming villages. The eight *subaks* in the sample were selected from sites spanning the full length of the Sungi River, from the uppermost reaches to the sea (average geographic distance is 13.9 km). While the upper *subaks* are about the same size as the 13 Gunung Kawi *subaks*, several of the lower *subaks* are much larger. Thus, our sample of *subaks* encompasses a range of contrasts, including ages, sizes, and regions. The third group comprises 100 random samples from each of the nine administrative districts on the island (Map 17.I), to provide context for the *subak* samples. All sampling protocols were approved by the Human Subjects Committee of the University of Arizona and the Eijkman Institute for Molecular Biology.

Genetic markers and data analyses

The Y chromosome polymorphic sites in our survey included 71 single nucleotide polymorphisms (SNPs) and 12 short tandem repeats (STRs) published by Karafet *et al.* (2005). Sequence data for the hypervariable segment 1 (HVS1 – 519 bp) of mtDNA were analyzed with the SEQUENCHER software program. Parameters of within-population diversity, including Nei's (1987) haplotype diversity (h), which is based on the frequency and number of haplogroups, and the mean number of pairwise differences among haplogroups, population genetic structure indices, and relationships between genetic and geographic structure by the Mantel test were estimated by using the ARLEQUIN 2.000 software (Schneider *et al.* 2000). The standardized measure G'_{ST} (Hedrick 2005) was calculated to compare the levels of differentiation between Y-chromosome and mtDNA data. Median-joining (MJ) networks (Bandelt *et al.* 1999) were constructed by using the NETWORK 2.0c program. For network calculations STRs were weighted according to their repeat number variances. The reduced median output was used as input for the median-joining network.

Genetic structure of Balinese subaks

Genetic diversity based on mtDNA and Y-chromosome data for all populations are given in Table 17.2. The trend for all three genetic systems demonstrated lower diversity in the Gunung Kawi region, compared with Tabanan and Bali as a whole. For Y-chromosome SNP markers in the Gunung Kawi *subaks*, the average h and p values were 0.52 and 1.99, respectively. These very low diversity values may be explained by the fact that 7 out of 13 Gunung Kawi *subaks* possess only one to three predominant haplogroups belonging to lineage O. The Tabanan *subaks* had substantially higher Y-SNP diversity (0.67 and 2.86, respectively for Nei's *h* and *p*). Nine different geographic regions of Bali showed an intermediate *h* (0.65) and the highest *p* (2.99) values. Diversity values for 12 Y-chromosome STRs also showed a general decline in *h* and *p* values for *subaks* in the Gunung Kawi region compared with those for Tabanan *subaks* and nine geographic regions in Bali. The finding of *both* Y-SNP and Y-STR diversity reductions is important because the tandem repeat markers do not suffer from a potential SNP's ascertainment bias (Hammer *et al*. 2001; Jobling and Tyler-Smith 2003). The first hypervariable segment of the mtDNA (519 BP) once again revealed significantly reduced variation in Gunung Kawi. Given the archaeological data indicating an older age of Gunung Kawi *subaks* compared with Tabanan, these results are consistent with a smaller effective population size for the Gunung Kawi region. This supports the hypothesis that Gunung Kawi *subaks* were established as small communities over a long period of time, perhaps experiencing sequential founder effects as predicted by the budding deme model (Fix 2002). Moreover, since migrants comprised a biological kin group, migration may actually increase local genetic differentiation (Fix 2004).

To further investigate the putative effects of serial founder effects on the Gunung Kawa *subak* system, we compared diversity parameters of the older (Bayad, Pujung, Sebatu, and Timbul) and younger *subaks* (Jati, Jasan, Bonjaka, and Tegal) of Gunung Kawi. As predicted by the budding deme model, the mean diversity in the younger Gunung Kawi *subaks* was lower than that in the older *subaks* in all parameters except pairwise differences (*p*) among mtDNA HVS sequences (Y-SNPs: 0.644 versus 0.411 for *h*, 2.49 versus 1.55 for *p*; Y-STRs: 0.933 versus 0.929 for *h*, 6.36 versus 5.16 for *p*; mtDNA: 0.926 versus 0.898 for *h*, 7.24 versus 7.39 for *p*). We also constructed a median-joining network for the most frequent haplogroup O-M95 in Bali (Plates 17.Ia and 17.Ib). The network of the O- M95 haplotypes in older *subaks* showed a notable microsatellite differentiation with several reticulations and without single shared haplotype (Plate 17.Ia). The majority O-M95 chromosomes in the younger *subaks* were connected in a simple way with one haplotype shared by all four *subaks*, and with seven haplotypes found in more than one population (Plate 17.Ib).

A budding deme model also predicts an increase in genetic differentiation among subpopulations as the process continues over time (Fix 2002). The F_{ST} values for the Gunung Kawi *subaks* were notably higher for all three genetic systems than those for Tabanan *subaks* and the nine randomly collected samples in Bali, indicating a significant degree of genetic differentiation within Gunung Kawi region (Table 17.3). For Y-SNPs Gunung Kawi exhibited a high F_{ST} value (0.141), nearly twice as high as for the regional Bali sample (0.075). Interestingly, Tabanan *subaks* were not significantly differentiated from one another. The same trend was observed for Y-STRs; however, genetic differentiation for Tabanan *subaks* was statistically significant (Table 17.3).

The Bali regions exhibited significant population structure for both Y-SNPs and Y-STRs (Table 17.3), but not for mtDNA ($F_{ST} = 0.008$, $P = 0.097$). Many studies of

Table 17.2 Genetic diversity parameters based on Y-SNP haplogroups, Y-STR haplotypes and mtDNA HVS1 sequences for individual populations

Subaks	Y-SNP						Y-STR						mtDNA					
	N	n	h	SE	p	SE	N	n	h	SE	p	SE	N	n	h	SE	p	SE
Gunung Kawi subaks																		
Bayad	20	5	0.62	0.11	2.31	1.32	20	13	0.93	0.04	6.31	3.12	20	12	0.93	0.04	7.51	3.66
Bonjaka	21	6	0.65	0.10	3.03	1.64	21	14	0.95	0.03	6.21	3.07	21	10	0.87	0.05	7.72	3.75
Calo	23	4	0.64	0.09	2.04	1.19	23	16	0.96	0.02	6.09	3.01	22	11	0.91	0.04	7.42	3.60
Jasan	23	1	0.00	0.00	0.00	0.00	23	15	0.94	0.03	3.58	1.89	23	13	0.94	0.03	7.01	3.42
Jati	20	3	0.49	0.12	1.69	1.03	20	12	0.93	0.03	5.62	2.81	20	12	0.90	0.05	7.52	3.66
Kaja	20	3	0.51	0.04	1.90	1.13	20	13	0.93	0.04	6.09	3.03	20	9	0.89	0.04	7.07	3.46
Kebon	20	1	0.00	0.00	0.00	0.00	20	9	0.88	0.05	3.23	1.74	20	6	0.62	0.11	4.44	2.28
Kelod	20	3	0.58	0.05	2.75	1.52	20	15	0.96	0.03	6.45	3.19	18	10	0.90	0.05	6.57	3.26
Pakudui	19	6	0.74	0.09	3.02	1.65	19	12	0.94	0.04	6.67	3.29	18	6	0.81	0.07	10.10	4.84
Pujung	20	6	0.78	0.06	3.79	1.99	20	12	0.95	0.03	6.79	3.34	20	10	0.91	0.04	5.74	2.87
Sebatu	38	4	0.67	0.04	2.32	1.30	38	19	0.90	0.04	5.64	2.67	38	16	0.91	0.03	8.02	3.81
Tegal	23	3	0.50	0.08	1.48	0.93	22	10	0.89	0.04	5.25	2.64	23	10	0.89	0.05	7.30	3.55
Timbul	20	3	0.51	0.09	1.56	0.97	20	13	0.95	0.03	6.72	3.31	18	12	0.95	0.03	7.69	3.76
Mean			0.52		1.99				0.93		5.74				0.88		7.24	
Total	287	14	0.60	0.03	2.82	1.49	286	125	0.99	0.00	6.36	3.03	281	72	0.96	0.01	7.85	3.67
Tabanan subaks																		
Apit Yeh	7	3	0.67	0.16	2.38	1.47	7	6	0.95	0.10	5.95	3.23	7	7	1.00	0.08	9.33	4.89
Bena	20	5	0.75	0.07	3.54	1.88	20	15	0.97	0.03	7.60	3.70	18	12	0.95	0.03	7.95	3.88
Gadon	20	7	0.64	0.12	2.82	1.55	17	14	0.99	0.02	6.76	3.34	19	16	0.98	0.03	7.92	3.85

continued...

Table 17.2 continued

Subaks	Y-SNP					Y-STR							mtDNA						
	N	n	h	SE	p	SE	N	n	h	SE	p	SE	N	n	h	SE	p	SE
Jaka	10	2	0.47	0.13	1.87	1.16	10	7	0.96	0.06	5.78	3.02	10	7	0.91	0.08	6.29	3.26
P.Akitan	10	4	0.78	0.09	3.51	1.95	10	6	0.91	0.08	6.28	3.25	10	7	0.91	0.08	7.56	3.85
Sungi	20	6	0.73	0.07	2.60	1.45	20	15	0.98	0.02	6.84	3.36	20	11	0.92	0.04	7.73	3.76
Tungkub	20	6	0.73	0.07	3.59	1.90	20	18	0.99	0.02	6.99	3.43	18	14	0.97	0.03	8.07	3.93
Uma Poh	13	3	0.62	0.08	2.62	1.49	13	12	0.99	0.04	6.55	3.31	12	7	0.83	0.10	8.79	4.36
Mean			0.67		2.86				0.97		6.59				0.93		7.95	
Total	120	15	0.69	0.04	3.03	1.59	118	90	0.99	0.00	6.91	3.27	114	58	0.98	0.00	8.32	3.88
Geographic regions in Bali																		
Badung	11	4	0.49	0.18	2.40	1.41	11	10	0.98	0.05	5.85	3.03	11	9	0.96	0.05	9.24	4.60
Bangli	9	3	0.67	0.10	2.89	1.67	9	5	0.81	0.12	6.50	3.40	9	9	1.00	0.05	7.50	3.87
Buleleng	9	2	0.22	0.17	0.89	0.68	9	9	1.00	0.05	4.78	2.58	9	8	0.97	0.06	7.83	4.03
Denpasar	8	4	0.64	0.18	3.25	1.87	8	8	1.00	0.06	6.57	3.47	7	7	1.00	0.08	10.00	5.21
Gianyar	25	5	0.71	0.05	3.83	1.99	25	23	0.99	0.01	7.26	3.52	23	17	0.97	0.02	7.84	3.79
Jembrana	4	4	1.00	0.18	4.00	2.52	4	4	1.00	0.18	7.67	4.53	4	4	1.00	0.18	7.17	4.26
Karangasem	12	5	0.80	0.09	4.23	2.26	12	12	1.00	0.03	7.74	3.88	9	8	0.97	0.06	9.06	4.61
Klungkung	12	4	0.74	0.08	3.82	2.07	12	10	0.95	0.06	7.38	3.71	12	9	0.95	0.05	8.56	4.26
Tabanan	10	2	0.53	0.09	1.60	1.03	10	7	0.87	0.11	5.80	3.03	10	10	1.00	0.04	8.07	4.09
Mean			0.65		2.99				0.96		6.62				0.98		8.36	
Total	100	11	0.69	0.04	3.27	1.70	100	77	0.99	0.00	7.06	3.34	94	81	1.00	0.00	8.66	4.04

N: number of individuals; n: number of haplotypes; h: gene diversity; SE: standard error; p: mean number of pairwise differences

Table 17.3 F_{ST} parameters for Y-SNP haplogroups, Y-STR haplotypes and mtDNA HVS1 sequences

	Y-SNP		Y-STR		mtDNA	
	Fst	p	Fst	p	Fst	p
Gunung Kawi (N = 13)	0.141	0.000	0.061	0.000	0.086	0.000
Tabanan (N =8)	0.009	0.274	0.024	0.000	0.052	0.000
Bali (N = 9)	0.075	0.011	0.034	0.000	0.008	0.097

p: p-value; N: number of individuals.

local populations have shown the similar pattern, which has been attributed to sex-biased migration associated with the common practice of patrilocality (Seielstad et al. 1998; Jorde et al. 2000). (But for alternate findings and explanations see Destro-Bisol et al. 2004; Wilder et al. 2004; Wood et al. 2005.) Interestingly, we found a higher F_{ST} value for mtDNA variation than for Y-STR variation in Gunung Kawi and Tabanan *subaks*. Because the interpretation of genetic differentiation based on measures of F_{ST} is complicated by its dependence on levels of genetic diversity associated with different loci (e.g. see Table 17.3), we computed a standardized measure of genetic variation described by Hedrick (2005). This measure (G'_{ST}), which is related to the widely used G_{ST} parameter, allows more appropriate comparisons between loci with different mutation rates. G'_{ST} estimates showed similar levels of differentiation for mtDNA and Y-STR data in the Bali region (mtDNA G'_{ST}/Y-STR G'_{ST} = 1.054), while Gunung Kawi and Tabanan *subaks* demonstrated higher population structuring for Y chromosome (0.828 and 0.890, respectively). Moreover, within Gunung Kawi region Y-chromosome differentiation was higher for Y-SNPs and Y-STRs in older *subaks* (0.167 and 0.069, respectively) than in younger *subaks* (0.103 and 0.055, respectively), while mtDNA was less differentiated in older *subaks* (0.060) than younger *subaks* (0.072). These results are consistent with the predictions of the budding deme model: the level of endogamy is higher for males because of the strong tendency for patrilocality in rice-growing villages, while females migrate more often, albeit at only a low rate.

Genetic and geographic variation over short areas

To test for associations between genetic and geographic variation in Bali we performed Mantel tests (Table 17.4). Genetic distances were calculated based on haplogroup or haplotype frequencies, without taking into account their allelic content and the molecular distances between the haplogroups and haplotypes. Geographic and genetic distances were not correlated for Y chromosome and mtDNA data in Tabanan or Bali as a whole. In contrast, Y-STR variation was highly correlated with geographic distances in Gunung Kawi (r = 0.541), as was mtDNA variation (r = 0.361). While the Y-chromosome association was highly statistically significant, the mtDNA correlation was not (Table 17.4). These results are especially noteworthy because the geographic distances among the

Table 17.4 Mantel test: correlation between geography and genetics, and between mtDNA and Y-chromosome genetic distances

	Correlation coefficient r	p
Gunung Kawi (N = 13)		
mtDNA – geography	0.361	n.s.
Y-SNP's – geography	–0.001	n.s.
Y-STR's – geography	0.541	0.000
Y-STR-mtDNA	0.629	0.000
Y-SNP-mtDNA	–0.067	n.s.
Tabanan (N = 8)		
mtDNA – geography	–0.046	n.s.
Y-SNP's – geography	0.060	n.s.
Y-STR's – geography	–0.189	n.s.
Y-STR-mtDNA	–0.159	n.s.
Y-SNP-mtDNA	–0.046	n.s.
Bali (N = 9)		
mtDNA – geography	–0.227	n.s.
Y-SNP's – geography	–0.050	n.s.
Y-STR's – geography	–0.164	n.s.
Y-STR-mtDNA	–0.223	n.s.
Y-SNP-mtDNA	0.133	0.278

n.s. not significant

Gunung Kawi *subaks* are very small (averaging 3.2 km). Not surprisingly, genetic distances based on slowly evolving Y-SNPs did not demonstrate any association with geography ($r = -0.001$).

To investigate the correspondence between paternal and maternal genetic variation, we also estimated correlation coefficients among different loci. The results indicate a strong correlation between Y-STR and mtDNA structure in Gunung Kawi ($r = 0.629$), possibly reflecting the same events in population history. In contrast, there was no positive correlation among Y-chromosome and mtDNA genetic distances in Tabanan or the geographic regions of Bali ($r = -0.159$ and $r = -0.223$, respectively).

Summary

The genetic analyses presented here provide several clear insights into the origins and expansion of the *subaks*, all of which are consistent with a kin-structured budding model of gradual expansion carried out by rice farmers. In this model, demographic pressure drives increases in population size, and downstream budding of the *subak* system. *Subaks* located at the furthest positions upstream on their respective irrigation systems demonstrate greater levels of genetic differentiation and diversity, suggesting that they must have been built before their downstream neighbors. The evidence from the Y chromosome is consistent with key features of the budding deme model: patrilocal residence with very little movement on the landscape except for occasional micro-movements to nearby daughter settlements. The older the *subak*, the more evidence for this pattern. Evidence from mtDNA is consistent with the contemporary observed pattern of patrilocal residence and preferential village or *subak* endogamy, but occasional marriages outside the *subak*. Again, this pattern is most strongly evidenced in the oldest villages, and scales with time. The all-Bali sample shows none of these patterns.

We conclude with the observation that the budding model imposes a very restrictive set of constraints on the genetic structure of farming communities in Bali. These include strong founder effects accompanied by genetic drift and directional micro-movements; more structure in patrilineages than matrilineages; and a strong contrast between *subaks* versus background relatedness of the whole population. These are not the patterns expected under the alternative scenario of state-controlled expansion of irrigation – that is, the rajahs transporting whole villages to newly constructed irrigation areas, or alternatively bringing settlers from nearby villages.

Acknowledgements

This work was supported by the National Science Foundation grants BCS 0083524 and 043224 to J.S.L., M.F.H. and T.M.K.). Research in Indonesia was sponsored by the Eijkman Institute for Molecular Biology, the Indonesian Institute of Science, and the Indonesian Ministry of Agriculture. Many researchers contributed to the archaeological, ethnological and ecological research that led to the budding model for *subak* expansion; their contributions will be evident from the references cited below. In no particular order they include I. Wayan Alit Arthawiguna, Sang Putu Kaler Surata, James N. Kremer, Vernon Scarborough, I Wayan Ardika, Gusti Ngurah Aryawan, Daniel Latham, Lisa Curran, Wayan Sumarma and Nyoman Widiarta. The authors are grateful to J. Watkins for his comments.

References

Ardika, I.W. (1986) *Hak Raja atas Tanah pada masa Bali Kuno*, Denpasar: Fakultas Sastra, Universitas Udayana.

Ardika, I.W. (1994) *Pertanian pada masa Bali Kuno: Suata Kajian Epigrafi, Laporan Penelitian*, Denpasar: Universitas Udayana.

Atmodjo, S.K. (1986) 'Some short notes on agricultural data from ancient Balinese inscriptions', in S. Kartodirdjo (ed.) *Papers of the Fourth Indonesian-Dutch History Conference, Yogyakarta 24–29 July 1983*, vol. 1, *Agrarian History*, pp. 41–2, Yogyakarta: Gadjah Mada University Press.

Bandelt, H.J., Forster, P. and Rohl, A. (1999) 'Median-joining networks for inferring intraspecific phylogenies', *Molecular Biology and Evolution*, 16: 37–48.

Bellwood, P. (1996) 'Hierarchy, founder ideology and Austronesian expansion', in J.J. Fox and C. Sather (eds) *Origins, Ancestry and Alliance*, pp. 18–40, Canberra: Australian National University.
Christie, J.W. (1992) 'Water from the ancestors: irrigation in early Java and Bali', in J. Rigg (ed.) *The Gift of Water: Water Management, Cosmology and the State in South East Asia*, pp. 7–25, London: School of Oriental and African Studies, University of London.
Destro-Bisol, G., Donati, F., Coia, V., Boschi, I., Verginelli, F., Caglia, A., Tofanelli, S., Spendini, G. and Capelli, C. (2004) 'Variation of female and male lineages in Sub-Saharan populations: the importance of sociocultural factors', *Molecular Biology and Evolution*, 21: 1673–82.
Fix, A.G. (2002) 'Colonization models and initial genetic diversity in the Americas', *Human Biology*, 74: 1–10.
Fix, A.G. (2004) 'Kin-structured migration: causes and consequences', *American Journal of Human Biology*, 16: 387–94.
Geertz, C. (1980) *Negara: The Balinese Theatre State in the Nineteenth Century*, Princeton, NJ: Princeton University Press.
Goris, R. (1954) *Inscripties voor Anak Wungçu, Prasasti Bali I–II*, Bandung: C.V. Masa Baru.
Hammer, M.F., Karafet, T.M., Redd, A.J., Jarjanazi, H., Santachiara-Benerecetti, S., Soodyall, H. and Zegura, S.L. (2001) 'Hierarchical patterns of global human Y-chromosome diversity', *Molecular Biology and Evolution*, 18: 1189–1203.
Hauser-Schaüblin, B. (2003) 'The precolonial Balinese state reconsidered', *Current Anthropology*, 44: 153–81.
Hedrick, P.W. (2005) 'A standardized genetic differentiation measure', *Evolution*, 59: 1633–8.
Hurles, M.E., Sykes, B.C., Jobling, M.A. and Forster, P. (2005) 'The dual origin of the Malagasy in Island Southeast Asia and East Africa: evidence from maternal and paternal lineages', *American Journal of Human Genetics*, 76: 894–901.
Jobling, M.A. and Tyler-Smith, C. (2003) 'The human Y chromosome: an evolutionary marker comes of age', *Nature Review Genetics*, 4: 598–612.
Jorde, L.B., Watkins, W.S., Bamshad, M.J., Dixon, M.E., Ricker, C.E., Seielstad, M.T. and Batzer, M.A. (2000) 'The distribution of human genetic diversity: a comparison of mitochondrial, autosomal, and Y-chromosome data', *American Journal of Human Genetics*, 66: 979–88.
Karafet, T.M., Lansing, J.S., Redd, A.J., Reznikova, S., Watkins, J.C., Surata, S.P.K, Arthawiguna, W.A., Mayer, L., Bamshad, M.J., Jorde, L.B. and Hammer, M.F. (2005) 'A Balinese Y chromosome perspective on the peopling of Indonesia: genetic contributions from pre-Neolithic hunter-gatherers, Austronesian farmers, and Indian traders', *Human Biology*, 77: 93–114.
Kulke, H. (1986) 'The early and the imperial kingdom in Southeast Asian history', in D.G. Marr and A.C. Milner (eds) *Southeast Asia in the 9th to 14th Centuries*, Canberra: Research School of Pacific Studies, Australian National University.
Lansing, J.S. (2005) 'On irrigation and the Balinese state', *Current Anthropology*, 46: 305–6.
Lansing, J.S. (2006) *Perfect Order: Recognizing Complexity in Bali*, Princeton, NJ: Princeton University Press.
Lansing, J.S. and Miller, J.H. (2005) 'Cooperation games and ecological feedback: some insights from Bali', *Current Anthropology*, 46: 328–34.

Nei, M. (1987) *Molecular Evolutionary Genetics*, New York: Columbia University Press.
Raffles, T.S. (1817) *The History of Java*, vol. 2, London: Black, Parbury & Allen.
Scarborough, V.L., Schoenfelder, J.W. and Lansing, J.S. (1999) 'Early statecraft on Bali: the Water Temple Complex and the decentralization of the political economy', *Research in Economic Anthropology*, 20: 299–330.
Scarborough, V.L., Schoenfelder, J.W. and Lansing, J.S. (2000) 'Ancient water management and landscape transformation at Sebatu, Bali', *Bulletin of the Indo-Pacific Prehistory Association*, 20: 79–92.
Schneider, S., Roessli, D. and Excoffier, L. (2000) *ARLEQUIN ver. 2.000: A Software for Population Genetic Analysis*, Geneva: Genetics and Biometry Laboratory, University of Geneva, Switzerland.
Seielstad, M.T., Minch, E., and Cavalli-Sforza, L.L. (1998) 'Genetic evidence for a higher female migration rate in humans', *Nature Genetics*, 20: 278–80.
Stein Callenfels, P.V. van (1926) *Epigrafica Balica*, pp. iii–70, The Hague: Verhandelingen van het Bataviaansch Genootschap LVI.
Wilder, J.A., Kingan, S.B., Mobasher, Z., Pilkington, M.M. and Hammer, M.F. (2004) 'Global patterns of human mitochondrial DNA and Y-chromosome structure are not influenced by higher migration rates of females versus males', *Nature Genetics*, 36: 1122–5.
Wood, E.T., Stover, D.A., Ehret, C., Destro-Bisol, G., Spendini, G., McLeod, H., Louie, L., Bamshad, M., Strassmann, B.I., Soodyall, H. and Hammer, M.F. (2005) 'Contrasting patterns of Y chromosome and mtDNA variation in Africa: evidence for sex-biased demographic processes', *European Journal of Human Genetics,* 13: 867–76.

18 The effect of history and life-style on genetic structure of North Asian populations

Tatiana M. Karafet, Ludmila P. Osipova, and Michael F. Hammer

Introduction

Siberia occupies the greatest part of North Asia from the Urals in the west to the Pacific watershed in the east and from the Arctic Ocean in the north to Kazakhstan, Mongolia and China in the south. This territory encompasses a 13 million km^2 area and is generally subdivided into West Siberia, between the Ural Mountains and Yenisey River, Central Siberia, between the rivers Yenisey and Lena, and East Siberia, between the Lena River and the Pacific coast. Because of its geographic position, Siberia forms an important geographic link between the Asian and North American continents and between North Asia and the Japanese archipelago. Siberia is among the few places in the world where, until recently, most people lived a foraging lifestyle. Siberian economic and cultural patterns are traceable to Paleolithic and Neolithic subsistence strategies (Rychkov and Sheremetyeva 1980). Population density in Siberia has historically been quite low, partly because of resource limitations, and traditional Siberian life-ways reflect common features of hunter-gatherer existence throughout much of the Arctic and sub-Arctic ecosystems. Thus, it has been postulated that surveys of genetic variation in indigenous groups (such as those in Siberia) will provide the opportunity to investigate aspects of population structure that have characterized humans from the Pleistocene to the present (Birdsell 1973; Cavalli-Sforza 1986). Surveys might also help test archaeological and language-based hypotheses about the history of Siberian populations.

The first Siberian Paleolithic archaeological site was discovered more than a century ago, in 1871 (Derev'anko 1998a). Despite this, the field still abounds with controversy and unsolved problems about the chronology of the initial peopling of northern Asia, the nature of its ancient human populations, the origins and migrations of local prehistoric cultures, and the expansion of populations into the New World. The archaeological record suggests that the early peopling of Siberia was a complex, lengthy process with at least four proposed source regions: Central Asia, Mongolia, North China, and southern Russia/eastern Europe (Derev'anko 1998a; Okladnikov 1981, 1983; Vasil'ev 1993). The earliest C^{14}-dated Asian Upper Paleolithic industries occur in the Altai Mountains of southwest Siberia at 43,300 ± 1600 years BP (Goebel *et al.* 1993; Kuzmin and Orlova 1998).

The recorded history of Siberia begins (apart from some references in early Chinese works) with its invasion by the Russians in the late 16th century. By then the ethnic and linguistic composition of its native population was more complex than now (Levin and Potapov 1964). Today 31 different populations are indigenous to Siberia, of which 26 are considered to be small ethnic groups. These small groups comprise only 2 per cent of the total population in Siberia. There are currently approximately 35 indigenous languages recognized in Siberia, although some are moribund or have recently become extinct. The majority of Siberian peoples speak different languages of the Altaic and Uralic language phyla (Anderson 2004). Languages of Chukotko-Kamchatkan (or Chukchi-Kamchatkan) linguistic family are spoken by the populations in northeast Siberia (Fortescue 2005). Siberian Eskimos speak the Yupik language belonging to the Eskimo branch of the Eskimo-Aleut language family (De Reuse 1994). Two Siberian languages which have not been shown to be related to any other language are Nivkh (Gilyak) (Gruzdeva 1998) and Ket (Vajda 2004). Although differing in their origin, language, and culture, most Siberian populations are characterized by common economic activities, typically hunting, fishing, reindeer breeding, and cattle herding. These traditional occupations are closely linked to nomadic and semi-nomadic ways of life. Most Siberian indigenous groups also share a number of common socio-cultural features such as clan structure, polygamous marriages, the levirate, and a high level of endogamy.

Previous genetic studies consistently showed a high degree of between-group heterogeneity for Siberian populations, often attributed to low population densities (Cavalli-Sforza *et al.* 1994; Novoradovsky *et al.* 1993; Posukh *et al.* 1990; Rychkov and Sheremetyeva 1980; Sukernik *et al.* 1986; Szathmary 1981), reduced genetic diversity within populations (Pakendorf *et al.* 2002), significant relationships among genetic and geographic or linguistic variation (Cavalli-Sforza *et al.* 1994; Crawford and Enciso 1982; Uinuk-Ool *et al.* 2003), and a clear difference between eastern and western Siberian populations (Karafet *et al.* 1994; Osipova *et al.* 1996; Sukernik *et al.* 1978; Szathmary 1981). Different Siberian populations demonstrated genetic affinities with peoples of Americas (Derenko *et al.* 2001; Karafet *et al.* 1997, 1999; Lell *et al.* 1997, 2002; Santos *et al.* 1999; Schurr *et al.* 1999; Shields *et al.*1993; Starikovskaya *et al.* 1998; Torroni *et al.* 1993), and East Asia (Su *et al.* 1999; Zerjal *et al.* 1997, 1999).

The NRY has been proven to be an excellent tool for tracing paternal ancestry, detecting between-group variation and for reconstructing the history of human migrations (Hammer and Zegura 1996). We present Y chromosome data from the North and Central Asia in the context of the three questions: (1) the population structure of Siberian foraging groups: (2) the relationship among gene pools, languages, and cultures; and (3) the early colonization of Siberia.

Material and methods

Populations and genetic markers

Twenty Siberian populations with a total of 957 males were analyzed for 71 Y chromosome binary polymorphisms. In addition, we included a total of 527 males from 10 surrounding populations. These 30 populations were subdivided into seven geographic groups: Northwest Siberia, Southwest Siberia, Central-South Siberia, Northeast Siberia, Central Asia, East Asia, and European Russia (Map 18.I). Linguistic affiliations, sample sizes, genetic diversity statistics, and three-letter codes are given in Table 18.1. Many of the samples analyzed here were included in our previous study (Karafet et al. 2002). New samples from the Teleut population were collected by T.M. Karafet and L.P. Osipova during 2003, while additional genomic DNA from the Chelkans were provided by O.L. Posukh.

The polymorphic sites in our survey included a set of 62 previously published binary NRY markers (Karafet et al. 2002). Additionally, we genotyped six polymorphisms (M25, M73, M78, M124, M214, M269 reported by Underhill et al. (2000) and Cruciani et al. (2002), P30, P47 (YCC 2002) and one novel polymorphism, defined as P63. We refer to each haplogroup using the appropriate capital letter followed by a dash and the name of the terminal mutation that defines a given haplogroup (see YCC 2002 for a complete description of this short-hand 'mutation-based' nomenclature).

Statistical methods

Population genetic structure indices, the Mantel test, measures of haplogroup diversity including Nei's heterozygosity (h) and the mean number of pairwise differences among haplogroups (p) were estimated by ARLEQUIN 2.000 software (Schneider et al. 2000). Geographic distances were calculated between populations from latitude and longitude data for the sample sites. The matrix of pairwise linguistic distances among populations was constructed according to the method described by Excoffier et al. (1991) and Poloni et al. (1997). We performed nonmetric multidimensional scaling (MDS) (Kruskal 1964) on Slatkin's linearized Φ_{ST} distances using the software package NTSYS (Rohlf 1998). Spatial autocorrelation analysis was performed using the autocorrelation index for DNA analysis (AIDA) (Bertorelle and Barbujani 1995). We used a method developed by Harpending and Ward (1982) to estimate the relative contribution of genetic drift and founder effect versus gene flow in causing population differentiation. The ANTANA program computed these distances from the centroid (Harpending and Rogers 1984). The mean and standard deviation of the time to the most recent common ancestral (TMRCA) Y chromosome sequence, as well as the ages of each of the mutations, were estimated using the program GENETREE (Bahlo and Griffiths 2000; Karafet et al. 1999).

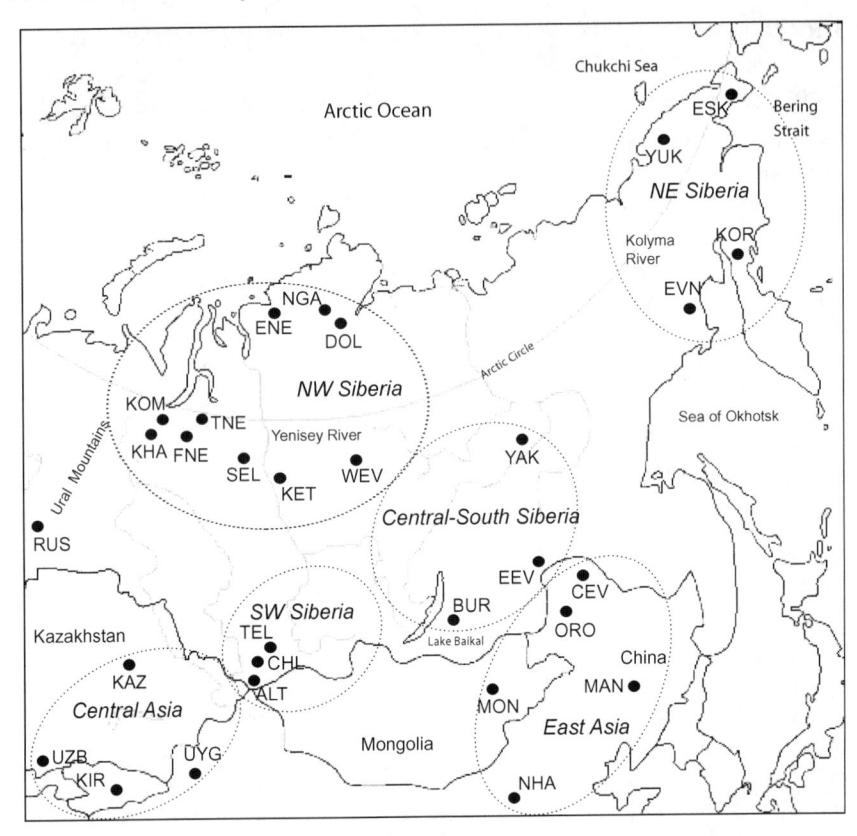

Map 18.1 Map showing the approximate geographic positions of 30 populations sampled in this study (see Table 18.1 and text for names and sizes of population samples). The populations are grouped into six geographic areas.

Results

Geographic distribution and diversity of NRY haplogroups

Figure 18.1 shows the evolutionary relationships of Asian Y chromosome binary lineages. The 24 haplogroups are present in the 20 Siberian populations. The vast majority (96.8 per cent) of Siberian Y chromosomes belong to only 4 of the 18 major lineages. The most frequent haplogroup, N-M178 (22.6 per cent), was found in 16 of the 20 Siberian populations. Interestingly, the distribution of N-M178 haplogroup is limited almost entirely to northern Eurasia and is absent or only marginally present in other regions of the world. Two sister-haplogroups, N-P43 and N-P63, were prevalent in Northwest Siberia (31.3 per cent), marginally present in Central-South and Southwest Siberia, and absent in Northeast Siberia. The majority of N-P43 and N-P63 chromosomes (90.4 per cent) occur among the Uralic-speaking populations in Northwest Siberia. Only the Selkups did not fit this pattern. Haplogroup Q chromosomes of the Siberian samples were distributed

Table 18.1 Sample composition, linguistic affiliations, and genetic diversity for 30 populations

Population	Linguistic affiliation	Sample size	h ± SE	p ± SE
Northwest Siberia (NWS)		533		
1. Forest Nentsi (FNE)	Uralic (N. Samoyed)	88	0.54 ± 0.02	2.12 ± 1.19
2. Tundra Nentsi (TNE)	Uralic (N. Samoyed)	59	0.47 ± 0.06	1.69 ± 1.00
3. Entsi (ENE)	Uralic (N. Samoyed)	9	0.42 ± 0.19	2.11 ± 1.29
4. Nganasans (NGA)	Uralic (N. Samoyed)	38	0.15 ± 0.08	1.12 ± 0.75
5. Selkups (SEL)	Uralic (S. Samoyed)	131	0.52 ± 0.04	2.63 ± 1.42
6. Komi (KOM)	Uralic (Finno-Ugric)	28	0.65 ± 0.06	3.11 ± 1.66
7. Khants (KHA)	Uralic (Finno-Ugric)	47	0.68 ± 0.03	4.00 ± 2.03
8. Dolgans (DOL)	Altaic (Turkic)	67	0.78 ± 0.03	6.53 ± 3.12
9. Western Evenks (WEV)	Altaic (Tungus)	18	0.65 ± 0.09	5.43 ± 2.74
10. Kets (KET)	Yeniseian (Isolate)	48	0.12 ± 0.06	1.08 ± 0.72
Central-South Siberia (CSS)		194		
11. Eastern Evenks (EEV)	Altaic (Tungus)	78	0.64 ± 0.04	3.97 ± 2.01
12. Yakuts-Sakha (YAK)	Altaic (Turkic)	35	0.11 ± 0.07	1.00 ± 0.69
13. Buryats (BUR)	Altaic (Mongolian)	81	0.61 ± 0.04	4.82 ± 2.38
Northeast Siberia (NES)		76		
14. Yukaghirs (YUK)	Uralic (Yukaghir)	11	0.82 ± 0.06	5.56 ± 2.89
15. Evens (EVN)	Altaic (Tungus)	31	0.60 ± 0.09	4.09 ± 2.10
16. Koryaks (KOR)	Chukchi-Kamchatkan	12	0.80 ± 0.08	6.20 ± 3.17
17. Eskimos (ESK)	Eskimo-Aleut (Yupik)	22	0.64 ± 0.08	3.62 ± 1.91
Southwest Siberia (SWS)		154		
18. Altai-Kizhi (ALT)	Altaic (Turkic)	98	0.72 ± 0.04	5.66 ± 2.74
19. Chelkans (CHL)	Altaic (Turkic)	12	0.62 ± 0.12	3.94 ± 2.12
20. Teleuts (TEL)	Altaic (Turkic)	44	0.73 ± 0.03	5.06 ± 2.50
East Asia (EAS)		304		
21. Chinese Evenks (CEV)	Altaic (Tungus)	40	0.85 ± 0.04	6.18 ± 3.00
22. Oroqens (ORO)	Altaic (Tungus)	23	0.49 ± 0.10	1.51 ± 0.94
23. Manchu (MAN)	Altaic (Manchu)	52	0.88 ± 0.03	5.36 ± 2.63
24. Mongolian-Khalks (MON)	Altaic (Mongolian)	145	0.82 ± 0.02	5.67 ± 2.73
25. Northern Han (NHA)	Sino-Tibetan	44	0.80 ± 0.05	3.52 ± 1.83
Central Asia (CAS)		164		
26. Kazakhs	Altaic (Turkic)	30	0.88 ± 0.04	5.74 ± 2.83
27. Uzbeks	Altaic (Turkic)	54	0.93 ± 0.02	6.63 ± 3.18
28. Uyghurs	Altaic (Turkic)	67	0.93 ± 0.02	6.00 ± 2.90
29. Kirghiz	Altaic (Turkic)	13	0.62 ± 0.14	4.69 ± 2.46
European Russia (RUS)		59		
30. Russians (RUS)	Indo-European	59	0.77 ± 0.04	5.20 ± 2.55

For more information on linguistic affiliation see Greenberg (2000), Ruhlen (1991).

400 Tatiana M. Karafet et al.

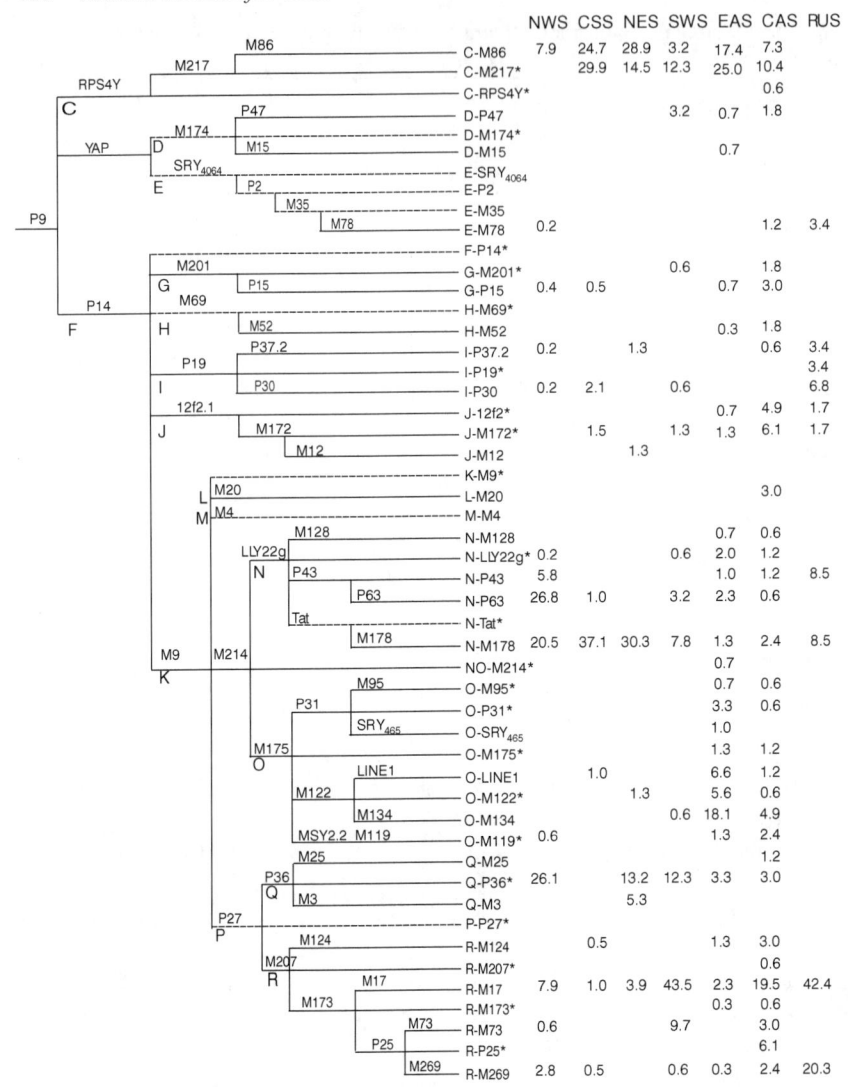

	NWS	CSS	NES	SWS	EAS	CAS	RUS
C-M86	7.9	24.7	28.9	3.2	17.4	7.3	
C-M217*		29.9	14.5	12.3	25.0	10.4	
C-RPS4Y*						0.6	
D-P47				3.2	0.7	1.8	
D-M174*							
D-M15					0.7		
E-SRY4064							
E-P2							
E-M35							
E-M78	0.2					1.2	3.4
F-P14*							
G-M201*				0.6		1.8	
G-P15	0.4	0.5			0.7	3.0	
H-M69*							
H-M52					0.3	1.8	
I-P37.2	0.2		1.3		0.6		3.4
I-P19*							3.4
I-P30	0.2	2.1		0.6			6.8
J-12f2*					0.7	4.9	1.7
J-M172*		1.5		1.3	1.3	6.1	1.7
J-M12				1.3			
K-M9*							
L-M20						3.0	
M-M4							
N-M128					0.7	0.6	
N-LLY22g*	0.2			0.6	2.0	1.2	
N-P43	5.8				1.0	1.2	8.5
N-P63	26.8	1.0		3.2	2.3	0.6	
N-Tat*							
N-M178	20.5	37.1	30.3	7.8	1.3	2.4	8.5
NO-M214*					0.7		
O-M95*					0.7	0.6	
O-P31*					3.3	0.6	
O-SRY465					1.0		
O-M175*					1.3	1.2	
O-LINE1		1.0			6.6	1.2	
O-M122*			1.3		5.6	0.6	
O-M134				0.6	18.1	4.9	
O-M119*	0.6				1.3	2.4	
Q-M25						1.2	
Q-P36*	26.1		13.2	12.3	3.3	3.0	
Q-M3			5.3				
P-P27*							
R-M124		0.5			1.3	3.0	
R-M207*						0.6	
R-M17	7.9	1.0	3.9	43.5	2.3	19.5	42.4
R-M173*					0.3	0.6	
R-M73	0.6			9.7		3.0	
R-P25*						6.1	
R-M269	2.8	0.5		0.6	0.3	2.4	20.3

Figure 18.1 Evolutionary tree for the 50 Y-chromosome lineages defined by 53 of the 71 markers employed in this survey. Major clades are labeled with large capital letters. The names of the markers are shown along the branches of the tree while lineage names are shown at the right. Lineage names with an asterisk refer to internal nodes of the tree. Dashed lines reflect lineages shown to provide phylogenetic context.

primarily across Northwest and Northeast Siberia. The vast majority of haplogroup Q chromosomes occurred in only two Siberian populations, the Ket and the Selkup, with frequencies of 93.8 and 66.4 per cent, respectively. Haplogroups C-M217* and C-M86 were widely spread throughout Siberia and Central Asia and were concentrated mainly in Altaic-speaking populations. Of the 205 C-M217-bearing chromosomes in the 30 populations in this survey, all but 17 occurred in Altaic-speaking groups. Chromosomes from the R lineage in Siberia primarily carried the M17 mutation. Haplogroup R-M17 (with a Siberian frequency of 11.9 per cent) was primarily a Central Asian lineage (Karafet *et al.* 1999; Wells *et al.* 2001; Quintana-Murci *et al.* 2001) found at relatively high frequencies in Southwest Siberia, Central Asia, and among European Russians, at moderate frequencies in some Northwest Siberian populations, and at low frequencies throughout Central-South Siberia, Northeast Siberia, and East Asia. With the exception of R-M73 and R-M269 (with a frequency of 1.9 and 1.8 per cent, respectively) all of the remaining lineages were present at frequencies of less than 1 per cent in Siberia. Many populations in Siberia were characterized with predominance of only one or two haplogroups. No single polymorphism was unique to Siberia, and unlike Native American populations (Karafet *et al.* 1999; Zegura *et al.* 2004), Siberian populations were not characterized by specific founder haplogroups.

NRY haplogroup diversity values for each of the 30 populations are given in Table 18.1. In Siberian populations both diversity statistics exhibited reduced genetic diversity, typical for hunter-gatherer groups (Oota *et al.* 2005). These relatively low average diversity values may be explained by the fact that most Siberian populations possess only one or two predominant haplogroups, and these lineages are often one- or two-step mutation neighbors. However, when Siberia as a whole is compared with other major regions of the globe, its *h* value (0.86) was higher than those in South Asia, Europe, or the Americas and its *p* value (6.06) was higher than that of any non-African region except Central Asia (Hammer *et al.* 2001; Karafet *et al.* 2001, 2002). Interestingly, when considering only the 20 individual Siberian populations, the mean *h* value was 0.55 and the mean *p* value was 3.59. In the resulting MDS on Y chromosome data 20 Siberian populations formed four clusters (Figure 18.2). Six out of eight Uralic-speaking populations from NWS grouped together on the right side of the plot. Three Altaic-speaking populations from SWS clustered with CAS populations and Russians. The small third cluster was comprised of the Ket and Selkup. Populations from CSS and NES formed a loose cluster with Dolgan. The Sakha (= Yakut) were an extreme outlier, while the Eskimo occupied an intermediate position.

AMOVA analysis and Mantel tests

Very high levels of variation from population to population characterizes Siberian populations. The Φ_{ST} value for the sample of 20 Siberian populations was 0.42 (Table 18.2), indicating a significant degree of differentiation within Siberia. Among-population differentiation in Siberia is higher than that reported for any world populations including Africans (Cruciani *et al.* 2002; Wood *et al.*, 2005).

402 Tatiana M. Karafet et al.

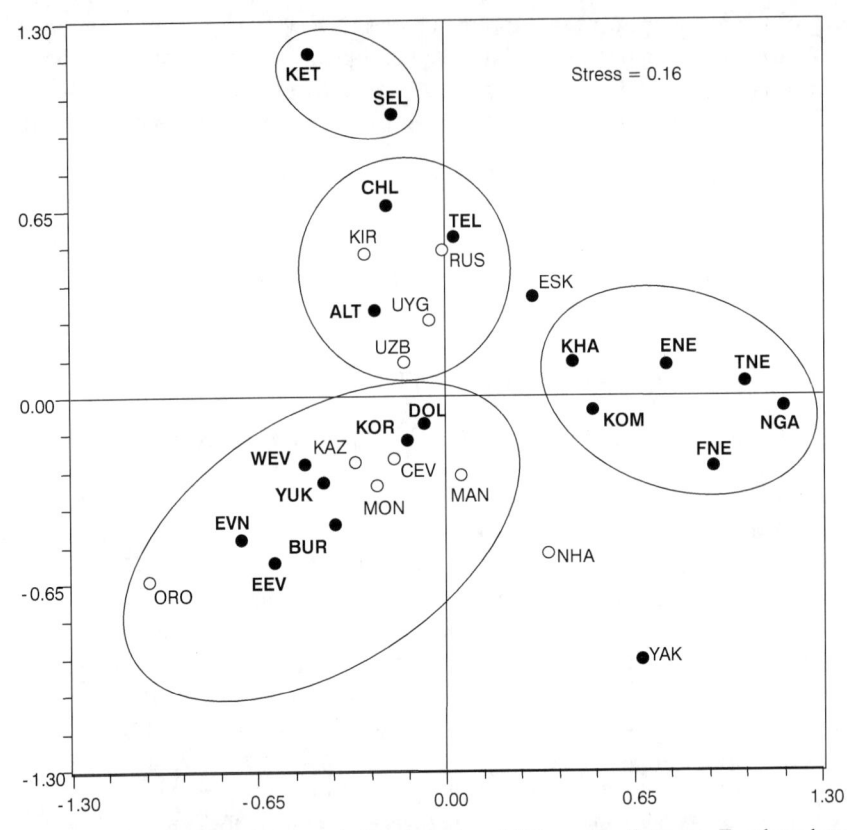

Figure 18.2 MDS plot of 30 populations based on ΦST genetic distances. For three letter population codes, see Table 18.1. Siberian populations are shown as solid black circles, while other populations are shown as open circles.

Table 18.2 Analysis of molecular variance (AMOVA)

Group	No. of populations	No. of groups	Within populations Variance (%)	Φ_{ST}	Among populations within groups Variance (%)	Φ_{SC}	Among groups Variance (%)	Φ_{CT}
All populations	30	1	64.73	0.35				
Siberia	20	1	57.73	0.42				
Geographic groups[a]	20	4	55.00	0.45	30.89	0.36	14.11	0.14
Linguistic groups[b]	20	5	55.00	0.45	32.48	0.37	12.52	0.13

All Φ statistics p values are less than 0.02.
a NWS, CSS, NES and SWS groups (see Table 1);
b Uralic, Altaic, Chukchi-Kamchatkan, Eskimo-Aleut, Yeniseian (see Table 1).

To assess the levels of genetic diversity within and among linguistic families and geographic regions, we divided 20 Siberian populations into four geographic groupings, and into five linguistic families. The Φ_{ST} value rose to 0.45 in both cases. The geographically and language-based Φ_{CT} values were 0.14 and 0.13 respectively.

To test the cause of association between genetic, linguistic, and geographic variation we performed Mantel tests (Table 18.3). Similar to our previous results (Karafet et al. 2002), genetic and geographic distances among Siberian populations did not reveal any significant correlation (r = –0.047, P = 0.67). In contrast, genetics and language were significantly correlated (r = 0.208, P = 0.006). Moreover, the partial correlation between genetics and language, with geography held constant, demonstrated an even stronger relationship (r = 0.235, P = 0.003). Thus, 6 per cent of the variance in the genetic data was explained by language, while only 0.6 per cent was determined by geography. To examine whether the two extreme outliers according to geography and language (Selkup and Yakut, see Figure 18.2) may have affected our results, we repeated the Mantel test excluding these populations. Linguistic correlation increased to 0.346, while correlation with geography remained negligible (–0.023). We also performed the Mantel test including 10 additional populations. The correlation between genetic and geographic distances was still non-significant (r = -0.040 P = 0.658), while the correlation between genetics and language remained significant (r = 0.200, P < 0.001).

AIDA analysis of Y-chromosomal variation

Although the Mantel test correlation analysis between genetic and geographic distance did not reveal any significant association, spatial autocorrelation analysis (AIDA) rejected the null hypothesis of random geographic distribution of NRY haplogroup frequencies. AIDA was independently run two times, initially

Table 18.3 Correlation and partial correlation coefficients between genetics, geography, and linguistic distances

Distance comparison	Correlation coefficient		
	30 populations	20 populations	18 populations[a]
Genetics and geography	–0.040	–0.047	–0.023
Genetics and geography, geography held constant	–0.122	–0.122	–0.155
Genetics and language	0.200**	0.208*	0.346**
Genetics and language, geography held constant	0.230**	0.235*	0.375**
Geography and language	0.358**	0.320**	0.332**

Notes
a excluding Yakuts and Selkups.
Significance level: * 0.01 > p > 0.001, ** p < 0.001.

404   Tatiana M. Karafet et al.

including all populations available and then separately analyzing Siberian populations. A very high positive autocorrelation at distance 0 was observed for the 20 Siberian populations (Figure 18.3a), indicating that individuals within the same populations in Siberia resembled each other. This result is consistent with the small number of haplogroups and low diversity indices in individual Siberian populations. A significant negative peak at the 5400 km distance class was followed by an upward fluctuation. Such a pattern is referred to as 'long distance differentiation' in classical spatial autocorrelation studies (Barbujani *et al.* 1994; Sokal *et al.* 1989). The pattern for the 30 population analysis (Figure 18.3b) was clearly clinal and exhibited a decrease of autocorrelation indices from significantly positive to significantly negative as geographic distance increased.

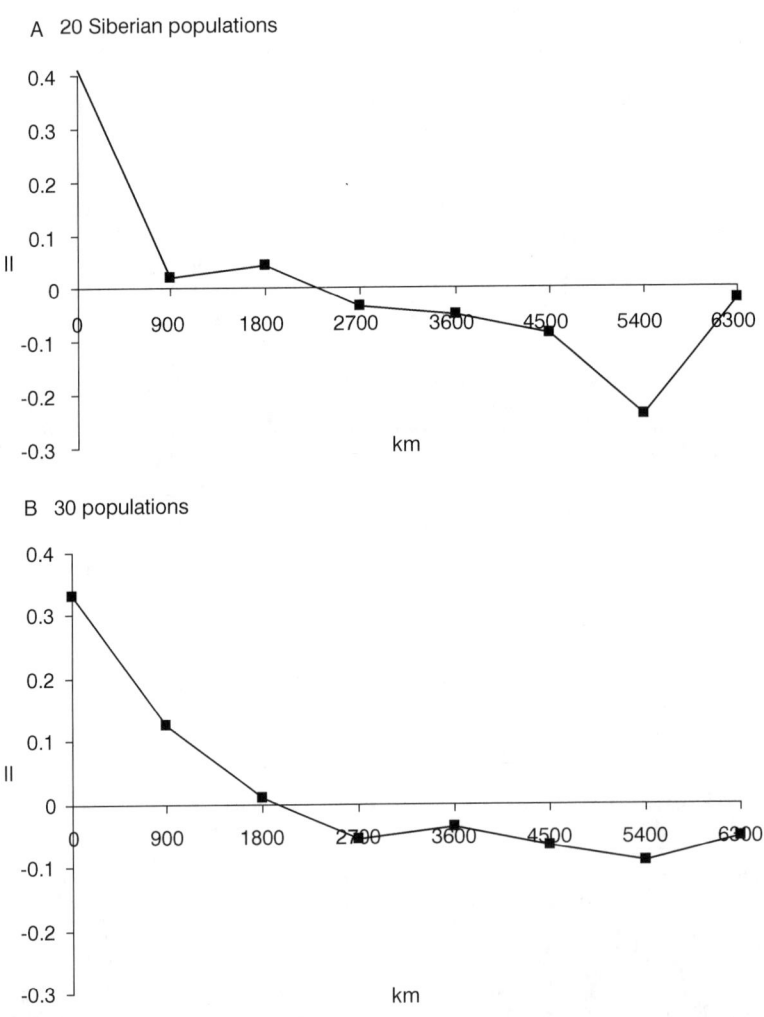

Figure 18.3 Spatial autocorrelation plots: A) 20 Siberian populations, B) 30 populations.

Genetic diversity versus distance from the centroid

A plot of the haplogroup diversity against distance from the centroid (r_{ii}) is shown in Figure 18.4. Theory predicts that the more distant the populations are from the centroid, the lower heterozygosity they will exhibit under assumptions of equal population size and the absence of gene flow from an external source (Harpending and Ward 1982). Those populations that have undergone systematic migrations will show higher heterozygosity than predicted by regression on r_{ii}. Conversely, those groups that are more isolated will show lower than predicted heterozygosity. All Siberian populations except the Koryaks and Teleuts exhibited lower than predicted heterozygosity, suggesting smaller effective population size and/or less gene flow among populations. Central Asian populations, the Manchu, and the Chinese Han showed an excess of diversity compared with predictions from the theoretical regression line, and have probably experienced substantial gene flow.

Discussion

NRY genetic structure of Siberian populations

Our results show that Siberian populations are characterized by a very low degree of gene diversity. Siberian hunter-gatherer groups also exhibit a considerable amount

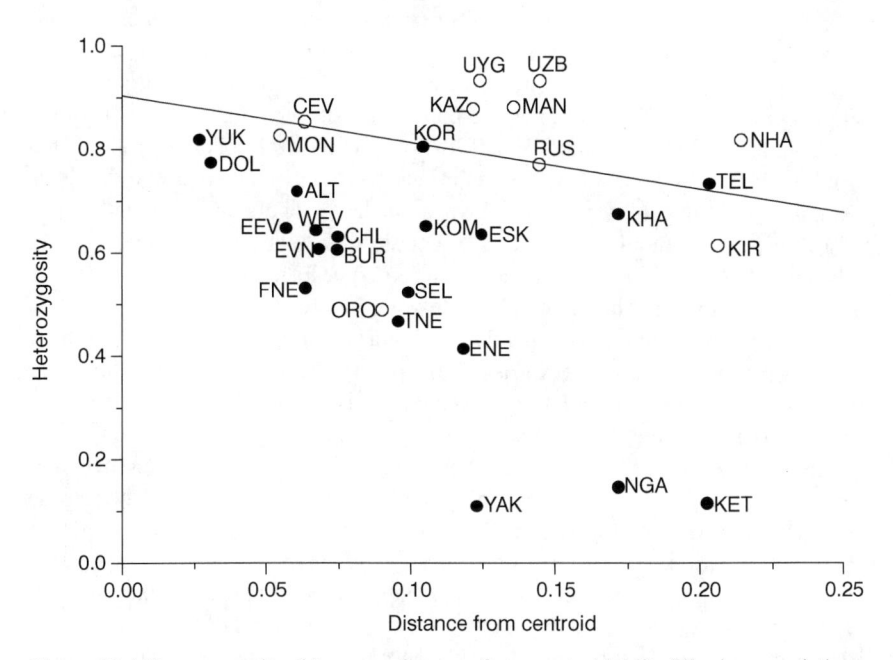

Figure 18.4 Heterozygosity (h) versus distance from centroid (rii). Siberian populations are shown as solid black circles, while other populations are shown as open circles. The solid line represents the theoretical regression line as described in Harpending and Ward (1982).

of NRY differentiation (Φ_{ST} = 0.42). When comparing these results with similar analyses of global populations, it can be seen that this degree of differentiation is higher than for any region of the world (Cruciani *et al.* 2002; Hammer *et al.* 2001; Wood *et al.* 2005). Another unusual pattern of genetic structure in Siberia is the high level of among-populations within-groups variance relative to the among-groups variance.

What processes have shaped the pattern of highly reduced diversity within populations but moderate diversity for the region as a whole? Do elevated levels of differentiation among populations correlate with significant variation within geographic and linguistic groups in Siberia? The pattern of low genetic diversity and high population differentiation might be explained by genetic drift and/or founder effects in small-sized and isolated populations (Sanchez-Mazas *et al.* 2005). Indeed, genetic drift is a major factor of population structure in Siberia due to the low population densities of Siberian native groups. Just after the Russian invasion in the 17th century, approximately 227,000 indigenous people of Siberia (Forsyth 1991) were distributed over a territory exceeding 13 million km². This average density of 0.017 individuals per km² is one of the lowest estimates for any hunter-gatherer population (Fix 1999; Hassan 1981). The graph of heterozygosity versus distance from the centroid (Figure 18.4) revealed a deficiency of genetic diversity among Siberian populations greater than predicted from the theoretical regression line.

If we assume that differentiation of Siberian populations arose by genetic drift only, then approximation of the time of divergence can be calculated by using the equation $Fst = 1 - \exp(-t/N)$, where exp is the exponential function, t is the time in generations, and N is the effective population size for males (Cavalli-Sforza and Bodmer 1971). Estimates from 17th-century archival documents suggested that the effective size of Siberian populations was approximately 250 individuals (Rychkov and Sheremetyeva 1980). If we assume a male effective population size of 125 individuals, under hypothesis of equilibrium with no gene flow it would take just 1362 years (or 68.1 generations when 20 years per generation is used) to reach this parameter. This time is definitely an underestimate since the equation supposes populations independently evolving from a single origin without intermigration. Siberia was never isolated from adjacent territories and probably witnessed a number of population movements. Historical population movements and the expansions clearly influenced population structure of Siberian indigenous groups. Karafet *et al.* (2002) used nested cladistic analysis to understand whether the geographic distribution of Y-haplogroups were due to restricted gene flow (population structure processes) or historical events operating at the population level (colonization, range expansions, past fragmentations). It was shown that most of these signals involved historical events operating at the population level. HLA data also demonstrated that multiple migrations or recolonization left strong signals on the genetic structure of Northeast Asian populations (Sanchez-Mazas *et al.* 2005).

If genetic drift and short-range dispersals were the key factors shaping spatial variation of NRY structure in Siberia, isolation by distance might be expected.

Spatial autocorrelation analysis of Siberian populations revealed strong patterning of genetic variation compatible with a clinal distribution (Figure 18.3). The observed pattern might be due to a series of founder effects taking place in a phase of population expansion, followed by local gene flow (Barbujani et al. 1994). Loss of genetic variation through repeated founder effects has been invoked as the likely cause of clines in several studies of natural populations (Fix 1999). When the clines extend over long distances and originate from fairly large initial gene frequency differences, they will be remarkably stable over time (Wijsman and Cavalli-Sforza 1984).

A variety of cultural and demographic factors have also influenced the paternal genetic structure of Siberian populations. For NRY polymorphisms due to inheritance by paternal lineage this differentiation is expected to be strongly elevated by cultural factors such as clan systems, polygamy, and the levirate. Siberian local residence groups were organized on the basis of kinship and clan affiliation. Each local camp or band (the level of organization most important for hunter-gatherer communities) is a group of people who might be related matrilineally, patrilineally, or bilaterally. Because most Siberian populations practiced patrilocality, people in a band were usually paternally related. Every band, therefore, could potentially be responsible for a strong founder effect detectable in Y-chromosome data. Our preliminary results based on mtDNA and Y-chromosome sequence data demonstrated a pattern of higher male than female population differentiation in Siberia (Karafet et al. in preparation). We also observed a reduction in male effective size relative to female effective size. Interestingly, a greater skew in the effective sex ratio was observed among the Forest Nentsi who are known to practice polygyny with a higher frequency than the other populations in Siberia. Through simulations using an island model of population structure, we showed that differences in Y versus mitochondrial F_{ST}'s may be attributed both to skews in the effective sex ratio as well as differential male and female migration rates.

In this study we attempted to evaluate the contribution of linguistic and/or geographic affiliation in the genetic structure of North Asian populations. A two-level AMOVA analysis was performed on Siberian populations combined in accordance with geographic and linguistic criteria. A hierarchical analysis of variance revealed that Φ_{CT}, the parameter that estimates among-group differentiation, was considerably lower than Φ_{SC} (an estimator of variation among populations within a group) (Table 18.2). Unlike Siberia, global Y-chromosome data showed the opposite pattern: groups were more different among themselves than were populations within these groups (Cruciani et al. 2002; Hammer et al. 2001; Poloni et al. 1997). The highly polymorphic and informative GM system also revealed higher genetic variability between linguistic groups than among populations within groups in East Asia (Poloni et al. 2005). It seems likely that both geography and language might be used as a predictor of the genetic affinity among Siberians. However, Mantel tests showed the existence of NRY genetic patterns correlated with language, but not geography in Siberia (r = 0.208 versus r = –0.047). This result is not surprising when history of Siberian peoples with extensive population movements is considered. The greater mobility of hunter-gatherers is a strategy to maximize the yield of sparsely distributed natural resources (Hassan 1981). There is also evidence of recent resettlements and population size reductions due to famine and epidemics in Siberia. Another reason for a weaker association between geography and NRY variation in Siberia may be the occurrence of extensive genetic drift.

In summation, we infer that intra- and inter-generational genetic drift (resulting from high population mobility and small population size, respectively) were the key evolutionary forces leading to high levels of genetic differentiation observed among Siberian foraging groups. Genetic drift was elevated by cultural factors, common in Siberia. Directed dispersals, range expansions, and long-distance colonizations determined by common ethnic and linguistic affiliation have most probably been of great importance in fashioning the genetic landscape of Siberia.

Early peopling of Siberia

The great boreal forest or taiga of Siberia was established in essentially its present character early in the Pleistocene and was never wholly displaced. During the Late Pleistocene most of Siberia was free of continental ice sheets and mountain glaciation was quite limited. There were no natural obstacles such as continental or large mountain glaciers to prevent human migrations toward and within Siberia (Kuzmin and Orlova 1998). The earliest dated North Asian Upper Paleolithic industries occur in the Altai Mountains in southwest Siberia ($43,300 \pm 1600$ years BP). Paleolithic industries, originally developed in the Altai region subsequently (i.e. from 34,000 BP to 21,000 BP) colonized southern Siberia including the Sayan Mountains, the Angara River basin, the Trans-Baikal and Mongolia (Derev'anko 1998b; Goebel 1999). Early Upper Paleolithic stone tool industries were centered on the production of macroblades similar to points found in initial Upper Paleolithic industries in Levant and eastern Europe (Goebel 1999; Kuzmin and Orlova 1998), suggesting continued ties between Siberia and western Eurasia during that time. There is no evidence for the long-distance migration of the first Siberian hunter-gatherers facilitating the distribution of exotic raw materials (Goebel 1999).

The Siberian climate began to warm shortly after 18,000 years ago. Coincident with this change is an appearance of microblade technologies with the earliest sites occurring in the Yenisey River basin (Kuzmin and Orlova 1998). The origin of the Siberian microblade industry is unclear. Many sites in Mongolia, North China, Japan, and Korea contain evidence for this core type. Many scholars find analogies between these industries (Derev'anko 1998b). Whether they represent the evolution of microblade technologies out of local ancestors or trace migrations from farther south and east cannot be determined conclusively with the available archeological evidence (Goebel 1999, 2003, 2004). By 11,000 years ago microblade sites occur everywhere from the Ural Mountains to the Pacific Ocean and from Inner Mongolia to the high Arctic. Late Upper Paleolithic people seem to have formed small groups of highly mobile hunter-gatherers. There is clear evidence of transport of material over great distances. Goebel (1999) has suggested rapid recolonization and possible replacement of early Siberian Upper Paleolithic populations by microblade-making humans from the Lake Baikal, Yenisey River, and Lena River basin regions.

According to our present data, native Siberian populations had four major founding haplogroups (C, N, Q, and R). The ages of haplogroup P (the haplogroup that contains Q and R) and haplogroup C (29,900 ± 4200 and 27,500 ± 10,100 years old, respectively) are consistent with the age of the Siberian Upper Paleolithic. This estimate of the age of haplogroup C agrees with that of Bergen *et al.* (1999) (27,000–33,000 years) which was based on the variance in repeat numbers at nine Y-chromosome STRs. The age of the M45 marker that also defines the haplogroup P was estimated by Wells *et al.* (2001) as 40,000 years old based on six Y-STRs. Archeological evidence suggests that the Altai Mountains were the first habitat of anatomically modern humans in Siberia. Both haplogroups C and P are found in the Altai at substantial frequencies (Figure 18.1) and haplogroup P might represent the oldest lineage in this area. The analyses of twelve Y-STR loci indicate that haplogroup P is about three times more diverse (considering the variance in STR repeat numbers) than haplogroup C in the Altai (0.964 versus 0.292, respectively). The candidate source populations for haplogroup P most likely include Central Asian populations – the most diverse in Eurasia (Hammer *et al.* 2001; Wells *et al.* 2001). Our conclusion is consistent with the inference of Wells *et al.* (2001) that early settlement of Central Asia 40,000–50,000 years ago was followed by subsequent migrations into Europe, India, and Siberia. This finding also supports archeological evidence for a Central Asian source of the first colonization of anatomically modern humans in Siberia. The first Siberians, with a macroblade industry and carrying NRY haplogroup P, might have settled in the Altai region and subsequently moved to the east. Unlike haplogroup P, the highest Y-STR diversity associated with haplogroup C chromosomes was found in East Asia,[1] followed by Siberia and Central Asia (0.954, 0.732, and 0.413, respectively). Mongolia and North China might represent the source of clade C in Siberia.

The most frequent haplogroups in Siberia belong to N lineage: N-M178*, N-P43 and its sublineage N-P63 (Figure 18.1). Although N chromosomes are numerous and widely distributed in Siberia, Y-STR diversity associated with haplogroup N (0.29) is much lower than diversity of P and C lineages (1.15 and 0.63, respectively). The ages of M178 and P43 mutations were estimated as 3,500 ± 300 and 2,180 ± 105 years old, respectively. The LLY22g mutation which defines haplogroup N may be as old as 6910 ± 1480 years, suggesting that the expansion of the N-P43, N-P63 and N-M178* haplogroups probably occurred much later than the first migrations of anatomically modern human into Siberia. Haplogroups N-P43 and N-M178* may have entered Siberia from Mongolia and North China (Zerjal *et al.* 1997), and later spread west and northeast within Siberia. N-P63 chromosomes are extremely rare outside Siberia and most probably originated in western Siberia – the place of the highest frequency of this mutation.

In summary, our data suggest that first migration(s) of anatomically modern humans to the Altai Mountains from Central Asia brought haplogroup

P Y chromosomes, and these people later dispersed throughout the southern part of Siberia and Mongolia. They also produced the early Siberian Upper Paleolithic stone tool industries that were centered on macroblade technology. Another migration (or most probably, multiple migrations) from Mongolia and/or North China to the Baikal region may have been associated with carriers of haplogroup C. These mobile hunter-gatherers with a microblade industry initially colonized southern Siberia, and then the sub-Arctic and Arctic zones. Later population movements from Central Asia and eastern Europe, Mongolia and North China brought NRY haplogroups R and N.

Acknowledgments

We thank Olga L. Posukh for collecting Chelkan samples from Altai Region. This research was supported by the National Science Foundation through grant OPP-0216732 to MFH and TKM.

Note

1 Y-STR diversity associated with haplogroup C chromosomes in East Asia was based on a population size greater than presented in this chapter.

References

Anderson, G.D.S. (2004) 'The languages of Central Siberia: introduction and overview', in E.J. Vajda (ed.) *Languages and Prehistory of Central Siberia*, pp. 1–119, Amsterdam: John Benjamins.

Bahlo, M. and Griffiths, R.C. (2000) 'Inference from gene trees in a subdivided population', *Theoretical Population Biology*, 57: 79–95.

Barbujani, G., Pilastro, A., De Domenico, S. and Renfrew, C. (1994) 'Genetic variation in North Africa and Eurasia: Neolithic demic diffusion vs. Paleolithic colonisation', *American Journal of Physical Anthropology*, 95: 137–54.

Bergen, A.W., Wang, C.Y., Tsai, J., Jefferson, K., Dey, C., Smith, K.D., Park, S.C., Tsai, S.J. and Goldman, D. (1999) 'An Asian-Native American paternal lineage identified by RPS4Y resequencing and by microsatellite haplotyping', *Annals of Human Genetics*, 63: 63–80.

Bertorelle, G. and Barbujani, G. (1995) 'Analysis of DNA diversity by spatial autocorrelation', *Genetics*, 140: 811–19.

Birdsell, J.B. (1973) 'A basic demographic unit', *Current Anthropology*, 14: 337–56.

Cavalli-Sforza, L.L. (1986) *African Pygmies*, Orlando, FL: Academic Press.

Cavalli-Sforza, L.L. and Bodmer, W.F. (1971) *The Genetics of Human Populations*, San Francisco, CA: W.H. Freeman.

Cavalli-Sforza, L.L., Menozzi, P. and Piazza, A. (1994) *The History and Geography of Human Genes*, Princeton, NJ: Princeton University Press.

Crawford, M.H. and Enciso, V.B. (1982) 'Population structure of circumpolar groups of Siberia, Alaska, Canada, and Greenland', in M.H. Crawford and J.H. Mielke (eds) *Current Developments in Anthropological Genetics*, vol. 2, pp. 51–91, New York: Plenum Press.

Cruciani, F., Santolamazza, P., Shen, P., Macaulay, V., Moral, P., Olckers, A., Modiano, D., Holmes, S., Destro-Bisol, G., Coia, V., Wallace, D.C., Oefner, P.J., Torroni, A., Cavalli-Sforza, L.L., Scozzari, R. and Underhill, P.A. (2002) 'A back migration from Asia to Sub-Saharan Africa is supported by high-resolution analysis of human Y-chromosome haplotypes', *American Journal of Human Genetics*, 70: 1197–214.

Derenko, M.V., Grzybowski, T., Malyarchuk, B.A., Czarny, J., Miscicka-Sliwka, D. and Zakharov, I.A. (2001) 'The presence of mitochondrial haplogroup X in Altaians from South Siberia', *American Journal of Human Genetics*, 69: 237–41.

De Reuse, W.J. (1994) *Siberian Yupik Eskimo: The Language and its Contacts with Chukchi* (Studies in Indigenous Languages of the Americas), Salt Lake City, UT: University of Utah Press.

Derev'anko, A.P. (1998a) 'A short history of discoveries and the development of ideas in the Paleolithic of Siberia', in A.P. Derev'anko (ed.) *The Paleolithic of Siberia: New Discoveries and Interpretations*, pp. 5–12, Urbana and Chicago, IL: University of Illinois Press.

Derev'anko, A.P. (1998b) 'Human occupation of nearby regions and the role of population movements in the Paleolithic of Siberia', in A.P. Derev'anko (ed.) *The Paleolithic of Siberia: New Discoveries and Interpretations*, pp. 336–51, Urbana and Chicago, IL: University of Illinois Press.

Excoffier, L., Harding, R.M., Sokal, R.R., Pellegrini, B. and Sanchez-Mazas, A. (1991) 'Spatial differentiation of RH and GM haplotype frequencies in sub-Saharan Africa and its relation to linguistic affinities', *Human Biology*, 63: 273–307.

Fix, A.G. (1999) *Migration and Colonization in Human Microevolution*, Cambridge: Cambridge University Press.

Forsyth, J. (1991) 'The Siberian native peoples before and after the Russian conquest', in A. Wood (ed.) *The History of Siberia: From Russian Conquest to Revolution*, pp. 69–91, London: Routledge.

Fortescue, M. (2005) *Comparative Chukotko-Kamchatkan Dictionary* (Trends in Linguistics, 23), Berlin: Mouton de Gruyter.

Goebel, T. (1999) 'Pleistocene human colonization of Siberia and peopling of the Americas: an ecological approach', *Evolutionary Anthropology*, 8: 208–27.

Goebel, T. (2003) 'The Middle to Upper Paleolithic transition in Siberia', *Anthropological Papers of the University of Alaska*, 26: 94–113.

Goebel, T. (2004) 'The early Upper Paleolithic of Siberia', in J. Brantingham and K. Kerry (eds) *The Early Upper Paleolithic East of the Danube*, pp. 162–95, Berkeley, CA: University of California Press.

Goebel, T., Derevianko, A.P. and Petrin, V.T. (1993) 'Dating the Middle-to-Upper-Paleolithic transition at Kara-Bom', *Current Anthropology*, 34: 452–8.

Greenberg, J. (2000) *Indo-European and its Closest Relatives: The Eurasiatic Family. Grammar*, Stanford, CA: Stanford University Press.

Gruzdeva, E. (1998) *Nivkh*, Munich: Lincom Europa.

Hammer, M.F. and Zegura, S.L. (1996) 'The role of the Y chromosome in human evolutionary studies', *Evolutionary Anthropology*, 5: 116–34.

Hammer, M.F., Karafet, T.M., Redd, A.J., Jarjanazi, H., Santachiara-Benerecetti, S., Soodyall, H. and Zegura, S.L. (2001) 'Hierarchical patterns of global human Y-chromosome diversity', *Molecular Biology and Evolution*, 18: 1189–203.

Harpending, H. and Rogers, A. (1984) *ANTANA: A Package for Multivariate Data Analysis*, Bosque Farms: H. Harpending & A. Rogers.

Harpending, H. and Ward, R.H. (1982) 'Chemical systematics and human populations', in M. Nitecki (ed.) *Biochemical Aspects of Evolutionary Biology*, pp. 213–56, Chicago, IL: University of Chicago Press.

Hassan, F.A. (1981) *Demographic Archaeology*, New York: Academic.

Karafet, T.M., Posukh, O.L. and Osipova, L.P. (1994) 'Results and perspectives of human population studies in Siberia', *Siberian Journal of Ecology*, 2: 105–18.

Karafet, T., Zegura, S.L., Vuturo-Brady, J., Posukh, O., Osipova, L., Wiebe, V., Romero, F., Long, J.C., Harihara, S., Jin, F., Dashnyam, B., Gerelsaikhan, T., Omoto, K. and Hammer, M.F. (1997) 'Y chromosome markers and trans-Bering Strait dispersals', *American Journal of Physical Anthropology*, 102: 301–14.

Karafet, T.M., Zegura, S.L., Posukh, O., Osipova, L., Bergen, A., Long, J., Goldman, D., Klitz, W., Harihara, S., de Knijff, P., Wiebe, V., Griffiths, R.C., Templeton, A.R. and Hammer, M.F. (1999) 'Ancestral Asian source(s) of new world Y-chromosome founder haplotypes', *American Journal of Human Genetics*, 64: 817–31.

Karafet, T., Xu, L., Du, R.F., Wang, W., Feng, S., Wells, R.S., Redd, A.J., Zegura, S.L. and Hammer, M.F. (2001) 'Paternal population history of East Asia: sources, patterns, and microevolutionary processes', *American Journal of Human Genetics*, 69: 615–28.

Karafet, T.M., Osipova, L.P. Gubina, M.A., Posukh, O.L., Zegura, S.L. and Hammer, M.F. (2002) 'High levels of Y-chromosome differentiation among Native Siberian populations and the genetic signature of a boreal hunter-gatherer way of life', *Human Biology*, 74: 761–89.

Kruskal, J.B. (1964) 'Multidimensional scaling by optimizing goodness of fit to a nonmetric hypothesis', *Psychometrika*, 29: 1–27.

Kuzmin, Y. and Orlova, L.A. (1998) 'Radiocarbon chronology of the Siberian Paleolithic', *Journal of World Prehistory*, 12: 1–53.

Lell, J.T., Brown, M.D., Schurr, T.G., Sukernik, R.I., Starikovskaya, Y.B., Torroni, A., Moore, L.G., Troup, G.M. and Wallace, D.C. (1997) 'Y chromosome polymorphisms in Native American and Siberian populations: identification of native American Y chromosome haplotypes', *Human Genetics*, 100: 536–43.

Lell, J.T., Sukernik, R.I., Starikovskaya, Y.B., Su, B., Jin. L., Schurr, T.G., Underhill, P.A. and Wallace, D.C. (2002) 'The dual origin and Siberian affinities of Native American Y chromosomes', *American Journal of Human Genetics*, 70: 192–206.

Levin, M.G. and Potapov, L.P. (1964) *The Peoples of Siberia*, Chicago, IL: University of Chicago Press.

Novaradovsky, A.G., Spitsyn, V.A., Duggirala, R. and Crawford, M.H. (1993) 'Population genetics and structure of Buryats from the Lake Baikal region of Siberia', *Human Biology*, 65: 689–709.

Okladnikov, A.P. (1981) *The Paleolithic of Central Asia*, Novosibirsk: Nauka (in Russian).

Okladnikov, A.P. (1983) 'The Paleolithic of Mongolia in the light of the new studies', in R.S. Vasil'evsky (ed.) *Late Pleistocene and Early Holocene Connections between Asia and Americas*, Moscow: Nauka (in Russian).

Oota, H., Pakendorf, B., Weiss, G., von Haeseler, A., Pookajorn, S., Settheetham-Isida, W., Tiwawech, D., Ishida, T. and Stoneking, M. (2005) 'Recent origin and cultural reversion of a hunter-gatherer group', *Public Library of Science (PLoS) Biology*, 3: 536–41.

Osipova, L.P., Posukh, O.L., Ivakin, E.A., Kriukov, Y.A. and Karafet, T.M. (1996) 'The gene pool of native inhabitants of the Samburg tundra', *Genetika*, 32: 830–6 (in Russian).

Pakendorf, B., Morar, B., Tarskaia, L.A., Kayser, M., Soodyal, H., Rodewald, A. and Stoneking, M. (2002) 'Y-chromosomal evidence for a strong reduction in male population size of Yakuts', *Human Genetics*, 110: 198–200.

Poloni, E.S., Semino, O., Passarino, G., Santachiara-Benerecetti, A.S., Dupanloup, I., Langaney, A. and Excoffier, L. (1997) 'Human genetic affinities for Y-chromosome P49a,f/TaqI haplotypes show strong correspondence with linguistics', *American Journal of Human Genetics*, 61: 1015–35.

Poloni, E.S., Sanchez-Mazas A., Jacques, G. and Sagart L. (2005) 'Comparing linguistic and genetic relationships among East Asian populations: A study of the RH and GM polymorphisms', in L. Sagart, R. Blench and A. Sanchez-Mazas (eds) *The Peopling of East Asia*, pp. 252–72, London and New York, NY: RoutledgeCurzon.

Posukh, O.L., Wiebe, V.P., Sukernik, R.I., Osipova, L.P., Karafet, T.M. and Schanfield, M.S. (1990) 'Genetic study of the Evens, an ancient human population of Eastern Siberia', *Human Biology*, 62: 457–65.

Quintana-Murci, L., Krausz, C., Zerjal, T., Sayar, H., Hammer, M.F., Mehdi, S.Q., Ayub, Q., Qamar, R., Mohyuddin, A., Radhakrishna, U., Jobling, M.A., Tyler-Smith, C. and McElreavey K. (2001) 'Y-Chromosome lineages trace diffusion of people and languages in Southwestern Asia', *American Journal of Human Genetics*, 68: 537–42.

Rohlf, F.J. (1998) *NTSYS-pc: Numerical Taxonomy and Multivariate Analysis System*, New York: Exeter Software.

Ruhlen, M. (1991) *A Guide to the World's Languages, Vol. 1: Classification*, London: Edward Arnold.

Rychkov, Y.G. and Sheremetyeva, V.A. (1980) 'The genetics of circumpolar populations of Eurasia related to the problem of human adaptation', in F. Milan (ed.) *The Human Biology of Circumpolar Populations*, pp. 37–80, London: Cambridge University Press.

Sanchez-Mazas, A., Poloni, E.S., Jacques, G. and Sagart L. (2005) 'HLA genetic diversity and linguistic variation in East Asia', in L. Sagart, R. Blench and A. Sanchez-Mazas (eds) *The Peopling of East Asia*, pp. 273–96, London and New York: RoutledgeCurzon.

Santos, F.R., Pandya, A., Tyler-Smith, C., Pena, S.D., Schanfield, M., Leonard, W.R., Osipova, L., Crawford, M.H. and Mitchell, R.J. (1999) 'The Central Siberian origin for Native American Y chromosomes', *American Journal of Human Genetics*, 64: 619–28.

Schneider, S., Roessli, D. and Excoffier, L. (2000) *ARLEQUIN ver. 2.000: A Software for Population Genetic Analysis*, Geneva: Genetics and Biometry Laboratory, University of Geneva, Switzerland.

Schurr, T.G., Sukernik, R.I., Starikovskaya, Y.B. and Wallace, D.C. (1999) 'Mitochondrial DNA variation in Koryaks and Itel'men: population replacement in the Okhotsk Sea–Bering Sea region during the Neolithic', *American Journal of Physical Anthropology*, 108: 1–39.

Shields, G.F., Schmiechen, A.M., Frazier, B.L., Redd, A., Voevoda, M.I., Reed, J.K. and Ward, R.H. (1993) 'MtDNA sequences suggest a recent evolutionary divergence for Beringian and northern North American populations', *American Journal of Human Genetics*, 53: 549–62.

Sokal, R.R., Harding, R.M. and Oden, N.L. (1989) 'Spatial patterns of human gene frequencies in Europe', *American Journal of Physical Anthropology*, 80: 267–94.

Starikovskaya, Y.B., Sukernik, R.I., Schurr, T.G., Kogelnik, A.M. and Wallace, D.C. (1998) 'MtDNA diversity in Chukchi and Siberian Eskimos: implications for the genetic history of Ancient Beringia and the peopling of the New World', *American Journal of Human Genetics*, 63: 1473–91.

Su, B., Xiao, J., Underhill, P., Deka, R., Zhang, W., Akey, J., Huang, W., Shen, D., Lu, D., Luo, J., Chu, J., Tan, J., Shen, P., Davis, R., Cavalli-Sforza, L.L., Chakraborty, R., Xiong, M., Du, R., Oefner, P., Chen, Z. and Jin, L. (1999) 'Y-chromosome evidence for a northward migration of modern humans into Eastern Asia during the last Ice Age', *American Journal of Human Genetics*, 65: 1718–24.

Sukernik, R.I., Karafet, T.M. and Osipova, L.P. (1978) 'Distribution of blood groups, serum markers and red cell enzymes in two human populations from Northern Siberia', *Human Heredity*, 28: 321–7.

Sukernik, R.I., Osipova, L.P., Karafet, T.M., Wiebe, V.P. and Posukh, O.L. (1986) 'Genetic and ecological studies of aboriginal inhabitants of North-Eastern Siberia. 2. Polymorphic blood systems, immunoglobulin allotypes, and other genetic markers in Asian Eskimos. Genetic structure of the Bering Sea Eskimos', *Genetika*, 22: 2369–80 (in Russian).

Szathmary, E.J.E. (1981) 'Genetic markers in Siberian and northern North American populations', *Yearbook of Physical Anthropology*, 24: 37–74.

Torroni, A., Sukernik, R.I., Schurr, T.G., Starikovskaya, Y.B., Cabell, M.F., Crawford, M.H., Comuzzie, A.G. and Wallace, D.C. (1993) 'MtDNA variation of aboriginal Siberians reveals distinct genetic affinities with Native Americans', *American Journal of Human Genetics*, 53: 591–608.

Uinuk-Ool, T.S., Takezaki, N. and Klein J. (2003) 'Ancestry and kinship of Native Siberian populations: the HLA evidence', *Evolutionary Anthropology*, 12: 231–45.

Underhill, P.A., Shen, P., Lin, A.A., Jin, L., Passarino, G., Yang, W.H., Kauffman, E., Bonné-Tamir, B., Bertranpetit, J., Francalacci, P., Ibrahim, M., Jenkins, T., Kidd, J.R., Mehdi, S.Q., Seielstad, M.T., Wells, R.S., Piazza, A., Davis, R.W., Feldman, M.W., Cavalli-Sforza, L.L. and Oefner, P.J. (2000) 'Y chromosome sequence variation and the history of human populations', *Nature Genetics*, 26: 358–61.

Vajda, E.J. (2004) *Ket* (Languages of the World, 204), Munich: Lincom Europa.

Vasil'ev, S.A. (1993) 'The Upper Paleolithic of northern Asia', *Current Anthropology*, 34: 82–92.

Wells, R.S., Yuldasheva, N., Ruzibakiev, R., Underhill, P.A., Evseeva, I., Blue-Smith, J., Jin, L., Su, B., Pitchappan, R., Shanmugalakshimi, S., Balakrishnan, K., Read, M., Pearson, N.M., Zerjal, T., Webster, M.T., Zholoshvili, I., Jamarjashvili, E., Gambarov, S., Nikbin, B., Dostiev, A., Aknazarov, O., Zalloua, P., Tsoy, I., Kitaev, M., Mirrakhimov, M., Chariev, A. and Bodmer, W.F. (2001) 'The Eurasian heartland: a continental perspective on Y-chromosome diversity', *Proceedings of the National Academy of Sciences USA*, 98: 10244–9.

Wijsman, E.M. and Cavalli-Sforza, L.L. (1984) 'Migration and genetic population structure with special reference to humans', *Annual Review of Ecology and Systematics*, 15: 279–301.

Wood, E.T., Stover, D.A., Ehret, C., Destro-Bisol, G., Spendini, G., McLeod, H., Louie, L., Bamshad, M., Strassmann, B.I., Soodyall, H. and Hammer, M.F. (2005) 'Contrasting patterns of Y chromosome and mtDNA variation in Africa: evidence for sex-biased demographic processes', *European Journal of Human Genetics*, 13: 867–76.

YCC (The Y Chromosome Consortium) (2002) 'A nomenclature system for the tree of Y chromosomal binary haplogroups', *Genome Research*, 12: 339–48.

Zegura, S.L., Karafet, T.M., Zhivotovsky, L.A. and Hammer, M.F. (2004) 'High-resolution SNPs and microsatellite haplotypes point to a single, recent entry of Native American Y chromosomes into the Americas', *Molecular Biology and Evolution*, 21: 164–75.

Zerjal, T., Dashnyam, B., Pandya, A., Kayser, M., Roewer, L., Santos, F.R., Schiefenhovel, W., Fretwell, N., Jobling, M.A., Harihara, S., Shimizu, K., Semjidmaa, D., Sajantila, A., Salo, P., Crawford, M.H., Ginter, E.K., Evgrafov, O.V. and Tyler-Smith, C. (1997) 'Genetic relationships of Asians and northern Europeans, revealed by Y-chromosome DNA analysis', *American Journal of Human Genetics*, 60: 1174–83.

Zerjal, T., Pandya, A., Santos, F.R., Adhikari, R., Tarazona, E., Kayser, M., Evgrafov, O., Singh, L., Thangaraij, K., Destro-Bisol, G., Thomas, M.G., Qamar, R., Mehdi, S.Q., Rosser, Z.H., Hurles, M.E., Jobling, M.A. and Tyler-Smith, C. (1999) 'The use of Y-chromosomal DNA variation to investigate population history: recent male spread in Asia and Europe', in S.S. Papiha and R. Deka (eds) *Genomic Diversity: Applications in Human Population Genetics*, pp. 91–102, New York: Plenum.

19 Y-chromosome phylogeography in Asia

Inferring haplogroup origins and polarity of haplogroup dispersion

Peter A. Underhill

Introduction

Asia encompasses considerable territorial expanse, geographic compartmentalization and ethnic diversity (Blench 2005). Correspondingly, the patterns of extant genetic diversity often recapitulate these themes (Cavalli-Sforza et al. 1994; Cavalli-Sforza and Feldman 2003; Underhill 2003), providing an independent line of ever developing and independently reproducible empirical evidence amenable to multidisciplinary hypothesis testing that is essential to a fuller understanding of the panorama of human history.

The aim of this chapter is to present perspectives regarding inferences of various migrations of anatomically modern humans within Asia based upon the evolutionary trajectory of molecular diversification associated with the haploid non-recombining Y-chromosome (NRY). A review of the totality of perceived migrations in Asia is beyond the scope of this chapter. Rather, instructive examples are presented, as well as some first principles concerning how to interpret patterns of genetic variability leading to deductions regarding potential geographic centers of the origins and directionality of spread of phylogenetic NRY haplogroups. Like its haploid maternally transmitted counterpart, the mitochondrial DNA genome, the patterns of paternally transmitted NRY differentiation provide one representation of the evolution of modern populations and their migration pathways (Underhill et al. 2001). The application of haploid molecular phylogenetics to human population genetics is now well established owing to substantive progress in defining the major architectural and hierarchical features of the haploid phylogenies. This provides a different and instructive alternative to traditional genetic census surveys using either protein polymorphisms or DNA sequence variations based upon allele frequencies of various unlinked genetic polymorphic genomic constituents.

The pioneering work of Hennig (1966) developed the fundamentals of modern phylogenetics. These principles form the foundation for the creation of haploid molecular genealogies and their interpretation. The NRY genealogy represents perhaps the quintessential example of Hennig's phylogenetic and underlying phylogeographic doctrines. The most critical insight by Hennig was that the best explanation for the distribution of characters depended upon the decisive fact that only synapomorphous characters define truly monophyletic taxa in which a most recent common ancestor can be discerned. Thus, phylogenetic characters can be attributed to either ancestral or derived character states. The unequivocal sequential accumulation of derived (synapomorphic) alleles in a binary marker based molecular genealogy accurately defines the various cladistic relationships found within a genealogy, be it molecular or other trait-based data. Each cladistic node reflects the appearance of a most recent common ancestor that follows the previous variety. Therefore, regarding the NRY genealogy, every Y chromosome with the same derived character state or allele descends from a single common paternal ancestor located within the temporally relative branching pattern of the Y-chromosome genealogy. Since the nucleotide changes that define the various nodes of the genealogy are assumed to reflect unique events, they often cluster within distinctive geographic space, displaying the phylogeography of haplogroup relationships. As time elapses, some descendents within a particular cladistic haplogroup may migrate from this ancestral homeland. By assessing the distributions of haplogroups one can trace the dispersal of Y chromosomes with common heritage and, by inference, the spread of populations. Thus patterns of genetic variation within those populations not maintained in total isolation often reflect both the consequences of local *in situ* diversification plus input from constituents from external regions resulting in signals of gene flow and hybridization.

An example of how the conception of ancestral and derived phylogenetic relationships may depend upon the extent of molecular information available at a certain point concerns the topic of the origin of the polymorphic Y chromosome Alu insertion (YAP = DYS287). This YAP insertion occurs in Africa at high frequency and is also observed at considerable frequencies in Japan, Tibet, and Andaman Islanders. This curious disjunct distribution has intrigued population geneticists and adherents of phylogeography. On the basis of just nine binary markers including YAP and SRY4064 (= M40) which occurs at 100 per cent within the African YAP representatives but not the Asian YAP samples, the Asian chromosomes may be assumed to be ancestral to the M40 derived Africans. In that case one may conclude that the YAP insertion first arose in Asia and that some descendents migrated back to Africa (Hammer *et al.* 1998). However, the discovery of the derived M174 single nucleotide marker in Asian YAP chromosomes (Underhill *et al.* 2000; Underhill and Roseman 2001) showed that the Asian YAP chromosomes are not necessarily ancestral relative to the Africans. In fact a plausible scenario is that the YAP insertion first originated in Africa and some descendents later migrated to Asia where the haplogroup D-M174 subsequently evolved and replaced the earlier Asian YAP lineage. Meanwhile, a YAP representative remained behind in Africa and later evolved into the haplogroup E-M40 clade. Further support for this African origin of YAP model comes from the discovery of some precursor derived YAP chromosomes in Africans that lack both the M40 and M174 mutations (Weale *et al.* 2003). While the back to Africa migration by YAP chromosomes can be disputed, a clear unequivocal signal of such an event exists in the form of haplogroup R1-M173 chromosomes (Cruciani *et al.* 2002).

Since the contemporary genetic landscape reflects the net effects of an accumulation of multiple gene flows during the entire period of occupation, including repetitive demographic expansions and periodic contractions, the known structures of the molecular genealogies, their irregular geographic distributions, and degree of associated subsequent differentiation provides clues to the various episodes of human migrations (Underhill 2003). Implicit in the NRY trees structure is the simple but important fact that bifurcations localized more within the interior nodes of the genealogy record more ancient molecular divergences, while branching occurrences nearer the canopy of the gene tree reflect more recent evolutionary events.

Depending upon which phylogenetic level of binary marker molecular characterization the haplogroup data are resolved to experimentally in a population census, the relative temporality of the diversification patterns and their geography can be characterized. This fundamental concept provides a foundation upon which inferences regarding the timing of gene flows and by extension the movement of peoples and cultures are formulated. As more and more binary markers are added to the NRY genealogy, not only are known nodes reinforced but, more importantly, previous apparent independent clades can either be united by newly characterized DNA sequence changes or split into distinctive sister sub-clades imparting genetic distance between clades previously viewed as terminal clades with common heritage and apparent similar histories. While the overall underlying framework of the tree is likely to persist, because it seems unlikely that any major subdivision is entirely missing, it is important to recognize that any current version of the NRY genealogy may be viewed as a temporary representation of the structure. Thousands of yet undiscovered NRY binary mutations must exist. As they are uncovered and appropriately 'treed', our knowledge of the NRY genealogy remains to expand and be refined. Interpretations of the phylogeographic, temporal, and polar nature of various haplogroup dispersals must be tempered with the fact that unknown relationships exist, underscoring the fact the NRY tree of binary haplogroups is not static but growing with the high likelihood of presenting new perspectives in the future. This cautions us against temptations to over-interpret the data and prematurely extrapolate current (but incomplete) knowledge of NRY diversity to hypotheses and models based upon non-genetic data such as linguistics, palaeo-climatology, and archeology. While reflective of an overall human history, some gene histories may vary from one another and molecular narratives will not always be in lockstep agreement with other types of data.

Concepts and methods

The NRY data used in the examples presented were taken from papers involving populations from present-day Turkey (Cinnioglu *et al.* 2004), India and Pakistan (Sengupta *et al.* 2006), as well as a compilation of East Asian data gleaned from a variety of specified primary studies (Underhill 2005) that involved over 3700 samples from 74 populations and/or ethnic groups which were normalized to 12 informative binary haplogroups (C*, C2, C3, D, F, K, M, N, O1, O2, O3 and P).

Localizing geographic origins of haplogroups

There are two fundamental approaches to this issue. One longstanding approach, that has been applied to genetic data in general, is that the region of highest frequency of a specific allele or character state may reflect its geographic origin. This approach may not be accurate in all situations, however, especially when uncertainty exists as to which allelic state is either ancestral or derived. Phylogenetics, however, permits accurate deduction of the informative derived (synapomorphic) state for which understanding its putative geographic origins is considerably more instructive regarding affinity and migration.

The other metric useful for inferring geographic origins of genetic variants involves the concept of identifying the region of highest diversity. In the case of NRY haplogroups, the origin could very well be that region that contains the highest assemblage of associated sub-cladistic diversity. This concept can be extended to inferences regarding the likely geographic origins of specific NRY haplogroups by employing the analysis of more mutable short tandem repeat (Y-STR) loci (i.e. microsatellites) that are linked to a specific collection of chromosomes within a common haplogroup. The region where the Y-STR variation is highest within a specific haplogroup would provide a perspective on the possible origin of that haplogroup within the data set from which other representative members or their ancestors radiated, taking with them only a subset of the Y-STR variation found in the putative source region. While both approaches have their merits and represent the best that can be accomplished practically speaking with any current version of molecular genealogical data, precautions should be taken when evaluating such frequency or associated diversity data. For example, it should always be kept in mind that the potential of regions of higher frequency and/or higher molecular diversity may also be a result of demographic growth, rather than longest time since origin. If high frequency haplogroups have low associated microsatellite variety, then it is likely that the data reflect a very recent and considerable increase in numbers of descendents. Alternatively, regions of high Y-STR variety can also be a result of very high effective population size even over a rather short period of time, or of multiple inputs from numerous different external source regions, somewhat artificially creating a false appearance of apparent temporal antiquity. The genetics viewed in isolation from other non-genetic evidence cannot distinguish between the extent of observed accumulated diversity over elapsed generational time versus the high diversity being a consequence of recent gene flow of haplogroup linked Y-STR lineages from divergent ancestors belonging to the same binary marker defined haplogroup. This is where the consideration of alternative non-genetic knowledge, such as palaeo-climate and archeological matter can help the geneticist best choose between the two possible agencies (i.e. highest frequency or highest diversity) that could have shaped the observed diversity patterns.

Here, spatial surface maps of both binary haplogroup frequency and haplogroup associated microsatellite variance distributions for the India and Pakistan samples were computed following the Kringing procedure (Delfiner 1976) using Surfer Systems Golden software.

Results

As previously stated, the pattern of genetic variation in a region or population is often a consequence of *in situ* indigenous diversification coupled with gene flow from external regions. Figure 19.1 shows a representation of this phenomenon using NRY haplogroup data from India, Pakistan, and East Asia (Sengupta *et al.* 2006). The currently defined haplogroup compositions are as follows; Pakistan (23), India (21), and East Asia (14). Considerable haplogroup sharing (overlapping sectors) exists between the populations but elements of individuality of haplogroup representation are also visible. Specifically, seven haplogroups are shared amongst all three regions, with India and the Indus Valley region (Pakistan) sharing the most (11), consistent with their geographic proximity and the general inappropriateness of employing recent political boundaries to reflect distinctive group membership at the genetic level. However, Pakistan has four autonomous haplogroups relative to the others. Other subtler haplogroup composition distinctions are also displayed.

Localization of NRY haplogroups

The small effective population size of Y chromosomes relative to the autosomal genome constituents (one to four, respectively, in randomly mating populations) accentuates the consequences of genetic drift and founder effect (Underhill 2003). This fact often results in irregular distributions of haplogroups with geography and contributes to the observation that NRY haplogroups are generally strongly related to geography.

Using an analysis of NRY haplogroup diversity and frequency, it has been proposed that genetic diversity in East Asia first arose in the south then radiated

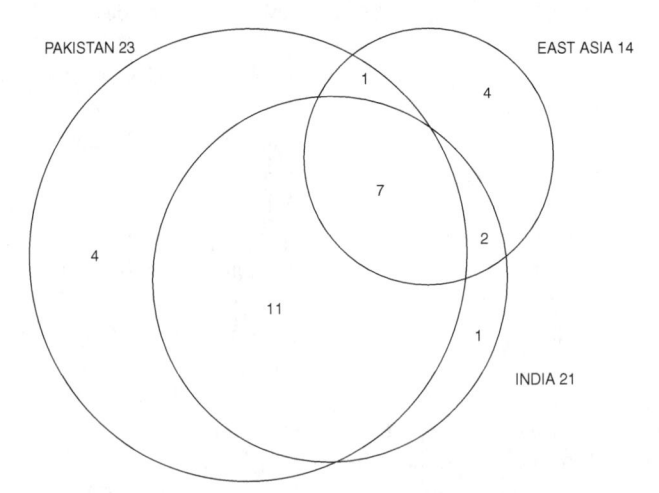

Figure 19.1 Representation of numbers of shared and independent Y-chromosome haplogroups in India, Pakistan and East Asia (Cambodia, Siberia, Japan, China). Data from Sengupta *et al.* 2006.

northwards (Su *et al.* 1999; Shi *et al.* 2005). This is consistent with the 'southern route' proposal of an initial migratory route of modern humans to Asia (Stringer 2000; Flemming *et al.* 2003) that has recently been bolstered by mtDNA analysis (Macauley *et al.* 2005)

Polarity of haplogroup spread

Additional insights can be gained when linked polymorphic microsatellite (also referred to as short tandem repeat, or STR) loci are assessed within specific Y-chromosome binary haplogroups. The degree of affiliated microsatellite diversity provides an additional metric that addresses the issues of the age of microsatellite accumulation within a set of samples that have common haplogroup ancestry, as well as an inference of the net directionality of haplogroup dispersal across the landscape. An example of this concept is the distribution of haplogroup J2-M172 chromosomes in Asia Minor (Cinnioglu *et al.* 2004). Within the political boundaries of modern-day Turkey, the frequency distribution of M172 derived chromosomes averages around 25 per cent and displays a random distribution with no apparent clinal pattern. However, a statistically significant decline of haplogroup J2-M172 related microsatellite variance with increasing latitude was observed. This genetic cline of microsatellite (Figure 19.2) correlates with the distribution of early Neolithic sites, which are concentrated within the southern sector of Anatolia (Roberts 2002). This statistically significant reduction in microsatellite variance northwards may reflect that these haplogroup J2-M172 defined chromosomes first diversified within the southern tier during the early phases of sedentarism possibly associated with the early transition to agriculture, with a subset of this diversity subsequently expanding geographically northwards, taking a reduced degree of microsatellite diversity with it, as well as increasing in frequency to similar levels found in southern Turkey.

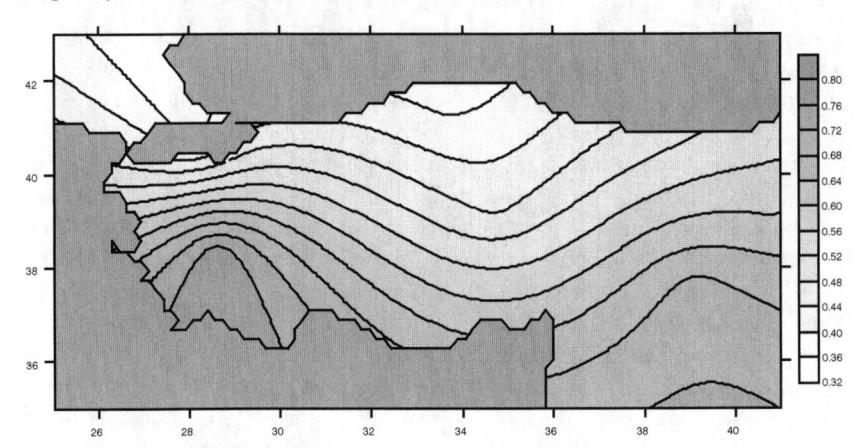

Figure 19.2 Spatial south towards north cline of associated 10 loci microsatellite mean variance of haplogroup J2 chromosomes in Turkey. Data from Cinnioglu *et al.* 2004.

Discussion

It is important to recognize that spatial frequency and spatial diversity maps of haplogroups involve considerable extrapolation between geographic locales where samples were actually collected. Although more sampling density and molecular resolution are always better, comprehensive population genetic molecular data are innately limited because of the considerable effort and cost involved in such surveys. It is always easier to contribute criticism than actual reproducible data. Obviously, future higher sampling density would most likely generate refined maps with finer detail on a more micro-geographic scale. In addition, both types of maps, i.e. frequency verses diversity, may not always mirror one another. An example of this situation involves haplogroup H2, defined by the M52 SNP. This haplogroup displays considerable frequency in the Indian subcontinent (over 40 per cent in some regions). The regionalization of this haplogroup to South Asia and its virtual absence elsewhere demonstrates that it is of indigenous origin somewhere within India. The co-presence of the ancestral haplogroup F*, from which the derivative haplogroup H-M69 originated, bolsters the deduction that haplogroup H2 arose *in situ* within the Indian subcontinent. In addition, sometimes regions of highest haplogroup frequency do not always coincide with regions of highest microsatellite diversity. Figure 19.3a, b presents haplogroup H2 frequency (panel 3a) and microsatellite variance (panel 3b) as an example. The highest variation is in the west, with a decreasing cline eastwards with the highest frequency occurring towards the east, indicating that a subset of H2 chromosomes probably moved eastward, then expanded demographically.

While the current maps display general trends that are likely to be representative, it is important to keep in mind that such maps represent the overall *net* picture of haplogroup distribution of chromosomes. Such landscapes are a snapshot in time and thus can be a composite of multiple past movements. Equally important is the realization that the level of molecular haplogroup resolution of the data being analyzed must be considered. At the major clade level (deeper within the phylogeny), one spatial pattern will appear, while when more derived sub-clades are mapped, the origin and trajectory of these may differ. Haplogroup L-M20 provides an example of this feature. Haplogroup L representatives span the Mediterranean basin, Anatolia, across western and southern Asian. Figure 19.4a shows frequency data for haplogroup L chromosomes from Turkey, Pakistan, and India. The region of highest frequency is near the Indus Valley, a plausible homeland for this ancient haplogroup. However, it is prudent to recognize that not all L representatives have recent common ancestry. Recently it was shown (Sengupta *et al.* 2006) that the vast majority of known L representatives apportion to three main sub-clades, namely L1-M76, L2-M317, and L3-M357, each with its own distinctive geographic region of maximum frequency. Figure 19.4b shows the spatial frequency map of haplogroup L1 that displays a cline radiating out of coastal western India, suggesting that this was possible center of origin and net demic expansion.

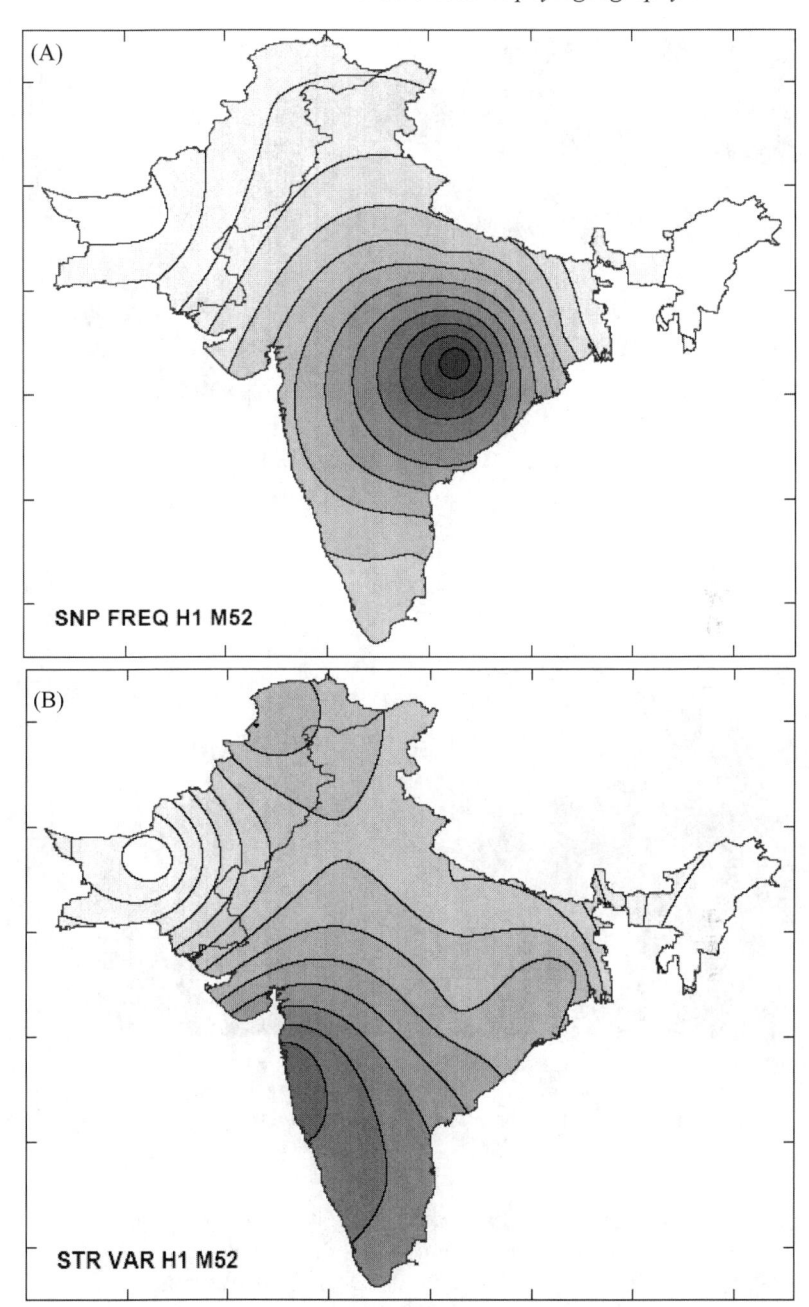

Figure 19.3 Spatial frequency distribution map of haplogroup H2-M52 chromosomes (A) and spatial distribution map of haplogroup H2 associated microsatellite variation averaged across 10 loci (B). Data from Sengupta *et al.* 2006.

424 Peter A. Underhill

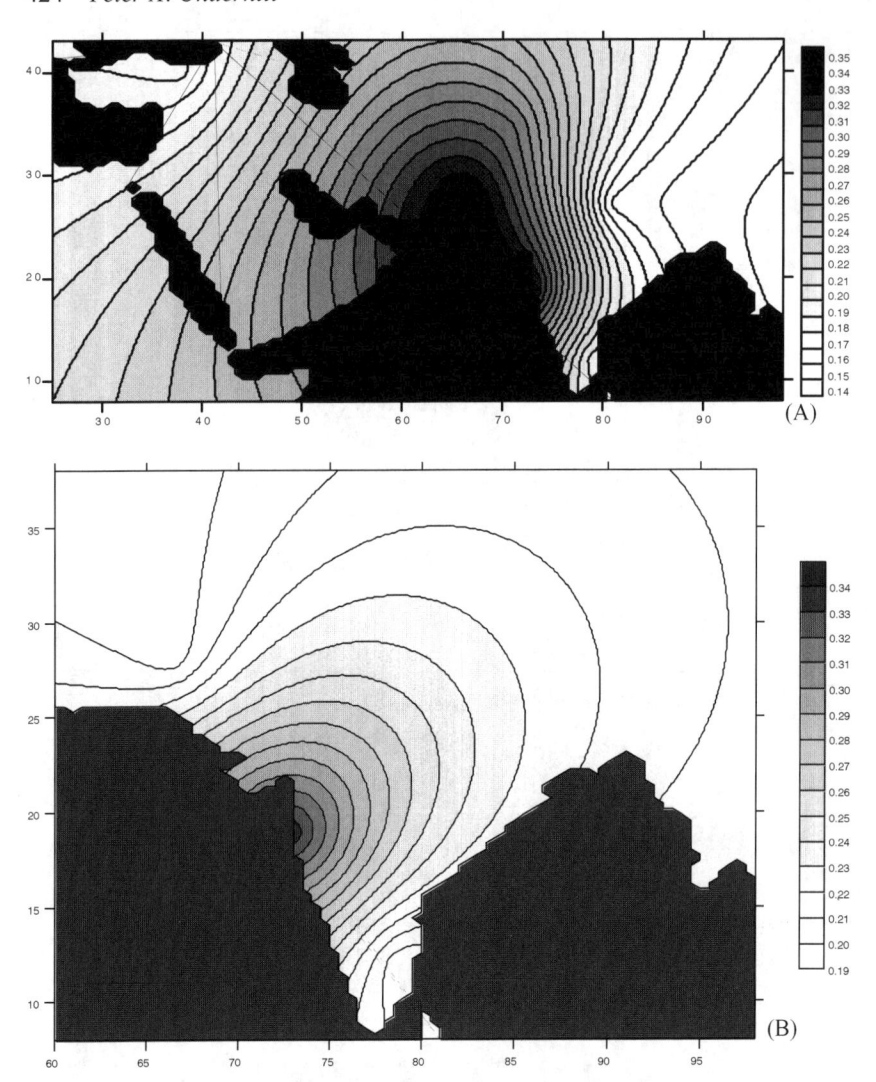

Figure 19.4 Spatial frequency distribution map of haplogroup L-M20 chromosomes (A) and spatial distribution map of sub-haplogroup L1-M76 chromosomes (B). Data from Cinnioglu *et al.* 2004; Sengupta *et al.* 2006.

As more molecular resolution is achieved for the Y-chromosome phylogeny and larger scale genotyping surveys conducted, the patterns of the regionalization of haplogroups will be more precisely displayed. Thus overarching conclusions attributing one migration to one haplogroup, especially when haplogroups are defined at deeper levels in the phylogeny, must be resisted. As molecular resolution of Y chromosomes increases using synapomorphic binary markers relevant to the geographic regions under study, the phylogeographic landscape will become more and more reflective of the associated human history.

References

Blench, R.M. (2005) 'From the mountains to the valleys: understanding ethnolinguistic geography in Southwest Asia', in L. Sagart, R.M. Blench and A. Sanchez-Mazas (eds) *The Peopling of East Asia: Putting Together Archaeology, Linguistics and Genetics*, pp. 31–50, London: RoutledgeCurzon.

Cavalli-Sforza, L.L. and Feldman, M.W. (2003) 'The application of molecular genetic approaches to the study of human evolution', *Nature Genetics*, supplement 33: 266–75.

Cavalli-Sforza, L.L., Menozzi, P. and Piazza, A. (1994) *History and Geography of Human Genes*, Princeton, NJ: Princeton University Press.

Cinnioglu, C., King, R., Kivisild, T., Kalfoglu, E., Atasoy, S., Cavalleri, G.L., Lillie, A.S., Roseman, C.C., Lin, A.A., Prince, K., Oefner, P.J., Shen, P., Semino, O., Cavalli-Sforza, L.L. and Underhill, P.A. (2004) 'Excavating Y-chromosome haplotype strata in Anatolia', *Human Genetics*, 114: 127–48.

Cruciani, F., Santolamazza, P., Shen, P., Macaulay, V., Moral, P., Olckers, A., Modiano, D., Destro-Bisol, G., Holmes, S., Coia, V., Wallace, D. C., Oefner, P. J., Torroni, A., Cavalli-Sforza, L. L., Scozzari, R. and Underhill, P. A. (2002) 'An Asia to Sub-Saharan Africa back migration is supported by high-resolution analysis of human Y chromosome haplotypes', *American Journal of Human Genetics*, 70: 1197–214.

Delfiner, P. (1976) 'Linear estimation of non-stationary spatial phenomena', in M. Guarasio, M. David and C. Haijbegts (eds) *Advanced Geostatistics in the Mining Industry*, pp. 49–68, Dordrecht: Reidel.

Flemming, N.C., Bailey, G.N., Courtillot, V., King, G., Lambeck, K., Ryerson, F. and Vita-Finzi C. (2003) 'Coastal and marine palaeo-environments and human dispersal points across the Africa–Eurasia boundary', in C.A. Brebbia and T. Gambin (eds) *Maritime Heritage*, pp. 61–74, Southampton: Wessex Institute of Technology Press.

Hammer, M. F., Karafet, T., Rasanayagam, A., Wood, E.T., Altheide, T.K., Jenkins, T., Griffiths, R.C., Templeton, A.R. and Zegura, S.L. (1998) 'Out of Africa and back again: Nested cladistic analysis of human Y chromosome variation', *Molecular Biology and Evolution*, 15: 427–41.

Hennig, W. (1966) *Phylogenetic Systematics*, Urbana, IL: University of Illinois Press.

Macaulay, V., Hill, C., Achilli, A., Rengo, C., Clarke, D., Meehan, W., Blackburn, J., Semino, O., Scozzari, R., Cruciani, F., Taha, A., Shaari, N.K., Raja, J.M., Ismail, P., Zainuddin, Z., Goodwin, W., Bulbeck, D., Bandelt, H.J., Oppenheimer, S., Torroni, A. and Richards, M. (2005) 'Single, rapid coastal settlement of Asia revealed by analysis of complete mitochondrial genomes', *Science*, 308: 1034–6.

Roberts, N. (2002) 'Did prehistoric landscape management retard the post-glacial spread of woodland Southwest Asia?', *Antiquity*, 76:1002–10.

Sengupta, S., Zhivotosky, L.A., King, R., Mehdi,, S.Q., Edmonds, C.A., Chow, C.T., Lin, A.A., Mitra, M., Sil, S.K., Ramesh, A., Rani, M.V.U., Thakur, C.M., Cavalli-Sforza, L.L., Majumder, P.P. and Underhill, P.A. (2006) 'Polarity and temporality of high resolution Y-chromosome distributions in India identify both indigenous and exogenous expansions and reveal minor genetic influence of central Asian pastoralists', *American Journal of Human Genetics*, 78: 202–21.

Shi, H., Dong, Y.L., Wen, B., Xiao, C.J., Underhill, P.A., Shen, P.D., Chakraborty, R., Jin, L. and Su, B. (2005) 'Y-chromosome evidence of southern origin of the East Asian-specific haplogroup O3-M122', *American Journal of Human Genetics*, 77: 408–19.

Stringer, C. (2000) 'Coasting out of Africa', *Nature*, 405: 24–6.

Su, B., Xiao, J., Underhill, P.A., Deka, R., Zhang, W., Akey, J., Huang, W., Shen, D., Lu, D., Luo, J., Chu, J., Tan, J., Shen, P., Davis, R., Cavalli-Sforza, L.L., Chakraborty, R., Xiong, M. Du, R. Oefner, P.J., Chen, Z. and Jin, L. (1999) 'Y chromosome evidence for a northward migration of modern humans in East Asia during the last ice age', *American Journal of Human Genetics*, 65: 1718–24.

Underhill, P.A. (2003) 'Inferring human history: clues from Y-chromosome haplotypes', in *The Genome of Homo Sapiens, Cold Spring Harbor Symposium of Quantitative Biology*, 68: 487–93.

Underhill, P.A. (2005) 'A synopsis of extant Y chromosome diversity in East Asia and Oceania', in L. Sagart, R. Blench and A. Sanchez-Mazas (eds) *The Peopling of East Asia: Putting Together Archaeology, Linguistics and Genetics*, pp. 297–313, London: RoutledgeCurzon.

Underhill, P.A. and Roseman, C.C. (2001) 'The case for an African rather than an Asian origin of the human Y-chromosome YAP insertion', in L. Jin, M. Seielstad and C. Xiao (eds) *Recent Advances in Human Biology*, vol. 8, *Genetic, Linguistic and Archaeological Perspectives on Human Diversity in Southeast Asia*, pp. 43–56, Rivers Edge, NJ: World Scientific.

Underhill, P.A., Shen, P., Lin, A.A., Jin, L., Passarino, G., Yang, W.H., Kauffman, E., Bonné-Tamir, B., Bertranpetit, J., Francalacci, P., Ibrahim, M., Jenkins, T., Kidd, J.R., Mehdi, S.Q., Seielstad, M.T., Wells, R.S., Piazza, A., Davis, R.W., Feldman, M.W., Cavalli-Sforza, L.L. and Oefner, P.J. (2000) 'Y chromosome sequence variation and the history of human populations', *Nature Genetics*, 26: 358–61.

Underhill, P.A., Passarino, G., Lin, A.A., Shen, P., Foley, R.A., Lahr, M.M., Oefner, P.J. and Cavalli-Sforza, L.L. (2001) 'The phylogeography of Y chromosome binary haplotypes and the origins of modern human populations', *Annals of Human Genetics*, 65: 43–62.

Weale, M.E., Shah, T., Jones, A.L., Greenhalgh, J., Wilson, J.F., Nymadawa, P., Zeitlin, D., Connell, B.A., Bradman, N. and Toomas, M.G. (2003) 'Rare deep-rooting Y chromosome lineages in humans: Lessons for phylogeography', *Genetics*, 165: 229–34.

Wen, B., Li, H., Lu, D., Song, X., Zhang, F., He, Y., Li, F., Gao, Y., Mao, X., Zhang, L., Qian, J., Tan, J., Jin, J., Huang, W., Deka, R., Su, B., Chakraborty, R. and Jin, L. (2004) 'Genetic evidence supports demic diffusion of Han culture', *Nature*, 431: 302–5.

20 Understanding yak pastoralism in Central Asian Highlands

Mitochondrial DNA evidence for origin, domestication and dispersal of domestic yak

Xue-bin Qi, Han Jianlin, Roger Blench,
J. Edward O. Rege and Olivier Hanotte

Introduction

Today a large human population inhabits the Central Asian Highlands, a vast area characterized by high elevation and cold climate. They are principally pastoralists or agro-pastoralists whose religion and culture are heavily influenced by Tibetan Buddhism (Blench 2001; Joshi 1982; Kreutzmann 2002; Liu *et al.* 1989; Sherchand and Karki 1996; Tshering *et al.* 1996; Wiener *et al.* 2003; Zhang 1989). The earliest prehistoric human occupation on the Qinghai-Tibetan Plateau may date back to *cal.* 25,000 BP to the Upper Pleistocene (Huang 1994; Madsen *et al.* 2006). Aldenderfer and Zhang (2004) review the various published dates, the methods used to establish them and the controversies surrounding them. Reliably dated sites are still very few and most dates are founded on typologies which are themselves controversial.

Recent surveys around the Lake Qinghai basin suggest that the upper elevations were only exploited seasonally by foragers and that it was only with the pastoral Neolithic that all-year-round occupation was possible (Brantingham *et al.* 2003; Madsen *et al.* 2006). However, the first major human occupation phase is thought to have begun *cal.* 20,000 BP (Zhang and Li 2002; Zhang *et al.* 2003), possibly following the peaking of the Last Glacial Maximum at about this period. A second phase began in mid-Holocene times, *cal.* 7,500 BP (Huang 1994), eventually leading to permanent human occupation of the Plateau about 4000–5000 BP (Tong 1990; Aldenderfer and Zhang 2004). Su *et al.* (2000) argue that Y-chromosome analysis of current Sino-Tibetan speaking populations suggests that the Neolithic inhabitants of the upper-middle Yellow River basin about 10,000 BP were likely the ancestors of modern Sino-Tibetan populations in the Himalayas and the Qinghai-Tibetan Plateau. Such a view is now highly controversial, with recent molecular surveys among highland populations suggesting the reverse, namely that the genetic diversity of these isolated populations is very high and that the region might be a source region for the Sino-Tibetans (Kraayenbrink *et al.* 2006).

The yak, *Poephagus grunniens*, a member of Bovini tribe, is endemic to Central Asia and well adapted to the cold and high altitude environment. Yak pastoralism is widespread in the Central Asian Highlands. With a current total population size of 14 million, the domestic yak constitutes one of the most important domestic animal genetic resources in the region and plays an indispensable role in the life of pastoralists and agro-pastoralists (Wiener *et al.* 2003). The geographical distribution of the domestic yak extends from the southern slopes of the Himalayas in the south to the Altai and Hangai Mountains of Mongolia and Russia in the north, and from the Pamir Plateau and Tien-Shan (Tianshan) Mountains in the west to the Qilian Mountains in the east (Figure 20.1). The wild yak, which once roamed throughout the Qinghai-Tibetan Plateau, still survives in remote areas of the Plateau and the Kunlun Mountains, although the total population is less than 20,000 animals and many of those may have suffered partial introgression from domestic yak (Guiquan 1996; Schaller and Wulin 1996). Both domestic and extant wild yak are thought to have originated from a so-called 'ancient or primitive yak'. Fossil evidence unearthed in the Pleistocene layer suggests that such anterior types were extensively distributed over northeastern Eurasia in the late Tertiary period (2.5 million years ago) (Cai 1989; Olsen 1990; Wiener *et al.* 2003).

At present, the mean heights of the Himalayas and Qinghai-Tibetan Plateau are 6100 and 4000 meters, respectively, although before the mid-Pleistocene period they were under 4500 and 2000 meters (Tang and Hare 1995). The persistent uplifting of the Himalayas and the Qinghai-Tibetan Plateau during the Quaternary has dramatically changed the palaeoenvironment in these areas. Forest on the Qinghai-Tibetan Plateau was replaced by alpine meadow, and animals (including the wild yak) became adapted to the higher altitude of the Qinghai-Tibetan Plateau following their migration from Northeastern Eurasia (Wiener *et al.* 2003).

The date and centre of yak domestication as well as the dispersal routes of yak pastoralism remain largely speculative. Textual references point to the beginnings of domestication in the Northern Qinghai-Tibetan Plateau by the ancient 'Qiang' people (a collective name for ancient nomadic people in Western China), with the establishment of yak pastoralism in the late Neolithic, *cal.* 5000 BP (Liu and Peng 1989; Wiener *et al.* 2003; Zhang 1989), i.e. several thousand years *later* than the domestication of cattle. The claim by Zeuner (1963) that yak domestication could have occurred at the same time as the domestication of cattle, in the Neolithic, around 10,000–8000 BP is not supported by any archaeological or genetic data.

Where this domestication took place remains unclear. The hypothesis of the Northern Qinghai-Tibetan Plateau area was largely based on archaeological findings as well as the fact that the majority of wild yak are found today within this region (Liu and Peng 1989; Wiener *et al.* 2003; Zhang 1989). This area is presently largely inhospitable to human habitation, although geomorphological and vegetation change makes it possible that it was formerly more attractive. An alternative centre of domestication in the Eastern Qinghai-Tibetan Plateau has also been proposed (Qi 2004).

The dispersal routes from the putative centre of domestication to the occupation of current yak territories also remain speculative. One view is that the current northern yak territories, in what is now Mongolia and Russia, were established following a westward migratory route that first occupied an area known as the 'Pamir Knot' covering the Pamir, the Hindu-Kush Mountains, the Trans-Karakoram Mountains, the Kunlun Mountains, and the Tien-Shan Mountains. During the 13th century it expanded further northwards to Southern Siberia (Felius 1995; Zhong 1996). However, it is also possible that yak pastoralism spread directly northwards across the present Gobi Desert before the region became hyper-arid, driving away its resident populations (Figure 20.1).

The rapid development of molecular biology in the past decade has made many molecular markers available for unraveling the major evolutionary issues on the origin, domestication, and dispersal of domesticated animals and plants. Analyses of mitochondrial DNA (mtDNA), with its characteristics such as maternal mode

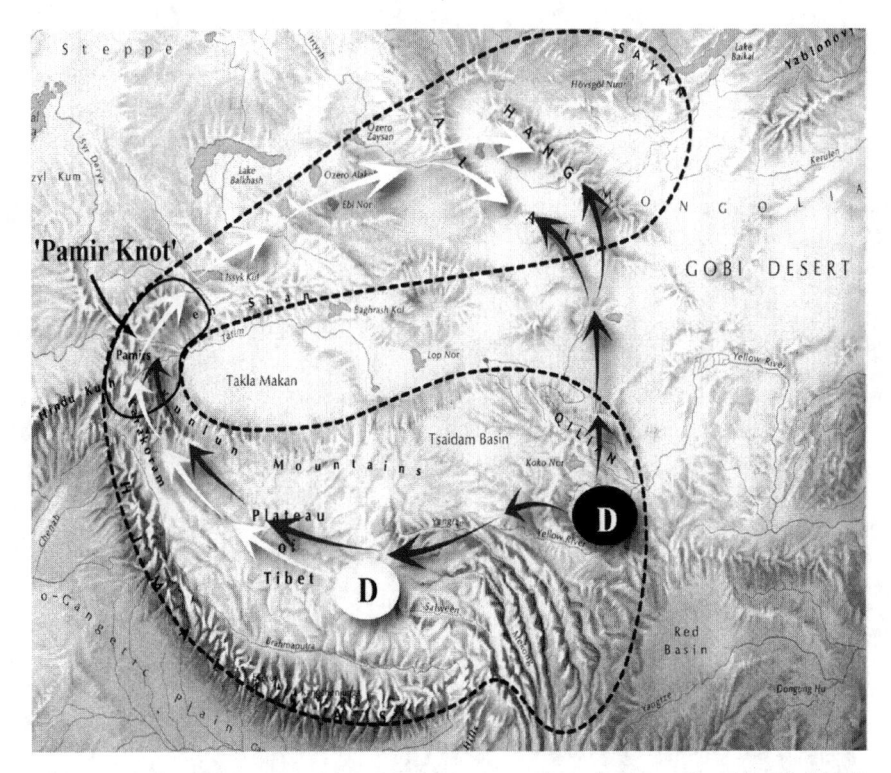

Figure 20.1 The current distribution of yak pastoralism in Central Asian Highlands (highlighted area). The letter D represents putative centres of domestication of yak and the arrows represents dispersal routes by which the domestic yak occupied the current 'Pamir Knot' and Mongolian and Russian territories. The white dispersal represents the 'traditional' view for the domestication and dispersal of domestic yak (Cai 1989; Wiener *et al.* 2003; Zhang 1989; Zhong 1996) while the 'dark' route is the one presented in this chapter using molecular information.

of inheritance, high substitution rate, and lack of recombination, have become a powerful tool in evolutionary genetics. By elucidating the contemporary geographical distribution of major mtDNA lineages across the geographical distribution of a domestic species, we can expect to gain deeper insight into a wide range of issues such as the origin, domestication, and demographic history of the species (see Bruford et al. 2003 for review). For example, analyses of mtDNA control region (D-loop) variations in European, African, and Indian cattle have provided convincing evidence for independent domestications of taurines (*Bos taurus*) and zebu (*B. indicus*) in two separate locations (Loftus et al. 1994). In addition, analyses of mtDNA D-loop variations also support the origin of European cattle in the Near-East (Troy et al. 2001) and a possible African source of taurines supporting independent origin of pastoralism in the two regions (Bradley et al. 1996).

Autosomal microsatellite DNA fragments are another class of molecular marker extensively used in evolutionary and population genetic studies of livestock species. They are characterized by a core sequence of tandemly repeated units with a length of 2–6 base pairs (bp). Microsatellites exhibit a high level of allelic variation, and are found in large numbers, relatively evenly spaced throughout the genomes of all eukaryotic organisms. They have been increasingly used in the past decade to address population genetic issues such as genetic relationship and differentiation of livestock breeds/populations (see Baumung et al. 2004 for review), but also more recently to unravel the origin and/or dispersal of pastoralism (Cymbron et al. 2005; Hanotte et al. 2002). For example, Hanotte et al. (2002) analyzed the geographic patterns of allelic variations at 15 microsatellite loci in 50 indigenous cattle populations throughout the entire African continent. They were able to show that the earliest cattle in Africa probably originated from a single geographic area within the African continent, but that genetic influences from the taurines in the Near East and Europe as well as the zebu from Indian subcontinent can also be identified in modern African cattle. The early dispersal of cattle to the southern part of the African continent most likely followed an eastern route rather than a western one, in agreement with the earliest archaeological dates for pastoralism in Eastern, Central, and Southern Africa.

Until now, however, molecular genetic studies have been rare in yak, with only a few populations characterized using autosomal microsatellite DNA markers (Dorji et al. 2002; Minqiang et al. 2003; Xuebin et al. 2002, 2005), a couple of molecular genetic studies assessing the level of cattle introgression into yak populations (Jianlin et al. 2002; Xuebin et al. in preparation) and a single study on mitochondrial DNA variation in four yak populations (Bailey et al. 2002).

We recently examined in detail genetic variation at the complete mtDNA D-loop (897 bp) and cytochrome *b* gene (1140 bp) sequences of 29 representative domestic yak populations spanning the entire geographic region of the species (Figure 20.2). Our purpose was to address the origin, domestication, and dispersal of the domestic yak, as well as the genetic relationships among these populations (Qi 2004; Xuebin et al. in preparation). By examining the contemporary geographical pattern of mtDNA diversity across the entire region, we expected to discover whether modern-day domestic yak originated from a single or multiple

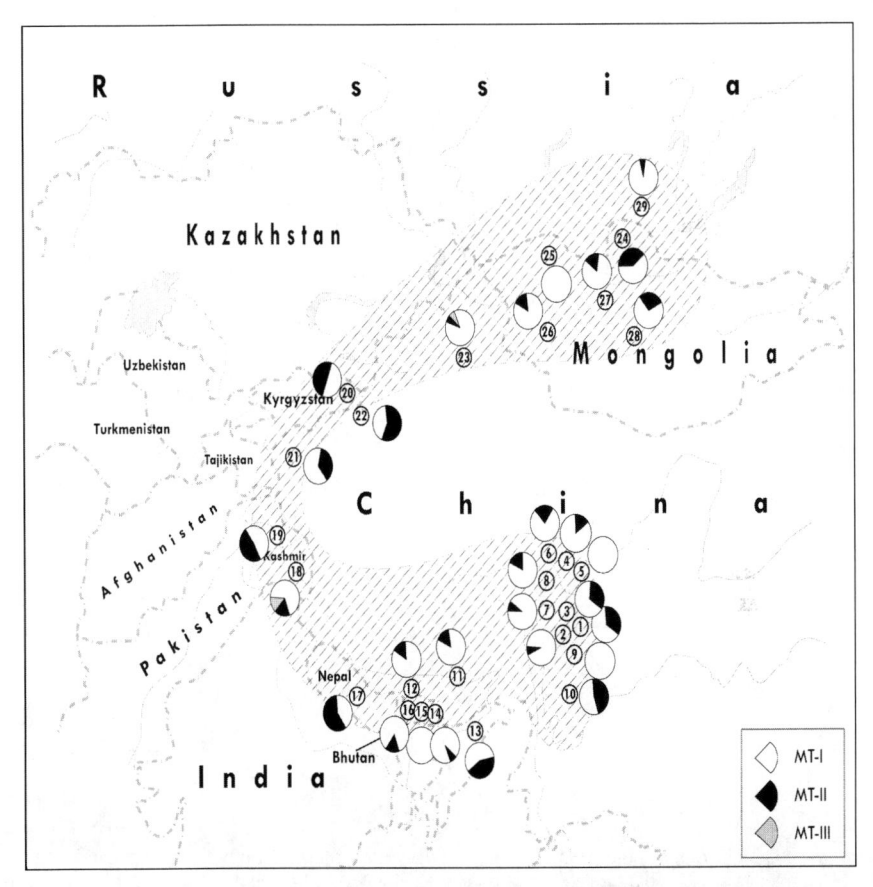

Figure 20.2 The sampling sites for this study. The pie graph represents the distribution of three yak mtDNA lineages in domestic yak populations. Population names: 1 Luqu; 2 Maqu; 3 Xiahe; 4 Tianzhu Black; 5 Tianzhu White; 6 Sunan; 7 Jianzha; 8 Datong; 9 Maiwa; 10 Jiulong; 11 Jiali; 12 Pali; 13 Northeast Indian; 14 East Bhutanese; 15 Central Bhutanese; 16 West Bhutanese; 17 Nepalese; 18 Northwest Indian; 19 Pakistani; 20 Kyrgyzstan; 21 Kashi; 22 Aksu; 23 Bazhou; 24 Hovsgol; 25 Ubs; 26 Gobi Altai; 27 North Hangai; 28 South Gobi; 29 Buryatia.

domestication event(s), where and when such event(s) took place and how yak pastoralism spread through the entire Central Asian Highland region.

Domestication of yak

The complete D-loop of mtDNA was sequenced for a total of 428 yak samples from 29 populations collected in China, Bhutan, Nepal, India, Pakistan, Kyrgyzstan, Mongolia, and Russia (Figure 20.2 for sampling locations). One hundred and thirteen haplotypes with polymorphisms at 87 sites including six insertion/deletions (indels) were identified. As illustrated in Figure 20.3,

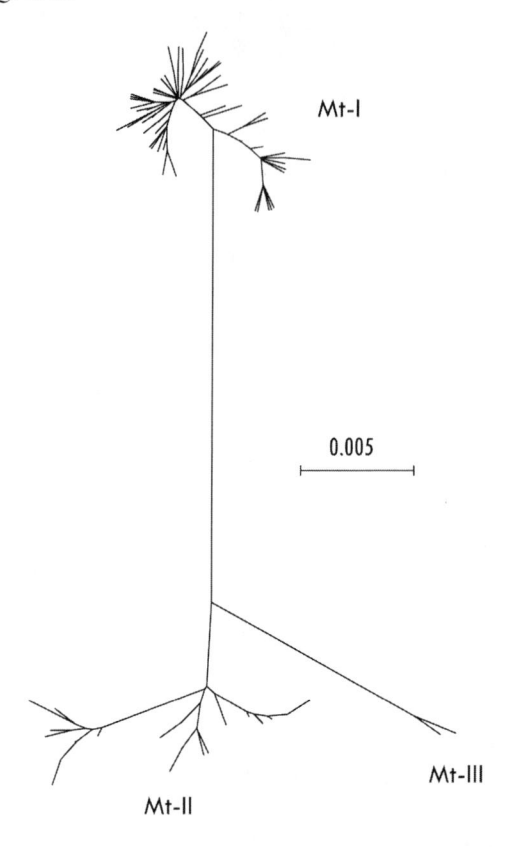

Figure 20.3 Unrooted neighbour-joining phylogeny of domestic yak constructed with 113 mtDNA complete D-loop haplotypes identified in 428 yak samples collected from 29 representative domestic yak populations across entire yak distribution.

phylogenetic analysis clusters these domestic yak D-loop haplotypes into three divergent mtDNA lineages: Mt-I, Mt-II, and Mt-III, with Mt-II and Mt-III being more closely related to each other than to Mt-I.

The mean sequence diversity within yak mtDNA lineages is 0.0051 (Mt-I), 0.0064 (Mt-II), and 0.0035 (Mt-III) (Table 20.1). The values of Mt-I and Mt-II are similar to those observed within taurines (0.0062) and zebu (0.0057). The mean sequence divergences between yak mtDNA lineages range between 0.0218 and 0.0471 nucleotide substitutions per site (Table 20.1). When a substitution rate of 3.1×10^{-4} nucleotide substitutions per site per year or 1 bp substitution per 3243 years, as estimated for the cattle/bison complete D-loop sequences, was applied (Qi 2004; Xuebin *et al.* in preparation), a divergence time of 63,000–136,100 BP was obtained between the yak mtDNA lineages. However, because D-loop sequence might evolve at different rates across lineages (Ingman *et al.* 2000), we also sequenced the complete cytochrome *b* gene for 19 complete

Table 20.1 Mean mtDNA D-loop sequence divergences within and between yak mtDNA lineages and their approximate divergence time

	Mt-I	Mt-II	Mt-III	Bison bison
Mt-I	0.0051	119,600	136,100	308,000
Mt-II	0.0414	0.0064	63,000	264,000
Mt-III	0.0471	0.0218	0.0035	276,000
Bison bison	0.1066	0.0913	0.0955	0.0064

Shown are the sequence divergences within yak mtDNA lineages (on the diagonal), the sequence divergences between yak mtDNA lineages (below the diagonal), and the divergence time between yak mtDNA lineages (above the diagonal).

D-loop haplotypes representing the two major yak mtDNA lineages (Mt-I and Mt-II). The mean cytochrome *b* gene sequence divergence between Mt-I and Mt-II is 0.007 substitutions per site. These sequence divergences correspond to a divergence time of 95,000 BP when a substitution rate of 8.4×10^{-5} nucleotide substitutions per site per year or 1 bp substitution per 11,902 years (estimated for cattle/bison complete cytochrome *b* gene sequences) was applied (Qi 2004; Xuebin *et al.* in preparation).

Overall, a typical signature of population expansion is observed at Mt-I lineage (Tajima's $D = -1.631$, $P = 0.018$; Fu's $Fs = -25.308$, $P = 0.000$), while the Mt-II lineage seems to have not been experiencing a similar overall population expansion since domestication (Tajima's $D = -0.117$, $P = 0.524$; Fu's $Fs = -6.829$, $P = 0.029$) (Xuebin *et al.* in preparation). Multiple star-like phylogenies within lineage Mt-I are observed (Xuebin *et al.* in preparation), suggesting that multiple founder haplotypes have contributed to this lineage. The age of the founder haplotypes in Mt-I lineage was estimated to be 5158 ± 1355 BP, assuming the mutation rate of bovine D-loop as of 1 bp in 3243 years (Qi 2004; Xuebin *et al.* in preparation). This suggests that the domestic yak population started to expand around 5000 BP. This molecular dating of the domestic yak population expansion is in accordance with archaeological evidence that yak domestication may have taken place around 5000 BP (Liu and Peng 1989; Wiener *et al.* 2003; Zhang 1989).

The Qinghai-Tibetan Plateau was not entirely covered by an ice sheet during the latest glaciation in the second half of the Pleistocene (Zhang and Li 2002). Wild yak populations could have survived in distinct refugia, leading to differing mitochondrial DNA lineages. Following the end of the glaciation period, these wild yak populations could have intermixed before domestication, leading to several mitochondrial DNA lineages in today's domestic yak populations following a single domestication event. Alternatively, multiple domestication events may have happened in separated geographic areas from genetically distinct wild yak populations, each at the origin of at least one of the three mitochondrial DNA lineages observed in this study.

To assess the presence of single or multiple domestication event(s) in yak, we examined the geographic distribution and diversity of the three mitochondrial DNA lineages. We grouped the 29 yak populations in four geographic areas: the

Chinese Qinghai-Tibetan Plateau (12 populations, n = 164), Mongolia and Russia (6 populations, n = 91), the Eastern Himalaya (6 populations, n = 77) and the Western Himalaya (5 populations, n = 96). See Figure 20.4 for the grouping of the yak populations in four regions. Geographically, the Chinese Pali yak borders with Bhutanese yak but is isolated from other Chinese yak populations, therefore we grouped Chinese Pali yak into the Eastern Himalayan group. Lineage Mt-I is present in 326 samples and in all 29 yak populations, with the highest haplotype diversity found in the Chinese Qinghai-Tibetan Plateau area and the lowest in the Western Himalayan area, while the Eastern Himalayan area and Mongolian and Russian yak populations exhibited an intermediate haplotype diversity (Figure 20.4 and Table 20.2). Mt-II lineage is less common and present in only 25 yak populations (n = 97). Mt-III lineage is very rare and only found in four Northwest Indian yak samples and one Chinese Bazhou yak sample (Figure 20.2), and it is therefore excluded from the following analysis and discussion.

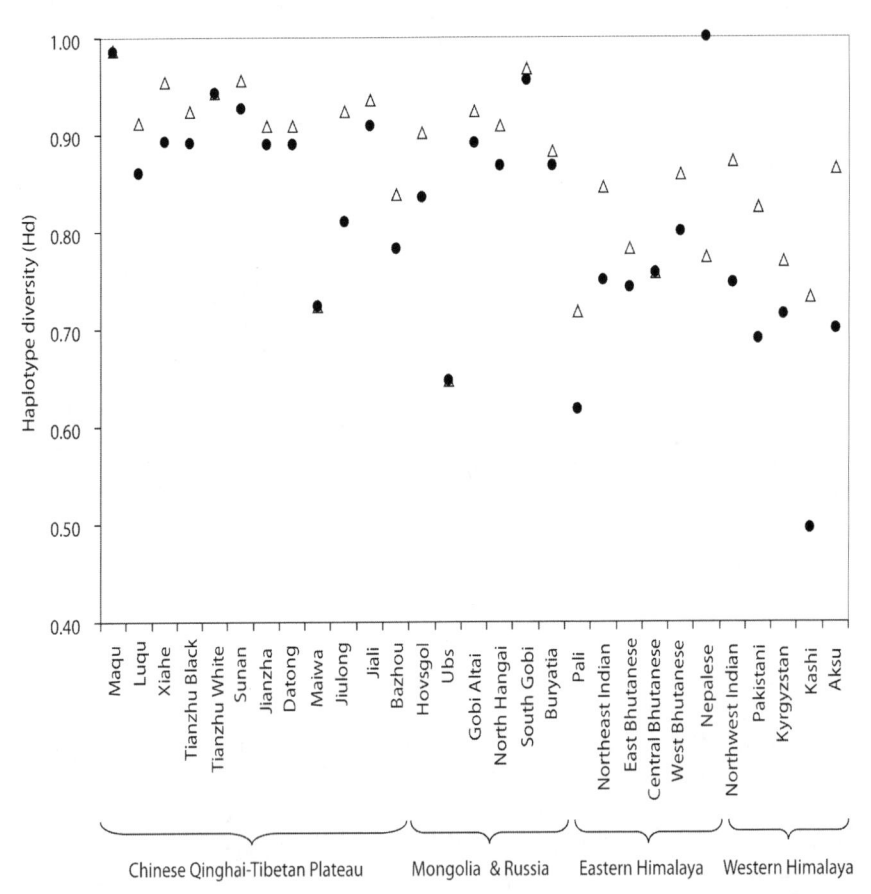

Figure 20.4 The mtDNA D-loop haplotype diversity (Hd) observed in 29 domestic yak populations. The signs 'Δ' and '●' represent the Hd calculated based on all mtDNA lineages and Mt-I lineage alone, respectively.

Table 20.2 The mtDNA diversity in four geographic areas of domestic yak

Population	N	H	Hd	SD (Hd)	π	SD (π)	Tajima's D	Fu's Fs
Mt-I lineage								
Qinghai-Tibetan Plateau	136	45	0.906	0.019	0.0036	0.0002	−1.554*	−25.618**
Eastern Himalaya	59	24	0.848	0.043	0.0029	0.0003	−1.4727	−15.5888**
Western Himalaya	56	10	0.690	0.062	0.0019	0.0003	−1.044	−5.016*
Mongolia & Russia	75	16	0.876	0.018	0.0046	0.0004	−0.1202	−2.143
Overall	326	71	0.882	0.015	0.0035	0.0002	−1.631*	−25.308**
Mt-II lineage								
Qinghai-Tibetan Plateau	27	13	0.897	0.038	0.0048	0.0003	−0.113	−4.581*
Eastern Himalaya	18	6	0.719	0.093	0.0028	0.0007	−0.815	0.136
Western Himalaya	36	7	0.679	0.062	0.0042	0.0005	0.915	0.956
Mongolia & Russia	16	5	0.800	0.057	0.0039	0.0007	0.561	0.923
Overall	97	22	0.880	0.018	0.0050	0.0002	−0.117	−6.829*

N = number of samples; H = number of haplotypes; Hd = haplotype diversity; π = nucleotide diversity; SD = standard deviation. Tajima's D (Tajima 1989) and Fu's Fs (Fu 1997) statistics are used to test population expansion; * $P < 0.05$; ** $P < 0.01$.

The total number of haplotypes is not statistically different among yak populations within or between geographic areas ($P = 0.79$). However, we observe a higher frequency of Mt-II lineage in the Western Himalayan area (37.5 per cent) compared to the Chinese Qinghai-Tibetan Plateau area (16.5 per cent), the Eastern Himalayan area (23.4 per cent), and the Mongolian and Russian yak populations (17.6 per cent), while Mt-I lineage is most commonly observed in all areas. This difference of frequency between the two lineages is a first indication of the possible presence of two distinct geographic centres of origins for the mitochondrial DNA lineages observed today in domestic yak. To further assess this possibility, we analysed the diversity of the observed haplotypes in different geographic areas. Table 20.2 summarizes the mtDNA D-loop haplotype diversity and Tajima's D (Tajima 1989) and Fu's Fs (Fu 1997) statistics for population expansion among four geographic areas. The Western Himalayan area showed the lowest Mt-II haplotype diversity among four geographic areas with the highest Mt-II haplotype diversity being observed in the Chinese Qinghai-Tibetan Plateau area. Among four geographic areas, only the Chinese Qinghai-Tibetan Plateau area showed a significant population expansion. The higher frequency of Mt-II lineage with the least haplotype diversity and without a population expansion observed in the Western Himalayan area may suggest the occurrence of recent bottleneck(s) or founder event(s) in those yak populations. Such demographic phenomena could account for the lack of a clear geographic pattern of genetic diversity and may have played an important role in reshaping the genetic landscape of domestic yak.

Two possible geographic areas of domestication have been proposed on the Qinghai-Tibetan Plateau: the Northern Qinghai-Tibetan Plateau (Liu and Peng 1989; Wiener *et al.* 2003; Zhang 1989) and the Eastern Qinghai-Tibetan Plateau (Qi 2004). Few domestic yak are currently found in the Northern Qinghai-Tibetan Plateau, a today largely inhospitable area to human settlements. Figure 20.4 shows that the highest mtDNA haplotype diversity is present in Eastern Qinghai-Tibetan Plateau populations (e.g. Maqu, Luqu, Xiahe) with lower diversity found in the Jiali and Pali, the two yak populations closest to the Northern Qinghai-Tibetan Plateau putative centre of domestication. Our molecular findings therefore do not support the Northern Qinghai-Tibetan Plateau as a centre of domestication of yak, but rather point to the Eastern Qinghai-Tibetan Plateau, a purely pastoral area. However, it should be pointed out that only two yak populations close to the Northern Qinghai-Tibetan Plateau putative centre of domestication were examined.

The results obtained here support the idea that the divergent maternal lineages Mt-I and Mt-II found in modern yak populations follow from a single domestication event, around 5000 BP, possibly in the Chinese Eastern Qinghai-Tibetan Plateau, and at least three divergent mtDNA lineages which survived at different refugia may have been recruited and reproduced successfully. However, the location of the centre of domestication would be more secure if data for more populations along the Northern Qinghai-Tibetan Plateau were available. Similarly, the date of domestication could be more accurate if there were a better calibration of bovine mtDNA mutation rates using complete mtDNA sequence and archaeozoological material.

Movements and migration of domestic yak

It is assumed that neutral genetic diversity in livestock populations would decline during the course of dispersal from the centre of their origin, with the least loss of genetic diversity in populations closest to the centre of domestication. Autosomal microsatellite and mitochondrial DNA markers provide a powerful tool to address these questions (e.g. Troy *et al.* 2001; Hanotte *et al.* 2002). The traditional view is that yak dispersed from their centre of domestication in the Qinghai-Tibetan Plateau, reaching Mongolian and Russian territories by migrating through the Pamir Knot (Figure 20.1). A migration northwards through today's Gobi Desert from the centre of domestication in Qinghai-Tibetan Plateau is also theoretically possible. We therefore tested for the route(s) by which domesticated yak might have dispersed out from the putative center of origin on the Qinghai-Tibetan Plateau. If this was via the Pamir Knot, today's Mongolian and Russian yak populations would have exhibited the lowest haplotype diversity, and the Pakistan, Kyrgyzstan, Kashi and Aksu populations (Western Himalaya) an intermediate level. Alternatively, a direct northern migration may be characterized by a lower diversity in the Western Himalaya region compared to Mongolia and Russia.

We fail to see a decline of mtDNA haplotype diversity in domestic yak populations versus geographic distance from either the Northern or the Eastern

Qinghai-Tibetan Plateau along a single migratory route (Figure 20.5, A; and Figure 20.1, white route).

Instead, as illustrated in Figure 20.5, a significant decline of mtDNA haplotype diversity was visible along two separate routes: a westward migratory route via the 'Pamir Knot' (represented by Northeastern Indian, Pakistani, Kyrgyzstan, Kashi, and Aksu populations), passing through the Himalayan and Kunlun Mountains; and a northward migratory route for Mongolian and Russian yak populations passing through South Gobi and Gobi Altai Mountains in Mongolia (Figure 20.1, dark route). These findings provide strong genetic evidence that the dispersal of domesticated yak followed two separate migratory routes from the Eastern Qinghai-Tibetan Plateau (Figure 20.1, dark route). That is, the domestic yak dispersed to the 'Pamir Knot' by following a westward route passing through the Himalayan and Kunlun Mountains and to Mongolia and Russia by following a northward route passing through Mongolian South Gobi and Gobi Altai Mountains.

Pastoralism and the dispersal of Tibetan-Burman populations

Although the Himalayas were probably exploited by low density foragers since the Early Pleistocene, the introduction of yak pastoralism must have been crucial to developing year-round sustainable occupation in the higher-altitude zones. The Himalayas today are also the centre of linguistic and genetic diversity for the Sino-Tibetan language phylum (van Driem 2001) and it is likely that this diversity reflects both ancient low-density forager populations and the impact of incoming yak pastoralists. Van Driem (1998) has argued that the culture responsible for the Majiayao Neolithic (dated to 3900–1800 BC) in Gansu moved westward through Sichuan into Tibet and the Himalayas around 5000 BP and that this can be identified with the Western Tibetan-Burmans (Bodish, Lepcha, etc.). If such people were yak pastoralists, this would correlate well with the loss of genetic diversity westwards of Qinghai. The median levels of genetic diversity amongst Mongolian (Bynie 2004) and Russian (Dmitriev and Ernst 1989) populations suggest that transfer of yak pastoralism northwards must have been at an early period rather than in medieval times. Since there are no Sino-Tibetan populations in this region, there would probably have been an early transfer to Altaic speakers. The climate of the Mongolian Plateau has deteriorated severely in the last 5000 years, and it may well be that the adoption of the yak helped *in situ* populations to adapt to climate change in the mountains north and west of Mongolia and the adjacent Altai.

Conclusion

At least three divergent maternal yak lineages survived at different refugia and may have been recruited or were reproductively successful and contributed to the formation of the earliest domesticated yak population with the divergent maternal lineages found in present day domestic yak populations likely the result of a

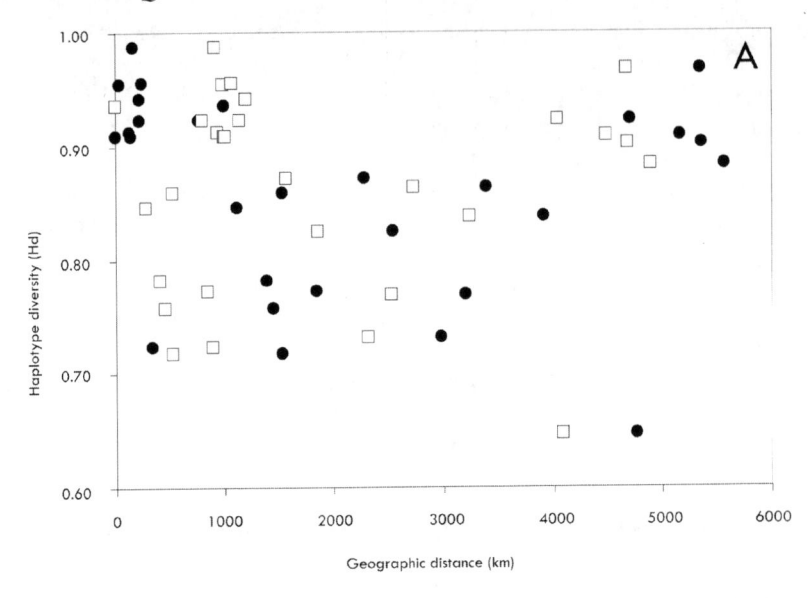

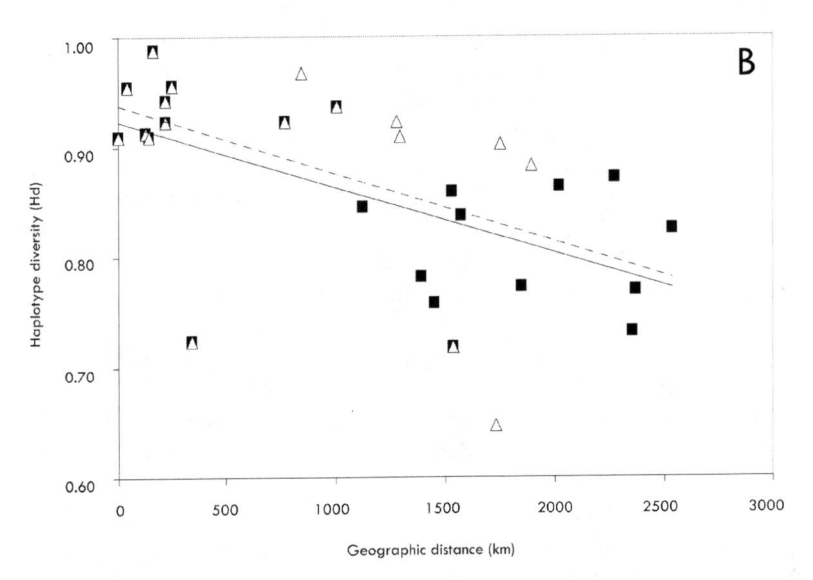

Figure 20.5 Regression of mtDNA D-loop haplotype diversities versus geographic distances in domestic yak populations. (A) The mtDNA haplotype diversities versus geographic distances along a single dispersal route (white route in Figure 20.1): '□', from the Northern Qinghai-Tibetan Plateau (represented by Jiali) r = 0.027, p = 0.888; and '●', from the Eastern Qinghai-Tibetan Plateau (represented by Maqu) r = 0.031, p = 0.361; (B) The mtDNA haplotype diversities versus geographic distances along two separate dispersal routes (dark route in Fig. 20.1) from the Eastern Qinghai-Tibetan Plateau (represented by Maqu): '■' and solid line, westward, r = -0.63, p < 0.01; and 'Δ' and dashed line, northward, r = –0.44, p = 0.06.

single domestication event. Yak-based pastoralism is also probably responsible for the all-year round occupation of high alpine pastures in the Himalaya and may be connected with the establishment of particular Tibetan-Burman populations in this region.

Acknowledgements

The authors are grateful to Shi-xin Tao, Jiang Hu, Yu-lin Liang, Zheng Ni, Ci-ren Tashi, Yu-cai Zheng, Guang-hui Zhong, Xiao-ling Mao, Cheng-lie Liu and Zhong-lin Lu (China), B. Lkhagva and D. Badamdorj (Mongolia), T. Dorji (Bhutan), L. Sherchand (Nepal), T. Phuntsog and M. Ali (India), M. Afzal and A.N. Naqvi (Pakistan), K. Kachkynbaeva and T. Cholponkulov (Kyrgyzstan), and I. Chekarova (Russia) for providing samples or assistance in the process of sampling. This study was funded by ILRI program grants from the United Kingdom, Japan, The European Union, Ireland and France, and unrestricted funding from other donors to the CGIAR. Xue-bin Qi was a PhD candidate jointly supported by graduate fellowships from ILRI and Lanzhou University, China during the course of this study.

References

Aldenderfer, M. and Zhang Y. (2004) 'The prehistory of the Tibetan Plateau to the seventh century A.D.: Perspectives and research from China and the West since 1950', *Journal of World Prehistory*, 18: 1–55.

Bailey, J.F., Healy, B., Jianlin, H., Sherchand, L., Pradhan, S.L., Tsendsuren, T., Foggin, J.M., Gaillard, C., Steane, D., Zakharov, I. and Bradley, D.G. (2002) 'Genetic variation of mitochondrial DNA within domestic yak populations', in H. Jianlin, C. Richard, O. Hanotte, C. McVeigh, and J.E.O. Rege (eds) *Proceedings of the Third International Congress on Yak*, 4–9 Sept. 2000, Lhasa, Tibet, PR China, Nairobi: International Livestock Research Institute (ILRI), pp. 181–9.

Baumung, R., Simianer, H. and Hoffmann, I. (2004) 'Genetic diversity studies in farm animals – a survey', *Journal of Animal Breeding and Genetics*, 121: 361–73.

Blench, R.M. (2001) *Pastoralism in the New Millennium* (Animal Health and Production Series, 150), Rome: FAO.

Bradley, D.G., MacHugh, D.E., Cunningham, P. and Loftus, R.T. (1996) 'Mitochondrial diversity and the origins of African and European cattle', *Proceedings of the National Academy of Science USA*, 93: 5131–5.

Brantingham, P.J., Ma, H., Olsen, J.W., Gao, X., Madsen, D.B. and Rhode, D.E. (2003) 'Speculation on the timing and nature of Late Pleistocene hunter-gatherer colonization of the Tibetan Plateau', *Chinese Science Bulletin*, 48: 1510–16.

Bruford, M.W., Bradley, D.G. and Luikart, G. (2003) 'DNA markers reveal the complexity of livestock domestication', *Nature Reviews Genetics*, 4: 900–10.

Bynie, B. (2004) *Mongolia: The Country Report on Animal Genetic Resources*, Ulaan Baatar: MOFA.

Cai, L. (1989) *Sichuan Yak*, Chengdu, PR China: Sichuan Ethnic Press.

Cymbron, T., Freeman, A.R., Isabel Malheiro, M., Vigne, J.D. and Bradley, D.G. (2005) 'Microsatellite diversity suggests different histories for Mediterranean and Northern European cattle populations', *Proceedings. Biological Sciences*, 272: 37–1843.

Dmitriev, N.G. and Ernst, L.K. (1989) *Animal Genetic Resources of the USSR* (FAO Animal Production and Health Paper, 65), Rome: FAO.

Dorji, T., Goddard, M., Perkins, J., Robinson, N. and Roder, W. (2002) 'Genetic diversity in Bhutanese yak (*Bos grunniens*) populations using microsatellite markers', in H. Jianlin, C. Richard, O. Hanotte, C. McVeigh and J.E.O. Rege (eds) *Proceedings of the Third International Congress on Yak*, 4–9 Sept. 2000, Lhasa, Tibet, PR China, Nairobi: International Livestock Research Institute (ILRI), pp. 197–201.

Felius, M. (1995) *Cattle Breeds: An Encyclopedia*, Doetichem: Misset Uitgeverij.

Fu, Y.X. (1997) 'Statistical tests of neutrality of mutations against population growth, hitchhiking and background selection', *Genetics*, 147: 915–25.

Guiquan, C. (1996) 'Status of the wild yak in the Qinghai-Tibetan Plateau', in *Proceedings of a Workshop on Conservation and Management of Yak Genetic Diversity*, 29–31 Oct. 1996, Kathmandu: International Centre for Integrated Mountain Development, pp. 61–5.

Hanotte, O., Bradley, D.G., Ochieng, J.W., Verjee, Y., Hill, E.W. and Rege, J.E.O. (2002) 'African pastoralism: Genetic imprints of origins and migrations', *Science*, 296: 336–9.

Huang, W.W. (1994) 'The prehistoric human occupation of the Qinghai-Xizang Plateau', *Gottinger Geographische Abhandlungen*, 95: 201–9.

Ingman, M., Kaessmann, H., Paabo, S. and Gyllensten, U. (2000) 'Mitochondrial genome variation and the origin of modern humans', *Nature*, 408: 708–13.

Jianlin, H., Ochieng, J.W., Rege, J.E.O. and Hanotte, O. (2002) 'Low level of cattle introgression in yak populations from Bhutan and China: Evidences from Y-specific microsatellites and mitochondrial DNA markers', in H. Jianlin, C. Richard, O. Hanotte, C. McVeigh and J.E.O. Rege (eds) *Proceedings of the Third International Congress on Yak*, 4–9 Sept. 2000, Lhasa, Tibet, PR China, Nairobi: International Livestock Research Institute (ILRI), pp. 190–6.

Joshi, D.D. (1982) *Yak and Chauri Husbandry in Nepal*, Kathmandu: His Majesty's Government Press.

Kraayenbrink, T., de Knijff, P., van Driem, G.L., Opgenort, J.R.M.L., Jobling, M.A., Parkin, E.J., Tyler-Smith, C., Carvalho-Silva, D.R., Tshering, K., Barbujani, G., Dupanloup, I., Bertorelle, G. and Tuladhar, N.M. (2006) 'Language and Genes of the Greater Himalayan Region', *OMLL Volume* (in press) available at http://www.le.ac.uk/ge/maj4/himalayas.html.

Kreutzmann, H. (2002) 'Recent results of yak research in Western High Asia', in H. Jianlin, C. Richard, O. Hanotte, C. McVeigh and J.E.O. Rege (eds) *Proceedings of the Third International Congress on Yak*, 4–9 Sept. 2000, Lhasa, Tibet, PR China, Nairobi: International Livestock Research Institute (ILRI), pp. 76–86.

Liu, Z.B. and Peng, Z.K. (1989) 'Chronology of Chinese yak development', in *Chinese Yakology*, pp. 4–20, Chengdu: Sichuan Scientific and Technology Press.

Liu, Z.B., Wang, C.Z. and Chen, Y.N. (1989) 'Yak resources and qualified populations in China', in *Chinese Yakology*, pp. 36–77, Chengdu: Sichuan Scientific and Technology Press.

Loftus, R.T., MacHugh, D.E., Bradley, D.G., Sharp, P.M. and Cunningham, P. (1994) 'Evidence for two independent domestications of cattle', *Proceedings of the National Academy of Science USA*, 91: 2757–61.

Madsen, D.B., Ma, H., Brantingham, P.J., Gao, X., Rhode, D., Zhang, H. and Olsen, J.W. (2006) 'The Late Upper Paleolithic occupation of the northern Tibetan Plateau margin', *Journal of Archaeological Science*, 20: 1–12.

Minqiang, W., Weigend, S., Barre-Dirie, A., Carnwath, J.W., Zhonglin, L. and Niemann, H. (2003) 'Analysis of two Chinese yak (*Bos grunniens*) populations using bovine microsatellite primers', *Journal of Animal Breeding and Genetics*, 120: 237–44.

Olsen, S.J. (1990) 'Fossil Ancestry of the yak, its cultural significance and domestication in Tibet', *Proceedings of the National Academy of Science Philadelphia*, 142: 73–100.

Qi, X.B. (2004) 'Genetic diversity, differentiation and relationship of domestic yak populations: a microsatellite and mitochondrial DNA study', PhD thesis, Lanzhou University, PR China.

Schaller, G.B. and Wulin, L. (1996) 'Distribution, status, and conservation of wild yak *Bos grunniens*', *Biological Conservation*, 76: 1–8.

Sherchand, L. and Karki, N.P.S. (1996) 'Conservation and management of yak genetic diversity in Nepal', in *Proceedings of a Workshop on Conservation and Management of Yak Genetic Diversity*, 29–31 Oct. 1996, Kathmandu: International Centre for Integrated Mountain Development (ICIMOD), pp. 47–56.

Su, B., Xiao, C., Deka, R., Seielstad, M.T., Kangwanpong, D., Xiao, J., Lu, D., Underhill, P., Cavalli-Sforza, L., Chakraborty, R. and Jin, L. (2000) 'Y chromosome haplotypes reveal prehistorical migrations to the Himalayas', *Human Genetics*, 107: 582–90.

Tajima, F. (1989) 'Statistical method for testing the neutral mutation hypothesis by DNA polymorphism', *Genetics*, 123: 585–95.

Tang, H. and Hare, J.M. (1995) 'Lithic tool industries and the earliest occupation of the Qinghai-Tibetan Plateau', *The Artefact*, 18: 3–11.

Tong, E. (1990) *Zhong guo xi nan min zu kao gu lun wen ji* (Collected Papers on Ethnoarchaeology in Southwest China), Beijing: Cultural Relics Publishing House.

Troy, C.S., MacHugh, D.E., Bailey, J.F., Magee, D.A., Loftus, R.T., Cunningham, P., Chamberlain, A.T., Sykes, B.C. and Bradley, D.G. (2001) 'Genetic evidence for Near-Eastern origins of European cattle', *Nature*, 410: 1088–91.

Tshering, L., Gyamtsho, P. and Gyeltshen, T. (1996) 'Yaks in Bhutan', in *Proceedings of a Workshop on Conservation and Management of Yak Genetic Diversity*, 29–31 Oct. 1996, Kathmandu: International Centre for Integrated Mountain Development (ICIMOD), pp. 13–24.

van Driem, G. (1998) 'Neolithic correlates of ancient Tibeto-Burman migrations', in R.M. Blench and M. Spriggs (eds.) *Archaeology and Language*, 2nd edn, London: Routledge, pp. 67–102.

van Driem, G. (2001) *Languages of the Himalayas: An Ethnolinguistic Handbook of the Greater Himalayan Region Containing an Introduction to the Symbiotic Theory of Language*, Leiden: Brill.

Wiener, G., Jianlin, H. and Ruijun, L. (2003) *The Yak*, 2nd edn, Bangkok: Regional Office for Asia and the Pacific, Food and Agriculture Organization of the United Nations.

Xuebin, Q., Jianlin, H., Lkhagva, B., Chekarova, I., Badamdorj, D., Rege, J.E.O. and Hanotte, O. (2005) 'Genetic diversity and differentiation of Mongolian and Russian yak populations', *Journal of Animal Breeding and Genetics*, 122: 117–26.

Xuebin, Q., Jianlin, H., Rege, J.E.O. and Hanotte, O. (2002) 'Y-chromosome specific microsatellite polymorphisms in Chinese yak', in *Proceedings of 7th World Congress on Genetics Applied to Livestock Production*, 19–23 Aug. 2002, Montpellier: INRA (Institut National de la Recherche Agronomique), vol. 33: pp. 509–12.

Zeuner, F.E. (1963) *A History of Domesticated Animals*, London: Hutchinson.

Zhang, D.D. and Li, S.H. (2002) 'Optical dating of Tibetan human hand- and footprints: An implication for the palaeoenvironment of the last glaciation of the Tibetan Plateau', *Geophysical Research Letters*, 29: 1–3.

Zhang, D.D., Li, S.H., He, Y.Q. and Li, B.S. (2003) 'Human settlement of the last glaciation on the Tibetan plateau', *Current Science*, 84: 701–4.

Zhang, R.C. (1989) *China Yak*, Lanzhou: Gansu Scientific and Technology Press.

Zhong, J.C. (1996) *Yak Genetics and Breeding*, Chengdu: Sichuan Scientific and Technology Press.

Index

9-base-pair deletion *see* 9-bp deletion
9-bp deletion 359, 365; in Africans 361;
    Asian type 361; in Bougainville 368;
    in Malagasy 367; in New Britain 368;
    origin date 362
Φ_{CT} 402, 403, 407
Φ_{ST} 397, 401–2, 406

Abkhazo-Adyghean 231
ablation of upper lateral incisors 139
aboriginal languages of Taiwan 161; 186
Aceh-Chamic 175
Acehnese 175
acorns 63, 71, 73
acupuncture 282
Aetas 323
Afroasiatic 7
agricultural dispersal 241
agricultural intensification 70
agriculture: emergence in China 51;
    evolution in Lower Yangtze 69; origin of 40–1; rice 40–1
Agta 35
Ahka 317
AIDA analysis 403–4
Ainu 268
Aldenderfer, M. and Zhang Y. 427
Alligator sinensis 139
Altai Mountains 395
Altaic 106, 113–16, 396; agricultural component 115; historical linguistics 277; lack of early written records 281; laterals, reconstruction of 270; lexical matches with Chinese 258–61; linguistic unity 263; loans in Old Chinese 256–7; sound-changes 273; suprasegmentals 273
Altaic hypothesis, methodological criticisms of 281
Altaic proto-language 265
Altaicists, diversity of views amongst 276–7
Ambon 365

Amis 185, 189, 313, 334, 352; genetically related to the Puyuma 326; genetic profile 121; losing genetic diversity 326
AMOVA analysis 401–3
Amygdalus (Prunus) persica 64
Amygdalus davidiana 64
Anaro 33; artefacts 33, 34; c^{14} dates 33
Anaro hilltop site 31
Anatolia 421, 422
Andaman Islanders 367
Andaman Islands 11
Andarayan 32
Angami 287

Apatani 287
apricot stones 63
archaeobotany: data 73; research in China 41–3
archiphonemes of neutralization 266, 271
Arunachal Pradesh 299; Tani-speaking subgroups 300
Asian medical praxis 282
Assam 287; population levels 292; slash-and-burn hills 287
Assam valley 288
Assamese 295
Asumboa 190
Atayal 161, 182, 192, 211, 313, 317, 334, 352
Australian Aborigines 326
Austric hypothesis 134, 171
Austroasiatic 10, 106, 117–19, 133, 171, 192, 240, 322; Bugan 106; in China 118; families 118, 224; fragmentation of 119; speakers, genetics of 117; time-depths 118
Austronesian 10, 106, 120–1, 133, 240, 322; dispersal 165; expansion 163–5; external affiliations 120; genetically related to Chinese 134; geographical distribution 120; geographical spread 314; inheritance relationships 165; language differentiation 315; language phylogeny

314; lexicostatistical classification 189; macrophylum 134; phylum size 120, 313, 334; primary branches 314; speed of dispersal 176; subgroups in Taiwan 349
Austronesian genealogical tree 174–7
Austronesian languages: dispersal of 358; distribution map 24; geographical distribution 357; groups 162; Oceanic subgroup 358; origin of 357–9; phylogeny 149, 229; size of family 357; spread by colonizers 358; subgrouping 175; subgroups 357; in Taiwan 25
Austronesian origins; 'Express Train' model 23–5; 'Out of Taiwan' model 23–5
Austronesians: mtDNA 356–69; origins of 328; Taiwan's role in spread of 329
Austro-Tai 116, 171, 212
Avery, J. 224
awns 53; reduction of hairs on 58

Babuza 211, 212, 313
Bai 109, 110, 124
Bailangge 109
Baiying 95
Bali: DNA study 376–92; data analysis 386; DNA samples 385–6; farmer cooperation 382–4; genetic distances 390; genetic drift 392; irrigation 376; matrilineages 385; patrilineages 385; topography 376; Y-STR variation 390–1
Balinese-Sasak-Sumbawa 175
Bali-Vitu 167
Bangladesh 296
Banpo 88, 95
Bantu 9
Baric 225
Barito languages 175
barley, in Near East 58
Barnes, G.L. 111
Basay 212, 313
Bashidang 41, 61
Basque 7, 231, 232
Batan Islanders, mtDNA analysis 350–4; Batan Island 25, 28, 29
Batanes Islands 26–33, 37, 150, 317, 349
Batanic 313
Be 116
Beinan culture 29
Beixin culture 67; Beixin-Dawenkou culture 139, 140
Bellwood, P. 36, 133, 134, 137, 241, 349, 384
Bellwood, P. and Hiscock, P. 177
Benedict, P.K. 116, 171, 225
Bengali dialects 296
Bentley, J.R. 276
Betsileo 367
Bezanozano 367

Bhutan 297, 431
biallelic markers 363
binary haplogroups, NRY tree of 418
Bismarck Archipelago 26, 37
Blust, R.A. 119, 120, 165, 166, 172, 174–5, 189, 190, 191, 212, 228, 314
Bodic 225
Bodo-Kachin 255
Boehmeria nivea 32
Bogan 118
Bolyu 118
bone artefacts 66
bone indentification methodology 84–5
Borneo 26, 365
Boro 296
Boro-Garo 296, 297; as origin of river names 298
Bos indicus 430
Bos taurus 430; African source of 430; domestication of 430
Bottle gourd 64
bottleneck 113, 125, 326, 329, 368, 435
Bowring, R. and Kornicki, A. 274
Brahmaputra corridor 295
Brahmaputra River 287; importance for trade 296
Brahmaputran 222
broomcorn millet *see* millet
Bubalus 67
Buck, P. 369
Budai 185, 192, 211
Budai-Labuan-Taromak 211
budding deme model 385–91; genetic differentiation of subpopulations 387
Bugan 106, 119
Bukit Tengkorak 35
bulliforms 61; first appearance of 72; phytolith variation 61
Bunun 189, 192, 211, 313, 317, 328, 334, 352
Burma 116
Burmese 107, 232; genetic relationships 220
Burmic 225
Burushaski 231, 232
Buxinhua 119

C^{14} dating 212
Cagayan Valley 25, 26, 28, 29, 32
Caioxieshan 68
Cann, R. 361
Caoxieshan 67
Capell, A. 164
carbonized grains 315
carriages, associated with horse bones 96, 97
cattle: domesticaton of 86; earliest in Africa 430; origin of European 430
Caucasian 9
Caucasus languages 231

Cavalli-Sforza, L.L. 37
CCR2 allele polymorphism 124
cemeteries 69; platform 70
CEMP *see* Central/Eastern Malayo-Polynesian
Central Asian Highlands 427; pastoralist/agro-pastoralist population 427
Central/Eastern Malayo-Polynesian 176
Ch'ang-pin 121
chaff 47
Cham Empire 120
Chang, K.-C. 315
Changpin culture 329
Chaolaiqiao 25, 29, 34
Chatham Islands 360, 362
Chen, X.C. 93
Chengbeixi 41
Chengtoushan 41, 61
Chengziya 95
Chepang 229
chestnuts 72
chickens, domestication of 86
China: linguistic prehistory, theories of 219; peopling of 124–5
Chinese numerals, Japanese borrowing of 212
Chinese: 'Common Chinese' 109; etymological dictionary 255; genetically related to AN 134; genetic relationships 220, 221; historical phonology 256; lexical matches with Altaic 258–61; morphological simplicity of 222; relationship with Tibeto-Burman 212; migration to Taiwan 313
Chinese–Korean bilingual dictionary 273
Chino-Tibetan 220
Choerospondias axillaris 64
Chukotko-Kamchatkan 396
Chuoden 60
Chuvash Turkic 268
Cishan 50, 91–2, 111, 112; date of 91; pig bones 91
Cishan-Peiligang culture 136, 137, 138, 240
climate warming, effect on Yangzi basin 72
clines 407
coalescence times 336, 342, 344, 352
Coix sp 64
comparative phonology 190
consonant symbols 280
consonant system: Bunun 184; Formosan languages 188; proto-Paiwan 186; proto-Tsouic 184
constructed proto-forms 236
cord-marked pottery 25, 29, 34, 111, 119
Corded Ware culture 121
correlation coefficients 320, 391, 403
correlation geographic/linguistic 403
craft specialization 70

culms 47
Cust, R. 220
Cyclobalanopsis 65, 72

D-loop 95, 334–5, 339, 341, 350, 432, 434, 438
Dabenkeng culture *see* Dapenkeng
Dahezhuang 95, 96
Dahl, O.C. 172
Daic 7, 9, 11, 106, 116, 116–17, 219, 221, 240
Dali 109
Dapenkeng 25, 32, 136, 228
Dashanqian 95
Da-Shun, G. 112
data acquisition difficulties 422
dating issues 212
Dawenkou 67, 228, 240
Daxi culture 41
demic diffusion 37
demographic expansion 4, 124
Dempwolff, O. 170, 228
Dene-Caucasian 231
Dene-Daic 232, 239
dentition, pig jaw 92
Dhimalish 222
dialect chains 300
Diamond, J.M. 23, 358
Diaotonghuan 41, 85
diet composition analysis 85
Diffloth, G. 118
Dimolit 34
Ding, J.C. 123
divergence time, 362, 432, 433
diversity patterns, agencies of 419
Dixon, R.M.W. 164
Dlod Blungbang 377, 380
DNA: East Asian, specificity of 123; extraction 335; non-coding regions 376; phylogeny 85; sequence analysis 335
dogs 85; earliest domesticated animal 86
domesticated grain crops, characteristics of 52–3
domestication 84; of animals 84; of cattle 50, 86; of cereals 235; of crops 52; as distinct from cultivation 52; of dogs 86; of goats 86; of horses 86, 93–9; of water buffalo 67; of O. japonica 137; of pigs 34, 49, 87–93; of rice 42–7, 50–7, 70–1; of chickens 86; of sheep 86; of taurines 430; of water buffalo 49, 50; of yak 428, 431–5; of zebu 430
domestication syndrome 51, 53
Driem, G. van 12, 108
Dumézil, G. 231
Dumi 232
Dyen, I. 172, 189

446 Index

East Asia haplogroup data 420
East Asian proto-language 240
East Asian theory 228, 240, 241
Easter Island 357, 362
Eastern Qinghai-Tibetan Plateau 436
EDAL 263–9; antipathy to loanwords 282; reliance on Martin 272
Edmondson, J.A. and Solnit, D.B. 116–17
Egerod, S. 223
Ehret, C. 9
endogamy in Siberia 396
Enemish 150
'entangled bank' model 358, 359
Epstein, H. 84
equine veterinary praxis 283
Equus caballus przewalskii 94, 95, 96
Eskimo-Aleut 396
Eskimos, Siberian 396
Etymological Dictionary of the Altaic Languages see EDAL
etymological studies 190
Euryale ferox 63, 64, 65
evulsion of teeth 140, 145, 152
'Express Train' model 35–7, 315, 359, 358, 360

F_{CT} 316
F_{ST} 387, 390
Faliscan 238
fallen leaves model 108, 233
fallow periods, synchronization of 382
farming societies, diffusion of 314
farming/language dispersal hypothesis 133–4
FATK see Formosan Ancestor of Tai-Kadai
female languages 222
female lineages, study through time 356
Fengtian 33
Fengtian nephrite 34
Ferrell, R. 121
Fiji 26, 363
Filipinos, genetic relationships 354
Forbes, C. 220
Forest Nentsi 407
Formosan aborigines: dispersal/migration scenario 216; early dispersal 213–16; origin of 212–13; recent despersal 216
Formosan languages 116, 120, 161, 313, 349; age of 192; Central (Tsouic) group 215; classification of 213; diversification of 120; Eastern group 215; extinct 313; Formosan Ancestor of Tai-Kadai 151; Formosan hypothesis 173; Formosan-Philippine 171, 172; languages extant 182; main branches 192; more diverse than elsewhere 211; Northern group 215; numerals 146; phonetic correspondences 187; reconstructed consonants 188; single genetic subgroup of Austronesian 182; Southern group 215; written documents 211
founder effect 420; in Siberians 406, 407
founder haplotype in yak lineages 433
founding dispersal 133
Fox, J. 384
foxnuts 63, 65
foxtail millet 133–4, 315; and STAN hypothesis 134–5; coterminous with STAN macrophylum 134
Frellesvig, B. 11
Frontier Tracts 289
Fu's Fs statistic 435
Fuguodun 228
Fujiamen 95, 96
funerary accompaniments 84

G_{ST} 386, 390
Gan 109
Gaoshan 106
Garo Hills 289
Gébelin, C. de 235
gene: diffusion 6; diversity 320; flow 4, 6, 53, 327–8, 397, 405–7, 419, 420; pool, 88, 326, 329, 343, 351, 353, 354
genealogical continuity 163
genealogical tree 166
genetic: dating 7; differentiation 316, 320, 387, 390, 392, 408; distances 320, 350; divergence of rice culitvars 137; pool 326, 328, 329; sampling 13; structure 7, 124, 319–25, 335, 385, 386, 392, 397, 405, 406, 427; studies of Taiwan 315
genetic drift 420; in Bali 392; and genetic diversity 322; intra- and intergenerational 408; in Siberians 406
genetic variation: and settlement models 356; causes of 420
genetics, synthesis with archaeology and linguistics 105
glottochronology 4, 9, 237, 306
GM: comparison of populations 322; frequency estimation 316; haplotype distributions 317, 319; haplotype frequencies 317, 318, 319; polymorphism 316, 319; variability in Taiwan 329
goats, domestication of 86
Gobi Altai Mountains 437
Gobi Desert 429
Gobineau, A. de 222
Gongduk 108, 227
grain assemblages, dominated by immature grains 58
grain gathering, timing of 54
grain measurement 51, 55, 57, 60
grain, evolutionary development 60
Gray, R. 4

Greater Subak of the Pamos Apuh Temple 380
Greenberg, J.H. 9, 11, 12
Grube, W. 223
Gunung 377
Gunung Kawi 377, 378, 379, 384, 385; radiocarobon data 378; sedimentology 378
Guo, J. 123
Gurung 297

Hainan 5
Hakka 109, 313
Han 106
haplogroups: analysis 337; ancestral 422; coalescence dates 343; foudning 409; geographic origins 419; phylogeography of 417; regionalizaton of 424; relationships 417; spatial maps 422; spread of 421
haploid molecular phylogenetics 416
haplotype diversity in yaks 434
Hardy–Weinberg equilibrium (HWE) 317
harvesting knives 67
harvesting: at Hemudu 57–62; of immature crops 53, 54, 61; with sickles 69, 71; timing of 67; wild rice 54, 57
Hattic 231
Hawaii 360, 362
Hawaiian 169, 170
head-hunting 303
Hedrick, P.W. 390
Hegel, G.W.F. 306
Hemudu 40, 42, 46, 47–9, 87, 88, 140, 228, 240; plant species 64; rice harvesting 57; storage pits 65
Hennig, W. 416
heterozygosity 405
Hexi 137
Himachal Pradesh 297
Hindu-Kush Mountains 429
historical-linguistic comparison 274
HLA: alleles 326; analysis 363; data 406; HLA-DRB1 326; loci 363; polymorphisms 328; variants 363
Hlai 116
Hmongic 112
Hmong-Mien 106, 112, 125, 133, 141, 240, 322, 323
Ho Nte 112, 141
Hoanya 211, 212, 313
Holocene migrations 40
Homo erectus 121
Hongshan culture 112
horse bones: late Pleistocene sites 94; Neolithic sites 95; Shang Dynasty 96–7

horse: as draught animal 94; domestication models 93; domestication of 86, 93–9; riding 94; terms in east Asia 115
Houghton, B. 220
houses, subterranean 145
hPhags-pa 266, 267, 279, 280
Hrusish 227
Hsien-jen-tung 119
Hsinchu 145
Hu 118
Huanbei 96, 98
Huayuanzhuang 89
human evolution 357
human immunoglobulins, GM polymorphism of 316
human major histocompatibility complex *see* HLA
human migration episodes 418
human mitochondrial genomes, family tree of 356
human populations, variation in 357
Humboldt, W. von 222
Hunanese 110
Hungarian 268
hunter-gatherers: California 65; Holocene 65
Hurles, M. 8
Hurrian 231
husks 53
HVS-I analysis 353
HVS-I matrix of haplotype frequencies 336
hypervariable region 359–60, 365

Iban 190
IgG immunoglobulins 316
Illič-Svityč, V.M. 237
incisors, ablation of 139
India 418, 431; haplogroup data 420
Indo-Chinese model 107, 221, 223–4; Indo-European 106, 121–2; outliers in China 121
Indonesia 25, 357; mtDNA variation in 363–7
Indus Valley 420
inheritance in languages 189
international phonetic alphabet 267
inter-population diversity 316
irrigation in Bali 376; archaeology 377; Gunung Kawi 377–9; irrigation systems: creation and management of 376; social management of 385; technology 385
Irwin, G. 369
Island Melanesia 25, 35
Island Southeast Asia 358
isolation by distance 123, 406
Itbayat 25, 28, 33, 336
Itbayaten population 28
Ivatan 28, 317

448   *Index*

Jaintia   289, 294
Janhunen, J.   10, 115, 274–5
Japanese: Altaic origins of   255; Altaic word forms   254; comparison with Korean   263, 265, 284; historical phonology   255, 265; Japanese scholarship   263–5; vocalization   266
Java   365
JC polyomavirus   123
jhum   287
Jiahu   61, 66, 89, 138
Jiali   436
Jinggouzhi   95
Jinghpaw   232, 238
Jingpho   297
Jomon Japan   65–6

Kachinic   222
Kairiru   161
Kamarupan   240
Kam-Tai   143
Kanakanabu   184
Kara, G.   284
Karen   220, 240, 255
Karenic   225
Karkar Island   5
Karuo   136
Kate, L. ten   236
Kaulong   190, 191
Kavalan   185, 186, 211, 212, 313, 328
Kazakhstan   395
Kemiehua   119
Kern, H.   229
Ket   396
Ketagalan   313
Khalkh Mongol   114
Khasi   289, 294
Khasi States   294
Khasi–Jaintia people   295
Kho-Bwa   227
Khoesan   7
Kiranti languages   226, 297
Kivisild, T.   123
Klaproth, J. von   107, 219, 220
Koch   296
Kon Keu   118
Korean   106, 122; Altaic word forms   254; classified as Altaic   264; comparison with Japanese   284; historical-linguistic comparison with Japanese   263–84; linguistic-historical link with Japanese   265; phonology   266; transcription of cognates   278; vocalization   266
Korean-Japanese   10, 254, 271
Koryaks   405
Kra-Dai   106, 219, 221, 230, 240
Kringing procedure   419

Kuahuqiao   40, 41, 42, 46, 47, 49, 50, 57, 58, 60, 61, 66, 86, 92–3; date   92; plant species remains   64
Kuanhua   119
Kuhn, E.   224
Kuki-Chin   223, 297
Kuki-speaking people   301
Kulon   313
Kulung   226
!Kung bushmen   65
Kunlun Mountains   429, 437
Kuroshio Current   33
Kweichow   116
Kyrgyzstan   431

Labuan-Taromak   211
Ladaki   297
Lagenaria siceria   64
Lai   118
Lake Baikal   409
Lake Qinghai   427
Lakhimpur   291; history of   293
language: confusion with race   221; diversity   7; intertwining   165; phyla of China   106; shift   5, 163; typology   222
languages: density of   298; genealogy of   166; high density   307; low density   307; speed of change of   306
language families: ages of   192; genetic relationships between   212; time depths   133
Lanyu   26, 29
Laoniupo   96
Laos   113, 116
Lapita   25, 26, 34, 36, 358, 360
Late Neolithic Elites   111
late Pleistocene sites, horse bone distribution   94
Latin   238
Lena River   409
Lepcha   223, 229
Lepsius, C.R.   223
lexical comparison   236
lexical divergence   237
lexical matches, between Chinese and Altaic   258–61
lexicostatistics   4, 9, 191, 237; analysis   190; calculations   192; classification   192; Swadesh list   189
Lhokpu   136
Liangzhu   41
Liangzhu culture   50, 67, 70
Limaish   150
Limbu   232
linear enamel hypoplasia   88, 89
Lingjiatan   69
linguistic comparative method   166
linguistic differentiation, distance-based   133
linguistic diversity, and genetic variation   356

linguistic inheritance 174
linguistic patterns in China 105–22
linguistics, synthesis with archaeology and genetics 105
livestock: in China 99–104; neutral genetic diversity in 436 ;origins 84, 85–6
localization of NRY haplogroups 420
Logan, J. 219
Lolo-Burmese 124, 240
Lombok 365
Longqiuzhuang 58, 60
Longshan 228
Lonqiuzhuang 50
'look-alike' forms, whether loanwords or cognates 282
Ludao 26, 29
Luilang 148, 313
Lung-K'eng 121
Luojiajiao 88
Lushai 229, 232, 233, 238, 304
Lushai Hills 289

Mackay Memorial Hospital 316, 335, 349
macroblade technology 410
macrophylum 134; Austronesian/Austroasiatic 134; STAN 134, 138
Madagascar 357, 363; maternal lineages 370; mtDNA variation in 367
Madak 164
Madurese 175
Maga-Tona 211
Mahatao 29
Majiabang culture 40, 43, 50, 58, 60, 66, 140, 228
Makatao 211
Malagasy 175, 367
Malay 190, 191
Malayo-Polynesian 23, 25, 146, 150, 161, 171, 175, 228, 314, 334, 349; dispersal of 25, 35; geographical distribution 357; hypothesis 173
Malayo-Sumbawan 175
male languages 222
Mallory, J.P. and Mair, V.H. 122
Mamanwas 323
Manado 365
Manchu 116
Mandarin 109, 313
Manggarai 161
Manila hemp 32
Manipur 295, 301
Manipur State 289
Mantel test 390, 391, 397, 401–3, 407
Maori 169, 170
Mariana Islands 26, 34
Marrison, G. 303
marsupials 176
Martin, S.E. 265–9

Marx, K. 306
Mason, F. 224
Matauran 211
maternal lineages in Madagascar 370
Matisoff, J.A. 107, 111, 225, 230
matrilineages in Bali 385
Mavolis 28
MDS 321; of Southeast Asia populations 324; results on East Asian populations 323; results on South Chinese dialect speakers 323; in Taiwanese populations 320; and Taiwanese population segregation 322; on Siberian Y chromosome data 401, 402
measurements: rice grain 137; skeletal 84
Meghalaya 295
Meitei 297, 304
Melanesia 357, 358; Polynesian outliers in 368
Melanesian peoples, genetic diversity 358
Merina 367
metatypy 164, 176
metrical development of rice 56
MHC see HLA
Miaoli 145
Miao-Yao 9, 106, 133, 192; see also Hmong-Mien
microblade industry 410
microblade technologies 408
Micronesia 164, 357
microsatellite differentiation 387
microsatellites 363, 430
Middle Korean 266, 267; hPhags-pa-based orthography 273; orthography 267; writing system 279
migration, Holocene 40; sex-biased 390; to Taiwan 193
migratory direction 165
Miller, R.A. 10
millet 66, 71, 91, 235; carbonized grains of 91
millet farmers 139
milling stones 65
Min 109, 142
Minigir 167
Minnan 313, 317, 322
Miri 292
Mishing 292
Mishmi languages 297
mitochondrial DNA see mtDNA
Mizo-Kuki-Chin 233, 240
mKhar-ro 136
molecular biology of East Asian populations 123; dating 329; genealogies 418; variance indices 336
Moluccas 35, 362
Mon-Annam 220
Mongol 277, 284

Mongol Empire 267
Mongolia 395, 431
Mongolian 254
Mongolic 10, 113
Mongolic languages 114–15
mongongo nuts 65
Mon-Khmer 106, 118, 224
morphogenetic change in plants 51
morphological observations 84
morphometric data 58
morphometric variation of modern rice 55
Motu 167
Mountain, J.K. 123
mtDNA 85, 334, 356, 368, 416; African type 368; in anthropological research 356; Asian type 361, 365; continental Asia variation 124; correlation with Y-STR in Gunung Kawi 391; diversity in Taiwanese aborigines 365; diversity in the Pacific 359–61; diversity in the Solomon Islands 368; diversity in yak 435; east Asian lineages 334; haplogroup distribution in Yami and Batan 351; highland PDG lineages 370; inherited maternally 356; markers, analysis of 357–9; paternal inheritance and recombination 357; Polynesian type 361, 365; sequences 35; Southeast Asian lineages 368; variation in Indonesia 363–7; variation in Madagascar 367
mtDNA haplogroup: A 337; A–G 334; B 337, 341, 344, 361; B4 334, 365, 367, 368; B4a 337, 342, 365; B4a1a 342, 344, 345, 351, 353; B4a2 353; B4b 341; B4b1 352; B4c 341; B4c1b 352; B5 368, 370; B5a 341; C 121, 337; D4 337; D5 337, 351; E 337, 340–1, 352; E1 351; E1a 352; E2 352; F 339–40, 370; F1a 340; F1a1 352; F1a1b 351; F3b 340, 351; F4b 352; G 337; H 121; L 121; M 334, 367; M7 123, 337, 340, 344; M7b1 351; M7b3 352; M7c 337; M7c1a 351; M7c1c 351, 353; M8 337; M9 337; N9 334; R9 334, 337, 339–40, 344; Y 316; Z 337
Muish 230
Müller, F.M. 220
multidimensional-scaling analysis see MDS
Munda 118, 224, 291
Musa textilis 32

Na-Dene 232
Naga 287; culture 301; Naga Hills 289; population density 294; war against the British 303;
Naga languages 297, 305; diverse array of 303; map 302; similairity of sounds in non-Naga Languages 304

Nagaland 301
Nagsabaran 34
Naidi Phase 349
name 106
Nanguanli 315
Nan-Kuan-Li 136, 215
Nanri 145
Nanshacun 95
Negrito 163
Nei's heterozygosity test 397
neo-grammarians 263, 284
Neolithic China, synthetic chronology 71
Neolithic dispersal process: dating of 35–7; directionality of 34
Neolithic population dispersal: C^{14} dating 26; into Indonesia and Oceania 25–6
Neolithic transitions for rice and *Setaria* 137
Nepal 431
nested cladistic analysis 406
neutral genetic diversity 436
New Zealand 357, 358
Nichols, J. 10, 11
Niger-Congo 7, 120
Nilo-Saharan 7
Nivkh 396
non-recombining Y-chromosome see NRY
Norman, J. 109; and Mei, T. 141–3
North Asia 395; initial peopling of 395
North Caucasian reconstruction 234
North East Frontier Area (NEFA) 299
North-East India, British census of 1931 287; population densities 289–91; populations of 287; Tibeto-Burmese language subgroups 297
Northern Philippine, archaeology 25–6
NRY 416; differentiation 416; genealogy 418; geographic origin of haplogrooups 419; localization of haplogroups 420–1; tree 418
NRY haplogroup: C 409, 410; C-M86 401; C-M217* 401; D-M174 417; H2 422; H2-M52 423; H-M69 422; J2-M172 421; L1-M76 422, 424; L2-M317 422; L3-M357 422; L-M20 422, 424; M40 417; M172 421; M174 417; M178 409; N 409, 410; N-M178 398; N-M178* 409; N-P43 398, 409; N-P63 398, 409; O 387; P 409; P43 409; Q 401, 409; R 409, 410; R-M17 401; R-M73 401; R-M269 401
nuclear DNA 44, 356, 365
Nuclear Polynesian 170
Nuclear Polynesian merger 174
numerals: Austronesian phylogeny 149; in Formosan languages 146–7; innovation in 146, 148; isoglosses of 148; post-Proto-Austronesian innovations 328
Nusa Tengaras 362

nut-based economies 63–6
nuts 71

oak 72
Oceanic languages: cognate vocabulary 168; genealogy 166; kin terms 168; sound correspondences 169; and Taiwan languages 161
Ohalo II 65
Ojibwa 57
Old Chinese 221, 226, 254; Altaic loans 256–7; borrowings from Korean-Japanese 254; ideogrammatic script 238; long vowels 226; as an older stage of Sinitic 227; phonology 254; reconstruction 236; syllabary 227
Old English 166
Old Japanese 265; compound-noun morphology 272; phonetics 272; phonology 272; vowel system 266
Old Koguryo 279
Olo 164
Olsen, S.J. 93
O-luan-pi II 121
Oota, H. 124
Oppenheimer, S.J. and Richards, M. 8
Orissa 57, 291
Oryza indica 44, 44–6, 48, 51, 55, 133, 137
Oryza japonica 43, 44–6, 48, 51, 55, 133, 137; domestication 137
Oryza javanica 43, 44–6
Oryza nivara 43, 44–6
Oryza officinalis 61
Oryza rufipogon 44–6, 55, 61, 67, 135; differentiation 138
Oryza sativa 44–6, 61, 135
Oryza spontanea 44–6
Oscan 238
Ostapirat, W. 11, 116, 151–2, 171
'Out of Taiwan' model 35–7

paddy fields 68
Pa-Hng 112
Paiwan 161, 186, 192, 211, 313, 334, 351
Pakanic languages 119
Pakistan 418, 431; NRY haplogroup data 420
Paleolithic industries 408
Pali 436
Palyu 118
Pamir 429
Pamir Knot 429, 436, 437
Pamos Apuh 380, 385
PAN numeral system 146
panicles 47
Papora 211, 212, 313
Papua New Guinea 357, 358
Papuan languages 164; diversity of 358

pastoralism: and Tibeto-Burman dispersal 437; yak 428–9
paternal genetic structure of Siberians 407
patrilineages in Bali 385
patrilocality 390, 392, 407
Pazeh 146, 148, 183, 192, 211, 212, 313, 317
peach stones 63, 65
Peiligang 111, 112
Peiros, I. 172
Pelasgian 232
Peñablanca Caves 28
personal pronouns, borrowing of 212
pest control measures 382–4; effectiveness off 382
Philippine languages 173
Philippines 25, 37
phonemes, velar-spirant and laryngeal 279
phonetic orthography, hPhagspa-based 281
phonological matches 236
phyla expansion 125
phylogenetics 419; analysis 357; haploid molecular 416; trees 3, 166; yak mtDNA 432; Y-chromosome
phylogeography 5
phylogeography of haplogroup relationships 417
phytoliths 51; size variation 62
pidginization 164
pig 34, 84; Cishan 91; domestication of 87–93; jaw dentition 92; second domesticated animal 86
Pingtan 145
Piper methysticum 369
Pituish 149
plant domestication pathways 42
platform cemeteries 70
plough tips 50, 67, 70
Poephagus grunniens 428
politeness shift 172
Polygonaceae 64, 65
polymorphic Y chromosome Alu insertion *see* YAP
Polynesia 357; genetic links with Taiwan 363; settlement of 358
Polynesian motif 344, 361, 365, 370, 371; in Indonesia 369; in Madagascar 367; in Melanesia 368; mean divergence times 362; in the Melanesian archipelago 368; origin date 362
Polynesian: genetic homogeneity 358; origins of 362; outliers in Melanesia 368; settlement trajectory 369; triangle 358
Poppe, N. 10, 268–74
population: density and village size 293; expansion 407, 433, 435; genetics 4, 239; grouping 323; movements 175; Siberia 395

452 *Index*

post-Proto-Austronesian 328
Pott, A.F. 222
pottery, red-slipped 25, 29, 34; Yangshao 115
Poyang Lake 41
pre-Mien 113
Prevosti's distance 323
principal component analysis (PCA) 336, 337, 339; three-dimensional 336
Pritsak, O. 277–80
proteins 13, 315, 316;
Proto-Altaic 237, 254, 268; correlation with Sino-Tibetan 256; correlation with Yangshao 256; evidence for 269
Proto-Altaic 9
Proto-Atayal 183
Proto-Austric 119
Proto-Austronesian 25, 136, 171, 190, 192, 213, 228, 256; in coastal China 192; dispersal 213; etymological dictionary 189; grammar 189; homeland 148; modificaton of consonant system 186; subgrouping 213, 214
Proto-Batanic 192
Proto-Central Pacific 192
Proto-Chinese 192
Proto-Daic 117
Proto-East-Asian 240, 241
Proto-Formosan 166; consonant system 186; lexiostatistics 189; separation from Proto-Austronesian 189
Proto-Formosan-Philippine 173
Proto-Hmong-Mien 113
Proto-Japanese, isolation from proto-Korean 273
Proto-Kam-Tai 143
proto-language lists, use in lexicostatistics 191
Proto-Malayo-Polynesian 166, 190; verbal system 172
Proto-Mongolian 255
Proto-Nuclear Polynesian 170, 177
Proto-Oceanic 169, 170
Proto-Paiwan 186
Proto-Philippines 116
Proto-Romance 238
Proto-Rukai 184, 185
Proto-Sino-Tibetan 111, 112, 254; comparative dictionary of 255; disintegration 256; lexicostatistical classification 255
Proto-STAN 136
Proto-Tai 143
Proto-Tai-Kadai 171
Proto-Tibeto-Burman 221
Proto-Tsou 188
Proto-Tungus-Manchu 255
Proto-Turkic 255
Proto-Uralic 237

Proto-Western Malayo-Polynesian 166
Prunus armeniaca 64
Prunus davidiana 64
Prunus mume 64
Przyluski, J. 224
Puluqic 150, 151
Puluqish 150
Puyuma 185, 192, 313, 317, 334, 351
Pyu 240

Qauqaut 313
Qiang people 428
Qiangic 240
Qianzhangda 96
Qinghai-Tibetan Plateau 427
Qingliangang culture 228
Qinweijia-Qijia 95–6
Quercus 64, 72

race, confusion with language 221
rachis, tough 53, 60
Raffles, Sir Stamford 377
Rafinesque, C.S. 237
Rakwaydi Phase 349
Ramstedt, G.J. 264–5
Rarotongan 169, 170
red deer 89
regional environmental change 73
regionalization of haplogroups 424
Reid, L.A. 11
Renfrew, C. 133, 241
Reranum Cave 28, 29, 31, 34; pottery 30
reticulation patterns 298
rice 235, 315; 'ancient' cultivars 48; 'ancient cultivated rice' variety 55, 58; collecting by hunter-gatherers 71; deposits 47–9; developmental trajectory 58; distribution map 45; domestication of 41–6, 50–7; early Chinese 51; effects of charring on grains 57; harvest yields 55; harvesting 57; measurements 61; metrical development 56; panicle maturation 55; phylogenetic analysis 43; pre-domestication cultivation 67; production 70–2; proportion of grains and spikelets 59; shattering 57; species compared 46, 59; speed of domestication 53; and STAN hypothesis 137; vulnerability to pests 382; wild rice 43–6, 51; *see also* individual species
rivers, as arteries for trade 296
roe deer 89
Roglai 120
Rukai 161, 184, 211, 213, 215, 313, 328, 334, 351
Russia 431
Rutgers, R. 232

Saaroa 184
Sabah 25
sacrifice 86
Sadiya Frontier Tract 299
Sagart, L. 10, 11, 110, 116, 120, 228, 230
Saisia 352
Saisiat 148, 192, 212, 313, 334, 352
Salar 114
Sama Bajaw 175
Samoa 25, 35, 37
Samoan 161, 169, 170
sampling in genetics 13, 124, 126, 351, 386, 422, 431
Santal 291
Sapir's principle 314
Sarikoli 121
Savidug jar burial site 31
Schott, W. 223
sea gypsies 175
secondary product revolution 70
Sedik 182, 313
serum proteins 316
Setaria 134, 136
Setaria italica 133, 152; archaeological sites 135
settlement models and genetic variation 356
sex-biased migration 390
Shang Dynasty, animal bones found 96
Shang period 86
Shantaisi 87
shared innovation in languages 170
She *see* Ho Nte
sheep, domestication of 86
Shengwen 111
Sherpa 297
Shiratori, K. 264–6
short tandem repeats *see* Y-STR
Siamese-Chinese family 224
Siberia 395; climate history 408; early peopling of 408; history of 396; low population densities 396; Paleolithic and Neolithic subsistence strategies 395; population density 395; Upper Paleolithic industries 395
Siberian 396
Siberian DNA study 397–409; evolutionary tree 400; results 398–405; sample composition 397–8; statistical methods 397
Siberian microblade industry 408
Siberians: clan structure 396; endogamy 396; foraging lifestyle 395; founder effect 406, 407; genetic drift 406; heterozygosity 405; low diversity indices 404; NRY genetic structure 405; paternal genetic structure 407; polygamous marriage 396; predominant haplogroups 401; small number of haplogroups 404; spatial autocorrelation plot 404
Sibsagar 291
sickles 67
Sihanaka 367
Sikkim 297
Sinitic 7, 108–9, 225; directional spread 111, 125; linguistic ancestors of 227; primary subgroup of Sino-Tibetan 107; reconstruction of older stages 238; surname patterning 123; underlying populations 125
Sino-(Tibetan)-Austronesian 110
Sino-Austric 239
Sino-Austronesian 110, 212, 227; compared with Sino-Caucasian 236–9; reconstruction 234
Sino-Austronesian theory 228, 230, 241
Sino-Bodic 225, 233, 240
Sino-Bodic–Sino-Tibetan debate 226
Sino-Caucasian 110; compared with Sino-Austronesian 236–9; reconstructions 233, 234; semantics 234
Sino-Caucasian theory 228, 231–7, 232, 239, 241
Sino-Tai 212
Sino-Tibetan 9, 106, 106–12, 125, 133, 255, 322; archaeological correlates 110; chromosome analysis of 427; classification of 126; divisions of 225; etymology 256; external affiliations 110; genetic correlates 110–12; historical phonology 256; internal classification 107; languages in phylum 107; number of speakers 106
Siraya 313, 317
Siyu 94
skeletal measurements 84
Slavic accentuation 226
'slow boat' model 334, 358
social differentiation 70
social stratification 69
Society Islands 360
Solomon Islands, mtDNA diversity in 368
Songze culture 43, 66, 67, 70
Sophora sp. 64
sound correspondences 167; New Britain languages 167
South Halmahera/West New Guinea 161, 171, 176
Southern Tibeto-Burmans' 124
spades 66; development 67
spatial autocorrelation 404
spatial maps of haplogroups 422
species, abrupt apearance of 84
spikelet 53, 57
Spriggs, M. 26

Index

STAN expansion model 139–53; coastal expansion 140–1; diversification in Taiwan 146–50; first expansion and first split 139–40; hypothesis, and rice 137; language genealogy 144; macrophylum 134, 138, 152; out of Taiwan 150–2; passage to Taiwan 145–6; and Yue language 141–5
Starosta, S. 213, 226, 240
Starostin, G. 114
Starostin, S. 9, 110, 228, 231, 236, 254; and Dybo, A. and Mundrak, O. 263
stilt houses 141
subaks 376–92; diversity parameter comparison 387; DNA analysis results 386; endogamy 392; ethnographic study of 380; genetic diversity parameters 388–9; genetics of 384–92; genetic structure 386; history 384–5; levels of cooperation within and between 382; microsatellite differentiation 387; population structuring 390
subsistence strategies 61
Sulawesi 26, 35
Sumerian 232
Sundanese 175
Sunget 29, 31 349; artefacts 32
Sungi river 386
Surma Valley 288
Sus philippensis 34
Sus scrofa 87; subspecies in China 88
Sus scrofa nigripes 87
Sus scrofa raddeanus 87
Sus scrofa ussuricus 87
Swadesh, M. 4

Tabanan 378, 386
Tagalog 161
Tahitian 169, 170
Tai 220
taiga 408
Tai-Kadai 106, 116–17, 133, 143, 150, 171, 192, 322, 323; genetically related to AN 150; subgroup within AN 151
Taiwan 357; as Austronesian homeland 145, 146; Austronesian languages in 25; Austronesian subgroups 349; B4a lineages 334; Chinese migration to 313; dispersal from 25–6; first peopling of 328; genetic continuity of population 322; genetic links with Polynesia 363; genetic studies of 315; GM genetic patterns 327; GM variablility 329; limited haplotype and nucleotide diversity 342; mtDNA lineages 342; mtDNA variations 334; population segregation 322; role in spread of Austronesians 329; time depths 329
Taiwan ethnic groups: dispersal C^{14} dating 212; dispersal dates 211
Taiwan languages, and Oceania languages 161
Taiwanese aborigines: average genetic distances 323, 325; B4a lineages 335; differentiation from East Asian populations 316; gene diversity 320; genetic heterogeneity 316; genetic relationships 354; GM data 317; haplogroup distribution 351; haplogroup frequencies 338; heterogeneity of 325; maternal ancestry 344; maternal lineages 334; mtDNA analysis 335–44, 350–4; mtDNA diversity 365; mtDNA lineages 343; paternal lineages 334; relationship to non-Taiwanese populations 323
Taiwanese populations: comparison with East Asian populations 322; gene diversity levels 327; genetic diversity of 325
Tajik 121
Tajima's D statistic 367, 435
Takia 5
Talasea obsidian 35
Tamang 297
Tanan dialect 215
Tangut-Bodish 240
Tani 287, 297, 307; dialect chain 299
Tanshishan 141
Tao 349
Taokas 211, 212, 313
Tapenkeng Culture 121, 215
Tarim Basin mummies 122
Taroko 313, 317
Tawala 167
tea gardens 291
tektek 380
Teleut 397, 405
terminal clades 418
Thai 116
Thailand 113
thalassaemia 359
Thao 192, 313
Thurgood, G. and LaPolla, R.J. 108
Tianluoshan 47, 73
Tibetan 107, 223; genetic relationships 220
Tibetan Buddhism 427
Tibeto-Burmans, dispersal of 437
Tibeto-Burman 106, 107, 240, 255; diversity of vocabulary and grammar 227; language groups 296; pinioned 221–7, 230; reconstruction 229; relationship with Chinese 212; subgroups 222
Tibeto-Burman hypothesis 219–21
Tibetoid language group 297
Tien-Shan Mountains 429
tillage 67
TMRCA 8, 340, 397

Toba Batak 161
Tocharian 121
Tolai 167
Tolsma, G. 232
Tonga 25, 26, 35, 363
tonic languages 220
tooth evulsion 140, 145, 152
tooth morphology 85
Torongan Cave 28, 29, 31, 33, 34; pottery 30
transhumance 115
Trans-Karakoram Mountains 429
Trapa bispinosa 64, 65, 73; *Trapa* sp. 64
'tribal' languages 296
Trobiawan 313
Trobriand Islands 370
Trubetzkoy, N. 231
Trung 136
Tsang, C.H. 121
Tsat 5, 120
Tseng-p'i-yen 119
Tsou 145, 161, 184, 192, 213, 313, 317, 334
Tsouic group 184
Tsuchida, S. 183, 215
Tujia 109, 110, 124
Tungus 277, 284
Tungusic 10, 113, 115, 116
Tungusic-Korean 125
Tungus-Manchu 254
Turanian 227
Turanian theory 220, 223
Turkey 418
Turkic 10, 113, 254, 268, 277, 284
Turkish, Crimean 114
Turkic-Altaic cognates 265

Uma 161
Umbrian 238
unidirectional evolution of Chinese 109
Upper Paleolithic industries in Siberia 395
Ural-Altaic 264
Uralic 396, 398
Urartaean 231
Urmelanesisch 170
urn burials 145
Uyghur 114, 122

Vanuatu 368
Vietnam 116, 357
village size and population density 293
voiced velar or laryngeal consonant 273
Vovin, A. 276

Waic languages 118
Wakhi 121
Walu-Siwaish 150
Wang, W.S.-Y. 105
Wang, X.J. and Song, P. 93

Wang, Y.T. 93
waste from dehusking episodes 57
water buffalo: domestication of 67; hunting of 67
water chestnuts *see Trapa bispinosa*
water sharing 380–4
Waxianghua 110
Weidun 69
Western Bengal 291
Western Malayo-Polynesian 353
Western Palaungic 118
Western Polynesia 36
wetland farming plots 67
wet-rice plains 287
wheat 58
Whitman, J. 11, 275–7
wild plant food production 66, 71
Witsen, N. 221
Wolff, J.U. 172
Wu 109
Wulff, K. 224

Xiang 109
Xianrendong 41, 72, 85
Xiaoshuangqiao 96
Xie, C.X. 93
Xinan Guanhua 110
Xinglonggou 50, 89, 90
Xinglongwa 89–91, 90; animal species found at 90; first phase 89; pig remains 89
Xinjiang mummies 121–2
Xitou 141

Y chromosomes 334, 359; AIDA analysis 403–4; Alu insertion *see* YAP; binary polymorphisms 397; phylogeny 424
yak 428–38; dispersal of domesticated 436; domestication events 433; domestication location 436; domestication of 428, 431–5; establishment of pastoralism 428; geographic distribution of 428; haplotype diversity 434; maternal lineages 437; migratory routes 437; molecular genetic studies of 430; mtDNA diversity 435; mtDNA lineages 432, 433; mtDNA samples 431; population expansion 433; populations 434; spread of pastoralism 429
Yami 313, 317, 349; genetic relationships 354
Yamphu 232
Yangshao 88; culture 256
Yangshao culture 112, 139, 240
Yangtze river archaeological sites 41–3
Yangtze: development of agriculture model 70; plant cultivation and domestication 70

Yanshi city 96
Yao languages 113
YAP 417; insertion, in Africa 417
Yenisey River 408, 409
Yenisseian 231, 232, 235
Yí languages 109, 139
Yinxu 86, 96, 97
Y-STR 363; correlation with mtDNA in Gunung Kawi 391; variation 419; variation in Bali 390–1
Yuan J. and An J.A. 93
Yuanshan culture 29
Yuchanyan 72
Yuchisi 89
Yue 109; and STAN expansion model 141–5
Yupik 396

zebu, domestication of 430
Zengpiyan 85, 88
Zeuner, F.E 428
Zhang, C.S. 94
Zheng Xuan 142
Zhou Chinese 109
Zhou, B.X. 93
Zizania aquatica 57